An American Ordeal

Syracuse Studies on Peace and Conflict Resolution
Harriet Hyman Alonso, Charles Chatfield, and Louis Kriesberg
Series Editors

Charles DeBenedetti

An American Ordeal
The Antiwar Movement
of the Vietnam Era

Charles Chatfield
Assisting Author

Syracuse University Press

Copyright © 1990 by Syracuse University Press
Syracuse, New York 13244-5160
All Rights Reserved

First Edition 1990

99 98 97 96 95 94 93 92 91 90   6 5 4 3 2

Permission of the authors is gratefully acknowledged for the use of quo-
tations from Daniel Berrigan, "America Is Hard to Find," in Berrigan,
America Is Hard to Find (New York: Doubleday, 1972) and W. D. Erhart,
"A Relative Thing," from *To Those Who Have Gone Home Tired: New &
Selected Poems* (New York: Thunder's Mouth Press, 1984).

The paper used in this publication meets the minimum requirements
of American National Standard for Information Sciences—Permanence
of Paper for Printed Library Materials, ANSI Z39.48-1984.

LIBRARY OF CONGRESS CATALOGING-IN-PUBLICATION DATA

DeBenedetti, Charles.
An American ordeal : the antiwar movement of the Vietnam era /
Charles DeBenedetti, Charles Chatfield, assisting author. — 1st ed.
    p.   cm. — (Syracuse studies on peace and conflict resolution)
        Includes bibliographical references.
ISBN 0-8156-0244-8 (alk. paper). — ISBN 0-8156-0245-6 (pbk. :
                alk. paper)
    1. Vietnamese Conflict, 1961–1975—Protest movements—
        United States.   2. United States—History—1945–
            I. Chatfield, Charles, 1934–   .   II. Title.
                        III. Series.
                DS559.62.U6D43   1990
            973'.923—dc20   89-21922
                                    CIP

Manufactured in the United States of America

For Sandy, Laura, and David

Until his untimely death in 1987, Charles DeBenedetti was a Professor of History at the University of Toledo. Active in peace education and social concerns, he lectured throughout the country and contributed articles to such journals as *The Historian, American Studies,* and *Peace and Change.* He was the author of *Origins of the Modern American Peace Movement, 1915–1929* (1978) and *The Peace Reform in American History* (1980) and the editor of *Peace Heroes in Twentieth-Century America* (1986).

Charles Chatfield is a Professor of History at Wittenberg University. He is the author of *For Peace and Justice: Pacifism in America, 1914–1941* (1971), *Peace Movements in America* (1973), and *The Radical "No"* (1974). He has also served as coeditor of numerous volumes, including *The Americanization of Gandhi* (1976) and *Peace Movements and Political Cultures* (1988).

Contents

Part One
The Reconstruction of the Peace Movement, 1955–1963

Part Two
The Construction of an Antiwar Movement, 1963–1965

Part Three
The Contest for the Center, 1966–1970

Contents

Part Four
The War and the American Way,
1970–1975

Reflections

Illustrations

Illustrations

Preface

Dear Anita—Did you ever have something to say and feel as if the whole side of the wall wouldn't be big enough to say it on and then sit down on the floor and try to get it on a sheet of charcoal paper—and when you had put it down look at it and try to put into words what you have been trying to say with just marks—and then—wonder what it all is anyway—

> —Georgia O'Keefe to Anita Pollitzer, 13 December 1915, in Jack Cowart and Juan Hamilton, *Georgia O'Keeffe* (Washington, D.C.: National Gallery of Art, 1987), 146.

This is an interpretive history of the effort of American citizens to promote a foreign policy contributing to peace, and of how that effort became transformed into a movement in opposition to the war in Vietnam. It was researched and worked out by Charles DeBenedetti. Tragically, just when he was ready to give the book its final form, the author was struck by a massive brain tumor. It came with violence in October 1986, and it took him on his forty-fourth birthday, 27 January 1987.

On the morning of 11 October my wife and I visited him and his family at St. Vincent Medical Center, Toledo, Ohio. When we entered the room, Chuck (as he was known to family and friends) was on his feet. He was dressed, stood as tall and straight as ever, and although he seemed tired, he did not appear incapacitated. He was the affable and courteous friend I'd known for many years. We talked generally among the family members and had two brief conversations alone.

In our private discussions Chuck was lucid and focused, although his search for words was more deliberate than usual and his energy limited. He was intensely anxious that his book should be completed. I assured him that I would see it through. I ventured that my challenge was to discover his interpretation and bring it out. "Your project is a precious child," I said, "and I am conscious that it is *your* child. My role is like that of a doctor at birth." He nodded his understanding and smiled his appreciation of the simile. His smile always had an interior quality, reflecting the resonance of a thought within him. He recalled our long-standing collaboration, and he wanted to think of us as "doing this thing together."

"Chuck," I said, "you are a good Catholic." He smiled again, genuinely pleased at the thought. "You will understand my meaning if I say that I'll need your continued help."

"You'll have it," he responded.

Was there anything in particular he wanted to say about the project? "Only to bring out the excitement: bring the story to life," he said.

That conversation defined the twin challenges of this work. On the one hand there was my friend's injunction to "bring the story to life," and on the other the fact that the book would not be written the way either of us would write it independently, yet would not exactly be a collaboration, either. My effort throughout has been to discover his interpretation and to bring it to life.

The reader deserves to know something about the process of revision. Charles DeBenedetti left us with a massive research base, a manuscript of approximately 1,100 pages, and a loosely arranged and partial bibliography. About 840 pages of manuscript were in what might be called finished first-draft form: that is, they were complete, fluent, and documented. The final two chapters were fairly complete, although at some points they trailed off into rough notes, and the documentation was often ambiguous. DeBenedetti anticipated cutting the manuscript by about half, as he told me on two occasions. That meant fundamental rewriting.

My procedure was first to prepare a detailed outline of the manuscript, and next to reduce that outline in stages so that the structure and themes would become clear. I then proceeded to restructure and rewrite the book chapter by chapter in an effort to make the narrative as coherent and accessible as possible, to develop the insights that had accumulated as the story had been constructed, to modulate the tonality of the whole, and to add a concluding reflection. The revised version served to identify the technical tasks of validating data and sources, checking the account against recent scholarship, referencing citations, and preparing the final manuscript for publication.

In all this I have been helped by a community of people committed to Charles DeBenedetti and the things for which he stood. At the special initiative of his close friend William Hoover, chairman of the Department of History, the University of Toledo arranged with Wittenberg University to reassign me in the fall of 1987 and spring of 1988 to work on the book. This was essential, and I am grateful to my colleagues in both institutions for the opportunity. Professor Hoover was indefatigable in providing support, and the faculty of history at Toledo were understanding and encouraging. The project benefitted, too, from the technical services of the University of Toledo computer center and from the unfailing cooperation of Paula Ashton, who had typed most of DeBenedetti's original manuscript.

Thomas Wellock and Gary Madryzkowski were assigned to this project as research assistants by the Department of History of the University of Toledo. Tom reviewed and indexed the original and first drafts, and he researched innumerable details. Gary assisted with the research, provided technical assistance, and proofread the final version. Their assistance has been invaluable.

Gary Hess of Bowling Green State University and Ronald Lora of the University of Toledo read the manuscript in various stages and provided valuable suggestions. Lawrence Wittner of the State University of New York at Albany and Robert Cohen of the University of Toledo helpfully critiqued the last version. Melvin Small of Wayne State University reviewed part of DeBenedetti's draft and also my version and provided an advance galley of his *Johnson, Nixon, and the Doves* (New Brunswick, N.J.: Rutgers Univ. Press, 1988), and Mitchell Hall of Central Michigan University shared his Ph.D. dissertation, "Clergy and Laymen Concerned About Vietnam: A Study of Opposition to the Vietnam War" (Univ. of Kentucky, 1987).

It was possible to illustrate this volume only with the cooperation of the Fellowship of Reconciliation, the Swarthmore College Peace Collection, the War Resisters League, and of those persons who permitted their work to be used. Each picture is credited to its source and, where possible, photographer. An effort was made to locate all known photographers, and I will appreciate having contact with those whom I could not reach.

I am indebted to the editorial staff of the Syracuse University Press, which made a special commitment to this volume, and especially to Cynthia Maude-Gembler and Joyce Atwood, who far exceeded their editorial responsibilities in the care which they gave it. I particularly appreciate the copyediting skill and sensitivity to language of Bettie McDavid Mason, who also gently shepherded Peter van den Dungen and me through the preparation of *Peace Movements and Political Cultures* (Knoxville: Univ. of Tennessee Press, 1988).

From the painful moment when it became clear that her husband would not be able to see his book through, Sandy DeBenedetti has been totally committed to its completion. Much more, she had been altogether supportive throughout the years of research and writing. She knew firsthand the labor and dedication on which the original manuscript was grounded. She shared personal sacrifices in anticipation of its publication. For that and for her encouragement in this work, Sandy has my deep gratitude. She will understand, in turn, the sincerity with which I acknowledge appreciation to my wife, Mary, for her sustaining support.

All of us who shared in the preparation of this book and those who read it are most indebted to Charles DeBenedetti himself, and to the movement whose excitement and life he both shared and interpreted.

Springfield, Ohio   Charles Chatfield
May 1989

Abbreviations

ADA	Americans for Democratic Action	IDA	Institute for Defense Analysis
AEC	Atomic Energy Commission	IPC	Indochina Peace Campaign
AFSC	American Friends Service Committee	LID	League for Industrial Democracy
ARVN	Army of the Republic of Vietnam	M2M	May Second Movement
		MIA	Missing in Action
AWOL	Absent Without Leave	MNC	Movement for a New Congress
BEM	Business Executives Move for Vietnam Peace	Mobe	National Mobilization to End War in Vietnam
CADRE	Chicago Area Draft Resisters	NAACP	National Association for the Advancement of Colored People
CALC	Clergy and Laity Concerned		
CCCO	Central Committee for Conscientious Objectors	NAG	National Action Group
		NAM	New American Movement
CIA	Central Intelligence Agency	NARMIC	National Action/ Research on the Military-Industrial Complex
CND	Campaign for Nuclear Disarmament		
CNVA	Committee for Non-Violent Action	NCAWRR	National Coalition Against War, Racism, and Repression
CORE	Congress on Racial Equality	NCNP	National Conference for a New Politics
CP	Communist Party		
CPF	Catholic Peace Fellowship	NCCEWVN	National Coordinating Committee to End the War in Vietnam
CPS	Civilian Public Service		
CSFW	Campaign to Stop Funding the War	NLF	National Liberation Front
FBI	Federal Bureau of Investigation	NPAC	National Peace Action Coalition
FCNL	Friends Committee on National Legislation	NSA	National Student Association
FOR	Fellowship of Reconciliation	PCPJ	People's Coalition for Peace and Justice
HUAC	House Un-American Activities Committee	PL	Progressive Labor
		POW	Prisoners of War

Abbreviations

PPT	People's Peace Treaty	UAW	United Automobile Workers
PRG	Provisional Revolutionary Government	UWF	United World Federalists
RYM II	Revolutionary Youth Movement II	VDC	Vietnam Day Committee
SANE	National Committee for a Sane Nuclear Policy	VIVA	Voices in Vital America [or Victory in Vietnam Association]
SCLC	Southern Christian Leadership Conference		
SDS	Students for a Democratic Society	VMC	Vietnam Moratorium Committee
SLID	Student League for Industrial Democracy	VVAW	Vietnam Veterans Against the War
SMC	Student Mobilization Committee to End the War in Vietnam	WILPF	Women's International League for Peace and Freedom
SNCC	Student Nonviolent Coordinating Committee	WRL	War Resisters League
		WSA	Worker Student Alliance
SOS	Summer of Support	WSP	Women Strike for Peace
SPU	Student Peace Union	YPSL	Young People's Socialist League
STDN	Set the Date Now		
SWP	Socialist Workers Party	YSA	Young Socialist Alliance
TTP	Turn Toward Peace		

An American Ordeal

Introduction

A darkening cloud of war gathered almost imperceptibly in the decade after 1955, and the storm broke before its magnitude was recognized. Its center was in Indochina, but it engulfed America. For ten years more it churned across the nation, charging every internal conflict with high tension and obscuring the issues which defined national identity. In the roiling darkness a Catholic priest wrote from hiding that America was "hard to find."

The priest was part of the antiwar movement, an amorphous and pervasive social current that connected the war in Vietnam to domestic struggles. The movement was both a cultural and a political phenomenon, and in that duality lay its central paradox: its cultural power compromised its political effectiveness. It gave cultural dissonance a political import more surely than it affected public policy. Nonetheless, it was part of the political process, for it was locked in a struggle with the government over how the people would define their values, institutions, and destiny.

This is the story of the antiwar movement and of the war in America. It could be called a story of the Vietnam War on the home front. But it is more truly an account of the conflict in the American interior—in church meeting halls, city streets, college campuses, editorial offices, electoral campaigns, congressional halls, and divided families—where most Americans struggled among themselves over the Vietnam War.* This is also the story of those who challenged that war. As a whole more antiwar than peace-seeking, their movement was a loose alignment of elements which changed in style, tactics, and thrust during the era. It altered partly in response to political and international circumstances and partly in relation to the personal ethos of its participants as they wrestled with the meaning of the war and the society.

The movement involved only a few dozen organizations in 1960, over twelve hundred a decade later. Most of them were local and ephemeral. Numbers never were an accurate index of the antiwar movement, either

*This study assumes that the antiwar movement was a social movement, as defined by the historical sociologist Charles Tilly, insofar as it was "a sustained *interaction* in which mobilized people, acting in the name of a defined interest, make repeated broad demands on powerful others via means which go beyond the current prescriptions of the authorities." "Social Movements and National Politics," in Charles Bright and Susan Harding, eds., *Statemaking and Social Movements: Essays in History and Theory* (Ann Arbor: Univ. of Michigan Press, 1984), 313; emphasis in the original.

in organizations or in demonstrations. Although antiwar dissent gained continuity from a core of activists, insofar as it was organized at all, its components were not primarily membership organizations. There never was a single directing agency, common leadership, or ideology. Only at a few points was there even a formal coalition, and then it was but partial. Highly eclectic, protesters employed tactics ranging from letter writing to bombings, from prayer vigils to self-immolations. Improvisational, they experimented with organized lobbying, electoral politics, mass demonstrations, teach-ins, vigils, and nonviolent civil disobedience. The measure of the movement was its influence, not the number of its adherents. Probably the very diversity of dissent increased its outreach, for its leadership permeated the society from the most elite and conventional to the most antisocial elements.

The American antiwar movement was at once a product of history and a process that made history. As a process, the movement was a highly charged force for change that galvanized some American citizens to challenge their government's nuclear weapons testing and then its policy in Southeast Asia. As a product, the movement was the latest expression of a long tradition of citizen peace activism that was organized around issues such as international disarmament and opposition to great-power interventionism. The Vietnam War was the catalyst for changes in peace advocacy, as well as in the nation, but in order to appreciate this fact it is necessary to locate the movement's prewar sources and to follow its course beyond the formal termination of war in 1973. Otherwise, we are left with only the stereotypes formed in the period of most intense conflict—images that obscure the continuity between seeking peace and confronting war.

In 1955 the movement appeared as a fresh form of peace advocacy familiar in American history. Seizing on the perceived threat from nuclear testing in order to advocate alternatives to Cold War confrontation, a coalition of liberal internationalists and radical pacifists developed new organizations and tactics. By the time of the nuclear test–ban treaty of 1963, the coalition had been influenced also by a revitalized radicalism, identified in the North with the New Left and in the South with civil rights activists. By then it had acquired the internal differences and the distinctive ethos which would characterize opposition to war in Indochina.

With the government's escalation of military involvement in Vietnam in the first half of the 1960s, the coalition was gradually transformed into an antiwar movement. It defined the issues on which policy would be debated for a decade. It provided a focus for citizens who felt uneasy about the war, and it attracted new constituencies of discontent which strengthened the movement's left-wing cast. When President Lyndon Johnson definitively committed the nation to war in 1965, he faced a loosely organized opposition ready to contest him for the support of the nation's political center.

As the war expanded in scope, intensity, and cost over the next two years, antiwar dissidents improvised a wide range of actions which forced the war issue into the public arena, generated organized opposition to intervention, pressed the administration to make ever-larger claims for the war, and fragmented the movement itself. Protest moved into the streets. Early in 1968 the ferocity of the communist Tet offensive triggered a change of war strategy and imposed limits on U.S. military commitment. In the midst of mounting domestic disorder, antiwar liberals pressed the war issue in electoral politics; but their chosen vehicles, the McCarthy and Kennedy campaigns, collapsed and left them on the political margin. About the same time, radicalism as a driving force of organized protest began to wane, and militant extremism spun off on the periphery.

The antiwar movement declined early in the Nixon presidency, but it regrouped to mount massive demonstrations in the fall of 1969. Exhausted and fragmented, though, it was unable to capture or mobilize the widespread public protest evoked by the administration's invasion of Cambodia the following spring. The politics of confrontation seemed to have played out, despite a brief resurgence in the spring of 1971. Although war dissenters still challenged government policy, they increasingly worked within established political institutions responding to war-weariness among the public.

Gradually leadership returned to political liberals until, with the 1972 presidential campaign of George McGovern, the war issue was brought fully within the political system. By the end of the year, Congress itself appeared ready to confront the Nixon administration. That contest was preempted by the Paris peace accord of January 1973, but shortly afterward the issue of presidential authority emerged as the Watergate syndrome. Antiwar dissidents linked the constitutional issue to the war, first on behalf of withdrawal from military engagement and, after the peace agreement, in opposition to a widening air war over Indochina and continued aid to the regime in Saigon.

The shifts in the emphasis and tactics of antiwar protest were largely a result of its intersection with political institutions. In particular, stridency and militancy in protest were related to the obduracy of the Johnson and Nixon administrations: confrontation was a product of the interaction of committed dissent and an unresponsive government. Insofar as the political system accommodated criticism in electoral and congressional politics, protest tended to flow within established channels.

Rapid transformations in organized protest were also a product of its relationship to American society. Like the larger culture of which it was a part, the antiwar movement of 1955–1975 was a diverse and dynamic enterprise that changed dramatically in its composition, assumptions, and purposes. Especially in the 1960s the United States experienced sharp challenges to important cultural norms—traditional religious beliefs, scientific objectivity, white and male dominance, adult standards of behavior, the assumption that poverty was a normal part of society, the notion of a Cold War mission, and the liberalism of consensus. As each of these became organized, it added to a plethora of social movements which were related to one another only tenuously, if at all. The demand to end the war and the concomitant challenge to established authority aligned several of these dissident elements.

On the one hand, the vision of a broad coalition for social change provided the antiwar movement with an incisive, radical cutting edge. Leading activists believed that national values and institutions had been distorted by a Cold War emphasis on maintaining order by force, which in turn was repressing pressures for social justice, whether in the Third World or in the United States. It was in this sense that the antiwar movement was related to other social and cultural protests of the decade. On the other hand, the eclecticism of antiwar protest made it especially vulnerable to fragmentation. Its leaders disagreed over whether to pursue a single-minded challenge to war or to develop a broad coalition for social change. They were divided by the eddies of controversy carried in the cultural currents that fed into the antiwar movement. They were burdened by stereotypes grounded in the reality of their uneasy association with radicals and counterculture figures, fixed in popular mythology by the media, and exploited by the supporters of administration policy. Thus, the organized movement developed a dual identity that was the source of its strength as well as its weakness. As a cultural force it vibrated with resilience and adaptability, energizing people with ideas, criticisms, political alternatives, and values. As a political force it remained embarrassingly weak, and this contributed to its disillusionment and despair. In spite of its appeal among church people, organized women, traditional peace workers, intellectuals, students, and assorted leftists, it remained largely on the political periphery. Movement leaders helped to rally a shattering cultural rebellion that altered the course of American politics and foreign policy; but the society for which many of them yearned remained "hard to find."

Fundamentally, the war was always about America. From start to finish in the arguments over intervention, the welfare of the Vietnamese people was secondary. Pro-war citizens maintained that the war was necessary to contain Asian communism far from America's shores. Policymakers referred to Vietnam as a "showcase" of nation building, a "proving ground" of successful counterinsurgency, or a "test" of America's will to prevail in the greater Cold War. Although critics of the war, on the other hand, argued that intervention thwarted the emergence of an independent Third World and many of them showed a poignant concern for the people of Indochina, even they argued mainly that the war effort hurt the United States. Antiwar activists habitually charged that the war weakened prospects for Soviet-American détente, destabilized the international order, smeared the nation's image as a positive force, wasted chances for domestic reform, and subverted national values and institutions. The war was in Indochina, but the ordeal for the antiwar movement and the citizens it sought to mobilize was in and over America.

Part One

The Reconstruction of the Peace Movement, 1955–1963

One

Regenerating Concern

"Year 1 of something far worse"

As air raid sirens shrieked, the president of the United States and fifteen thousand government employees fled the capital city in the first evacuation of Washington since the British invasion in 1814. The nation had been surprised by an atomic attack, the president announced. Nearly fifteen million people had already been killed or injured in strikes upon sixty-one cities. Martial law was invoked. Governmental authorities set defense programs in motion, the Agriculture Department lifting acreage allotments on major crops for the duration, and the Treasury revealing plans to freeze debts and ration money. Trading on the New York Stock Exchange halted. Two-thirds of the population of Bangor, Maine, including hospital patients and school children, were evacuated into the countryside, while elsewhere millions of people hurried into underground shelters. "Operation Alert" was on.

The emergency was simulated, of course, but it did take place on 15 June 1955. Designed to refine plans for civil defense in a nuclear age, it was not reassuring. President Dwight Eisenhower confessed afterward, "We found more complications yesterday than I believed possible."[1] Civil defense authorities promised to rectify problems through a more elaborate program.

The whole operation was improbably naïve, like something out of *Alice in Wonderland,* but it was real enough to expose a pervasive sense of vulnerability in the United States. There were other symptoms in 1955. In Europe the Soviets erected the Warsaw Pact military alliance to counter the integration of a rearming West Germany into NATO. In the Middle East the Baghdad Pact aligned the U.S. and Britain with the northern tier of Arab states to contain Russian influence, but the revolutionary Egyptian regime of Gamal Abdel Nasser began to court Soviet support in order to isolate Israel and assume pan-Arab leadership. In Asia the forces of

9

U.S. allied Nationalist China on the islands of Quemoy and Matsu were shelled by communist Chinese, eliciting a threat from Washington to use atomic weapons.

Most ominous of all, destructive new weaponry portended a terrifying new dimension in Soviet-American conflict: a series of atomic tests in Nevada throughout the spring was followed by H-bomb tests in Russia; the Navy launched the world's first nuclear-powered submarine and acknowledged plans for a solid-fuel, submarine-launched missile system; the Air Force successfully exploded a nuclear-armed air-to-air missile at 30,000 feet; and American scientists developed a miniature atomic bomb, which frightened Congress into offering rewards for information on the smuggling of small nuclear weapons and bomb-grade material into the United States.

Meanwhile, the unprecedented power of the hydrogen bomb and the health hazards from atmospheric fallout began to sink into public consciousness. In February the Atomic Energy Commission confirmed the fact that above-ground testing yielded both an immediate health danger and likely genetic damage. The *New Republic* warned that the technology of destruction had taken an "immense leap" forward, "one that dwarfs even that signaled by the dropping of the first atomic bomb in 1945." Times had changed. It was no longer "Year 9 of the Atomic Age, but Year 1 of something far worse."[2] Americans might be vulnerable after all.

On the other hand, as if in counterpoint to a growing threat, there were signs of a relaxation in Soviet-American tensions that raised hopes for a negotiated settlement of superpower differences. Stalinism was criticized in Russia and McCarthyism declined in America. It was agreed to remove occupying troops from a neutral Austria. A negotiated settlement in Vietnam seemed to have shifted the contest there from military to political force. National leaders from many former colonies met in April at an Asian-African Conference in Bandung, Indonesia, and declared their intention to guide the majority of the world's people around the volatile superpower confrontation. They talked of third-camp internationalism, stressed their interest in economic liberation and development, and appealed for an end to atomic weapons testing.

Early in 1955, Eisenhower built on the acclaim he had won two years earlier for his proposal to transform weapons competition into cooperpation on nuclear energy with an "atoms for peace" program. In March he named Harold Stassen as special White House assistant for disarmament, prompting even veteran critics to rhapsodize over America's new "Secretary for Peace" and the administration's elevation of conciliation over conflict.[3] In May, Soviet negotiators at the UN disarmament subcommittee meeting in London unveiled a new proposal that hinted their willingness to accommodate long-standing Western demands for international control and inspection. That month Eisenhower received a White

House report which recommended renewed efforts to regulate the arms race, perhaps starting with a verifiable test-ban agreement. Vera Micheles Dean, research director of the Foreign Policy Association since 1928, caught the tentative drift of events. The world teetered "on the razor edge between disaster and a vast surge into a creative future," she explained. Imaginative and determined leadership might yet lead the world "out of the wilderness of atomic slaughter and into the promised land of peacetime atomic productivity."[4]

Midway in the year Eisenhower made a special peace appeal at the UN, and a month later he met in Geneva with Soviet president Nikolai Bulganin and premier Nikita Khrushchev, British prime minister Harold Macmillan, and French premier Pierre Mendès-France in the first postwar "summit" conference of superpower leaders. Catching the spotlight, the president proposed negotiations on an "open skies" treaty arrangement that would reduce Soviet-American arms through regular aerial inspection of one another's territory. Neither the prospect of open skies nor the summit conference drew the Soviets into early and ambitious negotiations, but both encouraged hope for a peaceful resolution of the Cold War and lent legitimacy to more assertive citizen peace efforts.

The events of 1955, contributing alternately to anxiety and hope at the time, appear in retrospect as evolving patterns in foreign policy. President Eisenhower's overarching concern was to improve and stabilize relations with the Soviet Union and to lessen the prospects of war. He was in this sense a peace-seeker. He was also determined to contain Soviet influence, however, assuming that peace required balanced force as well as the accommodation of interests. A methodical man, he had completed a systematic review of overall policy alternatives by the summer of 1953 and had somewhat modified the policy of containment.

Under the Truman administration the policy of containing the Soviet Union with flexible responses on a shifting perimeter had become increasingly militarized. It projected a worldwide set of alliances ringing the communist bloc (which by 1949 included China), the creation of a strong and militarily integrated Europe, and the reconstruction of a powerful U.S. armed force. It assumed that the UN would be a pliable instrument with which to check Sino-Soviet expansion. The Korean War provided great impetus to the policy of military containment. During its course there emerged a national consensus for a kind of Pax Americana, a revolutionary development for a nation hitherto reluctant to intervene even temporarily outside its hemisphere.

The Korean War, as it became prolonged and indecisive, also produced a modification of containment that contributed to the arms race. Eisenhower campaigned for the presidency on a promise to bring an end to the war, and his commitment crystalized into the position that U.S. military action abroad must be restricted. He also wanted to limit military spending in the interest of a strong economy. Accordingly, the strategy of containment was adapted by replacing the threat of conventional war with the threat of atomic warfare—so-called "massive retaliation." The emphasis on a strong European defense system continued and regional alliances received greater emphasis, but the basis of unilateral deterrence shifted to American nuclear superiority. The difficulty was that the Soviet Union could not long accept nuclear inferiority and was, in fact, working to close the gap. Insofar as his administration relied on unilateral deterrence to enforce containment, therefore, the president had to defer his apprehension to the development of nuclear capacity. That was the meaning of the weapons tests and technological innovations of 1955. Eisenhower's achievement was perhaps that he resisted hardening the arms race, even though he could not contain it.

There was another difficulty in the containment policy inherited by the Republicans. It implied that the contest with Russian and Chinese communism was to be waged on a global scale, a perception reinforced by communist leaders, who gave a Marxist twist to disparate developments throughout the world. Both Sino-Soviet and U.S. strategists attached their rivalry to national and regional conflicts that had their own dynamics. Increasingly, the Cold War was waged by proxy, through political influence, economic assistance, and covert action. The Eisenhower administration significantly expanded the capacity and foreign policy role of the Central Intelligence Agency (CIA) and other agencies outside the State Department, in part to circumvent international law and Soviet responses and in part to avoid disrupting national and congressional consensus. By 1955 the White House could view covert operation as an acceptable risk, for the CIA had placed pro-American governments in power in Iran (1953) and Guatemala (1954). Such operations may have been handled responsibly by Eisenhower, as historian Robert Divine has argued.[5] They nonetheless presaged a foreign policy and constitutional ordeal which began to unfold in Vietnam in 1955. There the CIA authorized covert operations against the North, while in the South the United States took over the French role in military training and nation building. To the administration, American intervention in Indochina seemed as moderate an investment as simulated civil defense. Yet Southeast Asia, no less than the nuclear arms race, was mined with unexpected dangers and trials for the nation.

"This chance must not be allowed to slip through our fingers"

As millions of New Yorkers took shelter in Operation Alert, a handful of pacifists gathered in City Hall Park and refused to participate. Twenty-eight of them were arrested. The arraigning magistrate gave them a tongue-lashing, and nineteen were subsequently found guilty of violating the state's civil defense law, which mandated participation in civil defense exercises. A trivial incident? Perhaps; but surely civil defense routines were trivializing the awesome, and this small protest was a kind of overture to a broad attempt to confront the malaise of Cold War anxiety.

In 1955 a number of peace-minded citizens responded to the combination of growing military threat and apparent international accommodation by promoting U.S. initiatives for disarmament and a negotiated end to the Cold War. Their efforts were not yet coordinated, but they initiated a movement which would mushroom and metamorphose for two decades. These peace advocates had disparate backgrounds and approaches, but in general they represented two wings with deep roots in an historic American peace movement: liberal internationalists and radical pacifists. Divided and often disputatious, liberal and pacifist leaders would find themselves at odds in the 1960s, but at the outset they subsumed their differences to their common sense that international conditions were becoming both militarily ever more dangerous and politically more promising.

The larger and less cohesive number of them were liberal internationalists. They included liberal Democrats, like New York financier James P. Warburg, who favored negotiations over confrontation in Soviet-American rivalry and demanded a more aggressive U.S. crusade against hunger and want in the developing world. There were longtime supporters of the League of Nations and the United Nations, like Annalee Stewart of the Women's International League for Peace and Freedom. There were also world federalists, like writer-editor Norman Cousins, who decided after 1945 that the UN was too modest a means toward real world order and argued for a federal world government. Some were atomic scientists, like physicist Eugene Rabinowitch, who argued in the aftermath of Hiroshima for international control of atomic energy. Others were social and political critics, like journalist I. F. Stone, who believed that Washington's commitment to victory in the Cold War thwarted liberation in the Third World and democratic reform in America. Among them were pacifists, like Quaker leader and Nobel Prize laureate Clarence Pickett, who rejected war on principle.

The roots of liberal peace advocacy went back to nineteenth-century preoccupations with free trade, international law, and arbitration. By the twentieth century an interest in world order attracted professional people to well-funded peace societies. With the First World War this concern was converted to support for a League of Nations and Wilsonian internationalism—a world ordered collectively under law and morality. The League and the World Court became rallying points for increasingly political efforts in the 1920s. Following a bitter national debate in the late 1930s over intervention in the European war, leaders from the League of Nations Association (1923) with allied liberals successfully popularized the UN during World War II, eventually forming the United Nations Association (1941).[6] Their efforts on behalf of the UN were an extension of a theme underlying internationalism in the United States: it was thought to be a distinctly American responsibility to bring peace and order to the world.

The First World War also stimulated the organization of the Women's International League for Peace and Freedom (WILPF, 1919) by women from several nations who had sought in vain to check the conflict while it raged. Throughout the interwar period WILPF lobbied for international reconciliation from an office in Geneva, popularized disarmament, and provided an agency through which well-informed women in Europe and North America could express themselves on international affairs. Two of its leaders became Nobel Peace Prize laureates—Jane Addams (1931) and Emily Greene Balch (1946). Although many of its members were, like Addams, absolute pacifists, its programs reflected liberal internationalism. In 1955, WILPF had not regained its prewar peak of 50,000 members, but it had national chapters in sixteen countries and was expanding to the Third World. It provided a network through which some 4,500 peace-minded women in the United States and their counterparts abroad could address issues such as the arms race, and it was a major international nongovernmental organization.

The apprehensions and visions generated by Word War II yielded two other organizations central to liberal peace advocacy in 1955. Horrified by the devastation of Hiroshima and Nagasaki, and sensitive to the danger of proliferating nuclear weapons, scientists formed a series of groups which by 1946 had become the Federation of American Scientists. The Federation linked some two thousand scientists in a program of stopping the arms race, and its *Bulletin* was widely read outside the scientific community. About the same time, a number of organizations were founded in the hope of making the UN into an organization more truly capable of enforcing a lawful world order. Several of them joined to form the United World Federalists (UWF, 1947). Within two years the UWF had some forty thousand dues-paying members in over seven hundred local chapters and an array of sponsors in the intellectual and political elite. In the late 1940s, supranationalism enjoyed widespread support, measured in terms of polls, citizen groups, and resolutions passed by state legislatures.[7]

As the Cold War hardened at the end of decade, UWF membership plummeted—down by over half in 1952—and its leadership was put on the defensive. The political activity of scientists likewise waned.[8] The notion of world government narrowed to a proposal for a federation of Western democracies, a 1930s idea revived by the Atlantic Union Committee, and even that was put off to a distant future as the United States shouldered the responsibility of containing communist expansion. Only gradually did it become apparent that in the early Cold War, as Harold Josephson has observed, "American policymakers ... used the rhetoric and symbols of pre–World War [II] internationalism *principally* to win support for the expansion of U.S. power" and unilateralist foreign policy.[9] By the mid-1950s, internationalism was in disarray and many of its proponents were Cold Warriors. For those who were not, the nuclear arms race offered an issue around which to rally.

Liberal peace advocates could be identified by those to whom they looked for inspiration, people like Norman Thomas and Norman Cousins; by the magazines to which they subscribed, journals such as the *Nation,* the *New Republic,* the *Christian Century,* or the *Bulletin of the Atomic Scientists*; or by the various organizations they supported, notably the United World Federalists, the Federation of American Scientists, and the Women's International League for Peace and Freedom. Advancing various analyses and prescriptions, they neither shared a single understanding of the Cold War crisis nor offered a common solution for it. They were simply people of liberal temperament who wanted the United States to lead the nations away from an ongoing competition for armed superiority, to minimize international tensions and organize a consensual world order through negotiations and conciliation. Norman Thomas caught the flavor of renewal in 1955 when he wrote, "Never was I surer than now that practically and emotionally, lovers of peace must concentrate on their drive for controlled disarmament."[10]

Thomas was still vigorous at seventy-one. He dominated a rostrum with his six feet two inches of height and his command of fact seasoned with wit, and he was one of the nation's most respected public speakers. It had not always been so. Coming from a conservative Ohio family of ministers and missionaries, he had been exposed to the reality of social despair only when he worked in New York immigrant parishes. He encountered progressive thought there and at Union Theological Seminary. During World War I, Thomas crossed over from reform to dissent, challenging American intervention and defending the rights of conscientious objectors to military service. He joined the Socialist party because of its unequivocal antiwar stand and because socialism offered a way to apply the Social Gospel to the roots of injustice which he identified with war. That was not a popular stand, and the party was devastated by repression and factionalism.

Attracting liberal and intellectual support after the war, Thomas stood as a Socialist candidate in several local elections and in 1928 ran as the party's presidential candidate. He renewed that campaign every four years through 1948, using it as a platform from which to critique three administrations. Threading his way through internecine party conflicts, he subordinated Marxist dogma to his vision of collective social values.

In the late thirties he organized a coalition against American intervention in European war, but after Pearl Harbor he accepted the inevitability of war while advocating a postwar order based on internationalism and social justice. He was skeptical of formulas based on either world government or a consort of great powers. Neither seemed to take into account the economic and social revolutions which, he believed, were about to sweep through the world. Thomas adamantly opposed Stalinism, but he believed that containment had to be flexible, especially in the Third World, where confrontation would stifle the force of inexorable change until it was unleashed with violence. He worried about the arms race because of the propensity for power to become an end in itself. Although he had marshalled the Socialist party for a generation, Norman Thomas articulated essentially liberal values.

Many peace advocates were motivated, as Thomas was, by the values of liberal religion, and in fact a few religious groups were harbingers of the peace movement's renaissance. Early in 1955 peace-seekers in the national Methodist Conference inaugurated a "prayer chain" for peace, while the General Assembly of the Presbyterian Church commended the value of "dynamic peaceful competition."[11] Typically, given almost forty years of continuous peace action, Quakers in the American Friends Service Committee (AFSC, 1917) issued the sharpest faith-based challenge to the pursuit of peace through armed preeminence.

In a landmark statement, *Speak Truth to Power,* the AFSC declared that modern military preparations possessed such awesome destructive power that they were self-defeating in two crucial ways: armaments could no longer protect people from external threats without disastrous harm; and the pursuit of ever more destructive weaponry only aggravated national insecurity at the expense of individual freedom. "Man simply cannot make peace and prepare for war at the same time," said the Friends' statement, "any more than he can simultaneously support and oppose revolutions." The choice before modern peoples was no longer only between communism and democracy. The AFSC committee which wrote the pamphlet was pacifist, but it neatly summarized the disposition of liberal peace advocates: "the real choice lies between continuing to deal with international problems on the old basis of military power and attempting to deal with them on the new and revolutionary basis of nonviolence."[12]

A few liberals proposed more concrete critiques of the prevailing Cold War. Thus a former American ambassador to India, Chester Bowles, warned against both Soviet adventurism in the Third World and anticommunist extremism in America. Bowles called upon the U.S. government to take greater risks for "drastic and comprehensive" disarmament and also to employ more aggressive social and economic reforms toward "a complete democratic revolution at home and in the developing world."[13] Norman Cousins, editor of the *Saturday Review of Literature,* concentrated on the nuclear threat. He brought it home by directing a campaign to provide reconstructive surgery in New York City for twenty-five young Hiroshima women disfigured in the world's first atomic attack.

The urbane Cousins had become full editor of the *Saturday Review* in 1942 at age twenty-seven, two years after joining the staff and scarcely a decade after graduating from Columbia Teachers College. By this time he had assimilated the idealism of Emerson and Gandhi. From a wide-ranging study of ancient Greek city-states and American constitutionalism, he had generalized the notion that world federalism was a logical and necessary culmination of the nation-state system. This idea he pursued assiduously during World War II in the concrete form of the United Nations. His satisfaction with the UN was rudely shaken, however, by the nuclear destruction of Hiroshima. "Modern Man is Obsolete," he wrote in his most famous editorial, and world federalism was now urgent. Cousins participated in the formation of the UWF and became one of its vice-presidents. When the organization was choked down by McCarthyism, he took on its presidency, trying to rally people back to its vision. "Seven years ago, when world law was mentioned, people said it was too soon," he complained in 1952. "Now when it is mentioned, they say it is too late."[14] On the contrary, Cousins insisted, world government was precisely most relevant in the nuclear age.

Indeed, the issue of nuclear arms provided leverage for liberal peace-seekers. It attracted the most potent element among them—those scientists who criticized the escalating arms race and called for negotiated disarmament. In 1954 physicist Ralph Lapp and others called attention to the dangers of radioactive fallout from atmospheric nuclear testing and derided Washington's attempts to minimize the gravity of the issue. In July of the following year, British philosopher Bertrand Russell released a statement signed by him, the late Albert Einstein (who had died on 18 April), and nine other prominent scientists, which called upon super-power leaders "to acknowledge publicly" that modern weapons threatened "the continued existence of mankind" and made peace imperative to biological survival. Gravely, the Russell-Einstein appeal urged people to think creatively about a problem that was "stark and dreadful and inescapable: Shall we put an end to the human race; or shall mankind renounce War?"[15] Forty Nobel Prize–winning scientists issued a similar statement, warning that it was "a delusion if governments believe that they can avoid war for a long time through the fear of these weapons."[16] The Federation of American Scientists called for an international test-ban treaty and extensive disarmament agreements, and a group of Soviet and American scientists began to discuss the possibility of joint meetings to address the common crisis. Within two years, at Pugwash, Nova Scotia, the scientists initiated a series of scientific conferences on the social dangers being produced by their own rational inquiries.

Although liberal peace advocates were in some measure moralists, they were mainly reformers. They feared that American democracy was succumbing to a disastrous "apathy or fatalism" that permitted faith in superior nuclear weaponry to become the "real national religion" at the expense of any alternative formulation of national interest or security.[17] Moreover, they believed that peace required a process of social and economic change that was best promoted through American support of international agencies and multilateral cooperation—through UN peace-keeping efforts instead of unilateral American intervention in world trouble spots, through technical and economic aid rather than military assistance. At most, peace liberals hoped for a reformed world order that might constrain national rivalries, temper Soviet-American antagonism, and open the way for orderly disarmament. At least, they opposed the continuing escalation of the nuclear arms race. Most of them were suspicious of ideologies. Few were interested in a mass movement. They were inclined to use the means of persuasion and advocacy within established institutions. Having been virtually cut out of the mainstream of political life by the conversion of many liberals to the aggressive prosecution of the Cold War and by the attacks of right-wing McCarthyism, liberal peace advocates seemed almost restless to return to the public forum in 1955.

They did not expect much from the Democratic party, smarting from Republican charges of disloyalty and treason while harboring liberals committed to a kind of Pax Americana. The party clung in the mid-fifties to core constituencies among southern white conservatives, ethnic Roman Catholics, and anticommunist AFL-CIO labor leaders. Its left wing included a broad spectrum of liberals, including such prominent intellectuals as John Kenneth Galbraith and Arthur M. Schlesinger, Jr., who extolled the progressive tradition of Franklin D. Roosevelt and the droll style of former Illinois governor Adlai Stevenson. They favored pragmatic solutions to social problems and rejected out of hand authoritarian ideologies. Associated especially in Americans for Democratic Action (ADA, 1947), they endorsed the containment of communism and a kind of New Deal for areas emerging from colonial rule.

The peace concerns of Democratic liberals appeared problematic, particularly as the party's left came under pressure from a rising lobby of ambitious southern and western politicians and their corporate sponsors. Goaded by leading liberals such as former world federalist Thomas Finletter, this promilitary faction came forward in the middle fifties as the fresh voice of pragmatic liberalism, warning of alleged Soviet expansionism and calling for massive federal arms expenditures in order to move the country beyond Eisenhower's alleged complacency. In the summer of 1955, Senator Stuart Symington (D-Mo.) charged that the Soviets had established a dangerous "bomber gap" over the United States, and Senator Henry Jackson (D-Wash.) demanded a crash program for the development of intercontinental ballistic missiles. Peace liberals chafed under this latest twist in the politics of pragmatic liberalism. The "Democrats are still a cold war party," wrote journalist I. F. Stone in October, "and the prospect of their return to power at this time is appalling."[18]

Accordingly, liberal peace advocates reentered politics by supporting Eisenhower's attempts to relax superpower tensions. The Geneva summit conference aroused unreal hope. "Suddenly," gushed the *Christian Century,* "it looks as though something approximating a general peace ... can be attained. This chance must not be allowed to slip through our fingers!"[19] Lauding the president as a champion of true peace, the United World Federalists announced their support of his initiatives.

"We mean to speak now with the weight of our whole lives"

The smaller but more cohesive wing of the resurgent peace movement consisted of pacifists, including those who refused to participate in Operation Alert. They were radical in the root sense of the word—fundamental. They rejected war absolutely, refusing on principle to sanction or participate in it. In that sense, their pacifism was rooted in a tradition which stretched back throughout Christian history but was most explicitly represented by the Anabaptist sects and the Society of Friends (Quakers). It was the position of religious nonresistants in the early nineteenth-century American peace movement, and it had been partially secularized in twentieth-century war resistance and conscientious objection.

The word *pacifism* was coined in 1901, in fact, to identify advocates of peace generally. During and after World War I, especially in England and the United States, the word was narrowed to refer to those who rejected war altogether. In truth, however, many of those to whom the restricted definition was applied were also peace advocates in the more general sense. They were grounded in a tradition with roots in Quakerism, or in classic liberalism and liberal religion, one which had evolved an orientation to social reform. The pacifist community included, therefore, liberal internationalists and reformers who identified peace with justice and basic social change. Throughout the interwar period these pacifists actively promoted international cooperation and domestic reform. Pacifists active in the peace movement (but by no means most pacifists) shared this liberal orientation toward social issues along with their radical rejection of war on a personal level.

Meanwhile, a few pacifists, committed to both peace and social justice, elaborated a philosophy of nonviolence which drew on the work of the Indian liberation leader Mohandas Gandhi. In particular, they espoused disciplined, nonviolent direct action to reshape social values and institutions, and they sought to adapt it to the American scene. By 1955 there was an incipient form of pacifism with a politically radical nuance. Its adherents differed from traditional pacifists, whose absolute repudiation of war and military service did not extend to activism, and also from liberal pacifists, whose efforts for social reform did not extend to direct action or civil disobedience. Radical pacifists were not necessarily revolutionaries. They repudiated violence, and their activism was consonant with selective reform. Humankind does not live by definitions, however, and the ambiguity associated with the word *radical* would become associated with the word *pacifist*.

"Inner-directed persons," in the parlance of the time, radical pacifists had little use for directive leaders or formal organizations. They looked instead for inspiration to exemplary figures, notably to Abraham J. Muste. Lean and lanky at seventy, utterly unassuming but serenely self-confident, Muste had been labeled by *Time* magazine the "Number One U.S. Pacifist" during World War II, when he had pled indiscriminately for justice— for the victims of the Nazi holocaust and the German civilians targeted in Allied firebombings, for opponents of conscription and Japanese-Americans held in relocation camps, for international order and black civil rights. Even his opponents conceded his utter integrity and undaunted vision. His friends relished his sense of humor and love of baseball but worried when his few tattered suits were falling apart.

Six years after his birth, Muste's Dutch family immigrated to America and settled in Michigan. A. J. (as he was widely known) grew up there, deeply imbued with the Dutch Reformed piety of his parents and later of Hope College. At the same time, his mind was inquiring and his spirit restless. While on the east coast for training at New Brunswick Seminary, he absorbed the Social Gospel and socialist thought. He moved from Dutch Reformed to Congregational and Quaker ministries during World War I but found his true congregation in a small band of socially conscious pacifists. During the 1920s he directed Brookwood Labor College, a training school for union leaders. In the depression years he moved directly into labor organizing and headed the American Workers party, which he merged with the Trotskyist Workers party of the United States. The pacifist witness against all violence became tenuous in his crusade for social justice. By 1936 he was thoroughly exhausted, and friends raised funds to send him and his wife to Europe to recuperate. Suddenly cut apart from the turmoil in America and seeing the rising violence in Europe, Muste experienced a revelation which restored his religious and pacifist compass. He returned to the United States committed to Christian nonviolence without in the least foregoing his penchant for radical social transformation.

Indeed, he insisted that the pursuit of peace and justice would be corrupted unless it was pursued nonviolently. In this spirit, he welcomed Gandhian models of social action, nurturing them within the black civil rights movement, and he rejected the militaristic polarization of the Cold War. Articulate in speech and writing, Muste could reason with intellectuals; experienced in radical movements, he could rally activists; self-consciously prophetic, he could distinguish vision from reality. He did not act the part of a hero. He just modeled what he believed, and his radical pacifism was the more accessible for that.

Although pacifists did not define themselves in terms of organizational loyalties, there were four groups of particular importance to them in the mid-1950s: the Fellowship of Reconciliation, the American Friends Service Committee, the War Resisters League, and the Catholic Worker Movement.

The latter two were the smaller and more radically pacifist. The War Resisters League (WRL) was founded in 1923 as the American branch of an international association which sought to move from individual conscientious objection to collective, public resistance to war. The War Resisters International was a home for a few democratic socialists and anarchists in Europe and the United States who rejected violent and manipulative political strategy during the interwar years. In World War II the WRL became a support group for conscientious objectors whose orientation was anarchist and secular, and from them came a strong emphasis on revolutionary civil disobedience in the late 1940s. The WRL neither held meetings nor formed local groups among its twelve hundred members, relying for influence instead on the effort of a handful of people in a single office at 5 Beekman Street, New York, to organize protest actions and publicize their views. The Catholic Worker Movement was a tiny but tenacious fellowship begun in 1933 by itinerant French mystic Peter Maurin and journalist Dorothy Day. From a social service center on Manhattan's lower East Side, it extended its doctrine of prophetic love to the repudiation of war, and its loving concern for social outcasts to Catholic conscientious objectors. It measured its outreach by readers of Day's penny-a-copy *Catholic Worker* and by the examples of its leaders.

The Fellowship of Reconciliation (FOR) began in 1915 amidst opposition to World War I, and it served as a community of support for conscientious objectors to that war. Thereafter it promoted social justice and internationalism, opposing war and other forms of violence. It was in the FOR, to cite an example, that an American version of nonviolent action was first hammered out by Muste and others. The Fellowship was sustained by an essentially Christian vision and was the principal association for a wide range of absoute pacifists: its twelve thousand members explicitly pledged neither to take part in war nor to "sanction military preparations." It operated from a converted mansion high above the Hudson River in Nyack, New York.

The American Friends Service Committee also originated in World War I, initially to provide alternative service for conscientious objectors from the Society of Friends. Its Quaker orientation led it to other forms of social service and reconciliation after the war and from domestic to international action. Indeed, its extraordinary relief work during and after World War II earned it a Nobel Peace Prize in 1947. It was supported mainly by private contributions, and the measure of its influence was its programs and outreach rather than membership. Whereas the FOR was a fellowship of pacifists, the AFSC was a service agency imbued by a Quaker and pacifist ethos. Its offices were appropriately located in Penn's city, Philadelphia. Closely related to the AFSC through Quaker networks was the Friends Committee on National Legislation (FCNL) in Washington. Also supported by private contributions rather than by a membership, the FCNL had developed in the 1930s into an efficient political lobbying organization.

The AFSC and the FOR occupied a special place in the regenerating peace movement of the 1950s. Both had been active in the internationalist and anti-intervention campaigns of the thirties and had engaged in political action. Both had supported internationalism in the world federalist era of the 1940s. Each was on the one hand an expression of the liberal Social Gospel emphasis on political engagement for peace and justice and, on the other, an agency of the pacifist conscience. Each served traditional pacifists, whose witness against war was individual, and also radical pacifists disposed to direct social action. Both organizations were thus liberal in approach and pacifist in belief (a similar tension prevailed in WILPF, although it was not formally a pacifist organization). This distinctive quality prepared them to mediate among the fragmenting elements of the antiwar movement in the 1960s—and to be strained in the process.

Radical pacifists opposed all military preparations, defended individual conscientious objection to conscription, and argued for the decentralization and democratization of global power and resources. They believed that Washington and Moscow were both responsible for the Cold War, and they called for an immediate halt to the arms race through unilateral and negotiated disarmament. They welcomed popular nonviolent revolutions in the Third World, believing that self-determination and justice was the most reliable way around the superpower conflict. Muste and others promoted this alternative as the Third Camp position, a universal movement of liberation rather than the formation of a regional block.

Drawn to the defense of the powerless, radical pacifists believed that peace required individual acts of resistance to challenge arbitrary authority based on violent force and open the way for physical and spiritual liberation. Peace meant saying "No to power," Muste wrote, and *"action now"* for the emancipation of "all individuals from domination, whether military, economic, political, or cultural." It meant work for human liberation and global reconstruction "on the basis of love and not power."[20] Third World peoples should be liberated from the neo-imperialist dominance of former colonial powers. Western peoples should be liberated from the alienation of modern corporate and bureaucratic society. Apathetic white Americans should be freed from their political passivity, and black Americans from the evil of racial segregation.

When a few pacifists at the University of Chicago began to challenge segregation with nonviolent techniques during World War II, Muste was quick to recognize the potential of nonviolent action in the American civil rights struggle. He supported James Farmer, Bayard Rustin, and others as they expanded their efforts into a national Congress of Racial Equality (CORE, 1943).[21] Most of the early CORE members were FOR pacifists. They scored isolated victories in the North and West and challenged segregation on interstate buses with a 1948 Freedom Ride into the upper South. Gradually, they built a base of experience and organization until the sudden advance of the nonviolent civil rights movement in the mid-fifties concentrated new attention on radical pacifism and hastened its development. In December 1955, after Rosa Parks was arrested for refusing to leave her seat in the whites-only section of a municipal bus, the black community of Montgomery, Alabama, rose up in a remarkably disciplined nonviolent protest that soon elevated a young Baptist minister named Martin Luther King, Jr., to leadership. At his side during the months of struggle were advisors from the FOR and CORE.

The Montgomery black protest mushroomed from a bus boycott into a wide-ranging attack upon the whole structure of racial segregation, from a local quarrel into a full-blown nonviolent movement to secure black civil rights in voting, educational opportunity, and equal access in public accommodations. Peace activists joined with many other change-minded Americans to throw resources and bodies behind the black struggle. From Richmond to Little Rock, whites often reacted with violence, and yet the movement pressed forward irrepressibly. Through it pacifists grasped the possibility of a radically different society obtained through nonviolent change. In the process, radical pacifism was transformed into a political force which eventually linked the civil rights and antiwar movements.

It was not that historic outcome which motivated radical pacifists in 1955. Unabashedly, they were moralists responding to their immediate sense of duty and utopians resolved to act upon their dreams. Author and social critic C. Wright Mills, although not a pacifist, appreciated that feeling when he wrote, "What the powerful call utopia is now in fact the condition for human survival."[22]

Peace required justice, radical pacifists believed, and the liberation of people from arbitrary, coercive authority had to be embodied in the authenticating individual act. That conviction had led a small group of pacifists to undertake civil disobedience during Operation Alert, 15 June 1955. Inspired by Ammon Hennacy and Dorothy Day of the Catholic Worker Movement, the group included several WRL leaders, A. J. Muste of the FOR, and Orlie Pell, president of the U.S. Section of WILPF. Although arrested and found guilty, they were not imprisoned because the judge, as he explained, did not want to make martyrs of them. They did not think of themselves as martyrs. Pell wrote, rather, that her decision to stand up against the laws of the state finally touched her "directly as a person." After twenty years of citizen peace activism, the criminal decision not to hide from a simulated atomic bomb forced her to confront her "*innermost* self," and to conclude, "deep down inside: here I stand— I can do no other."[23]

In an attempt to give a voice to people like Orlie Pell, a handful of democratic socialists, anarchists, and radical pacifists developed a monthly journal under the leadership of David Dellinger. Then forty-one, Dellinger gave the hope of social transformation a pacifist twist. Born into a socially prominent Massachusetts family of colonial heritage, he had graduated from Yale and studied at New College, Oxford, and Union Theological Seminary. Something in him rebelled at conventionality, however, including support for World War II. Imprisoned for resisting the draft, he was one of several pacifists to challenge prison and draft rules with nonviolent action. Dellinger interpreted this as a token of resistance to a repressive political system. In 1945 he established *Direct Action,* a small journal which promoted democratic socialism and abjured violent revolution. The thin ranks of radical pacifists were slightly augmented then by a few social commentators, notably Trotskyist literary critic Dwight Macdonald, who had become disillusioned with revolutionary socialism but remained dissatisfied with conventional liberalism. Encouraged, Dellinger helped to organize a Committee for Non-Violent Revolution in hopes of giving form to radical pacifism, but little came of it. He was living out his views in the collective obscurity of a cooperative community in Glen Garden, New Jersey, in the winter of 1955–56 when *Liberation* was founded. A minor editor and writer, fervent in the pursuit of both social justice and personal righteousness, skeptical of coercive government to the point of anarchism, Dave Dellinger was poised to become the William Lloyd Garrison of the antiwar movement of the 1960s. Whether or not he intended it, even the name of his little journal recalled Garrison's *Liberator.*

Eclectic and utopian, the new journal was designed to be a forum for ideas and reports on the "political fundamentalism" of nonviolent revolutionary politics and active individual resistance.[24] Its contributing authors ranged from Dorothy Day to Michael Harrington and included historian William Hesseltine, political scientist Herbert Kelman, novelist Norman Mailer, and urban historian and critic Lewis Mumford, among others, but its editorial board was drawn rigorously from the WRL.[25] *Liberation* protested both the "political slavery" of Soviet-style Marxism and the crying social inequities of western capitalism. Its editors had little faith in technology and a strong attachment to the "direct participation of all workers or citizens in determining the conditions of life and work." They believed that the danger of war required individual, immediate "withdrawal of support" from the military preparations of the world's two major power blocs. "Whatever differences may exist between Communist and 'free world' regimes, in this decisive respect they are *equal* threats, two sides of the *same* threat to survival of civilization. The H-bomb is not an instrument of peace in the hands of one and of war in the hands of the other."[26]

The founders of *Liberation* presumed the need for a "here-and-now revolution" that would begin as an individual lived "in his own life" a "union of politics and religion" on the assumption that "the problems of changing society and of changing ourselves are inseparable."[27] Contending that the deed is always mightier than the sword, the editors proclaimed that it was time for experimental, nonviolent "personalist action" against "all the ways in which human beings are regimented and corrupted, dehumanized and deprived of their freedom."[28] They approached peace through the liberating power of revolutionary nonviolence: "What matters to us," they wrote, "is what happens to the individual human being—here and now."[29]

Liberation signalled a new moment in American radical culture and politics. It gave radical pacifism a revolutionary wing, and it crystalized many of the differences between radical pacifists and other peace advocates, thereby defining the terrain on which the evolving antiwar movement would fragment between 1955 and 1975.[30]

The differences within the movement were sometimes personal and even accidental. Mainly, however, they were immediate, pointed, and profound. Whereas liberal peace advocates sought through informed criticism to strengthen America's international leadership for peace, radicals considered the U.S. government as culpable as any other power for the inequity and instability in the world. Whereas liberals stressed international law and order as instruments for peace and justice, radicals would resort to the liberation and empowerment of disadvantaged people. Whereas liberals argued for policy change in Washington, radical pacifists called for the transformation of the very structure of wealth and power in America and the world. Whereas liberals called for electoral action and citizen lobbying, radicals demanded a personal commitment to non-violent direct action and civil disobedience against unjust social structures.

Perhaps most basically, whereas liberals tried to build a political basis for policy and even institutional change, radical pacifists intended to transform America's core ideals and governing consciousness. At this stage of history, radicals maintained, "The very presuppositions on which human relationships are based must be revolutionized." Questions of war and peace entailed far more than shifts in existing political relationships or the displacement of ruling groups. They required fundamental change. Toward that end radical pacifists promised, "We mean to speak now with the weight of our whole lives."[31]

Two

Coalescing Organization

"The time has come for a fresh examination
of the main issues"

Prospects for influencing national policy turned first on the question of atmospheric nuclear testing. That issue, with attendant concerns about health and genetic hazards, invaded the national consciousness in the spring of 1954, when debris from a U.S. hydrogen bomb test in the western Pacific fell upon Japanese fishermen aboard the *Lucky Dragon* and awakened widespread fear over the wind-borne dangers of atmospheric fallout. The Atomic Energy Commission (AEC), which had been formed that year to oversee American nuclear development, tried to discount popular anxiety as both U.S. and Soviet diplomats rejected an Indian proposal for a "truce" on the testing of new weapons.

Critics bristled at the superpowers' soothing claims. Several atomic scientists protested that continued testing would produce a significant increase in cancers and birth defects. Pleaded journalist I. F. Stone, "If there is still a peace movement left in America, this must be its platform. As a first step away from mutual destruction, no more tests."[1]

Early in 1956 established peace organizations like WILPF as well as ad hoc groups urged the cancellation of America's scheduled Pacific test series. The issue became political in April, when Democratic presidential candidate Adlai Stevenson called for a ban on H-bomb tests. President Eisenhower dismissed Stevenson's proposal as "theatrical," and Vice-President Richard Nixon thought it subversive. Backed by public opinion opposed to the test-ban idea, the administration insisted that any steps toward disarmament must follow prior Soviet-American agreement on mutual inspection and verification. The White House position hardened in August, when the Russians resumed testing. Eisenhower denounced that, and the Soviets responded by proposing an international test ban agreement, which the administration interpreted as a communist ploy.

Undeterred, Stevenson pressed his proposal for a test-ban treaty. In October, encouraged by growing popular concern over an increase in carcinogenic strontium 90 in milk supplies and consequently in children's bones, the Democratic candidate declared that the thermonuclear testing question constituted the key to more peaceable international relations. He promised that "the first order of business" of his presidency would be an international agreement ending H-bomb tests and an effort to end the "madness" of striving for a preponderance of terror weapons.[2]

Although Stevenson lost decisively in the November elections, his emphasis upon nuclear fallout and a test ban contributed to the resurgence of citizen peace activism in at least two ways. First, sizable numbers of veteran peace-seekers, concerned with fallout and encouraged by what Robert Divine has called Stevenson's "remarkable feat of public education," decided to organize with a vigor not seen since the world federalist crusade of the late 1940s.[3] Second, growing opposition to atomic testing encouraged the country's peace activists to mount a broad challenge to America's role in the nuclear arms race, its larger Cold War strategies, and the military orientation of U.S. foreign policy. Citizen peace advocates saw the need for a test-ban treaty and an end to the fallout menace in both substantive and symbolic terms. Substantively, they viewed fallout as an indiscriminate attack upon uncounted innocents. Symbolically, they treated the test-ban issue as a politically viable step toward Soviet-American disarmament.

Thus, although the resurgent peace movement was organized around the test-ban issue, its larger purpose was to challenge the arms race. "An ending will never be possible until a beginning is made," maintained the *Christian Century* early in 1958. A test-ban agreement was a minimal beginning: "It is not the whole way to nuclear disarmament, but it is the necessary first move."[4] About the same time, George Kennan, the influential foreign policy analyst who had first articulated containment theory, appealed for a great-power disengagement and a political settlement in Europe. "The time has come," he wrote, ". . . for a fresh examination of the main issues" dividing Washington and Moscow and driving "everyone deeper and deeper into the hopeless exertions of the weapons race."[5]

The time was not yet propitious for innovation. Successive domestic and international crises in 1956 put a premium on safe politics. In the United States a civil rights movement unrolled to challenge racial segregation in Montgomery buses and Little Rock schools, while angry and often violent white opposition flared. Abroad, the German question remained unsettling. Russian premier Nikita Khrushchev denounced the terror of Joseph Stalin's generation-long rule and unleashed a wave of uncertainty within international communism which aggravated the estrangement of Beijing from Moscow. In the Middle East war broke out in October when Egypt closed the Suez Canal and was attacked by Britain,

France, and Israel. Unexpectedly, America and Russia were aligned on a demand for an immediate cease-fire and allied withdrawal. Shortly, mass uprisings against communist rule erupted in Poland and Hungary, resulting in brutal Soviet suppression with the United States helpless to intervene.

Tacitly but plainly, Washington and Moscow accepted their respective positions in Europe and shifted their rivalry to the Third World, where the rise of the anticolonial, revolutionary nationalism appeared to both powers as a challenge and an opportunity. In January 1957 the president proclaimed the so-called Eisenhower Doctrine: the U.S. government was prepared to intervene militarily in the Middle East to preserve the status quo allegedly endangered by Soviet-sponsored aggression.

Then international tensions seemed to wane, providing an opening for fresh attempts at citizen peace activism. From San Francisco, for example, young Robert Pickus organized a program called Acts for Peace. Formerly peace secretary for the Chicago office of the AFSC, Pickus developed a coordinated program for a dozen pacifist and nonpacifist organizations to introduce peace issues on a community level in local groups ranging from the Chamber of Commerce to parent-teacher associations. On a national level a network of scholars, including sociologist Kenneth Boulding and mathematician Anatol Rapaport, launched the *Journal of Conflict Resolution* at the University of Michigan, opening a new field of peace research that would focus social scientific inquiry upon "the greatest problem of our time—the prevention of war."[6]

The nuclear issue—atmospheric testing and the related arms race—remained the fulcrum of peace activism. In England pacifists, peace workers, and leftists assembled the Campaign for Nuclear Disarmament (CND), contending that "mere vague condemnation of atomic weapons is not enough, and that some definite action must be taken."[7] Within a year they massed ten thousand people to walk from a nuclear weapons research facility at Aldermaston to London in the first of an annual series of English and American Easter peace marches. Moreover, in preparing for the march, CND organizers developed a symbol that fixed the semaphore symbols for the letters *N* and *D* in white against a black background within a circle. The background signified eternity, the circle the world, and the letters their cause. The antinuclear origin of this "peace" symbol would be lost in its ubiquity during the Vietnam era.

In the United States, meanwhile, citizens stepped up demands for an atmospheric test-ban agreement. Norman Cousins made a personal visit to Dr. Albert Schweitzer, appealing to him to speak out on the issue. On 23 April the Swiss-born physician, whose lifework in serving the people of French Equatorial Africa had established him as the most widely respected humanitarian of his time, issued a "Declaration of Conscience," in which he protested the health hazards of nuclear fallout and called for a general test ban. Building on Schweitzer's appeal, Linus Pauling, a Nobel laureate in chemistry, orchestrated an international test-ban petition which eventually won over eleven thousand signatures from scientists in forty-nine countries. By June a couple of thousand Americans had signed, and on their behalf Pauling submitted the statement to Eisenhower.[8]

While Pauling organized scientists, Nevil Shute touched the heart of the public with a novel prefaced by T. S. Eliot's haunting lines:

> In this last of meeting places
> We grope together
> And avoid speech
> Gathered on this beach of the tumid river . . .
>
> *This is the way the world ends*
> *This is the way the world ends*
> *This is the way the world ends*
> *Not with a bang but a whimper.*

Unlike John Hershey's *Hiroshima,* Shute's *On the Beach* did not recount the destruction and chaos of a nuclear attack, only death on the wind and quiet human responses to the inevitable. An American submarine is stranded in Australia after a nuclear war. Human life in the northern hemisphere has been extinguished, and the charged atmosphere drifts southward. "There's no hope at all, is there? For any of us?" an Australian woman says to her husband, who replies, "Nobody gets over this one, dear."[9] *On the Beach* sold a hundred thousand copies within six weeks of its publication, was serialized in forty newspapers, became a forceful Stanley Kramer movie, and evoked the deep anxiety of many Americans over lingering death by fallout. Encouraged by evidence of popular concern, church groups, peace organizations, and political figures called for a ban on atmospheric atomic testing.

Nonetheless, the president insisted that he would consider a test ban only as part of a larger, safeguarded disarmament package. Other officials turned more aggressively upon the critics. Commissioner Willard Libby of the AEC attempted to refute Schweitzer's fears about fallout, but he attracted fresh attention to the physician's concern. Congressman Lawrence Smith (R-Conn.) charged that protest against atmospheric testing was communist in origin, and the Senate Internal Security Subcommittee announced plans to subpoena Pauling in order to determine possible communist involvement in the scientists' petition. In a press conference Eisenhower charged that the test-ban efforts were apparently "organized," although not by any "wicked" organization. The newsweekly *U.S. News and World Report* was less discriminating. In a story entitled "What's Back of the 'Fall-Out' Scare," *U.S. News* detected a "pattern which suggests that much of the agitation against British and American tests is Communist-inspired."[10]

Eisenhower was closer to the truth. An organized movement in favor of a test ban was taking shape early in 1957, chiefly through the efforts of established peace activists. Early in the year the AFSC peace education directors in Chicago and New York, Lawrence Scott and Robert Gilmore, spurred radical pacifists and peace liberals to mobilize fresh citizen activism against the arms race and the larger Cold War. A number of peace liberals such as Norman Thomas and radical pacifists such as A. J. Muste met on 22 April in Philadelphia, where they agreed upon the need for a dual approach that would address the concerns of both major peace factions: one to mobilize radical pacifists for direct action against the arms race, and a second to rally popular opinion against atmospheric fallout and for disarmament and a strengthened world order. It was understood that older, established peace organizations such as the FOR, WILPF and the AFSC would support both approaches.[11]

There emerged over the next several months two new agencies: the Committee for Non-Violent Action (CNVA) and the Committee for a Sane Nuclear Policy (SANE). Originally conceived as ad hoc groups, neither was built upon any detailed constitutional formulas, nor were they joined in any formal way. They were closely linked through both the joint participation and personal ties of a few leaders and a common interest in "some organic and spiritual relationship."[12] They constituted the twin engines of an accelerating peace movement.

First meeting as the Nonviolent Action Against Nuclear Weapons, CNVA originated in the determination of radical pacifists "to go beyond words," to undertake direct action against the expanding arms race.[13] Its opening action centered on the U.S. nuclear tests scheduled for the government's Nevada test site in early August. After weeks of planning under project director Larry Scott, thirty pacifists gathered for vigils outside the Las Vegas offices of the Atomic Energy Commission. With substantial media attention, they initiated disciplined civil disobedience on 6 August, the twelfth anniversary of the Hiroshima bombing. Eleven were arrested for trespassing as they tried to enter the gates of the test site at Camp Mercury, seventy miles northwest of Las Vegas. Quickly tried, convicted, and released with suspended sentences, they returned to the entrance of the test site for a prayer vigil. The white light of the first explosion in the test series convinced them that, as one recalled, "our intuition, our feeling, and our senses were right. We knew that we could never rest while such forces of evil were loose in God's world."[14]

Stimulated by the Nevada Project, three hundred participants from eight pacifist organizations conducted an eleven-day Prayer and Conscience Vigil in Washington in November in an attempt "to use spiritual resources to change the heart of the Eisenhower administration."[15] They marched around the White House, distributed leaflets at the AEC offices, and turned out for speeches by writer Lewis Mumford and others, but they could not reach the people in power. Twice in 1957 peace activists from WILPF and the AFSC tried to submit to the president petitions bearing the names of some thirty thousand people opposed to the continuation of atmospheric testing. Both times they were refused admission to the White House grounds and had to deposit their petitions with guards at the gates.

Meanwhile, the small coalition of radical pacifists and peace liberals created the Committee for a Sane Nuclear Policy. In order to provide an organizational focus, they enlisted Norman Cousins and Clarence Pickett (executive secretary of the AFSC when it shared the 1947 Nobel Peace Prize with the Friends Service Council in London). By June they were able to convene a group of leaders from the fields of literature, business, science, religion, and labor who agreed to initiate "a broad ad hoc committee" to spearhead a national citizens' campaign for a test-ban treaty.[16] Cousins and Pickett headed a steering committee, and Homer Jack, a Unitarian minister long active in national peace efforts, was designated executive secretary.

Frequently called "nuclear pacifists," the varied leaders of SANE understood that the fear of fallout from atmospheric testing was merely "a loose thread in the arms race, by which you might begin to unravel the larger fabric."[17] They wanted to take apart the whole cloth, to open a way for genuine disarmament. And yet, unlike the radical pacifists protesting at Nevada test sites, SANE leaders did little throughout the summer. In September, Pickett noted the inaction and reiterated a question that had been posed in the spring: were the existing peace organizations "doing a sufficient job to stop nuclear weapons tests or is there a genuine need for a national organization and finances and personnel?"[18]

Before Pickett and his friends could answer their own question, the arms race itself provoked a response. Early in July weapons engineers in the Nevada desert detonated their most powerful explosion yet; but fallout was reportedly kept to a minimum, and the administration expressed pleasure in its progress toward a "clean" bomb. Two months later, the AEC supervised the country's first underground atomic test and thus demonstrated a way of reconciling continued weapons development with an end to atmospheric tests. The *New York Times* military affairs writer, Hanson Baldwin, reported that (thanks largely to the influence of Harvard professor Henry Kissinger's *Nuclear Weapons and Foreign Policy*) U.S. nuclear strategists were seriously considering a major shift from the doctrine of massive retaliation to a strategy of fighting limited nuclear wars with scaled-down atomic weapons. In September, just as a new fleet of B-52 superbombers came into service in the American strategic arsenal, Soviet rocket experts successfully tested the first intercontinental ballistic missile. Then, on 4 October the Russians shocked the world by launching the first earth-orbiting space satellite, Sputnik—a feat that dramatized Moscow's capacity to deliver nuclear death to any spot on the planet in minutes.

President Eisenhower tried to play down the significance of the Soviet space achievements, but Democrats and impatient Republicans such as Nelson Rockefeller called for a tremendous increase in U.S. military spending and a commitment to win the space race. Around Thanksgiving, reports leaked out of Washington that the Gaither commission, a blue-ribbon group appointed to evaluate American defense, had recommended an enormous increase in American military expenditures, including a huge national fallout shelter program. Although the commission's extravagant proposal for civil defense was rejected by the White House, its report added to the pressure for increased military spending.[19]

Peace liberals were spun around by the storm of events. Homer Jack of SANE noted that Sputnik had aggravated "a frightening conformity" in favor of greater security through intensified weapons competition. Pointing to the Gaither commission report and other demands for increased arms buildup, Jack reported that "Peace forces in Washington are unusually glum and see little hope." I. F. Stone agreed. Contemplating the significance of Sputnik, he concluded that nothing had changed "but the magnitude of our potential for mass murder."[20]

Gathering in October, the members of the ad hoc SANE committee decided to issue a *New York Times* advertisement, written mostly by Cousins and signed by prominent liberals such as Eleanor Roosevelt and Walter Reuther, appealing for an end to testing and for action to create a working world community. The ad elicited such surprisingly high levels of grassroots enthusiasm and financial contributions that the committee was finally persuaded to establish the national membership organization they had avoided. There was, after all, a constituency ready to concentrate "people's elementary sense of realism" against the continuing arms race.[21]

Cousins and Pickett became cochairmen of the new organization, which opened an office in New York. The staff scrambled hard to keep up with demands for literature and offers of support. Within a few months, there were 130 local chapters and a membership of 25,000, mostly traditional pacifists, world federalists, Stevenson Democrats, and diverse political leftists in New York, Chicago, and San Francisco. The name, National Committee for a Sane Nuclear Policy, had been suggested by prominent psychologist and author Erich Fromm, and it aptly underscored the committee's determination to "expose the insanity" of pursuing security through a nuclear arms race. The imperative of the moment, declared longtime internationalist James T. Shotwell, required "a national campaign to regain sanity."[22]

SANE's potential for leadership was implicitly compromised at the outset. On one level it included the many national notables who lent their names to the creation of an ad hoc test-ban committee. On another it involved social activists from local peace and social reform operations who wanted a nationally coordinated test-ban campaign. Tension between the two constituencies was predictable, but their differences took on an usually sharp edge because some leaders suspected that local activists, especially those in the San Francisco and New York metropolitan areas, were either former communists who had quit the party following Khrushchev's denunciation of Stalinism or individuals uncritically sympathetic to Soviet policies. Even in the early stages of SANE, Larry Scott had worried that its organization was too loose. An ad hoc committee could not set standards for local affiliation and would be vulnerable both to communist infiltration and to charges of being a communist front, he warned. The national officers were concerned about the politics of local workers, although they resisted tight control, because they were determined to build an antitesting campaign of unquestioned political independence. "Our own position," Cousins explained to SANE's executive secretary, Trevor Thomas, "is ... to strengthen America's relationship with other peoples through the creation of a nuclear policy that can serve as a basis for world leadership."[23]

Subtle but sharp, the division within SANE over the structure of the organization and the role of alleged Soviet sympathizers within it was held in check through the rest of the 1950s. Then it erupted in 1960 and weakened the organization for the next eight years while hapless SANE activists tried to come to terms with the changing nuclear arms race and U.S. intervention in Vietnam. Robert Gilmore would be involved in SANE's 1960 crisis, but after the first year of organization he sensed only achievement and potential. SANE was rolling forward, he thought, like a "wave of concern which answers the need of doing what needs to be done."[24] By 1958, proponents of a reduction in Cold War tensions and a test-ban agreement were organized to press their case more aggressively and in a variety of ways.

Deterrence as "a pseudo peace"

Washington announced plans for a new series of atomic tests in the spring. In England, the Campaign for Nuclear Disarmament took to the streets in protest, and people also marched between New Haven and Washington. Norman Thomas, Linus Pauling, Bertrand Russell, and fifteen others filed suit in a Washington federal district court in an attempt to stop U.S. atomic testing. Naming government officials as defendants, they charged that the 1954 Atomic Energy Commission Act unconstitutionally contravened the human rights provisions of the UN Charter and that lawsuits (an identical one was filed in the Procurator's Office in Moscow)

were necessary "so that citizens might prevent officials of their governments from continuing actions that endanger us all."[25]

Radical pacifists challenged testing, too. Late in March, Albert Bigelow,
a World War II naval officer who had become a Quaker and CNVA activist,
tried to sail his thirty-foot ketch, the *Golden Rule,* into the U.S. atomic
test site at Eniwetok atoll. It felt "cowardly and degrading for me to stand
by any longer," he recalled, "to consent, and thus to collaborate in atrocities" as depraved "as the experiments performed by Nazi M.D.s on
concentration camp victims without their consent."[26] Hastily, the AEC
prohibited the unauthorized entry of civilians into the Pacific test range.
When Bigelow and his crew defied the AEC order and sailed toward the
restricted zone, they were arrested and jailed in Honolulu. Observing
this in Hawaii was Earle Reynolds, a former U.S. government employee
who had been a member of one of the first study teams in Hiroshima
after the bombing. There he had built a forty-eight-foot yacht, the *Phoenix,* which he had sailed around the world with his wife, Barbara, and
their two children. Although homeward bound, the Reynoldses elected
to complete Bigelow's voyage. They sailed into the AEC test zone, were
intercepted, and Earle Reynolds was arrested.[27] In the summer CNVA
resumed the challenge it had initiated in Nevada the year before. This
time there was civil disobedience at missile sites near Cheyenne, Wyoming, and Omaha, Nebraska. At the Cheyenne base, a number of activists
tried to block traffic by sitting in the gateway of the base. A University
of Chicago graduate student, Ken Calkins, suffered a broken pelvis when
struck by a gravel truck while contesting the road, and his injury was
compounded by a fine for trespassing.

The pacifists' sea-borne incursions and land-based actions, like the
"fallout suits," seemed quixotic and futile, naïvely proposed and incapable of tracking the country's larger apathy. And yet peace-seekers felt
impelled to act. "What can men do when no one listens to the shouting?"
asked the *Christian Century.* "They can picket, they can write poems,
they can sail boats into Pacific fallout zones, they can debate—and they
can go to court."[28]

Throughout the spring, an atmospheric test-ban treaty was endorsed
by numerous individuals and organizations, including Eleanor Roosevelt
and Albert Schweitzer, the Americans for Democratic Action and an ad
hoc group of 140 Protestant clergy and theologians. Senators Ralph Flan-
ders (R-Vt.), Hubert Humphrey (D-Minn.), and John Sparkman (D-Ala.)
publicly called for test-ban negotiations through the UN, while Adlai Stevenson lauded the reappearance of the idea in national fora. "Since
when," wondered the *Nation,* "has a political issue provoked so much
motion, as well as emotion, in mankind?" More and more people "have
grasped the profound significance of the thermonuclear blast and the
dreadful fall-out. They feel it already, so to speak, in their bones."[29]

Not everyone. Americans polled by Gallup supported a test-ban treaty by a margin of only 13 percent and substantially opposed a unilateral halt in testing.[30] While the president retained a statesmanlike demeanor, elsewhere the debate sometimes became ugly. Representative Francis Walter (D-Pa.) charged that Norman Thomas and the other plaintiffs in the "fallout suits" were communist sympathizers, while prominent New York City minister Daniel Poling suggested that SANE's demands were pro-Soviet in origin. More circumspectly, AEC chairman Lewis Strauss alleged that antitesting protests were inspired by a "kernel of very intelligent and deliberate propaganda," seeded presumably by foreign agents.[31] When Bertrand Russell said that he would prefer to live under communist rule than have the world suffer the devastation of thermonuclear war, he fueled a quarrel over the question of "better Red than dead" that debased the value of debate for the next several years. In the last analysis, however, the issue was political rather than rhetorical because the executive branch retained the initiative in foreign policy.

Late in 1957, Polish foreign minister Adam Rapacki had proposed to reduce Cold War tensions through a mutual agreement on a neutral, nuclear-free zone in Central Europe. The following March the Soviets announced an immediate suspension of atmospheric testing and invited the U.S. and Britain to join in their lead. The American government, dismissing the Russian test suspension as a propaganda "gimmick," reiterated its determination to continue testing for the development of a radiation-free "clean" bomb. In fact, the administration was developing a negotiating position as a basis for calling a joint Soviet-American technical conference on detection which convened in July. On 31 October, after nine months of the most prolific atomic testing in history, an international diplomatic conference gathered in Geneva to consider a test-ban agreement. With the beginning of the laborious negotiations came a de facto moratorium on testing that lasted until September 1961.

Negotiations and the moratorium somewhat defused the disarmament campaign in 1959. Liberals, although they sponsored a number of marches and meetings, seemed almost to be reduced to listening for the government's progress: at one conference the featured speaker was U.S. negotiator James J. Wadsworth, who reported on the desultory Geneva talks. Radical pacifists directed their civil disobedience to the arms race itself. In the course of a summer-long campaign of local organizing, CNVA activists were arrested when they tried to enter a Strategic Air Command base near Omaha. Eastward at Groton, Connecticut, others picketed, leafletted, and even tried to board a missile-launching submarine. At Fort Detrick, Maryland, still others initiated a two-year vigil against germ warfare. Their commitment against nuclear arms was patently deep; but, like the liberal peace advocates, they were effectively deprived of their key issue. The test-ban was off the public agenda and on the conference table.

The timing was critical, because it allowed freer play for a trend which would subsume disarmament issues in a generalized critique of the complacency of Eisenhower's America. It began as social and moral commentary from a broad spectrum of liberals. In the spring of 1956, bellwether historian and social critic Arthur M. Schlesinger, Jr., suggested the need for a "qualitative liberalism" that would rally Americans around "a revitalized sense of the public interest" through collective action to problems of education, urban planning, medical care, and other questions involving "individual dignity, identity, and fulfillment in a mass society."[32] Significantly, Schlesinger made no reference to international issues or alternative Cold War policies. Sixteen months later, however, the Russians' Sputnik space shot ignited liberal attacks upon Republican passivity in foreign as well as domestic affairs and eventually paved the way for John Kennedy's presidential campaign with its promise to get the country "moving again."

Accordingly, while peace activists recommended restraint and negotiations, the larger body of American liberals seized upon popular fears of slipping behind the Soviets through inertia and advocated an intensified American arms buildup as well as increased federal domestic spending for education and other programs vital to the national security. Harvard economist John Kenneth Galbraith urged in *The Affluent Society* (1958) that Americans must redirect their investments from private pleasures into public centers of strength, or risk losing the whole of their wealth and power to more disciplined rivals. A best-seller, his book offered a leitmotif for liberals eager to rally America to new crusades. Galbraith wrote about economic culture, not international relations; but his prescriptions to strengthen the public sector and to govern with purpose were easily translated into a formula for Cold War success.

The governing equation in this respect became mutual deterrence and arms control. Prominent Democratic liberals such as Senator Henry Jackson attacked the strategy of massive retaliation. They said that it was dangerously inflexible and lacked credibility. In its place they would put a system of mutual deterrence. Eschewing disarmament as utopian, they promoted arms control as a way to manage the arms race so as to maintain a stable balance of terror. Arsenals were not to be dismantled. On the contrary, the U.S. should have tactical nuclear weapons and the capacity to fight a limited nuclear war. Theoreticians Thomas Schelling and Morton Halperin later explained that arms control was "a means of supplementing unilateral military strategy" by prior agreement on certain issues with potential adversaries. "The aims of arms control and the aims of a national military strategy should be substantially the same."[33] By the time they wrote, arms control as an instrument of effective deterrence had become conventional wisdom in mainstream liberalism.

The stakes in the Cold War seemed to be rising. In July the president ordered American marines into Lebanon. Shortly afterwards, the Soviet and American governments locked again over Berlin, and Sino-American relations were strained once more over the offshore islands of Quemoy and Matsu. All this only encouraged demands for greater military preparations. The White House, trying to hold down military spending and balance the budget, found itself on the defensive against charges that it was letting military capacity slip by default. A January 1958 Rockefeller Brothers Fund report recommended sharp increases in military spending and an extensive civil defense network. Through his *Time-Life* empire, publisher Henry Luce called for a massive shelter program. Democratic critics, including Stevenson and former president Truman, attacked the administration for its niggardliness in funding military defense. In a telling sign of his sensitivity, the president ordered a full Pentagon investigation of charges made in August by Senator Richard Russell (D-Ga.) that the White House was sponsoring a study of surrender in a future nuclear war. Russell referred to *Strategic Surrender* by Rand analyst Paul Kecskemeti, which, it turned out, was neither sponsored nor funded by the government. Nor would there be any such official study. On 27 August, Eisenhower signed legislation that prohibited any planning for surrender in the next great war.[34]

The law did not allay pressure for more aggressive pursuit of the Cold War. New York Republican governor Nelson Rockefeller, a political newcomer with clear presidential ambitions, vigorously opposed proposals for a test-ban agreement and crusaded instead for a crash program in civil defense shelters. A prestigious group at the Johns Hopkins University advised the Senate Foreign Relations Committee that Russia's increasing missile superiority might render the country vulnerable to Soviet attack or blackmail in the next decade. Angry and frustrated, the president lashed out at critics for exaggerating the country's military weakness, charging at one point that a "munitions lobby" eager for fatter government contracts was behind the demands for a greater military buildup.[35]

Liberal peace advocates in SANE were appalled by the whole spectacle. Lewis Mumford blasted deterrence as an exercise in "protective extermination." Rather than relaxing international tensions, peace liberals complained, deterrence was emerging as the justification for an implacable arms race which was eclipsing all other Soviet-American differences and becoming the main source of mutual insecurity. Arms control was equally self-deluding. It was a recipe for regulating war preparations. Wrote physicist Eugene Rabinowitch, deterrence was "a pseudo-peace."[36]

More was at stake than disarmament—never really part of the liberal canon. The last vestige of Wilsonian internationalism seemed to be slipping away unnoticed. In 1958, at the same time as *The Affluent Society* achieved public acclaim, internationalists Grenville Clark and Louis Sohn published *World Peace Through World Law,* a landmark proposal for building the UN into a truly world authority and resuscitating the world government movement. Political liberals would have none of it. A few tested UWF stalwarts like Norman Thomas and James P. Warburg praised the Clark-Sohn work, but the new appeal for a reformed world order was largely ignored. The test-ban issue notwithstanding, mutual deterrence seemed to have won a consensus that crossed liberal-conservative lines. For world order the nation would continue to rely on the unilateral extension of American economic and military power with the help of key allies and the sanction of a still pliant United Nations.

Established internationalist organizations such as the United Nations Association of the United States and the United World Federalists stagnated. Articulate liberals who were also internationalists became further isolated. The orientation of American peace activism began to change. With the decline of the long-standing concern for firmer forms of world order, the way was open to more radical appeals for peace through popular self-determination and revolutionary liberation.

A "collection of dissatisfied intellectuals"

Domestic radicalism subsisted in the mid-fifties for the most part in such shopworn Marxist sects as the Communist party (CP), the Trotskyist Socialist Workers party (SWP), and the social democratic League for Industrial Democracy (LID). Numbering only a few thousand adherents, these veterans of the Old Left waited more or less in expectation of capitalism's collapse while they argued bitterly over the true route through the apocalypse. Their ranks were breached by a generation of infighting and battered by a decade of Red Scare politics. Their organizations had no influence or appeal, serving mainly as a foil for subversive-seeking politicians and a kind of nursing home for ideas whose time never came. They hardly presaged a cutting edge of social change.

With the Old Left awash in futility, an independent radicalism emerged in the 1950s. In part, it was a variant of the so-called New Left in Britain, in part a version of the liberal emphasis on moral fiber announced by Schlesinger. It drew on fresh critiques of American society, however, notably from psychologist and social philosopher Paul Goodman, historian William A. Williams, sociologist C. Wright Mills, and cultural philosopher Herbert Marcuse. It attracted a small core of young people who had little patience for the continuing ideological quarrels of the thirties but were acutely interested in the ideas and analysis propounded in publications such as *I. F. Stone's Weekly* (1954), Irving Howe's *Dissent* (1954), the *Monthly Review* (1955), and *Liberation* (1956). There was as

yet no new radical tradition, only a fresh interest in political questions
and a mood of dissatisfaction with old answers—an ambiguous rallying
point for a "collection of dissatisfied intellectuals" to whom both Marxist
dogmatism and liberal realism seemed morally sterile.[37]

Young activists began to connect with one another, encouraged by
civil rights campaigns and the antinuclear testing movement. Some of
them converged in local, multi-issue organizations such as the student
political coalition SLATE, developed early in 1958 at the University
of California, Berkeley. Others came together in national, single-issue
groups such as Student SANE, established on scattered campuses in the
fall (often at the urging of students in the Young People's Socialist League,
or YPSL). Still others identified with new centers of left-wing intellectual
criticism such as the notable historians' study group at the University of
Wisconsin, Madison, which sponsored the influential new journal *Studies
on the Left* (1959).

The concerns of the new radicals varied from personal life-style to
campus, domestic, and international issues, although few individuals encompassed that range. The sources of radical inspiration and its lines of
thought were disparate. Many student radicals related to the utopian
anarchist Paul Goodman, whose *Growing up Absurd* (1960) interpreted
bureaucratic structures as repressive and elevated the quest for personal
authority. Like young historian Staughton Lynd, some radicals found inspiration in the existential politics and utopian experimentalism of radical pacifist A. J. Muste. Like war-resister and socialist David McReynolds,
some looked to Norman Thomas in the cause of disarmament and overseas disengagement. Like University of Michigan student Thomas Hayden,
some of them responded to Jack Kerouac's 1960 book, *On the Road,*
which glorified an open-ended approach to life that was unconventional
in a career-tracking generation. Most incipient radicals disparaged the
existing social order and felt intensely that the times demanded action.
Most of them also believed that Marxist modes of analysis, once freed
from old left dogmatism, would give direction to change. Beyond that,
at the outset they had little in common. In fact, to call them radicals is
to accept the convention by which they distinguished themselves from
mainstream liberalism, with which they were dissatisfied.

Few of them came forward initially in response to issues of war and
peace, or located themselves within the organized peace movement; but
the renascent radicalism of the late 1950s began to affect peace activism
in at least three ways. Precisely because the new radicals eschewed both
the existing Soviet communist model and the American capitalist one,
they provided fresh support for a neutralist, so-called Third Camp orientation to international affairs. Because they rejected orthodox Marxist
theories of history, they could focus on specific issues. Moreover, their
intense desire for fundamental change and their emphasis on personal

action contributed to more aggressive peace activism. Theirs was "a leftism liberated from the Marxist sects of the Depression years," recalled Michael Walzer, "but without, for the moment, any sort of popular base; a critical and worried but also an engaged and adventurous leftism."[38] One of the earliest expressions of the new mood was the Student Peace Union (SPU), through which the organized peace movement was opened to a student constituency that within a few years would transform it and bring it closer to emerging radicalism.

The SPU started at the University of Chicago, as had CORE a generation earlier. It formed around young Quaker activists Kenneth and Ele Calkins. Influenced by Bradford Lyttle, AFSC peace education director in the city and a CNVA leader, they and some other Chicago students had been involved in the 1958 Cheyenne action.[39] Ken was a volunteer worker for the AFSC and a member of the FOR, the CNVA, and the Socialist party. He and Ele sponsored informal meetings for Chicago area pacifist and left-wing students, hoping to stimulate them to work for disarmament and a strengthened UN and to take some "personal responsibility for building a just and peaceful world."[40] In April 1959 the students formed a regional student organization and in October, with help from the FOR, they held an intercampus convention. Within a year they had twelve chapters in the Midwest (the strongest affiliates were at Oberlin and Antioch) and perhaps 120 members, mostly religious pacifists, ban-the-bomb liberals, and leftists from the anti-Soviet Young People's Socialist League.

The Calkinses' Woodlawn apartment turned from an occasional meeting place to an organizational headquarters, with a consequent loss of privacy. For a time, they were compensated by the enthusiasm of the small band of students who hoped they could give isolated campus peace activists a sense of participation in a larger movement. Perhaps a "new era" could be constructed on the understanding that "what happened in Hiroshima can happen in Chicago or Moscow."[41] Perhaps their nation could help to build a less explosive world. Although quite prepared to criticize Soviet policies and the evils of communism, the SPU youth believed that their "primary duty" was to make their own country "right" and that "as individuals" they were obligated to act.[42]

Inspiration for action came from the South. On 1 February 1960, four black students from North Carolina A & T College protested lunch-counter segregation at the local Woolworth dime store by sitting in their places, although unserved and unwanted. Inadvertently, they prompted widespread nonviolent direct action protests against racial discrimination. Thousands of people, mostly black college students, conducted sit-ins in several southern towns and cities, while hundreds of northern white sympathizers picketed local stores of the Kresge, Woolworth, and Walgreen chains. "Never again during the decade," Clayborne Carson has written," "would the proportion of students active in protest equal the level reached at southern black colleges during the period from February to June 1960."[43]

Riding the tide of activism, veteran civil rights worker Ella Baker called two hundred student activists to an April meeting at Shaw University in Raleigh, North Carolina. There they established the Student Nonviolent Coordinating Committee (or SNCC, as its title was formalized in an October convention) in order to channel the new student militancy into the larger drive for civil rights. Loosely organized but bent on action, SNCC presaged the reform impulse of the early sixties: it was spontaneous and individualistic, committed to fundamental social and political change as a moral duty, and indifferent to the ideological quarrels of the past.

Through CORE and the FOR, SNCC was also associated with radical pacifism. Bayard Rustin was a leader in both groups, and in 1958 and 1959 he had orchestrated large youth demonstrations for school integration—in one, an estimated twenty-five thousand young people had rallied in Washington. CORE had organized direct action, too, and its membership and income were soaring. It placed field-workers in Greensboro within days of the outbreak of the sit-ins. As the movement spread, CORE activated contacts throughout the South and organized supportive picketing elsewhere in the country. By mid-year its staff had tripled and it had some fifty local chapters. Pacifists besides CORE founders Rustin and James Farmer were directing the movement, notably Martin Luther King, Jr., Ralph Abernathy, and James Lawson (southern secretary of the FOR). SNCC itself espoused radical pacifism in its initial statement of principles: "We affirm the philosophy or religious ideal of nonviolence as the foundation of our purpose, the presupposition of our faith, and the manner of our action. Nonviolence . . . seeks a social order of justice permeated by love."[44]

Radical pacifism thus animated the militant civil rights movement; but the reverse also was true: Gandhi was being Americanized in the South. The successful application of nonviolent direct action on a large scale in the United States greatly strengthened the morale and organization of radical pacifists who were, in fact, taken with increasing seriousness by the public. Moreover, by 1964 there had developed a significant literature on active nonviolence and Gandhi which included not only theoretical works but also a detailed manual for direct action in civil rights as well as all other nonviolent protest.[45] The experience refined in civil rights was critical in positioning radical pacifism within the changing peace movement.

Stimulated by black student activism in the South, white students elsewhere found a ready-made agency of activism in the SPU. The organization grew at a rate that its leaders termed "simply fantastic." "Everywhere we strike," wrote Calkins, "we strike fire."[46] Gradually, the Midwestern group reached out. Calkins had close ties with Robert Pickus, who also had been at Cheyenne, and especially with Dave McReynolds, who was on the WRL staff (and who hoped that students and radical pacifists could move the socialists to a stronger stand on peace issues). Calkins' friend Allan Brick had founded the College Peace Union in New England, and in an August 1960 meeting at the FOR headquarters, the two organizations were merged.

The SPU became national. Its membership increased to some two thousand by the summer of 1962, and the budget grew from about $1,000 to more than $22,000.[47] The organization was tapping an inchoate and restless mood which became political as it was articulated. A few Harvard and Radcliffe students had formed a group called Tocsin, initially to enlist support for peace politics. Far more restrained than their name implied, they were oriented to analysis and debate, and they associated with liberal advisors such as David Riesman and H. Stuart Hughes. The more they thought about nuclear deterrence and connected it to larger issues of the Cold War, though, the more they were inclined to act and the greater was their contact with like-minded students. These included members of Student SANE which, especially in New York City, was wracked by repercussions from the controversy over exclusion of alleged communists from the national organization. As the SPU picked up fallouts from Student SANE, often with the encouragement of Homer Jack, its leaders got an introduction to the intricacies of radical sectarianism. Their group was not oriented to the formulation of radical theory. On the one hand, most of its campus chapters remained quite autonomous. On the other, it had incorporated a Third Camp position which assumed independence from both world blocs and, to some extent, precluded debates on the merits of either of them. Nevertheless, the process of extending the organization was dialectical: every encounter with another group involved argumentation and analysis which strengthened the young people's sense of their own competence in foreign affairs. They were giving themselves a Socratic education.

The national headquarters in Chicago was moved to a house on the edge of the black ghetto and became a precursor to the political collectives of the 1960s. Increases in the budget prompted expanded programs, with the result that the SPU was always in debt. Young activists lived in voluntary poverty, dependent on contributions or savings. They subsisted on junk food. Because staff and facilities were minimal, space was cramped and normal routines were ignored. The house was a kind of way station for youthful transients with political or simply personal connections. There was camaraderie and tension, good talk and dull. National Cochairman Philip Altbach recalled that it was "like something out of the Russian anarchist movement of the 1840s."[48] In the intensely focused idealism of the small SPU clan, the most ordinary elements of life became entirely peripheral. It would take a decade to learn that the converse was also true: a life of concentrated idealism fell outside the purview of the average American.

Even before the SPU moved out of their apartment, Ken and Ele Calkins had become concerned about the erosion of their own life-style, particularly after the birth of their daughter. They moved to New York, passing leadership to younger hands in Chicago—notably Mike Parker and Philip Altbach, who were twenty and nineteen, respectively. Parker developed close ties with the Young People's Socialist League, as did Altbach with adult peace organizations and David Fink with religious ones. Altbach even made contact with the British Campaign for Nuclear Disarmament in London, from which he brought back a bag of pins bearing its "chicken track" symbol. The national SPU adopted the logo as its own, explaining that "like the cross and fish in early Christianity, it is simple and easily remembered. It can also be drawn or painted quickly."[49] Henceforth, the symbol conveyed the moral energy which linked, however tenuously, the civil rights and student peace campaigns.

That initial burst of energy impressed contemporaries. It led C. Wright Mills to conclude that "we are beginning to move again," and to christen the movers an American "New Left."[50] Sensing opportunity in the times, the Trotskyist Socialist Workers party established the Young Socialist Alliance (YSA) in April 1960 to win American youth for revolutionary Marxism. More important because more indigenous, some eighty leaders of the left, including Norman Thomas and James Farmer, gathered at New York's Barbizon-Plaza Hotel in June to initiate what might be called the Students for a Democratic Society in formation. It was appropriate that Thomas attended, for he had been active in the campus work of the League for Industrial Democracy during the 1920s, when it launched the Student League for Industrial Democracy (SLID). In the following decade the Student League had merged into the American Student Union, which collapsed in the wake of the Hitler-Stalin Pact. Resurrected, the SLID had remained a largely paper organization until 1960, when, hoping to catch the wind of student activism, the parent League reconstituted its youth division as Students for a Democratic Society (SDS) and launched it at the Barbizon-Plaza. The fanfare there was more hopeful than merited. SDS could claim but 250 members that summer. For two years it seemed to be "stuck together with staples and dreams," as Jack Newfield recalled.[51] Gradually it was rebuilt from within until in 1962 a fresh constituency asserted itself at Port Huron, Michigan, and defined SDS as the independent representative of a new and student left. The Barbizon-Plaza meeting was therefore a kind of presentment. It reflected, if a bit prematurely, a fresh vitality in the radical tradition, which in turn would affect the makeup and tone of the peace movement.

A meeting earlier in 1960 suggested that the liberal base of the movement also was in flux. At the invitation of AFSC chairman Stephen Cary, a couple of dozen of the nation's senior intellectuals gathered at Bear Mountain, New York, in March. They included psychologist Erich Fromm, sociologists David Riesman and Lewis Coser, historian H. Stuart Hughes, and language analyst S. I. Hayakawa. Several pacifists were conspicuous among them, including Muste, Cary, Gilmore, Pickett, Meacham, and Pickus. The conferees were responding to the same congeries of domestic and foreign events that had opened a sense of urgent possibility for student activists. The senior intellectuals as well dismissed old ideological quarrels. They agreed that reliance on deterrence for security reflected "a deep malaise from which . . . both the Western and Communist blocs suffer." Moreover, they linked creative innovation in international relations to "decentralized control" by citizens over their own society: America's role in the world was an expression of its national identity.[52]

Those present at Bear Mountain agreed to establish Committees of Correspondence, "something less than an organization, but more than an episodic relationship between friends" (Sidney Lens, at least, aspired to create a Fabian Society for the 1960s). The AFSC hoped that the network would counter hawkish propaganda in the media and government. The title was taken from a movement during the American Revolution— a choice made to underscore confidence in the role of intellectual exchange. Insisting that "fundamental changes were necessary in our world if the planet was to survive," the conferees advocated continued abstinence from nuclear testing, rapprochement with China, economic conversion from military to civilian production, and leadership in the social and economic development of the Third World. America's choice was not between total surrender or total annihilation, they insisted. "The question before the United States today is whether to abandon all initiative in the international situation and continue to be guided by the logic of deterrence and the arms race; or to take up the initiative once again and experiment imaginatively and courageously."[53] Some liberals outside the academy agreed. Michigan Democratic governor G. Mennen "Soapy" Williams sponsored a conference in support of intensified U.S. disarmament efforts, while thirty-eight prominent Americans—including two trade union leaders and Robert R. Nathan, chairman of Americans for Democratic Action—urged the Eisenhower administration to effect a total ban on atomic testing.[54] Easter week demonstrations for peace and disarmament were the largest ever.

Reinhold Niebuhr, the most respected voice of neo-orthodox Protestant liberalism and ethical realism, edged toward the Bear Mountain Conference position. The overriding reality, he wrote, was that the nuclear arms race itself was "a time bomb under our vaunted security." Both the United States and the Soviet Union faced the danger of atomic war from miscalculation, not by intentional provocation. Accordingly, slogans such as "bargaining from strength" and "deterring attack by the prospect of massive retaliation" had become "irrelevant." Niebuhr felt the need for a fresh approach. In the winter he endorsed a comprehensive nuclear test-ban treaty. His close friend and ally, John C. Bennett, explained that although he was not yet a nuclear pacifist, he could not put his faith in deterrence as an instrument of peace "much longer if there is no control of the arms race."[55]

Arms control was of course an ambiguous concept not inconsistent with deterrence, but the comprehensive test ban had acquired a symbolic value that connoted disillusionment with the arms race itself. The underlying problem was the search for national purpose, which preoccupied Americans in 1960. The specific question was whether or not it was any longer realistic to conduct the Cold War on military terms. Niebuhr's caveat was especially significant because his thought had provided the ethical linchpin of the political realism which had driven the liberal pursuit of Cold War policy since the late 1940s. Realism as the criterion of foreign policy was not vulnerable in 1960—the dominant voices of liberalism were urging military buildup and a Pax Americana.[56] But reality was subject to varying constructions, and this would become increasingly important to the antiwar movement of the 1960s, as liberal realists filled something of the void left by the decline of internationalism.

"At the very moment when the system appears impregnable to the realist, it often turns out to be vulnerable to the quixotic"

In the meantime, the liberal base in the peace movement was weakened when SANE came apart in midyear. The immediate context was another Cold War reversal for the United States: the U-2 incident. The immediate issue was how to treat allegations of communism in the organization.

Early in May the Soviet Union claimed to have shot down an American U-2 spy plane, allowed President Eisenhower some time to deny that the United States was involved in air surveillance, and then revealed that it had captured the CIA pilot, Francis Gary Powers, who acknowledged his spy mission on Soviet television. Khrushchev, blustering about Soviet retaliatory power, had Eisenhower trapped in an obvious attempt at deception. Trying to cover his humiliation, the president defended the overflights as vital to America's defense and promised to continue them. Khrushchev abused Eisenhower verbally at the Paris summit conference later that month, leaving him on the defensive and the conference in shambles.

The incident was one of several setbacks for the administration. Anti-American student demonstrations in Tokyo obliged the Japanese government to withdraw an invitation for Eisenhower to visit the country. Anti-American rioting broke out in Turkey. Student mobs in South Korea helped to overthrow the right-wing regime of U.S. ally Syngman Rhee. Another allied regime deteriorated in South Vietnam. In the Caribbean, differences between Washington and Havana sharpened. Central Africa became more volatile following Belgium's withdrawal from the Congo. Soviet-American disarmament negotiations slowed to a virtual standstill, and on 11 July an American RB-47 reconnaissance plane was shot down in the Bering Strait. Within a few weeks, wrote journalist Theodore White, "American statecraft reeled through a period of chaos and humiliation" that was without precedent or relief.[57]

There were new accusations of Soviet subversion, as an FBI official charged that attempted communist infiltration of key American institutions was at a record level, and in this context Senator Thomas Dodd (D-Conn.) challenged SANE. In May, just before a test-ban rally of twenty thousand persons in New York, Dodd proclaimed in the Senate that the moratorium on testing was playing into Soviet hands. The next day he brought New York SANE leader Henry Abrams before the Senate Internal Security Subcommittee, which he temporarily chaired. Abrams took the Fifth Amendment rather than respond to questions regarding his communist affiliation. Shortly afterward Norman Cousins, as cochairman of SANE, confronted Abrams and then dismissed him. Late that month Cousins and Norman Thomas got the board of directors to declare that communists, or "individuals who are not free because of party discipline or political allegiance" to apply the same standards of criticism to all governments, were "barred from any voice in deciding" SANE policies and programs. More bluntly, Cousins explained that membership in the Communist party was "incompatible with association with SANE." Speaking for himself and Clarence Pickett, he added, "We do not think it is possible to mount a powerful peace movement in the United States if we take a contrary position on this issue."[58]

Those actions only fanned controversy. The allegations of communist influence became public, along with a bitter division within SANE over the issue of civil liberties and related procedural questions. The whole affair was the more difficult because it was largely symbolic: internal staff analysis concluded that there was no appreciable communist influence to purge.[59] Several members withdrew from leadership roles, protesting the organization's failure to confront the congressional witch-hunters. Prominent among them were Robert Gilmore, Stewart Meacham, Linus Pauling, and A. J. Muste. Gilmore complained that the exclusion of people because of their political beliefs constituted an intolerable attack upon civil liberties and reinforced the political intolerance which was "epidemic in the world." Muste conceded that any peace organization appearing to be an agent of the Soviet Union would be politically irrelevant, but he warned that any people who could be "intimidated and terrorized by Dodd or whomsoever are not going to build a peace movement." It was necessary to apply the same standards to U.S. policymakers as to their Soviet counterparts, he argued. SANE's position showed that liberals could not undertake the "radical criticism of the U.S. politico-economic regime . . . that will have to take place in it, if nuclear war is in fact to be averted." The organization's leaders persisted in asserting that "the 'enemy' is still over there," Muste charged. "They do not fully and clearly accept the thesis that 'war is the enemy' and must be resisted in all its forms in every land."[60] He withdrew from SANE's Greater New York Committee.

Muste's comments suggested that the division within SANE went beyond the tension between civil liberties and the strategy of keeping the organization's public image untainted. That was real enough and, indeed, controversy over exclusionism—keeping out potentially subversive elements—would plague the antiwar movement of the 1960s. But underlying that issue were differences about American society. For liberals like Cousins, the nation had but to be roused to an appreciation of its values and real interest in order to take on authentic world leadership. For radical pacifists like Muste, American leadership was compromised by vested interests and warped values within the society. The division between the two men was a matter of emphasis, and their shared concerns were so strong that disagreement was painful.

SANE's attempt to detach itself from anyone suspected of pro-Soviet views precipitated disastrous internal fractures but failed to halt charges that it was compromised. Claiming that he had uncovered "serious Communist infiltration" of several SANE chapters, Dodd called upon the national organization to conduct an even broader "purge" of suspected communists, and in mid-October his Senate subcommittee released a report reiterating its charges of communist penetration of the test-ban movement.[61]

Weakened and defensive, SANE reorganized and tried to confront resurgent pressure for military strength. Sanford Gottlieb, director of the Washington, D.C., branch, had been named political action director in February. A Brooklyn, New York, native, Gottlieb had served in the navy during World War II. He had completed college at Dartmouth and thereafter had studied at the University of Paris, and he brought to SANE the orientation of a political scientist. From his office in the capital he had persuaded a number of religious pacifist and liberal peace groups to cosponsor a 1960 Campaign for Disarmament.

The goal was to interject the theme of "Security Through World Disarmament" into the presidential campaign. At Gottlieb's inspiration, sympathetic citizens wrote letters, visited with the representatives of candidates, and organized public meetings. The campaign continued after the divisive spring. Before the platform committee of the Democratic party, Norman Thomas advocated universal disarmament, and television personality Steve Allen represented SANE before the Republican party platform committee. The organization attracted some 2,500 Chicagoans to a rally in October. Its leaders struggled to present "a clear and dominant voice in at least one of the major parties."[62] As the *Christian Century* put it in August, "Fifteen years of suspension over the fires of nuclear hell is long enough. It is time for a change."[63]

All these efforts made only the slightest impact on the 1960 presidential campaign. Both Nixon and Kennedy prescribed easily digestible formulas for complex global realities. Defending the general course of the Eisenhower administration, Nixon called for the continuation of "Peace without Surrender." Kennedy exaggerated the so-called missile gap and condemned the administration's alleged complacency. He claimed that the Republicans had defaulted on the promise of American life and had lost the initiative to Russia in the contest for international preeminence. Kennedy embraced the full range of the liberal foreign policy agenda. He endorsed the creation of a national peace agency to study and promote alternatives to war. He announced plans for a Peace Corps, through which technical and educational work in underdeveloped parts of the world could serve as an alternative to compulsory military service. More stridently, and throughout the campaign, he promised "a coherent and purposeful national strategy backed by strength."[64] Like Nixon, he promised to press the Cold War harder from Quemoy and Matsu to Cuba and Berlin.

By the time that Kennedy eked out an election victory in November, few peace activists believed the Democrats would chart a fresh course toward a negotiated end to the Cold War and real disarmament. Most of them agreed with the *Nation* that the whole presidential campaign had been "a nauseating exhibition" which left the peace question still "the great undebated issue" of the day.[65] Their frustration was compounded in the autumn by fresh indications that the arms race was rapidly intensifying. The Navy launched the world's first atomic-powered aircraft carrier and placed on patrol in the Atlantic the first of a new class of American submarines armed with sixteen nuclear-tipped Polaris missiles. The AEC opened a new series of underground atomic tests. After three years of frantic buildup, the size of the American nuclear weapons stockpile had tripled, from 6,000 to 18,000 weapons, and the number of Soviet targets designated for destruction had risen to 2,500. American nuclear strike capability was expanding in what David Rosenberg has called the "tendency toward excess."[66]

The appearance of destructive new weaponry, combined with the apparent irrelevance of the 1960 presidential campaign, reinforced apprehensions in the peace movement of a drift toward mass destruction.

Popular endorsement of military strength might have been interpreted as confidence in unilateral deterrence, of course; but it was represented as fatalism by those for whom nuclear arms were intrinsically threatening. In the postelection view of the Roman Catholic journal *Commonweal,* "the most dismaying development of the last few years" was the general "belief that nuclear war is inevitable."[67] Norman Cousins had already warned that a "curious sense of paralysis" gripped political sensibilities and represented the most confounding fact of modern American life.[68] People seemed to feel "politically and intellectually impotent," some activists felt. "Well, that is the question," sociologist Nathan Glazer concluded. If fear and inertia were so overwhelming, "if there is no way for the informed intelligence to penetrate into public opinion, Congress, the bureaucracies, and the institutions, then we may really be doomed."[69]

Even when based on the threat of nuclear war, the politics of persuasion had not seemed to work, and peace activists apparently were left with the politics of individual, symbolic action. Citizens organized by SANE and WILPF marched from Princeton, New Jersey, to New York City in the name of disarmament; two hundred Cornell University faculty and students demonstrated on behalf of a test-ban treaty; and Bradford Lyttle of CNVA coordinated a San Francisco to Moscow Walk for Peace to call attention to the international scope of the arms race. Beginning in December 1960, about ten pacifists trekked to the East Coast, accompanied by others along the way, and flew to London, where they were joined by European peace walkers en route to the German Democratic Republic and Poland. From there they flew to Moscow. Reaching Red Square on 3 October, they conducted a vigil and challenged Russian citizens to protest the policies of their own government. Here and there, the *Nation* observed, people were "beginning to walk if not march," modest in numbers but confident in "a new realism, a new understanding . . . that the only way to reduce an issue of the staggering complexity of disarmament to manageable proportions for the individual is to encourage him to express his concern by some act which will elicit the interest and perhaps the support of others."[70] Such a conviction had motivated some five hundred people who refused to take shelter during the sixth annual Operation Alert in May. They rendered the New York State civil defense law effectively unenforceable. City police randomly arrested twenty-six people, and various college officials disciplined participating students, but the authorities did not try to break up the major demonstration at City Hall Park.

Pacifists were thrilled. Veteran war resister Jim Peck declared that the civil defense protest was "as phenomenal as the southern sit-ins," and A. J. Muste applauded the uprising against conformity as an indication that "people, including students, want to *act.*"[71] New York state officials grudgingly agreed. The show of deliberate disobedience, reinforced by popular apathy and a general sense of fatalism in the face of nuclear threat, was becoming too widespread to challenge at an acceptable cost. Within two years, the state's civil defense practice program was quietly suspended. Leaders in annual civil disobedience to Operation Alert, notably Muste and Dorothy Day, could conclude that five years of effort and individual acts had reduced "the staggering complexity" of at least the civil defense issue to "manageable proportions."

By 1960 the American peace movement had been reconstituted. It had grown rapidly on the issue of atmospheric testing, but it had not effectively popularized its larger agenda of disarmament and a negotiated end to the Cold War. Indeed, the politics of persuasion and advocacy of its liberal wing had yielded disappointment and frustration. Perhaps the time was not ripe. In any case, there was no longer any expectation for an immediate breakthrough on the government level or through the political process. The momentum of the movement shifted a bit to the radical pacifist wing, with its emphasis on individual acts of moral protest. The experience of southern black protest suggested that such actions could have a collective impact—that "at the very moment when the system appears impregnable to the realist, it often turns out to be vulnerable to the quixotic."[72] Throughout the 1960s that hope would increasingly infuse the peace movement and its antiwar successor.

Three

Making a Transition

"Dr. Spock is worried"

The peace movement remained in flux through the Kennedy years. Because its various elements defined themselves as peace advocates in relation to the arms race, specifically atmospheric nuclear testing, their relevance to policy decisions continued to depend very much on the fortunes of the Cold War, over which they had no control. The test-ban treaty of 1963 deprived liberals of their chosen issue, while racial violence that year knitted radical pacifists and the student New Left together. The challenge to policy in Vietnam came from this unstable grouping of critics who were characterized mainly by the attitudes with which they viewed their society and the ideals against which they measured themselves.

John Fitzgerald Kennedy exuded idealism. Tough idealism. His demeanor was gracious, his rhetoric uplifting. He promised forward movement and innovation. His foreign policy followed Eisenhower's in principle, departing in style and organization. The young president accepted global confrontation with the Soviet Union but went beyond his predecessor in building military capability. The alleged missile gap on which Kennedy had campaigned turned out to be a fiction. Instead of reassuring the administration, this discovery increased its priority for conventional military power, in part an extension of the flexible response called for under mutual deterrence and in part a response to the fact that confrontation was shifting to the Third World. Military capacity was extended by government sponsorship of arms sales abroad; it was consolidated under the systematic Secretary of Defense, Robert McNamara; and it was diversified with special attention to counterinsurgency. Covert operations continued and became more difficult to control. At the same time, though, the administration prepared to deprive the Soviets of the opportunity to exploit endemic discontent in the Third World by offering greater U.S. resources for controlled social and economic development through programs such as the Peace Corps and the Alliance for Progress.

While the White House prepared for the long term, it was challenged by a series of immediate crises. In April 1961, Kennedy was embarrassed by his disastrous attempt to land fifteen hundred anti-Castro Cuban exiles at the Bay of Pigs. Early in June he was further sobered at a summit meeting in Vienna where Khrushchev not only promised to support wars of "liberation" but also threatened Berlin. Upon returning to Washington, the president called up 25,000 national guard and reserve troops and asked Congress for a $3.1 billion supplemental military appropriation and an expanded civil defense shelter program. On 13 August, East German authorities sealed off their section of Berlin behind a hideous wall, initiating another great-power crisis that lasted well into the autumn. Moscow broke the three-year moratorium on atmospheric tests and detonated a score of nuclear blasts, including one that was three thousand times more devastating than the Hiroshima bomb. The White House denounced the Soviet action, resumed underground testing, and prepared for an extensive test series of its own in the spring. Kennedy's policy of firmness had the support of most Americans. Congress overwhelmingly approved the president's request for military increases, including for the first time a major shelter program.

Some people wanted to go further. Republican conservatives set out to orient their party to clearer support of private enterprise, opposition to black protest, and victory in the Cold War. "Every time we have stood up to the Communists they have backed down," explained Senator Barry Goldwater (R-Ariz.). "Our trouble is we have not stood up to them enough," nor persuaded them "that we would rather follow the world to Kingdom Come than consign it to Hell under communism."[1] Aggressive conservatism gained ground in the Republican party, especially in the South and West, flanked by a militant radical right which included such diverse elements as the Young Americans for Freedom, the John Birch Society, and the paramilitary Minutemen. Corporate sponsors and local right-wing groups funded special schools on communism and television shows that warned of the Red threat. The prevailing political emphasis became firmness, toughness, and strength. Any hint of negotiated agreements smacked of subversion if not sedition. The worst thing that America could suffer was not a devastating great war, declared Richard Nixon, but rather "defeat without war." Like Goldwater, the former vice-president called for a global strategy of victory.[2]

An intensifying Cold War and an aggressive radical right, together with persisting civil rights demonstrations, seemed only to bolster peace activism. A few days after the abortive Bay of Pigs invasion, pacifists conducted a two-week fast and vigil outside CIA headquarters in Washington, protesting Kennedy's Cuban policy and demanding economic and technical aid for the Cuban people. Shortly afterwards, nearly twenty-five thousand people in more than a dozen cities conducted Easter walks for peace which constituted the largest single peace action since the 1930s. In New York radical pacifists again challenged civil defense, whereas a number of intellectuals created the World Law Fund (1961) in order to disseminate internationalist ideas.[3] SANE officially broadened its agenda from atmospheric testing to disarmament, a stronger UN, and economic conversion from military to social spending.

Peace advocates were trimming their sails in the face of the prevailing conservative winds of 1961, though, even as they mounted an ambitious attempt to build a broad-spectrum peace coalition—Turn Toward Peace (TTP). The new program was envisioned by Robert Pickus, Robert Gilmore, Norman Thomas, Sanford Gottlieb, and others as a clearinghouse for pacifist and internationalist organizations, liberal groups, and labor organizations that would lobby for policy changes to "break the present disaster course" of world politics.[4] They hoped to construct a "politically effective peace movement" which might rebuild confidence that international issues could be resolved through the democratic process. Accordingly, they rallied twenty-eight organizations and individuals, including Eleanor Roosevelt, Walter Reuther, and Martin Luther King, Jr., to launch the coalition in the spring. From Pickus' office in Berkeley, TTP crafted position papers on matters ranging from China to UN reform, always with a sharp sensitivity as to "WHY these policies offer the best chance for peace and the survival of free societies, given even the most pessimistic evaluation of Soviet intentions." Thomas promised that TTP did not in any way stand for "mental, moral and physical surrender to communism."[5] Rather, it wanted to apprise the American people of alternate approaches to security in a hostile world where reliance on war posed an even larger threat to democracy than did Soviet ambitions. Like the CNVA pacifists then carrying their plea for an end to the arms race to Moscow, TTP sought to transcend the Cold War.

In the fall, while TTP organized with deliberation, Women Strike for Peace (WSP) spread spontaneously. The women's organization began in Washington, D.C., where children's book illustrator Dagmar Wilson and three of her suburban neighbors felt desperate to "do something." It occurred to them to call specifically on American women to voice their desire for a test-ban treaty, negotiated international disarmament, economic conversion, and a moratorium "AT ONCE on name-calling on both sides."[6] That sounded more like mothers than strikers, and yet the idea took hold. Contacted through networks of SANE and WILPF sympathizers, well over twenty-five thousand women demonstrated across the country on 1 November in support of the appeal: "End the Arms Race—Not the Human Race." Wilson and her associates were excited by the magnitude of the response. They decided to continue the WSP although, familiar with the bitter SANE quarrel over communist association, they declined to establish formal criteria for membership. Anyone who showed up at a WSP rally was a member "in good standing," an activist explained.[7]

The WSP supporters did share one distinctive sensibility—the belief that women are uniquely fitted to speak for the survival of the species. Self-consciously feminine and mothering (a critic termed it "maternal emotionalism"), WSP activists like University of Michigan sociologist Elise Boulding believed that it was "a woman's work to make the whole world a home." Declared Boulding, "I am not now and never have been a feminist, but one thing I will say for women, they know that there are no miracles except the one ultimate miracle of the seed of life."[8] Women should nurture and protect that seed. According to contemporary public opinion analysts, popular sentiment paralleled Boulding's belief. Two sociologists noted in a 1962 study of college student attitudes on war and peace that young women took positions more frequently than did young men. In view of the gender split, these researchers speculated, it was likely that future antiwar opposition in America most likely would operate "in large part [as] a feminine responsibility—today as in the time of Lysistrata."[9]

Peace organizations continued to multiply with the new year, as Soviet-American relations improved. Columbia University sociologist Amitai Etzioni initiated the Council for the Gradualist Way to Peace, and a number of pacifists and clergymen formed a short-lived Peace Hostage Exchange Foundation, hoping to exchange citizens between rival states as guarantees against surprise attack and war. A more enduring, Cambridge-based study group of doctors, the Physicians for Social Responsibility, issued a report in the *New England Journal of Medicine* which detailed the horrendous medical implications of a modern atomic war and derided civil defense planning. Hoping that "the combination of the sweet voice of reason and substantial campaign contributions might very well do the job," atomic scientist Leo Szilard tried to get scientists, scholars, and politicians to lobby for some common grounds of agreement with their Soviet counterparts. At the same time he tried to persuade twenty thousand people to commit 2 percent of their income to the cause. In June, although well short of his goal, he established two groups which a few months later merged to form the Council for a Livable World. Ever optimistic, Szilard promised that the Council would become "the most effective public interest lobby that ever hit Washington."[10]

Optimism attracted over four thousand college students to Washington on 16–17 February 1962 to urge their government to reorient its policies from confrontation to conciliation.[11] It was the largest peace mobilization in the history of the capital before 1965 and the apex of the student peace movement. The demonstration had been proposed and largely organized by Todd Gitlin and Peter Goldmark of Tocsin in tenuous alli-

ance with the Brandeis Student SANE. It was somewhat reluctantly co-
sponsored by SPU, Student SANE, SDS, and YPSL, all working through
an ad hoc "Turn Toward Peace Student Council." Well-dressed students
from fifty-seven colleges in seventeen states lobbied from Capitol Hill to
the State Department. They marched to Arlington Cemetery to lay a
wreath at the Tomb of the Unknown Soldier, and they displayed a fine
sense of impartiality by picketing the Soviet embassy. In sharp contrast
to later demonstrators, they waved no banners and made few speeches.
Thinking of themselves as liberal realists, the young people avoided moralism. They simply addressed the irrationality of civil defense efforts,
unchecked atmospheric testing, and uncontrolled arms competition.

Their measured approach attracted few sympathizers. Most members
of Congress ignored them, and city churches and colleges were so afraid
of being tagged as subversive that they refused to provide sleeping or
meeting space for the youths. The warmest welcome came from the
White House. While students picketing in the snow received coffee, courtesy of the president, their leaders inside were served cookies and hot
chocolate by officials who seemed "condescendingly neutral."[12] National
Security Advisor (and former Harvard College Dean) McGeorge Bundy
lectured them on the difficulties of achieving verifiable arms control, and
other presidential advisors explained that the real problem was at the
Pentagon. Unwelcome anywhere else, the students closed their mobilization with a rally near the Washington Monument, where Norman
Thomas and others congratulated them for their efforts and urged them
on to further action. The site probably conveyed more than the speakers'
words: the students were out in the cold, small in number, excluded
from the centers of power, and listening to politically marginal figures
tell them to struggle on behalf of symbols like the grey monument that
loomed above them.

Spring brought warmth and an announcement from Kennedy that the
government was preparing a series of thirty-six atomic tests over a six-
month period, a record of sorts. The next day, 4 March, some five thousand people defied a recently passed New York City ordinance banning
demonstrations in Times Square in order to hold a sit-in protest against
testing. Police waded roughly into the crowd, arresting over forty people
and injuring many. City officials excused the police behavior as an aberration. Dave Dellinger thought it foreshadowed the coming cost of
militant action.[13]

There were other actions. The Student Peace Union demonstrated at
the United Nations as WSP members picketed the White House and AEC
headquarters. The American Association for the United Nations joined
the many organizations petitioning the president to cancel the test series.
Faculty groups from Cornell, Yale, and several midwestern colleges sponsored newspaper ads asking for cancellation. The tests were held, and

protest continued. In June, Linus Pauling and Clarence Pickett joined an antitesting picket line outside the White House before entering the gates for a presidential dinner honoring them and other Nobel Prize laureates. More aggressively, radical pacifists made two abortive attempts to sail the vessel *Everyman* into the Pacific atomic test site before they were arrested.

Perhaps most significant for the future of the movement, the protests that spring enlisted pediatrician Benjamin Spock, author of the most widely-used child care book in America. Deeply moved by the medical implications of atmospheric testing for children's health, Spock joined SANE and contributed his name and picture to a widely reproduced advertisement: the tall doctor looked benevolently down at a little girl over the caption, "Dr. Spock is Worried."

"Time out for another tranquilizer, then back with renewed zest to the fray"

Although these events were evidence of widespread dissent in the spring of 1962, they did not add up to a coherent movement. They indicated only ambition. Thus leading peace liberals hoped to build a liberal-labor coalition that would overhaul U.S. foreign policies and help bring the Cold War under control, and they believed that Turn Toward Peace was the most promising means of doing that. Michael Harrington predicted that if TTP worked, it would produce "a politically responsible American movement for peace" and "a decisive breakthrough" in national politics.[14]

Other activists proposed to channel rising peace sentiment into a broader movement toward some "new politics" of fundamental change. This was the significance of the Port Huron Statement of the Students for a Democratic Society. Since the summer of 1960, Al Haber had cultivated a new constituency for SDS. His goal was leadership, not numbers. As an activist at the University of Michigan, he had recruited the talented editor of the university's student newspaper, Tom Hayden. Together they linked up with politically-oriented student leaders such as Paul Booth at Swarthmore and Rennie Davis and David Potter at Oberlin. The idea was to create a network of campus nerve centers. Haber provided the design, but Hayden provided the critical initiative.

Tom Hayden, then twenty-two, had been reared in and outgrown a traditional Catholic culture in Michigan. Keen, articulate, and personable, he was a natural student leader. In the summer of 1960 he had hitchhiked to California, where he encountered the fresh burst of student activism at Berkeley and the residue of student encounters with the House Un-American Activities Committee (HUAC) in May. He covered the Democratic national convention for his school paper and then plunged into the politics of both the National Student Association and the Michigan campus. By this time his writing had a midwestern populist ring. Haber had just set up shop in New York, and he prevailed upon Hayden, after his graduation, to be SDS field secretary with an office in Atlanta, where his wife, Casey, could work in the civil rights movement. Thus, in the fall of 1961, Hayden learned firsthand about the black democratic revolution while Haber lay the basis for a white student network. Toward the end of the year the small core of SDS recruits met and agreed to develop a "manifesto" from which they would develop a program in a convention the following June at a Port Huron, Michigan, labor camp. Hayden mainly drafted the statement. From the time of its adoption, the new student constituency owned SDS, much to the discomfort of its sponsor, the League for Industrial Democracy.

Hayden and his friends broke with the LID and with all the old formulas, but their statement was radical only in that it was comprehensive and that it emanated from youth. It was a distillation of current social criticism, a highly integrated analysis of the agenda for their generation: every problem was related to all others. Clearly, the challenges of racism and the nuclear arms race intruded most forcefully on their consciousness, but these were understood to be symptomatic of a pervasive disparity between the liberal values they espoused and the society of which they were a part.

The Bomb (nor even atmospheric testing) was not the point for the young SDS; it was but a manifestation of a policy that included deterrence, Cold War anticommunism, and intervention in the Third World. Foreign policy was fully dealt with in the Port Huron Statement, but it was linked to everything else because "every effort to end the Cold War and expand the process of world industrialization . . . is bound to establish greater democracy in America." Conversely, an authentic foreign policy would be guided—and achieved—by a vigorous "democracy of individual participation." That was the point: fraternity, honesty, and participation in decision-making to the ends that every person could achieve the fullest potential in an interdependent society and every nation could aspire to its own goals in an interdependent world. SDS did not see itself as exclusively a peace organization, but the authors of the Statement believed that peace abroad and justice at home would be best served by extending what they called "participatory democracy."[15]

For all the grandeur of its conceptions—Harrington's politically responsible coalition for peace or Port Huron's cutting edge of democratic reform—activism stalled noticeably in the middle of the year. Student SANE disintegrated, while the parent organization seemed to lack a clear sense of purpose. The FOR went "into the doldrums," and SPU leaders complained that the student movement was dying "in a vacuum—in the absence of an adult movement."[16] Leaders variously attributed the decline to the competing attraction of civil rights activism, the apparent easing of international tensions, or distracting local encounters with the radical right. Some reported simple organizational fatigue.

Ennui fed on division within the ranks. Differences over the viability of American institutions and the very means and ends of peace-seeking sharpened during 1962, and the already tenuous coalition of peace advocates became further strained. Radical pacifists associated with *Liberation* warmed to the New Left critique of conventional politics. Psychologist and social philosopher Paul Goodman had been writing for the magazine since the mid-1950s. "The Cold War cannot be altered by ordinary political means" of petitions, parties, or voting, he insisted. It was time to move "nonviolence beyond the narrow confines of symbolic protest to action that will have a real impact on history" and "change the course of events." People must choose, explained Dave Dellinger, "between being liberals who limit expression of our idealism to activities and goals which minimize personal risk . . . and being radicals who concentrate on historical exigency rather than on personal safety."[17] Liberal peace advocates naturally chafed under such jibes. Harvard sociologist David Riesman discerned "a strong element of cynicism and even of nihilism" within the "anarchist wing," along with a disturbing "contempt for parliamentary forms."[18] Even harsher criticism came from Roy Finch, a pacifist who had quit the *Liberation* editorial collective to protest its uncritical support for Castro's revolution. The radicals' preoccupation with personal resistance and spontaneous action made for a grand "emotional togetherness" and "folk-songy oneness," Finch conceded; but it encouraged an "atmosphere of cultism" which invited political manipulation and discounted programs that might appeal to ordinary people.[19]

The alternative to moral confrontation was, of course, to work within the political system through organized lobbying and electoral action. Perhaps two dozen self-proclaimed peace candidates stood for national office in 1962. Some, like Chicago labor organizer Sidney Lens, campaigned in order to build up support for the 1964 elections. Others angled for Democratic votes in hopes of strengthening themselves within the party, as did Harvard University historian H. Stuart Hughes, who sought nomination for the national senate seat vacated by John F. Kennedy. Conducting campaigns "as diverse and unorganized as the peace movement itself," peace candidates argued variously for an end to atmospheric nuclear testing, expansion of the Arms Control and Disarmament Agency, and economic conversion from military to social spending. There was otherwise nothing in common among the campaigns of groups such as New England PAX, the Chicago Voters for Peace, or the Ann Arbor Voters Voice for Peace.[20]

Those feeble electoral efforts were countered by the conservative cast of national politics on both international and domestic issues. The civil rights movement was checked on many fronts, despite great effort and risk. Several black churches in Alabama were bombed during the winter, and a yearlong campaign failed to desegregate the town of Albany, Georgia. Early in the fall the first enrollment of a black student at the University of Mississippi provoked a violent reaction. Federal marshals provided round-the-clock protection to James Meredith, while hundreds of Ole Miss students and supporters went on a prolonged rampage until regular army troops and guardsmen restored order at bayonet point. Southern Democratic segregationists joined conservative Republicans in a counter-offensive against black activism and the "no-win" foreign policy of the Kennedy administration: the White House was going too far at home, and not far enough abroad. Senator James Eastland (D-Miss.) charged that federal authorities had provoked the Ole Miss riots by mistreating the students, while Senator John Tower (R-Tex.) asked Congress to declare formally that the U.S. aim in the Cold War was for "victory."[21] Campaigning for the California governorship, Nixon claimed that incumbent governor Pat Brown was soft on communism; the Republican National Committee charged liberal House Democrats with advocating a foreign policy of "surrender"; and Goldwater singled out disarmament specifically as a "great Communist-inspired deception."[22] Sweeping in its breadth and intensity, aggressive conservatism permeated the national political atmosphere and chilled campaigns based on international negotiations and accommodation.

Any hopes for electoral success still nursed by peace liberals in the fall shrivelled fatally during the Cuban Missile Crisis. After weeks of unsettling rumors, the White House announced in mid-October that the USSR was installing intermediate-range ballistic missiles in Cuba. Terming the Soviet missiles an intolerable threat to American security, President Kennedy insisted upon their removal and imposed a naval blockade (politely termed a "quarantine") around the island. After first denying the existence of the missiles, the Soviets explained that they were defensive weapons installed at the request of Premier Castro, who feared a new invasion. The Soviets rejected Washington's demand for removal of the missiles, and they refused to recall supply ships headed toward Cuba and the American naval line. The world braced for a collision.

Anxiously, peace activists rallied. On 23 October a WSP contingent picketed the White House and eight hundred women marched on the UN Plaza, appealing for international intercession and an end to the U.S. blockade. SANE called for an "immediate military disengagement" under UN supervision, a reciprocal halt to the U.S. blockade and Soviet missile construction, and the mutual withdrawal of U.S. missiles from Turkey and Russian missiles from Cuba under UN guarantees.[23] Meanwhile, around the country there were isolated actions in support of a UN-supervised solution. With a few exceptions, dissidents demonstrated without harassment. It was as though the crisis was so encompassing that dissent scarcely mattered.[24]

Certainly activists felt helpless, irrelevant, and sometimes panicky. On 26 October, for instance, a few demonstrators in the capital picked up a rumor that Cuba was to be bombed. Shaken by the "possibility of an immediate nuclear holocaust," individuals began to think about evacuating the city with their families. Most of them decided "that it would be better to die on the job, urging negotiation."[25] Shortly, reports trickled in that the crisis had passed. The Soviets chose not to challenge the U.S. blockade and opened negotiations over the removal of their weapons.

The missile crisis affected the peace movement in several ways. Most immediately, it undercut the electoral campaigns of the eight peace candidates still in the field. Cornell University law professor Harrop Freeman, who was running as Liberal party candidate for an upstate New York congressional seat (and who actually supported Kennedy's blockade of Cuba), got barely 3 percent of the popular vote. In Massachusetts, H. Stuart Hughes received what his campaign manager called "a stunning low vote" of fifty thousand. Despite the victories of some major party candidates in whom peace advocates had confidence, Norman Thomas concluded dryly that the fall election was "not one greatly to encourage the fragmented peace movement."[26]

On another level, peace activists reflected on the implications of the missile crisis for world politics and their own roles. They were more than ever clear that the UN was indispensable and that nuclear weapons had to be controlled, if not eliminated. They felt much less confident in the value of their own efforts. Those few who had demonstrated believed that their actions had been "as good as could be expected," perhaps even "courageous." They conceded, though, that their protest had been "belated and largely irrelevant."[27] The hard fact was "that we came near being blown up," admitted one SDS activist, "and that our almost total impotence to avert the crisis had its effect on all of us."[28] Peace leaders scavenged the experience for its lessons, mostly reinforcing their own predilections. Women in WSP decided that the fight against the Cold War required an even greater emphasis on *"communication."* Liberal pacifists argued for a movement toward world order beyond the radical "dogmatic, utopian demand for total, unilateral disarmament." SDS members concluded that "the priority today, as never before, is power."[29] Whatever their strategic preference, however, peace workers were obliged to acknowledge that at the gravest moment of crisis they had been ineffective. The prognosis for the future, wrote Catholic priest Thomas Merton, was for "a lull, a time out for another tranquilizer, then back with renewed zest to the fray."[30]

In the longer run, the missile crisis contributed to U.S. and Soviet policies which led to a ratified partial test-ban treaty in September 1963.

For peace liberals the treaty became the tranquilizer Merton prophesied, but not before their own efforts unexpectedly combined with a shift in international relations to produce an atmospheric test ban.

Khrushchev covered his loss in the Cuban escapade with the line that Soviet restraint had prevented war, and the Soviets reemphasized peaceful competition with the West. Kennedy emerged from the crisis with an enhanced reputation for firmness and restraint. Politically vindicated by standing up to the Russians, he was in a position to bend. The two leaders exchanged letters, agreeing on the importance of controlling the arms race, but negotiations on a test-ban treaty remained deadlocked through the following winter. At Eastertime peace organizations conducted their now traditional appeals for a test-ban. They were stimulated by the proclamation of the encyclical *Pacem in Terris* by Pope John XXIII, a landmark of explicit Catholic endorsement for peace-seeking, but no one sensed movement.

Meanwhile, early in April, Norman Cousins flew to Russia on a mission of citizen diplomacy. Cousins was well known to the Russians. He had sponsored the Dartmouth Conferences of American and Russian intellectuals and had represented the Pope to Khrushchev in December 1962 on behalf of a Catholic cardinal interned under Stalin. Acting on a suggestion from Secretary of State Dean Rusk, he met with Khrushchev at the premier's Black Sea estate in April. In the course of a long conversation, Cousins explained the U.S. test-ban coalition and conveyed the president's good faith in negotiations. The Russian leader seemed to accept that and indicated his receptivity to new initiatives.[31]

The conversation, which Cousins recounted in detail for Kennedy, reinforced the president's resolve to speak decisively for détente in a major address at the American University in June. Acknowledging that both powers had "a mutually deep interest in a just and genuine peace and in halting the arms race," Kennedy appealed for a reexamination of the Cold War. "If we cannot end now our differences, at least we can help make the world safe for diversity. For in the final analysis our most basic common link is that we all inhabit this planet. We all breathe the same air. We all cherish our children's future. And we are all mortal."[32] The Soviets accepted Kennedy's gambit, and limited test-ban negotiations resumed in earnest. A treaty prohibiting atmospheric but not underground atomic testing was signed on 25 July.

Peace liberals turned to the task of securing ratification. Cousins had implied to the Russians, after all, that the test-ban coalition would help the president get public support. Acting on an administration suggestion, he helped to form an independent Ad Hoc Committee for a Nuclear Test Treaty in order to rally a broad cross section of Americans. Cousins concurred with the president's view that the treaty should not appear to be "solely a liberal cause" and cautioned that SANE "was not quite what was needed in terms of a specific mechanism aimed exclusively at a nuclear test ban."[33] Accordingly, SANE yielded a measure of leadership in the campaign for ratification of what had been its very raison d'être. Public opinion shifted gradually and then decisively. On 24 September the Senate overwhelmingly ratified the Partial Test-Ban Treaty. The seven-year campaign through which organized peace effort had been shaped was over.

Upon returning to Washington in September after a month's vacation, I. F. Stone confessed that he felt like "a Rip Van Winkle . . . pleasantly awakened to a world he never expected to see." Stone observed that even the White House was "speaking the language one heard earlier only from fringe groups like SANE which seemed to be crying in a nuclear wilderness."[34] SANE leaders hailed the treaty as their "greatest moment." Massachusetts businessman and peace liberal Jerome Grossman revelled in the "summer of victories," and the *Bulletin of the Atomic Scientists* contended that the "old order of priorities is being revised in America."[35]

The satisfaction of peace advocates was premature. Although they had organized an impressive coalition and had persistently kept the issue of nuclear testing before the public, they had played only a marginal role in securing the treaty and none in shaping it. In the end they had campaigned on the administration's terms and under the auspices of a national committee more than on their own recognizance. They had acquiesced in the limited objective of banning atmospheric tests in deference to their concern for a brake on the arms race and had campaigned for a bilateral treaty in lieu of a more highly developed international system. In a December 1962 article on the administration and the missile crisis, journalists Stewart Alsop and Charles Bartlett had described the prowar "hawks" and the pronegotiation "doves" who had fluttered about the White House during policy-making discussions. Happily, they reported, the two species gradually merged as a consensus of "hoves" and "dawks."[36] The subsequent test-ban treaty, although a testimony to the reorganized peace movement, represented a consensus in support of the administration more than a victory for doves. Understandably, many activists wavered between feelings of enthusiasm and irrelevance. After adrenalin, the tranquilizer.

"'The heart' of the American problem"

With the test-ban treaty ratified, many rank-and-file peace workers concluded that "peace has been declared" and scattered into related reform enterprises or into the Democratic party. One estimate put the membership of national peace groups at perhaps 85,000, and another concluded that even with hundreds of groups on the local level, peace advocates involved a maximum of 150,000 American families.[37] The student peace movement collapsed. The SPU membership waned rapidly, and its budget, over $22,000 in 1961–62, dropped a third by June 1964, when the organization dissolved.[38] Women Strike for Peace settled on "a kind of plateau," with smaller affiliates "dying out" and general interest drying up.[39] Turn Toward Peace already had failed to achieve any significant growth, and now it collapsed into internal quarrels over national coordinator Robert Pickus' attacks on radical pacifists and leftists as being naïvely one-sided in their criticism of American foreign policy.

As it redefined itself after 24 September, SANE mirrored the dilemma and direction of liberal peace advocacy. Although it had been sidelined somewhat by a more broadly representative ad hoc committee in the final push for a test ban, the very intensity of that campaign had elevated the organization's prominence. Cousins and some other leaders wanted to disband the organization on the grounds that its first purpose had been realized. In reply, the majority argued that SANE should take advantage of an emerging détente and escalate its efforts toward general disarmament and a strengthened UN. Cousins and Pickett were succeeded as cochairmen by Benjamin Spock and H. Stuart Hughes, and Homer Jack was followed by Donald Keys as executive director. SANE was more than ever committed to public information and political action. Thus, toward the end of 1963, it was represented by Sandy Gottlieb on a Peace Politics Clearing House which identified candidates meriting support for their positions on the arms race and related international issues. Meanwhile, Cousins became honorary president of the United World Federalists, and, in the following year, there were persistent efforts to merge the UWF and SANE. The plan was derailed early in 1965 when the organizations divided sharply over how to respond to the escalating war in Vietnam.[40]

In 1963 the issues were still generalized: disarmament without the focus offered by atmospheric testing and détente without an immediate crisis. Throughout the established peace movement there was a spate of meetings, correspondence, and articles addressing the problem of direction. Indeed, the difficulty was compounded by the awareness of numerous leaders that the issues of peace, disarmament, civil rights, economic justice, and human welfare all were interrelated. The questions raised since 1955 by a resurgent peace movement seemed peripheral, and advocacy was apparently off the streets. Liberal peace advocacy retained its organizational structure following the test-ban; but it tended increasingly toward education, electoral politics, and lobbying, and away from public protest.

Radical pacifists and social radicals of the New Left were very much involved with public protest, but the issue was domestic—civil rights. Expanding the militant nonviolent tactics of 1960–61, SNCC had attempted a new "jail-in" tactic in 1962, trying to overwhelm the criminal justice system with nonviolent activists. Other black and white protesters picketed, boycotted, marched, and sat in against segregation at lunch counters, park benches, and playgrounds throughout the South that year. In May, CORE launched a series of Freedom Rides to challenge segregation in interstate travel. Bus-borne activists were attacked by white mobs in Alabama and Mississippi with such viciousness that the federal government dispatched seven hundred federal marshals in their defense.

The civil rights movement spread into the nation's cities, and it became increasingly ambitious, impatient, and provocative. Martin Luther King, Jr., and the Southern Christian Leadership Conference (SCLC) opened winter demonstrations in Birmingham, Alabama. Violence mounted until, after two bombings in the black community, thousands of blacks disrupted the city's business district one May night before they were dispersed by police and national guardsmen. The Kennedy administration sent mediators from the Justice Department to Birmingham and drafted a major civil rights bill intended to desegregate public facilities in enterprises involved in interstate commerce.

As the bill bogged down in Congress, protest flared. Powered by a sense of what King called "somebodiness," blacks demonstrated in the streets and sometimes scrapped with police or local white youths in big cities from Chicago to Seattle as well as in smaller towns like Dearborn, Michigan, and Lincoln, Nebraska.[41] Interracial clashes in the South were not only more frequent, but the police there were more inclined to disperse demonstrators with dogs, fire hoses, and tear gas. Still, the hope for nonviolent racial change persisted. In late August an unprecedented coalition of civil rights groups, labor unions, and religious groups rallied over 200,000 people to a huge March on Washington, where they heard Martin Luther King, Jr., proclaim his "dream" of an integrated America. Even this, the most massive and moving democratic spectacle in modern American history, failed to enlist Congress behind the civil rights bill or to constrain the rising spiral of violence.

Racial crisis blended distrust of authority and deepening polarization into a politics of impatience and suspicion that dominated national life for the following decade. The phenomenon was manifest among segregationist whites. As civil rights activism continued, despite official intimidation and night-riding terrorism, southern political leaders accused federal authorities and the national news media of stimulating racial animosities. Some segregationists branded demands for racial change as subversive. Various white leaders accused King of being a communist, a charge that the FBI went to great lengths to validate (failing that, the Bureau decided in December 1963 to neutralize King as a black leader by means of threats and blackmail). Governor George Wallace of Alabama routinely attacked civil rights protesters as "communist-inspired" or the dupes of unspecified but suspect "left-wing groups," and warned that common folk were "fed up" with their demonstrations and demands.[42]

Civil rights activists themselves began to polarize over the validity of American institutions. While desegregation leaders such as King and CORE's James Farmer pressed more aggressively for the nonviolent reconstruction of Jim Crow America, Malcolm X and black nationalists questioned the value of integration and argued for black racial pride. In 1963 that was still a matter of emphasis. The civil rights movement was not truly split at this point, but elements within it felt alienated from the national society.

Political violence persisted: W. L. Moore killed near Attalla, Alabama; Medgar Evers gunned down in Jackson, Mississippi; four children and two adults killed by a bomb during a church service in Birmingham. An ugly mood spilled over to other arenas of protest. In October UN Ambassador Stevenson was spat upon and struck by anti-UN activists in Dallas and Chief Justice Earl Warren was attacked in New York City. In mid-November, after months of domestic tension, journalist James Reston declared that the president's problem was not so much how he might win reelection in 1964 as how he might govern the country.[43] A week later John F. Kennedy was dead.

The peace movement reflected the crosscurrents swirling through the nation, including black protest itself. Peace liberals like Sandy Gottlieb of SANE wanted to forge stronger links with militant nonviolent activists in groups such as CORE in order to connect the "peace, Negro, labor, and other groups" in "a coalition of peace" that emphasized a national program of jobs, freedom, an end to the Cold War, disarmament, and the conversion of the American economy from military to civilian purposes.[44] Radical pacifists, on the other hand, contended that nonviolent protest succeeded only when it went beyond moral appeals and disrupted existing social structures. War Resisters League leader Dave McReynolds concluded that peace activists, like black protesters, needed to think in terms "of massive social dislocation." They would halt the war machine only when they "jammed its gears" with mass direct actions.[45]

Liberals and radical pacifists clashed in 1963 on a second and recurring issue—exclusionism in the movement. Assailing groups that welcomed "anyone, communist or not, who is for peace," Norman Thomas warned against confusing "Khrushchev with Tolstoy" or judging him "by far more lenient standards than we judge President Kennedy."[46] SANE leaders warned members against joining demonstrations that suggested support for "pacifist, radical pacifist, anarchist, and Soviet apologist positions," and Robert Pickus of TTP attacked the "blind, ritual ANTI-anti-communism" of various leftists and radical pacifists.[47] For their part, radical pacifists meanwhile adopted the New Left emphasis on inclusiveness—cooperation with anyone who shared their goals. Enchanted by dreams of a new popular front on the left, Muste and his friends complained that exclusionism was an unacceptable concession to the hysterical, red-baiting forces in Cold War America.

The orientation of key radical pacifists was converging with a shift in the New Left toward the "politics of insurgent protest" and the promise of building a new-style peace movement within a broader front of left-wing change. This tendency was typified by the Students for a Democratic Society. Moving beyond the liberal assumptions of its Port Huron Statement, SDS proclaimed the need for a radical opposition "boring from below" among the urban poor, disaffected blacks, and disenchanted students to create systemic change.[48] The overriding need was for fundamental reform, but the immediate struggle was between "established liberalism and a new radicalism" whose "defining characteristic" was grassroots struggle against racism, unemployment, and poverty.[49] This perception led several SDS leaders into local community organizing.

Significantly, their new position statement contained few references to international affairs. SDS leaders argued that their version of radicalism would constitute "a 'peace movement,' even if the advocacy of foreign policy alternatives were not a major feature of its program." Radical domestic change assumed the "fundamental reordering of priorities of our society." The SDS leaders insisted: "The evils manifest in American society—unemployment, economic insecurity, segregation, the threat of nuclear war—cannot be attacked piecemeal, because they are symptoms of one disease, not separate and distinct maladies."[50] The illness was corporate liberalism; the cure was to support socialism and neutralism abroad and to broaden the basis of decision-making power at home. That meant a social revolution, although it did not imply violent confrontation. A few articulate radical pacifists, particularly those associated with *Liberation,* found the New Left orientation attractive.

In question was the very purpose of domestic change and international détente. *Progressive* magazine voiced the liberal view that "the heart" of the American problem was "to develop WITHIN our own society the superiority of our free way of life over the totalitarianism of the Communist system."[51] New Left radicals agreed on the primacy of domestic change, although they were skeptical about the capacity of established institutions to effect it. Similarly, both liberals and radicals welcomed détente, and both anticipated that it would increase U.S. interest in the Third World; but they drew different conclusions. Norman Thomas represented peace liberals who viewed détente as a rational attempt by Moscow and Washington to cope with new realities such as Chinese expansionism and global polycentrism. In this view, the danger was that great-power recklessness in the Third World might escalate "small conflicts" into a nuclear collision.[52] Radical pacifists and SDS activists, on the other hand, did not view Third World conflicts as in any way small. They regarded détente as the first step in Washington's mounting determination "to prevent, forestall, or suppress" popular revolutions. Absorbed in the domestic politics of race and poverty, the new radicals were "profoundly American-centered." They feared that Washington's new fascination with counter-insurgency abroad would thwart change at home.[53] They hoped to check interventionism by reordering American society.

In 1963 all this seemed pretty abstract, even ethereal. Its influence was limited to a small coterie in the peace and civil rights movements and to rhetorical sparring on the left. Sooner than anyone suspected, however, the makeup and motifs of the peace movement would affect American life, as the meaning of intervention was tested in Vietnam.

"There was no way to join; you simply announced or felt yourself to be a part of the movement"

By the time that Indochina policy became a public issue, the proponents of a comprehensive test-ban treaty, disarmament, and disengagement from the Cold War had constructed a peace movement which bridged their two major factions—liberal peace advocates and radical pacifists. They were alive to elements in American culture which would affect the peace movement more than they could expect: changes in liberal thought, the rise of student-led protest, the emergence of a new radical left, and the challenge of a militant (although nonviolent) civil rights campaign. They were perhaps less cognizant of another influence they would shortly feel, the growth of a counterculture. Already the peace advocates had carried their concerns into the public arena in a variety of ways: attempting to inform and persuade, seeking electoral and legislative influence, and dramatizing issues through protests and civil disobedience.

They represented a loose alignment of peace organizations: older ones such as the FOR, AFSC, WRL, and WILPF; and new ones, notably SANE, CNVA, and the SPU. Their constituency and concerns overlapped those of civil rights groups such as CORE and student activists in SDS. Peace advocates were professionals, students, intellectuals, and pacifists—men and women who came together as "a very specific response to the unique moral and political problems posed by the Bomb."[54] Most of them were commonsense realists, hardly ideologues. One researcher found that peace activists were "overwhelmingly middle-aged, college educated, and politically liberal" people from existing social networks, such as political clubs and church groups, whose paths converged after they had experienced a change in their attitudes toward war and peace issues during youth or early adulthood. Some were "'cause' people." Many were liberal pacifists who coupled their absolute rejection of war with political efforts, and a few were radical pacifists who espoused direct action and civil disobedience. Collectively, they were unusual in that they exhibited acute alienation from prevailing power structures at the same time as they expressed great confidence in their capacity to change those structures.[55]

Often called "nuclear pacifists," these peace advocates believed that systematic preparations for a great-power nuclear war were not morally or politically tolerable. They assumed that in order to check those preparations they had to reach the hearts and minds of the American people. Unlike the internationalists of the 1940s, they did not have to persuade the public to become involved in world affairs; they were more concerned with changing the terms of involvement. They directed their effort to the nation's foreign policy rather than to the organization of a new world order, and accordingly they challenged the way Americans thought about national values and interests. They sought to convince their fellow Americans that the main threat to the nation came less from international communism than from the Cold War itself and the weapons, governmental duplicity, and citizen passivity it engendered.

The movement was still in formation in 1963, unknowingly in transition from peace advocacy to war opposition; but it is possible to discern even then several shared emphases. These were the motifs which distinguished the peace movement of the 1950s from its historic antecedents and which set the tone it would project in opposition to the Vietnam War. Variations on these themes help to delineate the lines on which the antiwar movement would fracture during the ordeal of challenging the national consensus.

There were essentially three. One was the *motif of madness*—the sense that organized twentieth-century life was devolving into institutionalized insanity. A second was the *motif of moral deadness*—an apprehension that the Cold War and arms race were crushing democratic participation and critical moral judgment in policymaking. Closely related was a secondary theme, sensitivity to manipulation and deception. Finally, there was the *motif of personal morality,* often played out in symbolic actions and not infrequently in civil disobedience. In combination, these themes composed the changing style of the peace and antiwar movements.

The Motif of Madness Peace activists identified themselves as SANE quite deliberately. The title was the mirror image of the insanity they felt to be the distinguishing characteristic of their time. "I saw the best minds of my generation destroyed by madness."[56] So began Allen Ginsberg's "Howl," but the theme of irrationality was not confined to beats. It was pervasive. It was dramatized by Eugene Ionesco in the theater of the absurd, and was parlayed in satire by *MAD,* one of the most popular serial publications of the decade. Even Secretary of Defense Robert McNamara's definition of U.S. nuclear strategy as mutual assured destruction was quickly understood, in the acronym-crazy spirit of the times, to be MAD.

Intellectually, the theme emerged as social critics tried to come to terms with the three largest facts of their lives: Nazism and the Holocaust, the Cold War and McCarthyism, and the nuclear arms competition—itself symptomatic of technology beyond human control. Obsessed with the irrationality of mass man since the rise of Nazism, a number of European and American social analysts, including Theodor Adorno and Erich Fromm, contended that modernization was alienating individuals from the larger social fabric, leaving large numbers of people vulnerable to manipulation by demagogues. Studies of the Communist party in America by Lewis Coser and Irving Howe and reflections on it by Clinton Rossiter, Daniel Bell, and others implied that Marxism tapped adherents' fanatical need for absolutes. The threat of irrational mass politics was brought home to intellectuals by McCarthyism and its wholesale claims of disloyalty and internal subversion. Social critics like Eric Hofer warned against the zealotry of "true believers" whose spiritual emptiness made them prime recruits for authoritarianism. Irrationality was not an incidental feature of modern life, it seemed. Rather, it was becoming characteristic of mainstream politics in the industrial world.[57]

A distinctive characteristic of peace activism after 1955 was that it subordinated traditional arguments about economic causes of war to a concern over the politics of irrationality. Neither liberals nor radicals could conceive of the menace of the nuclear arms race in any other way; neither could avoid the metaphor of madness. In his widely read book, *The Sane Society,* Fromm worried whether Cold War America could yet "be converted to sanity—or [would] use the greatest discoveries of human reason for its own purposes of unreason and insanity?"[58] Was it foolish to talk of disarmament in a world of atomic bombs? Robert Pickus countered: the overriding "fact that stares men in the face today is that *an armed world in this age is itself madness.*"[59] Norman Cousins charged that nuclear strategists trafficked in "the language of madmen." A. J. Muste added that the arms race was the "activity of lunatics" whose faith in national defense through the deterrent power of mutual annihilation was "an extreme expression of the mental sickness" gripping world politics in a state of "mass hypnosis, mass hysteria or catalepsy."[60] Warned Lewis Mumford, "We are now facing something worse than war: we are threatened with an outbreak of compulsive irrationality" because of the fear introduced into international affairs. In the face of this murderous absurdity, argued Catholic Workers, the moral person must obey "the strict obligation to say 'No' to the madness."[61] C. Wright Mills agreed that there was no other choice. A "crackpot realism" of "military metaphysics" dominated policymaking processes in both Russia and America, he wrote, and modern peoples were "at a curious juncture in the history of human insanity: in the name of realism, men are quite mad."[62]

Although peace liberals and radical pacifists shared a common apprehension of political irrationality, they differed about its source and import. Liberals like Cousins were frightened by the spectre of mass man. They saw McCarthyism as a crazy aberration in American politics, one that showed the danger of popular movements and the need for humane, rational leadership. Instinctively they believed that there was a limit to irrationality. When asked about rumors of U.S. military escalation in Vietnam, Norman Thomas responded to an Indian journalist in 1963 "that I was willing to risk my reputation for knowing my own country by saying that I did not think in spite of all the talk ... that the U.S. would risk war employing its own men and facilities in Southeast Asia. It would be a kind of military madness."[63] The point, for liberals, was to educate the public, persuade the elite, and reason with policymakers about the implications of both mass fear and confounding technology.

Radical pacifists, on the other hand, tended to view McCarthyism and the arms race as symptomatic of a larger madness in the bureaucratic structures of modern industrial society ("Moloch whose mind is pure machinery," as Ginsberg put it[64]). Political and economic systems operated with a kind of cold and inhumane calculation, the logic of their own organizational priorities, they thought. The result was a politics of the absurd. It was a *Catch-22* system, to borrow the title of a 1955 novel by Joseph Heller. Rather than try to win over the policymakers, radical pacifists and New Left radicals turned to people they thought were untainted by the corrupting logic and structures of modern industrialism—especially southern blacks and Third World peoples. For this purpose they valued especially individual acts of obstruction and resistance which would expose the inhuman illogic of institutions and which would demonstrate that individuals could affect issues seemingly beyond control. The point, for radicals (pacifist and political) was to empower people by raising their consciousness and confidence in action.

The Motif of Moral Numbness. A second motif in the peace movement of the early 1960s was a preoccupation with alienation and moral numbness. Closely related to the first theme, it too was reflected in social criticism throughout the Eisenhower years. Wrote Lewis Mumford, "We must conquer our moral numbness and inertia: the state that since 1945 has enabled us, in America, to accept the indiscriminate extermination of human life, by atomic and bacterial means, as the conceivable act of a sane government engaged in war."[65] C. Wright Mills added that the "key" moral and political fact of the times was the absence of "any truly debated alternatives" to the belief that America would prevail in the Cold War through the ceaseless accumulation of weapons of ever-increasing destructive power. Without any serious discussion over ways toward survival, the American people "are becoming politically indifferent; they are being rapidly transformed into masses; and these masses are becoming morally as well as politically insensible. . . . They are not radical, not liberal, not conservative, not reactionary. They are inactionary. They are out of it."[66] Complained Albert Bigelo (skipper of the *Golden Rule*), "We stand benumbed, morally desensitized by ten years of propaganda and fear. How do you reach men when all the horror is in the fact that they feel no horror?"[67]

Peace advocates feared that the Cold War and the nuclear arms race were creating "a broadening chasm between the citizen and the decision-making process."[68] Scientist Ralph Lapp complained in 1962 that the number of Americans concerned with the arms race was "pitifully small."[69] "The arms race is dangerous enough," read that year's circular for the February mobilization of students, "but the absence of debate among legislators *and among the American people at large is also cause for alarm.*"[70] That was a basic theme in the Port Huron Statement: the political system was generating no real alternatives in the face of increased urgency. Specifically addressing students, the SDS paper warned, "Apathy about apathy begets a privately constructed universe."[71] This view corresponded to the apprehension of radical pacifists lest "extraordinary apathy" and "moral passivity" were corroding the values of individual freedom and working democracy.[72]

Sensitivity to moral numbness became more acute as Nazi war criminal Adolf Eichmann was captured, tried, and then executed. Seized in Argentina by Israeli agents in 1960, he was tried in Jerusalem for his role in the destruction of European Jews. In his own utterly ordinary way, Eichmann defended himself on the grounds that he was ignorant of the Nazis' larger policies and that he was merely a soldier following orders. He was diagnosed as medically sane, found guilty, and executed in 1962. The whole episode was an extended morality play that opened issues such as obedience, authority, and institutionalized insanity. Its import troubled American peace activists for whom the analogy to the Nazi holocaust was a nuclear one. Thomas Merton began to develop a serious peace concern during those years, and he made the connection explicit. A moral and political paralysis gripped America, he wrote. It was "a psychology of evasion and helplessness" and "pseudo-Christian obedience" that was nothing more than "the obedience of an Eichmann."[73] The fact that Eichmann was found to be sane compelled thoughtful people to consider, Merton added, that perhaps in a world of bureaucratized obedience "it is precisely the SANE who are the most dangerous." The Catholic priest had linked the motifs of madness and numbness, and the implications were clear, if unnerving: "We can no longer assume that because a man is 'sane' he is therefore in his 'right mind.'"[74]

According to leading peace-seekers, the centralization and bureau-cratization of decision-making required for modern warfare were generating what Ralph Lapp called a "new priesthood" of scientists and technocrats. Conversely, it was breeding a frightening "moral passivity" among Americans, an indifference to the values of life and democracy. Preoccupied with the need for physical security through political conformity and arms acquisitions, American democracy seemed to be locked on a course in which it "would betray its values in order to protect them."[75]

This observation left peace advocates with a special responsibility. They not only had to attack the Cold War, they also had to rescue America's very democratic process. Quaker pacifist Stewart Meacham concluded that "the reason that there is a new kind of peace movement today is not so much that people are frightened by the threat of nuclear destruction as that they are terrified at being lost as people. The deepest problem we face is not to escape physical destruction, but to regain a sense of the meaning and worth of our lives. The peace movement will achieve power only as it helps restore us to ourselves."[76] "In our minds," declared the leaders of the Student Peace Union in 1960, "the danger to civilization from the arms race is just as much because of the shift in our whole value system as it is because of the threat of annihilation."[77] Less than two years later, that position became a central thesis of the Port Huron Statement.

Growing sensitivity to manipulation and deception in public life contributed to the motif of moral numbness and accented concern for the integrity of national values and institutions. Like other themes, this one distinguished the peace advocates of the early 1960s from their predecessors. Suspicion of official manipulativeness derived from many sources. It was partly an extension of a long-standing intellectual interest in propaganda—that management and control of information refined by the government during World War I. The suspicion of official sources was heightened by the memory of deceit, such as communist and fascist information control techniques. Widespread familiarity with the writings of George Orwell, recent experience with the deceptive politics of McCarthyism, and misinformation from the AEC during the test-ban debate further exacerbated the distrust of official information.

Moreover, manipulation was in the air. Fascination with the power and pervasiveness of mass consumer advertising techniques was illustrated by enthusiasm for Vance Packard's 1957 best-seller, *The Hidden Persuaders,* and by revelations in 1959 that a series of popular television quiz game shows had been rigged. The real $64,000 Question became: whom can you trust? The U-2 incident and Eisenhower's exposure in May of the following year compromised a national figure thought to be above deception. Not that anyone questioned the president's personal morality;

but perhaps officials absorbed in a protracted crisis like the Cold War lied as a matter of course. Arthur Waskow, then a Ph.D. candidate at the University of Wisconsin, recalled ten years later that the U-2 affair had filled him with a "very strange mixture of shame and sorrow and fear (shame at the nation's weird upside-down moral reaction—why didn't Powers shoot himself, etc.—fear at what I thought was a major shift of the chances in favor of war) all concentrated on a feeling that the flag meant much less to me than it ever had before."[78]

The same month as the U-2 incident, nearly a thousand young people confronted the House Un-American Activities Committee at the San Francisco City Hall, protesting the committee's high-handed search for subversives in northern California. Violence ensued, resulting in injuries and arrests. The committee confiscated television footage in order to produce its own version of the incident, which portrayed the dissidents as dupes of international communism. That film, *Operation Abolition,* was widely distributed over the next few years by right-wing groups. It was countered by an American Civil Liberties Union version, *Operation Correction,* and the whole affair intensified suspicions of official deception.[79] Within the peace movement of 1963 the motif of moral numbness and manipulation evoked a strong commitment to act on behalf of democratic institutions. During the Vietnam War, reaction to moral numbness would divide many activists from one another and distance some of them from their society.

The Motif of Personal Morality. The third motif of the movement was in some respects the converse of the first two. This was the expression of personal idealism, couched in terms of individual action or dissident communities. In the SDS formulation, "a new left must transform modern complexity into issues that can be understood and felt close up by every human being."[80]

It is clear that in the peace movement, as in civil rights, commitment to social change often followed from a conversion-like personal experience—some critical episode that shattered one's sense of personal security and vision of moral order.[81] Norman Cousins, for example, first became involved in active opposition to the arms race when, in August 1956, a group of Washington University scientists convinced him that the danger of fallout was far greater than the AEC acknowledged. This moved him to "an enlarged understanding of the need to bring nuclear testing under control."[82] Benjamin Spock had a similar experience. The language with which such liberals as these described their conversion to activism conveyed their rationality and their faith in humankind and progress.

For others the response was visceral. Albert Bigelow recalled that as a naval commander in the Pacific he had been "absolutely awestruck" by the atomization of Hiroshima. "Intuitively," he recalled, "it was then that I realized for the first time that morally war is impossible." As a high school student in Palo Alto, California, Joan Baez rebelled at a requirement to take part in school defense drills, read some of her father's physics texts, and concluded: "The idea that it would help to take cover from a nuclear bomb was just crazy. I wouldn't do it."[83] Dorothy Hutchinson, who as president of WILPF protested at AEC Washington headquarters, remembered a feeling of horror as she discovered during discussions with agency officials that the "men at the top" felt no qualms over their daily planning for wholesale death. Like "the people who served Hitler," she wrote, they felt no sense of "responsibility for the decisions they carry out," no "willingness to contemplate the consequences of their actions."[84] These experiences were no doubt shared by many Americans. What set activists apart was their decision to respond with personal action.

That was more than a political calculation. It was an affirmation of moral responsibility and personal worth. Activists with strong religious orientation assumed that the peace question fundamentally was "a moral and spiritual problem." The Cold War crisis was "a crisis of man's spirit," Merton explained. "It is a great religious and moral upheaval of the human race, and we do not really know half of the causes of this upheaval."[85] Secular activists were less prone to phrase their concerns in Merton's terms, of course, but they also were in search of "a meaning in life that is personally authentic."[86] Far more than liberals and adults, pacifists and young people expressed the need for political communities that could fulfill their personal need for meaning, and many of them sought such community in the peace—and then the antiwar—movement.

During the 1960s the term "movement" became ever more inclusive. It encompassed many communities in which individuals were related through a sense of social cause. Typically these were action-oriented groupings of people committed to racial justice, economic justice, community participation, women's liberation, and an end to the war in Vietnam. Cultural communes and counterculture groups could be included insofar as they were rationalized in terms of social purpose. Some groups, like SDS, had a sophisticated political rationale; but most did not. Few had a defined membership. What cohesion they had rested on personal identification with some collective cause. All were subsumed in "The Movement," which simply indicated identification with allied communities of purposeful change. Increasingly the term "movement" became self-descriptive: "There was no way to join; you simply announced or felt yourself to be a part of the movement—usually through some act like joining a protest march." Defying any notion of organization, the Movement came to signify "a mood, a mode of life."[87] The sense of tribal belonging, of mystic sharing and communal purpose, would be powerfully reified in the tension of unpopular or even dangerous activity during the Vietnam years.

The sense of purposeful togetherness, of community in action, was one element that helped to integrate the rising New Left in the peace and antiwar movement. With Merton and the pacifists, the New Left of the early 1960s sought to promote more than the politics of change in Cold War America. It aimed, as one sympathizer put it, "to infuse life with a secular spiritual and moral content, to fill the quotidian with personal meaning and purpose." It sought "meaning and purpose in a society that offered very little of either."[88]

Although becoming a force in its own right, the new and student left was drawn to the radical pacifists of the peace movement because of several shared emphases. New Left activists were enthusiastic about direct action on the community level. Like radical pacifists, they also held Washington and Moscow equally responsible for the Cold War. They were encouraged by Third World revolutionary movements and disparaged the anticommunist fears of Cold War liberals. Indeed, they mistrusted conventional politics. As John Patrick Diggins, Irwin Unger, and others have observed, the New Left arose from the confluence of economic affluence, political powerlessness, and cultural anxiety and alienation that characterized the experience and feelings of a significant minority of the country's middle-class youth.[89] Moralistic but pragmatic, the young radicals felt contemptuous of old ideologies and established institutions. They preferred a personal ethic of action to traditional politics and shared a vague but strong sensibility: they were participants in a social movement that would change America for the better.

The New Left and the reconstructed peace movement were independent attempts to redefine American values and institutions. In 1963 each was a small part of a larger search for national definition. As they intersected in the following half decade, each would affect the other and the Movement as a whole. Moreover, each would be touched by yet another current in American life—the rise of an articulate counterculture.

Already in 1955 there had been indications of fresh cultural vitality: the reappearance of the Weavers stimulated interest in folk forms of social protest music; Elvis Presley began his meteoric rise; the film *Rebel Without a Cause* turned the late James Dean into a minor cult figure; and the founding of the *Village Voice* focused attention on a handful of cultural radicals. The new bohemians, perhaps a few hundred people in New York's Greenwich Village and San Francisco's North Beach, called themselves "beat" either because of their world-weariness or, more romantically, because their "inner search for wholeness, i.e., holiness" resonated to "the beat of jazz, heartbeat, the beat of the beatific vision" of "basic, original nature."[90]

Beat romanticism seemed to be "more a pose and an attitude" than a movement or ideology, more a lifestyle of withdrawal than a way of serious social change.[91] Ridiculing prevailing orthodoxies, beats extolled personal liberation through self-awareness and political withdrawal. They rejected the bourgeois American faith in hard work and material accumulation and sought an inner self with the help of jazz music, drugs, and freer sex. Their modest efforts received public attention, starting perhaps with a 1954 *New York Times* article, and then growing with the *Village Voice,* the 1956 publication of Allen Ginsberg's *Howl and Other Poems* (which by 1960 had outsold any other book of contemporary American poetry), and the appearance in 1957 of Jack Kerouac's best-selling rendition of romantic life, *On the Road,* soon followed by its film version. Late that year San Francisco newspaper columnist Herb Caen coined a word for the phenomenon and, to his surprise and the beats' chagrin, "beatnik" stuck.[92]

From the start, the beat rebellion was complicated by its connection with a hipster subculture of outcasts and misfits, whose line of descent was less in the bohemian countercultural tradition than in the urban demimonde of petty crooks, delinquents, and black street people. Hip was "the affirmation of the barbarian," explained writer Norman Mailer. It represented "a new breed of adventurers" who operated with "the sophistication of the wise primitive in a giant jungle."[93] Personified in characters like the leather-jacketed Marlon Brando of *The Wild One* and canonized in the writings of Mailer, hipsters were identified with beats because of their contempt for conventional life, their preoccupation with immediate sensual experience, and their assertion that both individual and social psychopathologies expressed a lofty truth beyond social convention. Whereas hipsters were visceral, lower-class hustlers, however, beats were cerebral bourgeois alienated by materialism. Whereas hipsters were apolitical and liable to serve as bullyboys in the ranks of any cause, beats were politically withdrawn but sympathetic to the left. Whereas hipsters lived in a world of commonplace violence (Mailer idealized it as "the catharsis which prepares for growth"[94]), beats were nonviolent in sensibility and practice. As the 1960s opened, the differences between beat and hip subcultures were blurred by the fact that together they were the only counterculture in motion.

Beat culture intrigued a few radical pacifists, notably those associated with *Liberation.* Like them, beats seemed to value authentic individualism and personal liberation, as well as human communities inspired by philosophical anarchism and democratic socialism. Like them, the beats cautioned would-be revolutionaries that they could not "create new structures" until they had "transformed consciousness" through the inner quest for self-knowledge and understanding.[95] Beats illustrated an important political proposition, concluded Paul Goodman: *"People can make it on their own,* without resentment, hostility, delinquency, or stupidity, better than when they move in the organized system and are subject to authority."[96] The system was the problem, and the individual was the solution.

On the other hand, radical pacifists could not identify with the beat preference for social withdrawal, political inaction, and the company of violence-prone deviants. That was what most defined their difference. Unlike beats, radical pacifists were civil disobedients rather than deviants. The pacifists lived to change the madness of modern American life, not to magnify it. And yet, if only as a style of rebellion, the beat phenomenon lent momentum to the radical pacifist cause of social transformation and thus edged into resurgent American peace activism. The import of this confluence was twofold. By the late 1960s the antiwar movement would become widely stereotyped with a counterculture image. Early in the decade, on the other hand, beat culture reinforced a politics of personal idealism thought to be capable of overcoming war and injustice, of liberating Americans from social alienation, moral numbness, and institutional madness. In 1963 these were but eddies in the backwaters of American culture. Shortly they would enter the main currents in opposition to a war across the Pacific.

From a Reconstituted Peace Movement to Antiwar Protest

The U.S. peace movement was reconstructed between 1955 and 1963 in protests against the atmospheric testing of nuclear weapons. Here, at a 1961 demonstration in New York City, were brought together the two wings of that protest: the Committee for a Sane Nuclear Policy (SANE), which sponsored the familiar "Dr. Spock is worried" ad, and the Committee for Non-Violent Action (CNVA) [Swarthmore College Peace Collection (SCPC)].

Above, demonstrators protesting civil defense drills are arrested at Grand Central Park, New York City, 2 July 1956 [Fellowship of Reconciliation (FOR), William Lusk and Alan Pesetsky]; below, Detroit citizens walk on 3 July 1958 against nuclear testing [FOR].

On 1 July 1959 pacifist leader A. J. Muste scaled a fence at the Mead Missile Base, Nebraska, in one of a series of CNVA-sponsored actions to dramatize the nuclear arms issue [SCPC].

Pacifists carried their protests to the Soviet Union in a San Francisco to Moscow Walk for Peace which began in California in December 1960 and entered Moscow in October 1961, led by Scott Herrick [War Resisters League (WRL)].

The coalition of groups which organized to ban atmospheric testing became the core of opposition to the Vietnam War, here symbolized by a New York City sign advertising an antiwar rally on 26 March 1966 in connection with the Second International Days of Protest [SCPC, copyright © Photo/Wallowitch by Edward Wallowtich].

Gathering opposition to the War, 1966

Opposition to the war came from a broad spectrum of citizens including trade unionists and women's groups demonstrating in New York City on 26 March 1966 [WRL, from *In the Teeth of War* (New York: The Fifth Avenue Vietnam Peace Parade Committee), 38, photos by Robert Parent].

By the time of the 1966 New York demonstration, the conflict had become a
confused war of symbols—religious ones, such as the quotation from Pope Paul VI
carried by an FOR contingent, and political ones, such as the slogans and the
American and communist flags carried by political opponents of the war [*In the Teeth
of War,* 39, photo above by Eli Finer, below by Robert Joyce].

Early critics of the war

Early critics included senators Wayne Morse and Ernest Gruening, as well as private citizens such as those shown here: (opposite, top) journalist I. F. Stone, (opposite, bottom) political scientist Hans Morgenthau (standing) and Sanford Gottlieb, director of SANE, and (above) the Reverend William Sloane Coffin and Norman Thomas [Stone and Coffin-Thomas photos copyright © Diana Davies; Morgenthau photo SCPC].

David Dellinger, Staughton Lynd, and Robert Parris Moses were splattered by red paint when they led a coalition Assembly of Unrepresented People in protest at the Capitol, 9 August 1965 [opposite, WRL], and the Bread and Puppet Theater made an appearance at a SANE rally in Washington that fall [above, SCPC].

By the spring of 1967 the antiwar coalition had the explicit support of Martin Luther King, Jr., seen here marching with Benjamin Spock in New York City on 15 April 1967. [photo copyright © John Goodwin]. King was assassinated a year later.

The Construction of an Antiwar Movement, 1963–1965

Four

Crystalizing Dissent

"A struggle" short of war

The reconstruction of a peace movement in the United States between 1955 and 1963 was paralleled by the growth of American presence in Vietnam. The reorientation of peace advocacy to war protest began as intervention was challenged during Kennedy's brief presidency, and by the end of Lyndon Johnson's first year in office the lines were drawn which would define the contest over the war. Intervention in Indochina was rooted in the same Cold War period that produced the issue of nuclear arms, but conflict in Vietnam antedated U.S. involvement.

Since late in the nineteenth century, Vietnam had been divided into three areas of French Indochina. In the south (Cochinchina) the French ruled directly, while elsewhere they exercised power through local rulers, despite Vietnamese resentment and occasional resistance.[1] During World War II, Indochina was occupied by the Japanese, but since France—itself then controlled by the Nazis—cooperated with Japan, the French colonial system was left more or less intact until the Japanese took direct control in March 1945. The wartime situation proved fertile ground for the growth of a liberation movement which built on nationalist agitation that had swelled in the generation prior to World War II. Because the French had consistently suppressed opposition, patriotic groups had become ever more revolutionary. The strongest of them was the communist front, organized and led by Ho Chi Minh, which during the last stages of the war dominated a broadly based nationalist coalition—the Vietminh. The communists exploited the turmoil to build a powerful political movement which contested the returning French. From 1946 to 1954 the conflict was a war, and the French finally cut their considerable losses by agreeing to withdraw, leaving the country temporarily divided between the communist-led Democratic Republic of

Vietnam in the North and the Bao Dai government which the French had installed in the South in 1950.[2]

The United States was not a party to these arrangements (defined by the Geneva Accords of 1954), but it was privy to them. The military conflict in Indochina coincided with the Korean War, and the two came to be linked in American policy as a single, massive threat posed by communist China and, by extension, the Soviet Union. The United States underwrote much of the French war effort and even considered direct intervention when the French faced defeat at the critical battle of Dienbienphu. With France's withdrawal, the Eisenhower administration became the patron of the Bao Dai government, to which Ngo Dinh Diem had been appointed as premier in 1954. The following year Diem won a referendum against Bao Dai, and then—with American support—he aborted a Vietnam-wide unification election scheduled for 1956 by the Geneva Accords. Thenceforth, the issue of legitimate government could be resolved only by preponderant and effective power. The question was essentially whether or not Ho's national aspiration would be thwarted by a viable government secured in the south. Eisenhower's sponsorship was conditional: South Vietnam would have to produce that viable regime. It would merit U.S. aid insofar as it could become militarily independent, economically stable, and politically more democratic. In an experiment in nation-building, Washington provided the Diem regime with a billion dollars in military and economic assistance between 1955 and 1960.

Few Americans noticed. Although press reports of authoritarian tendencies in the Diem government provoked some concern among citizens who followed policy during those years, few questioned the need to maintain South Vietnam against the expansion of Asian communism. In the last few weeks of 1960, members of the South Vietnamese armed forces staged a bloody but abortive coup against Diem. The incident raised questions about the narrow base of the Saigon government, the limited effectiveness of lavish aid, and the spread of noncommunist as well as communist opposition to Diem's rule. Some of America's most widely read news magazines observed that although the Ngo family's "dictatorial regime" had retained power, the "conditions that brought on the revolt remained." By supporting Diem, America might yet become "the real loser in Vietnam."[3] Then the issue slipped out of public attention.

The incoming Kennedy administration saw little alternative to aiding Diem against his internal opposition, which, in Washington's view, was concentrated in the communist-led National Liberation Front (NFL) and sponsored by North Vietnam. The NLF had been created late in 1960 out of the remnants of the Vietminh in the South and other opponents of the regime, and it had explicit support from the North. Although the sources of dissidence were far broader than the communist movement, the NLF focused the rebellion and was targeted, therefore, as the opposition. Indeed, Diem coined the word *Vietcong,* with which to label all insurgents as communist.

A decision on Vietnam came up just after the 17 April failure of the Bay of Pigs invasion and in the midst of another crisis in Laos, where a confused civil war involved the Cold War patrons. Kennedy eventually endorsed a compromise in Laos; but he would not relinquish South Vietnam, although he was reluctant to commit the nation to a major effort there. The president authorized the dispatch of four hundred Special Forces troops and the expansion of clandestine harassment and sabotage against North Vietnam by South Vietnamese agents under the direction of the CIA. In the fall, amid reports of a new Vietcong military initiative, the White House undertook a major assessment of its options. It received divided advice: General Maxwell D. Taylor and Walter Rostow recommended significant increases in military aid; Chester Bowles and W. Averell Harriman recommended restraint. The administration increased its commitment significantly, although not as fully as Taylor and Rostow asked.

U.S. aid, including Army helicopter companies, armored personnel carriers, and military advisors, enabled the 526,000-man South Vietnamese Army to take the offensive against an estimated 17,000 Vietcong guerrillas early in 1962. A new and enlarged military command for military operations and economic programs replaced the previous one. In an attempt to secure the countryside, a Strategic Hamlet program was devised: peasants were concentrated in so-called secure centers while troops scoured the area for Vietcong. U.S. aircraft began to defoliate jungle and woodland areas in order to destroy the guerrillas' cover, and napalm was introduced. Despite initial success, the South Vietnamese were back on the defensive by the end of the year.

Attorney General Robert Kennedy insisted that the administration was involved in a "struggle," not an undeclared war in Vietnam.[4] The increase in American troops (from 3,164 in December 1961 to 11,326 in December 1962) did not represent a commitment to combat, it was explained, but to "combat-type training missions."[5] When the Pentagon resisted issuing Purple Hearts to servicemen wounded in action in Vietnam on the grounds that it was not an official combat zone, the president issued an executive order authorizing the awards in what he called a "cold war" operation.[6] Republicans charged that Kennedy was covering up the extent of American military involvement in Vietnam but otherwise found little fault with U.S. policy.

Administration rhetoric disguised division in its ranks. It was getting contradictory advice, for some members of the foreign policy-shaping elite found fault with its policy. Thus Robert S. Browne, an economist with the U.S. Foreign Aid Program in Cambodia and Vietnam from 1955 to 1961, argued that a political solution in Vietnam was precluded by the corruption of the Ngos, and Senator Mike Mansfield (D-Mont.) added that reliance on them jeopardized U.S. policy. Dissent from the taciturn Montanan was particularly important because he was not only majority leader in the Senate but a trusted friend, whom Kennedy had sent to Vietnam to make an assessment. Formerly a professor of Far Eastern history, Mansfield was known as an authority on Asian affairs during his long tenure on House and Senate foreign relations committees. He had surveyed Vietnam in 1955 and had then supported Diem unequivocally. His criticism, more than that of iconoclastic Senator Wayne Morse (D-Oreg.), signalled the emergence of elite dissent on Vietnam policy.

Valued advisors in the academic community, notably John Kenneth Galbraith, Bernard Fall, and Hans Morgenthau, added cautionary advice. Fall, a French-born Vietnam expert, urged the government to treat the conflict as "a revolutionary war, that is, a military operation with heavy political overtones. To win the military battle but lose the political war could well become the U.S. fate in Vietnam."[7] Similarly, German-born Morgenthau warned Kennedy against depending on military responses in Vietnam. An eminent political scientist from the University of Chicago and a leading proponent of realism in foreign policy, Morgenthau urged the administration to force political reforms upon the Diem regime and to seek an internationally negotiated settlement in line with America's very limited interests in the area. Otherwise, he wrote, the United States was headed into another "Korean-type war" that was likely to continue for ten years and offer nothing more than a stalemate and enormous domestic frustration.[8]

From Vietnam, warnings were raised by a few newsmen. In July 1962 *New York Times* correspondent Homer Bigart concluded an extensive survey of the war by contending that the destruction of communist insurgency was a long way off, that the Ngo regime was better at alienating than winning the people, and that the U.S. government ought to reassess its economic aid programs and stress political reform. Shortly afterwards, François Sully of *Newsweek* reported that the war was currently "a losing proposition."[9]

Although privately still uncertain of his direction in Vietnam, the president seemed to brush off this advice. Reiterating the basic line of U.S. policy, he declared that Saigon's fall would trigger the collapse of all Southeast Asia to communism. Meanwhile, Secretary of Defense Robert McNamara and other U.S. officials criticized American newsmen for filing misleading reports from Vietnam. Saigon went beyond criticism. It barred U.S. journalists from various parts of the country and expelled François Sully and the National Broadcasting Company's John Robinson. Mme Ngo Diem Nhu, Diem's assertive sister-in-law, even suggested that

American journalists were "worse than Communists" because they parroted the opposition line with "a Western tone."[10] Thus the South Vietnamese anticipated an argument which would become integral to the official American line—that a public challenge to policy only played into communist hands.

Saigon's attacks upon the news media called attention to U.S. policy and to its critics. Until late spring 1963, Vietnam held relatively small importance for U.S. policymakers and the public, preoccupied with Berlin, Cuba, and Laos. Nonetheless, critics emerged. They included a few politicians like Mansfield, academics like Morgenthau, reporters like Sully, journalists like Walter Lippmann, democratic socialists like Norman Thomas, publishers like John S. Knight, ministers like Donald S. Harrington, black leaders like A. Philip Randolph and Bayard Rustin, radical pacifists like A. J. Muste, religious pacifists from the FOR and AFSC, Trotskyists from the Socialist Workers party, New Left radicals from SDS and SPU, female activists from the WILPF and WSP, and publicists from the *Nation* and the *New Republic*. Too assertive to be dismissed as a mood, they were too scattered and undemonstrative to rank as a movement. They were simply a mélange of skeptics proposing criticisms and alternatives.

Critics of intervention differed in many respects, but they agreed that an expanding war in Indochina would not improve the lives and fortunes of the Vietnamese people. Increasingly they complained about the oppressive corruption of the Diem regime, identifying it as the principal impediment to the U.S. goal of a legitimate government in the South. Some critics worried that continued conflict in Indochina only aggravated the Sino-American tension, precluding regional stabilization and global détente. Others imagined that U.S. policy, already being shielded from public debate, would sap the vitality of American democracy. Dissent was perhaps tentative in 1962, as was Vietnam policy itself. In the following year it would become strong enough to convey the outlines of a coherent critique. At the outset, however, it set the tone of opposition and stimulated the political strategy of the government's response.

In a November 1961 memorandum, McNamara warned that failure in South Vietnam "would stimulate bitter domestic controversies in the United States and would be seized upon by extreme elements to divide the country and harass the Administration."[11] Other officials agreed. In an effort to preempt criticism from the right while avoiding involvement in a new Asian land war, the White House cast about for alternatives. It avowed its opposition to a broader war, while it underwrote significant increases in the South Vietnamese armed forces and encouraged more aggressive attacks upon communist guerrillas and their North Vietnamese allies. It proclaimed its interest in a regional peace arrangement, although it evaded demands for multilateral negotiations for neutralization of the area. It pursued the goal of a viable, independent nation in the South, even as it assumed increasing responsibility for Saigon's defense.

These apparently inconsistent approaches had in common a political stance. During 1962 the Kennedy administration established a political guideline that would be respected by decision-makers for the next thirteen years: in its effort to ensure an anticommunist regime in Saigon, Washington would battle from the American political center, distinguishing itself from critics on the right and left. U.S. policymakers disagreed with opponents on the right, who would use nearly any means in order to maintain an anticommunist regime in Saigon, and they disdained critics on the left who argued that U.S. objectives for Vietnam were at least unattainable and at most immoral. National leaders made war from the political middle, confident that zealotry exists only in extremes. Vietnam became a struggle for the American center.

As 1963 opened, the administration still lacked clarity. U.S. military leaders in Saigon predicted imminent success, confident the "corner definitely has been turned" toward victory.[12] Whether from optimism or from concern about an overexpansion of U.S. resources, officials initiated plans to phase out the American military presence over perhaps two years. Relations between Washington and Saigon became ever more tense over the issue of political reform, and they all but snapped in the summer. On 8 May long-simmering Buddhist resentment toward Diem's Roman Catholic regime erupted in major demonstrations in the ancient imperial city of Hué. Government troops fired on protesters, killing nine and wounding fourteen. Suddenly, a religious challenge was transformed into national rebellion. The Buddhists issued a series of public demands and launched major new demonstrations. At noon on 11 June, a monk named Thich Quang Duc sat down in the middle of a downtown intersection in Saigon and allowed himself to be consumed by fire. The vivid scene of his death was carried around the world by the press and television. Two months later a second monk immolated himself.

Leaders in the Diem regime played down the internal challenge, charging that the protests were communist-inspired and deriding the self-immolations. The government also tried to crush the opposition directly. Security forces attacked Buddhist pagodas throughout South Vietnam on 21 August, arresting over fourteen hundred monks and sacking sacred buildings. The attack only broadened the protest. South Vietnamese military officers began to distance themselves from the regime and attempted to organize a coup with the full knowledge and support of the U.S. government.

Elite dissidence continued to develop in light of the administrations' quandary—unable to work with the Saigon government but unable to construct a viable South Vietnam without it. In March fifty-five prominent Americans, including Linus Pauling and Harvard sociologist Pitirim Sorokin, issued an open letter that urged the White House to heed proposals by Mansfield, Lippmann, and French president Charles de Gaulle to reduce U.S. commitment and to endorse an international conference on Vietnam under UN auspices. Two months later, another group of national figures, ranging from pacifist historian Roland Bainton to Marxist theoretician Paul Baran, published an open letter which warned Kennedy that America had become involved "in a conflict that it cannot win despite its tremendous power" and urged him to conduct "a painstaking reexamination" of U.S. policy with the goal of early disengagement.[13] Members of the liberal ADA urged the president to quit his escalation policy in Vietnam and to withhold further aid pending "basic, social, political, and economic reforms" including the formation of "a new, broadly-based nationalist regime" with popular support.[14]

Elements of the established peace movement began to shift their attention from Soviet-American rivalry to Vietnam. Early in 1963, leaders in the WSP announced that they had "a special responsibility" to alert Americans to "the dangers and horrors" of the war in Vietnam, since that was "the only place in which our own armed forces are actually engaged."[15] To the great discomfort of liberal organizers of the annual Easter marches for disarmament, a few activists carried signs protesting U.S. intervention, Bayard Rustin asked in vain that the signs be removed from the New York demonstration, whereas A.J. Muste used his scheduled speech to blast U.S. policy on Vietnam.[16]

In September, SANE's national board appealed for "graduated disengagement" from Diem, the neutralization of Vietnam, and the conclusion of "an overall political settlement with China." With the test-ban treaty in hand, the leaders observed, Vietnam now deserved to rank "high among SANE priorities."[17] Four weeks later, the Friends Committee on National Legislation—the Quaker lobby in Washington—opened a Vietnam Information Center that provided a new hub for the spreading liberal concern with the whole Asian crisis. Meanwhile, SPU and SDS activists organized demonstrations across the country to protest a month-long American tour by Mme Nhu.[18]

"How many more installments of this tragic war . . . will it take?"

By this time it was possible to discern the terms on which intervention would be challenged in the following decade. Disparate voices within the policy-shaping elite and among the loosely aligned peace groups contributed to a critique that was shaped between 1961 and 1963. Sharply mindful of the French failures in Indochina and Algeria and recalling the costs of Korea, policy dissidents repeatedly warned that the conflict could escalate into a vicious, counterrevolutionary race war ("America's Algeria"), a Sino-American confrontation ("another Korea"), or possibly World War III.[19] In that apprehension there were four lines of criticism.

The first was moral: it was politically fatuous and morally wrong for the United States to fight to the last Vietnamese on behalf of a noncommunist regime in Saigon against a communist-led revolution in the very shadow of China. Apparently assuming that, given the likelihood of Chinese support for North Vietnam, a war fully undertaken would be protracted, some early critics argued that the cost to the Vietnamese would outweigh the value of military victory. The self-immolation of Buddhist monks seemed to dramatize the repudiation of that war policy by sensitive Vietnamese. The introduction of napalm, chemical defoliants, and the forced relocation of peasants into "glorified concentration camps" called "strategic hamlets" provided symbols of a "dirty, cruel war." SANE's national council viewed it with "moral indignation."[20] Underlying opposition to intervention, then, was a feeling that the destructiveness of a protracted guerrilla war would be far worse for the Vietnamese than communist rule. This view was sometimes coupled to a fear of pointless American losses, and in any case moral concern for the people of Vietnam was a minority view in 1963, expressed by few critics.

A second and much more common line of criticism was that intervention was futile: the United States could not attain its goal of an independent, anticommunist South Vietnam. This argument was consonant with political realism, and it involved two considerations that were familiar to Kennedy's foreign policy advisors.

One was the old quandary: a self-sustaining nation could not be constructed without the cooperation of its government, and the government in power was not politically viable. Certainly that government was not legitimate in the view of most informed Americans. By far the most serious public protests against U.S. policy on Vietnam in 1963 focused less upon the war itself than upon the religious repression by the Catholic Ngos, whom the United States supported. On two occasions during the summer, an ad hoc Vietnam Ministers Committee of leading liberal Protestants such as Harry Emerson Fosdick, Donald S. Harrington, and Reinhold Niebuhr issued public statements calling for an end to U.S. aid to Diem's regime because of its persecution of Buddhists and smaller sects. Criticism intensified after Saigon's August attack upon the pagodas. In September the *Christian Century* insisted that "a new and religiously tolerant government in Saigon" was the only hope of preventing South Vietnam's fall to the communists, and Senator Frank Church (D-Idaho) and thirty-two cosponsors introduced a Senate resolution proclaiming that U.S. aid to the Diem regime "offends the conscience of the American people and should not be continued."[21]

The merit of the argument involved an assessment of the Diem regime itself and the political economy of the society. It is clear that in 1962–63 the administration and its critics became increasingly disillusioned with Saigon's capacity to rule. That was the thrust of criticisms by Mansfield, Fall, Morgenthau, and others in 1962: military success was not meaningful against a background of political disaster. Their argument became more telling with the Ngos' intransigence in the spring of 1963, and it was capped with the widespread rebellion of August. With characteristic bluntness, Wayne Morse called Diem a "police-state dictator."[22] As long as the problem was identified with a specific Vietnamese government, however—with Diem and his brother—there remained the tantalizing hope that another ruler would be more amenable to American advice and would merit U.S. support. That possibility was identified by Gail Paradise of SPU, who argued presciently that no anticommunist government could survive the negotiated settlements which alone could bring peace to Vietnam.[23]

Another factor in the calculation of feasibility was the capacity of the United States to sustain a major military commitment halfway around the globe. Determining policy involved an assessment of America's resources against its international interests. Thus Walter Lippmann objected to intervention because "the price of a military victory in the Vietnamese war is higher than American vital interests can justify." The preservation of an anticommunist regime was "an important secondary interest" for the United States, he wrote; but it was not "a primary vital interest."[24] A Mansfield study group warned the Senate that the contest was becoming a very expensive "American war" which "in present circumstances" was not justified by U.S. security interests.[25] This consideration, which was shared by Morgenthau and some other foreign policy realists, may have motivated the administration's 1963 projection of a phased withdrawal.

A third line of criticism involved a sense that intervention would be counterproductive to the national interest in regional and global stability. Southeast Asia was an area of concern to both realists and peace liberals. In this regard, the extended analyses of Mansfield and Lippmann, seconded by other prominent Americans in 1963, were especially pertinent. Both of them agreed with Kennedy and other policymakers at the time that Chinese expansionism was the main threat to the peace in the region. They urged Washington to meet the Chinese threat by effecting a multilateral commitment among the great powers, in the style of the 1962 Laotian agreements, to neutralize at least South Vietnam and at most all Indochina. They condemned proposals to increase America's military commitment to an anticommunist regime in South Vietnam as utterly contrary to Washington's primary concern with China, and they dismissed talk of winning the war in Vietnam as naïve. Any attempt to engage in combat would raise the problem of cutting off the Vietcong from its base of supplies in North Vietnam, Lippmann warned, and that problem could not be resolved without risking major war with North Vietnam and the possibility of Chinese intervention on the scale of another Korea and perhaps beyond.[26]

In a variation on this line of thought, the *New Republic* argued that the United States should quit the Diem regime and open discussions with Ho Chi Minh with the hope of bolstering Vietnamese nationalism as a means of containing Chinese ambition. "So long as America props up Diem," it reasoned, "Ho will share the militancy of Peking. But once Ho's country is united under his rule, he could become another Tito," who would be "most likely to serve America's primary purpose in Southeast Asia: stopping Chinese expansion."[27]

Peace liberals worried also that expanded war in Indochina would threaten the prospects for détente and control of the nuclear arms race. This apprehension was especially prevalent in SANE, and it was put explicitly by Norman Thomas: "To sacrifice progress in disarmament on which our hope of peace depends in the name of checking Communist interpenetration in a foreign land is sheer madness."[28] Not merely regional but also world stability was at stake in Vietnam.

On a fourth line of criticism, the concerns that generated opposition to Vietnam policy included apprehension about the direction and vitality of American ideals. Some dissidents complained about the utter "disappearance of debate" within American politics. It was "almost incredible," Thomas thought, that "there has been no ringing protest, no alternative suggestion of policy," from Congress or any major political institution.[29] Early accounts by reporters like Bigart and Sully, and White House attempts to dismiss them, exacerbated the problem. Month after month Kennedy sought to dispel charges, often from Republicans, that he was keeping information from the public and Congress. From the administration's reticence to discuss its still unformed policy flowed suspicions which later would congeal as a credibility gap.

Some critics contended that Washington's increasing involvement in a counterrevolutionary war against colored communists halfway around the world utterly contradicted America's liberal ideals. The *Nation* questioned the merit of intervention to preserve democracy, wondering: "Will the toll of American lives have to mount significantly before we can see that what we are attempting to do in South Vietnam is to suppress a genuine peasant insurrection, albeit one that is unquestionably aided by North Vietnamese Communists?"[30] Leaders of WILPF and other peace groups protested that the Strategic Hamlet program was "a clear violation of human rights" and "a conscious departure from the moral values supposedly being defended in the Cold War."[31] Indeed, it was observed, the contrast between Washington's growing involvement in Vietnam and its hands-off approach to the southern civil rights struggle suggested a perverse set of national priorities. With southern whites battling federal authority to prevent black self-determination, wrote I. F. Stone, "the fleet should be in the Gulf of Mexico and helicopters over Mississippi."[32]

For all their opposition to intervention, few policy critics called for immediate American withdrawal. Indeed, early dissidents explicitly opposed the idea of America's "scuttling out" of Vietnam and denied that they sought the "unconditional surrender of either side" in the conflict.[33] They called for America's graduated disengagement from the Diem regime—but not Southeast Asia—simultaneous with UN or other multilateral intervention. The only other alternative, they warned, was the spread of a protracted war of attrition in which people would "continue to be ground up to satisfy the American obsession."[34]

Morally wrong, imprudent and infeasible, counterproductive to national interests in regional and international stability, and antithetical to American ideals—on these lines intervention in Vietnam would be challenged in the following decade.

Already in 1963, lines were being drawn visibly across America. Mme Nhu's autumn tour of the United States was preceded by her description of Buddhist immolations as a "barbecue." She was thought to epitomize the Diem regime. The so-called Dragon Lady was challenged by silent pickets at the Universities of Michigan and Chicago and by placard-waving crowds at Harvard and Princeton. In contrast, she was cheered at Fordham and Georgetown and was lauded as a "fighting lady" at a dinner of Los Angeles County Republicans. At the University of North Carolina and elsewhere, demonstrations were thwarted by local hostility to peace activists.[35]

In the midst of her tour, events etched the lines more sharply. On 1 November a South Vietnamese military junta toppled the Diem regime. The hated president and his brother were assassinated. Some critics hoped that Diem's death might open the way to negotiations and disengagement "without abandoning South Vietnam to the Communists."[36] Others worried that it signified no more than "a changing of the troops" and would not affect the administration's overriding commitment to destroy insurgency and preserve an anticommunist regime.[37]

Washington, although claiming no detailed foreknowledge of the coup, had fully implicated itself in the generals' success and to that extent was more deeply committed than ever to Saigon. With Diem gone, moreover, the tantalizing prospect of a more malleable regime was raised, and Kennedy faced a new and now more sobering choice of policies. But on 22 November the president was shot to death in Dallas.

"Part of the Way with LBJ"

Two days after the assassination stunned the nation, Lyndon B. Johnson affirmed his intention to support the Kennedy programs, explicitly including military and economic support of South Vietnam. The administration ordered a fresh assessment of the situation there. As the new year opened, McNamara warned Congress that the situation was grave, with accelerated Vietcong action which was clearly linked to the Hanoi government in the North, and yet in mid-February he testified that the bulk of U.S. forces could be expected to leave Vietnam by 1965.

The Kennedy programs also included a wide range of domestic proposals which Johnson packaged as a prescription for a "Great Society." Civil rights legislation, its centerpiece, was given increased urgency by the acceleration of racial struggle in the first half of 1964. Late in April five thousand clergy supported the administration's civil rights bill in an Interreligious Convocation on Civil Rights in Washington, and Catholic-Protestant cooperation continued during the year. The interfaith alliance was not organized in any formal way, but it created a precious reservoir from which antiwar sentiment and action would be drawn.

More immediately, the racial struggle stimulated militancy and violence, which climaxed early in the summer. Two hundred black and white volunteers, mostly under SNCC auspices, organized voter registration in the Mississippi Summer project. Three of them disappeared at the outset—victims of abduction, beating, and murder by local law enforcement officers. The project provoked fearsome white resistance. By the summer's end the toll in Mississippi included six dead, eighty beaten, over a thousand arrested, thirty-five black churches burned, and thirty-one homes and buildings bombed. Blacks retaliated sporadically. Attacks on local police erupted in southern towns, and northern cities experienced riots and burnings. Late in July, three weeks after President Johnson signed the 1964 Civil Rights Act into law, a coalition of civil rights leaders called for a moratorium on demonstrations.

Escalating racial crisis stimulated the growth of right-wing politics. Established extremist groups, including the John Birch Society, grew steadily during the year, along with newer programs such as the telephone service "Let Freedom Ring" and Texas billionaire H. L. Hunt's radio "Lifeline." Governor George Wallace attracted dramatic support in Democratic presidential primaries in Wisconsin, Indiana, and Maryland. When he withdrew from the presidential race in July, he claimed to have "conservatized" both major parties on the race question.[38]

The Republican nominee was Barry Goldwater, a man of personal integrity but heavy-handed rhetoric. Professing opposition to discrimination, the Arizona senator attacked civil rights legislation and demonstrators alike. Acknowledging that bombs could not destroy communism, he attacked the administration for its alleged accommodation to it and called for a winning policy in the Cold War. Leading Republicans singled out Vietnam as a test of the will to resist communism: Goldwater talked about using atomic weapons to defoliate the South Vietnamese country-side; Nixon advocated air war against North Vietnam and communist-controlled parts of Laos; Governors William Scranton of Pennsylvania and Nelson Rockefeller of New York called for an all-out U.S. effort to thwart communist victory.

Johnson seized the center ground in the national debate on both do-mestic and foreign policy, as Kennedy had done. The president promised the Vietnamese that his purpose was "identical" with theirs: to protect South Vietnam "from the acts of terror perpetrated by Communist in-surgents from the North."[39] Both Secretary of Defense McNamara and Secretary of State Rusk repeatedly pledged U.S. support to South Vietnam in the spring and early summer. Washington significantly increased mil-itary aid to Saigon. At the same time, the president spoke the voice of moderation and restraint, rejecting calls for all-out military involvement and acknowledging the need for a political settlement. He asserted his belief in the priority of reason over force and warned that any dream of successful general war in the nuclear age was "impossible." America had a special responsibility to the next generation, Johnson told a group of visiting students, for that generation had "a rendezvous with peace."[40]

Like his predecessor, Johnson wanted to maintain a national consensus which would give him discretion in foreign policy. This seemed all the more important early in 1964 because of the fluidity of events in Vietnam. At the end of January, there was another military coup in Saigon. Deser-tions from the South Vietnamese armed forces increased, pacification efforts stalled, and the Vietcong made significant gains. Anticipating an extended conflict, the White House sought to contain both those impa-tient for victory and those skeptical about involvement. It felt the need, as several of its advisors agreed in June, "to prosecute an urgent infor-mation effort in the United States toward dispelling the basic doubts of the value of Southeast Asia which were besetting key members of Con-gress and the public." As Ambassador Henry Cabot Lodge told Demo-cratic foreign policy advisor W. Averell Harriman, "The most important single factor in the whole Vietnam problem is support from the American home front."[41]

The problem did not seem serious early in the year. Most Americans were "both cautious and confused" about Vietnam, according to one poll. One of four citizens did not even know the United States was in-volved in fighting, and two of three paid little or no attention. Those who followed policy replicated it in their preference for supporting a government in Saigon that would resist communism "with American advice and direction."[42] Frustrated antiwar critics blamed public indifference on the "smoke screen of spurious optimism and plain lies" manufactured by the administration or attributed it to the habitual entrusting of important international decisions to national leaders. All agreed that the Vietnam question, "although grave, has excited little public attention."[43]

It was without much notice, therefore, that skeptics converged into an identifiable opposition. They included U.S. senators, intellectuals, journalists, clergy, students, activist women, and veteran peace advocates. From the start, dissent resisted national organization or direction, and its very diversity and independence gave it resiliency and staying power.

Earlier criticism was consolidated to form the principal arguments that would sustain protest against U.S. intervention. Dissenters condemned the administration's military escalation and called for a negotiated settlement of what they regarded as a political problem. The war was a civil conflict, they insisted, one which could best be contained by a great-power political arrangement that would pave the way for Vietnam's emergence as an "Asian Yugoslavia."[44] A SANE-organized appeal signed by over five thousand academicians called upon the president to neutralize Vietnam as a step toward "a united front of the non-Chinese nations to establish countervailing power to Chinese influence in the region." Presenting the petition at a news conference, Hans Morgenthau declared his support for a communist Vietnam, "if Ho Chi Minh were willing to become the Tito of Southeast Asia." Like Lippmann, Morgenthau contended that America's interest in Southeast Asia would be best served by a multilateral arrangement that encouraged Vietnamese communists to go "Titoist, that is to say to remain Communist but not Chinese."[45]

Repeatedly, dissenters insisted that the U.S. had neither sufficient national interest nor moral cause to involve itself further in Vietnam's violence. They argued that U.S. involvement in war would kill hopes for domestic reform and international disarmament. A handful of skeptical senators, including Edward L. Bartlett (D-Okla.) and George Aiken (R-Vt.), warned against further escalation. Senator Mansfield privately cautioned the president against "another Korea."[46] Lippmann publicly warned that the notion of an American air war against North Vietnam was as foolish as it was immoral. It would reinforce Saigon's irresponsibility, he said, and it would show a "wanton disrespect for the opinion of mankind" that would "not go unpunished because we stop our ears. It would be our day of infamy." It would be blatant "outlawry," Senator Morse added, and "outlaws have a way of coming to a bad end, both for themselves and their countries."[47]

Dissidents dismissed the morality of fighting in Vietnam for freedom as pure cant, warning that the people there were "being destroyed in the process" of trying to save the country.[48] Such a war was "a blind alley," wrote I. F. Stone, "which is destroying faith in our government not only there but at home."[49] Morse scoffed at the idea of fighting on for the national honor: "I have heard of 'throwing out the baby with the bath water,' but never before have I heard it suggested that we should blow off heads to save face."[50]

The arguments had not changed, but Morse's language suggested that the tone of criticism had a sharper bite now. He called the administration's policy "stark, ugly imperialism." The normally restrained Lippmann characterized it as "catastrophic," and Senator Ernest Gruening (D-Alaska) said it would someday be "denounced as a crime." There was no justification "for murdering a single American boy in South Vietnam," Gruening told the Senate in March 1964, for the issue had now become "one of murder."[51]

Peace advocates initiated a round of public protests. Sponsored by nine peace groups, some five thousand people paraded through New York City that month, calling for the negotiated withdrawal of U.S. troops from Vietnam and the pursuit of a domestic war on poverty. Shortly afterwards, about two hundred women from WILPF and WSP spent a day in Washington to lobby for a diplomatic solution and the neutralization of Vietnam. In April their appeal was seconded in a petition to the president by thirty-three leading liberals, including Benjamin Spock and Stringfellow Barr.

At the same time, liberal peace advocacy continued the decline which had started with the Cuban Missile Crisis and had been accelerated with the test-ban treaty. It still lacked focus, and Vietnam remained a minor theme. Some activists moved into the civil rights movements and others drifted into Democratic party politics as the constituency of the peace movement shrank. SANE leaders complained of internal ennui and diminishing popular interest. The *Bulletin of the Atomic Scientists* experienced severe financial problems. The SPU closed its national office in June, emerging in the fall with only a rump organization. The three-year-old Turn Toward Peace fragmented further as Robert Pickus challenged activists he believed to be less critical of communism than of American policy. At an autopsy for the organization in June, Norman Thomas confessed that, in spite of great efforts, neither TTP nor other organized peace groups had sustained a genuine "peace movement, a great political force in the mainstream of American life." Instead, citizen peace-seekers wallowed in "confusion and apathy," uncertain over their next steps and unsure over their role in an era of great-power détente.[52]

New Left radicals in SDS were also immobilized on foreign policy, feeling that there was "precious little" they could do about it.[53] Many of them remained deeply involved in the civil rights struggle or were fully engaged in attempts to organize the urban poor. Some SDS activists criticized Washington's escalating military involvement and called for a new U.S. approach to the Third World that emphasized "aid through the UN rather than bayonets and napalm." But mostly they worried that America's growing involvement in Vietnam would ignite domestic right-wing attacks which would "threaten further the structure of democracy in our own country" as surely as Korea had fueled McCarthyism.[54]

In an exception to the rule of inertia in 1964, a few radical pacifists initiated public protests against conscription. On Armed Forces Day, twelve young men burned their draft cards to the applause of 150 demonstrators at an antidraft rally in New York City, sponsored by the SPU, WRL, Catholic Worker Movement, and CNVA. For the participants it was not then a question of war crimes or "the right of the people of Vietnam to self-determination." Said one of them: "The basic issue is my right of choice."[55] This civil libertarian position had always characterized anti-conscription efforts, but it had existed in tension with conscientious objection to foreign policy itself and to the draft as its instrument. The political side was epitomized by David Mitchell, who had been active in the SPU and CNVA as well as End the Draft (formed in 1963). Mitchell would be brought to trial in 1965 for refusing induction, initially in opposition to a foreign policy based on a capacity for nuclear war. During sixteen months of litigation, he would adapt his defense to the claim that the war in Vietnam violated the Nuremberg prohibition on citizens from committing crimes in the name of the state.[56] That this would be the direction of draft resistance was suggested in July 1964, when A. J. Muste and his comrades in the *Liberation* collective announced that they would distribute a "Declaration of Conscience" with which signatories could pledge their noncooperation in the U.S. war effort and their support for young men who refused military service in Vietnam.

About that time, a number of Catholic pacifists, including Jim Forest, Tom Cornell, Daniel Berrigan, and James Douglass, established the Catholic Peace Fellowship (CPF) as a nonmembership organization without dues or scheduled activities. Douglass had been engaged in graduate study at Gregorian University in Rome, where he had been a consultant on the theology of peace to several bishops during the Second Vatican Council. Forest became secretary of CPF; discharged from the Navy as a conscientious objector following the Bay of Pigs invasion, he had become managing editor of the *Catholic Worker.* Cornell, who became director of the CPF, had also been an editor of that pacifist journal as well as a CNVA activist, and he had burned his first draft card four years earlier. Working out of the New York offices of the War Resister League and affiliated with the Fellowship of Reconciliation, the CPF undertook some modest educational activities and took a special interest in aiding Catholic conscientious objectors. A future constituency for war resistance was implicit in the renewed opposition to the draft.

More explicitly, a constituency for antiwar protest gathered on the political left. Various activists seized upon Vietnam partly as a flagrant example of Washington's determination to crush revolutionary socialism and liberation in the Third World. They hoped also that the issue would help them to build campus constituencies and to emphasize the priority of domestic change. Probably some of them were compensating for their exclusion from the increasingly nationalistic black civil rights movement, where young white radicals who for years had supported civil rights activism found themselves shut out of decision-making roles. Youthful militants from the Old Left organized opposition to U.S. intervention in Vietnam the most diligently in early 1964, and they were the first to call for an immediate American military withdrawal. In mid-March, about four hundred students from several eastern colleges attended a New Haven conference on socialism, where strong feelings about the war surfaced. Some of the students supported Haverford College student and SDS member Russell Stetler in forming the Student Committee to Send Medical Aid to the Front of the National Liberation of South Vietnam in its "just struggle" against foreign rule.[57] Eighty-seven conference participants, inspired by a letter issued by French students opposed to the Algerian war, published an advertisement announcing their refusal to fight with U.S. armed forces "for the suppression of the Vietnamese struggle for national independence" and inviting other young men to join them in their opposition.[58] An ad hoc committee chaired by Stetler was formed at the New Haven conference to organize public protests on behalf of immediate American withdrawal from Vietnam. Its May Second demonstrations attracted nearly a thousand students in four cities. The informal committee was converted into the May Second Movement (M2M), which was largely dominated by the Progressive Labor Movement as a means of organizing youth. The M2M radicals often compromised themselves by their manipulative tactics, and they were sometimes indiscriminately grouped with the W. E. B. Du Bois Clubs of the Communist party; but they addressed feelings held by a substantial number of young Americans free from any communist influence.[59]

The demand for unilateral U.S. military withdrawal, initially from political radicals of the Old Left, set off a sharp debate which established a dividing line between radical and liberal critics of U.S. policy for the next five years. Antiwar radicals in the spring of 1964 called for an immediate disengagement not only as a matter of moral right but more especially as "a revolutionary demand ... linked to a continuing campaign against U.S. intervention anywhere at any time." They wanted to assemble an anti-imperialist movement, not merely an antiwar initiative.[60]

The great majority of antiwar critics, on the other hand, rejected the demand for immediate withdrawal as politically infeasible, dishonorable in view of Washington's past commitments, and contrary to America's role as a dependable Pacific power checking Chinese expansion. Speaking for SANE, Homer Jack dismissed the notion as "simplistic" and sure to produce "more problems than it solves."[61] Gail Paradise of SPU complained that disengagement without a negotiated settlement and internationally supervised reconstruction would merely lead to the imposition of Vietcong "terrorism and slaughter."[62] Painfully, religious pacifists in the FOR and the AFSC were moved to agree. Widely respected FOR executive secretary Alfred Hassler confided to friends that the "most obvious" pacifist answer for Vietnam was immediate U.S. withdrawal, but the most likely consequence would be "a bloodbath" of anticommunist Vietnamese and a communist expansion throughout Southeast Asia which would provoke renewed and even increased intervention by the United States. "In other words," he conceded, unilateral withdrawal was a "policy that is moral and right within a total framework that is immoral and wrong." It was an excruciating situation. For Hassler there was "literally no answer" to the Vietnam question that he might recommend or approve on the grounds of pacifist principle.[63]

The fact that even deep-seated skepticism about U.S. policy was scattered—without alternatives, focus, or organization—allowed Johnson a free hand during the presidential campaign of 1964. In the last days of July, the administration announced that an additional five thousand troops would be dispatched to Vietnam, raising U.S. forces to twenty-five thousand. A few days later, on 2 August, a U.S. Navy ship engaged North Vietnamese torpedo boats in the Gulf of Tonkin. The president threatened retaliation. Two days later the Navy reported another encounter in the Gulf. The president responded with a crushing air strike on North Vietnamese naval and oil facilities at Vinh—an eye for a tooth. Johnson kept on the initiative at home, too, winning quick and overwhelming approval from Congress for a Southeast Asia Resolution that authorized "all necessary measures" to repel any attack on U.S. forces and to "prevent further aggression."[64] The Gulf of Tonkin Resolution, as it came to be called, was the legal basis cited for subsequent escalation into war.

With this blank check in hand, and with the retaliatory air strike behind him, the president completely undercut Goldwater's campaign. His response to the Tonkin Gulf crisis was backed by 85 percent of the polled population, and public approval of his handling of the Vietnam issue rose from 42 to 72 percent.[65] Having demonstrated firmness in the face of apparent provocation, Johnson vowed his determination neither to pick nor to avoid a bigger fight in Vietnam. That was dissimulating, since by autumn there was a secret consensus in the administration that the war would have to be widened by U.S. air strikes against North Vietnam early in the new year—just the policy Goldwater was advocating in public. As Khrushchev slipped from power and communist China exploded its first atomic bomb, the Republicans could only become more unacceptably strident. Goldwater charged the administration with being "soft on Communism," while Nixon referred to vice-presidential candidate Hubert Humphrey as "a very dedicated radical."[66] The White House conceded the extreme right to its opponent and commanded the overwhelming center.

There was, for all practical purposes, no independent left and no alternative for Johnson's dovish critics. A few of them, notably the *Progressive* and I. F. Stone, voiced skepticism about the administration's Tonkin Gulf policy.[67] There were scattered protests, and on 25 August about four hundred radical pacifists from CNVA, WRL, and the Catholic Worker Movement held a day-long vigil at the Democratic national convention in Atlantic City in order to express concern about "the kind of war being waged" in Vietnam.[68] Although opponents of war challenged Johnson's belligerence, they were in an untenable position: the president assiduously cultivated the image of restrained strength, while Goldwater epitomized hawkishness. Accordingly, Benjamin Spock led an ad hoc committee of Scientists and Engineers for Johnson-Humphrey, and other liberals fell in line. Even New Left radicals backed the ticket, albeit reluctantly. Some SDS activists agreed to go "Part of the Way with LBJ," and radical pacifists argued that Goldwater's defeat was "imperative, if we are to have the opportunity for continuing the struggle for a better world."[69] With support from the left and center, LBJ won a decisive election victory.

In Vietnam nothing was clear. Intrigue plagued the government throughout the American presidential campaign and continued afterwards. Beset by discontented junior officers, unhappy Buddhists, and rival military factions, Saigon stumbled through attempted coups and military failures. Before the year ended, the military dissolved the provisional legislature created by a new constitution, and despite U.S. objections the action was supported by the more-or-less ruling General Nguyen Khanh.

The American administration worked through a major reassessment of policy following the election. By December the only question was how and when to proceed directly against North Vietnam. Despite pleas from the Joint Chiefs for a massive air offensive, the administration opted for gradually escalated air attacks which it deferred because of the instability in Saigon.[70]

There was some dissent within administration circles. George Ball argued forcefully against mounting an air war on the North, and Mansfield advised the president in December that the prospective cost of expanding the war was "appalling" and that it would compromise the very goal of an independent South Vietnam "since it would require such a vast United States involvement as to negate the meaning of independence." The nation's best hope, he argued, was a negotiated settlement and "ultimate withdrawal."[71] That was also the formulation of liberal peace advocates. The national board of SANE orchestrated a campaign of petitions, demonstrations, and lobbying for a political settlement and the "eventual disengagement" of American as well as *all other foreign powers*" from Vietnam.[72]

Scorning the liberals' emphasis on de-escalation and negotiations, WRL leader Dave McReynolds charged that they were "less worried about the crime of what we are doing in Vietnam than the danger the war might get 'escalated' and thus hurt some Americans." Radical pacifists were for negotiations, McReynolds maintained, and for neutralization of the region. "But first of all, and most of all, we are for the immediate withdrawal of all U.S. military forces and military aid."[73] When they first used the term "immediate withdrawal," radical pacifists insisted, they did not mean it in a literal sense. Rather, they wanted a clear political decision to pull military support out of Vietnam "as expeditiously as possible" and would accept only *"negotiations on that basis."*[74] Inevitably, this position antagonized antiwar liberals, and it frustrated an attempt by six pacifist organizations, including the FOR, WRL, and AFSC, to put together an antiwar coalition in November.

Nonetheless, a number of leading religious pacifists and radicals called for nationwide demonstrations as the first step in a "continuing campaign of nonviolent action" for an immediate cease-fire in Vietnam and the "earliest possible withdrawal" of U.S. troops.[75] On 19 December nearly two thousand people took to the streets in nine cities. While folksinger Joan Baez and others led about six hundred demonstrators around San Francisco's Union Square, Norman Thomas, A. J. Muste, and A. Philip Randolph pilloried U.S. policy, and Phil Ochs sang his "Talking Vietnam Blues" to a thousand people chilled by subfreezing weather in New York.

Two weeks later, on 30 December, I. F. Stone came to New York for a meeting with the SDS national council. Vietnam was not uppermost on the agenda: more current was the Berkeley Free Speech Movement; more substantive were community organizing projects in Chicago, Cleveland, and Newark. Stone appealed for action against the nation's deepening involvement in war. Extremely moved but divided over the right course of action, SDS leaders debated the Vietnam question for seven hours. Its intrinsic importance impressed them, and besides, as their national secretary, C. Clark Kissinger, saw, the issue was a key to student organization. Todd Gitlin proposed a draft-refusal campaign, but the council chose instead to sponsor an Easter demonstration in Washington. They would be the sole sponsor and they would not exclude anyone. They would demand U.S. troop withdrawal "on the ground that the war is causing untold harm to the people of Vietnam, and is also damaging American democracy."[76] The New Left was on board.

The SDS decision to hold an antiwar Easter march in 1965 signalled the emergence of a new style of antiwar opposition out of the preexisting peace movement. The unilateral call preempted the annual demonstrations for détente and disarmament, and the refusal to cosponsor the march with other groups reflected a rejection of the traditional coalition practice of discouraging participation from the far left. Concerned first with changing American society, SDS leaders were not interested in building a new peace movement. They were eager, however, to overcome what they saw as the irrelevance of the old one, and to encourage the formation of an anti-imperialist phalanx in its place. With I. F. Stone, they believed that "the basic problem is not in Vietnam but in the U.S.A."[77]

By the end of 1964, there was a significant base of dissent from Vietnam policy, although there was not yet an organized opposition. On the whole, critics were not yet so alienated from policymaking authorities that they were prepared to support more active, concentrated, and sustained protest. Dissent had already acquired four lasting characteristics, however. First, it was thin but broad, formally disorganized yet expressing disparate antiwar sentiment in the country. Second, the opposition was animated (but not dominated) by activists from the country's peace movement and was legitimated (but not led) by members of its policy-shaping elite. Third, in spite of its essentially moderate makeup, the challenge to official policy had begun to take a left-wing cast for several reasons, including the decline of liberal peace activism after 1962, the convergence of a radical left on the war issue in 1964, the emergence of a defining issue in "immediate withdrawal," and the cultural change and social polarization in American life of the early sixties.

Finally, antiwar dissent was riven by incipient division that originated in a complex of personal, political, and ideological differences, all compounded by the fact that every antiwar faction had its own reasons for protesting Washington's policy. Pursuing separate agendas, the dissidents who first inspired antiwar opposition looked upon Vietnam as an opportunity as well as a crisis. For elite critics like Lippmann and peace liberals from SANE, for example, the escalating war was an opportunity to promote a less bellicose approach toward China and a broader view of great-power relationships. Radical pacifists found an occasion for individual resistance to militarism, while social radicals from the Old and New Left saw in Vietnam an issue that offered them access to young people and, somewhat later, workers and blacks.

At the outset, antiwar critics of all persuasions—liberals and radicals, pacifist or not—confronted the challenge which held them together but dogged them throughout the years of war. Fundamentally, they had to convince the American people and their leaders that the United States could accept a loss; that the national interest would gain more by accepting limitations than by pursuing illusive and Pyrrhic victory. The "real tragedy and the real dilemma" for the American people, wrote one critic, was that they were "in Vietnam to win the war. But they cannot win the war. They can succeed only in doing what the French did, prolong the agony till the final withdrawal must come."[78] The war "cannot be won by the United States," declared the *New Republic*: "It can only be won by the Vietnamese." Washington's problem was that it was the Vietnamese communists who were winning. The only victory for America in Vietnam, agreed the *Nation,* was in "finding an honorable way out." And that could come only at a price. Americans would have to "pay something" for the "grievous mistake" of intervening in Indochina, wrote Walter Lippmann in December 1964.[79] They would pay—either with their pride through a political settlement or with their lives in an extended war. Plainly, antiwar critics wanted the country to accept its error and suffer its pride.

The basic problem was not in Vietnam, they agreed, but in the United States. Operating from radically different plans and assumptions, various people came together during 1964 to devise a makeshift antiwar opposition upon nothing more than their common hostility toward Washington's Indochina policy. Their government was enmeshed, but not formally at war, in Vietnam. Opposition had crystalized, but it was not yet a movement.

Five

Consolidating Opposition

"Our problem is in America, not in Vietnam"

Lyndon Johnson was anxious to get on with the Great Society as he took office in his own right, but he was nagged by the challenge of communism in Indochina. Joan Baez reminded him of it at a gala originally intended for Kennedy, when she mentioned the war and sang "The Times They Are A-Changin'."[1] How much things were changing, no one could then guess. In his State of the Union message Johnson warned that the security and national ideals of America were at stake in Vietnam. Three presidents had promised support to a "friendly nation" which had asked for help against communist aggression, he recalled, and he was not about to break that pledge.[2] The president did not suggest what would be required to keep it.

His critics had raised questions of great import. Was China an expansionist threat? If so, as even most liberals did, was it best contained by a southern regime dependent on the United States or by an independent, albeit communist, Vietnam? Was it possible to create in South Vietnam a viable and militantly anticommunist government? Was American interest in international stability best served by unilateral military action in Asia or by multinational diplomacy? What military objectives were attainable and what would success cost Vietnam and the U.S., respectively? What was motivating American policy—strategic analysis, cultural ethnocentrism, a bent toward militarism, corporate capitalism, or some combination of these and other factors—and was this a valid expression of national interests and ideals? Should containment facilitate change in the world or hold the line? Were communist systems malleable at all? Would intervention align the United States with the forces of national independence and social change or place the country athwart them?

Here in the mid-1960s was material for a national debate, but that debate was not held in any sustained way. The political right did not regard such questions as debatable. The administration avoided them in order to maintain a consensus of the center that would support its domestic programs and leave it free reign in foreign policy. Congress went along. In the absence of a parliamentary challenge, antiwar critics invented a sustained protest movement among citizens who felt politically discontented and morally disfranchised. The opposition concentrated on intervention in Vietnam, but it divided over the meaning of its own effort. Indeed, the abiding irony of the Vietnam issue in 1965 was that Washington's sudden and deceptive escalation of the war fueled an antiwar movement that fractured the more it proliferated.

The Vietcong struck U.S. forces at Pleiku on 6 February. That was the excuse Johnson needed to inaugurate air war against North Vietnam. He ordered an immediate retaliatory strike across the Seventeenth Parallel, ostensibly to protect American noncombatant ground forces. On 24 February the Air Force initiated regular bombing raids on military and industrial targets in the North. The operation, called Rolling Thunder, was described as a policy of "sustained reprisal."

Spurning international appeals to halt the bombing and negotiate, the State Department explained the bombing as a response to "aggression from the North."[3] Early in March two battalions of marines were placed near Danang to defend the air base there, and they soon opened combat forays into the nearby countryside. As it became clear that the air war (3,600 individual missions in April alone) was having no appreciable effect on the deteriorating military situation in the South, pressure mounted within the administration to commit ground troops to open warfare. By the end of April, it was agreed to dispatch forty thousand troops in order to forestall a major Vietcong victory. Without explaining that, the president asked Congress for $400 million to support military operations. In mid-June there were fifty-four thousand American troops in Vietnam, some of them were engaging in combat, and the president's closest advisors were wrestling with the next steps.

In retrospect, the response to Pleiku constituted what historian George C. Herring has called a "watershed" of American military commitment; but throughout the spring the administration claimed that there had been no change in policy.[4] In fact, the White House did not want to submit the issue to debate: it did not want to arouse the North Vietnamese; it did not value public judgment on complex problems; and it did not want to jeopardize support for its domestic programs. It also assumed that the main threat to its control of foreign policy came from the militant right wing. The president and his top advisors did not take seriously what they termed the "Fulbright-Mansfield-Church School" of thinking, and they but bristled at the jibes of "fleabite professors."[5] They were not eager to alienate their leading critics, though, and so they heard out public dissenters like Walter Lippmann and insiders like George Ball and Clark Clifford. Indeed, the president agreed to a brief bombing pause in May out of deference to the demands of elite critics. When nothing followed from that initiative, he became all the more convinced that McGeorge Bundy had been right at the outset: "None of the special solutions or criticisms put forward with zeal by individual reformers in government or in the press is of major importance," his National Security Advisor had promised, "and many of them are flatly wrong."[6]

Privately, the president shared his aides' suspicion that people "like Lippmann, Morgenthau, Fulbright and marching students do great damage by creating false hopes in unfriendly breasts" in Moscow and Hanoi.[7] Publicly, Johnson refused to excoriate the dissidents that spring, however, and he declined to label them as appeasers. After all, he declared, the right to dissent was precisely what America was fighting for in Vietnam. On a more practical level, his liberal foreign policy critics were among the strongest supporters of his domestic policy. Public controversy could shatter the political center on which the administration depended for all its plans. Accordingly, the president interpreted the air war as a retaliation for an unprovoked attack, an alternative to combat, and a firmness that would yield lasting peace grounded on an independent South Vietnam. In this sense, the policy goals governing "sustained reprisal" did indeed remain constant.

By not fanning popular support for war, the administration left dissidents with maneuvering room. Its early attempt to manage news in order to wage the conflict with "as low a level of public noise as possible" also aggravated prevalent suspicion of government deception, which strengthened its critics.[8] Although Americans rallied behind presidential initiatives like the bombing, popular opinion during the spring was confused and contradictory, eager for success but reluctant to pay for it. In late January, for instance, Gallup pollsters found that 81 percent of the population favored an international conference to effect "some kind of acceptable and peaceful compromise." The February air strikes were backed by two-thirds of people polled; but six weeks after the start of the air war, Gallup determined that American sentiment was "widely diversified," with opinion evenly split (42-41 percent) between those who favored sending more troops and those who wanted immediate negotiations.[9] Even allowing for the vagaries of polling, these results suggested the volatility of public opinion. The antiwar movement gained and maintained life as it tapped a deep substratum of popular doubt.

The lack of consensus on or clarity about the administration's purpose in Vietnam provided an opening for challengers. By this time, numerous dissidents had learned to trust their own judgment in the course of the test-ban campaign. Others had gained self-confidence in confronting the moral legitimacy of the prevailing authority through the civil rights movement. With U.S. military escalation, some citizens normally reluctant to question the foreign policy decisions of officials suddenly took a critical interest in Vietnam, and they made no apologies for their lack of formal expertise. As a Catholic nun put it, "Even if we cannot make a complete judgment on all social, economic and military factors, we can still make a moral judgment on the war's basic inhumanity."[10] The day after Pleiku was attacked, and while B-52s pounded North Vietnamese targets, SDS leaders announced their antiwar Easter march on Washington. The elements of opposition were in motion.

Opinion polls to the contrary notwithstanding, the more than fifteen hundred telegrams sent to the White House after the air responses of early February were more than twelve-to-one against the president's decision. The reaction was "sharply different" from that which followed the Tonkin Gulf bombings, McGeorge Bundy cautioned the president, and it indicated that "we have an education problem that bears close watching and more work."[11] The administration continued to receive about eighteen hundred Vietnam-related messages per week, with antiwar sentiment predominating by ratios of six- through twelve-to-one. The letters were "literate, judicious and reasoned," Bundy was told, with women outnumbering men and with emphasis on the immorality of the war, the need for a negotiated settlement, and complaints that Johnson was following the discredited Goldwater approach.[12] Antiwar petitions and advertisements followed the same pattern. Over four hundred participants at a New York commemoration of Pope John's encyclical *Pacem in Terris* released a joint letter of protest in February, and local dissidents from Seattle to Boston pooled their resources to purchase newspaper advertisements.

In Washington, critics lobbied against escalation. Mansfield and Lippmann privately shared their reservations with the president and his top aides. Senators George McGovern (D-S. Dak.) and Frank Church and a few others protested publicly. Over three hundred women from WILPF and WSP gathered in a Washington's "Mothers' Lobby" between 8 and 10 February, confronting legislators with demands for a negotiated settlement and the "dignified withdrawal" of U.S. forces from Vietnam.[13] The AFSC and FCNL canvassed congressional sentiment, while representatives from SANE and ADA met occasionally during the late winter with either White House officials or the president himself. Their exchanges were polite and perfunctory.

Antiwar liberals made little headway in the face of the private obduracy and public ambivalence of the administration and in the absence of strong congressional opposition. Government officials either said that they "felt sorry for people who had no faith in our government" or vowed that, while they shared the same goals as the dissidents, they had access to precious nuggets of "secret information" that justified their course.[14]

After ten days of lobbying in Washington, AFSC peace education secretary Stewart Meacham concluded that it was "almost impossible" to penetrate the defenses and convictions of U.S. policymakers.[15] Besides, liberals' support of the administration's domestic programs muted their criticism of its foreign policy. Most of them seemed to expect that the war would end soon anyway, and all wanted "to maintain some influence with the President without incurring his wrath" in what was expected to be a two-term White House.[16]

Scattered dissidents protested directly. About five hundred student radicals in the San Francisco area announced a grandiose plan to trigger "mass-resistance" among students. Catholic priest Daniel Berrigan, with other pacifists, declared himself to be "in peaceable conflict" with the state.[17] The six-month-old "Declaration of Conscience," pledging "conscientious refusal to cooperate" and nonviolent means "to stop the flow of American soldiers and munitions to Vietnam," was revived (by April it had 4,500 signers).[18] At the United Nations Plaza on 13 February about 3,000 citizens protested the U.S. air war.

Largely spontaneous protests throughout the country were reminiscent of the early civil rights movement. At SDS headquarters in Chicago early in March, Paul Booth found that "every day's mail brings word of a demonstration or two we'd never heard of."[19] His view was distorted by the fact that he was getting word only of citizen protest, of course; but even veteran peace activists marvelled at "the upsurge of student demonstrations" and the formation of "various ad hoc committees and organizations not usually considered in the mainstream of the peace movement."[20] Yet spontaneity had its cost. On 16 March the antiwar dissent numbered its first martyr: in mute testimony to her anguish over the war, an eighty-two-year-old Quaker—a member of WILPF and a refugee from Nazi Germany—doused her body with gasoline and set herself afire on a Detroit street corner.

Two days later, while Alice Herz lay dying in a hospital, an event at the nearby University of Michigan inaugurated the most significant form of dissent that spring: the "teach-in." There had been a few dozen antiwar protests on college campuses during the late winter. Some of them were locally initiated. Others were organized by the Universities Committee on Problems of War and Peace, a three-year-old peace group based at Wayne State University, whose members shared an academic and political concern about the Cold War. Campus dissent received national attention, though, when a number of University of Michigan faculty members hit on the idea of a teach-in to focus attention "on this war, its consequences and ways to stop it."[21]

Inspired by the "freedom schools" and other self-help efforts pioneered in the civil rights struggle, the idea appealed to dissident academics like sociologist William Gamson, mathematician Anatol Rapaport, anthropologist Marshall Sahlins, and economist Kenneth Boulding as the most useful way of communicating their moral discontent with U.S. war policy in a forum of reasoned inquiry. Clearly, the teach-in was a protest rather than a debate; and yet it was also a shrewd means of energizing the university without disrupting it, since it was substituted for a proposed faculty strike. Through the night of 24–25 March, and over the opposition of Michigan governor George Romney and other politicians, more than 3,000 students and faculty members flowed through the University's Angell Hall, participating in lectures, debates, and discussion groups. At least twice, the crowd was forced outside briefly by bomb threats. The next morning about 600 people remained for a concluding rally on the library steps in twenty-degree weather. For some students and faculty it was the highlight of their university years, a night when "people who really cared talked of things that really mattered."[22]

The Ann Arbor teach-in got national coverage and was rapidly emulated. One of its speakers addressed a similar convocation of 2,500 at Columbia University the following day. Within a week Vietnam teach-ins were held on at least 35 more campuses, and by the end of the school year the idea had spread to some 120 schools. Raising the Vietnam issue did not always elicit opposition to the administration or support for antiwar dissidents. When 30 picketers protested the U.S. air war at Kent State University in early February, they were dispersed by an angry crowd of 150 prowar students. A teach-in at the University of Wisconsin provoked 6,000 students to sign a letter supporting the president's policy. A quarter of the Yale student body did the same thing. For all the talk about campus protest and antiwar teach-ins, student opinion roughly paralleled that of adults, with hardly 24 percent of them arguing for negotiation or withdrawal.[23] In any case, University of Michigan faculty members began to negotiate with McGeorge Bundy for a national teach-in. By mid-April an ad hoc Inter-University Committee for a Public Hearing on Vietnam was formed, and 15 May was set for a program involving the country's leading campuses.

Dissent from professors disconcerted Lyndon Johnson and his aides more than that from students. The president had "both envy and contempt for academics," historian Melvin Small has concluded, and he was very sensitive to their approval. "Like them or not," he regarded intellectuals as important.[24] So did McGeorge Bundy. The intellectual elite was the backbone of ADA, reached deep into the Democratic party, and was almost coterminous with opinion-shaping commentators. Bundy had been urging the White House to address the Vietnam policy frontally for some time, but it was the dissent signalled by the first teach-ins which prompted the president's Johns Hopkins address of 7 April—"the first major example of the impact of antiwar and other dissenting activities on the making of foreign policy during the Vietnam War."[25]

As campus protests mounted thereafter, government leaders tried to counter them. In May a team of civilian and military officials was dispatched to midwestern universities to defend administration policy, but the program was singularly ineffective and it was dropped in favor of less formal visits by government officials. College men were recruited to work as civilian aides in Vietnam during the summer on the theory that upon their return to campus they would be effective spokesmen. Covertly, the administration helped to raise $25,000 in private funds which was channeled to Michigan State University political scientist (and former advisor to Saigon's security forces) Wesley Fishel in order to convert the American Friends of Vietnam (founded in 1955) into a nationwide prowar speaker's bureau and information center. Part of that effort involved the creation of campus groups. Such efforts were grounded in the assumption of White House officials that the *"basic difficulty"* was that supporters were "largely silent and either unorganized or disorganized."[26]

The 1965 teach-ins were significant, in fact, more because of their very organization than for their novelty or the extent of student protest. They legitimatized dissent at the outset of the war. The vacuum of understanding which they exposed created a market for information. What analysis there was became widely available, notably Bernard Fall's *The Two Viet-Nams,* I. F. Stone's critique of the State Department's White Paper, Robert Scheer's *How the United States Got Involved in Vietnam,* and later in the year Fall's and Marcus Raskin's *The Viet-Nam Reader.* Moreover, the 1965 teach-ins served to identify a coterie of academic experts who challenged national policy, helped to make connections among them, and established them as an alternative source of information and understanding. A similar development began quietly in Washington, where the FCNL and other peace groups sponsored meetings with American and foreign experts for national organizations and members of Congress.[27] In the long run, the development of cohesive, alternative expertise on Vietnam would have its effect.

In the spring of 1965, however, it was clear that the administration had the support of the country's major opinion-shaping agencies. Antiwar activists quickly realized their limited effectiveness. The nationwide demand for peace was the greatest since the early days of the test-ban campaign, one of them observed, but the whole effort added up to no more than "a very impressive marshalling of what are at best meager resources."[28] Reported SANE, "The silence in Congress has been deafening," with a few senators for de-escalation and all others "circumspect to the point of paralysis."[29] Popular reaction to the war debate likewise seemed confused or indifferent. The U.S. air war against North Vietnam reminded the *Nation* of "the happy days of unchecked imperialism, when the Royal Air Force could bomb Indian villages and no one cared but the Indians." It was "extremely difficult to foresee a mass campaign under present conditions," ventured Sidney Lens. "The average citizen has been beguiled into believing that the bombing of North Vietnam will lead to negotiations and peace very quickly."[30]

Antiwar activists felt doubly frustrated early in 1965 because they valued the president's support on civil rights. In the Alabama industrial town of Selma, Martin Luther King, Jr., and the Southern Christian Leadership Conference were battling for enfranchisement. Local and state police there responded to black street meetings and marches with tear gas and electric cattle prods, while elsewhere in the state white mobs and Klansmen set upon and killed northern white civil rights volunteers. Outraged, thousands of clergymen descended on Alabama for a landmark march from Selma to the capital at Montgomery, and blacks and whites demonstrated throughout the country. Johnson put the presidency behind the civil rights crusade. Addressing the country in a nationally televised address to Congress on 15 March, he called for immediate legislation in support of black voting rights, promising that "we shall overcome" a national heritage of racial hatred and injustice.[31]

Three weeks later the president again seized high ground at the Johns Hopkins University, where he announced that he was willing to engage in "unconditional discussions" with any government to end the war and to inaugurate a $1 billion program for the economic development of the Mekong River valley. After the speech White House insiders reported "a sharp reversal in the heavy flow of critical mail."[32] Johnson also reaffirmed support for an independent South Vietnam, but dissenters like Lippmann and William Fulbright praised the address for the conciliatory tone they wanted to hear. Most critics remained skeptical. Pacifists in the FOR and AFSC and liberals in SANE and ADA welcomed the shift in spirit but saw no real policy change, and radicals condemned the president's new pose as deceitful. Johnson's proposals were designed to make "obstinacy look like conciliation, . . . its war look like peace," complained SDS leaders. He was "conning Americans now as he did all through his peace-hawking campaign."[33]

The president's tolerance of dissent and the ambivalence of his Vietnam policy that spring helped to accentuate long-standing tensions between liberal and radical antiwar critics over their purposes and expectations. Peace liberals in groups such as SANE, ADA, and AFSC sought to create a climate that would facilitate negotiations by relating as much as possible to "a 'Mr. and Mrs. America' position." They rejected demands for both escalation and immediate withdrawal, lobbying for an internationally negotiated settlement that would preserve an independent South Vietnam while containing Chinese expansionism. "We must be effective," declared SANE's Donald Keys, and this meant to offer responsible alternatives within the framework of decision-making.[34]

On the other hand, SDS activists were more interested in building a broad movement for radical social change than in directly influencing Washington. University of Michigan graduate student Richard Flacks had collaborated with Tom Hayden in 1963 to draft a sequel to the *Port Huron Statement,* which they entitled *America and the New Era.* Flacks argued that the nation had to "choose between devoting its resources and energies to maintaining military superiority and international hegemony or rechanneling those resources and energies to meeting the desperate needs of its people."[35] Since making such a choice required fuller popular participation in defining the national interest, he added, the political process had priority over specific policy. Accordingly, SDS members could be found working for civil rights, university reform, the empowerment of the poor, and the liberation of black South Africans from apartheid. Few concentrated upon Vietnam. Seeing the war as but one more American injustice, young radicals viewed Vietnam mainly as a means of mobilizing various "insurgency groups" to "challenge the very powers that make the policies we oppose."[36] Although sincere in opposing the war, they did not expect to affect it so much as they hoped that it would accelerate left-wing activism.

Tensions between liberals and radicals began to crystalize over the SDS April march on Washington. From the inauguration of Rolling Thunder, people began to abandon the annual spring disarmament programs in favor of the only planned demonstration against the war. In calling it, SDS organizers Paul Booth and Todd Gitlin avoided the issue of unilateral withdrawal by advocating only that the U.S. get out of Vietnam. They had resolved, though, not to exclude from the march any dissidents with unpopular political tendencies (meaning communist), nor to police the march against controversial peace proposals (meaning immediate withdrawal). They thus raised the old, intractable issue of exclusionism within the peace movement.

Peace liberals like Norman Thomas, disturbed by SDS's implicit acceptance of communist and Vietcong sympathizers, complained that it could be used to validate right-wing charges that antiwar dissidents were less interested in peace than in a communist victory. At the instigation of Bayard Rustin and Robert Gilmore, a number of peace leaders (including Thomas and Muste) met in New York City to review plans for the scheduled demonstration. On the eve of the march, they issued a statement which praised the "healthy shift" in U.S. policy implied in the Johns Hopkins address and called for "an independent peace movement, not committed to any form of totalitarianism nor drawing inspiration or direction from the foreign policy of any government."[37] The innocuous midnight advisory, publicized the next day, inflamed SDS leaders who remembered their bout with the LID, but it had little impact on the demonstration.

SDS leaders had hoped for ten thousand participants. About twenty thousand people, mostly young and casually dressed, pressed into Washington on Easter Saturday, 17 April, in the largest single antiwar demonstration yet organized in America.[38] The crowd encircled the White House with a picket line and then moved to the Washington Monument. Folksinging by Judy Collins, Joan Baez, and Phil Ochs alternated with speeches by I. F. Stone, black civil rights leader Robert Parris Moses, and Yale University historian Staughton Lynd. "The times they are a-changin'," sang Collins, and her listeners wanted to believe it. In the featured address Senator Gruening called for an immediate bombing halt and the opening of peace negotiations, but SDS president Paul Potter won the most applause when he urged activists to use the Vietnam issue, "the symptom of a deeper malaise," to forge "a massive social movement" toward America's radical reconstruction.[39] Clearly, the participants were moved. Singing the civil rights anthem, "We Shall Overcome," the throng marched down the Mall, eighty abreast, to the steps of the Capitol, where they presented proposals ranging from immediate withdrawal to negotiations through a new Geneva conference. After a brief debate about the wisdom of conducting massive civil disobedience at the Capitol, the demonstration broke up quietly in the late afternoon.

The news media were sufficiently impressed by the size and seriousness of the Easter demonstration that they gave national coverage to SDS and the student antiwar movement.[40] The leaders of the protest were themselves so enthusiastic that on the night of the march they debated the possibility of building a radical reform movement around the Vietnam issue, but they could not commit themselves. SDS returned to its primary agendas of community organizing and university reform, half convinced that the war issue would prove to be ephemeral. "Where would we be," asked a member opposed to full-blown antiwar activism, "if peace were to break out tomorrow?"[41] In retrospect, the question throws the naïveté of initial responses to the war into bold relief. "We really screwed up," Paul Booth later reflected. "We had the opportunity at that meeting to make SDS *the* organizational vehicle of the anti-war movement."[42] For the time being, the initiative was left with liberals, and they were very much on the defensive.

At the end of April, the Johnson administration ordered the first of an eventual twenty-three thousand U.S. marines to the Dominican Republic in order to establish a conservative junta battling against the reform government of Juan Bosch which it had displaced. A few politicians and intellectuals, including Senator Wayne Morse and historian Henry Steele Commager, protested Johnson's intervention, but the great body of Americans backed the president's decisive action. Even critics of Vietnam policy such as Mansfield and Gruening accepted it.

The Caribbean action was nonetheless part of a package—a comprehensive response to the perceived threat of communist revolution anywhere. Earlier that month the White House had authorized another twenty thousand marines for South Vietnam and had approved General William Westmoreland's request to modify their military mission from providing base security to offensive action against Vietnamese guerrillas. The strategy was to apply military power to defeat the communists by "depriving them of victory."[43] The United States would win when the communists accepted failure. Publicly, the administration denied any change in the American role in Vietnam until 8 June, when a State Department press spokesman casually announced that U.S. forces were "available for combat support" and, in effect, confirmed the fact that the United States was involved in another Asian land war.[44] On 11 June, South Vietnamese military officers Nguyen Cao Ky and Nguyen Van Thieu replaced the civilian government with a regime that brought the first sign of political stability in twenty months but offered no immediate prospect of military success. In the meantime, the U.S. air war against North Vietnam continued unabated, aside from the brief pause in May. Communist forces only struck harder, and South Vietnamese forces crumbled faster. The U.S. government wrestled with the alternatives.

With policy apparently still fluid, a few members of the policy-shaping elite yet hoped to contain escalation. They preferred what Lippmann called "strategic retreat" to "scuttle and run" or becoming "bogged down in a large land war on the Asian mainland" in order "to save face."[45] Lippmann and some others urged the government to hold "one or more highly fortified strongpoints with certain access to the sea," in order to signal both determination and willingness to negotiate.[46] Thinking of themselves as political realists and disdainful of irregular politics, dissenters who felt close to the administration refused to align themselves with assertive activists. None of them had any interest in being, as George Ball once put it, "a hero of the yippies" or one "of those fatuous intellectuals who felt that issues were better settled in the streets than through established organs of government."[47] Like Senator J. William Fulbright (D-Ark.), whose reservations about Vietnam were aggravated by intervention in the Dominican Republic, they nonetheless overestimated their personal influence with the president.

Dissent was augmented, meanwhile, from two sources which did not share that illusion: the cultural and religious communities. Leading figures in the new but influential *New York Review of Books* circulated an antiwar petition, and the president of the American Academy of Arts and Letters, Lewis Mumford, denounced U.S. policy in Vietnam at the Academy's annual May meeting. The country's premier poet, Robert Lowell, publicly rejected an invitation to a White House Festival of the Arts a few weeks later, citing his "dismay and distrust" over the administration's Vietnam policy.[48] During the Festival, author Dwight Macdonald and *Newsweek*'s cultural affairs editor Saul Maloff solicited signatures to an antiwar petition. They got little support, but they enraged the president. Scarcely containing his anger, Johnson snapped, "Some of them insult me by staying away and some of them insult me by coming."[49]

Discontent was reflected also in liberal religious circles. With support from the FOR, an Interreligious Committee on Vietnam sponsored a number of mass mailings and newspaper advertisements in April, promoting a military cease-fire and negotiations.[50] Early in May it sponsored an interfaith delegation of 60 Christian and Jewish clergy who visited Washington to appeal for peace, and a week later 550 clergymen lobbied Congress for a negotiated settlement. The following month an interfaith group of religious leaders organized by the FOR visited Vietnam. Upon their return they condemned "the sinister character of the war" and called for negotiations through a new Geneva conference.[51] Meanwhile, Reinhold Niebuhr, John C. Bennett, and their editorial associates in *Christianity and Crisis* assailed Johnson's Vietnam policy and called for a negotiated settlement among all parties and "reconciliation between the U.S. and China."[52] That statement carried special weight because the journal had been established in 1940 to oppose liberal Protestant pacifism and support armed U.S. intervention in Europe as a matter of ethical realism. Now its founders were joining pacifists to challenge Asian intervention on both moral and realistic grounds.

Liberal peace advocates tried to rally public opinion. A SANE rally on 8 June attracted eighteen thousand people to New York's Madison Square Garden. Having declined to sponsor the April rally and eager to show their respectability, SANE organizers insisted that "none of the publicity should use the word protest."[53] At the Garden, speakers Wayne Morse, Benjamin Spock, Norman Thomas, and others called for a unilateral U.S. cease-fire, negotiations among all warring parties, and UN supervision of a Vietnam peace settlement. Only SDS leader Clark Kissinger broke from the liberal line, declaring from the platform that the war was neither irrational nor mistaken. On the contrary, he said, Vietnam was part of a pattern of U.S. counterrevolutionary interventionism that demanded not merely policy change in Vietnam but "the radical reconstruction of American foreign policy." Kissinger was closing in on his liberal hosts. "Our problem," he insisted, "is in America, not in Vietnam."[54] That was the essence of the radical challenge. Beyond all the rhetoric and cultural baggage with which it was often obscured, the crux of the Vietnam issue was to locate the problem.

"A new, radical alignment for peace"

By the time of the SANE rally, the teach-ins had gone national, and they too reflected a division in antiwar understanding. The Inter-University Committee for a Public Hearing on Vietnam, formed in the wake of the campus programs in March, sponsored a national teach-in at Washington's Sheraton Park Hotel on 15 May, which, for three and a half hours, reached over 100,000 people through television links to a hundred campuses. For more than fifteen hours, Vietnam was debated by scholars from major universities, including historian Arthur M. Schlesinger, Jr., and Soviet affairs specialist Zbigniew Brzezinski speaking for the administration and Bernard Fall, Seymour Melman, and Hans Morgenthau arguing against it. The feature of the event was to have been a debate between McGeorge Bundy and George Kahin of Cornell University, an expert on Southeast Asia, but at the last minute Johnson sent his national security advisor on a mission to the Caribbean—backhanded testimony to Johnson's apprehension of public debate. Bundy did appear opposite Morgenthau three weeks later on a national teach-in moderated by broadcast commentator Eric Severeid of CBS-TV. Dissent had become "more respectable," and this did not please the president.[55]

It did satisfy the organizers of the teach-in. Arguing merely for "responsible debate," they endorsed no "particular scheme for settling the situation in Vietnam."[56] Some activists criticized the national programs, however, for domesticating dissent and converting the spontaneous protest at the heart of the campus teach-ins into "a glorified faculty meeting of the Establishment."[57] Within days, the national teach-in project was divided between a "Loyal Opposition" trying to reorder U.S. foreign policy, and a moral and political challenge to the nation's priorities.[58] The program broke apart a few months later; it was the first of many efforts to crack under the pressure of interpreting the war.[59]

Mounting division within the movement was vividly dramatized at the University of California, Berkeley on 21–22 May, when over twenty thousand people participated in a thirty-six-hour marathon teach-in. Berkeley had been in turmoil during the fall of 1964, when students transformed their interest in civil rights into a full-fledged challenge to campus authority. Their demand for the right to solicit support on campus for political action had mushroomed into the Free Speech Movement and an attack on the university administration, which radical students interpreted as epitomizing "the greatest problem of our nation—depersonalized, unresponsive bureaucracy."[60] The university had been responsive enough to mollify most students, until the escalating war offered a new vehicle for protest. The opportunity seemed particularly clear to "impish, iconoclastic" Jerry Rubin, who had been active in the Free Speech Movement.[61] Working out of Rubin's apartment, a few students teamed up with faculty members such as mathematician Stephen Smale to form an ad hoc Vietnam Day Committee (VDC), a strange concoction of radical pacifism, student protest, civil rights activism, leftist politics, and cultural bohemianism peculiar to the Bay Area.

There was no attempt to balance the program with government representatives; the Berkeley teach-in was designed as a protest, not a debate. In a sense, it was a drama. Although VDC was contemptuous of established peace groups, it also disdained exclusionism. Speakers represented the range of "American Opposition," from thoughtful Norman Thomas to existentialist novelist Norman Mailer, and they included Ernest Gruening, Isaac Deutscher, Staughton Lynd, Robert Parris Moses, and David Dellinger.[62] The roster leaned leftward.

For two days antiwar liberals and radicals voiced the need for a coordinated antiwar movement while they skirmished over the meaning of the war, the nature of American society, and approaches to social change. Radical pacifists and left-wing radicals argued that Vietnam was a war of American aggression that could be ended only by immediate U.S. withdrawal. Contending that the war was being made by liberals, the radicals called upon antiwar advocates to quit the "liberal-labor-Negro coalition" of the Democratic party and join civil rights activists, student militants, and other proponents of radical change in a self-styled, "new, 'do-it-yourself'" revolution.[63] Vietnam had to be saved by redeeming America, they insisted. Antiwar liberals, on the other hand, rejected the radical analysis—Robert Pickus called it "so much pure crap."[64]

The phrase was a kind of intellectual direct action. Pickus was a radical pacifist who had responded to the ethical currents of his Jewish tradition by seizing on the Quaker concern with war. He had encountered Gandhian leaders in India en route home from a 1957 Fulbright year in London. He had participated in direct action projects at missile sites in Nevada and California and had handled the West Coast organizing for the 1961 San Francisco to Moscow Walk. If his ideals were those of a radical pacifist, his politics were nonetheless those of a liberal realist. Stationed by the army in Sweden during World War II, he had come in contact with European exiles whose idealism the Nazi *Wehrmacht* had broken. What he had seen reinforced his mistrust of romantic idealism and his appreciation of the degree of freedom structured into American society. Subsequently, as a student of Hans Morgenthau and Leo Strauss at the University of Chicago, he had imbued the tenets of realism in the service of international order. Pickus had developed a distinctly clear intellectual position, and the San Francisco to Moscow project exemplified it: to challenge the romanticizing of violence, whether in the rhetoric of containment or communist revolution.

His goal was to alter U.S. Cold War policies, not to challenge the American system, and that was the perspective of the liberals at the Berkeley teach-in. They portrayed Vietnam as an international problem that would best be addressed by changing U.S. policy to multilateral negotiations and military disengagement. Declared Norman Thomas, "I am interested in peace," and that "does not require us to hate America" or to undertake its radical transformation.[65]

The brouhaha at Berkeley was only a prelude to the larger division of American pacifism during the summer of 1965. With the war escalating and domestic tensions rising, pacifists broke into opposing liberal and radical factions that quarrelled over the meaning of Vietnam, America, and nonviolence. On one level, they differed about questions such as the desirability of immediate withdrawal from Vietnam and the wisdom of closer collaboration with various left-wing groups. Militant pacifists like Dellinger, for example, insisted upon immediate withdrawal and supported SDS and others of the New Left in collaborating with the full range of radicals. Liberal pacifists like Alfred Hassler of the FOR, on the other hand, had reservations about unilateral withdrawal and feared that organizational inclusiveness would leave uncritical activists vulnerable to political sectarianism.

At a deeper level, the division between radical and liberal pacifists involved long-standing differences over the meaning of nonviolence and the question whether or not American institutions could be redeemed. Concluding that the United States was a principal source of global injustice and violence, radical pacifists sought to revolutionize the country in combination with discontented blacks, students, and others who rejected prevailing authority and sought to build an extraparliamentary opposition through parallel institutions in community unions, new political parties, and, eventually, "a new continental congress."[66] *Liberation* radicals believed that America could be saved only through a revolution of individual nonviolent resistance and collective democratic action, and that Vietnam could be saved from America only through the resistance of the Vietcong. Liberal pacifists argued, on the other hand, that the problem was not so much America as war itself, and they proposed to attack the war system by promoting impartial nonviolence rather than revolution. Pacifists must aim, said Pickus, "not at polarizing, but at permeating the society" with alternative values. They must aim not to support one side or another, but to oppose the war. Their preference for the peace of reconciliation led some liberal pacifists to support the Buddhist "Third Force" in Vietnam, which stood for peace in opposition both to the U.S.-sponsored Saigon regime and the communists, even as they admitted with Hassler that "there literally may be NO MORAL solution" to America's armed intervention.[67]

A. J. Muste remained above the controversy—not aloof, but beyond it. "My attitude on all these things is frankly an experimental one," he once confided. "I don't want to be separated from these young elements at this stage. At the same time, I am not at all sure whether a truly viable New Left or revolutionary movement is going to develop. For the time being, I am going to take each situation as it comes along, analyzing it very carefully."[68] Muste had confidence in the democratic values of SDS leaders and was certain that pacifists must work in all nonviolent ways to bring an immediate end to the war in Vietnam. The development of sharp differences within the movement was to be expected, he cautioned, but not turned inward.

Tension among pacifists in the summer of 1965 was born of philosophical differences enormously aggravated by a feeling of helplessness on the verge of a war which, they all agreed, would be disastrous. Division and anguish left the core of domestic antiwar activism fragile. Within the movement, as in America, the contest of the next half-decade would be for the center.

The quarrel among pacifists also dramatized another dilemma that would be felt by nearly all antiwar activists: how could they oppose U.S. military intervention without giving succor to the totalitarianism it was supposed to contain? In one sense, the dilemma was artificial. Plainly, the great majority of antiwar critics were aroused in reaction to U.S. policies, and they rejected suggestions that their protest abetted communist military success. When prowar politicians accused domestic dissidents of prolonging the war by their criticism, Walter Lippmann replied that the very accusation conveyed the "self-delusion" of American omnipotence and omniscience. It assumed, he wrote, that other governments made their policies according to "how they read the Gallup poll in the United States" and that "as compared with foreigners, we are always right and never wrong. If therefore we agree among ourselves, none can withstand us because none should withstand us, and we shall and must prevail."[69] Historian Henry Steele Commager characterized the charge of abetting an enemy as "a form of blackmail" intended to drown out all criticism, and Dave McReynolds turned the argument around by claiming that antiwar activists protested government policy "not because *we are 'anti-American,' but because the government is*."[70]

Undeniably, a minority of antiwar dissidents favored the communist cause in Vietnam. Dellinger tried painstakingly to square his support for the Vietcong guerrillas with his commitment to revolutionary nonviolence, to distinguish between the "*struggle* of the National Liberation Front," which he approved, from its violence, which he could not endorse.[71] The fringe group May Second Movement identified with the ideology of China's Chairman Mao Zedong, and it simply cheered the Vietcong for their struggle in righteous battle; but this sentiment (and even Dellinger's rationalization) was by far a small exception to the sensibility of the growing antiwar movement.

If the dilemma was artificial in the sense that it did not reflect the position of most dissenters from the war, however, it was no less real in that it was widely posed for them. They were routinely and indiscriminately vilified as articulate fools or communist dupes. Editorialists complained that by encouraging the Vietcong to miscalculate the nation's will, critics were prolonging the war, if not promoting international communism. Senator Dodd's Internal Security Subcommittee promised to detail communist sources of the springtime teach-ins. In New Jersey the announcement by historian Eugene Genovese of Rutgers University that he would welcome a Vietcong victory became a major issue in the gubernatorial race. Reaction to dissent was altogether tangible at the local level, where counterdemonstrators frequently confronted antiwar protesters. Thus seventy-five dissidents who tried to protest during an ROTC ceremony at Cornell University became the targets of jeers and eggs from some four thousand students. A clear majority of Americans regarded the teach-ins as the work of radical troublemakers, according to a Harris poll. Indeed, most respondents saw campus dissent not as a healthy sign of democracy in action, but rather "as a harmful activity while U.S. troops are fighting abroad."[72]

The Johnson administration remained outwardly tolerant of domestic criticism. Temperamentally incapable of recognizing the legitimacy of wartime opposition, the president fretted, "How can an American Senator or an American newspaperman or an American student tie the hands of our fellow American military men? Are they duped; are they sucked in?"[73] Politically, though, Johnson felt compelled to tolerate antiwar criticism rather than to inspire an attack upon dissidents that might flare into a right-wing resurgence, bury the Great Society, and possibly fragment the Democratic party. His aides spoke of a "growing and potentially dangerous chasm" between "intelligent" critics and the government.[74] Angry and frustrated, the president vented his feelings in a Cabinet meeting:

We are confronted with a dilemma, unquestionably, that it is difficult to face up to, as a result of the extremes of McCarthyism and the extremes of Goldwaterism. The people have more or less put the Communist menace on the back burner. You immediately become a dangerous character or suspect if you express strong feeling about our system and some question about the activities of Communists as a result of these two other extremes.

I don't want us to get into that dangerous position. I love this system, and I don't want us to either be addicts of some other system or tools of some other system. The thing that troubles me more about our government than nearly anything else is that I will see a line from Peking, Hanoi and Moscow . . . about a month ahead of the time I see it here. I see it being openly espoused by so-called devotees of our system. It is almost taken in text.[75]

He did not see any way of avoiding the dilemma.

The president's frustration was compounded as the racial crisis roiled on. With black voting nearly legislated, Martin Luther King, Jr., announced that the civil rights movement was shifting its attention to black economic liberation. He unveiled a program targeting Chicago as the site of a new challenge to discrimination in the urban North. While tense but peaceful demonstrations continued in towns from Americus, Georgia, to Springfield, Massachusetts, there were incidents of armed violence between whites and blacks throughout much of the South, and an ominous new pattern of rioting by black youths against local police spread to other parts of the country. Urban disorder occurred with increasing scope and ferocity. Despite the historic Voting Rights Act, which Johnson signed on 6 August, the momentum of racial violence carried to the black Los Angeles ghetto of Watts in the middle of the month. There a five-day spasm of street rioting, gunfire, and looting subsided only after 34 people died, 1,032 required hospital treatment, and 13,900 national guard troops were called in.[76]

The civil rights and antiwar movements intersected briefly that summer. King called for a negotiated settlement of the war and considered joining some teach-ins and antiwar rallies. SNCC activists in McComb, Mississippi, urged blacks to resist the draft and refuse to fight for the freedom of white America in order to "kill other Colored people."[77] A prompt backlash of criticism from otherwise sympathetic white liberals and proadministration black leaders such as the National Urban League's Whitney Young undercut any immediate prospect of fusing the antiwar dissent and civil rights advocacy. Most black antiwar dissidents, including King, reemphasized the black agenda and tried to make a separate peace with the president.

All this time, political radicals had been working on the assumption that racial discontent was a symptom of repressed disaffection among a large class of Americans who, despite economic and cultural differences, were deprived of power by the way the society was structured. American radicals were few in number (one observer estimated the national total of active radical leftists at 12,000 in 1965), and those who identified with the New Left were fewer. Even so, they were an important constituency of the antiwar movement. A number of them dreamed of building "a countercommunity, Another America" among the country's students, blacks, and poor.[78] They assumed also that those "dispossessed" could achieve cohesion and power by fusing, as Dellinger put it, "individual conscience with immediately relevant mass political action."[79] The first step would be to identify the disparate elements as a class by bringing them together, and this idea was discussed in radical circles during the spring and early summer, as involvement in Vietnam escalated. Staughton Lynd gave form to the notion in his Berkeley Vietnam Day speech. Like Dellinger and Robert Parris Moses, he identified the war as the willful policy of an unrepresentative, bureaucratic elite. Lynd suggested convening a "new Continental Congress" in which the war might be the "immediately relevant" issue from which to forge a new style of politics that could bypass the party system.[80]

The Assembly of Unrepresented People, 6–9 August, was an expression of this combination of neo-Marxist analysis and romantic hope. It originated in a meeting initiated by the Washington Action Project late in June, and it was designed to attract people who were willing to renounce the U.S. war effort and to cooperate in social reform. The plan was to combine antiwar action with workshops on various social issues in order to lay the basis for a united front of the left.[81] The Assembly was a mélange of perhaps two thousand Quakers, radical pacifists, Maoists, Trotskyists, community organizers, poverty workers, and student radicals. On the first day they marked the twentieth anniversary of Hiroshima with a silent vigil at the White House. Then the crowd divided into workshops on topics ranging from free universities to the elimination of the House Un-American Activities Committee. The Assembly closed on 9 August, the anniversary of Nagasaki, with an 800-person march from the Washington Monument to the Capitol, where a declaration of peace was read and 350 demonstrators were arrested at a sit-in and jailed. Muste, Joan Baez, and a few others meanwhile met with staff people at the White House. There were "some very limp young men" at the meeting, an aide reported sardonically, but "no crockery was broken."[82]

Sponsors of the Assembly concluded euphorically that it had produced "a new radical alignment for peace" that was "anti-imperialist as well as antiwar."[83] Others were not so impressed. SDS leaders distanced themselves from the new left-wing front. Jack Newfield, a charter member of SDS and assistant editor of the *Village Voice,* could see why. The Assembly seethed with tensions between blacks and whites, he reported, between those who wanted to bear religious witness against Vietnam and those who wanted to use the war to build a radical political movement, and "between freedom and authoritarianism." For all the talk of the unrepresented, no one spoke for the poor. For all the talk of nonviolence and organizing the masses, no one could miss the "incestuous" in-group nature of the proceedings and the "irrational militancy" of the "hyper-militants and the authoritarians."[84]

The so-called new radical alignment for peace was simply the National Coordinating Committee to End the War in Vietnam (NCCEWVN, sometimes referred to as NCC). In the wake of the Berkeley teach-in, the Vietnam Day Committee had become formally organized. Cochaired by Jerry Rubin and Stephen Smale, VDC chose to sponsor fall International Days of Protest which would be conducted not only at home but also abroad. The international emphasis was largely Rubin's idea. It was rejected by Old Left groups which Rubin courted (the SWP and the YSA), and he then arranged for a workshop on national Vietnam action at the Assembly. In the course of seemingly interminable discussions among a shifting collection of participants, Rubin's proposal was adopted, and the NCCEWVN was created as a planning agency. The question was where to locate it and with what responsibility. When it became clear that SDS would not provide office space in Chicago, the new organization was placed in Madison, Wisconsin, with Frank Emspak as national coordinator. It was to be a clearinghouse for news and information from national and local antiwar groups—some independent and others fronts for left-wing bodies. The fractious radical antiwar groupings in the workshop denied any decision-making authority to the NCCEWVN, although they made it the executive agency for the mass protest which Berkeley's VDC already had set for 15–16 October.[85] By that time, the United States was at war in earnest.

After months of criticism and protest, and having experienced responsiveness, indifference, and rejection, most antiwar activists still seemed persuaded that the great majority of Americans had "no *heart* for the war in Vietnam, and no illusion" that it would succeed.[86] In the face of their own unpopularity and political weakness, they concluded, they must somehow shred what they took to be the nation's illusions and reach its heart. In that sense, their problem truly was in America.

It "really is war"

The Vietnam War never was declared; it was reported in stages and after the fact. In May and June large units of Vietcong defeated South Vietnamese forces, the Army of the Republic of Vietnam (ARVN), in pitched battles. The situation was deteriorating rapidly, and the Joint Chiefs, Secretary of Defense McNamara, and Walt Rostow of the State Department, among others, urged the president to give the U.S. military command more resources and a freer hand. In late July he authorized saturation bombing in the South and a further escalation of the air war in the North, although short of Hanoi. He also agreed to deploy immediately fifty thousand new ground troops in Vietnam and promised the Pentagon fifty thousand more. In fact, the commitment of forces was virtually open-ended, because U.S. strategy changed from securing enclaves to aggressive "search and destroy" movements against the Vietcong.

In a televised press conference on 28 July, Johnson announced that troop strength in Vietnam would be raised from 75,000 to 120,000 and that draft calls would be increased. This "really is war," the president said. "It is guided by North Vietnam and it is spurred by Communist China. Its goal is to conquer the South, to defeat America, and to extend the Asiatic dominion of communism."[87] He called upon Americans for support, and he got it. Congress responded with such overwhelming endorsement that he observed dryly, it was "mighty hawky."[88] Popular opinion was altogether supportive, although analyst Samuel Lubell cautioned that the national mood "seemed dominated by resignation rather than enthusiasm, by concern rather than confidence over any early solution."[89]

There were scattered protests, notably a campaign in the Bay Area, where activists from the Berkeley VDC and Women Strike for Peace challenged the movement of troops to the Oakland Army Terminal for shipment to Vietnam. On three occasions a few hundred demonstrators blocked the rail line until they were scattered by local police and oncoming locomotives. "We didn't have a prayer of stopping those troop trains," one protester admitted, "but people ... could see that we cared enough to take a chance. It made people THINK."[90] As a matter of fact, most Americans did not think much of antiwar protesters.

They began to think more about the war, though, because it was becoming Americanized. Supplies and support forces filled Saigon and choked the transportation system. Parts of the countryside were being saturated with bombs and napalm. The lavish use of firepower began to take its heavy toll of civilians. American planes bombed targets ever deeper into North Vietnam, and the U.S. Air Force began to experience losses. The war of attrition implied by "search and destroy" became a war against North Vietnam; but the United States, whose forces increased to nearly 185,000 during the fall, brought fighters into line only half as rapidly as its enemy.

The Vietcong attacked U.S. bases in October, and the next month heavy combat in the Ia Drang valley left 240 U.S. dead in one week. Secretary of State Rusk grimly declared that "serious fighting" lay ahead.[91] By the end of the year, 1,350 Americans had been killed in action. Not only did U.S. casualties become significant, but the warfare was viewed directly through television. Sweeping the countryside near Danang in the company of U.S. television news crews, American troops pumped nonlethal gases into tunnel complexes to flush out enemy forces and, in one of the earliest and most vivid battlefield scenes recorded for home viewing, marines entered a village and ignited thatch-roofed peasant huts with their cigarette lighters. Increasingly over the next few years, scenes of such tactics would evoke international protest and domestic qualms.

At the outset, however, popular support for the war rose in proportion to the fighting and larger draft calls. Louis Harris reported in mid-September that his polls showed "a dramatic shift" in favor of administration policy, with 67 percent approving of Johnson's handling of the war. Although 25 percent favored negotiations, the same percentage wanted to carry the ground war into the North. A solid majority expected extended fighting.[92] Three weeks later, Harris found that public support for the war continued to grow "sharply," while preference for negotiations and withdrawal fell to 11 percent. "If anything," he observed, "the most hotly debated issue among Americans was whether they should first carry the ground war North or destroy the Vietcong in the South."[93]

Although disheartened by the U.S. escalation, critics like Walter Lippmann kept urging the president to adopt a defensive strategy, while forming a South Vietnamese government that could negotiate a truce. A few of them grew so skeptical of White House promises that they became personally estranged from the president, most notably William Fulbright. A Rhodes scholar and former university president with a broad sense of history, Fulbright had established himself as a leading internationalist in the House in 1942 and in the Senate four years later. His internationalism was of the realist school, like Morgenthau's, and in the 1950s he became increasingly worried about the militaristic and ideological thrust of containment. Despite his mounting reservations to Vietnam policy, the Arkansas senator had gone along with Kennedy and Johnson, even shepherding the Tonkin Gulf resolution through the Senate in 1964. Johnson, who valued Fulbright's loyalty and his influence as chairman of the Senate Foreign Relations Committee, tried to persuade the senator that his views were taken seriously. By late July, however, Fulbright had become disillusioned with the president as a result of his committee's investigation of intervention in the Dominican Republic. In the context of fresh escalation in Vietnam, he "suddenly realized that Johnson had used and manipulated him."[94] The subsequent break between the two men would contribute significantly to the antiwar movement, although for the time being Fulbright merely cautioned restraint, hoping for a negotiated settlement and gradual withdrawal.

Meanwhile, antiwar discontent within the academic community stumbled. In mid-September, leading figures in the teach-in movement met at the University of Michigan, hoping to reinvigorate the program. Instead, they argued desultorily over details such as whether to function as consulting experts or to organize a new, broad-based protest movement. Did it matter, anyway, in view of the irrelevance of expert debate and informed discussion to the administration's determined escalation of war? There was no answer and no consensus on action, and the teach-in project lapsed. Its leaders had finally faced the possibility that, as historian Christopher Lasch wrote, "no amount of persuasion will change the central fact of American politics—the fact that there is no opposition party, no political opposition at all to the rhetorical but enormously effective demand that we stand up to the Communists, resist 'aggression,' avoid another 'Munich.' "[95]

Activists had been making that point for months. The country did not need a Vietnam teach-in so much as "an American teach-in," wrote Cornell University economist Douglas Dowd, for "the real problem is the source, which is to say the state of affairs in this country, of the Vietnamese war."[96] In a series of events that fall, the incipient antiwar movement tried to address the problem at home; but its efforts only dramatized the anomaly of the movement.

SANE had gone its own way when it refused to endorse the April SDS march on Washington, and SDS had declined to take the mantle which its march had won. The vacuum in leadership was underscored by the summer's Assembly of Unrepresented People, from which a loose alignment of radical activists had emerged in support of the International Days of Protest, scheduled for October. The demonstration became the nominal responsibility of the infant NCCEWVN, although the initiative actually was assumed by local antiwar groups, especially Berkeley's VDC and New York's Fifth Avenue Vietnam Peace Parade Committee. Somehow they pieced together the largest single citizen protest yet.

They succeeded insofar as organizational principles were subordinated to the single cause of checking the war. SANE, for example, reversed its spring position to the point that it encouraged local chapters to cooperate in demonstrations, although it expressed strong reservations about the NCCEWVN. Similarly, in New York a committee was formed of individuals who reflected a broad range of antiwar organizations but officially represented none of them—from the Communist party, Old Left, and militant pacifists of *Liberation* to the AFSC, WSP, and the liberals of SANE. In fact, the principal organizer in New York was Henry Abrams, whom Norman Cousins had fired from SANE in 1960. The Fifth Avenue Peace Parade Committee, as it came to be known, worked out of the CNVA-WRL offices at 5 Beekman Street, under the conciliating influence of A. J. Muste. It managed to slip past debates over immediate versus ultimate withdrawal with its slogan, "Stop the War in Vietnam NOW."

The International Days of Protest engaged nearly a hundred thousand people in eighty cities and several nations: eleven protesters were jailed in Madison, Wisconsin, after they tried to make a citizens' arrest of the commander of a nearby air force base; twenty-five demonstrators walked through a hostile crowd in Salt Lake City, Utah; seventy-five demonstrators carried American and UN flags and placards two abreast in Boulder, Colorado. At the Ann Arbor draft board, thirty-one students sat in while seven hundred people marched in their support. Across the country more than fourteen thousand protesters were incited by VDC militants in two days of chaotic attempts to occupy the Oakland Army Terminal before they were turned away at the city limits by four hundred police and sheriff's deputies.

In New York City three hundred dissidents gathered on 15 October for a "Speak-Out" at the armed forces induction center on Whitehall Street, and they cheered when twenty-two-year-old David Miller ceremoniously burned his draft card in the first open defiance of a stringent new federal law.[97] On the next day over twenty thousand people participated in the Fifth Avenue Peace Committee's march to the UN Plaza. Some sang. Others chanted. Most walked in silence. But the full range of dissidents, from Maoist students to Orthodox Jewish rabbis, voted with their bodies in support of ending intervention "NOW." Though divided about the meaning of the war, in the face of its unfolding madness, they shared a sense of purpose.

Radical pacifists like Muste, who was absorbed in plans for a new united front on the left, were exultant: in the absence of parliamentary opposition, the people were creating their own. Others were less sanguine, although no less committed. "We won't end the war," said one California student. "Bobby Kennedy, or someone like that, will have to end it. But we've got to do something."[98]

The marchers did at least provoke popular resentment: Fifth Avenue Peace Parade marchers in New York were attacked with fists, eggs, and red paint; in Austin, Texas, two hundred antiwar demonstrators were threatened by the Ku Klux Klan and attacked with water bags by Young Republicans; in Cleveland, four hundred antiwar demonstrators were challenged by an even larger number of counterdemonstrators who provoked street fights, burned an antiwar banner, and "made so much noise that the program had to be curtailed."[99] A Committee to Support American Fighting Men rallied fifteen hundred students in a prowar rally at Claremont College, and six members of the Hell's Angels motorcycle gang broke through police lines in Oakland, beating up some demonstrators at a street sit-in. When draft-card burner David Miller appeared on a radio talk show in Manchester, New Hampshire, he had to be escorted away by police in order to protect him from an angry mob.

Hostility reverberated through the press and politics of the nation. At best, thought *Life* magazine, the October protesters were "chronic show-offs" who failed to realize that "this remote and cruel war is a last stand for democracy or freedom or even that the destiny of the U.S. is at stake."[100] At worst, declared *Time* in the week following the marches, how these "Vietniks" behaved "seemed to bear out" a fresh Senate Internal Security Subcommittee report which concluded: "The control of the anti-Vietnam movement has clearly passed from the hands of the moderate elements who may have controlled it at one time, into the hands of Communists and extremist elements who are openly sympathetic to the Vietcong and openly hostile to the United States."[101] In the Senate the October demonstrations were described as "tantamount to insurrection" and the protesters as "auxiliaries of the Communist psychological warfare effort . . . engaged in international war in the United States."[102] "Every protest will cause the Communists to believe they can win if they hold on a little longer," said Senator Richard Russell (D-Ga.). Agreed liberal Senator William Proxmire (D-Wis.), "It is this wish—this gross misreading of the attitude of the American people—which more than anything else is keeping the war going, in spite of our immense power superiority and our solid military victories. It is this which is preventing peace."[103] Attorney General Nicholas Katzenbach announced on 17 October that the Justice Department would launch an immediate investigation of groups suspected of encouraging violation of the draft laws, starting with SDS.

Spontaneous support for Johnson's war spread across the country. The U.S. Junior Chamber of Commerce announced plans to counter the protests. The *Trenton Times* inaugurated a letter-writing campaign intended to pledge the nation's faith to GIs in Vietnam. New York City officials scheduled a Support America's Vietnam Effort day on 30 October, in which over 25,000 patriots marched behind 5 Medal of Honor winners past a reviewing stand lush with prominent politicians. American colleges and universities competed with one another in support of the president's war policy: nearly 16,000 Michigan State University students signed a petition supporting the president's position; 2,000 University of Michigan students and 175 Harvard Law School students telegraphed their support to the White House; students at the University of Chicago rejected a proposal to censure U.S. policy by a ratio of three-to-one. Any doubts of student loyalty were dispelled by a Gallup poll at the end of the month reporting that young people between the ages of twenty-one and thirty supported the war effort at higher rates than did their elders.[104]

Popular resentment only reinforced the belief of some antiwar activists that Vietnam marked the failure of American democracy, and it alienated them still further. The FOR's *Fellowship* magazine had warned in March that the Four Horsemen of the Apocalypse had been replaced by Apathy, Frustration, Sloganism, and Bestiality.[105] The motif of moral numbness, articulated in opposition to nuclear arms, had been transferred to the Vietnam war.

To Berkeley radicals Vietnam showed conclusively that the American people "have lost control of the government" and had become objects to be ignored or manipulated, utterly excluded from any "role in the decisions which affect their lives."[106] The extreme left increasingly tended to see itself as a saving remnant within a collapsing system, and it sought inspiration in some historical example of a tiny minority that acted correctly and courageously in the face of governmental contempt and popular hostility. Its leaders rejected the civil rights movement as a precedent on the grounds that, unlike the blacks, no major segment of the American population suffered directly from the society's complicity in evil. Instead, antiwar radicals became attracted to the analogue of Nazi Germany: the Eichmann motif. This development provided a striking study in counterpoint. While the administration referred to Vietnam in terms of the appeasement symbolized by Munich, antiwar radicals reaffirmed the Nuremberg doctrine of personal responsibility to resist evil. While the administration saw in Ho Chi Minh a new Hitler, radicals found in the government new Eichmanns. While the administration proclaimed a saving war against Communism in Asia, radicals warned against budding fascism at home.

The moral analogy yielded a "terrible predicament."[107] Living by what they called "a post-Nuremberg ethic," antiwar radicals increasingly saw themselves less as a domestic opposition than as an internal resistance. Asked one, "If the American people haven't awakened to the Vietnam horror by now, when will they? In other words, is there a point at which the horrors have become so obvious that those who have not recognized them by then never will; and efforts at education then should stop, and the aware minority should recognize itself as one and go on to determine how, with small numbers, it can begin to wreck the machine, not just as conscientious but ineffective protesters to it?"[108] That was not communist manipulation. It was the agony of rigorous moralism, and it offered a premonition of the 1968 Battle of Chicago.

"We are not all of a mind on this"

In the fall of 1965, radical moral commitment was expressed in opposition to the draft. Attention was drawn to the conscription issue in October, when Attorney General Katzenbach promised to investigate the antidraft movement. Michigan state Selective Service officials revoked the draft-exempt status of thirty-one students arrested in the draft board sit-in that month, and in December, Selective Service Director General Lewis B. Hershey threatened to use reclassification as a weapon against college dissidents. In the meantime, government draft calls went out to over thirty-six thousand men, the largest number since the spring of 1952, and the Central Committee for Conscientious Objectors reported that it had received the highest number of requests for draft-related information in its seventeen-year history.

The draft was a ready-made issue for radicals eager to stress the "way in which the war touches people personally and unjustly."[109] Hershey had designed the system as a way of managing human resources, but the selection process left gaping loopholes for the rich and college-educated and also rejected the very poor and unskilled. The result was a conscription "disproportionately comprised of men from the lower-middle/working classes."[110] To the early moral outrage of the war itself was added, therefore, the social inequity of fighting it. Several SDS leaders reiterated their support for local antidraft organizing. Its national secretary, Paul Booth, challenged the Johnson administration to allow young Americans "a free choice" between Vietnam and America by making "service to democracy" at home "grounds for exemption for the military draft."[111]

Seeing conscription as the immediate symbol of the war, a number of New York pacifists scheduled a major draft-card burning ceremony in

Manhattan's Foley Square for 28 October. This was not an attempt to "wreck the machine." It was to be a "major symbolic act of renunciation of the war in Vietnam and U.S. militarism generally." The project organizers rejected the support of nonpacifist antiwar radicals because of their concern that the demonstration be "clearly pacifist and not confused by the presence of various left wing elements."[112] The scheduled ceremony fizzled badly. Four young men had been prepared to burn their draft cards and stand in solemn witness with their supporters. Instead, they were lost in an unruly crowd of jostling reporters, photographers, hecklers, and police. Dorothy Day felt "an extraordinary tension" in the street, "the most miserable mob scene ever." The pacifists called off the action and rescheduled the draft-card burnings for 6 November.[113]

Norman Morrison burned himself first. A thirty-two-year-old father of three, Morrison was a Pennsylvania-born Presbyterian who had attended the College of Wooster before turning to Quakerism and a simple life of service in the Society of Friends and the civil rights movement. He became involved in various antiwar activities around his Baltimore home, experiencing the anguish of that "terrible predicament"—being unable to do anything to stop the carnage. On the morning of 2 November, he read an account by a French priest who, describing the bombing of his Vietnamese parishioners, cried out, "I have seen my faithful burned up in napalm." Morrison also read a newspaper appeal to write legislators in protest. He had done that. "What else can we do?" he asked. Late in the afternoon, cradling his eighteen-month-old daughter in his arms, he walked to the river entrance of the Pentagon. Hardly fifty yards from Defense Secretary McNamara's office, he doused his body in kerosene and struck a match. Instantly he was engulfed in flames. Passing Pentagon workers snatched up the child before she was injured, but they could do nothing for the father. Morrison was declared dead on arrival at Fort Meyer Hospital. To his wife of ten years he had written, "Know that I love thee but must act for the children of the priest's village."[114]

Four days later, the New York City draft-card burning ceremony proceeded on schedule and with better planning. Supported by fifteen hundred sympathizers, including A.J. Muste and Dorothy Day, five pacifists appeared on a platform in Union Square, properly attired in suits and ties. After observing a moment of silence in honor of Norman Morrison, each read an individual statement of conscience. Then together they extended their cards into a single flame. Before the cards could ignite, a young man with a fire extinguisher bolted from the crowd and doused the pacifists and their cards. One of the group later recalled that the incident seemed "rather amusing" and "a very creative act for a right-winger."[115] Finally the pacifists burned their soggy cards, as hundreds of angry New Yorkers chanted across police barricades: "Give Us Joy, Bomb Hanoi!" and "Burn Yourselves, Not Your Cards!"[116]

Their hatred overwhelmed Roger LaPorte. A twenty-two-year-old Catholic Worker from upstate New York who had once studied for the Trappist monastic life, LaPorte could not comprehend the depth of anger directed at his pacifist friends. They later surmised that he sought to protect them by absorbing the surrounding violence. Whatever his motives, they were so deeply felt that early in the morning of 9 November he sat in the UN's Hammarskjöld Plaza, emptied a two-gallon gasoline container, and immolated himself. Burned over 95 percent of his body, he was rushed to Bellevue Hospital, where he told aides, "I'm a Catholic Worker. I'm against war, all wars. I did this as a religious action." He died thirty-three hours later, after making what the attending priest called "the most devout act of contrition I have ever heard."[117] Rumors spread that there was a "suicide club" of pacifists who planned one self-immolation per week until the war ended, and pacifist leaders released statements that, while respecting the integrity of Morrison's and LaPorte's deaths, discouraged further human sacrifices and emphasized rather the need to live for peace.[118] Attention returned to conscientious objection to the draft, which would become a major field of service for pacifists, campus counselors, and liberal clergy.

That autumn, conscription was still grist for left-wing contentiousness. Some SDS activists argued that the antidraft program distracted from efforts against the war itself. A local organizer complained that the campaign had no real basis anyway; it was "a product of mass fiction, generated by the press and the administration."[119] Extremists in the May Second Movement rejected alternative service as a form of collaboration with the government, and they ambitiously vowed to establish a nationwide network of "Independent Anti-Draft Unions."[120] Trotskyists in the SWP hoped that dissent could be sown within even the armed forces. NCCEWVN activists complained that the draft issue was palpable, "like an albatross" that weighted down antiwar organizing efforts and enabled the administration "to convince everybody that our main objective is to be a bunch of professional draft dodgers."[121]

"We are not all of a mind on this," Joan Levenson told Jerry Rubin. "People seem to have forgotten that there are other issues in the peace question and that the adult community is not interested, not to say alienated" from the radicals' draft quarrel.[122] Indeed, rhetoric and symbolic acts reinforced the picture drawn by the Senate Internal Security Subcommittee—that control of the antiwar movement had passed from moderate elements to communists and extremists. The committee was wrong on two counts: no one was in control of the antiwar movement, and its liberal wing was active, if less noticed than the radicals.

Some liberals sought to put the Vietnam War in a broader Asian context. Thus, representatives of ADA met at the United Nations with Ambassador Arthur Goldberg, appealing for a unilateral U.S. bombing halt, negotiations among all warring parties, and a UN-sponsored all-Asian peace conference. That had been ADA policy since February, when it had encouraged letters and wires to the White House, warning that America was "falling into a V.C. trap" by letting guerrillas determine its Asia policy.[123] In fact, ADA mirrored national liberalism: it was seriously divided on both domestic and foreign policy issues. Except for the bombing, which virtually all factions opposed, the liberal community was split between those who accepted the continuation of liberal resistance to communism and those who sought a fresh approach to foreign policy, between most who sought to advise the administration and some who would challenge it. Negotiating the issue in an all-Asian context hedged the liberal division. Representative Donald Edwards (D-Calif.), elected ADA national chairman in April, was strongly opposed to the war, but the organization was not willing to yield its advisory role. Even Johnson's sharp escalation in July did not elicit criticism; as yet ADA was hobbled by the belief that it "needed Johnson much more than he needed the ADA."[124]

Under these circumstances, liberal initiative fell to SANE, which had been organizing its own antiwar demonstration since late August. Sanford Gottlieb persuaded a group of prominent liberals to call a march on Washington for 27 November in order to promote a cease-fire, a unilateral bombing halt, and negotiations among all belligerents. SANE leaders stressed "responsible criticism" that would enlist "the broadest possible participation of all who favor a negotiated settlement."[125] Hoping to attract sizable student support, they tried to keep radical activists involved but at arm's length. They pointedly omitted radical critics like Dellinger and Lynd from the list of sponsors, and they ignored the radical demand for the immediate withdrawal of U.S. troops. On the other hand, SANE discouraged but did not prohibit signs calling for immediate withdrawal. Radical leaders felt put off but not estranged. Most of them believed that SANE was making a serious effort to reach leftist groups, and they were alert to reports that Martin Luther King, Jr., was about to lead civil rights activists into open antiwar protest through SANE and its related liberal organizations, potentially a step toward a "new radical alignment for peace." In any case, radicals could not repudiate the liberal demonstration without contradicting their own commitment to inclusiveness. Grudgingly, a cross section of radical antiwar activists in the NCCEWVN agreed in mid-September to support the SANE march on the grounds that no one element "really represents 'the movement.'"[126]

Liberals regarded the march as a critical thrust toward the political center. "If this effort, supported by the 'moderates' of the peace movement ... is not successful," warned FCNL director Edward F. Snyder, "leadership may well pass to extremist groups on the left, and there may be a hardening of attitudes toward negotiating a solution."[127] Sandy Gottlieb, who was coordinating the march, saw it the same way. He rejected any plans for civil disobedience, explicitly discouraged communist participation in the march, and urged marchers to carry signs and flags approved by the sponsors. In "this super-heated atmosphere," he explained to one radical antiwar leader, "we just want to give as little ammunition as possible to the opposition."[128] Veering between radical leftists and proadministration liberals, the SANE group inevitably antagonized elements on both sides. Radical pacifists attacked the march's emphasis on negotiations, while unhappy liberals (notably historian and ADA leader Arthur M. Schlesinger, Jr.) saw little value in any kind of public protest, and prominent democratic socialists like Irving Howe and Michael Harrington criticized the policy of nonexclusionism.[129] Nonetheless, the antiwar liberals managed to steer a middle course that got the march under way.

March organizers spent ninety minutes discussing Vietnam with presidential aide Chester Cooper on the afternoon of 27 November, as some thirty thousand people circled the White House, then proceeded onto the grounds of the Washington Monument for speeches and songs. It was the largest antiwar demonstration yet convened in the nation's capital, and certainly the most respectable. Aside from a few hecklers and a small contingent chanting "Hey, hey, L.B.J., how many kids did you kill today?" (the first time that was heard[130]), the crowd was concerned and polite. Dr. Spock, Coretta Scott King, and others detailed the domestic and international costs of the war. SDS president Carl Oglesby attacked the "corporate liberalism" which, he said, had brought on a counterrevolutionary war and could be overcome only through a broad, multiissue movement for real democracy. Did he sound anti-American? "Don't blame me for that! Blame those who mouthed my liberal values and broke my American heart."[131] The young radical got an ovation, but the elder statesman Norman Thomas most succinctly captured the tone of the day: "I'd rather see America save her soul than her face."[132]

Parallel actions took place around the country. Usually low-key and often unrecorded, they got little national attention; but they were perhaps an indication of early and unconnected discontent with the war among average citizens. Gottlieb concluded modestly that "an acceptable image" had been restored to antiwar dissent.[133] The *Christian Century*'s assessment was sober: the march had been "a good deed in a bad time" and "a candle shining in a deepening darkness."[134] The image was apt in view of popular attitudes reported by Gallup that month. Hardly 1 percent of those polled said that they felt moved to demonstrate over Vietnam, and most of those said they would like to demonstrate in support of U.S. policies.[135]

Still, organizing the demonstration had helped antiwar liberals to define a platform: an immediate end to U.S. bombing of North Vietnam, a military cease-fire, and the opening of negotiations among all warring parties (including the Vietcong). Now the "crucial problem," they agreed, was to give dissent a political thrust. Spock pressed Senator Robert F. Kennedy (D-N.Y.) to assume leadership of the antiwar cause, but he received little encouragement from the New York senator or other politicians with whom he met. Indeed, liberals found it increasingly difficult to get a hearing in Washington. Many of them felt that their criticism had "reached the point of diminishing returns" within the government, and that public protests were "defeating their own purpose [and] . . . hardening the opposition."[136] Given these conditions and the cooperation on the march with New Left leaders, there emerged a liberal version of the new alignment for peace—the National Conference for a New Politics (NCNP).

"New politics" meant harnessing the ambitions of young radicals for immediate reform to the liberal confidence in electoral action—street politics and electoral work. The idea was explored at a meeting on 28 November at Washington's Shoreham Hotel called by Paul Booth and H. Stuart Hughes under the auspices of the Center for the Study of Democratic Institutions. The conferees were New Left radicals and sympathetic liberals drawn from SANE, SDS, SNCC, and similar organizations. They settled on little except an agreement to establish a National Conference for the continued discussion of fusing "'movement" and 'liberal' styles and goals . . . into a new sort of elective politics," but that effort in itself was significant in view of the polarization within the fragile antiwar protest.[137]

As liberals sought to consolidate their efforts, radicals made their most serious attempt to launch "a conscious left peace movement" when they held the first convention of the three-month-old NCCEWVN.[138] The meeting was scheduled for Washington, 25–29 November, so that activists could support SANE's antiwar march. "The first Party Congress of the 'New Left'" (as it was sarcastically dubbed) drew over fifteen hundred participants from about a hundred local and national antiwar organizations, including several southern black civil rights workers. A dozen workshops and a few plenary sessions were designed to refine the structure of the NCCEWVN and develop a new program of common action.[139] It didn't work, and the conference quickly deteriorated into a marathon ideological argument of the old style, punctuated by charges of manipulation and elitism.

The haze of debates and deals demoralized everyone. "Factions, maneuvers, caucuses, deals, parliamentary procedure and parliamentary disruption flew about like bats in a dark cave," remembered one participant, and were sped along by "divisiveness, power-seeking, demagoguery, and egotism."[140] Boggled by ideological code words and sectarian infighting, most participants fell back in anger or apathy. The convention succeeded only in setting dates for further antiwar street demonstrations: 12 February 1966 was designated to emphasize the links between the antiwar and civil rights movements (although black participants had dismissed the convention as irrelevant); and 25 and 26 March were identified as the Second International Days of Protest. In neither case could the delegates specify a national program. Jerry Rubin cheerfully exclaimed, "We survived," but few other participants could laugh off the radical failure to influence national debate on war policy or even to make peace among themselves.[141] "This is what we are fighting for in Vietnam," one participant said bitterly, "—our way of life, so that 1,000 radicals can play political games over a five day weekend and not get into worse trouble."[142]

There was more to it than political gaming. Behind the scenes was a bitter factional contest for leadership of numerous local antiwar committees that had been organized in the wake of the April demonstration. SDS still was not leading on the war issue. Into the vacuum plunged the constituents of the NCCEWVN: notably the Communist party and Du Bois clubs, which exercised a dominant influence at the coalition's Madison headquarters, and the Trotskyists in the Socialist Workers party and its Young Socialist Alliance, tentatively allied with Jerry Rubin's VDC in Berkeley. Frank Emspak and the national NCCEWVN sought a broad, multi-issue organization concerned with civil rights, poverty, and university reform, and they had the support of the CP, whose strategy called for electoral activity. The YSA wanted a single-issue coalition for immediate withdrawal from Vietnam. Each wing worked for weeks in advance to obtain control of the convention. In Washington the Trotskyists were defeated on substantive issues and in several parliamentary maneuvers, and they convened a separate caucus to constitute a national organization of local committees favoring immediate withdrawal. SDS played virtually no role in the convention, and Rubin's VDC waffled. The NCCEWVN leadership prevailed at the expense of failing to define a coherent radical position on the war and of confusing independent delegates.[143]

Resentment surfaced in a meeting of people from the South. "All that's happening is that people are being manipulated," said one. There was general agreement and some discussion of organizing to present their own concerns, but that only elicited more frustration: "It makes me mad to think we have to organize these folks to listen to us." This southern delegation was composed mostly of black, working-class people who had come to Washington in the hope of organizing around the connection of peace and freedom which they felt in a gut sense. Their reaction reflected the pain they had experienced in a racist society and the paternalism foisted on them not only by that society but also by the cadres of northern whites who came south in solidarity with them. Their frustration also had something to do with the fact that blacks were being beaten in Selma while marines were landing in Danang. Here it was again. "I'm mad at this whole convention," one of them exploded. "I feel I'm being used."

Then the discussion sharpened. The convention politicos were talking incessantly about organizing against the war, but they hadn't identified enough with the people to get beyond abstractions. "In the South we've organized around pain," someone explained. "With the middle class you're dealing with people who deny they're in the midst of pain. . . . What you've got to do if you're ever going to get at them as humans is . . . to get them to affirm their pain."[144] What more could be said? In the midst of the November debacle, a few people who knew what they cared about had nailed a problem that would haunt the antiwar movement for a decade: how to relate authentically to middle- and working-class America. As the people of the nation felt their own pain, identified it with the war, and concluded that it wasn't worthwhile, they would abandon the effort. Until enough Americans experienced the war painfully, there could be no common reference point for an antiwar movement. It would continue to fragment on the periphery of the commonwealth.

The NCCEWVN fiasco also reflected a countercultural trend that had its sources in the earlier beat and hip movements and was fortified with the kind of celebration of life and love which Paul Goodman had proposed in *Growing up Absurd* (1960). By mid-decade there was a perceptible loosening of mores, especially among young people. Reflecting a pervasive mood and fed by attendant fads, a vaguely definable youth subculture began to emerge. Its leitmotif was experimentation, its symbols "grass" and rock. Musically it ranged from Joan Baez through Bob Dylan to the Grateful Dead, from "Where Have All the Flowers Gone?" to "The Eve of Destruction." It encompassed bohemian individualism and communal values, escapism and a search for authenticity, self-centeredness and a rejection of those cultural patterns in which were embalmed ancient hypocrisies such as racism, conformism, and status computed by wealth. In some measure it touched young people everywhere, even if it transformed relatively few lives. The youth culture found a ready response among radical pacifists' orientation to questions of life-style, and it began to pervade the antiwar movement in 1965.

Its many dimensions and contradictions were difficult to reconcile but real enough to elicit apprehension, especially when they were etched by the media as an emerging hippie counterculture (the word "hippie" was invented late in the year) that extolled hallucinogenic drugs, acid-rock music, and sexual liberation. A national phenomenon, the counterculture had become attached to radical politics in the Bay Area by the fall, and it expanded into a so-called romantic left that found a political tendency in the cult of youth.[145] In the next few years, innumerable radical leftists with a real concern about Vietnam identified with various forms of counterculture; but their connection came to be epitomized for the nation by

outrageous appearance, bizarre forms of protest, and revolutionary apoc-
alypticism that alienated them from the very America they proposed to
change. The association also drained and disrupted the radical wing of
the antiwar movement itself, even as early as the NCCEWVN conference.

In Oakland on 20 November, VDC sponsored a march that drew over
eight thousand people into raucous street actions, clashes with police,
and vandalism of automobiles and buildings that together achieved a new
level of unreality. Prior to the demonstration it considered a scenario
drafted by poet Allen Ginsberg, which would have flooded the streets
with grandmothers, babies, flowers, and rock music sound tracks. In case
of "heavy anxiety," Ginsberg cautioned, the marchers would sit down
and begin mass calisthenics or a predetermined mantra. He suggested
either "The Lord's Prayer," "Three Blind Mice" or "The Star-Spangled
Banner."[146] As a tactic to defuse conflict, Ginsberg's plot was clever. As
theater it satirized conflict itself. Captivated by the spreading infatuation
with the absurd, some SDS activists cheered the emergence of a "hippy-
politico blend" which they predicted would "add a whole new dimension
to the radicalism of this latest stage of American revolutionary movements."[147] Even opposition to the war had become infused with the motif
of madness.

For days prior to the march, VDC leaders debated over demonstration
tactics and self-defense (one proposal called for the use of sharpened
flagpoles). They admitted that their commitment to nonviolence was
merely tactical: "Our opposition is not necessarily opposed to all war,
but rather to a military subjugation of the newly emerging nations."[148]
Longtime sympathizers were appalled. Veteran pacifists Roy Kepler and
Ira Sandperl denounced the Committee for pushing "hatred and, if need
be, overt violence," while critical radicals repudiated VDC's infatuation
with mass street actions.[149] Calling for greater community organizing
efforts, one of them announced that he was "tired of being in a Marching-
And-Talking-To-Yourself-At-Rallies Society." If "carrying signs in a clump
is the only way to feel we're a movement," he declared, "we're in
trouble."[150]

Late in December, SDS held its annual meeting in Champaign-Urbana,
Illinois. Although distanced from political extremism as the Illinois prai-
rie is separated from the California Bay, SDS reflected the new strain of
"emotional anarchism" as it tried to cope with a surge of growth and to
define a coherent program.[151] It failed on both counts. The organization
had been swamped by numerical success. It had succumbed to what
Todd Gitlin later called its "internal frailties"—an undefined ideology of
participatory democracy which worked only when it reflected close personal relationships, and an experimental program which was appropriate
only when its leadership and membership approximated each other.[152]
The many new members were neither grounded in a close study of social

theory—not even SDS theory—nor experienced in social action. The national office had come apart in pursuit of decision by consensus. The organization's multi-issue orientation was strained by its extreme diversity. The SDS convention broke into special-interest factions, including a separatist women's workshop, while its members failed to develop a new anti-Vietnam strategy. "No one knows what to do really" about the war, said one participant, and people were "losing their grip thinking about it."[153]

No one knew what to do. Paul Potter worried that the SDS ethic of taking personal responsibility for social change would be swamped by an ideological identification with revolution abroad. Some activists concluded that the antiwar movement was too small, politically vulnerable, and single-issue oriented. It never would work. In fact, the war would end, even if the protesters did "nothing at all," in two or three years, when the sheer weight of increasing U.S. casualties would "turn public opinion against it."[154] As it was, it seemed as though there was "no chance of stopping the war," no matter what strategy was pursued. "I feel like a veteran of the resistance," wrote Frances Prevas, "and the resistance has lost."[155] Perversely, some dissidents concluded, as one put it, that antiwar effort was "*an essential ingredient of the war effort*: our protest activities, in the context of contemporary American life, convert more people into the war consensus than into the antiwar movement." Agreed another, "The government will not suppress us if it is smart . . . it will contain us and use us."[156]

There was some truth to both statements. Government leaders professed their respect for freedom of speech, asked critics to direct their complaints to Hanoi, and tacitly encouraged the proadministration sentiment. Cities and civic organizations sponsored marches and ceremonies in support of the government, and collected hundreds of tons of gifts and millions of messages for GIs in Vietnam. College students and faculties were especially forthcoming: thousands of them signed petitions and held vigils in support of the administration, and collected blood for use in Vietnam. Likewise, public support for administration policy rose to a new high, with 71 percent of those polled in December agreeing on the need to hold the line and keep fighting.[157]

Support for the war effort was accompanied by growing resentment of dissidents, as though popular frustration with the war had found an accountable lightning rod and explanation. Harris reported in mid-December that popular hostility toward antiwar critics was so deep that one-third of Americans believed that citizens did not have the right to demonstrate against the war, and that only one-fourth were willing to concede the underlying sincerity of anti-Vietnam demonstrators. The great majority of people, especially the less educated and less privileged, believed instead that antiwar demonstrators were either motivated by personal exhibitionism, communist manipulation, or a desire to avoid the draft.[158] Radical rhetoric and the free association of the counterculture, both highlighted in the media, no doubt contributed to this impression. Vietnam *really was a war* now, and the majority of Americans resented people who seemed to take the business of war or the national values lightly.

There were some direct and punitive attacks upon the dissidents and many symbolic rejections of them. Thus the Des Moines, Iowa, school board banned from classes a handful of students who wore black armbands to school out of mourning for U.S. war dead, the Reverend Billy Graham criticized antiwar dissenters from a Houston pulpit, and a Texas congressman announced plans for legislation that would make antiwar demonstrations an act of treason. The "manic phase" was now in movement, warned the *Nation.* "Let the hysteria expand, and it will be surprising if they do not regard all opposition as traitorous."[159]

Insofar as polls were indicative, a growing number of Americans expected military success. In late November, when asked how they expected the war to end, 30 percent of those questioned said that they expected a Korean-like stalemate and 29 percent anticipated a U.S. victory. The number who said that they expected the war to end in a communist victory or American withdrawal was statistically so small that it did not even register in the polling figures.[160] Those anticipations projected the assumed error and irrelevance of antiwar protest into the future. Small wonder that many of its participants questioned the future of their own movement.

During the formative period from February to August 1965, the antiwar movement acquired its salient characteristics: its layers of often disconnected dissent in various strata of society; the tenuous relationship to its liberal and radical wings, their deep-seated differences, and the immediate issues that provoked their division; its association in popular opinion with an iconoclastic subculture; a hostile public itself divided over foreign policy; a national administration seeking to retain a consensus of the center—all this, and intense frustration in the face of a war that would violate cherished values and national visions. All this by the summer, when the country became openly committed to war.

In the following months, protest grew and became more organized. It also was increasingly fragmented, not only between its liberals and radicals but among them. By the end of the year protest was pervaded by a sense of frustration, not to say a foreboding of futility, which exaggerated all its differences. It is impossible to recapture that feeling in retrospect because a later generation knows what the tiny minority of dissenters could hardly hope in December 1965—that their efforts would expand with an escalating war and would in some measure affect its course.

From Protest to Confrontation and Political Action

By 1967 opposition had turned to resistance, especially to the draft. Volunteers worked in the New York office of the Resistance, surrounded by posters emblematic of the time [photo copyright © Diana Davies].

Draft resistance began as a symbolic act, like the burning of draft cards by
Tom Cornell, Marc Paul Edelman, Roy Lisker, and David McReynolds at Union
Square, New York City on 6 November 1965 [above, courtesy of Neil Delmar
Haworth], but it broadened to include the mass turning in of draft cards with
the support of adults, seen here in New York City in October 1967 as part of a
Stop the Draft Week. A similar action in Oakland, California, turned into
violence [below, copyright © John Goodwin].

Resistance to the draft and the war was dramatized by seizing and either
pouring blood on draft files or burning them, as in this action of the
Reverends Philip and Daniel Berrigan at Baltimore, Maryland, in the fall of
1968 [FOR, *Fellowship* (March 1969), 5].

In the face of an apparently unresponsive government, war resistance became confrontational, notably in the "Confronting the Warmakers" demonstration at the Pentagon, Washington, D.C., 21 October 1967 [FOR, Minoru Aoki].

The antiwar movement was never solely confrontational. Most dissident citizens, like those seen here in a SANE-sponsored 1966 demonstration for voters' action in Washington, D.C., challenged the war through actions designed to influence politics [SCPC, Robert Parent].

After the Tet offensive early in 1968, the presidential campaign of Eugene McCarthy [above, copyright © John Goodwin] mushroomed, drawing Robert Kennedy into the race and leading Lyndon Johnson to withdraw from it, which encouraged activists such as the University of Pennsylvania students seen below, after Johnson's announcement on 31 March [copyright © the *Guardian,* photo by Martin Smith]. The campaign itself became confrontational at the Democratic convention the following summer.

Although chastened, activists returned to the campaign against the war in the early months of the Nixon administration, their determination mirrored in the face of Jim Peck and in the poster he held at a spring demonstration in 1969 [copyright © John Goodwin].

Activists concentrated nationwide attention on the war in the Moratorium of 15 October 1969, and moved on to massive demonstrations the following month. On 13 November Pete Seeger sang to 2,000 people at Duffy Square in New York City. "Someone released a dozen doves from a cage," he recalls, "and one alighted on my head, so I lifted my cap, and the bird stayed on it" [photo by Ezio Peterson courtesy of Pete Seeger].

That day, 13 November, over 45,000 individuals began a solemn procession from Arlington National Cemetery to the Capitol, each bearing a placard with the name of an American killed or a Vietnamese village destroyed [SCPC, Lana Reeves]. Two days later about half a million protesting citizens marched up Pennsylvania Avenue and filled the Mall in Washington, D.C. [SCPC, courtesy of Theodore B. Hetzel].

The Nixon administration's policy of withdrawing U.S. troops and Vietnamizing the war defused protest for a time, but spontaneous protests erupted in the wake of the invasion of Cambodia and the shooting of students at Kent State University in the spring of 1970. Demonstrations in front of Philadelphia's Independence Hall protested "a new and bigger war," on 8 May 1970 [SCPC, courtesy of Theodore B. Hetzel].

With the war being "Vietnamized" and the issues still hard to discuss, the conflict in America continued to be largely over national images, here dramatized by an inverted U.S. flag—the universal symbol of distress—waved by demonstrators atop a Washington, D.C., war memorial in April 1971. [SCPC, courtesy of Theodore B. Hetzel].

The antiwar religious community was important in sustaining protest, as in this CALC march in Washington, D.C., February 1970, with Al Krebbs of the *National Catholic Reporter,* Richard Fernandez, Rabbi Abraham Heschel, and Robert McAfee Brown [above, SCPC]. On 19 April 1971 antiwar Vietnam veterans marched past the Lincoln Monument to inaugurate a series of demonstrations in the capital [below, WRL].

In the so-called MayDay actions of 1971, activists tried to use nonviolence to tie up traffic in the capital [above, photo copyright © John Goodwin], resulting in the often indiscriminate arrest of some 7,000 citizens who were detained in the Washington Coliseum and RFK Stadium [WRL, Lana Reeves].

Protest normalized in politics

War protest was normalized in the 1972 presidential campaign of George McGovern [above, SCPC], but it had already been carried into the 1970 campaign which resulted in the election of congressional dissidents such as Robert Drinan and Bella Abzug. Drinan is seen here (opposite, top) with a delegation of antiwar lobbyists [FOR, *Fellowship* (winter 1973), 17]. Abzug is shown on a 1972 fact-finding mission to Paris, where she presented a copy of her forthcoming book, *Bella!* to Mme. Nguyen Thi Binh of the Provisional Revolutionary Government [SCPC].

Following the peace accord of January 1973, and amidst the spreading Watergate scandal, activists lobbied against continued U.S. military aid to the Thieu regime of South Vietnam, whose repression they dramatized with "tiger cages" that simulated the pens used to hold political prisoners, such as this one set up at the Capitol [FOR].

The campaign to end all U.S. intervention in South Vietnam climaxed with the Assembly to Save the Peace Agreement, 25–27 January, 1975, in Washington. Not so much a demonstration as a major lobbying effort, the Assembly was a last gathering which brought together many of the threads and individuals in the antiwar movement, including folksinger Joan Baez [copyright © the *Guardian*]. Three months later, the war was over.

Part Three

The Contest for the Center, 1966–1970

Six

Raising the Stakes

"The antiwar movement is . . . something
that has been happening to America"

Toward the end of 1965, White House advisors urged President Johnson to order a pause in the bombing of North Vietnam. Robert McNamara and others argued that this would put pressure on the Soviets to facilitate negotiation and might even split the North Vietnamese and the Vietcong. Most important, they contended, a pause would demonstrate the president's sincere desire for peace and solidify popular support for the war. Sensing that public endorsement was broad but soft, opinion analysts assured Johnson that most Americans approved administration policy but warned: "If we are to have public support for our policies—if we are to blunt mounting frustration—it is absolutely essential that the public be constantly assured that we are doing all we can to get an honorable negotiated settlement. A majority does not now believe it."[1] Beginning on Christmas Eve, the United States curtailed its air war while its emissaries carried word abroad that the administration wanted a settlement.

Diplomatic activity but clarified the impasse behind the fighting. Washington would halt its bombing only if North Vietnam reduced its military commitment, and it ruled out negotiations which implied the inclusion of communists in a South Vietnamese coalition government. Hanoi, for its part, would begin peace talks only if the United States first halted the bombing and agreed to settle the future of Vietnam in accordance with the NLF political program.

With differences thus frozen, bombing was resumed at the end of January. The war intensified throughout Vietnam, raising the stakes for each side in the conflict there—and at home. In the first seven months of the year, over 50,000 people died in battle, including 2,691 Americans. Warplanes penetrated North Vietnam to the Chinese frontier. Mao Zedong warned that the United States was risking new war with China, and he unleashed a massive cultural revolution which included anti-American xenophobia.

Americans exposed their own phobias. The majority of newspapers backed the president's war policy (the *New York Times* was a notable exception), and many criticized him for not waging the war aggressively enough. In his first open break with the administration, Senate minority leader Everett Dirksen (R-Ill.) said that the United States needed a clear military victory before it could enter any peace talks. Public opinion polls intimated an aggressive spirit born of popular frustration with the war and apprehension of prolonged conflict. The country was shifting into "a 'get it over with' mood," reported Louis Harris: "A sense of 'travail without end' is straining both the patience and normal optimism of the American people."[2]

In the first half of 1966 opposition to the war began to show a breadth and vitality that far surpassed its limited organizational base. With no agreed upon leaders or central directorate, citizen activists created a social movement as they improvised and sustained attacks on the war from church pulpits or Senate seats, on campus greens or at business offices, in the streets or behind editorial desks. They had in common only the conviction that escalation of the war was somehow threatening basic American interests and values. A few years later Jerome H. Skolnick would conclude: "the antiwar movement is not a fixed group of people; it is something that has been happening to America."[3] People made it happen spontaneously, although organized groups gave it visibility.

A few members of the policy-shaping elite began to express second thoughts about the war. During the president's so-called peace offensive, fifteen senators and seventy-six representatives formally asked for an extension of the bombing pause in the hope of stimulating negotiations. In the Senate, Aiken and Mansfield were very critical of Vietnam policy in a report for the White House following a world tour, George McGovern (D-S. Dak.) became more outspoken in his criticism, and Eugene McCarthy (D-Minn.) made his first formal attack on the war. A month after the resumption of bombing, McGeorge Bundy left the administration. Both George Kennan and James Gavin, a retired army general and former ambassador to France, warned that the U.S. was dangerously overextended and urged Washington to stop bombing the North. General Matthew Ridgeway agreed. With endorsements from people like Kennan and Gavin, the idea of establishing defensive enclaves offered a rallying point for antiwar critics within the establishment and a means of avoiding both immediate withdrawal and danger of war with China through further escalation.

The Chinese had been on the minds of the congressional authors of the joint letter to Johnson, and they were a serious concern to McNamara.

"I believe that when we resume bombing . . . ," he told the president in January, "we'll be in air battles with Hanoi aircraft—next year we'll battle Chinese aircraft."[5] Working from a different perspective, William Sloane Coffin had also concluded the previous summer that China was the key to Vietnam. With the support of prominent Democrats, the Yale University chaplain put together the Americans for a Reappraisal of East Asian Policy to advocate U.S. recognition of the People's Republic of China, admission of communist China to the UN, and a negotiated settlement in Vietnam in an all-Asian context. Political activist Allard Lowenstein was hired to organize campus chapters across the country. The group developed a program on 20 October that combined local teach-ins through a national telephone hookup featuring, among others, Norman Cousins and China expert John King Fairbank of Harvard. It also placed a full-page ad with twenty-five hundred signatures in the *New York Times*. The Beijing route met resistance, however, both from those who opposed communist China and from those who saw it as peripheral to the U.S. war in Vietnam.

The danger of a confrontation with the Chinese surfaced again with the resumption of bombing in 1966. It worried Senator Fulbright, who found a national forum for his deepening opposition to the president's policy. The senator had been studying the issue assiduously under the tutelage of Bernard Fall. Fully prepared and very anxious, Fulbright endorsed open hearings by the Senate Foreign Relations Committee early in February on the administration's $415 million supplement aid request for South Vietnam. For six days the committee hearings were televised live to a nationwide audience by two major networks. Johnson hastily arranged a dramatic meeting with South Vietnamese president Nguyen Cao Ky in Honolulu, probably to divert attention from the hearings.[6] In Washington, meanwhile, Secretary of State Rusk and retired general Maxwell Taylor, former ambassador to Vietnam, argued that the war was necessary to halt communist aggression and establish U.S. credibility. Kennan and Gavin urged a "defensive strategy" in keeping with the nation's limited interests in Southeast Asia and its larger global commitments.[7] Various antiwar critics insisted that "the Vietnam debate is in reality the great China debate."[8] The problem was not so much the war in Vietnam, Lippmann wrote, as in getting Washington off its "collision course with China."[9]

Although the Fulbright hearings were not quite the "Great Debate on U.S. foreign policy" which *Life* magazine called them, they did open the ambiguities, contradictions, and uncertainties of administration policy to deliberative review and lent legitimacy to dissent.[10] Indeed, on 19 February, Senator Robert Kennedy proposed negotiations directly with the Vietcong, although he then backed off to advocate only a Saigon regime which would include "discontented elements" that would not portend "domination or internal conquest." Kennedy was looking for a "middle

ground" between escalation and withdrawal.[11] Similarly, Arthur M. Schlesinger, Jr., and John Kenneth Galbraith urged the president to withdraw
to a defensive enclave from which the communists might be convinced
to negotiate, knowing that "whatever our error in getting in, we cannot
easily be shoved out."[12]

Critics such as these failed to address the essential conflict in negotiating positions that separated Washington and Hanoi. They challenged
the administration's strategy for getting into negotiations but minimized
the substantive issues involved. The war was fought basically over the
political status of Vietnam south of the Seventeenth Parallel, and the
differences between the United States and North Vietnam were fundamental. In some measure, concern about China and global U.S. interests
diverted analysis from the obdurate problem of Vietnam itself. Insofar as
critics attempted to offer policy alternatives, their positions no less than
the government's involved ambiguity, contradiction, and uncertainty. Like
the president, his liberal critics in 1966 tended to see the Vietnam issue
as one lending itself to an American-designed solution.

Liberal dissent grew especially among the clergy early in the year,
building on the fear of further escalation and on a record of interfaith
cooperation achieved in the civil rights struggle. William Sloane Coffin
was pivotal in making the connection. Having served as a liaison officer
to the Russian army during World War II and as a Russian affairs specialist
for the CIA during the Korean War, he had brought to Yale in 1958 a
Niebuhrian combination of worldly realism and prophetic Christianity.
Early in his tenure as chaplain he became involved in international social
service and the Peace Corps, and he was arrested three times for challenging segregation in the south. Since Coffin was in close touch with
the network of clergy which had supported the civil rights struggle, he
was positioned for leadership in that constituency as he trained his moral
indignation on the war in Vietnam during 1965.

In October of that year, A. J. Muste complained to John C. Bennett that
the National Council of Churches and denominational agencies seemed
to be "simply marking time."[13] By the end of the month, an ad hoc group
called Clergy Concerned About Vietnam had been organized in New York
under the leadership of the Reverend Richard Neuhaus, Rabbi Abraham
Heschel, and Father Daniel Berrigan, and the following month it sponsored a study forum on Vietnam for five thousand area clergymen. By
the end of the year, the World Order Study Conference of the National
Council of Churches had passed resolutions comparable to SANE's, and
the FOR, the Catholic Peace Fellowship, and the Union of American He-
brew Congregations had taken issue with U.S. policy. Moreover, when
Berrigan was asked in November to sever his ties to antiwar groups and
then was sent to South America in a kind of vocational exile, reaction
was strong and ecumenical.

Leading clergy began to build on their fall initiative. At the urging of Richard Neuhaus, pastor of St. John the Evangelist Lutheran Church in New York, several prominent leaders met in John Bennett's apartment on 11 January and formed a National Emergency Committee of Clergy Concerned About Vietnam.[14] By the end of the month, the Committee had a prestigious board, predominantly Protestant but with significant Jewish leadership from Rabbi Heschel and a Catholic presence in Daniel Berrigan, who was recalled to the United States in the spring.[15] Coffin was named executive secretary, and he volunteered a week of organizing around the country, while a cadre of seminarians working out of an office at the National Council of Churches made phone contacts with clergy, many of them formerly active in civil rights. Within a few weeks the Committee built a strong national network of local committees which spun off in their own antiwar actions.

The Committee emphasized political realism, with an occasional moral critique of the war. Recommending persuasion and traditional political action, it hoped to accumulate "that massiveness and momentum which enabled the clergy to help turn the tide in the civil rights struggle."[16] Its leaders explicitly opposed the idea of immediate withdrawal, denied any pacifist proclivities, and promised that they were organizing only on an emergency basis. Rabbi Heschel explained, "We came into being specifically to provide a religious comment on the war that would not be allied to the traditional peace movement and that did not stem from a body . . . committed to its own continuation beyond the cessation of the present crisis."[17] By April, though, interest from lay people and the further escalation of the emergency led the committee to change its name to Clergy and Laymen Concerned About Viet Nam—a National Emergency Committee (CALC) and to prepare for a long struggle.[18] The antiwar movement had enlisted a constituency with direct access to the American center.

There were numerous expressions of religious concern. The religiously pacifist FOR activated its contacts abroad to form the International Committee of Conscience, which called for an end to the violence in Vietnam. At the White House, theology students from twenty-five seminaries conducted a two-week vigil for peace negotiations. The United Church of Christ and the American Jewish Congress urged unconditional negotiations among all parties, including the Vietcong. Moreover, Christian realists associated with *Christianity and Crisis* explicitly broke with the administration. Calling for an end to the violence, John C. Bennett commended a political settlement that would not "depend upon the defeat of the other side."[19] Reinhold Niebuhr agreed, warning that continued escalation would result in "physically ruining an unhappy nation in the process of 'saving' it."[20]

Dissent began to draw in other constituencies as well. A number of distinguished lawyers and law faculty prepared an extensive memorandum making the case that the war was illegal. Several Chicago civic and professional leaders urged de-escalation on Johnson and the Illinois congressional delegation. In the first break in otherwise solid support for the war shown by the AFL-CIO, union leaders in the Amalgamated Clothing Workers of America attacked administration policy; shortly afterwards, a dissident labor faction called Trade Unionists for Peace rallied in New York City for a negotiated peace. Washington hosted a march by "Poverty Workers for Peace," including social workers and ex-VISTA volunteers, and Boston was the site of a fund-raising evening of chamber music promoted as "Fight McNamara with Mozart." Poet Robert Bly helped to organize American Writers and Artists Against the War, which brought together prominent writers and poets for "read-ins."

Some women in the movement began to see themselves as a distinct constituency, and feminism became associated with the antiwar movement of the 1960s (much as the women's rights movement had converged with opposition to World War I). Going beyond the inclusive demonstrations of WSP, women at a Berkeley rally in February asked men not to join them, arguing that "parallels can be drawn between treatment of Negroes and treatment of women in our society as a whole." They then protested at the Oakland induction center four days after two army nurses perished in a helicopter crash in Vietnam, the first American women to die there.[21]

War veterans began to participate. A hundred of them, flanked by three hundred supporters, marched to the White House on 5 February, where some returned their service medals and discharge papers in protest, and a week later, an Ad Hoc Committee of Patriots for Peace in Vietnam sponsored two days of demonstrations in Gainesville, Florida. Other small veterans' groups included Veterans for Peace, which included World War II men, and Veterans and Reservists to End the War in Vietnam. The February issue of *Ramparts* magazine featured charges by former Green Beret officer Donald Duncan that U.S. Special Forces routinely employed torture tactics and conducted forays into Laos. Far from defending democracy, Duncan said, the U.S. was imposing an anticommunist regime on a people whose aspirations were actually represented by the Vietcong. The story was sensational, but the ten-year veteran and holder of numerous medals was not; he carried a sober and disenchanting assessment to the college circuit.

Dissent, although thin, seemed to be broadening, and already in the spring of 1966 there was interest in harnessing it to electoral politics. This took the liberal wing of the movement beyond its frequent lobbying in the capital. SANE organized a National Voters Peace Pledge Campaign designed to gather grassroots pledge cards from individuals who promised to vote in the forthcoming congressional elections for candidates who favored the war's de-escalation and negotiations. The fledgling National Conference for a New Politics hoped for a coalition of New Left radicals and "post–Cold War" liberals in a "peace-race-poverty-oriented set of electoral campaigns" in the fall.[22] Although operating on different levels, SANE and the NCNP were responding to a common fact: antiwar dissidents had no serious national political leadership or party mechanisms. "We have to depend on local action," acknowledged Norman Thomas. There was no national political support for dissent, and no one was interested "in anything as apocalyptic as a 1968 challenge to Lyndon Johnson."[23]

Thomas lived to see the judgment day he did not expect; even as he wrote there was already surfacing the political crisis that would ultimately fell Johnson. It was identified by Leon Shull, ADA national director, who reasoned that "effective political action" was the "key" to the dilemma of being faced with an increasingly unpopular war that could negate liberal domestic policies. Candidates must somehow question the foreign policy of the administration and defend its programs at home.[24] The war was undermining the Great Society, not only in terms of funding and priority but because it was breeding disillusionment with the political system itself. The ADA repeatedly criticized escalation and urged negotiations, and its leadership—Galbraith and Schlesinger, for example—increasingly became opposed to the war. For the time being, however, the organization could not challenge the White House directly, precisely because it had grounded liberalism in the Democratic party, of which the president was the leader. It chose to attack the war but not the man responsible for it, and this led it perforce to local politics.

A particularly interesting race was that of California journalist Robert Sheer for the Democratic nomination from the seventh congressional district. Sheer was far to the left of ADA. He put the war at the forefront of an unconventional campaign, and he attracted the support of Jerry Rubin and some of his friends, whose VDC was in a "chaotic mess."[25] Their hope was that the Sheer campaign would revitalize the VDC. Their rhetoric was that it might build a radical third party addressing war, racism, poverty, and "the *quality* of life."[26] Rubin called this "nonviolent revolution" rather than politics, but he was bitterly contested by other Berkeley radicals who dreamed of massive civil disobedience and disruption. Barely avoiding an open split, the VDC broke into two factions and slipped into irreversible decline. Although Sheer lost the primary, he ran so strongly that his opponent modified his previously prowar position.

In the mainstream, meanwhile, SANE continued its electoral program. On 14 May it held a Peace Pledge Convention in Washington to publicize the fact that it had collected seventy-three thousand cards on which people pledged to vote only for peace candidates in the November congressional elections. The next day the organization rallied about twelve thousand people on the Mall, reaffirming its commitment to change U.S. policy through electoral action. These were thoroughly respectable-looking street dissidents—what Benjamin Spock called "the adult, moderately liberal, pro-humanity segment" of the American population.[27] They were the kind of people that SANE, the AFSC, ADA, and CALC counted on to support some hundred designated peace candidates who entered summer primaries in order to offer electoral alternatives to administration policy on the war. The political activists ranged in background from a Republican Wall Street investment broker to a Democratic Columbia University graduate student. The only thing they had in common was a desire to end the war without further escalation—that, and a general failure to make inroads in the primaries.

In mid-July, nonetheless, Shull and ADA staff member Curtis Gans met with leaders from some unions, the Council for a Livable World, SANE, and the Inter-University Committee to discuss collaboration against the war. Hoping for support from the AFSC, FCNL, and other liberal groups with antiwar positions, they agreed to support a dozen and a half designated candidates, for whom Gans would raise funds and prepare background materials. New York attorney Allard Lowenstein was present as a representative of the Inter-University Committee. That was appropriate because he had presided over and built up the National Student Association (NSA) in the early 1950s and had been responsive to student concerns as a dean at Stanford. A liberal activist who had thrown his enormous energy into causes ranging from antiapartheid efforts in South Africa to the 1964 voting campaign in Mississippi, Lowenstein commanded a remarkable network of contacts. Following the July meeting he participated in a debate on antiwar alternatives with Stanford student body president David Harris at the NSA congress at Urbana. There he encountered overwhelming student concern with the war and the radicals' disdain for the political system, which "propelled him into action."[28] Together with Gans, a founding member of SDS, Lowenstein began to mobilize his contacts among ADA, civil rights, and student leaders in an effort to marshal the system against the war.

Antiwar radicals derided those political efforts, even though they were themselves fractured and confused. Their confusion was perhaps inherent in the multiple strains of radicalism, and their fragmentation illustrated the distinctly local and grassroots base of antiwar protest in 1966.

There were direct actions in the winter. The largest of them took place on 23 February around New York's Waldorf-Astoria Hotel, where a liberal group called Freedom House was holding an award ceremony for President Johnson in honor of his efforts for peace and justice. Amid over four thousand demonstrators in the streets outside, A. J. Muste presided over an alternative award ceremony that paid homage to Julian Bond and various war resisters. Inside the hotel, pacifist Jim Peck, in black tie and tuxedo, joined a dinner table at the rear of the banquet hall. As Johnson began to speak, Peck stood on his chair and shouted, "Mr. President, Peace in Vietnam!" He was knocked to the floor and hustled out. Johnson barely noticed the commotion, but the event inaugurated a pattern in which over the following eighteen months antiwar demonstrators confronted the president in public appearances.[29]

The Waldorf-Astoria demonstration was organized by the Fifth Avenue Parade Committee, which originally had been formed only to coordinate New York activities in the first International Days of Protest. The Committee was revived in order to sponsor a large rally early in January which publicized the conclusions drawn by Tom Hayden, Staughton Lynd, and Herbert Aptheker from their trip to Hanoi. It organized a demonstration in Times Square when the bombing of North Vietnam was resumed. The Parade Committee was a coordinating body of individuals who reflected but did not officially represent some eighty organizations with conflicting ideologies and approaches. A. J. Muste's pragmatic conciliation was at its heart. His presence and the Committee's informal character made it possible to resolve tensions among its constituents in the interest of coordinating antiwar actions. Focusing on discrete events rather than broad programs was "the key to unity in the antiwar movement for the duration of the war," recalled Fred Halstead, a Trotskyist on the Committee's staff.[30] It was true on both local and national levels; but in the latter, where national organizations were involved, the political stakes were higher and cooperation was more difficult.

With many factions and little discipline, NCCEWVN leaders feuded bitterly during the winter over personalities, politics, and sectarian slogans. The dividing slogan was immediate withdrawal, of course, but that was divisive mainly because it was invested with the identity of some member groups (such as the YSA) but threatened others. The organization assumed a collective left which did not exist. It survived as a clearinghouse of ideas and information, thanks to a devoted local staff, while its members debated "whether we build a peace movement that may become radical or whether we are building a radical movement that is for peace."[31] They did not address the prior question of whether or not there ever was any prospect of a radical peace movement. Their ethos assumed a community of interests among disaffected citizens, but the reality was that discontent was a centrifugal force, in which the war was only one factor. Political ideology, racism, and sexism were others, and they too fractured the antiwar center.

Accordingly, the Second International Days of Protest, although nominally coordinated by the NCCEWVN, was evidence of local initiative rather than central organization. Thanks to the effectiveness of the New York Fifth Avenue Parade Committee, the East Coast demonstration on

26 March involved perhaps fifty thousand people, twice as many as the one in October. Local groups in the Bay Area bypassed the immobile VDC to stage a much smaller event in San Francisco. A broad coalition in Chicago drew some five thousand people to its demonstration, a sevenfold increase over the fall. Overall, the protest involved well over a hundred thousand demonstrators in eighty to a hundred cities in the United States and in a third of the world's nations.[32] In Philadelphia, newly formed groups of military veterans assumed a major role in antiwar organizing for the first time; in Cincinnati, Ohio, and Wilmington, Delaware, clergy conducted prayer ceremonies for the dead. Activists dealt with ever-present hostile counterdemonstrators in various ways: organizers in Rochester, New York, invited a representative of some prowar hecklers to the platform, successfully easing tensions; New York City leaders used unarmed marshals to help keep prowar demonstrators away from the antiwar marchers; and local SDS militants in Boston fought back when attacked at the Arlington Street Church. The call for protest was national, but the response was overwhelmingly local.

The response did not satisfy some radicals who were tantalized by visions of aggressive militancy. Despite his brief flirtation with third-party politics, Jerry Rubin wrote in April of a "liberation movement" that would overturn the existing order in America and redeem the oppressed of the world.[33] Some radical pacifists in CNVA concluded that the Cold War peace movement was not valid: "The War in Vietnam has changed everything."[34] It revealed the thrust of American imperialism, they thought, and it had to be challenged by a combination of personal resistance and collective action, with less regard for the proprieties of nonviolence. Articulate anti-imperialists such as Lynd and Dellinger had little faith in the political power of traditional demonstrations, lobbying, or pacifist witness. Theirs would be a "new nonviolence," fighting nonviolent "wars of liberation" against the status quo and for its victims as aggressively "as the Fidelistas in Cuba, the N.L.F. in South Vietnam, and S.N.C.C. in the South."[35] The practical implication was not particularly clear, although it tended toward civil disobedience, nor was nonviolence effectively squared with the Fidelistas or the NLF. Radicalism—even radical pacifism—was no more free from ambiguity, contradiction, and uncertainty than was antiwar or prowar liberalism.

The president himself seemed to be perplexed about the opposition. Privately he condemned antiwar activists for providing "great encouragement" to the enemy by projecting images of domestic division and weakness. He urged critics "to do their dissenting in private" in the conviction that public criticism "works against all our efforts in the war." The dissenters were "nervous Nellies," he said, people who "turn on their leaders and on their country and on our own fighting men."[36] Furthermore, Johnson felt personally affronted when old friends like Fulbright turned against him on the war issue, and he refused to consider concessions to Hanoi at least partly out of fear that it would "look like I'm reacting to the Fulbrights."[37] Presidential aides Jack Valenti and John Roche despised domestic dissidents, and they played upon Johnson's suspicion that, while superficially fragmented, the antiwar opposition actually functioned with cunning coordination. Fulbright, "the doves, the Lynd-liners, and the *Times* [were] all of a piece," Valenti warned, moving like volcanic lava in their demands for one concession after another until the whole game would be lost.[38] Advisors Harry McPherson and George Reedy, on the other hand, urged the president to recognize the distinctions that divided the antiwar movement, and to deal with each segment accordingly. Johnson declined to attack the antiwar dissidents frontally early in the year. Maintaining the appearance of strength and control, he sought to command the political center.

His attention was claimed by the war front, where U.S. effort intensified while the South Vietnamese government tottered on the verge of collapse. Discontented students, angry Buddhists, and even dissident military units challenged the military government of Nguyen Cao Ky, and at least five Buddhist women burned themselves to death in protest against the regime and its American patron. Ky's troops attacked hostile crowds in the streets of Saigon, and loyal marines flew to Danang and Hué to overcome regional opposition, while a ten-man junta alternated between naked force and promises of civilian rule.

The war exacted its toll in America. U.S. casualties steadily increased, until the rate of American war dead not only exceeded that of 1965 but also passed beyond the number of South Vietnamese soldiers killed in action. Reports spread of an increased incidence of GI drug abuse and of worsening tensions between the Vietnamese and Americans. By June, respondents in one poll were evenly divided when asked if they thought that the South Vietnamese even wanted U.S. forces in their country.[39]

Public support for the war was strong but volatile in the spring. Prowar sentiment was demonstrated by groups as disparate as inmates of the Atlanta federal penitentiary and Young Americans for Freedom. Sergeant Barry Sadler's "Ballad of the Green Berets" topped the popular record charts. Polls suggested that there was increased support for the intensified bombing of North Vietnam and for a blockade of Haiphong harbor. Still, popular approval of the president's handling of the war fell below 50 percent, although that may have reflected hawkish as well as dovish sentiments. More clearly reflective of rising antiwar sentiment was the increasing support for immediate withdrawal (although it was still a small minority) and the fact that a record one-third of those polled said that intervention had been a mistake.[40] Wrote a British journalist, American opinions on the war were changing "[more] radically than I would have believed possible." A writer for the *New Republic* agreed: "Make no doubt about it, the public is tired and sick of Vietnam, and we feel the thing is approaching some kind of a showdown."[41] As that comment suggested, Americans were already showing evidence of war-weariness: the effort no longer looked as easy as it had the year before.

Protest was no more acceptable than before, however, and it could be explained away as "an organized communist effort."[42] Some prowar enthusiasts took things into their own hands. Students burned an effigy of Senator Gruening at Ohio State University; Texas A & M campus police arrested students distributing antiwar leaflets and drove them eighty miles away with instructions not to return; the Rye, New York, school system fired a teacher because of his antiwar views. And there was violence. On 6 March the San Francisco headquarters of the Du Bois Clubs was destroyed by at least ten sticks of dynamite. Three weeks later, a Greenwood, Mississippi, church was burned to the ground shortly after it had hosted an antiwar prayer service. In early April the VDC headquarters in Berkeley was demolished in a bomb explosion that injured four students. Four weeks after that, the SDS Newark offices were ransacked, and office files and equipment destroyed.

Antiwar demonstrators were occasionally assaulted. After a mob of 150 high school students attacked four antiwar demonstrators trying to burn their draft cards at a Boston federal district courthouse, a city police captain commented, "Anyone foolish enough to commit such an unpatriotic gesture in South Boston can only expect what these people got."[43] Jim Peck reported that his attempt to speak at a SANE meeting on Long Island was aborted by counterdemonstrators who screamed with a hatred that reminded him of earlier freedom rides in the Deep South. Pleaded Frank Emspak of NCCEWVN, "One must try to realize that outside of New York City most communities are extremely hostile to the existence of any anti-war movement in their midst. Often it is almost impossible for anti-war groups to survive with a relatively mild position."[44] There were death threats and killings. On 4 March, a Catholic Worker was beaten to death outside a Rochester tavern by two youths angered by his antiwar views. Six weeks later, a civil rights and antiwar activist was shot ten times in the back in Richmond, Virginia, a slaying that police termed unmotivated. Soon thereafter, right-wing militants invaded the Detroit offices of the SWP with shotguns, killing Leo Bernard and wounding two other men.

It was "open season on dissenters," declared the *Christian Century*. Arthur Schlesinger, Jr., feared that a virulent new form of McCarthyism was moving across the country, and Senator Fulbright warned that Johnson's policy was fomenting "war hysteria."[45] Fulbright himself was denounced by Senator Goldwater for giving "aid and comfort" to the enemy. Staunchly, the Senate Foreign Relations Committee chairman used a prestigious lecture series at the Johns Hopkins School of Advanced International Studies to condemn "the arrogance of power" which, he felt, was overextending the nation abroad and consuming it within.[46] Fulbright's lectures raised the stakes of policy from prudence to fundamental values.

Indeed, the issue of morality was sharpened during the spring and early summer as napalm, painfully depicted in TV images of burning Vietnamese civilians, became a special symbol of the war. An important antinapalm campaign in California not only gave direction and momentum to the issue, but also suggested the confusion of class lines on the war. Dissidents led by clergy in Redwood City tried to halt the production of napalm at the United Technologies Center plant. Insisting that napalm production was a moral question, the Redwood City Committee Against Napalm solicited enough signatures to put the issue on a local referendum. When that was rejected by the city, they vainly pursued it through the courts and undertook direct action at the plant site. The small city was in turmoil for months. The campaign attracted national attention. Local leaders claimed that it had enlisted concerned, intelligent people and had overcome "the fear people had in this community of being identified with peace." They found also, however, that their crusade had split Redwood City along unfamiliar class lines. Upper-income people, whether Republican or Democrat, mostly backed the campaign; but "lower income people seemed to be indoctrinated and wouldn't listen."[47]

Antinapalm agitators were nonplussed—understandably so, for they were among the first to encounter what Louis Harris called a "new kind of class politics" in which affluent and more educated people endorsed "liberal" positions on Vietnam and racial matters while the white poor and less-educated resented racial change and dissent. There was no longer any reliable correlation between affluence and conservatism, Harris wrote, or between the lower middle class and liberalism. Partisan loyalties and established orthodoxies were becoming unstuck, and new social divisions were erupting that went "well beyond politics" and portended "a new era" in American life.[48] Something was happening to America. The phenomenon reoccurred in subsequent antiwar experience, although it was not effectively integrated in movement strategy.

The antinapalm campaign extended beyond the Redwood City referendum. On 3 May over three thousand people gathered in the California town for a rally that featured Senator Wayne Morse and SDS leader Tom Hayden. Three weeks later, a Citizens' Campaign Against Napalm led a demonstration outside the Rockefeller Plaza headquarters of the Dow Chemical Corporation, a major supplier of napalm ingredients to the government. When Dow officials rejected demands to abandon napalm production, the Citizens' Campaign called for a consumer boycott of Saran Wrap, a plastic household product made by Dow. Dave McReynolds told Dow officials that their arguments in defense of work on napalm "might have been written by a German businessman during World War II defending his actions in supplying the chemicals required by the death camps run by the Nazi government."[49]

McReynolds' remark both conveyed the moralistic cutting edge of anti-war dissent and reflected the motif of moral numbness. Radicals increasingly resorted to analogies between the Johnson administration and the Third Reich and, short of that, the metaphor of the Holocaust appeared more frequently. Washington's war policy showed "no sign of swerving from a final solution to the Vietnam problem," said one religious journal. It could only "be classified as genocidal," said another.[50] Antiwar liberals felt uncomfortable in accusing the United States of genocide, but they also found it increasingly difficult to contain their own moral outrage. Former State Department official and Asian expert Owen Lattimore wrote in anguish, "You reach a point where decent-minded people, because they are decent-minded, have to resist, or sabotage, or evade your policy."[51] That was the very scandal of Nazism, added Daniel Berrigan: there was no protest "and people acted as though life could possibly be normal" when enormous crimes were being done in their name.[52] For Berrigan this was no idle image: it led him surely toward civil disobedience as a moral America became ever harder for him to find.

"No way to relate"

The stakes in the war continued to rise. On 30 June, American planes bombed oil and industrial plants near Hanoi and Haiphong, and the North Vietnamese responded by threatening to put captured U.S. pilots on trial for war crimes. China opened its territory as a rear base for Hanoi and, with the Soviet Union, shunted large quantities of war equipment southward. American forces engaged Vietcong and North Vietnamese troops throughout South Vietnam. With a lavish use of firepower, the United States was inflicting inestimable destruction on both ally and enemy—hard to assess in part because of the difficulty of distinguishing friend from foe.

"I cannot recall," Senator Fulbright wrote privately, "when I have felt so depressed about our foreign relations."[53] John Bennett was finding it increasingly "difficult to be an American," and Lippmann fulminated that the president's actions signified a "claim to arbitrary power" that was at odds with "the sovereign principles of the American commonwealth."[54] Although public opinion rallied behind the president, the first concern of the people seemed to George Gallup to be "the desire to 'bring the boys home' as soon as possible."[55]

"Support Our Boys—Bring Them Home" placards appeared in spring demonstrations. If that seemed irresponsible to liberals concerned about the terms of policy change, it was exactly the point of the movement's left wing, where the Worker Student Alliance (WSA) and the Young Socialist Alliance were working closely with pacifists around A. J. Muste. Their singleness of purpose was publicized through the *Bring the Troops Home Now Newsletter* (Cambridge). Muste was convinced that only the stark desire to quit the war would elicit popular dissent. In April he and five other pacifists made a trip to Saigon in order to show their solidarity with Buddhist and other opponents of the warring regime.[56] Although they made contact with Thich Nhat Hanh and other Third Force leaders, their trip was cut short when they were summarily deported. The experience only redoubled Muste's resolve to organize demonstrations for August in order to obviate the usual summer lull in activism. Since the NCCEWVN resisted the idea, it was bypassed, and a call was issued from the Fifth Avenue Parade Committee and the *Bring the Troops Home Now Newsletter.* By June, though, the summer demonstrations were jeopardized by the very ebb in antiwar activism they were designed to counteract.

At that point the Parade Committee was contacted by three soldiers fresh from basic training at Fort Hood, Texas, who had made up their minds to refuse embarkation orders for Vietnam. The Committee came alive. It activated the national network of organizations, arranging for publicity and demonstrations which prevented the military from quietly burying the case of "The Fort Hood Three." This was the first episode in what came to be a practice of identifying civil disobedients according to place and number. It was a way of singling out the event and implying that it was one of a series of heroic if anonymous actions which anyone could do.[57] The case was a breakthrough for antiwar groups, especially the Trotskyist SWP, which were convinced that dissent could penetrate the army and ethnic groups (one of the men was black, another Mexican). It rejuvenated plans for the August demonstrations. Moreover, the incident demonstrated the leadership of the strong Fifth Avenue Parade Committee in the absence of a cohesive national coalition.

In an attempt to generate collective initiative, faculty who had been involved in teach-ins in the Cleveland area sponsored a consultation late in July for a cross section of movement groups.[58] The meeting was pervaded by a feeling of "pessimism and futility."[59] Discussion rambled for hours. It revealed three familiar factors that would continue to divide the movement: all-left inclusiveness, with its potential for disruptive action; the acknowledged weakness of radicals on the local level and their consequent desire to develop leadership through the visibility of national demonstrations (already in 1966 this orientation conflicted with liberal efforts to organize locally and through political channels); and a multi-issue emphasis in contrast to a single focus on the war. Muste urged a united mobilization in the fall, but the group could agree only to schedule another meeting at the end of the summer. The most they could hope for prior to the election was concerted actions, each being representative of a "particular locality."[60] No one advanced "any positive alternatives," reported Joan Levenson "except to fall into their own bags again, and just propose what their own group was doing."[61]

The next Cleveland consultation, 10–11 September, was larger but not much more decisive. Sociologist Sidney Peck of Western Reserve University emerged as the driving force in both meetings. In the second he was instrumental in getting any resolution at all, and that was merely to form an ad hoc committee which would conduct "an experiment in united timing" during 5–8 November under the innocuous theme "Sick of the War in Vietnam."[62] The committee worked out of the Fifth Avenue Parade Committee office. Its call for action straddled divisive issues: neither negotiations nor immediate withdrawal was mentioned, Vietnam was bracketed with human rights and economic justice, and the choice of emphasis, form of action, and policy on nonexclusionism were left to local prerogative.

At Cleveland, Robert Greenblatt, a young mathematics teacher from Cornell University, had wanted to believe that the time was ripe for more. Whereas in 1965 antiwar activists had naïvely assumed that "if only the American people were informed, something would change," he told the meeting, radicals now realized that policy change required an alteration of the decision-making process. What was needed was a massive mobilization of "all the groups and all the people in this country that have come to the recognition that there are things basically wrong, and that they must do something to change it."[63] During and after the consultation Greenblatt encountered the reality of old divisions and suspicions. The proceedings were indecisive. They were ignored by SNCC and other black militants, while SDS concluded that demonstrations were at "a dead end" and gave priority instead to local organizing in its national antidraft program.[64] Liberals worried about a political backlash from further street actions, and preferred to emphasize "routine, nitty-gritty precinct work . . . in the political party structure."[65]

The Cleveland meetings illustrated the fact that no one could organize and manage the full range of the antiwar dissent, partly for ideological reasons but mostly because of the very diffuseness of the opposition. This was an overwhelmingly local movement, built on the spontaneous initiatives of unconnected individuals and small groups. It was "a 'grass roots' development if I have ever seen one," observed AFSC peace education secretary Stewart Meacham. "There just isn't any way a centralized control group . . . could maintain the widespread public protest against the Vietnam war which has developed."[66] That defined the main operational dilemma for the antiwar movement. The local and decentralized nature of the dissent charged it with irrepressibility and variability, and yet these same attributes contradicted the hope for national organization and concentrated effort. The movement could not be controlled, but neither could it direct. Instead, it expanded and contracted, advancing and retreating in reaction to a war which itself could not be controlled.

In a real sense, the growing edge of the antiwar movement in the summer of 1966 consisted of diverse actions only scantily reported, if recorded at all: a Fourth of July rally at Independence Hall of five hundred pacifists lauding draft resisters and tax refusers as "contemporary American revolutionaries"; a walk from Valley Forge to Washington by twoscore Veterans and Reservists Against the War; a two-day fast in New York by the Reverend John Neuhaus and other CALC leaders; the boarding of the USS *Maddox* in San Francisco Bay by antiwar women; large Hiroshima anniversary marches in New York, Los Angeles, and San Francisco; a two-day demonstration at the Dow Corporation plant at Midland, Michigan; a solemn vigil outside a California mortuary where the bodies of GIs killed in Vietnam were prepared for shipment home; and questions raised in meeting halls and churches throughout the country.

Despite its prevalence, antiwar street activism seemed to be on the wane to *Time,* which commented that the movement, "which only recently was capable of producing a cacophony of complaint," realized that it was "not making much of an impression on anybody" and had begun "to lose heart."[67] *Time* did not recognize the local basis or the evolving rhythm of the movement, which would regularly experience a summer lull with the dispersal of college students. But in part, the magazine accurately sensed antiwar frustration. The movement was suffering from major internal complications, one of which involved its relationship to a fresh emphasis on black power.

The civil rights movement suffered sharp losses in financial and public support early in 1966, and the Johnson administration's civil rights program was stalled in Congress. With black impatience mounting, outspoken activists in SNCC and CORE talked about achieving racial justice through black pride and power. Their ethnic rhetoric and hints of mass action provoked a serious quarrel among the country's major black leaders. When the fiery Stokely Carmichael of SNCC called on the organization to exclude whites from leadership positions, Roy Wilkins of the National Association for the Advancement of Colored People (NAACP) attacked black power as "black racism" and Martin Luther King, Jr., sought to mobilize his supporters in resistance to it. "I am fighting the battle of my life," he told his friend Walter Reuther.[68]

The argument over black power became more volatile in the context of a rising spiral of racial violence. Across the land young urban blacks clashed with police and national guardsmen in the hottest summer yet of rioting, looting, and street violence, with the worst of it taking place on Chicago's West Side and Cleveland's Hough ghetto. Whites helped to intensify the crisis atmosphere. Black leader James Meredith was gunned down in Mississippi, where also King and other civil rights workers were attacked by a mob of some three hundred people. Blacks were shot from passing cars in Benton Harbor, Dayton, and Atlanta. Outside of Milwaukee, 500 national guardsmen were called out to protect 150 civil rights demonstrators from an angry mob of 2,000. Escalating along with the violence in Vietnam, the racial fighting and the militant emphasis on black power fractured the antiwar movement still further.

The spreading black nationalist sentiment had strained relations between black and white activists early in the year. On 6 January the Atlanta offices of SNCC released a statement denouncing the U.S. role in Vietnam and declaring its support for men refusing conscription. Issued three days after the brutal murder of Navy veteran and SNCC activist Samuel Younge, the SNCC statement declared that the killing was "no different than the murder of peasants in Vietnam," and condemned Washington's claim that it was fighting for freedom in Asia as "hypocritical" when it refused "to end the rule of terror and oppression within its own borders."[69] Bitter and uncompromising, the SNCC statement provoked a storm of patriotic indignation which, in turn, only hardened resentment in SNCC. "Be assured," one of its leaders wrote to a well-intentioned critic, ". . . that statement is but a first in a series in which we shall frighten and anger you."[70]

There was something of a parallel between the slogans "black power" and "bring the troops home now," but there was also a difference. Both evoked the pain of people without recourse and roused them to action. Neither addressed the complexities of achieving redress within the social and political order. "Black power" separatism was more than parallel to antiwar radicalism, however: it precluded cooperation with whites on the grounds that the war was distinctly a problem for black Americans. Ethnic independence bothered consensus-oriented liberals and those radicals who sought to align blacks in a multi-issue movement. It was accepted by A. J. Muste, who, with his usual equanimity, averred that "matters relating to the crisis in the civil rights movement ought to be kept out" of antiwar activities.[71]

For their part, radical black protest leaders felt estranged from the country's white leadership. In July, James Farmer and the national board of CORE called for America's immediate withdrawal from Vietnam, and SNCC urged American blacks "to organize for power" and evade military service in Vietnam (a position on which SDS concurred). The draft, Stokely Carmichael declared, was nothing more than "white people sending black people to make war on yellow people in order to defend the land they stole from red people."[72] Such views led twelve SNCC blacks to demonstrate at an army induction center in Atlanta against "the annihilation of Black men in the illegal racist war in Vietnam." They were arrested, and one was charged with insurrection, a capital offense in

Georgia.[73] For black power militants, estrangement extended to the antiwar leadership. "We're not inside the peace movement," SNCC leader Ivanhoe Donaldson declared in August. "It's basically all-white. There's no way to relate to that!"[74]

No doubt this seemed like an intramural debate to most Americans, for whom black power and war opposition both challenged national institutions and values. The prevailing mood was hostility to protest, and sometimes it was expressed in action. Officials at the Ohio State Fair in Columbus barred antiwar critics from setting up a booth on the fairgrounds. Workers in a Clyde, California, ordnance facility organized themselves in armed patrols in order to clear their town of antiwar demonstrators. An organizer in the Southwest reported that dissidents routinely experienced "threats, ostracism, and economic sanctions."[75] In Vermont twenty citizens became the target of eggs and obscenities, and their attempts to speak were drowned out by car horns, motorcycle engines, and cries of "Red! Red! Red!" It was just an exercise in everyday democracy, one participant said wryly: "ordinary men and women in the cradle of the Town Meeting."[76]

In mid-August the House Un-American Activities Committee was convened in California for hearings on a bill intended to punish Americans convicted of aiding any "hostile" foreign government or impeding the movement of military personnel and material. After taking testimony from friendly witnesses, the committee called up militants from the Progressive Labor Party and the Medical Aid Committee for Vietnam. Instead of invoking Fifth Amendment protections against self-incrimination, as had been the usual practice, the witnesses turned the hearings into a platform from which they affirmed their Marxist convictions and attacked U.S. foreign policy and HUAC. Their sympathizers in the audience heckled the committee members and disrupted the hearings. After four days and fifty arrests, congressional leaders persuaded the committee chairman to halt the charade.[77]

The affair was instructive: in HUAC a few militant activists had found a dramatic stage; but they had played into the role for which the committee had cast them. Bitterly, Dave McReynolds complained that the government had "very cleverly made US the issue in the Vietnam war rather than debating Vietnam itself."[78] The hearings reinforced the public image of protest against national values and institutions and obscured the whole point of serious opposition to the war. Opinion polls showed little enthusiasm for dissidents, and less for public protests. Even sympathetic citizens confessed their discomfort with the ongoing street protests. One New Yorker, for instance, recalled that she had decided to participate for the first time in an antiwar march, the 6 August demonstration, and had wafted down Fifth Avenue with other massed protesters "like the saved going off to Judgement Day." Before long, however, she was acutely embarrassed by the marchers' chants, the speakers' diatribes, and the extremists' pleasure in shocking onlookers with "Fuck War" placards and obscene rhymes. Silently, she found a bus and headed home, disturbed by the war and disgusted with demonstrations.[79] There was no way for her to relate to them.

"We Won't Go!"

People truly concerned to halt the war felt still more isolated during the fall. American troop commitments, ground engagements, casualties, and air attacks all escalated with an intensity that resulted in a total of 375,000 U.S. troops in Vietnam, and 5,008 American dead and 30,093 wounded for the year. Bernard Fall concluded that, unlike the limited war of Korea, the U.S. buildup was "at the present moment open-ended."[80] In contrast, Secretary McNamara predicted that the war would be over within a year, and the administration exuded confidence. Already in August, President Johnson had claimed that communist victory was impossible. Two months later he conferred with President Ky in Manila, announcing that the United States was prepared to quit South Vietnam within six months of a North Vietnamese withdrawal. The president then paid a surprise visit to U.S. forces stationed at Camranh Bay and promised that the nation would not betray them or their South Vietnamese allies. General Westmoreland sent assurances that the allied forces were winning the war, while President Ky predicted that the Hanoi government would fall within months and advocated war against China.

Within the American policy-shaping elite there were doubts. Edwin Reischauer, a former ambassador to Japan, came out in favor of de-escalation; and *New York Times* correspondent Neil Sheehan expressed his disillusionment in a widely reviewed essay, "Not a Dove, But No Longer a Hawk."[81] Prominent liberals connected to Senator Robert Kennedy cast about for alternatives to Johnson's policy. Schlesinger criticized escalation, while former aide Richard Goodwin proposed to form a committee around the slogan "No Wider War" in order to help the president adopt "the course of wise restraint." Goodwin promised that the committee would not advocate U.S. withdrawal, or "even a lessening of the war in the South."[82] It would simply oppose any larger war. Having urged a bombing halt and negotiations all year, the ADA national board voted unanimously to support Goodwin's project. The senator himself maintained a respectful distance, expressing his wish for moderation in the conduct of the war while criticizing antiwar dissidents for their impatience. A group of enthusiasts in New York opened a national office for a Kennedy-Fulbright ticket in 1968, but other antiwar activists ridiculed the well-modulated criticisms of the Kennedy liberals. Schlesinger's straddle made him look like a new creature, sneered I. F. Stone, "half dove, half hawk, and wholly opportunist," while Goodwin sounded "like a Patrick Henry saying 'Give me liberty or give me death—or give me some compromise so I can stand with the British.'"[83]

Disdainful of the liberals, radical activists were frustrated in their own efforts. Nothing constructive came of the "experiment in united timing" on 5–8 November. Perhaps 20,000 people nationwide participated in modest actions that emphasized the domestic costs of the war and the relationships among domestic social injustice, the violation of civil rights, and overseas intervention. Demonstrators rallied and held vigils, marched and prayed, but they failed to broaden or enlarge the antiwar movement. On the other hand, public opposition appeared to be curiously muted. "The shouts, obscene and otherwise, of the previous demonstration were gone," an activist reported from Texas.[84] People were not shifting toward the antiwar movement, and yet they seemed more hesitant to express support for the administration or its war. The common denominator seemed to be doubt.

The most notable result of the 5–8 November demonstrations—and one not anticipated—was to solidify public identification of antiwar activism with hippie counterculture. High on Beatles music and following a stage-prop "Yellow Submarine," about three thousand young bohemians gathered in downtown New York on 5 November and improvised (of course they would improvise) their own feeder march into the city's rally of ten thousand. They added a new dimension to the antiwar opposition, if only in popular perception. Flaunting outrageous clothing and hairstyles and proudly permissive in their attitudes toward individual personal behavior, sex, and drugs, hippies converted the seeming madness of their society into a rationale for joyous absurdity. They were a nonaggressive kind of youth cult, proudly individualistic but yet communal, materially secure but yet scornful of middle-class values. Arrayed in old clothes, preferably with a military motif, they rhapsodized about the superior wisdom of "Flower Power" and the need to "Make Love, Not War," while they enchanted younger people (and even some older ones) with calculated foolishness. In the spirit of hippie antipolitics, Jerry Rubin announced that he was for the Marxist tradition—"the revolutionary tradition of Groucho, Chico, Harpo and Karl."[85] To some antiwar activists, it made sense. "Appeals to conscience and to rational thought alone—essentially what we've been doing—may have been a mistake," declared one dissident.[86] It was time to challenge the country's cultural norms, and that was what hippies were all about.

Unfortunately for the dissidents, hippies cared more about the "feeling of 'freedom in being'" than for transforming political consciousness.[87] They were hardly prepared to turn the country against Lyndon Johnson. In January 1967, drawn by the promise of "the San Francisco Sound" of the Grateful Dead and other acid-rock bands, some 20,000 hippies gathered in a "Human Be-In" at Golden Gate Park to ingest a pharmacopoeia of drugs, project endless visions, and proclaim the war's end.[88] Antiwar dissidents were outraged. One complained that the student movement had literally "gone to pot."[89] The hippies could not have cared less, but their deviance made it easy to identify them indiscriminately with black power advocates and antiwar protesters as an antisocial periphery. The antiwar movement was distanced all the more from the political center.

There was no indication, however, that popular disdain of protest affected attitudes to the war. The large majority of Americans united on the need to support the war in order to maintain an anticommunist government in Saigon and effect an early American withdrawal. On another level, though, Americans were seriously divided over whether they might realize these ends most effectively by continuing military escalation or by de-escalating and negotiating, and they also split over Johnson's handling of the war. According to Louis Harris, "The key to understanding public opinion on this war is that the American people want to honor this country's commitment to the South Vietnamese, but would also like to see the war come to an honorable end as rapidly as possible. The dialogue today is not really between so-called 'doves' and 'hawks,' but rather over what might be the most effective way to win our limited objective and end the fighting."[90] The confounding fact, agreed Seymour Martin Lipset, was that the American people were "simultaneously doves AND hawks."[91]

Eager to win their way at the lowest cost, and anticipating the later policy of Vietnamization, a majority of Americans gravitated late in 1966 to the idea of having the South Vietnamese take over the burden of the fighting in combination with phased American withdrawal from it, even though two-thirds of them believed that the South Vietnamese could not resist the communists without U.S. troops.[92] Moreover, for most Americans, this was still a faraway and "painless" war, materially profitable and gratifying to their anticommunist sensibilities. Indeed, with the economy booming and relatively few families suffering losses, the United States scarcely appeared to be a country at war in the last months of 1966. Few were called upon to sacrifice, and fewer volunteered to do so. The country was bubbling with a "good-time-Charlie attitude," wrote the *Nation*, with the noise of antiwar dissidents overwhelmed by "the rock 'n' roll from a hundred million loud-speakers."[93]

The November off-year elections also suggested that the war remained a peripheral concern, or perhaps that doubts were not clearly formulated. In Dearborn, Michigan, voters passed an explicitly antiwar referendum, but elsewhere Vietnam was largely avoided. Few self-identified peace candidates and few proponents of escalation won contests, at least not clearly on their chosen issue. In California, Ronald Reagan, a former motion picture actor who had developed a right-wing posture, swept into the governorship in an emphatic show of voter dissatisfaction with incumbent Democrat Edmund G. "Pat" Brown, whereas in neighboring Oregon a liberal Republican and antiwar critic, Mark Hatfield, won a Senate seat with the help of Wayne Morse. In Congress, the Republican party rebounded from the devastation that it had suffered in 1964. Allard Lowenstein and Curtis Gans were not displeased: the election demonstrated that the president was a liability to his party, they concluded, and he was vulnerable to a challenge for the 1968 nomination. Jack Newfield pondered the deep cleavages bared in campaigns throughout the country, divisions between young and old, urban and rural, black and white. "I am not sure what this means," he wrote, "except that the irrational, the absurd, and the emotional are going to play a greater part in our politics."[94] In a way not yet evident, Lowenstein and Newfield were both correct.

Elements of the antiwar movement tried to regroup after the elections, meeting again at Western Reserve University on 26 November. This conference was dominated largely by the YSA, whose orientation to the single war issue prevailed. It fixed 15 April 1967 as the date for major spring demonstrations in San Francisco and New York, and it created a Spring Mobilization Committee to End the War in Vietnam to plan for them. Muste was to chair the committee with the help of Dave Dellinger, Robert Greenblatt, Sidney Peck, and Ed Keating, founder and publisher of *Ramparts*. A month later, about 250 young people met in Chicago, initially to consider a student strike against the war. Sidney Peck, Paul Booth, Bradford Lyttle of CNVA, and Fred Halstead of SWP were present, and the idea of a student strike gave way to the creation of a separate Student Mobilization Committee (SMC) in support of the April demonstrations. Linda Dannenberg's designation as executive secretary assured full cooperation with the adult group, since she had been on the staff of the Fifth Avenue Parade Committee. Still seeking an inclusive movement of the left, the leaders of the Spring Mobilization Committee reached out deftly for liberal involvement. At a meeting in mid-December, they set the goals of the demonstration in line with the position recently defined by SANE: a halt to U.S. bombings, a U.S.-initiated cease-fire, negotiations among all parties, and the "phased withdrawal" of U.S. troops.[95] As accommodating as they seemed to be, the radicals still viewed Vietnam as indicative of disorders in American society which required immediate reform. "Our motto," said organizer Robert Greenblatt, "might well be 'Action, not protest!' "[96]

The formation of the Spring Mobilization Committee provoked another round of quarrels in SANE over the question of collaborating with radicals in an inclusive antiwar movement. Benjamin Spock had defended exclusionism previously. Now, anxious to involve "moderate radicals" and militant youth with SANE, he urged his colleagues to act in a "less self-righteous, less intolerant, less antagonistic way" toward antiwar leftists and to seek "a brotherhood movement" of peace and civil rights organizations.[97] Homer Jack, among others, insisted that SANE occupied "the center and right of center" in American politics, working "somewhere between elite and mass." SANE was "very much action-oriented," Jack believed; but it could not survive within a larger coalition, with radicals "deeply alienated from the U.S. and/or frankly pro-Vietcong."[98] If effectiveness at the political center was a criterion, the dispute must have seemed sterile. On 8 December the organization had attracted 18,000 people to a rally at New York's Madison Square Garden; but the *New York Times,* certainly sympathetic to the critics, observed that "nothing new was said" in five hours of speeches lambasting the war in Vietnam.[99]

What more could be said? Trapped between the escalating war and their demonstrated ineffectuality, antiwar critics showed signs of deepening anguish and despair in the last weeks of 1966. A few accepted jail rather than the draft. Some abandoned the struggle. Others took their anger directly to those responsible for the fighting. Thus SDS activists surrounded Secretary McNamara's car during a 7 November visit to the Harvard campus and refused to let him proceed until he responded to their questions. Ten days later the chairman of the Joint Chiefs of Staff, General Earle Wheeler, was booed, interrupted, and ridiculed during a speech at Brown University. Newspaper editors across the country came down hard on the student dissidents, and former Kennedy aide Theodore Sorensen reprimanded them for their rudeness and "militant bad manners."[100] Other liberals struggled for a sense of perspective, the FOR's *Fellowship* explaining, "The conduct of the United States is so outrageously immoral, its evasions and lies so transparently obvious, and the political stupidity of its policies so widely remarked on, that our inability to affect the Administration's actions induces an almost frantic sense of frustration and near-hysterical search for some way out."[101]

Madness begets madness. A. J. Muste did not think the radicals hysterical, and he was less concerned about disruptive street actions than by the spreading sense of demoralization and hopelessness. Rhetorically he asked, "Did we really think the job would be easy and attained at a modest price?"[102]

Outside the circles of antiwar leadership, frustrated dissidents tried to convey their feelings as the year closed. Citizens in La Jolla, California, ran a newspaper ad asking their neighbors to write the White House and Congress in protest against the bombing of North Vietnam. Antiwar Nevadans wore black armbands. In Houston, women leafletted the offices of pediatricians and orthodontists, opposing war toys. Two dozen North Dakotans held a quiet march nearly 400 miles from Fargo. The WSP, meeting in Chicago, resolved to concentrate on the napalm issue. And in New York, members of the Bread and Puppet Theater staged a Christmas week nativity pageant featuring a napalmed, blood-drenched Jesus doll. Walking with the troupe through midtown Manhattan, a woman playing the role of Mary tried to lay the doll on the steps of St. Patrick's Cathedral, when a plain clothes detective snatched the toy and arrested her for loitering. A reporter noted that the police were unintentionally playing out the protesters' message: "As a nation we have lost Jesus."[103] Even when invested with theatricality, these acts were isolated witnesses. Of greater import was the development of organized draft resistance.

Peacetime conscription was a Cold War phenomenon in United States history, but by the time it was instituted there were strong precedents for conscientious objection to military service. Rejection of armed service on religious principle was accommodated during the Civil War, and it was incorporated into American law with the inauguration of the Selective Service System in 1917. The right of conscientious objection was initially limited to members of churches with creedal objections to all war service, exempting men only from actual fighting. The provisions were broadened somewhat as they were administered in World War I, although not without ambiguity and injustice. During World War II, the exemption was extended to anyone motivated by a well-defined religious principle, and the government set up a system of Civilian Public Service (CPS) camps, operated more or less in cooperation with churches and the FOR. The system had serious flaws, and in any case it did not provide for conscientious objectors who were motivated by secular philosophies or objected on principle only to selected wars. Indeed, some of the leading radical pacifists of the 1960s, including Dellinger and Peck, had chafed under CPS. Conscription expired in March 1947 but was reinstituted the following year. It was significantly modified in 1965, when the Supreme Court ruled that any deep-seated "religion," even if not church-related, was a legal basis for conscientious objection.

With the ever-growing draft calls of 1966, the number of youth resisting conscription increased, and it became clear that there was a potentially sizable body of young men who, while not actively protesting the war, would not willingly cooperate with it either. Not only eligible youth but also their parents, especially among the middle class, had a stake in the draft, as Jack Valenti advised Johnson in August: "Vietnam bugs the people right now—particularly those who have sons nearing draft age. I have talked with enough people to know that mothers and fathers of draft-age sons are totally blind to reason and logic. They just don't want their sons to go to Vietnam."[104] For some of those sons, the issue was clear: refusing to fight this war (or any war) was itself a civic duty. Numerous young men felt torn between the competing claims of their consciences and the nation, though, while many others simply declined to sacrifice their personal ambitions or security to military service in a war of questionable merit. In any case, they needed and often sought counsel and help.

Counseling was first provided by an established voluntary agency, the Central Committee for Conscientious Objectors (CCCO); by the National Service Board for Religious Objectors, traditional pacifist groups such as the AFSC, FOR, and CPF; and by some churches. By mid-spring the CCCO had opened a branch office in the Bay Area of California and had a staff of seven-plus volunteers in its Philadelphia headquarters. The eighth edition of its *Handbook for Conscientious Objectors* sold eleven thousand copies in less than five months and went into a second printing.[105] The *Handbook* was designed to serve the committed objector, not to challenge the draft system.

Conscription itself was questioned by SDS activists, who distributed a "Vietnam Draft Exemption" during three national tests administered in the spring by the Selective Service in order to identify draft-eligible males among students. Designed to test knowledge of Vietnam and of U.S. policy, the SDS exam attempted to build upon existing disaffection with draft inequalities, especially the privileged position of white middle-class youth and eligibility tied to academic rank; but it did not generate much interest, even at testing centers.[106] During the year, SDS continued to wrestle with the draft issue, provoked especially by Paul Booth and Carl Oglesby, but it could not develop consensus on a program. Antidraft activists protested through individual acts of refusal or demonstrations. Out of their actions and from meetings to evaluate them emerged local "We Won't Go" groups at Yale, Chicago, Cornell, and elsewhere, all of which were linked in an informal network of personal relationships.

Toward the end of the year, with the existing draft law due to expire on 30 June 1967 and a presidential commission already developing alternative proposals, opposition to the prevailing system converged from several sources. Liberals and civil rights leaders attacked the inequities of the draft and the disproportionate burden of service borne by the poor and nonwhite. Religious leaders responded to the moral quandaries of youth. Conservatives favored a universal compulsory service system as a way of breaking organized student dissent and disciplining youth through martial patriotism. Young people wanted a more predictable draft or, preferably, none at all. With growing hostility toward the existing system, radical pacifists and leftists were able to convert resentment of conscription into a draft resistance movement by investing personal choices with a political rationale.

Radical pacifists concluded that draft resistance involved more than an individual act of conscience or even a collective moral witness.[107] However individually motivated, and on whatever grounds, the *act* of refusing conscription involved a rejection of political authority. Even if permitted as an exception under law, that act implied a rejection of the government's foreign policy. Radical pacifists concluded, therefore, that resistance to the draft signified "a revolutionary political action" which related an individual's conscientious choice to a mass movement for radical social change.[108] Unexpectedly, the draft issue provided the link between political action and personal commitment and life-style for which radical pacifists had been seeking. That was a critical turning point for them.

The implications were quickly grasped by New Left and Quaker historian Staughton Lynd. Whereas his parents, sociologists Robert S. and Helen M. Lynd, had pioneered the study of community power structure, he had become involved in social struggle. During his tenure at Spelman College in Atlanta, he had directed the freedom schools of the 1964 Mississippi Summer project. Civil rights strategy was in flux then, and Lynd rejected traditional political approaches in favor of linking individuals who would challenge oppression directly. Chairman of the 1965 antiwar march on Washington, he had been active in forming NCCEWVN, but had come to recognize the impotence of that jerry-built organization. Beyond that, he had become skeptical of organizational politics. The slogan of genuine antiwar and antidraft resistance should be "We Won't Go," Lynd urged, because such a declaration asked people "to change their lives."[109] This was just the kind of commitment the whole antiwar movement now needed, radical pacifists agreed. With the war headed for a long haul, "protest shouldn't merely be integrated with politics, but somehow a whole new life style should be developed, one that 'illuminates' just about every minute of every day."[110] The familiar motif of personal commitment could be developed through a program in which many young people had a very personal stake, one which did not depend on national organizations.

With fresh enthusiasm, over five hundred antidraft activists met in a "We Won't Go" conference at the University of Chicago on 4 December. Although representative of a wide range of approaches, they nonetheless agreed to encourage and advance draft resistance as the first line of attack against the Vietnam war. Two weeks later, SDS members held their national convention in Berkeley, where they pledged to oppose conscription and support draft resistance. The SMC followed suit. Echoing Lynd's analysis, the SDS national secretary wrote that the new program could engage and transform "the lives of those involved despite the seeming impossibility of revolutionary social change."[111] The title of his report coined a slogan: "From Protest to Resistance." A new SDS button read simply "Resist." The movement needed "action, not protest," Robert Greenblatt had said in Cleveland. Organizing around the motto, "We Won't Go," political radicals and radical pacifists hoped to escalate opposition in pace with the enlarging war.

Seven

Sharing the Crisis

"To sustain momentum"

Two days before Christmas 1966, Catholic *Commonweal* pronounced the war "a crime and a sin" and urged the United States to withdraw, even at the cost of a communist victory.[1] What accounted for the persistent certitude of dissidents in the face of government authority and an apathetic if not hostile public? No doubt a core of them were sustained by sheer religious or ideological conviction. Even so, there was a larger current carrying dissent—the feeling that unfolding events exposed a crisis in American values. That sense was reinforced through the following year by activists' contacts with North Vietnam, as well as by a spreading disaffection at home, contradictions in the government's accounts, and testimony from independent observers.

Thus, on Christmas morning, *New York Times* associate editor Harrison Salisbury began a series of reports from North Vietnam in which he detailed the damage done to civilian areas by U.S. bombing and contended that American air attacks were only strengthening Hanoi's determination to fight on. Salisbury's account directly contradicted the president's insistence that the air war was destroying only military targets. Just after the holy day, an army captain and physician was charged with disobeying a lawful command because he had refused to teach medicine to Green Berets. He held that the Nuremberg trial precedent would make him liable for their crimes in Vietnam. Meanwhile, despite the Pentagon's denial that U.S. troops had committed crimes in Vietnam, a military court convicted and sentenced three marines to life imprisonment for killing civilians while on patrol near Tribinh. Grimly, Hans Morgenthau predicted that "the real moral heroes of this war" would be those officers who quit their commands rather than participate in the indiscriminate killing of civilians.[2] Strong language. For that distinguished political realist, as for antiwar moralists, national values and credibility were at stake.

This sense was strengthened as American activists made contact with Vietnamese. Like Salisbury, some of them were concerned to see for themselves. This was Dave Dellinger's purported goal in visiting North and South Vietnam in October 1966: there was a dearth of reliable information, especially on the North. Tom Hayden had gone in December, at least partly to be at the heart of events. Some wanted to link up with neutralist forces in South Vietnam, as Muste's group had done in April 1965. Others hoped to form a human bridge for diplomacy, which was the ostensible purpose of Lynd and Hayden's visit, or to deliver medical supplies as a mission of mercy. A few may have wanted to be supportive of the North Vietnamese, as their critics routinely charged. Most antiwar visitors to the North wanted to challenge the depiction of the Vietnamese as a ruthless enemy and to show that there were Americans who did not accept that image. Dellinger explored the countryside, where he recorded both widespread civilian devastation and the villagers' perplexed but determined response to it: "The more we hate the Americans the more we unite with each other," he was told.[3] Hayden and Lynd were deeply touched by the importance many Vietnamese attached to the self-sacrifice of their friend Norman Morrison. When they returned from their brief tour of duty in January 1966, they put their impressions in writing as *The Other Side*.[4] Although the antiwar visitors tended to overlook the potential for arbitrary rule in Hanoi, they at least documented the fact of tragic civilian destruction, the people's nationalistic dedication, and a popular sense of participating in the creation of a new society.

It was somewhat fatuous of the U.S. government to complain that the North was merely using its guests to showcase its claims, for the American embassy regularly did the same thing in the South. The administration's complaint that tours by antiwar activists played a part in the contest for the American mind was to the point, however, because that was their purpose. Obviously this was useful to the communists; but if one believed the war to be wrong, then it was also useful to the United States. And in America the war itself was precisely the issue. Whatever motives were involved, and they were mixed, the firsthand exposure of these citizen-diplomats reinforced their commitment, consolidated their leadership within the movement, and challenged the credibility of their government's war effort.

At one point in his visit, Salisbury found himself with four American women in a hotel cellar, waiting out a bombing raid together. The women included *Liberation* editor Barbara Deming, civil rights activist Diane Nash Bevel, and the wife of one of the Fort Hood Three. They had responded to an invitation from the Vietnamese Women's Union. When they returned home, their reports of widespread civilian casualties from

U.S. bombing raids were backed by the authority of Salisbury's dispatches. The administration tried to seize their passports. In January the eighty-two-year-old A. J. Muste visited North and South Vietnam with three colleagues, talked with President Ho Chi Minh in Hanoi, and returned to the United States calling for an immediate bombing halt. Critics called him a communist dupe. Sanford Gottlieb of SANE and Baltimore priest and civil rights activist Philip Berrigan secretly sought the State Department's encouragement to visit Hanoi "on an absolutely private and confidential basis" in an attempt to establish contact between the two governments. The government expressed little interest in their offer. It was in fact, as Gottlieb reported privately, "furious" with them for subverting the credibility of the administration's diplomacy.[5] State Department advisor Chester Cooper concurred in retrospect. Many of the Americans who visited North Vietnam were "very, very good people—nice people," he conceded; but it was "awfully hard to rely on them for any serious objective accounts of what was going on or really very difficult to use them as confidential channels. . . . Their discretion was suspect; their judgement was suspect; their emotional biases were suspect."[6]

The administration upped the ante in January 1967, launching Operation Cedar Falls into the so-called Iron Triangle, a communist military command base northwest of Saigon. After nineteen days, and despite engaging in no frontal battles, the Americans counted 72 dead and 337 wounded, and 720 confirmed enemy dead. The next month the U.S. began Operation Junction City in the Tay Ninh jungles, which by May resulted in 282 Americans dead and 1,576 wounded.[7] While 25,000 U.S. troops searched for infiltrators near the Cambodian border, U.S. planes made their first attacks on industrial targets north of Hanoi, close to the Chinese frontier. Already in early March, American weekly casualties reached a record 1,617, including 274 killed in action, while South Vietnamese civilian casualty rates passed beyond those of the South Vietnamese armed forces, averaging more than 2,000 per week. There was something very wrong about the war, wrote Jonathan Schell, a journalist who had covered the Operation Cedar Falls: "We are destroying, seemingly by inadvertence, the very country we are supposedly protecting." The logic of that catastrophe led him to conclude that "in the process of waging this war, we are corrupting ourselves."[8]

Schell's apprehension was not yet politic. About a dozen senators urged the president to halt the bombing and inaugurate negotiations, but only Eugene McCarthy said explicitly that the war was morally unjustified. Mansfield, returning from a trip to Vietnam in December, endorsed General Westmoreland's request for an additional 150,000 troops, although he urged a defensive position and backed Secretary McNamara's plan to construct a $4 billion infiltration-proof barrier between North and South Vietnam. Robert Kennedy kept his anguish largely to his inner circle. Fulbright reconvened the Senate Foreign Relations Committee to consider U.S. commitments abroad, and again he provided a platform for dissidents such as General Gavin and Ambassador Reischauer. The senator himself proposed direct talks between Saigon and the Vietcong on South Vietnamese self-determination and the eventual neutralization and reunification of all Vietnam. Like all other elite critics and most antiwar activists, Fulbright was still looking for some middle ground between escalation and withdrawal. Indeed, the leading antiwar critics in the Senate, prompted by Church and including Fulbright and Morse, issued a public statement warning Hanoi that there was no chance of U.S. withdrawal, that by far most Americans supported their government, and that the alternative to negotiation was further military escalation.

Most of the nation's newspapers endorsed the administration's policy in the winter and early spring. George Romney, a former Michigan governor and now a GOP presidential hopeful, declared his support of Johnson's policies. Nixon, also aspiring to the White House, urged intensified military effort and denounced Democratic dissenters in Congress. A Harris poll indicated that only small minorities of 12 and 18 percent, respectively, favored withdrawal or more escalation. The great majority of the people were prepared for a long effort in order to avoid "selling out" to the communists, but they accepted the idea of negotiating with the Vietcong or even establishing a coalition government with them. Popular approval of the president's handling of the war, an ambiguous indicator of sentiment, fell to a new low of 40 percent.[9]

Given the general but unenthusiastic popular support of the war, and considerable skepticism about Johnson's direction of it, antiwar activists placed great importance on disparate and spontaneous protests which occurred throughout the country in that winter of discontent. Sanford Gottlieb told other SANE leaders, "It is vital to sustain momentum, showing a new group opposing the war every week or two. One-shot affairs should be avoided. The President must be convinced that there is a groundswell of opposition to the war." Johnson must be convinced, Gottlieb continued, that millions of Americans were coming to conclude that the war and not the communists was corroding the "sanity and soul" of the nation.[10]

It was indeed possible to report every week or so a group that urged a bombing halt and negotiations: Business Executives Move for a Vietnam Peace (BEM), established by Baltimore insurance magnate Henry Niles; Washington Physicians and Other Health Workers for Peace in Vietnam; the Returnees Association of over four hundred former Peace Corps members and other veterans of voluntary service abroad; the Federation of American Scientists; the International Ladies Garment Workers Union; the ADA; fifty Rhodes scholars; three hundred members of the design profession; seventy-five guests at the National Book Award ceremonies who walked out on a speech by Vice-President Humphrey; a Beverly Hills organization called Another Mother for Peace, which flooded the White House with messages like the one in the child's scrawl, "for peddie saeckes give peace talks."[11] There were small weekly vigils for peace in about twenty towns and cities; a couple of hundred New York artists held exhibitions and performed antiwar plays and poetry readings in a "Week of the Angry Arts"; students at the University of Wisconsin conducted sit-ins against Dow corporate recruiters.

There were larger demonstrations too. At the end of January, CALC, with help from SANE and the AFSC, brought some 2,500 clergy and sympathizers from forty-seven states to the capital for a vigil and lobbying in two days of "education-action mobilization."[12] About two weeks later the WSP sponsored a march on the Pentagon by some 2,500 women. It started respectfully, with a quiet vigil; but when WSP demonstrators were denied a meeting with Secretary McNamara, several of them chanted and beat on the main doors of the building while others rushed past guards and provoked minor disruptions inside. These mothers and grandmothers, leaderless and angry that they had no access to responsible officials, just wanted to let "people know how mad we are."[13]

Martin Luther King, Jr., rapidly moved to the forefront of the opposition, contributing most to the antiwar momentum of the early spring. Although already on record as a critic of the war, King did not emerge as a prominent antiwar figure until 26 February, when in Los Angeles he called upon the country's "creative dissenters" to "combine the *fervor* of the civil rights movement with the peace movement . . . until the very foundations of our nation are shaken."[14] A month later, he and Dr. Spock led a Holy Saturday procession of 8,500 people down State Street to the Chicago Coliseum, where King again condemned the war; but his most memorable antiwar challenge was delivered at a CALC-sponsored meeting at New York's Riverside Church on 4 April.

His words were as measured as they were evocative: "I could never again raise my voice against the violence of the oppressed in the ghettos without having first spoken clearly to the greatest purveyor of violence in the world today—my own government," King said. He was speaking against national policy but on behalf of the nation, in the spirit of the 1957 motto of the Southern Christian Leadership Conference, "To save the soul of America." He addressed the contradictions and apparent deceptions of U.S. policy on Vietnam at length. He located primary responsibility with the United States, which held the initiative and could change its course. He expressed concern for American troops, warning that the country was adding "cynicism to death" by sending them to fight in a fictitious cause. Appealing to the people, he urged: "We are at a moment when our lives must be placed on the line if our nation is to survive its own folly. Every man of humane convictions must decide on the protest that best suits his convictions, but we must all protest." Pressing on, he declared that Vietnam was "a symptom of a far deeper malady" that led America to oppose the rightful revolutionary demands of freedom-seeking peoples throughout the world in the name of anticommunism and for the sake of privilege. Unless the nation experienced a "true revolution of value" and renounced militarism, racism, and economic exploitation, he warned, generations of concerned Americans would find themselves marching for people "beyond Vietnam," from Guatemala to South Africa.[15]

Because of his mythic stature and his organizational connections, the 1964 Nobel Peace Prize winner quickly established himself as a key figure within the antiwar movement during the spring of 1967. Eager to heal the fractures within the movement, he became a cochairman of CALC and lent his name to such disparate undertakings as the radical Spring Mobilization Committee, the liberal Negotiations Now! and the coalition project Vietnam Summer. He was not seeking "a mechanical fusion" between the civil rights and antiwar movements, King insisted. Rather, he saw them as a "kind of double action program" that were related not organizationally but, rather, in their mutual concern for justice and peace.[16] His own position was moderate: a bombing halt, a unilateral cease-fire, an enclave strategy, negotiations with the Vietcong, and a set date for the removal of all foreign troops from Vietnam in accordance with the 1954 Geneva Armistice Agreement. He explicitly rejected mass civil disobedience, disparaged confrontational rhetoric (not to mention carrying Vietcong flags), and opposed organized draft evasion because he believed that these tactics obscured the essential issue at stake for him. "I oppose the war in Vietnam because I love America. I speak out against it not in anger but with anxiety and sorrow in my heart, and above all with a passionate desire to see our beloved country stand as the moral example of the world." In sum, he declared, "This war is a blasphemy against all that America stands for." His country had "strayed away," and it was "time for all people of conscience to call upon America to return to her true home of brotherhood and peaceful pursuits."[17]

King's antiwar activism elicited a sharp backlash of criticism. Former ambassador Ralph Bunche and the *New York Times* complained that he was confusing the civil rights and antiwar causes (which he intended to relate). NAACP director Roy Wilkins disputed his contention that Vietnam was inhibiting black progress in America, and New York's Freedom House castigated him for what it interpreted as his linking civil rights with "the hate-America left" (which he was actually trying to distinguish from each other).[18] Vice-President Humphrey said publicly that King had made a serious misjudgment. White House aide John Roche privately told the president that King had "thrown in with the commies." Both would have to be destroyed, Roche added. "Essentially, the Communist origins of this operation must be exposed, the leaders discredited and the flag-burners and the draft-card burners jailed. This is not McCarthyism—McCarthy could not distinguish a Communist from a giraffe. It is a rigorous defense of what we have built from a bunch of nihilists, commies, and opportunists. It can *not* be done by HUAC—it should be handled by tough-minded liberals."[19] King was badly shaken—even stunned—by the ferocity of the prowar attack. Other dissidents were not surprised. "The Establishment has spoken," the *Nation* noted wryly, and the storm was "only beginning."[20] Sustained antiwar momentum was leading not to the conversion of the administration, as Gottlieb had hoped, but rather to confrontation with it.

By February, plans were well underway for the Spring Mobilization to End the War in Vietnam. The offices of the Fifth Avenue Parade Committee at 5 Beekman Street became inadequate, and additional space was found nearby. The Student Mobilization Committee moved in, but yet another office had to be obtained. There was always a great deal to be done in preparing a major demonstration: the terms of a call to negotiate; sponsors to enlist and funding to secure; permits to obtain and arrangements to make with authorities, speakers and entertainers to select and sign up; sanitary and sound equipment to contract and install; publicity to provide for local groups hundreds of miles away which might send participants; transportation and accommodations to coordinate; the media to cultivate. By 1967, organizers had learned also to train a corps of marshals that could direct the walk and handle hecklers. These tasks were all the more formidable when more than one site was involved, in this case New York and San Francisco. The event was the focal point, but its very organization and outreach was essential to the process of movement growth.

The 1967 Spring Mobilization was originally conceived of as a means of joining the whole antiwar movement in an action comparable to the 1963 March on Washington for civil rights and as a prelude to continuing collaboration. In practice, however, planning was impeded by differences of emphasis among leaders such as A. J. Muste, who envisioned a liberal-left antiwar coalition; Old Left veteran Sid Peck, who wanted to fashion a broad left-wing political movement; and radical pacifist Dave Dellinger, who proposed to "move beyond dissent and protest to actually stopping the war."[21] Problems were exacerbated when the Reverend James Bevel was hired as executive director. A top aide to Martin Luther King and director of the 1965 March on Selma, Bevel personified the goal of relating the civil rights and antiwar movements; but he alienated liberals already suspicious of the Mobilization scheme by his sometimes intemperate rhetoric (as when he called the war "a profound expression of the policy of genocide" on the NBC evening news).[22] Because of the political accent of Mobilization leaders and the lack of liberal involvement in planning, WSP declined to endorse the project. Antiwar activists "should be anti-Administration," it complained, "but not anti-American."[23] Similarly, FOR and SANE leaders refused to be official sponsors. Undeterred, the organizers kept referring to the Mobilization as "a new national center for the peace movement."[24]

Suddenly, on 11 February, Muste died of a stroke. The antiwar left lost not only its patriarch but the personality who had cemented its ill-fitting parts, and the whole movement lost one of the few people who commanded respect and attention across its breadth. "Who," wondered Michael Harrington, "can be instinctively, viscerally hopeful in the situation which exists right now?"[25]

The threat of violence commanded public attention that spring. Extremist radicals talked of ending war and racism through mass violence by organizing urban guerrilla contingents on the model of their new hero, Cuban revolutionary Ernesto "Ché" Guevara. A band of heavily-armed young black men calling themselves the Black Panther Party for Self-Defense marched on the California state legislature in order to protest gun-control bills and warned that they would resist Oakland police by any available means. Following a student's arrest in Nashville, black students at Fisk University fought a two-day pitched battle with police. Ghetto uprisings took place in Cleveland and San Francisco. Congress, apprehensive of violent civil unrest, voted $75 million to provide summer jobs for urban black youth, whereas the CIA started its Project Merrimac to secretly monitor the activities of certain "extremist groups," including WSP and SNCC (purportedly to protect Agency buildings during demonstrations in the Washington area).[26] Martin Luther King estimated in mid-April that some ten cities were "powder kegs" waiting to blow.[27]

In this atmosphere the Spring Mobilization to End the War in Vietnam opened on 15 April. Well over fifty thousand people marched down San Francisco's Market Street to Kezar Stadium for rounds of speeches, music, and a sense of purposeful belonging. Perhaps two hundred thousand—the organizers claimed twice that number—converged on New York's Central Park. The first contingent led off at about one o'clock, walking through rain and wind to rally at the UN, where the last participants arrived at six. Local chapters of the FOR, SANE, WSP and CALC came, despite the fact that their national organizations were not official sponsors. Thousands of people found a way to express unity beyond the divisions in their ranks and hope that belied Harrington's pessimism.

A WSP activist reported that she was "constantly astonished, yet again, at the disparate elements that a peace demonstration can encompass."[28] Participants included blacks and whites, hippies and church members, children and grandparents, military veterans and Vietcong sympathizers—even a small bridal party. In New York a group of Native Americans carried signs that appealed: "Americans—Do Not Do to the Vietnamese

What You Did to Us."[29] A Quaker elder observed, "The mobilization was so vast and amorphous that one could get a host of different reports on it from as many different individuals."[30] For some, it was a hippie "be-in," filled with psychedelic art forms and rock music; for others it was a day of militant opposition. For about 150 young men, including a uni-formed ex–Green Beret, it was an opportunity to burn their draft cards in a ceremony at Sheep Meadow in Central Park, which formally chris-tened the new draft resistance movement. Claimed one New Left activist, the demonstrations were "just the thing to pull the Movement out of the doldrums we have been in the last several months." A WSP leader agreed, elatedly concluding that *"people oppose the war, more deeply and more actively, than ever before."*[31] The Mobilization was far from representing popular opinion, but it flaunted the message that antiwar momentum had been sustained through the early spring of 1967.

"A three-front war"

Social critic Max Lerner warned shortly after the Spring Mobilization that Vietnam had become "a three-front war: the home-front battle of opinion in America, the ... battle of pacification in South Vietnam vil-lages, and the struggle over Sino-Soviet attitudes toward the war. ... The thing to note is that any modern limited war in which a revolutionary nationalism is involved is bound to be fought out in the area of opinion and conscience."[32] This was a precise and accurate assessment, although in a sense there were also three fronts in the United States: the admin-istration, hawkish critics who would expand the war, and dovish critics who would curtail it. Here the contest was a matter of judgment and morality. The conflict in America was not merely a front on which Hanoi waged war; it was independently the heart of the matter. The war was coming home, and it was beginning to engage the political center. The April demonstrations gave citizens venues for their disaffection: the crowds of hundreds of thousands were a truly popular response which activists elicited but could not have organized directly. As long as dissent had remained on the periphery, the administration could afford to dis-miss it as irrelevant. By the spring of 1967, the White House had become convinced that it had to respond in force.

The reports with which Salisbury opened the year had created a "trau-matic reaction" in the administration.[33] Johnson's liberal Democratic co-alition was strained in February by a sharp dispute over the war between the president and Robert Kennedy. It was further threatened as Martin Luther King accepted antiwar leadership, so much so that the president's press secretary reacted by sowing allegations that King had communist affiliations. In the wake of the Spring Mobilization, the White House marshalled its resources. It brought General Westmoreland back to rally the home front. It helped to organize demonstrations and a letter-writing campaign to support "Our Boys in Vietnam," creating for this purpose the National Committee for Peace with Freedom in Vietnam. Former presidents Truman and Eisenhower acted as honorary co-chairmen, but the fact that Nixon declined to be associated with the committee suggested how serious public disaffection had become.[34]

The Johnson administration countered its critics with two related themes: communists were at the center of the antiwar discontent, and protest encouraged the enemy to fight on. As the Mobilization got under way, the president announced that he was studying a new FBI report on communist involvement in the antiwar movement, and the next day Secretary of State Rusk claimed that antiwar demonstrators were supported by a "Communist apparatus" and were "prolonging the war rather than shortening it."[35] White House media aide Robert Kintner asked the Justice Department to cooperate with the *Washington Post* in preparing a report on "common planning" behind protest demonstrations for use either as a news story or as a special report by the attorney general.

In fact, the White House was pressing its intelligence officers to document subversive connections with antiwar groups, a case it could not yet make (and never would). The FBI launched a probe of SDS, SANE, journalists, intellectuals, and even authors of protest letters. Earlier the CIA had begun to monitor and infiltrate WSP, SANE, CORE, WRL, and various mobilization committees. Suspecting this, the judicious FCNL warned at midyear that CIA infiltration posed a "serious threat" to both the movement and "the very roots" of American society.[36] The Secret Service, the Internal Revenue Service, and the Justice Department also were involved. The government found plenty of activity, but no clear evidence of foreign influence or communist direction.

Whatever its source, the administration insisted, protest supported the communist cause. Westmoreland charged that antiwar demonstrations gave the enemy hope that it might win in America what it could not gain on the battlefield, and the commander of U.S. forces in the Pacific, Admiral U. S. Grant Sharp, held a Pentagon press conference to attack protesters for encouraging Hanoi and damaging "our over-all position."[37] At a Medal of Honor ceremony, the president declared that soldierly sacrifices were the price to be paid for domestic dissent. Ambassador Lodge in Saigon was encouraged to stress that dissent at home "bucks up Hanoi."[38]

The great majority of the nation's news media followed the administration's lead. *Time* scoffed at the "Vietniks and Peaceniks, Trotskyites and potskyites" who made up the Mobilization, while warning that they only encouraged Hanoi and prolonged the fighting.[39] Other commentators picked up on the same line or tried to diminish the significance of the demonstrations by emphasizing the small proportion of the people

they enlisted. There was, however, a new note of sophistication in editorial reaction to the springtime peace offensive. Some commentators
warned against the administration's heavy-handedness in dealing with
dissent, and a few journals developed elaborate distinctions between
responsible and irresponsible antiwar criticism. The *Denver Post* cata-
logued four distinctions between "responsible" and "irresponsible" dissent, for example. The *Christian Science Monitor* simplified the matter.
It was "one thing" to demand a bombing halt but "quite another" to
demand "an early and sharp end by America's one-sided withdrawal."
In any event, explained the *Detroit News,* Americans should "not collec-
tivize the kooks and peaceniks and those who have honest doubts or
conscientious objection."[40]

The administration's strategy of relating all protesters to the radical
fringe clearly was designed to put its opposition on the political margin.
In large measure the contest for the center was waged over national
symbols.

The American flag came to symbolize the war effort insofar as isolated
cases of flag-burning and the carrying of Vietcong flags were associated
with antiwar protests. The residents of Mount Lebanon, Pennsylvania, flew
the American flag in a mass protest against flag-burning, a sentiment
seconded by 347 faculty members at Washington State University. Actor
Chuck Connors carried a flag in a prowar parade, then handed it to
General Westmoreland for delivery to Vietnam. Prowar demonstrators in
Jackson, Michigan, capped a march by burning a Vietcong flag.[41] In the
summer, the House of Representatives passed legislation making it a
federal crime to mutilate or desecrate the American flag, punishable by
fines up to $1,000 and a year in jail. Meanwhile, manufacturers of flags
reported that sales surged to record highs following the springtime flag-
burning incidents. "People just didn't like what those beatniks did," said
one, and they wanted "to show their own colors this year."[42]

The identification of dissidents with beatniks and communists provided a convenient target for advocates of sharper escalation. Whether
or not the White House intended this, it was convenient for the president,
who felt threatened from the right in his effort to maintain a consensus
for limited war. Governor George Wallace advised the administration to
jail all the "traitors" who supported North Vietnam. A group called the
Support Our Servicemen Committee urged Congress to legislate penalties for giving "aid and comfort" to the nation's enemies, and a Cali-
fornia-based Victory in Vietnam Committee collected money to defeat
Senator Frank Church as part of its effort to break antiwar politicians.[43]
Outright attacks on dissenters multiplied in the summer.

Critics of the war did not feel threatened by hostility from the right
nearly as much as by apparent apathy in the political center. Their problem was effectively depicted in journalist Calvin Trillin's account of "the

war in Kansas." Citizens of Junction City cared about Vietnam only insofar as it affected their friends and businesses, Trillin found, and people in Wichita talked more about daylight savings time than about the Saigon government. Kansans expressed "virtually unanimous contempt" for draft-card burners; but they benignly accepted draft avoidance, and they were tolerant of antiwar critics. Local activists leavened their determination with caution. Holding meals of reconciliation and silent public vigils, antiwar Kansans tried to get at the "fantastic brute apathy" around them but doubted they could ever move the great majority of their neighbors, who preferred not to think about either protest or war.[44]

Apathy was mixed with ambivalence in a way that made public opinion both unstable and hard to assess. A poll in June suggested that nearly half the respondents had no clear idea of what the war was all about (under the circumstances, that could be interpreted as an informed and considered opinion).[45] Surveys the next month indicated that a plurality of 48 percent rejected the idea that the war had been a mistake but that most people rejected large increases in troop commitments by 49 to 40 percent (Harris) or 61 to 29 percent (Gallup).[46] Interestingly, in an early attempt to gauge the impact of television, three-quarters of those sampled favored military escalation after viewing the fighting, although visualizing the war may have merely reinforced a previously held orientation. What does seem clear is that between May and July popular support for military escalation was sustained but unstable, that the public expected a long war but wanted to get it over quickly, and that despite their willingness to endure fighting, Americans were losing confidence in the president's handling of the war (down to 33 percent in July). The idea of turning it over to the South Vietnamese began to sound attractive. Still ambivalent, public opinion was becoming vulnerable. Gallup concluded in May that a quarter of the population believed that the war was not morally justified, and Harris reported in July that 61 percent of the people he sampled felt personally affected by the war.[47]

Irreversibly, the war was coming home. Rightly or wrongly, more and more Americans were coming to conclude that their nation was being corrupted in the process. For Lutheran minister Peter L. Berger, the destructiveness of the war already had exceeded whatever purposes might have originally justified intervention. The war's "moral horror" had passed so far beyond political ambiguity, he wrote, that nothing could be worse "than what is taking place right now."[48] Journalist James Wechsler conceded that America might yet win the war in Vietnam, but only at the cost of "spreading moral civil war" at home.[49] "Indeed," added the *Nation,* "the more complete our military conquest, the more tragic becomes our loss in everything that counts in the long run."[50] Those were minority sentiments, but they did not come only from a radical fringe. They reflected a deep love for the country. They boded frustration and sadness, although not despair. Antiwar critics shared these feelings. Most of them, radicals and liberals alike, agreed with Robert McAfee Brown that the only answer to the escalation of the war was "the escalation of dissent."[51] Somehow, even the illusion of movement had to be sustained, they felt, not to convert the administration but rather to arouse the people.

The problem was how to organize. Superficially, a spirit of cooperation settled over the movement in the wake of the Spring Mobilization. In an attempt to link the liberal and radical wings of the movement, Arthur Waskow and Marcus Raskin, fellows of the Institute for Policy Studies in Washington, worked with liberal and left-wing intellectuals to incorporate the war in the multi-issue platform of the National Conference for a New Politics. Hoping to offer an alternative to both major parties in 1968, they projected a national convention on the so-called New Politics in Chicago over Labor Day weekend. Most activists concentrated on the single issue of the war.

In mid-May about six hundred young people, most of them delegates from college and high school groups, attended a planning conference in Chicago sponsored by the SMC, which had taken over from the NCCEWVN. The youths agreed to cooperate during the summer in efforts to reach out to adult constituencies, encourage local antiwar referenda, and support draft resistance. Most important, they adopted a plan for an October march on Washington. This idea became, in turn, the focal point of a broadly representative conference of about seven hundred adult activists who met in the capital the following week. Even SANE was represented. The meeting was organized in workshops which corresponded to the tactical alternatives open to the movement: mass public protest, popular persuasion and electoral politics, and draft resistance. Each approach represented a separate tendency and reflected plans already under way. Only the first—a major demonstration—required movement-wide sponsorship, and it was adopted along the lines proposed by the SMC. The twenty-first of October was designated for a mass protest in Washington on the theme, "Bring the Troops Home."[52] The ad hoc Spring Mobilization Committee was converted into the National Mobilization to End the War in Vietnam (or less formally, "the Mobe"). Until autumn, activists would variously promote political education through Negotiations Now! and Vietnam Summer and would encourage civil disobedience through resistance to the draft.

The very breadth of the Mobe divided liberal leadership. Benjamin Spock, who had cochaired the Spring Mobilization, again appealed to his colleagues in SANE to work more closely with antiwar radicals, especially youth. Privately, he felt that the board had "alienated them by looking down its nose at them."[53] In fact, it was they, not SANE, who were generating momentum, he said. Norman Cousins and other cautious SANE activists objected that the Mobe's inclusiveness accommodated the policy of unconditional withdrawal and the tactics of confrontation, both of which would polarize the country. During the spring the national board clarified SANE's approach as "policy change," in contrast to the "social protest" of the mobilizations; but at the same time it gave a larger governing voice to its local chapters, which were divided on the issue of cooperation in public demonstrations.[54] In particular, Gottlieb helped to initiate and fully backed Negotiations Now!—drawing together about twenty liberal political and religious organizations opposed to both administration policy and radical demands for immediate withdrawal.

The program was announced on 24 April at a New York City news conference with Martin Luther King, Jr., and ADA leader Joseph Rauh.[55] It was promoted especially by Gottlieb in SANE and John Kenneth Galbraith in the ADA, and by Robert Pickus, whose World Without War Council (1967) took over from the shattered Turn Toward Peace. Negotiations Now! was endorsed by leading liberals such as Reinhold Niebuhr, Arthur Schlesinger, Jr., and Victor Reuther (United Auto Workers) in an effort to create "a new coalition of conscience" that would move all belligerents in Vietnam "to end the killing" and effect "an honorable settlement of the war."[56]

The organizers projected an image of reason and fairness, hoping to rally the moderate American center to a policy along the lines proposed by UN Secretary-General U Thant on 14 March: an unconditional U.S. bombing halt, a reduction in fighting in South Vietnam, and internationally supervised elections in the South. Negotiations Now! sponsored ads and petitions to the president in an effort to stimulate "a groundswell of support for new peace initiatives."[57] Its sponsors wanted to contain the apparent drift toward political polarization, and yet they also claimed to provide a "sharp point of comparison . . . to the anti-American elements of the protest movement."[58] By their own admission it was already too late to avoid polarization, and they were attacked from both the right and the left.

Leaders of Americans for Democratic Action were divided. A minority of them, including veteran labor leaders Gus Tyler and David Dubinsky (assisted by White House aide John Roche), assailed Galbraith for antagonizing the administration and exaggerating the importance of Vietnam at the expense of other ADA concerns. Disturbed by Galbraith, the Tyler group was altogether antagonized by Allard Lowenstein, now a member of the board, and Curtis Gans, who had become ADA director of research and publication. Lowenstein had become thoroughly disillusioned with the administration by January and, with Gans and Leon Shull, had participated in the CALC-sponsored antiwar vigil at the end of that month. Thoroughly opposed to radical activists, Lowenstein was all the more convinced that opposition to the war had to be pursued vigorously within the system. He helped to organize a large teach-in at Harvard and put together a Campus Coordinating Committee, headed by theology students David Hawk (Union) and Sam Brown (Harvard), which mobilized protest from seminarians. At an ADA board meeting early in April, he spoke eloquently for a resolution drafted by columnist James Wechsler which threatened the president with loss of the organization's support unless he altered Vietnam policy. The resolution passed. Late in the spring a majority of the ADA national board condemned the president's war policy and proposed to support any candidate in the 1968 elections who promised to work for "restraint in the conduct of the war" and toward "its peaceful resolution on honorable terms." Galbraith, the new president, declared that he and his allies intended to "build the broadest possible base for dissent."[59] By July, Wechsler regarded ADA as "perhaps the chief rallying point" for antiwar liberals; but the quarrels there and in SANE continued throughout the summer, punctuated by sharp exchanges and angry threats, wrecking friendships, and sowing deep enmity.[60]

The day before Negotiations Now! was announced, Martin Luther King joined Dr. Spock, Carl Oglesby, and others at a news conference which unveiled an ambitious attempt to connect liberals and radicals in local antiwar community organizing: Vietnam Summer. Initiated in Cambridge and modelled after the 1964 Mississippi Summer project, the program was directed by Lee Webb, a former national secretary of SDS, and Richard Fernandez, who had become the executive officer of CALC the previous April. Fernandez had roots in both the peace and the civil rights movements. In college he had been most influenced by Bayard Rustin and Norman Cousins. He had participated in FOR and Turn Toward Peace events and had been arrested four times under SCLC auspices. Bringing vigor and efficiency to CALC, he hoped to move the organization to the political center through patient organizing.[61] Vietnam Summer offered an opportunity to mobilize a phalanx of students for that purpose. It would be "a program of teach-outs instead of teach-ins."[62] During the summer its full-time staff of eleven helped to coordinate the efforts of a hundred recruiters and some four thousand part-time community volunteers, particularly on the West Coast. It inspired neighborhood canvassing, petitioning, curriculum writing, and draft counselling—anything which might raise community consciousness on the war issue.

Theoretically, Vietnam Summer was designed to make a transition from a peace movement of students, Old Leftists, pacifists, and liberals to "a movement ... in contact with the majority of Americans opposed to the war on one level or another."[63] In practice, although it made the first inroads into some communities, the project encountered the hard facts of volunteer activism. People worked sporadically. Staff members were not consistent. Ideological animosities were all too predictable in a project more or less supported by the AFSC, SANE, SNCC, SCLC, and some factions of SDS. Antiwar liberals hoped that Vietnam Summer might harness radical activism to the work of mobilizing a middle-class voting bloc against the war, whereas radicals wanted it to marshal an independent political force around the demand for immediate U.S. withdrawal. Confounded by this division, and complicated by variations on it, Vietnam Summer was inherently compromised as a grassroots antiwar movement. Moreover, project volunteers encountered apathy in low-income neighborhoods and antipathy among the middle class. Undoubtedly, activists reported from the field, the greatest wish of Americans confronted with Vietnam was to be "left undisturbed."[64]

A third summer initiative, draft resistance, was designed precisely to disturb the country. Following the December "We Won't Go" conference in Chicago, students at Chicago, Wisconsin, and Queens College independently announced that they would not fight in Vietnam, adding to existing groups such as those at Cornell, Yale, and Stanford. In the spring they were joined by students at Princeton, Brown, and some other schools. By the time of the Spring Mobilization, there were almost thirty known campus groups, and more followed the April demonstration. Some moved beyond the campus—Chicago Area Draft Resisters (CADRE), "Support-in-action" in New York, and New England Resistance operating out of Boston. Groups variously recruited resisters, leafletted or picketed at induction centers, and provided draft counselling, sometimes cooperating with local FOR, AFSC, or SANE chapters. In the summer a newly formed Draft Resistance Clearinghouse in Madison estimated that nationally there were perhaps two thousand resisters, with a few thousand supporters in related groups, often as counselors on legal rights and ways of avoiding conscription. Sporadic and fragmented, draft resistance developed both as an expression of personal resistance to the war and as an act of revolutionary politics under the simple threat: "We Won't Go."

Organized draft resistance was only the most visible expression of the widespread rejection of conscription which began to break down the Selective Service System. Young men, especially from the upper and better educated classes, found innumerable ways to evade the draft. Vietnam became as much a war of individual survival in civilian life as it was on the battlefield. It was not possible to quantify the motives for avoiding combat service, whether conscientious objection on the grounds of religious or philosophical principle, political rejection of the Vietnam war, or self-centeredness. Differentiation did not affect the political import: conscientious objection, war resistance, draft avoidance and evasion—all reflected a collective repudiation of the war, although explicit resistance most conveyed a rejection of the government's authority to prosecute it.

In this respect, the resistance movement developed in two new thrusts in midyear: campus-based refusal was focused on a nationwide event, and an adult community was organized in support. The national movement was initiated at Stanford. There David Harris, the student body president who had debated Allard Lowenstein at the 1966 NSA convention, was living in a kind of commune which included Dennis Sweeney, who had become something of a protégé of Lowenstein's but had broken with him during the Mississippi Summer Project (and would assassinate him in 1980). Both of them were "consumed" by "moral outrage" over the war. Lennie Heller and a friend came over from Berkeley in March, and the four decided to invite other resisters to turn in their draft cards collectively on 16 October. There were no longer simply issues or problems, they concluded. "Beyond innuendo and beyond observation and conclusion, there is an act with the totality of our lives against the machines of the state. The act begins with a refusal to cooperate with conscription. As long as America continues to mean oppression, the act has no end."[65] Harris announced the projected collective draft refusal at the April mobilization in San Francisco. During the summer he "talked his way up and down the west coast," as Lynd recalled, while Heller activated young people eastward across the country. They called themselves "the Resistance."[66]

Meanwhile, various statements of support for draft resistance were circulating among adults, building on the 1964–65 "Declaration of Conscience." The most important version, "A Call to Resist Illegitimate Authority," was drafted by Arthur Waskow and Marcus Raskin.[67] The war in Vietnam was immoral and illegal, they argued, and therefore individuals had an obligation to resist the government prosecuting it. Their declaration perfectly caught the emerging thrust of draft resistance as a moral and civic duty. Moreover, it offered adults and women a way to volunteer their complicity in the civil disobedience of draft-eligible young men. Organizing as RESIST, its sponsors among left-wing intellectuals gathered signatures to the statement throughout the summer and published it in September. The community of support was to be linked with the resisters themselves by prominent adults who would receive the draft cards turned in during the October action and present them to the Justice Department.

The "Call to Resist" captured the mood of a number of intellectuals associated with the *New York Review of Books*—Noam Chomsky, for example, and Mary McCarthy, Mitchell Goodman, Paul Goodman, Andrew Kopkind, Arthur Miller, and Norman Mailer. For such writers the crisis in Vietnam was the crisis of the intellectual. Feeling intensely alienated from both the intransigent body politic and the war, they argued that resistance was the moral duty of intellectuals. As they tried to explain the failure of liberalism and the effectuality of radical politics, they concluded that popular apathy was symptomatic of a deeper malaise. Americans were conditioned by the very organization of their society to deny responsibility for the moral consequences of their institutions, they thought, and this denial had led to *"an extreme and dangerous dissociation of the personality"* from its existential, social context. It was therefore incumbent upon intellectuals to become engaged through at least symbolic action in order to preserve the very meaning of morality, of intentional choice. Thus Howard Zinn of Boston University argued for the "historian as an actor."[68] With others, he felt constrained to act, if only to affirm resistance to illegitimate authority.

No intellectual was more influential in this respect than linguist Noam Chomsky of the Massachusetts Institute of Technology. In a series of trenchant articles, he challenged not only Vietnam policy but also the liberal consensus on the Cold War.[69] It was one thing to contain aggression, he insisted, but quite another to try to bottle up the forces of revolutionary change. Vietnam was a case in point of the irresponsibility of intellectual apologists who were paralyzed by their own rhetoric and its apparent acceptance as a political consensus. Echoing Randolf Bourne's anger at the apostasy of intellectuals who uncritically supported World War I, Chomsky called upon his contemporaries to expose deception and exercise skepticism, even to the point of resisting authority. If they were to raise the consciousness of the nation, then by their very defiance the intellectuals would become fully integrated into the social process. The "Call to Resist" offered them a modicum of action.

The three national campaigns—Negotiations Now! Vietnam Summer, and draft resistance—gave antiwar activists a sense of movement in the middle of 1967. A sharp upsurge in local and individual protest during the summer was also important, though, because of its cumulative effect. Some actions were imaginative: dissidents in Tucson, Arizona, recalling that President Eisenhower had promised to fly to Korea to end the war there, raised funds by promising to buy president Johnson a one-way ticket to Vietnam; protesters cavorted across a mock battlefield east of Toledo, Ohio, in order to disrupt army war games; and Another Mother for Peace raised funds for Vietnamese civilian medical relief by selling cards that bore the words "War is Not Healthy for Children and Other Living Things."

Some protests were solemn. Activists in Grand Rapids, Michigan, canvassed, leafletted, and prayed; and two hundred people held a silent vigil on Independence Day near Lexington Green, Massachusetts. Some efforts were impressive. A group of California businessmen circulated a statement of "Individuals Against the Crime of Silence," which was signed by thousands of people, including Hans Morgenthau, Daniel Berrigan, writer Ray Bradbury, and Harvard political scientist Stanley Hoffman, and submitted the document to UN Secretary-General U Thant "as both a permanent witness to our opposition to the war in Vietnam and as a demonstration that the conscience of America is not dead."[70] Asian scholars at Harvard protested U.S. policy and called for military de-escalation, and Linus Pauling told a group of scientists that "every additional day of this evil war is an additional crime against humanity."[71] Dissent emerged within the Roman Catholic church when the Reverend Fulton J. Sheen, bishop of Rochester, New York, and one of the country's most widely admired religious figures, called for the withdrawal of U.S. troops from Vietnam, and when four other Catholic bishops endorsed Negotiations Now!

Some actions were dramatic. An Air Force Academy captain and an army captain refused to train men for Vietnam combat. The lead singer with a popular rock group, the Beach Boys, was indicted, and heavyweight boxing champion Muhammad Ali was stripped of his crown and sentenced to a maximum penalty of five years in jail and $10,000 in fines—both for refusing induction. In June, police employed brute force to break up a demonstration of several thousand protesters outside a Los Angeles hotel where the president was speaking. And on 19 August, navy veteran J. D. Copping burned himself to death in Panorama City, California, in anguish over the war.

Copping absorbed the despair that others resisted. From the perspective of those who opposed the war, his act was understandable only as a personal expression of the madness in society. They chose other actions which, however trivial, at least helped them to preserve some sense of balance. Jack Newfield caught their feeling: "If two years ago, someone told me that the Warren Report was incorrect, that the CIA was subsidizing the National Student Association and a dozen unions, that LBJ would adopt Goldwater's Vietnam policy, that actor Ronald Reagan would soon be governor of the largest state in the country, and that Congress would vote to throw out Adam Clayton Powell, I would have said such a person was insane. But all the impossibles became possible."[72]

The dissidents' effort to convince the country that the war was senseless was difficult to sustain, in the face of the hostility they frequently encountered. Sometimes intimidation was trivial, as when Joan Baez was banned from appearing at Constitution Hall. Often it was vaguely threatening, as in Phoenix, where leading activists received death threats from the right-wing Minutemen, or in Washington, where Abigail McCarthy reported that dissident politicians believed their phones were tapped.[73] Sometimes the threat was real enough, as when an activist was shot down in the streets of Austin, Texas; or the Los Angeles office of Vietnam Summer was firebombed; or the offices of Chicago's major antiwar groups were burglarized.[74] "Our time is Vietnam," Dave McReynolds wrote early in the summer. "Everything now revolves around Vietnam. . . . [It is] no longer a distant, bloodied, tedious spot half across the planet. Vietnam is here."[75]

Everything did *not* revolve around Vietnam that summer. Vietnam was subsumed in a pervasive mood of anger, uncertainty, and apprehension, and much of that was racial. Whites and blacks in the South fought pitched battles from Baton Rouge to Birmingham. In the North, racial violence commonly took the form of clashes between ghetto blacks and local police. There were at least 218 racial disturbances in 1967, and staccato bursts of mob violence—firebombings, lootings, and sniper fire—tore through black urban areas around the country. The loss of life and property damage was unprecedented. The erosion of national self-confidence was incalculable. In the middle of July, twenty-one people died during riots in Newark, New Jersey. Two weeks later 4,700 U.S. paratroopers were ordered into Detroit to help local police and National Guardsmen restore order with machine guns, tanks, and armored personnel carriers. Rioting there resulted in the death of 43 people, the destruction of nearly 600 businesses, and $85 million in property damage. SNCC leader H. "Rap" Brown warned that Detroit's agony would "look like a picnic" once blacks united nationally.[76]

Widely scattered and seemingly irrepressible, urban black riots were only the most obvious sign of the climate of hate and fear in the summer of 1967. Moderate civil rights leaders Roy Wilkins and Whitney Young were the targets of murder attempts, as was communist theoretician Herbert Aptheker. American Nazi party leader George Lincoln Rockwell was shot to death by a discontented subordinate. Razor-sharp anger was in the air. After an attack on the home of an NAACP official in Mississippi, the organization's state field director advised blacks to "shoot to kill" anyone found loitering suspiciously on their property, and Stokely Carmichael urged black Americans on to "total revolution" through urban guerrilla warfare.[77] Governor Romney worried aloud that the country did indeed verge on "revolt and revolution."[78] Gripped in the worst civil violence in memory, America seemed to be coming apart. "Vietnam is here," McReynolds had said in June. By August the phrase implied more than a political program: "Vietnam Summer" evoked a social condition.

Excited by the racial violence and Third World liberation ideology, antiwar radicals were polarized, as Todd Gitlin observed ruefully, between moods of "apocalyptic expectation and deep despair."[79] Staughton Lynd declared that antiwar organization in the ghettos was the "frontier of peace activity," and Tom Hayden added, "urban guerrillas are the only realistic alternative at this time to electoral politics or mass armed resistance."[80] Both may have been expressing their frustration rather than advocating specific programs, but cynicism was infectious. Leaders of the National Mobilization Committee held a press conference in August to declare that the scheduled October action in Washington would "obstruct

the war machine" and to proclaim their support for black ghetto uprisings. There was, they said, *only one struggle—for self-determination—
and we support it in Vietnam and in black America.*"[81]

The Mobe had stalled earlier that month, short on funds and without
a project director. At the outset its guiding spirits, notably Dave Dellinger,
Jim Peck, and Robert Greenblatt, had intended to include direct action
in order to escalate the movement into a "stage of structured confrontation." They intended to radicalize the demonstrators and to confront
the administration: "LBJ isn't going to know what's hitting him."[82] And
yet they also intended to mass a broadly inclusive demonstration. The
only way those goals could be reconciled was by including alternatives—
from verbal protest to direct action—from which participants could
choose, and this so unnerved the AFSC, SANE, and SDS that they declined
to affiliate. By August the October mobilization was mired in bitter factionalism and distracted by the competing summer programs. In desperation, the leadership made a hasty, fateful decision.

At Fred Halstead's suggestion, Dellinger phoned Jerry Rubin, who
agreed to head up the October demonstration. Rubin had changed from
the radical activist of the previous year to a cultural militant. He looked
and acted like part of the Berkeley street scene, and he promptly enrolled
Abbie Hoffman from bohemian Greenwich Village. Together, and to the
dismay of their radical colleagues in the Mobe, they began to give the
mobilization vitality with a counterculture twist. For one thing, they
seemed to think that black rebellion had radicalized Americans opposed
to the war. For another, they focused the demonstration on the Pentagon.
At a press conference late in the month, surrounded by activists from
WSP, CADRE, the NCNP, SDS, CORE, Vietnam Summer, and the Resistance,
Hoffman promised to levitate the building. That was all rhetoric, and
Hoffman admitted it. "There's nothing to explain about the war in Vietnam," he shrugged. "Those days are over. The time has come for resistance." Radicals were out of the protest business, Jerry Rubin promised.
"We are now in the business of wholesale and widespread resistance and
dislocation of American society."[83] Dellinger, devoted to both nonviolence
and mass action, managed to hold the coalition together on the basis that
the demonstration would provide a range of actions from lawful demonstration to peaceful civil disobedience. He was still talking about having come "from dissent to resistance," while Rubin was moving from
street theater to a circus of the absurd.

The provocative rhetoric of this vociferous but tiny faction accelerated
several processes already in motion in the middle of 1967. Good media
copy, it reinforced the image of the antiwar movement as a radical fringe
and pushed it further to the political margin. By antagonizing the American center, the militants aggravated cultural and political polarization in
both the country and the movement. They contributed to the excited

rhetoric of even some naïve liberals: physicist Jeremy Stone, for instance, remarked that there was room now "for any plausible act of resistance."[84]

At the same time, the militants' trendy rebelliousness was paradoxically conservative. Incapable of affecting immediate political realities, they persuaded themselves that political action was irrelevant. Richard Flacks, principal author of SDS's *America and the New Era,* speculated on roles for radicals from his position on the University of Chicago faculty. What was required, he suggested (anticipating Charles Reich's *The Greening of America* by three years), was the "transformation of the American consciousness" so that people could "take control of their own lives," delegitimize existing institutions, and thus pave the way for the coming revolution.[85] In Flack's New Left this formula still implied painstaking work for plausible reform through community action. Militant extremists formulated the position differently, however, so that cultural transformation was pursued in lieu of political change. This change of emphasis allowed radicals to move off in several directions. Some remained with the antiwar movement, contributing an almost transpolitical quality to it. Some simply withdrew to private lives. Others shifted toward movements like black power and women's rights that encouraged the politics of cultural symbolism. And still others disappeared into the hippie world of drugs, sex, rock music, and psychedelic rebellion, certain that it was "more possible to change private reality with LSD than America's reality with SDS."[86]

Dramatized in the Mobe's August press conference, the rhetoric of rebellion had already widened divisions within the country's pacifist community. Dave McReynolds and Charles Bloomstein quit the editorial board of *Liberation* at the end of June, complaining that under Dellinger it was no longer a collective and was moving toward the acceptance of violence "as a legitimate, even radical, alternative in the struggle against oppression."[87] That was not what they understood to be radical pacifism.

Pacifists were further divided in July, when a number of U.S. peace leaders, including Dr. Spock, Sidney Lens, Homer Jack, Alfred Hassler, and David McReynolds, met with four hundred international activists at a World Conference on Vietnam in Stockholm. The meeting was largely a stage for the five representatives of the NLF and North Vietnam: neutralist Buddhists were not even seated. Even so, it made a powerful impact on the Americans precisely because it seemed clear that the communists would negotiate for no less than ultimate victory. Any hope of a middle ground vanished, leaving American participants sobered by a clear choice between war and withdrawal. "Realism is painful," Jack concluded. Both negotiated compromise and a neutral Buddhist "third solution" in South Vietnam were illusory.[88]

Al Hassler, executive secretary of the FOR, clung to the idea of a negotiated U.S. withdrawal all the more firmly. His main concern was for the fate of the South Vietnamese. Hassler and others were very impressed by Buddhist leaders who were promoting a "third solution" in South Vietnam—a coalition of Buddhists and non-communist nationalists who rejected domination by either the U.S. or North Vietnam. Creating a link with the Buddhists had become a major thrust for the FOR. It offered a political expression of Hassler's heartfelt responsibility as a pacifist to condemn the violence of both sides. The FOR sponsored a U.S. and European speaking tour by poet-scholar Thich Nhat Hanh in 1966, and the following year it sponsored the publication of *Vietnam: Lotus in a Sea of Fire* and publicized his poignant book with a foreword by his American Catholic counterpart, Thomas Merton.[89] The Buddhist appealed for his people to be left to their own future, not cast in either a communist or an American mold. As Hassler came to see it during a trip to Vietnam that spring, the United States was so blinded by its determination to set up an anticommunist regime that it was helping to crush the very Vietnamese who could legitimate a noncommunist society in the South. He rejected the war effort unequivocally, but he resisted immediate withdrawal out of a deep concern for the Vietnamese and from a perspective grounded both in Christian pacifism and in the Buddhists' assessment of Vietnamese politics.

Other radical pacifists denied that Americans had a specific responsibility for noncommunist Vietnamese. Rather, they insisted, the first obligation of American peace-seekers was to press Washington for immediate withdrawal, which would allow the Vietnamese to settle their own future. Anything less was inhumanly destructive. Nothing more was politically feasible. Neither pacifists nor militarists in the U.S. could create a viable Vietnam. Dave McReynolds articulated this view. The core of serious peace activism, he insisted, consisted in understanding that "the future of Vietnam must be resolved by the Vietnamese without any further intervention from the outside."[90] Implicitly at least, McReynolds did not take the prospect of arbitrary communist domination as seriously as did Hassler—or the Buddhists. Explicitly, he regarded the "third solution" as another illusion which would only prolong the war and its devastation.

Thus, in their contest with the administration, deeply committed and respected pacifists such as Hassler and McReynolds came to differ over appropriate antiwar goals on fundamental, arguable grounds. Their difference became highly personal, and it was made all more volatile by the explosive national climate and intemperate language on the extreme left. Their clash, and similar arguments among others, cut into the morale and effectiveness of staff members in pacifist organizations. It further distracted the country's small pacifist community, which, in contrast to the militant radicals, felt keenly the poignancy of their limited influence against the enormity of the war. Beyond their differences, McReynolds and Hassler agreed that they were dealing with a "tragedy of psychotic proportion." They felt condemned by history to be living through a human crisis in which no course of action could "avoid containing profound evil, injustice, and violence."[91]

"At least it was something to do"

By the fall of 1967, President Johnson also was anguished and drained. The nation was in turmoil, his great consensus of the center and his vision of a Great Society breaking on the shoals of war. He had worked himself into an impasse from which he saw no escape. He had become ever more isolated as key aides had left in doubt—George Ball, Mc-George Bundy, Jack Valenti, Bill Moyers. On 3 August he had announced that another 55,000 men would be sent to Vietnam and had set a new ceiling of 525,000 GIs by 30 June 1968. The ground war now engaged well over a million men in bloody but inconclusive fighting. There was still no viable, independent regime in the South. American warplanes struck new targets in Hanoi, but controlled escalation had softened the North Vietnamese negotiating position only slightly. On one side the military pressed for an all-out effort, and they were echoed by political hawks, while on the other the Secretary of Defense argued for de-escalation leading to disengagement. The president held on in the center as both war and dissent intensified.

In September, under the combined pressure of domestic crisis and radical initiatives, the organized opposition fragmented still further. This became clear over Labor Day weekend in the first convention of the National Conference for a New Politics. The result of two years of discussion and planning, the meeting brought over 3,000 people from some 372 organizations to the Palmer House in Chicago. It was the largest gathering of the American Left since the 1948 Progressive party convention.

The "New Politics" convention purported to represent "the politics of ordinary people." It would work from the bottom up "to bring new people into politics—housewives into making foreign policy, Negroes into choosing sheriffs and writing laws, Vietnamese and Dominicans into deciding their own future instead of having the great powers decide it for them."[92] Unfortunately, no one knew what the "New Politics" meant in any practical sense. For some it was building a third party around a presidential ticket of Martin Luther King, Jr., and Benjamin Spock. For others it meant community organizing. For a few it implied immediate revolution. For Arthur Waskow, at least, it would put the politics of persuasion and election into a dialectical relationship with street action.

Under the glare of intense media interest, the NCNP opened with a rather pedestrian speech by King, who left the convention soon afterwards. Between plenary sessions the delegates formed caucuses and workshops, dominated by the country's racial crisis and their felt need to draw blacks into a biracial movement for radical domestic change. Indochina appeared to be a minor concern for most delegates, who dismissed it as a *"local issue"* or argued that they had really passed beyond Vietnam and were organizing to stop "the seventh war from now."[93] When a 150-member black caucus demanded that the convention adopt its thirteen-point declaration, which included condemnation of Zionism and immediate reparations to long-suffering American blacks, the meeting erupted in a prolonged floor fight which one observer characterized as "a scene worthy of Genet or Pirandello, with whites masquerading as either poor or black, blacks posing as revolutionaries or as arrogant whites, conservatives pretending to be communists, women feigning to be the oppressed, and liberals pretending not to be there at all."[94] After hours of debate, the majority of delegates caved in and approved the statement. The blacks then issued a new demand: they should receive voting power and official positions equal to that of the large white majority. Pandemonium again swept the convention until a majority of whites once more deferred in the belief that black America really constituted the cutting edge in the domestic drive toward radical change. Emotionally drained, the delegates finally closed the proceedings with a perfunctory set of resolutions that demanded immediate U.S. withdrawal from Vietnam and gave community organizing a higher priority than preparing for the 1968 election. The unreality of the convention was institutionalized three weeks later when a coordinating committee met in St. Louis and established the NCNP as a continuing organization chaired jointly by Dr. Spock and St. Louis black activist James Rollins.

Just after the Palmer House convention, forty antiwar radicals met with North Vietnamese and NLF representatives in Bratislava, Czechoslovakia. The consultation had been organized by the Czechoslovakian Peace Committee through Dave Dellinger and SDS leaders Tom Hayden and Nick Egleson. It drew "a motley cross section of the peace movement, ranging from poor people to ministers, from Dick Flacks to academicians like Christopher Jencks, from *New Republic* editor Andrew Kopkind to long-haired oracles of the underground press."[95] The Vietnamese rejected any suggestion of negotiations prior to U.S. withdrawal, and the Americans endorsed the communist analysis of events, pledging "unquestionable support."[96] Hayden was quoted after the meeting as saying, "Now we're all Viet Cong." If those were his words, they were ambiguous, although clearly he identified the North Vietnamese as victims of war.[97] At Bratislava he gathered a few people he could trust, mostly from SDS, for a trip to Hanoi. He included Rennie Davis because he believed that the experience would elicit from his friend a fuller concern for Vietnam, much as his own trip had propelled him into antiwar activism the year before. His hunch was correct. Hayden's primary mission in Hanoi was, however, to secure the return of some American prisoners of war, perhaps as a precedent for further releases and even to open up the diplomatic process, and in this too he was successful. After long and delicate negotiations, three POWs were released into his custody in Cambodia. During the long flight home he came to identify with them—three more victims of war.

Hayden thought of his venture abroad more as constructive engagement than protest; but, coming as it did on the heels of the NCNP convention, it seemed to defy public opinion and to defer to Hanoi. Both the Chicago and the Bratislava meetings provoked further division within the movement. Pacifists condemned the violent rhetoric at the Palmer House meetings and concluded that the NCNP was irrelevant to peaceful change. Some radicals attacked the convention as nakedly manipulative. Liberals interpreted Bratislava in the same way. It showed that leading leftists cared more about a communist victory than ending the war, wrote an ADA analyst, and they deserved to be recognized as "an obstacle— not an ally—to achieving peace in Vietnam." "It is indeed the worst of times," concluded another liberal: the NCNP was a disgrace to the movement, Bratislava was a humiliation, and there seemed to be no way of rectifying the twin disasters.[98]

The national board of SANE broke apart over both its relationship to Negotiations Now! and Dr. Spock's decision to cochair the NCNP. Several leaders threatened to quit the organization unless the baby doctor was disciplined, but Spock resigned as SANE cochairman first, fed up with what he called SANE's "fuddy-duddy" politics.[99] At the same time, a SANE contingent led by Robert Pickus and Mary Temple tried to merge SANE into the Negotiations Now! campaign which had been run largely from their West Coast office. When that failed, they quit the leadership, complaining that it was dominated by people who were "more anti-Washington than anti-war."[100] Despite losses from the right and the left, the board and its new chairman, H. Stuart Hughes, managed to hold the organization's center together through weeks of highly publicized wrangling. On 19 October, SANE emerged from its internal crisis with a coherent program, as the board encouraged members to support antiwar convention delegates and political candidates on the local level in preparation for the 1968 campaign. It was especially eager to support "the most peace-oriented contender" in the Republican primary battles, because it did not believe a Democratic nominee could defeat Johnson.[101] Liberal strategy was debated in ADA about the same time, and there too the outcome was ruled by the impression that the president commanded the party.

Antiwar liberals were embittered in the fall by a growing realization that the radical left which they resented was, in fact, part of a crisis in

American democracy. Their frustration was at "an absolute high," remembered Sandy Gottlieb.[102] The war only escalated, domestic tensions only sharpened, and nothing they did seemed to mitigate those two realities. A few of them decided to support unilateral withdrawal, concluding with Peter Steinfels that it would be better for the world, the U.S., and Vietnam "to 'lose' this war today . . . than to 'win' it fifteen years from now."[103] Most liberals still resisted immediate withdrawal; but they agreed that the issue was less Vietnam and more, in Norman Cousins' words, the American people's "moral reputation in the world and with their own institutions." Seymour Melman of SANE agreed: "[the] American issue is not the Vietnam war itself, but rather the system of policy and institutions which generate Vietnam wars."[104]

Independently of radical convention halls and liberal board rooms, dissent mushroomed. New groups were reported weekly, and now they included Vietnam Veterans Against the War and a few retired military officers, such as former Marine Corps commandant David M. Shoup, Rear Admiral Arnold E. True, Generals Samuel E. Griffiths and Hugh B. Hester, and Air Force General Lauris Norstad. Donald Luce, the director in Vietnam of International Voluntary Services, resigned (as did about a third of his staff) and returned home in order to reach middle-class America.[105] An editor of the *New York Times Magazine* inspired a Writers and Editors War Tax Protest that collected five hundred pledges to withhold a tax surcharge.

Direct action became more frequent in the streets. At least 110 public vigils took place weekly during the fall, from Miami, Florida, to Everett, Washington. Most people politely carried placards and issued leaflets to express their feelings, but some employed guerrilla theater to shock onlookers with reminders of Vietnam's everyday suffering. New federal regulations attempting to control demonstrations outside the White House were defied by a WSP group of more than 600 middle-class women who clashed with police. Again there were the stark, lonely immolations: in San Diego a thirty-six-year-old Buddhist woman, Hiroko Hayashi; in Los Angeles a fifty-five-year-old peace activist and mother of two, Florence Beaumont. She was "quite sane," Beaumont's husband told reporters, "but couldn't stand to live any longer under this thing."[106]

Popular discontent was reflected in institutional politics early in the fall. Michigan governor George Romney expressed his preference for a negotiated settlement, saying that he had been "brainwashed" into supporting administration policy during his earlier visit to Vietnam. The liberal Republican Ripon Society and a few GOP senators came out against further escalation. For the most part, however, disaffection was channeled through the Democratic party. Independent groups supporting antiwar candidates appeared in California, across the Midwest, and into Northeast. In Minnesota, the Young Democratic-Farmer-Labor Organization split from the national Young Democratic Clubs over the war. Robert Kennedy distanced himself still further from the White House. Congressman Morris Udall (Ariz.), a liberal Democrat, joined the congressional critics in October, and he reported strong constituent support. Indeed, politicians were noting shifts in public opinion that month. The number of people approving of Johnson's conduct of the war fell to a new low of 31 percent, while a record high 41 percent termed the war a mistake.[107] Moreover, analysts reported, people were increasingly doubtful about the value of further military efforts.[108] The "painless, nonsacrificial phase" of the war was over, explained Walter Lippmann, and the result was an increasingly virulent popular resentment toward increased taxes, draft calls, and inflation.[109]

The dissent that autumn ranged from opinion to protest, from demonstration to rebellion, and it was often keyed to draft resistance. In September, CALC announced a campaign to enlist people of all faiths in support of young draft resisters. The next month it released a "Statement of Conscience and Conscription" which acquired thirteen hundred signatures by February 1968.[110] Draft-counselling centers were organized by sympathetic clergy and lay people. Twenty-six prominent Catholic intellectuals jointly pronounced the war unjust and declared that Christians were "morally obliged to actively search out ways to oppose this war, through personal action, political pressure, and, if necessary, civil disobedience."[111] *Look* magazine carried an article by Protestant theologian Robert McAfee Brown, who reached the same conclusion. The American war effort was "evil, vicious and morally intolerable," Brown maintained, and he promised to counsel and abet draft resistance no matter what the cost.[112] He recalled by analogy the moral numbness of Christians in the face of Nazi Germany.

This was more than rhetoric; important issues were being raised. The ethics of conscientious objection was extended to civil disobedience, as a person's moral responsibility was broadened from withholding participation in military service to actively challenging the lawful organization of a war. In another sense, the grounds for conscientious objection were narrowed from universal principle to political judgment, as a person moved from a refusal to sanction any war to the rejection of this specific war.

The political dimensions of draft resistance were further extended to collective action on 16 October, when the Resistance sponsored a nationwide draft card turn-in designed to help "bring the war machine to a halt."[113] Over 1,100 young men destroyed or turned in draft cards, while female and adult sympathizers issued statements of support and complicity. In Boston, for example, 4,000 people attended an interfaith service at the Arlington Street Church where, following remarks by William Sloane Coffin and others, 87 men burned their cards over an altar candle and some 200 others turned theirs in. Smaller demonstrations were held in Cincinnati, at Philadelphia's Independence Hall, and at fifteen other regional centers across the country. Symbolic demonstration became a political statement, as a thousand individual witnesses added up to a collective act. Interpreting the action in Boston on the NBC-TV news, John Chancellor observed solemnly, "If men like this are beginning to say things like this, I guess we had all better start paying attention."[114]

In Oakland, the commitment to nonviolent personal disobedience which animated the Resistance gave way to undisciplined collective action and mob violence. On Tuesday, 17 October, about 3,500 radicals tried to shut down the army induction center after some 120 nonviolent resisters had been arrested there the previous day. Oakland police responded with an attack that hospitalized over 20 people. The Berkeley community was inflamed, and on Friday, 10,000 protesters confronted 2,000 Bay Area policemen at the center, provoking a melee that spread violence over a twenty-block area of downtown Oakland.[115] Meanwhile, 60 people were injured in Madison, Wisconsin, when a battle erupted between police and students protesting university war-related contracts and on-campus recruiting by Dow Chemical corporation. Within the movement the advocates of violence were widely accused of "delusions of grandeur, *machismo* posturing, even fascism," but the so-called mobile tactics of the Oakland riot became briefly legendary among militants.[116] Heady with the excitement of street action but reluctant to promote a bloodletting, radical leaders equivocated, talking about "nonviolent terrorism," or "unviolence," or "renunciation of nonviolence while still shrinking from a positive recommendation of violence."[117] In the charged atmosphere of the fall, those were arcane, obfuscating distinctions.

Inevitably, the spirit of disruptive disobedience permeated preparations for the 21 October March on the Pentagon which was also billed as "Confront the Warmakers." While the government and Mobe officials wrangled over arrangements for the demonstration through September, radical pacifists threatened that "the peace movement has developed a strong backbone and means to fight," and hippies dreamed about levitating the Pentagon and exorcising the demons in it or conducting "loot-ins" at nearby department stores.[118] Worried by irresponsible rhetoric, SANE, SDS, and WILPF declared that they would neither endorse nor repudiate the October action, and antiwar military veterans and religious leaders hotly reminded leftist militants that the Mobilization was a coalition formed to help end the war in Vietnam, not to begin revolution in America. Mobe leaders were briefly chastised. They softened their language, dropped inflammatory figures such as Rap Brown from the list of scheduled speakers, and agreed that participants would have a range of alternative actions from which to choose. WILPF came on board at the last moment.

Ground rules for the demonstration were agreed upon by early October. Innumerable details were worked out by Maris Cakers of the Workshop in Nonviolence and Brad Lyttle of CNVA. Excited protest leaders finalized plans for a mass demonstration on the Mall and either civil disobedience or outright resistance at the Pentagon. On the other side, the government ordered up six thousand federal marshals and troops, including contingents of the Eighty-second Airborne Division (which most recently had undertaken counterinsurgency operations in the Dominican Republic and Detroit). For the first time since the 1932 Bonus March, the federal government called upon its armed forces to protect the capital from its own citizens.

It all began quietly enough. The first of an estimated hundred thousand dissidents filtered into the Washington area on Friday, 20 October. In the afternoon a few went to the Justice Department, where William Sloane Coffin and members of the Resistance engaged in a bizarre exchange with officials who refused to accept a collection of turned-in draft cards for fear of being accomplices in a criminal action. At an evening fund-raising program in the Ambassador Theater, Norman Mailer swaggered through a speech and Robert Lowell whispered some readings. That night, dissidents scattered to thousands of homes where parents of young people such as David Bruce (whose father was the U.S. ambassador to Great Britain) and Mary McCarthy (whose father was a senator from Minnesota) lent not only their homes but their hearts and minds as well.

Late the next morning, a throng assembled at the Lincoln Memorial for the largest antiwar demonstration yet held in the capital. The weather was sunny and mild, reflecting the crowd's disposition. Children played. The Bread and Puppet Theater performed. Phil Ochs sang, as did Peter, Paul, and Mary. Rennie Davis displayed a fragmentation bomb he had obtained in Hanoi. There were interminable speeches. People visited friends from protests past. Families became separated. First-time visitors got lost. Mostly young and overwhelmingly white and middle-class, the crowd milled about in a spirit that suggested the carelessness of a summer picnic. Still, some people felt uncomfortable. "I'm not a marcher," recalled one demonstrator. "I'm not a marcher at all. I couldn't bear the idea of marching; but I did it. I mean, at least it was something to do—this horrible war had to be stopped!"[119]

At 1:30 P.M., under the cover of army helicopters and following a huge "Support Our GIs, Bring Them Home Now!" banner, some fifty thousand protesters walked slowly to the Arlington Memorial Bridge, across it, and into the north parking lot of the Pentagon. There the march broke down. The greatest number of people either milled about or sat down in the parking lot; but a group from New York calling itself the SDS Revolutionary Contingent rushed the building, and a number of militants tried to run up some service ramps, where they were repulsed by military police.

Without leadership or direction, most demonstrators became involved in sincere but aimless efforts. Some tried to win the troops over with talk of "flower power" and generational solidarity, or courted peaceable arrest. People sang, shrieked, or went limp in the arms of arresting federal marshals. A few cursed or flung missiles at the soldiers over the heads of front-line demonstrators. Troops responded in force, and protesters retreated, sometimes caught in clouds of tear gas, shaken by the very nakedness of the power that they had provoked. Well-meaning activists were stunned: "Did you ever suddenly realize that you were something your government needed protection against? Perhaps the first thing you do is laugh at the absurdity, the second is ask yourself why, the third is stop laughing."[120]

Early in the evening, a number of leaders, including Dellinger, Lyttle, and Noam Chomsky, committed civil disobedience by entering a proscribed area. They were arrested peaceably and trundled into waiting buses for shipment to jail, leaving Jim Peck to deal with the disorder. Others were arrested with violence. The largest number of demonstrators, uninterested in either civil disobedience or disruptive resistance, drifted back to Washington, while the remaining activists tried to rally their forces. After midnight, government troops and marshals employed classic counterinsurgency tactics to reoccupy the grounds of the Pentagon yard-by-yard—dispersing, arresting, and sometimes beating nonresistant demonstrators in intermittent advances into their ranks. Perhaps 750 protesters managed to remain on the grounds overnight, warmed by fires made from wrecked party chairs. Hardly 250 were left when their demonstration permit expired Sunday night. In all, 647 were arrested and 47 were hospitalized. The Pentagon remained intact and unlevitated.[121]

A few commentators defended the demonstration by noting the diversity of the dissidents, and their sense of sheer desperation, but most columnists, critics, and politicians blasted the demonstrators for vulgarity, violence, and sanctioning communist participation. Robert Kennedy mildly complained that violence was destroying the credibility of legitimate dissent, although he defended the demonstration itself. For NBC-TV commentator David Brinkley, the Pentagon march was "a coarse, vulgar episode by people who seemed more interested in exhibitionistic displays than any redress of grievances"; for Goldwater it was a "hate-filled, anti-American, pro-Communist and violent mob uprising."[122] Three Republican representatives declared that the March had been "cranked up in Hanoi," a view developed as fact by *U.S. News and World Report.*[123] Americans agreed by a three-to-one margin that antiwar demonstrations were "acts of disloyalty against the boys in Vietnam," encouraged the communists to "fight harder," and (by 70 percent) hurt the antiwar cause.[124]

Protests continued, nevertheless, as the year waned. The Reverend Philip Berrigan and three other radical pacifists created a symbolic act of nonviolent civil disobedience on 27 October, when they entered the federal customhouse in Baltimore, poured a mixture of their own and animal blood over draft files, and accepted arrest. A new wave of campus demonstrations was usually but not always disciplined, and there were widespread expressions of citizen dissent.

In mid-November, violence erupted in the streets when SDS activists staged a mass assault against Secretary Rusk's party at an appearance before the Foreign Policy Association in New York. Three weeks later, radical pacifists and student radicals inaugurated an ambitious "Stop the Draft Week" of protests in thirty cities, which resulted in three days of disorder and the arrest of some six hundred people. Hostile demonstrations against the president's appearances were so commonplace and powerful that he was obliged to stay in tightly secured areas. Outraged and frustrated, Johnson condemned protesters for their "storm-trooper tactics." The FBI stepped up its surveillance of dissidents, and the CIA initiated a new operation, Resistance, in order to infiltrate dissident groups and get "an overall picture" of what was happening.[125]

It did not require infiltration to detect spiraling anger and recrimination within the movement. Liberals were as incensed as the president by militant rhetoric and street violence. Wrote Catholic pacifist Jim Forest of the FOR, radicals were quite prepared "to martyr *others*" for the cause, but they only alienated the great body of citizens from antiwar leadership at a time when more and more Americans were losing faith in the administration's policy.[126] Michael Harrington insisted that moral clarity required the movement to work for peace in Vietnam and "not for victory for one side or the other," and ethical realism required it to calculate every action in terms of political effectiveness.[127]

Willfully, militants rejected politics for disruption. "The times tell me," said Carl Davidson of SDS, "what we have to do at this time is to destroy." Looking forward, Jerry Rubin promised that radicals would help "screw up this society" by disrupting the 1968 Chicago Democratic national convention.[128]

The society seemed to be coming apart. The war, poverty, race, and violence were erupting with synergistic power. "I hate the word crisis," wrote *Newsweek*'s Emmett John Hughes, "and yet ... there is a sharp scent of crisis in the American air, spreading and souring. A grim oracle is not yelling the word: a frayed people are feeling the fact. And it is a feeling—a tension in society and a stress among men—not known since the 1930s."[129] It seemed trite to talk of "crisis and gloom," said the

Christian Century. And yet it was "difficult to think of a moment since
the Civil War when such talk was more morally plausible." Lady Bird
Johnson felt that a "sort of poison" was spreading through the foundations of government—what *Time* called a "noxious atmosphere" enveloping Washington. Every day it became plainer, in the view of *Commonweal,* that the American people were destroying not only Vietnam,
but also their own society. That apprehension was seeping into the magazines of the cultural center. *Life* conceded that it was time for a bombing
pause and the *Saturday Evening Post* termed the war "a national mistake."[130]

There is a natural disparity in an open society between the time that
public opinion, or even mood, takes form and the time when it is institutionalized in politics. Normally, the political system provides for this
transition. Since at least 1965, the electoral and legislative channels of
decision-making had provided only a reluctant, partial agency for debate
and discussion of the escalating war in Vietnam. Accurate information
and assessment had been largely unavailable even within the administration. With a few exceptions, official Washington had accepted the merits of the war as a foregone conclusion and the marshalling of public
support as a public relations problem. One consequence of drawing this
conclusion had been the administration's exaggerated claims for military
success. Another was popular frustration.

Dissent and debate over the war had taken place largely outside the
political system—in journals, on college campuses and church pulpits,
and in meeting halls and the streets. The fact that the political process
was not fully responsive to discussion of Vietnam had fueled the antiwar
movement, informally as a constituency of concerned, apprehensive citizens and formally as organizations and loose networks which contended
among themselves. At the end of 1967, organized dissent was sapped by
internecine conflict, rendered trivial by the image of cultural iconoclasm,
and constrained by official charges of disloyalty, so that it was not an
effective agency of debate, even though it promoted and focused national
anxiety. Little wonder, then, that there was a brooding feeling of desperation inside the movement and outside among articulate commentators,
or that there was skepticism about the effectuality of American institutions.

Already, however, the system was beginning to respond. Countless
antiwar activists worked on local levels through the summer and fall,
sometimes in connection with SANE or the ADA but often independently,
to draft antiwar candidates and build peace caucuses for the 1968 party
conventions platforms. If there was a common thread to this activity, it
was provided by Allard Lowenstein and Curtis Gans, who fashioned what
became known as the "Dump Johnson" movement.

Lowenstein had become convinced early in the year that there would be no progress on Vietnam without a new but still Democratic president. If the political system were to work (and he believed firmly that it would), it followed that the Democratic party had to have an alternative to Johnson in 1968. As disaffection with the war spread, a growing number of liberals, especially in the Robert Kennedy circle, agreed with his analysis of the president and the war. They differed on the question of political strategy. Galbraith, Rauh, and others argued that an alternative candidate was required in order to build an anti-Johnson movement within the party, and no one was yet available. Lowenstein argued that an antiwar candidate would respond to the development of a strong demand for one.

With little encouragement from the liberal leadership, he and Gans pursued their notion of market-driven politics. The Campus Coordinating Committee was converted into ACT-68 to reach out to young people. More important, the two men crisscrossed the country to speak and orchestrate intraparty dissent. By August, Lowenstein had identified funding sources which enabled Gans to leave ADA and start a Conference of Concerned Democrats. They built constituency lists, largely from signatures on published antiwar petitions. They enlisted a student cadre from the NSA and put it to work organizing precincts and campuses. They sponsored rallies and more speaking tours. And all the while they badgered leaders such as Kennedy and McGovern to respond to the demand they were organizing.

In September the ADA board was badly split on political strategy. Lowenstein tried to get an explicit repudiation of Johnson's 1968 candidacy, but Rauh, Galbraith, and Schlesinger effectively countered with a proposal to organize a peace caucus at the Democratic convention. Gus Tyler and John Roche gleefully exploited their differences. Nonetheless, the demand for alternative leadership grew through the fall. Polls showed the president's political appeal behind Kennedy's. Political constituencies weighed in against Johnson, including local ADA chapters and dissident Democratic factions in a number of states, notably California. In November, middle-echelon labor leaders met in Chicago in the first National Labor Leadership Assembly for Peace, where Norman Thomas called on them to unite for political action against the war (it was Thomas's last public speech, for he suffered a stroke on the way home and died a year later). Still searching for a candidate who would respond to the market for change but still being rebuffed by a number of senators, including Kennedy and McGovern, the Dump Johnson crusaders finally persuaded a droll, ex–college professor and poet named Eugene McCarthy to take on the president in a few selected primaries.

After weeks of dodging reports of his availability, Senator McCarthy held a Washington press conference on 30 November and declared that he would contest the president for the Democratic presidential nomination in a campaign that promised to fix limits on the U.S. military commitment in Vietnam and seek a negotiated way out of the conflict. With a liberal reputation despite some conservative instincts, McCarthy declared that the war had become politically and morally disproportionate in its costs and therefore should be concluded. Vietnam represented only one factor in a "configuration" of problems that was inspiring a generalized "sense of political helplessness" and violent alienation, the Minnesotan contended.[131] He would address them all. Reserved and deliberate, McCarthy was hardly prepared to break away from the Cold War creed of liberal America. He opposed immediate U.S. withdrawal, favored an enclave strategy, and assumed the importance of America's global commitment to containment. Nonetheless, McCarthy alone offered a political alternative to Lyndon Johnson, and simply on that ground he attracted thousands of antiwar and social cause supporters.

Pundits seemed stunned. Antiwar liberals lauded McCarthy as a politician of singular courage to be willing to challenge an incumbent president for renomination. It had not been done in twentieth-century American politics. Actually, they believed that there was little choice. The expected contest between Johnson and Nixon—both viewed as prowar— would confirm the inability of the electoral system to provide an alternative to the prevailing drift, they feared. Given the pervasive spirit of violence and confrontation, the lack of an alternative could prove disastrous. McCarthy's candidacy offered antiwar citizens fresh hope, a cause worth championing. Few believed that he would gain the party's nomination, but the campaign offered something to do. Moreover, reflected the *Nation,* after nearly three years of war and racial violence, there was "a dimension of uncertainty about the present mood of the American electorate" which suggested that "almost anything *might* happen in 1968."[132]

Eight

Turning a Corner

A Test of Will and Purpose

Doubt, if not despair, was etched in Robert McNamara's spirit during the fall of 1967. It was not a failure of nerve. It was a question of purpose. The secretary of defense was torn between loyalty to his commander-in-chief and his own patriotic and professional responsibility. Throughout the year he had chafed over the bombing campaign and recommended changes in war policy. In August he had testified publicly to the Senate's hawkish Armed Services Committee that an escalation of the air war on North Vietnam would be illusory and futile. His view was rejected by the committee, but McNamara was in a position to know, and he had no vested interest in contradicting his president or his military. Exhausted and dispirited, he worked on in anguished ambivalence until the end of November, when his nomination to the World Bank was announced and it became plain that he had joined the silent opposition to the administration's policy. By that time some five hundred newsmen in Vietnam were exposing contradictions between the official accounts and the reality of the war. Roving the battlefields and the countryside, with access to Vietnamese intellectuals as well as American soldiers, they were reporting that the war was not going well.

The president would have none of it. Discounting press reports from abroad as biased and uninformed, he summoned the nation to persist. Discounting internal dissent as the work of an obstreperous minority, he welcomed the backlash that followed the October march on the Pentagon and subsequent disruptive antiwar demonstrations. The public seemed to be saying that "if this is what opposition to the war means, then count me out," Louis Harris would report in February.[1] White House insiders agreed already in November that "one of the few things that helps us right now is public distaste for the violent doves."[2]

That was a hasty conclusion. There was no evidence that public anger with the dissidents translated into outright support for the president or the war. Indeed, aside from a very few counterdemonstrations on 21 October, there was a noticeable lack of prowar enthusiasm. The usual hecklers were absent at the march on the Pentagon, and dissidents in smaller towns reported a marked decrease in overt hostility. It was "quite a striking thing to see," reported Harrison Salisbury. Following his December 1966 visit to North Vietnam, he had spoken in various parts of the country, fielding hostile questions and weathering personal attacks. By the fall of 1967, however, these criticisms "practically vanished," he observed, as though huge chunks of the American body politic had simply pulled away from the administration and its war.[3] In Washington, Under Secretary of the Air Force Townsend Hoopes sensed silence on the right, which he interpreted as "the first real evidence of a consequential shift in public sentiment on the war."[4] People had little use for antiwar protesters, but they also had less and less interest in waging Washington's war. *Good Housekeeping* concluded from a poll of its readers that women desperately wanted a "quick and final solution," preferably through military pressure.[5] George Gallup concluded that the American people wanted out. Their preferred exit was to turn the war over to the South Vietnamese, even though only 25 percent of the public believed that the Saigon government was strong enough to stand on its own after a U.S. withdrawal.[6]

The president understood the importance of public opinion. "Our biggest problem," he told a reporter, "is not with Ho and with the fighting out there. It's with our situation here. It is leading the enemy to believe that we might quit."[7] With public support fading and the military situation a stalemate, the administration launched a major effort to sell the war as a success and to discredit the antiwar movement.

On the eve of the March on the Pentagon, Secretary of State Rusk announced that the White House had secret evidence that the antiwar movement was communist-controlled. Shortly afterwards, the president arranged news leaks, including a meeting with a small bipartisan group from Congress on 24 October, intended to suggest that the CIA had documentary proof of the movement's communist sources. Itching to seize the offensive against his critics, the president met with his closest advisors on 4 November and ranted: "I'm not going to let the Communists take this government and they're doing it right now. . . . I told the Attorney General that I am not going to let 200,000 of these people ruin everything for the 200 million Americans. I've got my belly full of seeing these people put on a Communist plane and shipped all over this country. I want someone to carefully look at who leaves this country, where they go, why they are going, and if they're going to Hanoi, how are we going to keep them from getting back into this country."[8]

As the president well knew, his own security agencies had been looking carefully at the antiwar movement and its international connections. The FBI had been engaged in surveillance (and sometimes harassment) of dissidents for two years, and the CIA had begun to penetrate Washington-area peace groups in February 1967 through a proprietary company related to its Project Merrimac. In September the CIA had intensified its surveillance of the antiwar movement in a program aptly called Operation Chaos. Investigation concentrated initially on the Pentagon march and on international connections of organized protest. It turned into the CIA's most massive intrusion into domestic American politics—a seven-year campaign that monitored (and sometimes disrupted) over 1,000 organizations and 200,000 individuals while claiming a priority status equal to that of the Agency's spying on the Soviet Union.

On 15 November, CIA director Richard Helms submitted a preliminary report of this investigation to the president. The CIA team concluded at the outset that the antiwar movement was so diverse that it could not be characterized by any specific political or ideological labels. The CIA judged, moreover, that the leaders of the movement *"have close Communist associations but they do not appear to be under Communist direction."* More precisely, the report drew two key conclusions:

On the basis of what we now know, we see no significant evidence that would prove Communist control or direction of the U.S. peace movement or its leaders.

Most of the Vietnam protest activity would be there with or without the Communist element.[9]

The president refused to release this report, although pressed to do so by House minority leader Gerald Ford who, as a result of the president's private briefing, had claimed publicly that the October march was "cranked up in Hanoi." Instead, the administration continued to denigrate the antiwar movement as communist-inspired.

Meanwhile, on 2 November, Johnson brought to the White House a group of so-called Wise Men who had periodically advised him on the war since the summer of 1965 and asked them to review U.S. policy in light of the special need to rally a consensus at the center. The president's consultants concurred in his war strategy, and they agreed that "the principal battleground is in the domestic opinion," but they were at a loss to prescribe ways of building popular backing for the long haul ahead. General Omar Bradley blamed the media and a lack of patriotic slogans for the lagging public support, and diplomat Robert Murphy wanted to generate "a hate complex" against Ho Chi Minh and the North Vietnamese. In the end, however, the Wise Men agreed that "the single most serious cause of domestic disquiet about the war" was "the prospect of endless inconclusive fighting" that remained the core of prevailing administration strategy and Washington's only formula for success.[10]

With that in mind, they proposed that Johnson undertake two concurrent strategies. They suggested that in the short run the administration emphasize military progress and the "'light at the end of the tunnel' instead of the battles, deaths and danger." For the long haul, they proposed that the "only effective way of changing public attitudes at home" was "a redirection of strategy and emphasis" in the war to "make it plain that we are over the hump" in Vietnam and establish "a pattern of gradually decreasing cost that would be endurable for the *five or ten years*" that were required for victory. "If one thing is more clear than another," explained McGeorge Bundy, "it is that we simply are not going on at the present rate for that length of time, and since I think the Communists have proved more stubborn than we expected at every stage, I think that sooner or later we are going to have to find a way of doing this job that is endurable in cost for a long pull."[11] Paradoxically, Bundy and the other Wise Men endorsed the prevailing war strategy, but they could not suggest how to win the domestic struggle except by altering the strategy itself. Richard Nixon would adopt a long-term approach in line with what Bundy proposed, and he would call it Vietnamization.

Looking to the short run, the Johnson administration attempted to persuade the American people to hold tough for a victory in the offing. An interagency coordinating committee arranged for favorable news reports. White House aides assembled a group of prominent Americans in the Citizens Committee for Peace with Freedom in Vietnam in order to rally "the largely 'silent center'" behind the president, and they tried to sabotage the organizing efforts of antiwar liberals, especially in ADA.[12] U.S. Ambassador Ellsworth Bunker and General Westmoreland were brought to Washington in order to reassure the country that the end of the war was beginning "to come into view."[13] The president took off on a show-stopping, round-the-world trip late in December, attending the funeral of the Australian prime minister, carrying holiday greetings and official reassurance to U.S. troops in Korea, Thailand, and Camranh Bay in South Vietnam, and visiting the pope in Rome—all in an attempt to emphasize his confidence in the war's imminent and successful end. "The enemy is not beaten," Johnson declared on his return to the U.S. two days before Christmas, "but he knows that he has met his master in the field," and was clinging only to the hope "that our Nation's will does not match his will."[14]

On the other side, Arthur Schlesinger, Jr., had written in *The Bitter Heritage* that the problem was precisely to secure the *administration's* "will" to change its policy.[15] Richard Goodwin's *Triumph or Tragedy* and John Kenneth Galbraith's *How to Get Out of Vietnam,* were variations on the same theme, a kind of prolegomenon to the search for a Democratic candidate willing to extricate the country from the quagmire. That image, an Asian swamp into which the nation had almost inadvertently stumbled, had been established by David Halberstam even before the bombing campaign, and it dominated liberal criticism. Burdened with a Niebuhrian respect for the complexity and obscurity of events, many liberals had concluded with Schlesinger that the time had come "to decide," to yield in the interests of a stable democracy. Although they still advocated the middle course of negotiation, they urged the "resolute and courageous liquidation of unsound positions."[16] Going beyond the liberal intellectuals, and shifting from policy considerations to moral imperatives, the *New York Review* writers emphasized will, asserting that the role of the intellectual as custodian of morality was at stake. By making Vietnam ever more a test of will, both the president and his opposition had set the stage for confrontation in 1968.

More than will, purpose was at stake, although that fact would be obscured for another half dozen years. By the fall of 1967, a great deal of expertise had been marshalled to demonstrate that the administration's unrelenting analysis of Vietnam was wrong and that its policy was counterproductive. About the time the president left on his world tour, a conference of scholars and former ranking government officials was convened by the Carnegie Endowment for International Peace, the conservative fifty-eight-year-old dowager of the American peace movement. The consultants agreed that the national interest was not served by escalating the war, that bombing should be halted unilaterally, and that the NLF should be recognized in South Vietnamese politics. Similar advice came from Asian specialists: the very point of American policy in Vietnam was mistaken.[17]

New voices were raised with the new year. Nine leading religious journals issued a joint statement protesting administration policy and calling for peace. Six retired U.S. military command officers publicly urged de-escalation. Four sailors from the carrier *Intrepid* jumped ship in Yokohama, requesting political asylum for their antiwar views. Leonard Bernstein and Barbra Streisand opened a show called *Broadway for Peace '68* to raise money for antiwar congressional candidates. Dave Dellinger, Daniel Berrigan, and Howard Zinn travelled to Hanoi in order to escort three released Air Force prisoners of war home. Over five thousand women responded to a WILPF call and gathered across from the Capitol in the bitter cold of 15 January to cheer the protest of Jeannette Rankin, the eighty-seven-year-old Montana feminist who, as a member of Congress, had voted against the U.S. declarations of war in 1917 and 1941 (the latter time as a minority of one).[18] Three days later, in the warmth of the White House, singer Eartha Kitt stunned a meeting of leading American women by confronting Mrs. Johnson and attacking the war for wrecking the hopes of a generation of young Americans. The White House did not get the point. What disturbed Mrs. Johnson's social secretary was that Kitt had been cleared by the FBI without any record that she was either a "peace marcher" or engaged in "peacenik activity."

Dissenters were indiscriminately lumped together as peaceniks and dismissed out of hand.[19]

The next month CALC gathered over two thousand people in Washington for rallies, workshops, a prayer vigil in Arlington National Cemetery, and congressional lobbying. These events were organized around a four-hundred-page study of American military conduct in Vietnam, entitled *In the Name of America*. Seymour Melman had supervised the research, which amply documented the deterioration of moral standards of conduct and increasing violations of international law and complemented an earlier book edited by Richard A. Falk, *The Vietnam War and International Law*.[20] In May and November, the United States had been condemned for violating international law, not to say human decency, in inquiries held in Stockholm and Copenhagen under the auspices of the Bertrand Russell Peace Foundation. The Russell tribunal, as it was called, detailed the use of defoliants, napalm, phosphorous, and fragmentation bombs. Again, references to genocide and the Nuremberg trials appeared: the Eichmann motif, but this time prominently in the context of world opinion. In the United States the Russell tribunal was challenged, even by radical pacifists, because its inquiry was one-sided and relied heavily on North Vietnamese documentation. The CALC study, in contrast, employed impartial sources. Moreover, it was distributed to each senator and got significant newspaper coverage.[21]

The administration meanwhile intensified its attack on antiwar critics on 5 January, when the Justice Department announced in Boston that a grand jury had indicted Dr. Spock, William Sloane Coffin, Marcus Raskin, Harvard graduate student Michael Ferber, and novelist Mitchell Goodman on charges of conspiring to counsel young men to violate federal draft laws. The news came as a surprise to the defendants, none of whom really had known the others previously. Briefly, the antiwar movement pulled together. Martin Luther King, Jr., Dwight Macdonald, Linus and Ava Pauling, and many other sympathizers jointly released a statement of complicity with those under indictment. SDS, the Resistance, and other antiwar radicals sponsored demonstrations in their defense, while officials from SANE and the FOR announced their support. In apocalyptic tones typical of the times, theologian Harvey Cox predicted that the government was "now ready to stop at nothing," and radical pacifist Martin Jezer argued that the forthcoming trial would produce "a moral and political confrontation" that would finally force the American people to choose Johnson and war or the antiwar movement and peace.[22]

In this test of will, the administration continued to paint a bright picture: General Westmoreland declared that enemy forces were fading fast; the American official in charge of pacification asserted that two-thirds of the South Vietnamese lived in secured areas; and Ambassador Ellsworth Bunker said that prospects for an American victory were as good as he had ever seen them. The president reiterated the theme that his strategy was working and victory was around the corner.

Political dissent seemed to be muted. Senator Robert Kennedy, the rival that the White House most greatly feared, declared that, in spite of his differences with the president, he was prepared to support Johnson in the forthcoming elections. Senator Fulbright and the Senate Foreign Relations Committee, dissuaded by the White House from conducting a broad-ranging inquiry into America's Asian policies, instead undertook an investigation of the Tonkin Gulf crisis. Both Morse and Gruening kept up a drumfire of opposition; but they were easy to contain. So too, apparently, was Eugene McCarthy. Trailing by 63 to 17 percent in the first Democratic presidential preference poll, the Minnesota senator failed to gain ground in December or January. He had little support from other antiwar members of Congress, and less from party regulars. It was not much of a campaign. McCarthy even failed to enter the New Hampshire primary until early January, and then his efforts were so lackluster that he alienated and demoralized several backers. Low on funds and fast losing energy, McCarthy's campaign was reeling.

Americans seemed to be getting the administration's message. Polls indicated that they favored escalation over a military letup (if that were the choice) by a margin of 63 to 37 percent, a record approval for administration policy, and again the largest number of those polled hoped to force a successful settlement, if not an outright victory.[23] The president seemed to have a strong consensus in the political center. If the war were to be determined by the will of the American people, he was well positioned.

The people were willing, but they were not purposeful in this war. Only as long as the president could evoke the hope that his policy would yield a successful conclusion, it seemed, would he have their support. That hope was shattered at the end of January, changing the political scene in the United States and transforming the antiwar movement.

On the eve of Tet, the Vietnamese lunar New Year, 30 January, communist forces launched a major offensive throughout the South, attacking thirty-six of South Vietnam's forty-four provincial capitals and five of its six largest cities. Their troops even broke into the $2.3 million American embassy in Saigon, supposedly guerrilla-proof. At first the U.S. command believed that the offensive was a diversion intended to distract attention from Khesanh in northwestern South Vietnam, where 6,000 marines were defending a garrison astride the Ho Chi Minh trail. Then, regrouping and calling for fresh troops, U.S. military leaders organized a month-long counteroffensive that drove the communists out of the areas they had just taken. But American and South Vietnamese forces remained in a defensive position which had been won at enormous cost: dead were some 40,000 communist troops, over 1,100 Americans, and about 2,300

South Vietnamese soldiers; a million civilians fled as refugees and at least 12,000 were killed, including perhaps 3,000 who were massacred by Vietcong forces at Hué. Tet wrecked Saigon's pacification program and created new problems for an already overburdened regime. The size and ferocity of the offensive shattered the credibility of the Johnson administration, which had insisted for two months that the enemy was in disarray. As the U.S. counteroffensive proceeded, Westmoreland declared that the enemy had suffered a major defeat during Tet; but even Lyndon Johnson rejected the general's contention that "North Vietnam is crying for peace because of battle wounds."[24]

The president called upon Americans to meet the new communist challenge with determination. Congressman L. Mendel Rivers (D-S.C.) urged the use of even nuclear weapons to win the war, a position reportedly shared by a quarter of the people surveyed. ABC-TV news commentator Howard K. Smith and prowar newspapers including the *Chicago Tribune* and the *New York Daily News,* also pressed for more military pressure on North Vietnam. Initially, the people seemed to support more aggressive air and naval attacks on North Vietnam. They were shocked by the size and surprise of the offensive, however: it sharply contradicted the administration's previous assurance that the communists were under control. Moreover, disturbing new images tumbled out of the bitter fighting. The desperate battle at Khesanh was virtually serialized on TV. The picture of Saigon's police chief meeting a hand-tied youth identified as a Vietcong officer in the center of a battle-strewn street, raising his pistol, and firing point-blank into the man's head was etched into public consciousness. A U.S. Air Force officer explained that bombers had levelled the town of Bentre after it was occupied by Vietcong troops because it was necessary "to destroy the town in order to save it."[25] In a phrase, the airman confirmed the rationale which for two years antiwar dissidents had claimed lay behind the war. Grieved the *Christian Century,* "This is the genius of our war effort—to destroy Vietnam in order to save it. This is the logic of men maddened by murder. We have all been made murderers."[26] These incidents renewed questions about the credibility of the American and South Vietnamese governments and the morality of their campaign.

Increasingly, articulate voices such as those of the *Wall Street Journal, Life* magazine, and CBS-TV newsman Walter Cronkite concluded that it was time to deal with the war as a political and not a military problem. Robert Kennedy delivered his most bitter attack on administration policy. Silence was telling, too: Nelson Rockefeller declined to comment on the war issue; and Richard Nixon, after criticizing the administration for not striking hard enough against North Vietnam, began to distance himself from Johnson's war, arguing only that "new leadership" in America would successfully end the fighting in Vietnam.[27]

Liberal critics seized upon the Tet offensive as a way to emphasize the failure and ominous future of Johnson's strategy of escalation. Seeking an alternative, former University of California president Clark Kerr and Harvard University sociologist Daniel Patrick Moynihan used the established Negotiations Now! network to fashion a National Committee for a Political Settlement in Vietnam, lobbying for military de-escalation. Other liberals called on Johnson to begin the phased withdrawal of U.S. troops while turning the fighting over to the South Vietnamese, a course of action already popular in America. Still opposed to immediate, unilateral withdrawal, antiwar liberals took advantage of the nation's reaction to Tet to promote negotiations and military disengagement without abandoning Washington's anticommunist allies in the South. It would take them another eighteen months to conclude that they could not square the circle.

In the light of Tet, they were powerfully attracted to the McCarthy campaign. On 27 January, SANE gave the senator its first presidential endorsement. The vote in the national board was unanimous. Two weeks later, on 10 February, the ADA national board endorsed McCarthy's candidacy. The vote was about two-to-one, and endorsement was resisted by some who did not like his record or wanted to keep an option open for Kennedy, and by others who did not want to break with Johnson. It resulted in a few resignations, including three union presidents, but it also led to significant growth in membership and contributions. The ADA's position on the war and especially its endorsement of McCarthy significantly altered its composition, diminishing the influence of labor and adding younger members who challenged even the moderate Galbraith-Schlesinger faction.[28] An initial result of the Tet offensive, therefore, was to bring the war issue into open political debate within established institutions. On one hand, the tenuous balance of influences in the Democratic party was disrupted, making possible an explicit reevaluation of liberalism within the system. On the other, antiwar liberals and pacifists were incorporated into the political process. They lost a certain independent visibility thereby, and they were distanced still further from the radical fringe of the movement which, it became increasingly clear, was more opposed to established institutions than to the war itself.

Late in February a national poll registered for the first time a plurality (of 49 to 41 percent) for the view that troop commitment to Vietnam was a "mistake."[29] McCarthy's New Hampshire primary campaign finally took on life. Fresh money poured in, and cadres of young volunteers manned telephone banks and canvassed door-to-door. Democratic party regulars fought back hard, sometimes casting the challenger as a veritable communist stooge and the primary as virtually a referendum on American patriotism, but on 12 March the senator polled 42.4 percent of the vote. When write-in ballots and Republican crossovers were counted, the result was a stand-off. McCarthy's supporters were ecstatic. "I don't think any of us will ever feel the same kind of joy about bringing down a Goliath or making a point," one recalled. "It was a very aging experience."[30] It was also deceptive. The president got 49.5 percent of the vote as a write-in candidate, and postelection polls indicated that voting did not break down into clear lines on Vietnam policy. Still, McCarthy's achievement in New Hampshire undoubtedly caused waves in American politics. It made the war a bona fide political issue, and it revealed that Johnson was vulnerable.

Scenting that, and having been assured also that Johnson would neither relinquish control nor alter his policy, Robert Kennedy announced on 16 March that he would seek the Democratic presidential nomination on a platform of de-escalating the war and healing domestic divisions. His announcement triggered long-standing liberal resentment toward the apparent opportunism of the Kennedy family and threatened to split antiwar sentiment. Nonetheless, Kennedy, more than McCarthy, did seem to be a dissenter who wanted to win, a Democrat who had a real chance of gaining his party's nomination.

The Dump Johnson campaign had gotten more candidates than it had bargained for, and yet together they attracted the constituency that Lowenstein and Gans had sought to reach—the innumerable citizens who opposed the war or Johnson's handling of it but for whom even SANE was too radical. At the same time, both challengers enlisted the liberal wing of the organized antiwar movement—SANE, Another Mother for Peace (now 25,000 strong), WSP, WILPF, the AFSC, and others. Even Dr. Spock, although still tolerant of the radical left, felt clear that politics and religion offered the best channels of protest that year. Both McCarthy and Kennedy condemned the war as immoral and ill-advised but offered moderate policy alternatives: U.S. military de-escalation, South Vietnamese political reforms, and negotiations among all parties, including the Vietcong. Each restrained his personal criticism of the president. Neither advocated immediate withdrawal. In common, they interpreted Vietnam as the expression of a greater American crisis of spirit and leadership; but they offered two distinct styles of political salvation.

Fiery and visceral, Robert Kennedy campaigned hard in a number of primaries, using his family's money, his brother's memory, and a generation of political contacts to excite support among a remarkable combination of urban ethnics, ghetto blacks, and action-minded intellectuals. The campaign was a projection of the man. It was professionally organized, and it rolled out with the fervor and excitement of an evangelical tent show, ever in motion if not altogether clear about its destination.

The McCarthy campaign was a pole apart. Ice-cube cool, the Minnesota candidate summoned what he called "a constituency of conscience"—

well-educated, suburban middle-class businesspeople and professionals who ordinarily constituted the reform element in local party affairs.[31] His supporters were overwhelmingly adult and included large numbers of Adlai Stevenson Democrats, Jews, and issue-oriented liberals who were concerned not only about Vietnam but also about the declining quality of American life. When, in March, Jerome Grossman became administrative director in Washington, he found the organization "positively Byzantine" in factional intrigue.[32] He pulled it together for a time, but the campaign never did radiate from the candidate. On the contrary, said one close advisor, the aloof McCarthy had little to do with the development of his backbone constituency: "he led it—but he never created it."[33] It flourished like a "mushroom revolution," explained reporter Richard T. Stout. "A lot of little people in a lot of little places were doing a lot of little things."[34] It was a "joyful thing," remembered a Washington State housewife who had canvassed for McCarthy in Nebraska. "I just felt like for once in my life I felt strongly about something, not to be afraid to stand up in front of a group of people and tell them how I feel, and to sit down with people and feel I had something to give that was so important and so valuable."[35]

Even in its earliest stage, McCarthy's campaign was an expression of 1960s grassroots, participatory democracy. Together with Kennedy's, it expanded the political horizon to the extent that the notion of a New Politics was revived. Moreover, it provided a vehicle for the broad shift of public opinion that took place between mid-February and mid-March, when public support for the war shrank from a reported 74 percent to 54 percent, and the ratio of self-designated hawks and doves, once 61 to 23, was suddenly 41 to 42 percent.[36]

In Washington, meanwhile, the Tet offensive precipitated the first basic review of U.S. war policy in three years. The Joint Chiefs requested another 206,000 men for Vietnam, and that set off a crucial debate within the White House over the future of American commitment. Guided by incoming secretary of defense Clark Clifford, a high-level group of civilians and military leaders devoted the first week of March to an intensive review of the troop request. The debate, together with independent studies, convinced Clifford that further escalation would be counterproductive and that unilateral de-escalation leading to negotiations was required. In a separate assessment conducted for the president, Dean Acheson reached the same conclusion by 15 March, the day before Kennedy announced for the presidency. His view was independently seconded by the ambassador to the UN, Arthur Goldberg. Under pressure from Clifford, the president reconvened the group of advisors he had brought together in November, the so-called Wise Men, on 25–26 March. The whole review process was set against the background of the drama of Khesanh, where an isolated and desperate marine garrison was under attack. Although the siege was finally lifted by overwhelming air power, which left some 10,000 communists dead, the nighmarish spectacle permeated the month at the same time that opposition to the war was mounting within Democratic politics.

The presidential advisors concluded that the Pentagon had no strategy for winning the war within reasonable and necessary political boundaries and that American opinion was overwhelmingly against extending the current war strategy. Acheson told the president bluntly, "The Joint Chiefs don't know what they're talking about."[37] Clifford reported that the key people in the country's legal and business establishment were "no longer with us."[38] Moreover, along with other key advisors, he concluded that grassroots American opinion would rebel against throwing any more men into Vietnam unless there was a reasonable indication of imminent success. Indeed, said Cyrus Vance, unless popular impatience was pacified by some new initiative, "the mood in this country may lead us to withdraw."[39] The Wise Men recommended that the president reject the Pentagon's manpower request, de-escalate the war, and seriously seek peace negotiations: "We can no longer do the job we set out to do in the time we have left and we must begin to take steps to disengage," first by stopping the bombing in an attempt to "quieten the situation here at home."[40] The question was not a matter of will, they said; rather, it was a question of national purpose, which an open-ended commitment to war did not serve.

Johnson was initially shocked and angered by the March assessments. They not only revealed a massive defection within his inner circle and in the country as a whole, but they contradicted his whole understanding of the military and domestic situation. Gradually the president let himself be guided by his advisors. Toward the end of March, he denied all but a pittance of the original troop request, eventually establishing a new ceiling of 549,500 troops for Vietnam, and he reassigned Westmoreland. On the last day of the month, the president faced the nation on television. He reviewed the government's actions since Tet and its earlier efforts to negotiate peace. In a further attempt to spur responsible negotiations, he said, he was halting bombing north of the Twentieth Parallel. In closing, he dropped the explosive announcement that he would not accept a presidential nomination in 1968.

The nation turned a corner in Vietnam with Johnson's March address. It did not turn back from the goal of an independent South; it turned aside only from a strategy which had failed to achieve that objective. The administration accepted the paired realities that victory could not be satisfied by a limited war and that neither the national purpose nor public opinion could be satisfied by an open-ended military commitment in Vietnam. In opening negotiations, however, the United States government did not change its original intent. For nearly four more agonizing years, it would both talk and fight, in pursuit of the illusive goal of a bulwark against Vietnamese communism and the redemption of its original purpose. The strategy changed, but the policy—and therefore the central contradiction of the policy—had not altered.

"The war is not over!"

A few critics were quick to point out, in the immediate aftermath of the president's speech, that only strategy, not policy, was changing. I. F. Stone, for one, warned that Washington's decision to shift the burden of fighting to the South Vietnamese simply meant that the White House was trying to win through the peace talks what it had been "unable to win by military means, and that is an 'independent' non-communist South Vietnam."[41] For the next month antiwar activists tried to rouse people to the fact that, as they said, *the war is not over!*[42]

This proved to be a hard message to sell, because the country wanted to believe otherwise. The Resistance held its third national draft card turn-in on 3 April, but it generated fewer resisters than previous ones and little public interest. On 26 April the Student Mobilization Committee sponsored a national student strike involving perhaps a million students, although the organizers ruefully observed that it represented "minimal" commitment, since on many campuses students stayed out of classes without participating in war-related activities.[43] On the next day the National Mobilization Committee gathered over 100,000 people in New York to hear Coretta Scott King, Mayor John Lindsay, and other speakers urge action against a war that was far from over, but the crowd seemed docile if not passive, less interested in politics than in the occasion itself. In contrast to previous protests, with their emphasis on specific issues, this one epitomized the notion of "doing your own thing." It was "a combination of a left-wing Easter parade and a May Day affair where radicals and liberals show their numerical strength," recalled a radical commentator. "Now the antiwar movement is part of the American culture. . . . But the cutting edge of the protest is dulled."[44] In Chicago police fought with demonstrators, but less because of the demeanor of protest than because of the mood of the city's security force.

Within most of America the effect of Johnson's address was to strengthen a general conviction that, for all practical purposes, the U.S. involvement in Vietnam was ending. Trading on the New York Stock Exchange shot to record levels. Public approval of the president's conduct of the war increased from 38 percent to 57 percent following his 31 March address, and criticism subsided inversely.[45]

Americans did not expect peace to break out during the spring of 1968, but they did begin to treat the war as history. In some ways they began to see it less as a matter of fact than as a thing of the past. In this spirit, Richard Nixon aborted well-developed plans to enunciate his election-year position on the war in a major address, and he spent the rest of the year emphasizing the need for new national leadership that would avoid future Vietnams. He spoke of the war mostly in the past tense. Similarly, academic and international experts began to elicit "lessons" from Vietnam, conducting intellectual autopsies on the implied assumption that the issue was quite dead.[46] In a related way, Senator McCarthy and various Protestant clergy began to call for an amnesty for those Americans who had violated draft laws during the war. The amnesty question was important for both substantive and symbolic reasons, but its appearance in the spring of 1968 expressed the prevailing expectation that the war was winding down.

In the archetypical Middle American town of Millersburg, Pennsylvania, a visitor found that the question of what to do about war protesters was more bothersome than the question of the war. It wasn't that Millersburg folk were prowar; that wasn't the issue. The very notion of war protester had come to be synonymous with hippie—"a hairy youth with needle marks on his arm, wearing a blanket and flowers, who is more than likely also a Communist. A hippie does not believe in God, family, private property, good grooming, personal daintiness, Bing Crosby, Bart Starr or almost anything else that Millersburg believes in." People in Millersburg bitterly resented critics who challenged the government's right to make war and conscript men into service, although they tolerated draft avoiders and those who ignored the war. Indeed, many Millersburg citizens suggested that they supported the war because "the war protesters were against it."[47]

Conversely, college students increasingly seemed to assume that the war was wrong without feeling personal provocation. Most of America's 6.7 million college students were, like those at Iowa's Cornell College, acknowledged to be apolitical if not conservative. And yet, when Calvin Trillin visited Cornell during the spring, he found that the students' earlier prowar sentiment, which consisted of unquestioning patriotism and rote obedience to authority, had simply "melted away," as if the students there "began to think about the war and began to oppose the war at the same time."[48] Doubt about Vietnam policy seemed to become more accepted, as did the questioning of authority in general.

Indeed, a record number of college protests were staged in the winter and spring: antiwar teach-ins and marches, protests against ROTC programs, and picketing of recruiters from the CIA and Dow Chemical. Thousands of crosses were planted in the earth at Southern Illinois University and elsewhere to symbolize the war cost already incurred and yet to come. Most demonstrations were peaceful; the exceptions were the best publicized. Arsonists destroyed the naval ROTC building at Stanford, a bomb blast damaged Selective Service offices at Berkeley, and University of Wisconsin students pelted a car carrying draft director Hershey. Still, campus violence was more an expression of rebelliousness over local issues than a protest against the war. Most dramatically, Columbia University was convulsed in a searing struggle among white radicals, black militants, conservative students, and New York City police. The involvement of the local SDS chapter there projected Mark Rudd to prominence in the national organization, and Tom Hayden, who happened to be on campus, found himself in an occupied class building, able to make only a strained connection between the issues at Columbia and the war.

Student uprisings also took place in other countries. Major ones occurred in Poland, and a worker-student revolt disrupted France. A dramatic liberalization movement advanced in Czechoslovakia. Japanese higher education was strained by student activism. "The mood of the questioning has been worldwide," thought John Kenneth Galbraith. "Perhaps not since 1848 has there been anything so universal."[49] It may have been rebellion itself that Millersburg resented. Campus violence was but one aspect of a pattern of social disruption in which Vietnam was only a major contributing factor.

Racial tensions increased sharply with the new year. In the first weeks of 1968, blacks battled police from Tampa, Florida, to El Dorado, Arkansas; black and white gangs clashed in New York City streets; and police and national guardsmen fired point-blank into a crowd of protesting youths in Orangeburg, South Carolina, killing three and wounding forty. In fact, there were ten times as many race-related disturbances in America in the first three months of 1968 as there had been in the comparable period one year earlier, and everyone expected even worse to come. President Johnson warned in February that the country should expect "several bad summers" before it passed through its urban and racial crises.[50] Local authorities were less philosophical. Police in different parts of the country bought up so many antiriot weapons, including armored personnel carriers and chemical mace, that some black leaders charged them with stockpiling "war weapons."[51] In April the SCLC inaugurated a Poor People's Campaign to implement Martin Luther King's appeal for a campaign against poverty, discrimination, and the draining war in Vietnam. A shifting population of demonstrators encamped in a shantytown south of the Lincoln Memorial, making poverty altogether visible in the capital, while King was on the road trying to give form to the campaign. He headed toward Tennessee.

President Johnson almost certainly had in mind the broad pattern of civil disorder as well as division over the war when he told Vice-President Humphrey on 3 April that he had felt compelled to withdraw from the political race because "it was the only way ... to hold the nation to-gether."[52] Martin Luther King, Jr., was assassinated in Memphis the fol-lowing day.

The country erupted in another convulsion of violence. Some 75,000 federal troops and guardsmen joined thousands of local police to contain uprisings in over 110 cities that resulted in 711 recorded fires, the deaths of 46 people, the arrests of 200,000 others, and $67 million in property damage. In recorded racial violence April 1968 was second only to the previous July. Some residents of Washington, D.C., fled the city in the face of the worst disorders in the capital's history. Nashville suffered through five days of seeming guerrilla warfare, and Maryland's Republican gov-ernor Spiro Agnew outraged Baltimore black leaders when he attacked them for not preventing disorders in the city's black ghetto. Chicago's mayor Richard Daley ordered police to "shoot to kill" arsonists on the city's burning West Side. The city's police were still tense from black riots when about 10,000 antiwar demonstrators marched on 27 April, and they contained the protesters with an aggressiveness that left 21 in hos-pitals and another 72 in jail. It was a harbinger of things to come. Hur-rying to contain the national violence, Congress passed a civil rights act intended to outlaw racial discrimination in housing; but it added strict penalties upon anyone convicted of crossing state lines with intent to incite a riot.

In Vietnam, U.S. and allied forces conducted their largest offensive yet, deploying 110,000 men in an early April attempt to clear enemy troops from eleven provinces near Saigon. American losses were 1,100 during the two-week sweep. If the sacrifice was designed to strengthen the U.S. position at the peace talks scheduled to begin in Paris, it was to no avail. Shortly after negotiations between the United States and North Vietnam opened in early May, they broke down over the communists' demand for a total bombing halt and Washington's insistence that Hanoi show prior restraint. With the talks snagged, sharp new fighting broke out in the central highlands and south of the demilitarized zone, even as U.S. forces prepared to evacuate Khesanh, territory that Washington had pledged six months earlier to defend to the last. Within weeks, the Pentagon reported that fighting in Vietnam had achieved two records: the number of U.S. combat losses in Indochina exceeded those in Korea, and the Vietnam War surpassed the War of Independence as the longest in U.S. history.[53]

American pacifists mirrored the antiwar movement in the late spring of 1968, torn over how they might truly end the war and rebuild a divided America. Liberal pacifists in the AFSC supported electoral action against the war, although some regional leaders cooperated in demonstrative protest. In the FOR, Al Hassler continued to promote a "third solution" for Vietnam, although he was not optimistic, while Ron Young and others on the staff wanted more direct action and supported immediate withdrawal. Dave Dellinger joined political radicals in trying to fuse the youth and black liberation movements into a cutting edge for revolutionary change. Dave McReynolds, Stewart Meacham and others tried to find a responsible radical thrust, one that would not backfire in a conservative reaction. A handful of radical pacifists carried their understanding of nonviolent direct action to civil disobedience.

On 17 May, the brother-priests Daniel and Philip Berrigan and seven confederates entered a draft board near Catonsville, Maryland, removed 400 draft files to a nearby parking lot, and burned them with a homemade napalm concocted from instructions in a U.S. Army Special Forces manual. In a statement released after their arrest, the Catonsville Nine justified their action on the grounds that "some property has no right to exist" and mocked those who would attack them for their excessive zeal: "Our apologies, good friends, for the fracture of good order, the burning of paper instead of children, the angering of the orderlies in the front parlor of the charnel house. We could not, so help us God, do otherwise."[54] Conducted with guerrilla-like precision, the Catonsville action precipitated a quarrel over the propriety of even symbolic violence. Catholic theologian Rosemary Reuther criticized the Berrigans for practicing a political perfectionism that alienated more people than it attracted. Both Hassler and McReynolds agreed. The militant pacifists, for their part, could see no other way to dramatize the immorality of devastation waged without ethical purpose. A week after their raid, a federal judge sentenced Philip Berrigan to eighteen years in prison for pouring blood on draft files eight months earlier in Baltimore, and the venerable Dorothy Day wrote in what she intended to be a consoling letter, "I am convinced that sooner or later we are all going to end in a concentration camp."[55]

The apparent disintegration of the antiwar movement contributed greatly to the despondency of pacifists like Day. The movement itself was turning a corner, its direction hard to fathom. The weight of its respective elements was shifting, even among pacifists. Radicals scrapped among themselves as some of them practically abandoned the war. Antiwar liberals became absorbed in electoral politics, counting on the McCarthy and Kennedy campaigns to open prospects for political change.

By the time of the Catonsville action, peace negotiations were under way in Paris. David Halberstam predicted that America was in for a long and "painful period" and that the process of peacemaking would be "far more difficult than even the most pessimistic analysts admitted."[56] Like the journalist, most antiwar liberals realized that diplomacy would be long and difficult, and that the hated fighting would accompany the talking. For the moment, however, they did not know how to react. After three years of agitating, they had negotiations between Washington and Hanoi. Now they had reached the core of the political dilemma: how should American withdrawal relate to the redistribution of power in Vietnam? The great majority of antiwar dissidents still were reluctant to advocate outright withdrawal. With no substantive alternative, and unwilling to face the issue as a clear either-or choice—that was not, after all, their style—antiwar liberals trusted in the political process and, alternatively, Eugene McCarthy or Robert Kennedy.

McCarthy won the Wisconsin Democratic primary two days after Johnson withdrew from the race, and he headed out toward a string of bitter primary fights. Late in April, Vice-President Humphrey announced his candidacy, calling for the end of the war without "humiliation or defeat."[57] A few days later, Kennedy won the Indiana Democratic primary in a victory that was offset shortly afterwards by McCarthy's triumph in Oregon. Running neck and neck, the two raced toward the climactic California primary of 3 June, with Humphrey trailing a poor third. The contest for control of an already badly damaged party sizzled with bitter personal antagonism made worse in the country's general sense of crisis. What counted, however, was the final distribution of votes. When those came in, Kennedy won by a margin of 46 to 42 percent in a further demonstration of his appeal to an unusual cross section of ethnic groups, blue-collar workers, and white suburbanites.

In the early morning hours of 5 June, Kennedy delivered a victory speech to cheering supporters at the Ambassador Hotel in Los Angeles. Minutes later, he was gunned down. Hardly eight weeks after King died in Memphis, yet another advocate of change lay murdered in cold blood, allegedly by a lone gunman, in a crime whose loss extended beyond the victim. This time there were no riots. No disorders. The country sagged in ghastly stillness, as though the last lines of reason had been breached and the people rendered mute. It was unreal, nightmarish. Almost anything could happen in 1968, contemporaries had said.

The Battle of Chicago

The summer campaign became desultory following Kennedy's death, as though a flame had been snuffed out. The campaign did not prove to be an effective vehicle for antiwar activists. For one thing, other issues were pressing, including domestic unrest. On 19 June over 50,000 people played out Martin Luther King's dream of a multiracial movement against poverty, discrimination, and war as they marched in Washington on behalf of the Poor People's Campaign. The society remained short of the dream, and racial tension and violence erupted sporadically during the summer. A presidential Commission on Civil Disorders reported that white racism was at the root of the country's turmoil and warned of the emergence of two Americas: one affluent and white, one black and impoverished. Whether they were expected to deal with fundamental issues or merely to calm the country, politicians were under pressure to address domestic concerns.

Besides, Johnson's withdrawal from the race eliminated a symbolic target for generalized antiwar resentment, and his shift in strategy persuaded the great majority of Americans, including many peace-seekers, that Washington was moving toward an honorably negotiated settlement in Vietnam. Having become an open political issue after Tet, the war was again largely removed from serious debate by the negotiation process, much as in 1959 the test-ban issue had been lifted from American streets and meeting halls to the Paris conference table.

There was a lull both on the battlefield and in the peace negotiations. After devising ground rules for discussions, the diplomats in Paris became locked on substantive issues. The North Vietnamese demanded a total U.S. bombing halt and withdrawal of American support of the South Vietnamese government prior to serious talks. U.S. negotiators demanded that the communists show some sign of military restraint, the withdrawal of all North Vietnamese as well as American troops from South Vietnam, and internationally supervised elections in the South. Fighting in the countryside diminished, and the war became a standoff. North Vietnamese leaders shifted their strategy to prolonged conflict, while the Johnson administration resolved that it would "fight hard and wait" until international and battlefield conditions proved more favorable to an acceptable settlement. At a National Security Council meeting in May, Secretary of Defense Clifford idly scribbled among his notes a portion of an ancient Scottish ballad, which captured the current sentiment of the White House: "I am hurt, Sir Barton said. I am hurt, but I am not slain. Methinks I'll lie me down and bleed awhile, Then rise and fight again."[58]

The administration had at least the luxury of a national acquiescence. Attorney General Katzenbach told the cabinet: "We are in much better shape than any of us could have predicted [in March] . . . We are much better off, with far greater support at home and in the world."[59] Indeed, by August there seemed to be a national consensus for administration's decision to talk and fight. The substantial number of Americans who wanted to intensify the war in order to "get it over with" mainly referred to increased air and naval attacks against North Vietnam. Hardly a quarter of the people expected a settlement at Paris, and by far most anticipated an extended conflict.[60] More and more people were attracted to the idea of phasing withdrawal of U.S. troops in tandem with strengthening the South Vietnamese to defend themselves. Gallup noted that this approach had been the one most consistently favored over the previous two years, and he concluded that it had come to reflect a "rare uniformity of opinion."[61]

That popular preference was reflected on the campaign trails. By June, Richard Nixon, Hubert Humphrey, George Wallace, and Eugene McCarthy emerged as the leading presidential contenders. Their differences on future U.S. policy in Vietnam were nuanced. All opposed immediate withdrawal. All opposed further U.S. manpower commitments and favored a negotiated settlement. Each proposed a strategy by which America might yet hope to preserve an anticommunist regime in Saigon without further draining U.S. resources. Humphrey called for an immediate cease-fire and internationally supervised elections in the South. McCarthy demanded a total bombing halt and negotiations between Saigon and the Vietcong. Even Governor Wallace accepted the need for diplomacy. Nixon was nominated early in August on a platform calling for a negotiated settlement and self-determination. He added his wish that the South Vietnamese should take over more of the fighting. That proposal might have been problematic for Vietnam, but it was popular in America, where two-thirds of the polled electorate said they would vote for a candidate who would bring about the "de-Americanization" of the war.[62] The campaign headed for Chicago.

Antiwar liberals tagged along, their apparent inertia suggested by the image of Dr. Spock sleeping through parts of the great draft conspiracy trial. Judge Francis Ford refused to hear political arguments or statements of conscience, and the so-called Boston Five conducted their cases on technical points of the law. The whole affair became a "4-week chore," as Spock admitted.[63] Neither the trial nor the conviction of Spock, Coffin, Ferber, and Goodman aroused much interest. It certainly looked as though the movement was in a summer lull. A storm was forming, however, out of currents set in motion from the far left and from government security agencies.

Throughout the spring radicals had distanced themselves from liberals, from the war, and from one another. "Opposing the Vietnam war in 1968 is not a radical demand," contended the *National Guardian*. "It is a liberal demand," and quite irrelevant to the work of revolutionary anti-imperialism.[64] In part, that reflected sincere radical analysis: although McCarthy and Kennedy had condemned the war and changed the terms of negotiation, they emphasized gradual extrication from the quagmire rather than outright repudiation of counterrevolutionary interventionism. Partly, too, self-interest was involved. Worried about losing their supporters to the McCarthy presidential candidacy, radicals became more aggressive and provocative, eager to foment disruptive street actions around issues which, as Tom Hayden put it, would not be "co-optable" by liberal politicians.[65] Militancy further distanced the radical left from political reality, though, and aggravated its serious divisions. SNCC collapsed. The Student Mobilization Committee broke apart in bitter personal, racial, and ideological disputes after the April student strike and antiwar demonstrations. There were divisions in the WRL, with which CNVA had merged. The FOR was strained by staff members who advocated coalition with radicals and the policy of unilateral withdrawal, and the Resistance suffered from poor coordination, too few organizers, and defections by men who did not want prison after all.[66] The twenty-year-old *National Guardian* was ruptured in a fight between cultural radicals and old-line Marxists.

Hayden's SDS itself was in shambles. Its leadership was divided between the original New Left and a new coterie of officers, represented by Mark Rudd, who had risen on the strength of his role in the Columbia University confrontation. The new leaders were, in turn, prey to ideological factionalism. After the May Second Movement merged with SDS in 1966, the Progressive Labor people pressed their own agenda, organizing a Worker Student Alliance in 1968 for this purpose. They were fiercely contested by the national officers of SDS, for whom the issue of ideology was a question of control, but the leadership itself had become distanced from local chapters. Those varied greatly. By far most of them were challenging the war in conventional ways. It was in the few locals which had the most influence on the SDS national office—the University of Michigan and Columbia chapters, for example—that there appeared what historian Irwin Unger aptly called "a cult of violence . . . that paraded under the name of action politics."[67] In a kind of symbiotic relationship, these locals and the new national leaders had access to radical left publications and, thence, to the national media. Accordingly, the organization as a whole became invested with a coherent, militant image not at all representative of rank-and-file students. In June, SDS barely sustained a convention in which nihilists, anarchists, and pro-Chinese Progressive Labor cultists battled one another and the few serious New Left radicals remaining.

On the outrageous fringe of radicalism, Jerry Rubin and Abbie Hoffman spawned a Youth International Party of yippies on 16 January 1968, promising to promote the "Politics of Ecstasy" and win the "struggle for personal liberation" through living revolution.[68] The twoscore founders included Rubin's VDC pal, Paul Krassner, Alan Ginsberg, Phil Ochs, Country Joe and the Fish, and the Fugs. Their immediate plan was to lay the counterculture on Chicago in August and overcome war madness with comic relief. What made their party less than playful was its underlying theme. Ochs had described it as "merely an attack of mental disobedience on an obediently insane society. . . . And if you feel you have been living in an unreal world for the last couple of years, it is particularly because this power structure has refused to listen to reason. . . . Step outside the guidelines of the official umpires and make your own rules and your own reality."[69] In March, Rubin and Hoffman fantasized that they would disrupt the Democratic National Convention with a "Political Circus"—replete with sawdust, dancing bears, and a pig that would be nominated for the presidency and then eaten.[70] Doubtless, they would be the clowns. What did all that have to do with the war or an antiwar movement? "There is no such thing as an anti-war movement," Rubin proclaimed. "That's a concept created by the mass media to fuck up our minds. . . . I'm not interested in the so-called anti-war movement—I'm interested in Detroit, Newark, campus disruptions, everyone smoking pot, people learning to speak out and be different." If there were such a thing as an antiwar movement, Rubin would try to destroy it. He was out to teach people how to be liberated, "how to become Vietcong."[71] The yippies were playing games with America. There was a serious side to their sport, however, because in the summer of 1968 the radical left was rent asunder, leaving the extreme fringe with a semblance of form.

Indeed, the militant left crackled with fiery rhetoric and aimless violence. Calling for "power to the people," along with black nationalists, various radicals rebelled against leadership and structure, ricocheting from one action to another without purpose or direction. Hundreds of young people disrupted Vice-President Humphrey's campaign appearances in Los Angeles and Philadelphia, and in Berkeley violence between city police and street people escalated into three nights of major rioting. Militants called it progress.

With the left fast coming apart, radical leaders seized on the Democratic convention as an opportunity to rally their following, revive the demand for immediate U.S. withdrawal, and—a now familiar ploy—to stop "repression in the ghettos."[72] Actually, the idea of a demonstration in Chicago had been somewhat reluctantly approved by the Mobe coalition through March, when it was still presumed that Johnson would be the Democratic candidate and would provide a natural focal point for protest. Then the McCarthy and Kennedy campaigns claimed the energies of local SANE chapters, WSP, the AFSC, and similarly liberal groups, which were reluctant to invest heavily in a demonstration. Several movement leaders worried about the rhetoric of provocation. After the president quit the race, the point of a demonstration was blurred, and the plan was opposed on strategic grounds by groups as different as WSP and YSA.

By this time the Mobe had come to be run largely by Dave Dellinger, Robert Greenblatt, Rennie Davis, and Tom Hayden, and for them a mass, multi-issue protest seemed critical. In press conferences on 29 June, Dellinger and Hayden in New York and Davis in Chicago apparently acted on their own to announce that the Mobe would conduct marches and disruptive actions in Chicago. If the authorities provoked violence, they said, "we will physically protect our people and are already working on chemical deterrents."[73] At a coalition meeting in Cleveland three weeks later, they overrode objections to the Chicago action. Dellinger chaired the conference. He and Hayden had met with North Vietnamese representatives in Paris, meanwhile, and had become convinced that the U.S.

government was blocking negotiations there. Action seemed all the more urgent. Davis, the project director, explained that many groups would bring their causes to Chicago—yippies, the Poor People's Campaign, blacks, McCarthy supporters, even Lowenstein's liberal Coalition for an Open Convention. He projected the radical protest as part of a "vast, decentralized people's movement." It might invigorate the dormant Mobilization itself. On these vague terms, and despite some opposition, the Mobe approved action.[74]

Dellinger was convinced that confrontation could be nonviolent, as was CNVA organizer Bradford Lyttle. With Davis and Hayden they sought to organize an orderly protest. Their repeated attempts failed to obtain permits, however. Even the liberals in the Coalition for an Open Convention were denied a place, and they cancelled their plans. As convention time approached, it became clear that the radical turnout would be small. At this point Hayden sank into what he recalled as "the politics of resentment."[75] Courting certain resistance from the police, and without a solid coalition behind them, the Mobe leaders forged contingency plans. The freewheeling yippies simply set up their "political circus" in the midst of this foreboding uncertainty. With no other means of saving the collapsing left, and apparently with no other purpose, militant radicals rushed toward a volatile confrontation in Chicago.

The Federal Bureau of Investigation tried to hasten the collapse of radicalism. In May it launched a new Counterintelligence Program (Cointelpro) intended to "expose, disrupt, and otherwise neutralize" the New Left and its allies.[76] J. Edgar Hoover bristled at what he deemed to be "the depravity" of antiwar radicals. He instructed Bureau field offices to attack left-wing insurgency in several imaginative ways: exploiting personal conflicts among radical leaders; encouraging suspicions that some antiwar militants were FBI informants; sending anonymous letters to university officials, state legislators, and wealthy university donors that stressed the prevalence of "narcotics and free sex" among young radicals; getting "cooperative press contacts" to highlight the minority status of left-wing dissidents; setting radicals up for drug arrests; mailing anonymous advisories to the employers, neighbors, and parents of antiwar radicals and thus "forcing the parents to take action"; spreading "misinformation" about meeting dates and activities; and using stories, cartoons, and photographs—"Naturally, the most obnoxious pictures should be used"—to ridicule New Left activists through "friendly news media."[77]

At least some FBI field offices rose to the opportunity. Cincinnati Bureau agents invented anonymous letters designed to defame nearby Antioch College, a source of antiwar dissidence, and to bludgeon the college into reining in "those students who spend most of their time engaging in anti-social activity, protest demonstrations, and affiliation with subversive groups."[78] Agents in Albany, New York, devised a leaflet attacking local SDS activists. In San Antonio, agents drafted fictitious protest letters from parents to Governor John Connally and the University of Texas Board of Regents, assailing University administrators who were "permitting an atmosphere to build up on campus that will be fertile field for the New Left." Thus San Antonio agents warned Hoover, "If we can 'nip this in the bud,' it could prevent the development of another New Left such as that at Columbia University."[79] A responsible bureau of investigation would have distinguished among radical elements and cultivated a sense of proportion about them. On the contrary, Hoover's directive fit into a political pattern of indiscriminately associating all opposition. In another time, FBI harassment and the yippie circus might have been equally trivial and foolish. In the political heat of 1968 Chicago, they combined to reinforce the identification of antiwar activists with cultural iconoclasts, and to relegate them all to the political edge.

Democratic leaders tried to make Chicago secure for the largest political convention ever held in America, even not counting protesters. The convention was isolated in the International Amphitheater on the white south side of the city. The skies to 2,500 feet were declared off limits to unauthorized aircraft. Manhole covers in the street were sealed. One lane of traffic on the Dan Ryan Expressway, the world's busiest roadway, was set aside for delegates' buses, and redwood fencing was erected to protect the official visitors from the sight of boarded-up buildings and trash-strewn empty lots. Downtown, Mayor Daley and his Chicago machine were harried by a telephone installers' strike and worried about renewed ghetto uprisings. They put up a tough front against antiwar dissenters, refusing to grant parade permits and trying to impose nighttime curfews on public parks. Early in August a special commission investigating violence during the peace demonstration of 27 April reported that Chicago police had attacked citizens gathered in peaceable assembly without cause or provocation.

On that note, the first of perhaps 5,000 demonstrators began filtering into the city in advance of the 5,500 Democratic convention delegates. A like number of Chicago people, doubtless including some looking for trouble or just excitement, increased the ranks of protesters. There was a core of yippies and political radicals, but most activists were ordinary, if better-educated, younger people from the three-state Chicago area who simply felt a concern over Vietnam and domestic racial tensions. They encountered official hostility, personalized by the city's mayor. Ironically, Daley himself was keenly opposed to the war in Vietnam and had mentioned the idea of a presidential review commission to Kennedy in February.[80] But the mayor was not about to brook war in Chicago. He put its 12,000-man police force on twelve-hour shifts for the duration of the convention. On 20 August, the governor of Illinois dispatched 6,000 state national guardsmen to defend the city. Unperturbed, yippies took their presidential candidate, a 150-pound pig named Pigasus, to the Chicago Civic Center and turned it loose. The prank lent credence to rumors that radicals were planning to place LSD in the city's water supply and commit other criminal jokes. FBI director Hoover advised the president (wrongly) that Rennie Davis was planning to infiltrate black militants into the maintenance crew at the convention hall, where they would sabotage plumbing, electrical, and communications systems.[81]

The Battle of Chicago began on 25 August, when 150 police broke up a demonstrators' encampment in Lincoln Park with tear gas, nightsticks, and chemical mace. Regrouping the next night, protesters fought back with taunts, missiles, and a hit-and-run retreat through the North Side streets near Lincoln Park. The army dispatched 5,000 troops to the city. On 27 August, while protesters held a giant "unbirthday party" for Lyndon Johnson, Chicago police stripped themselves of their badges and attacked the crowds with clubs and mace. They singled out newsmen and photographers for special treatment, attacking journalists with such abandon that conservative writer Winston S. Churchill of Great Britain condemned the police as "brutal and mulish," and leaders of the country's major news organizations protested to City Hall.[82]

Four miles to the south, the convention met under tight security. The Democratic establishment maintained close control of the proceedings— arresting delegates who refused to show floor passes and harassing reporters who nosed around too freely. Allard Lowenstein recalled that the feeling on the floor was what one might find "in a police state." Going from the New York to the Wisconsin delegation seemed like "going on a mission from Toogaloo to Jackson," he said. "You never knew whether you'd get there or not." To reach the podium he had to go through a kind of "Checkpoint Charlie" and was frequently pushed around on the way by people who refused to show any credentials. Playwright Arthur Miller, a Connecticut delegate, called the convention "the closest thing to a session of the All-Union Soviet that ever took place outside of Russia."[83] Characteristically, for all the attempted control, the Democrats found enough room to argue, especially over the racial composition and voting loyalty of southern state delegations.

The convention process broke wide open on Vietnam. On 23 August, antiwar delegates from the McCarthy, Kennedy, and McGovern camps agreed on a platform plank that called for a total bombing halt, U.S. military de-escalation, mutual withdrawal, and efforts to "encourage" the South Vietnamese government into negotiating some "political reconciliation" with the Vietcong.[84] In a measure the coalition proposal vindicated the antiwar liberals' strategy of working through the political system. Unmoved, the platform committee rejected the dissidents' proposal in favor of a statement essentially endorsing the president's position on Vietnam, which a few days later, and after hours of acrimonious debate, the convention adopted. In a measure that outcome vindicated radical skepticism about the political system. On 29 August the delegates nominated Hubert Humphrey for president.

Downtown Chicago exploded that night. About five thousand demonstrators jammed Grant Park across the street from the delegates' quarters at the Hilton Hotel. Such leaders as there were could not agree on what to do. Dellinger called for a nonviolent march on the Amphitheater. Davis was felled when police clubbed their way toward a youth lowering the American flag. Hayden urged people to form small groups and scatter disruptively. The crowd started to move—to what, it was not clear. Although ringed by national guardsmen in jeeps strung with barbed wire and fogged by tear gas, people broke through the encirclement and fanned out into the Loop. At the Hilton, bathed in the eerie glow of spotlights and television news cameras, protesters taunted police with chants of "The whole world is watching." The police seemed not to care. Officers charged into the crowd, some shouting "kill, kill," wielding clubs, spraying mace, and making arrests indiscriminately. A large number of demonstrators were pressed up against the hotel until several were literally forced through its plate glass windows and into the laps of dining conventioneers. Police attacks on luckless people trapped on nearby Loop streets were arbitrary and brutal, and the downtown area was so saturated with tear gas that even Vice-President Humphrey in his twenty-third-floor Hilton suite suffered eye and skin irritation.

The whole Kafkaesque scene was televised to an incredulous nation. It was viewed at the convention hall, where Senator Abraham Ribicoff of Connecticut condemned the Daley machine for its "Gestapo" tactics. Other delegates held up signs equating Chicago with Prague, where Soviet tanks were already rolling in a crushing attack on the Czech liberalization movement. Daley had won the streets, but the cost was great. Over 1,000 people, including 192 policemen, were injured during the four days of street fighting, and 662 were arrested. The Democratic party faced the election campaign in disarray, and for many observers the future seemed to offer further street skirmishes and official brutality. "This is just the beginning," said Kennedy aide Richard Goodwin. "There'll be four years of this." More plainly than ever, I. F. Stone continued to insist, "The war is destroying our country as we are destroying Vietnam."[85]

"The Movement, like society, has run amok"

The antiwar movement crossed a watershed at Chicago. On one hand, the youthful New Left drive for change through grassroots democracy had been to some extent co-opted by the rebellious radical fringe and led into frontal confrontation with the defenders of established authority in the streets of the Loop. The response was heavy-handed and repressive, but it was apparently very satisfying to the majority of Americans. The political right was at least symbolically reestablished on the offensive that it had lost four years earlier in the Goldwater debacle, while the radical left was shattered.

On the other hand, the drive for change through electoral politics had led to the McCarthy-Kennedy-McGovern coalition position on Vietnam in the platform committee. The response had been heavy-handed, if not repressive, but it satisfied the party regulars. The incumbent administration was secure from the challenge that had mounted since the New Hampshire primary, while antiwar liberals were demoralized.

Todd Gitlin has observed that youthful radicals—as distinct from the militants on the fringe—were more dependent on liberals than either knew. "New Left radicalism was a vine that had grown up around liberalism, they had sprung from the same energy and soil of possibility, and although by now the two represented different cultures, different styles, different ideologies, like it or not they were going to stand or fall together."[86] The Battle of Chicago, as he reflected on it, taught him that. In the autumn of 1968, it reverberated through liberalism and radicalism, contributing to the disorientation of the former and symbolizing the repulse of the latter.

Few people and organizations protested against the misbehavior of the Chicago police. The prevailing mood was to stand behind the forces of order and denounce the dissidents and the news media. Public opinion polls indicated that 56 percent of the people approved of the way that Mayor Daley handled the convention disorders and that 71 percent thought that his security measures were justified.[87] Assuming that the riot was caused by protest, the FBI announced that it would look into the role of yippies and the Mobe; Spiro Agnew suggested that communists were to blame; and a HUAC subcommittee opened an investigation into the communist role in the convention disorders. Moreover, leading politicians blamed the "liberal, left-wing press" for the riot, as Governor Wallace charged, or for a "deliberate conspiracy" among the major television networks to distort their reporting of Chicago police behavior, as Senator Russell Long suspected.[88] Senator Goldwater simply acknowledged that he had been amused by the sight of the newsmen being beaten during the convention. So incensed with media coverage was Mayor Daley that he produced his own interpretation of events, which was broadcast over 142 television stations and 1,000 radio stations in mid-September.[89] Less sensationally, an official investigating commission concluded in November that the Chicago violence constituted essentially a "police riot." By then, however, the event had become fixed as a symbol of the righteous quelling of rebelliousness. The popular reaction to the Battle of Chicago convinced I. F. Stone, at least, that the right wing had "won the election even before the votes are cast."[90]

Chicago 1968 also proved that the radical dream of rallying the left by provoking the right was sheer fantasy, although initially the euphoria of having survived the battle confirmed Chicago militants in their eccentric version of reality. Naïveté had been a source of strength from the beginning of the New Left, Todd Gitlin would recall almost twenty years later. After Chicago, the movement's will and moral seriousness, unhinged from real possibilities, hardened into its own "cage."[91]

Distance only obscured reality for those who wanted to believe, and Berkeley street people rioted for two days in support of the Chicago protesters. When classes resumed in the fall, SDS membership reached a record 100,000 people in 500 chapters. One out of eight entering freshmen at Princeton signed SDS membership cards, while chapter meetings at the universities of Wyoming and Montana drew 60 to 100 students.[92] Jerry Rubin and Abbie Hoffman rocketed between campus speaking tours and HUAC committee meetings, wearing clothing fashioned after the American flag and calling for "two, three, many Chicagos."[93] Their notoriety was good stock, but it was not influence.

Although radicalism remained to some extent in vogue, it had lost its capacity to organize. National SDS leaders called upon students to strike classes on 4–5 November, but they were unable to shut down a single school. The demonstrations which militants had scheduled for early November fizzled badly. As collective efforts in nonviolent resistance evaporated during the fall, there were over forty acts of arson and bombings against ROTC and draft offices from Delaware to Oregon. "The Movement, like society, has run amok," thought Martin Jezer. "Fighting cops. Killing pigs. Hurray! Our vision for the future. A new age soaked in blood. I'm crying."[94] Such was the politics of despair. Within a visionary movement it had spawned militant radicalism which, frustrated, had become random motion.

Edging toward despair but still grounded in religious certainty, some radical pacifists (known now as the "ultra resistance" because of their sacrificial nonviolence) recapitulated Catonsville. On 24 September, fourteen Catholic activists raided five draft boards in Milwaukee and its suburbs, dragged ten thousand A-1 files in burlap bags to the base of a flagpole at a World War I memorial, burned them with homemade napalm, and waited in prayer and song for arrest. Their action resumed the radical pacifist challenge to the legitimacy of the government war effort, and it intensified the intrapacifist debate over the morality of property destruction. The Milwaukee Fourteen saw little purpose in debating. What mattered to them was the act. As Philip Berrigan put it, there was "no other human course except to say by one's life and one's acts, 'This is me against genocide in Vietnam, against thermonuclear paranoia, against Third World rape, against Black containment, against environmental ruin—against a society which defines itself as a technological tribe!"[95] Three weeks later the Catonsville Nine were each sentenced to eighteen years in jail. Among the others free on bail, Father Daniel Berrigan was expected to present himself at Danbury prison on 9 April 1970.

Political radicals meanwhile became ever more isolated. Black nationalists continued on their own way. Feminists struck out as well, getting national attention in a September demonstration at the annual Miss America competition in Atlantic city. Factions in SDS vied to appear the most extremist. Here and there, isolated radical militants taunted police and battled one another, becoming so fractious that even the normally ebullient *National Guardian* was forced to concede at the end of the year that "the radical movement is split as rarely before in the decade-long history of the modern left."[96] The SMC began to regroup, shorn of its radical component, and radical pacifists met in Philadelphia shortly after the Chicago convention in an effort to recapture nonviolence as a principle as well as a tactic.

The illusion of radical influence persisted, however, not only among the Rubins and Hoffmans of the country but also among their erstwhile opponents. FBI Director Hoover coordinated a steady new flow of surveillance reports on black nationalists and antiwar radicals, which he passed on to the White House and a half-dozen other national security agencies. Investigation was not enough for Hoover. He ordered field officers to take "immediate action" to publicize "the depraved nature and moral looseness of the New Left." They should alert the press to scheduled antiwar demonstrations "which might be immoral or obscene in nature"; they should write anonymous letters to the parents of youth involved in protests that featured "an obscene display." Hoover was out to protect American morals, not merely to investigate crime, and he seemed to believe that cultural deviation was the product of alien subversive forces. Antiwar militants were "influenced by domestic and foreign subversive elements," he wrote, and every resource of the Bureau would be employed "in order that no opportunity will be missed to destroy this insidious movement."[97]

Richard Helms, director of the CIA, knew better. In September he reported to the president that on the basis of an exhaustive agency investigation there was "no convincing evidence of control, manipulation, sponsorship, or significant financial support of student dissidence by any international Communist authority." The overwhelming majority of America's 6.3 million students were "politically apathetic," he said. Hardly 35,000 could be considered "hard core" radicals, and even those were poorly organized in "amorphous, polycentric" operations like SDS, which was "really little more than a collection of local chapters, not all of which respond readily to any leadership."[98]

Not satisfied, the president discussed the Helms report with his cabinet members on 18 September. Johnson and his senior advisors dismissed the CIA analysis and drew instead on their own personal experiences and received gossip. Secretary of Agriculture Orville Freeman, for one, recalled that during his travels through the country he had met "all kinds of people [who] tell me about Communist involvement in this thing." Dean Rusk confided that a member of an Ivy League university board of trustees had told him "that he has thirty Communists on his faculty." At length the president closed discussion of the Helms report. "I just don't believe this business that there is no support," he said. "I've seen it in my own school. I've seen them provoke and aggravate trouble. I know that Students for a Democratic Society and the Du Bois Clubs are Communist infiltrated, Communist supported and aggravated. Maybe they are not Communist led, but they are Communist agitated and aggravated."[99] The president and his aides could not explain confrontational dissent in any other way. It was not American. As Johnson's close advisor and former Health, Education and Welfare secretary, Joseph Califano, remembered years later, administration officials simply could not believe, despite all the available evidence, that the Vietnam war, "a cause that is so clearly right for the country, as they perceive it, would be so widely attacked if there were not some [foreign] force behind it."[100]

Dissent was generated by the war; but confrontation was an expression of dissonance which was more or less attached to the war. It was a symptom of a malaise which began to permeate the military itself. The armed forces encountered increasingly serious expressions of internal opposition and disaffection after 1967. Desertion rates increased. Riots in brigs and stockades became more frequent and violent. Racial tensions skyrocketed. The command structure was threatened in the field, and the call letters FTA, which could stand for either "free the army" or "fuck the army," became the code for resentment toward officers, military life, and the war.[101]

Although the disaffection was general, some troops dissented on principle. In February 1968, twenty GIs held a "pray-in" for peace on the chapel steps at Fort Jackson, South Carolina, and five were jailed when they refused to disperse. A twenty-five-year-old second lieutenant in uniform picketed against the war outside the White House and later was arrested when he refused to board a plane for service in Vietnam. A captain was sentenced to a year at hard labor and dismissed from the Air Force for refusing to train pilots for Vietnam. At Fort Lewis, Washington, the CND symbol—now known as the peace sign—was painted around the post and baked on cookies for distribution in the mess hall. Forty-three soldiers were arrested at Fort Hood, Texas, for protesting against being sent to guard Chicago. Reporters later accompanying President Johnson on a trip to that base were "stunned" when ranks of troops responded to his call to fight and die for freedom with a low moan of protest.[102]

Antiwar coffeehouses made their appearance at military installations around the country, prompting General Westmoreland, now Army Chief of Staff, to order a secret investigation of their activities. There was no secret. These were places where soldiers could be exposed to antiwar literature and discuss the war openly. The coffeehouse movement began late in 1967, and it flowered during the following summer, when the editor of *Ramparts* financed it through the Summer of Support (SOS, one of the more apt acronyms of the movement), often with the help of nonmilitant members of SDS. An antiwar GI press emerged. At first it was the work of veterans, like those who put out *Veterans Stars and Stripes for Peace* in Chicago, or of civilians like the publishers of the *Bond* in Berkeley. By mid-1968 and despite persistent harassment, GIs in service were putting out their own papers, including the defiantly named *FTA* at Fort Knox, Kentucky.

Indeed, antiwar sentiment was becoming as organized among GIs as it had become among veterans. When SMC called for rallies on 12 October under the slogan, "GIs and Vets March for Peace," groups of servicemen did participate. The one in San Francisco originated among GIs in that area and, by some estimates, drew five hundred active servicemen into a fifteen-thousand-person demonstration.[103] Active-duty soldiers also participated in demonstrations in Europe and Japan. A number of activists concluded that it was time to harness disaffection in the military to the movement. At a Chicago meeting in December, they agreed to sponsor GI-civilian demonstrations the following spring.

Civilians were already responding. Throughout 1968 the decentralized network of Resistance groups had shifted from demonstrative turn-ins or the burning of draft cards to unsolicited counseling about the draft and the war among men facing induction. Counselors reached innumerable men who then embarked on military service with a consciousness of their civil rights and questions about the war which they would not otherwise have had. Moreover, the ancient concept of sanctuary was revived on behalf of draft resisters and soldiers AWOL on principle, probably first in May at Boston's Arlington Street Church. In the summer at least two other churches tried to give sanctuary to AWOLs, one of them incurring police violence in the process. Students at four eastern colleges attempted to provide asylum in the fall.

By this time, CALC was exploring the possibility of a ministry for self-exiled resisters and deserters in Sweden, and it sent a delegation to Paris and Stockholm for that purpose. Its leaders had continued to support principled draft resistance, government prosecution notwithstanding, and they were promoting amnesty for all violators of draft and military laws. As these clergy ministered to military discontent, they, like the GIs who joined demonstrations and published antiwar papers, helped to make it more visible. The "Vietnam malaise is rotting out the shining heraldry woven by American fighters for two centuries," said *Life* magazine. "Almost imperceptibly, the closely woven fabric of military discipline is unraveling at the edges. Never defeated in war, the armed forces can't quite cope with the peace assault."[104] Discontent was endemic to warfare, but military dissent was an expression of dissonance in America.

Both the Resistance and the increasing involvement of veterans and GIs in antiwar activity contributed an element of realism and seriousness which helped to counteract and isolate the militant fringe. The national SDS dropped draft work in the spring of 1968 as it moved into confrontational politics, but several members who had been involved in its community organizing work earlier in the decade became involved in the Resistance and gave it a community-wide basis. In Boston and in Wisconsin especially, draft-counseling provided a vehicle for the original emphasis of the New Left.[105] Staughton Lynd and Michael Ferber, among others, found in community-based antidraft work an expression of not only the vision but also the spirit of community and tolerance from which SDS had so radically departed: "At meetings, no one is called cop-out, and individuals can oppose militant stands without being denounced as chickens. A tolerance exists, a sense of brotherhood, a lack of the radical status-seeking all too often found among most of the other New Left groups."[106] In a related way, GIs and veterans who risked speaking out against the war found themselves in a bonded group of peers who knew their risk and shared their travail. As they began to filter into the antiwar movement, they brought a kind of concreteness—an appreciation of warfare and of the power of the military system—and a devotion to American values which countered the abstract, nation-disparaging rhetoric of radical militants.

All the while, liberals struggled to recover from the Chicago Democratic convention debacle. Their organizational base was disrupted, and their confidence in the political process shaken. Anticipating this even before Chicago, Sandy Gottlieb had held a meeting with leaders from the FCNL, UWF, CALC, WILPF, the Council for a Livable World, and others to plan a grassroots campaign to "reorder national priorities."[107] Well to the left of these groups was Marcus Raskin's National Council for a New Politics. Mistrust of the Democratic leadership was shared by people from the Kennedy, McGovern, and McCarthy forces. A number of them attempted to forge a new alliance within the party. The first week of October, a New Democratic Coalition attracted to Minneapolis over two hundred would-be reformers, people such as Lowenstein, Gans, Gottlieb, Don Peterson, and Sam Brown, who had worked hard to dump Johnson on the war issue. They felt estranged from Hubert Humphrey. He seemed to represent the president, both because he had been nominated on the administration's war plank and because he was backed by the party's establishment. He symbolized the system they wanted desperately to reform. On the other hand, he had a long record as a committed liberal politician and, in any case, he was the only alternative to Richard Nixon, who was shadowed by his own anticommunist zeal and by the Republican right wing. The New Democratic Coalition was reduced to a long-range vision. While it deliberated, ADA's national board voted to endorse Humphrey, though with some reservations. Increasingly, antiwar liberals gravitated to the Humphrey campaign.

They were painfully slow in adjusting to the war's changing reality. Most of them hungered for domestic reconciliation and longed to believe that the war was truly winding down toward a settlement that would spare the country further humiliation. With diplomacy in place after years of effort, most antiwar liberals were not quite yet prepared to pass from pleas for military de-escalation and good-faith peace talks to the naked demand for immediate withdrawal. There was, to be sure, a lingering anxiety that I. F. Stone was correct in continuing to insist that the real U.S. purpose was *"to reduce the level of conflict to a point the American people will tolerate for a long pull without giving up the basic aim of restoring a South Vietnam under American control."* This was "the best the Establishment offers for the next four years," he wrote in late October, and a sure "recipe for new disasters."[108] That had been the prescription of the Wise Men as the alternative to disaster in March, of course, and in the fall it was apparently the position espoused by both Humphrey and Nixon.

Their contest turned only partly on the war issue. Vietnam was enmeshed in a web of racial tensions and barely articulated discontents. Not one of the major candidates staked out a clearly defined position on the war. Governor Wallace, the candidate of an American Independent party, claimed to favor a negotiated settlement; but his vice-presidential running mate, retired Air Force general Curtis LeMay, talked of bombing his way to victory. Vice-President Humphrey suggested that he would cease all bombing if he sensed any sign of moderation in North Vietnamese behavior, but he refused to support a coalition government in Saigon. Richard Nixon commanded an overwhelmingly early lead among voters who believed that he was the best prepared to end the war, and he refused to discuss Vietnam for most of the campaign, purportedly so as not to complicate the Paris negotiations.

Instead, he and Agnew joined Wallace in using the war as a symbolic issue with which to attack antiwar critics and other dissidents as destructive subversives. Picking up Wallace's call for "law and order," Agnew aggressively attacked domestic critics as communist-inspired agitators. They should be "cast out" of American life in the interests of national unity, he said, and a Republican administration would "define permissible limits of dissent." Protest was "out of control," he added, but the Republicans would correct that.[109] Some militants on the right couldn't wait for a new administration. Late in August, a half-dozen Minutemen tried to burn buildings at a farm community near Voluntown, Connecticut, which had served as a pacifist base for nonviolent action since the Polaris Action projects of 1962. A running gun battle with state troopers wounded one woman resident and four assailants.[110] There were other such incidents, and in September two men were indicted in New York on charges of plotting to murder 158 "active leftists."[111]

Then, with the election only a month away, Humphrey began to close ground rapidly. An imminent breakthrough in the Paris peace talks was rumored. Nixon declared that he intended both to reduce American military involvement in the war and to oppose any coalition regime in Saigon. He intimated that he had a secret plan to end the war. On 31 October, President Johnson announced a total bombing halt over Vietnam, hinting that negotiations were carrying the war toward an early conclusion. Johnson's move failed to carry Humphrey's surging candidacy to victory, however, and Nixon was elected with a 43.4 to 42.7 percent edge in the popular count and a more decisive 302–191 vote in the electoral college.

Voting analysts concluded that the American voters did not treat the presidential election as a referendum on the war, mostly because they perceived that Nixon and Humphrey stood "very close together" on the issue of escalation versus disengagement.[112] The voters were more explicit, however, in expressing their preference for a more conservative government. Harris pollsters found that nearly 70 percent of American voters considered themselves conservative or middle-of-the-road, and that the great majority of them believed that Nixon was of the same persuasion. Looking at the 59 percent tally garnered by Nixon and Wallace together, the Gallup polling organization reached the same conclusion: the nation's conservative forces were stronger than at any time in recent American history.[113] A month after Nixon's election, John Kenneth Galbraith voiced liberal apprehensions about the fate of the Great Society and the road to peace when he wrote a friend, "We're in for a rather dull, grim four years."[114]

Time magazine had said that anything might happen in 1968. At the end of 1967, that had been merely a facile remark. A year later it was a poignant one, for in the interval a commanding and combative incumbent stepped out of the presidential race, the country was convulsed in spasms of political violence and civil unrest, two outstanding national leaders were murdered, a war said to be nearing victory was stalemated in negotiations, the Democratic national convention erupted in violence, and peace in Vietnam came to depend on a Republican president who had built a reputation as a fighting anticommunist. In the process, the antiwar movement was transformed.

For three years, antiwar activists challenged the consensus of acquiescence on Vietnam at the political center of the country. They kept the issue alive. They criticized, dissented, protested, and demonstrated. Some of them rebelled. Cumulatively, they contributed to the making of a political and social crisis which, in the spring of 1968, led millions of people to conclude that the course of war in Vietnam had to be reversed. The communist Tet offensive did not break the American will to fight so much as it forced the people, and then the government of the United States, to reassess the nation's commitment in light of its purpose. As it became clear that the national interest could not justify an unlimited investment in the war, policymakers altered their commitment to victory. America was now on a new course in Vietnam, but Washington's options were reduced. The United States headed toward military disengagement and, implicitly, failure in its limited political objectives—but only implicitly, because the very opening of negotiations obscured the issues for the time being.

Given hope by the onset of peace talks and the appearance of more antiwar politicians, some liberals pulled back from concentrated peace activism and turned to other reform endeavors. They hoped to calm the domestic crisis. Others of them worked for peace through the electoral process, almost entirely in the Democratic party. For many of these activists, the Chicago convention and the election brought discouragement. Meanwhile, the same domestic crisis that enjoined restraint on liberals engaged some radicals in stronger reform efforts and excited other, more militant ones to increasingly extreme positions. The radical wing became ever more splintered, its vacuous extremity exposed in the Battle of Chicago. The reaction to the Democratic convention and the subsequent election suggested that the country had had enough of violence, iconoclasm, protest, rapid change, and war. The postelection mood was that of a nation drawing a deep breath. "Four dull years," Galbraith had said. That must have sounded altogether attractive to the Americans who constituted the political center, and not "grim" at all. The war was negotiable, wasn't it? Who was to say "no"? The antiwar movement had come unravelled, its radical wing devoid of purpose and its liberal wing lacking direction, if not will.

Nine

Redrawing the Lines

"The future of the antiwar movement now
depends on one man"

The impasse in Vietnam was symbolized in a disagreement over a configuration of furniture. When President Johnson stopped bombing the North at the end of October 1968, he also agreed to include representatives of both Saigon and the NLF in peace negotiations. South Vietnamese president Thieu, enraged by the inclusion of his internal opposition and encouraged by the prospects for a Republican administration, boycotted the talks for several days before he agreed to send a negotiating team to Paris under the titular leadership of Vice-President Ky. The arrival of the South Vietnamese and NLF delegations late in November produced a new diplomatic snag over the format of the Paris peace talks: the North Vietnamese and NLF contended that the talks were a four-sided affair; the United States insisted on two long tables that underscored the bilateral nature of negotiations; and the South Vietnamese resisted an American–North Vietnamese compromise for a circular table.

Walter Lippmann, among other analysts critical of the administration, understood the symbol. The dispute over physical arrangements mirrored the political problem: "how a government that is acceptable to us is to be maintained after our troops leave."[1] Even with a half-million troops and a punishing three-year air war, the United States had failed to guarantee the survival of the Saigon government. How did it now propose to achieve its purpose with less? For Lippmann that was a rhetorical question, and it pointed to another: what purpose now could be served by continued fighting? The answer depended on the new president.

Promising to bring the nation together again, Richard Nixon opened his first term on a honeymoon from serious criticism. A relative calm pervaded the country in the general expectation that America was headed out of Vietnam. The new president was determined to reconcile the inherently contradictory commitments to military withdrawal, the survival of an independent South Vietnam, and pacification of American politics which he had inherited from Lyndon Johnson. Like his predecessor, Nixon understood that America's strategic investment had come to involve the nation's prestige and credibility more than any substantive security interests. Unlike the Johnson White House, however, Nixon and his national security advisor, Henry Kissinger, interpreted the preservation of an anticommunist regime in Saigon as a fundamental prerequisite to their grand design for a new superpower condominium among Russia, China, and America. A lack of resolve in Southeast Asia, they contended, would weaken Washington's capacity to negotiate with Moscow and Beijing. Nixon understood as well as Johnson that Vietnam was tearing America apart. Unlike his predecessor, the new president was willing to go to great lengths in order to discredit domestic antiwar critics.

Nixon's personal approach to the domestic struggle over the war was shaped by at least three factors: an abhorrence of dissent; an obsession with undifferentiated domestic "enemies," and apprehension that American democracy lacked the will and character required to assert itself vigorously in the world.[2] Nixon detested disagreement, not to say dissent. According to White House aides, the president was incapable of confronting anyone with contrary views, even in his circle of advisors—at least, once he had chosen a course of action. His contempt for serious policy critics and street protesters (the latter he regarded as "trash" and "rabble," if not outright insurrectionists[3]) was naturally more acute. It reinforced an "us vs. them" mentality in the White House which set the stage for unusually divisive politics during his years in office. A man whose grudges vied with his suspicions, Nixon believed that the eastern establishment and the national news media were trying to destroy him, and he acted out his fears by projecting a "cult of the tough guy," which his aides took as a sanction for their undeclared civil war against opposition.[4] "Combat," Nixon once wrote proudly, "is the essence of politics." Some White House officials took his words quite literally. "Those who are against us we will destroy," promised one. "In fact, those who are not for us, we will destroy."[5] The "tough guy" image also affected relations with Hanoi, which Nixon wanted to keep off-balance, unable to count on his continuing to restrain U.S. military power.

His hatred of critics and his obsession with toughness reflected Nixon's own doubts over the moral health of America. Like all politicians, he routinely sang the praises of American democracy. Unlike most, however, he seemed to disdain its crucial mediating institutions, notably Congress, the news media, and the foreign policy bureaucracy, which he came to discredit and damage (at the outset, he and Kissinger transferred crucial policy-making power from the State Department to the National Security Agency). Although he frequently praised the good sense of the American people, Nixon privately doubted that very many of them understood key international issues, and he feared that they were prone to self-indulgence and softness in a world requiring discipline and obedience. A conservative moralist in a dissonant democracy, he intended to salvage those qualities of tenacity and "guts" that were vital to that peace which accompanied America's global primacy. This was the reason, no doubt, that Nixon felt so bitter toward antiwar critics who called for the open acceptance of American failure in Vietnam. They struck him not only as traitors but as agents of an alien belief system. Antiwar activists were not communists. They were worse. They were Americans whose attacks on the creed of global toughness represented an irresolution which for the president was the Achilles' heel of democracy. His task was not simply to save Saigon. It was to deal with Vietnam in such a way as to preserve America.

Johnson had not so much halted the U.S. air war on North Vietnam as he had shifted it southward and to Laos, where the rate of bombing tripled in the last three weeks of the year. Combat in Vietnam intensified with the new year. By April, when U.S. forces in Vietnam reached their peak of 543,000, the number of U.S. casualties was over 200,000. In February and April, communist troops launched sizable offensives, but they were contained by U.S. and ARVN forces, backed by the most concentrated air attacks in the history of warfare. With the battlefield situation unresolved, formal peace talks proved fruitless.

Negotiators in Paris, after a ten-week stalemate over seating arrangements, agreed on a system by which U.S. and South Vietnamese diplomats sat opposite their North Vietnamese and NLF counterparts (in April the title of the National Liberation Front was changed to the Provisional Revolutionary Government, or PRG); but the fundamental issues remained intractable. Washington required the mutual withdrawal of forces not indigenous to South Vietnam and guarantees of the South's independence under the incumbent regime. Hanoi insisted upon the withdrawal of U.S. forces, the removal of the Thieu regime, and a political settlement in South Vietnam as defined by the PRG. Negotiations remained stalled on the political issue.

Expecting little from the Paris peace talks, the administration at first tried to persuade the Soviet Union to pressure Hanoi into withdrawing from South Vietnam. When that approach failed, the president tried to frighten the North Vietnamese into accepting a dictated peace. Starting in March, Nixon ordered the beginning of a sustained and clandestine U.S. air war against alleged North Vietnamese supply routes and sanctuaries in Cambodia and Laos. The decision to launch a secret and unilateral war upon two neutral states was politically so dangerous and constitutionally so dubious that the White House went to extraordinary lengths to keep it secret not only from Congress and the American people, but even from many key military and diplomatic officials. The Air Force was ordered to maintain a dual record of the bombings—one full and accurate, and one for the public record which made no mention of Cambodia. Between March 1969 and June 1970, the American planes covertly dropped 100,000 tons of bombs on Cambodia (that was no secret to the communists or the Cambodians). When, in May, *New York Times* correspondent William Beecher broke the story of the president's secret air war, Nixon became so enraged that he organized a band of "plumbers" to seal the White House against future unauthorized disclosures of information. Thus, only months after his inauguration, Nixon was headed toward a rendezvous with Watergate.

During the winter months a number of things mitigated the chill of war. Early in the year the president promised to honor his predecessor's plans to return soldiers home, so that the only significant debate in Washington on the war seemed for a time to be the number and pace of withdrawals. By the same token, the president introduced plans to modify and then end the draft, and he put a new emphasis on the return of U.S. prisoners of war, a process normally associated with a war's conclusion. Public figures contributed to the sense that the war was winding down, as they had done in the weeks following Lyndon Johnson's address on 31 March. Indeed, various leaders in the outgoing administration began arguing about its errors, adding to the impression that Vietnam had passed into the realm of historical debate and controversy.

Ironically, by the style of their protest actions, some antiwar dissidents bolstered the notion that the war was over. AFSC activists held memorial services for the war dead, for example. For its February mobilization, which drew only about half as many people as the previous one, CALC issued a position paper anticipating social and political issues beyond Vietnam. In the National Mobilization Committee, Paul Potter talked about living in a "post war world."[6] Left-wing militants dismissed the war as a problem of the past (that is to say, for liberals), while antiwar liberals gave priority to other issues. A number of them hoped "to transform the Democratic Party" into a political instrument for disaffected minorities through the New Democratic Coalition, whose steering committee included Sam Brown, Sandy Gottlieb, and Curtis Gans.[7] Senators Morse, Gruening, and McCarthy had not returned to Congress. Newly elected Allard Lowenstein and other antiwar legislators gave Nixon a grace period.

Antiwar clergy in CALC maintained the best organized opposition to the war that winter, with over a hundred branches and a mailing list of twenty-five thousand, and yet even they found it difficult to concentrate their discontent once U.S. bombing of the North stopped and negotiations began. They pursued other aspects of peace, especially an end to the draft and amnesty for draft-law violators, and in February they inaugurated a ministry to military exiles in Sweden. In the spring they reached out to draft resisters in Canada. Religious pacifists in the FOR condemned the war, but they maintained their contacts with Vietnamese Buddhists, publicizing the "third solution" as an alternative to the repressive Thieu regime and the PRG, and they also promoted amnesty and aid to resisters. In the Resistance itself, the draft card turn-in waned as a tactic, and most groups disbanded, feeding members into other causes.

In lieu of a frontal challenge to the White House, there emerged a critique of the institutional sources of the U.S. intervention to the end that, as McGovern exclaimed, "there must be no more Vietnams!"[8] Thus liberals criticized the military-industrial complex and the national-security bureaucracy, demanding that American priorities be revised. With initiative especially from SANE and ADA, the Washington-based Arms Control and Disarmament Council was converted into a Coalition on National Priorities at the end of February. Arthur M. Schlesinger, Jr., summed up a theme common to its liberal sponsoring groups: "Nothing has distorted United States foreign policy more in recent years than the military insistence that every other interest be subordinated to their own."[9] A few liberal representatives sponsored a Congressional Conference on the Military Budget and National Priorities, 28–29 March, in order to protest military influence over U.S. foreign and domestic policies.[10] Similarly, CALC assailed the "economic military machine" allegedly sustaining an American empire.[11] In April it sponsored a protesting delegation at the stockholders' meeting of Dow Chemical. SANE, the FCNL, and new groups of university research scientists formed the Union of Concerned Scientists in order to challenge a proposed anti–ballistic missile system. In what came to be an important precedent, a number of graduate students at the Massachusetts Institute of Technology stopped their research on 4 March in order to underscore the importance of shifting "away from the present emphasis on military technology towards the solution of pressing environmental and social problems."[12] For liberals in and out of Congress, Vietnam remained a nagging sore early in 1969, but the immediate challenge was to learn from it and to redeploy the country's resources for domestic reconstruction.

Early in the spring the nation was distracted from Vietnam by the attention given to spreading campus unrest. With the threat of further ghetto uprisings real but subsiding, a wave of protest disturbed nearly 400 of the country's 2,500 college campuses. This disorder was more volatile, had a higher incidence of violence, and involved more frequent confrontations with police than that of the previous four years. Over 4,000 students were arrested on campuses from San Francisco State to

Swarthmore, while 7 percent of the country's schools reported violent protests involving property damage or personal injury.[13] Although the great majority of student protests were peaceful and orderly, there were enough disorders and clashes with police to arouse public anger—one poll reported that 82 percent of adults sampled demanded the expulsion of student demonstrators.[14]

Folk wisdom to the contrary, there seemed to be no significant relationship between campus protests and the vested concern of students with the draft.[15] In fact, only a minority of college students opposed U.S. policy on Vietnam, and only a small fraction of those who opposed it actively demonstrated against the war. Students raised so many issues—including instituting black studies and other curricula, participation in decision-making, and regulations of behavior—that it was difficult to generalize about campus demonstrations. Some observers did characterize student protest as being marked by an "intense individuality." Wrote one university official, young dissidents were "almost totally self-absorbed in their pursuit of liberation."[16] Although the quest often embraced the college or university community, its consequence for antiwar activism was paradoxical. Campus disorders and even the affectation of radicalism spread while the war issue subsided, and the link between the culture of personal rebellion and the politics of radical protest finally began to come apart. Whereas many students successfully challenged authorities in matters of racism, language, life-style, curricula, and other campus issues, relatively few now extended their protest to Vietnam itself.

In fact, personal protest triumphed at the expense of politics within the radical left itself, which disintegrated in a furor of sectarian division, angry rhetoric, and violent action, all aggravated by government infiltration and harassment. The motivating rationale of the early New Left had been the dream of fusing individual alienation and collective disaffection into a political force that would make America more free and democratic. This hope had been seriously compromised in 1968 by cultural rebellion and militancy on the radical fringe, and it largely dissolved during 1969–70. The trend was anticipated in a counterinaugural demonstration in January.

The groups still loosely aligned as the Mobilization Committee, enormously discouraged by the election, felt that they had to "serve notice" to the incoming president "that the war at home has not ended."[17] The difficulty was that the coalition was still led by Dave Dellinger, now with Paul Potter in lieu of Tom Hayden, who had secluded himself on the West Coast. Again the Chicago illusion that a provocative demonstration might rally the radical left around the war issue surfaced in the Mobe. Although the idea was quashed and a pledge to abjure confrontation was secured, there was enough ambiguity that some militants came expecting a fracas.

On the evening of Sunday, 19 January 1969, Dellinger led about eight thousand activists, mostly young, down Pennsylvania Avenue and over to a heated circus tent on the Mall for what was billed as a Counterinaugural Ball. While people huddled together to the beat of rock music and the drone of speeches, a group of New York militants briefly took over the Mobe's office. On Monday demonstrators lined sections of the inaugural parade route, chanting antiwar slogans and waving signs. Breakaway rowdies disrupted downtown traffic, broke windows, and skirmished with city police.

Without real purpose or direction, the counterinauguration was at best an exercise in ineptitude. The numbers were about what had been expected, and a few leaders felt that the effort had been worthwhile. Others disagreed sharply. "If the CIA had set out to produce a savage burlesque of the peace movement," wrote I. F. Stone, "it could not have done better."[18] Rennie Davis conceded the fiasco. Without means of controlling "guerrilla street activity," he declared, the Mobe should quit sponsoring mass actions because they were too "dangerous."[19] Militants in SDS came to the opposite conclusion—that too much self-restraint had been exercised—and they drew still more inward. Given the polarization within the movement, the Mobe declined to plan any major demonstrations in the spring. It proposed only to support local antiwar activity and to maintain its international contacts (basically that meant the North Vietnamese in Paris with whom Dellinger met in February and through whom a group of pacifists developed a Committee of Liaison which provided POWs with family contacts). In effect, the Mobe ceased to function.

Several groups stepped into the breach. One was the National Action Group (NAG) of dedicated pacifists which had been convened informally by the AFSC's Stewart Meacham after the Chicago convention in an effort to differentiate fundamental commitment from mere extremism. By December the still ad hoc NAG had developed into a pacifist caucus bent on sustaining principled nonviolent action in the wake of the collapsing radical left. It provided what discipline there was in the counterinauguration. It was in a way the Vietnam equivalent of CNVA in the test-ban era. At its New York meetings were found people with a considerable body of nonviolent theory and experience: Meacham of the AFSC; Dave McReynolds of the WRL; Richard Fernandez of CALC; James Bevel of SCLC; Tudja Crowder of SANE; Katherine Camp, president of WILPF; Paul Lauter of RESIST, who had been active in draft resistance since 1966, when he was an officer of SDS and a staff member in the Chicago AFSC; Brad Lyttle of the New England CNVA, who had participated in antinuclear projects as early as 1959; and William Davidon of Haverford College, who with Lyttle had accompanied A. J. Muste to Saigon in 1966; Muste's own secretary, Beverly Sterner; Otto Nathan, executor of Albert Einstein's estate and an active participant in the New York Parade Committee from its inception; and Allan Brick, Ron and Trudi Young, and Jim and Linda Forest of the FOR (Jim was one of the Milwaukee Fourteen). With a few others of like spirit who did not meet regularly—Staugton Lynd, for one—these friends linked pacifist and religious groups on issues such as amnesty and the revision of American priorities, but their first concern was to reactivate the antiwar movement.

From the end of January, the group began to plan four days of protest on Easter weekend in April. Although they agreed to coordinate a large number of local events, they concentrated on three or four cities which did not have New Left factions that would complicate and divide their efforts: they would encourage "100 flowers to bloom while planting 3 or 4 flowerbeds."[20] The pacifist organizations represented in NAG would provide staff for the project. Their emphasis would be on the unacknowledged escalation of the war. They would also support SCLC programs scheduled for the anniversary of Martin Luther King's death on 4 April, and, in response to a letter from Sid Lens, they agreed to support GI-civilian protests also scheduled for that weekend.

Those demonstrations had been scheduled by the GI-Civilian Antiwar Action Conference in Chicago on 28 December, which had made Fred Halstead of the SWA and the New York Parade Committee responsible for organizing them. In turn, Halstead recruited Lens. By mid-February it was clear that the Mobe would not coordinate the effort but that support would be forthcoming from NAG, WILPF, the strong Chicago Peace Council, the New York Parade Committee, Vets for Peace, what was left of the SMC, and a planning board of GIs. Thus, although the Nixon administration had still not shown its hand, various elements of the antiwar movement were regrouping.

During the "April Action" of Easter weekend they operated as an informal coalition. The SMC generated campus rallies, especially against ROTC, a few of which resulted in serious confrontations. The NAG coalition and the GI-Civilian committee rallied about 150,000 supporters in forty cities around the slogan "Resistance and Renewal" for the first coordinated antiwar protest of the Nixon presidency. Virtually all the actions were led by adults and, depending on local constituencies, included leafletting, guerrilla theater, teach-ins, parades, and festivals. Interfaith teams of pacifists conducted a seventeen-hour Good Friday vigil at Philadelphia draft boards, reading the names of the thirty-three thousand Americans killed in Vietnam. A seventy-two-hour vigil was held in downtown Akron, Ohio, and an ecumenical peace service drew eight hundred worshipers in Richmond, Virginia. New York's parade gathered perhaps a hundred thousand people, San Francisco's forty thousand. Chicago, Atlanta, and Austin, Texas, had their largest peace demonstrations yet. On Easter Sunday four young men were symbolically crucified on thirteen-foot crosses planted in front of the White House to express the conviction that "as long as this war continues, it is always Good Friday."[21]

Freighted with religious symbolism, the April Action was a welcome counterpoint to the bullyboy tactics spreading through the radical left, and it was evidence of continuing concern with Vietnam. Its demonstrations were the modest investment of a new working coalition. "The future of the antiwar movement now depends on one man—Richard Nixon," a protester said. "If he really plans to de-escalate the war, the peace groups will scatter to other issues or fall apart. If he doesn't, then he's in for a rough summer."[22]

The Nixon administration vacillated in the first half of 1969 between attempts to placate antiwar critics and plans to crush them. At one point, Henry Kissinger tried to reassure youthful skeptics of the administration's peaceable intentions. "Give us a year," he told seven student leaders. "No, I mean it. Come back here in a year. . . . If you come back in a year and nothing has happened," he said, "then I can't argue for more patience." One of the students observed that the Johnson White House had exhausted the government's credibility. Kissinger replied, "All I can do is ask you to trust us."[23] Unfortunately, students had little credit with the government either. The president and his top advisors believed initially that antiwar sentiment originated from opposition to the draft and continuing U.S. casualties—that most student dissidents simply wanted, as Nixon later put it, "to keep from getting their asses shot off."[24] The assumption was that cowardice could be appeased by reducing draft calls and bringing home the troops.

The White House also wielded threats, overtly from the Justice Department. On 29 March, eight activists who had been more or less involved in the Battle of Chicago were indicted by a federal grand jury. The defendants—the Chicago Eight—included Dellinger, Davis, and Hayden of the Mobe; Rubin and Hoffman; two men who had acted as demonstration marshals; and Bobby Seale of the Oakland Black Panthers, who had appeared in Chicago only at the last moment. The charges against them, conspiracy and traveling across state bounds "to incite a riot," were contrived for the purpose of stereotyping and curtailing the antiwar left. There were covert threats, too, as the government marshalled its principal security agencies. A so-called Committee of Six, which included Patrick Buchanan and Tom Charles Huston, was formed to encourage the Internal Revenue Service to harass liberal organizations such as the Brookings Institution and to starve them of federal grant support. About two thousand FBI agents were ordered to monitor the New Left, while other agents helped local right-wing groups and businessmen to disrupt local left-wing activism. The White House ordered the FBI to begin an "Inlet" program of political intelligence-gathering, and, after the secret bombing of Cambodia was disclosed, the Bureau was instructed also to conduct illegal wiretaps of several administration officials and journalists. By summer the National Security Agency was beginning to gather data on thousands of politically suspect citizens through Operation Minaret.

The CIA, meanwhile, was pressed to document links between overseas communists and the domestic antiwar movement. Late in the spring, after the agency reported for the third time in three years that it had no evidence of significant communist involvement in the antiwar movement, Huston told its officials to expand their investigation with a most "liberally construed" interpretation of communist.[25] When the CIA still could not produce appropriately damaging data, Operation Chaos chief Richard Ober ordered thirty agents to infiltrate various antiwar organizations. Like the other White House operations, the expansion of CIA spying involved elaborate precautions against public disclosure. It was no secret among the dissidents who assumed, correctly, that the real point was to destroy the antiwar movement by defining it as an alien, subversive force. In response, a coalition including the FOR, BEM, WSP, and some members of Congress considered ways of challenging political repression in Saigon and the suppression of dissent within the U.S. military, arguing presciently that "the only way the United States can continue its war policy in Vietnam is to increase suppression of dissent in Vietnam and at home."[26]

The long-awaited Nixon blueprint for Vietnam came in the midst of the government's covert activity. Early in May the PRG unveiled a tenpoint proposal for U.S. withdrawal and the war's conclusion. The president countered with the mutual, phased withdrawal of "non–South Vietnamese forces" and internationally supervised elections for the South Vietnamese "to determine their own political future without outside interference."[27] Nixon rejected demands for immediate U.S. withdrawal, and he called for public support for a gradual reduction of the American military presence on the grounds that this approach would "win a true and lasting peace" in Vietnam and the world. The president maneuvered to put his domestic critics on the defensive by alleging that the North Vietnamese had abandoned their hopes for a military victory and were now "counting on a collapse of American will in the United States."[28] Nixon thus perpetuated the illusions that had governed U.S. policy since he was vice-president: the United States could secure an independently viable, noncommunist regime in the South, and the North Vietnamese could be dissuaded from challenging it.

The American president rendezvoused with his South Vietnamese counterpart at Midway Island early in June, where he announced the withdrawal of 25,000 GIs in the first large-scale reduction of U.S. troop strength, part of a new "Nixon Doctrine" of limited U.S. involvement in revolutionary Third World wars. In Washington, Secretary of Defense Melvin Laird underscored the administration's intention to shift the combat burden to Saigon and declared that U.S. battlefield strategy had changed from "maximum pressure" to "protective reaction."[29] Within weeks, U.S. combat losses fell to their lowest level in two years, and they stayed low as the administration tried to conduct a military retreat that would still yield political victory.

Nixon's enunciation of war strategy revived dormant antiwar sentiment. Although a few Senate doves initially praised Nixon's plans, elite dissidents such as Clark Clifford, the former secretary of defense; W. Averell Harriman, the former chief U.S. negotiator at Paris; and Cyrus Vance called for speedier disengagement. The day after Nixon's address, eight antiwar members of Congress announced that they would introduce legislation calling for an immediate cease-fire in Vietnam and the withdrawal of 100,000 U.S. troops. The great majority of antiwar activists condemned the president's proposals as a prescription for open-ended war in Vietnam. Antiwar activists in Seattle greeted the first large-scale contingents of returning GIs with demands for the immediate withdrawal of all U.S. forces, and on Memorial Day thousands of dissidents throughout the country sponsored antiwar services in which they read the names of U.S. war dead in Vietnam and pleaded for an end to the carnage. In Washington, AFSC supporters endured jail and litigation in federal courts for their right to recount the death toll on the steps of the Capitol. "Obviously," wrote Daniel Berrigan shortly afterwards, "we are in for a very long haul on this war, and those who are trying even now to say no to it will be the ones who save whatever can be saved."[30]

The main burden of regenerating antiwar activism fell upon those liberals who had retreated from the Vietnam issue following the election. They now faced a clear, if formidable, challenge. Radical journalist Andrew Kopkind put it squarely to them immediately after Nixon's May address. The critical problem, he wrote, was that "the next logical demand is unilateral withdrawal," which constituted surrender to the communists, and "no liberal movement in the U.S. can yet accept that consequence."[31] Kopkind correctly assessed the dilemma facing many liberals, especially in Congress; but in the following months several liberal antiwar organizations, including WILPF, ADA, BEM, and the AFSC (SANE and WSP had already shifted their positions in December) demanded that the United States terminate its support of the Thieu regime and withdraw unilaterally from military action in Vietnam.

The resurgence of springtime activism culminated in the organization of two efforts—the Moratorium and the New Mobilization—which combined in the fall to rally the most potent and widespread antiwar protests ever mounted in a western democracy. In tandem their thrust was to generate a popular demand for either immediate departure from Vietnam or at least a fixed timetable for a total U.S. withdrawal.

The more explicitly liberal program was the Moratorium. It was not exactly Sam Brown's idea, but in large measure it was his and David Hawk's project. A native of Council Bluffs, Iowa, and president of the Young Republicans and the student body at Redlands University, Brown became active in the NSA, where he met Al Lowenstein. In 1964 he signed on in the Mississippi Summer Project. Then, after earning a graduate degree in political science, he enrolled in a Ph.D. program in divinity at Harvard. It was from there that Lowenstein recruited him to work with David Hawk in 1967 to mobilize seminarians against the war and then to form the Alternative Candidate Task Force. Both of them worked for McCarthy in the New Hampshire campaign. After King's death in April 1968, Brown went on to become a leader in the McCarthy organization, then returned to Harvard. Hawk meanwhile went to the Washington office of the NSA, where he mainly worked on antidraft projects. In the spring of 1969, with Brown's help, he organized a letter in which 253 student leaders from major universities vowed to refuse induction for service in Vietnam on the grounds that the war was immoral and unjust. The tone of the dissent was respectful, and, with the help of Lowenstein and McGovern, it got national attention. It was to a delegation of these students that Kissinger counseled patience.

In their interview the frustrated students encountered the problem which unsettled a number of Boston activists: how could a national movement be built that would penetrate the obdurate, self-contained White House? The germ of an idea surfaced one evening in a long conversation at a Brookline, Massachusetts, home from which Jerome Grossman took it to an executive meeting of MassPAX, a local antiwar group to which he was a major contributor.[32] What if a kind of national strike were called in case the war were not settled by a specific date? That one-day "deadline strike" could be extended by a day each subsequent month that troops were still in Vietnam. Just maybe it would snowball. Tested with a few moderate organizations, the idea drew only lukewarm support; but with the put-down at the White House fresh in mind, Brown and Hawk warmed to the notion and helped to refine it. The word *strike* was abandoned for fear of antagonizing segments of the middle-class constituency that the organizers intended to rally, and the action was instead labeled a "moratorium," a simple pause in business-as-usual for the purpose of reflection on and protest against the war.[33]

As the organizers of the moratorium acknowledged, the concept drew on four precedents: the 1967 Vietnam Summer experiment, various New Politics campaigns, the March halt in research at MIT, and traditional labor strikes. The plan was to begin a monthly antiwar escalation that would mobilize the broadest possible combination of antiwar citizens in "a legal and traditional protest action" which would have "a painful effect on all with power and influence."[34] The group wanted to generate a rising protest, "to make the forces in power 'hurt,'" until the government made "a firm commitment to a definite timetable for total withdrawal" or concluded a negotiated settlement.[35] There were to be no more token withdrawals, prolonged negotiations, or plans for a new Korean settlement. Likewise, the antiwar effort would not depend on a one-time demonstration or on its own constituency.

Moving ahead despite the fact that Lowenstein then opposed the idea, a Vietnam Moratorium Committee (VMC) was formed, with assurance of funding from Grossman. The core of organizers included Brown, Hawk, David Mixner, and Marge Sklencar. Mixner, who had not quite completed a B.A. in English literature, had been at the Chicago convention, where he had been shoved through a plate-glass window by police. In the following year he worked in Washington as a staff member of McGovern's commission on reform of the Democratic party. Sklencar, who had been an SDS leader in college, became active in the NSA and the 1967 effort to dump Johnson, and she helped to form the Conference of Concerned Democrats. She joined McCarthy's campaign staff, coordinating student work, and she also helped to organize Lowenstein's congressional effort. Following the election she taught for a Head Start program in Chicago until she joined the VMC. The four activists opened an office in Washington at the end of the school year, declared that their target date was 15 October, and proceeded to round up organizers and sponsors. Early in July, Hawk explained the project to a national conference of antiwar leaders in Cleveland.

The New Mobilization was born at that meeting, which had been called in yet another effort to form an antiwar coalition on the left. On the surface there was nothing in American radicalism to suggest that a fresh attempt would be any more successful than previous ones. Seething with hatreds, SDS met in its ninth and final national convention in Chicago late in June, only to break into hostile gangs. Delegates were offered a choice between Progressive Labor (PL) or the national office, and within the latter between Mike Klonsky's Revolutionary Youth Movement (by then RYM II) and the self-styled Weather Underground (after the Bob Dylan line, "You don't need a weatherman to know which way the wind blows"), in which Mark Rudd and Bernadine Dohrn were leaders. Women liberationists shouted for the destruction of male chauvinism, while Black Panthers mocked them with taunts of "pussy power."[36] Ironically, for an organization which had been founded on nonexclusionism, the national office faction forced PL out.

The spasm of disintegration was an extraordinary humiliation for the radical left. And yet, in a curious way, it freed many people from organizational ties with extremism. There still were radicals who responded to a personal core of social values rather than to self-indulgent action, and the resurrection of activism in the Easter demonstrations suggested that there might still be an authentic role for an antiwar left. Under the aegis of the AFSC and SWP, a cross section of independent leftists, radical pacifists, Trotskyists, and various liberals carefully organized a national consultation, again sponsored by the Cleveland Area Peace Action Council, for 4–5 July. The steering committee for this meeting was broadly representative but determined to create a more disciplined, responsible coalition than before, and its adult leadership set up the New Mobilization Committee to End the War in Vietnam.[37]

Pledging themselves to nonviolence, the New Mobe organizers agreed to concentrate on a national demonstration in Washington for 13–15 November, which would call for America's immediate withdrawal from Vietnam. The war was "the Pivotal Issue," New Mobe leaders agreed. It prevented reforms and was the key to the power elite within America. Pull "the Vietnam cinch-pin," they promised, "and the present tightly locked power structure of military and police repression, so profitable for those who make the profits and so crushing for those who struggle for liberation, will begin to come apart."[38] Presumably, the cause of revolutionary change would forge ahead, but the focus was on peace.

The New Mobe did not reckon sufficiently with the fact of confrontation in society or the force of cultural rebellion in the radical left. In May, police in Berkeley provoked seventeen days of sometimes bloody street fighting. The war had nothing to do with it, but resisting students did, and that was enough to link them with war protesters as "commies." Throughout the summer there was street violence and property destruction, both attacks on activists and actions directed against government agencies and war-related corporations. Radical infighting continued, too, as Mark Rudd, Bernadine Dohrn, and others fantasized about merging a revolutionary youth movement with working-class young people. Carl Oglesby complained about "vanguarditis." Staughton Lynd rued the attitude of a frustrated youth who exclaimed, "At least you can make yourself into a brick and hurl yourself."[39] The image of antiwar radicalism blended indiscriminately with that of random violence, such as the Charles Manson murders, and the "do-your-own-thing" communal harmony of the half-million youths at the Woodstock music festival in upstate New York. Since enthusiasts like Abbie Hoffman fused these disparate elements into dreams of a "Woodstock Nation" of peaceable but alienated youth—a unique "blending of Mao and marijuana"—the public could be excused for confusion.[40] Perhaps even the New Mobe could be excused, as it planned for a massive antiwar demonstration in the fall.

From the Oval Office, everything seemed secure. If the left mattered at all, its fragmentation only strengthened the administration's position.

Together with Vice-President Agnew, Nixon pursued his inaugural promise to "bring us together" by lashing out at the "self-righteous moral
arrogance" of the critics who constituted the "severest challenge" in
history to the integrity of American institutions.[41] Popular approval of
Nixon's handling of Vietnam climbed to a record level of 54 percent in
June.[42] Indeed, some right-wing elements even hoped for military victory,
given public support for the president's declared strategy, widespread
skepticism about the Paris peace talks, and a mood of patriotism suggested by the popularity of John Wayne's pro-war film *The Green Berets.*
Nixon had hopes for a political victory. Secretly, he ordered his aides to
draft a plan for drastic military escalation, code-named Operation Duck
Hook, and he privately issued an ultimatum to Hanoi that it quit the war
by 1 November or face a "savage, decisive blow."[43]

The president miscalculated on both counts. The North Vietnamese
did not respond to his threat, and popular support fell off significantly
during the summer. The prospect of a tax increase loomed in the context
of rising inflation. The war was not forgotten, and only its cost was clear:
Life magazine devoted eleven somber pages of a summer issue to the
photographs of 261 GIs killed in action during one week of fighting,
commenting that the country "must pause to look into the faces" of its
dead.[44] There remained an ambivalence in American attitudes to the war
that left them volatile and unpredictable as summer merged into fall.

The Fall Offensive: "All we are saying, is give peace a chance"

Ho Chi Minh died in September, and the U.S. government announced
a thirty-six-hour suspension of B-52 raids within South Vietnam, but
neither development seriously affected the battlefield or the negotiations.
Eager for early success, Nixon resolved to "go for broke."[45] He urged his
aides to accelerate plans for a devastating military escalation against the
North after 1 November in order to terrorize Hanoi into a dictated settlement. Playing upon his reputation as a ferocious anticommunist, the
president warned the North Vietnamese to consider him a "madman,"
capable of authorizing the kind of full and utter destruction that would
push them beyond their "breaking point."[46] The credibility of Nixon's
ultimatum depended on two things: Hanoi's ability to fight would have
to be broken by heavy U.S. bombing, a naval blockade, and the mining
of North Vietnamese harbors, but the military planners of Operation
Duck Hook could not promise that; and, moreover, domestic support had
to be reliable, but it was not. Even as Nixon planned a radical escalation
of the war during the early autumn, popular and political momentum
shifted toward the side of those dissidents who demanded a more rapid,
if not immediate, American withdrawal from Vietnam.

Antiwar sentiment had a clear focus in the 15 October Moratorium. Throughout the summer Brown, Hawk, Sklencar, and Mixner had worked primarily with student leaders, but after Labor Day the Vietnam Moratorium Committee gained precious support from older liberals and elite dissidents—for example, the *New Republic,* the Central Conference of American Rabbis, the New Democratic Coalition, BEM, ADA, and the liberal Republican Ripon Society. On 22 September it was endorsed by leading intellectuals, including John Kenneth Galbraith, Hans J. Morgenthau, and Noam Chomsky. Ninety-six percent of the Harvard faculty voted for it. The UAW and the Teamsters came out in its favor, as did an interfaith group of religious leaders. Twenty-four Democratic senators added their support, along with W. Averell Harriman, the dean of American diplomats. Moreover, endorsements came from leaders previously critical of the antiwar movement, such as Whitney Young of the NAACP, and Richard Cardinal Cushing, the Roman Catholic bishop of Boston. By October the organizing VMC had a full-time, paid staff of 31 and 7,500 field organizers. Worried CIA operatives who had infiltrated the headquarters warned their agency that the Moratorium was "shaping up to be the most widely supported public action in American history. Several of the "usual troublemakers" were involved, the CIA reported, but the real problem was that "prominent people regarded as loyal Americans have instilled the day with respectability and even patriotism."[47]

Indeed, Vietnam was now on the congressional agenda. On 25 September, Senator Charles Goodell (R-N.Y.) announced that he would sponsor a resolution calling upon the president to withdraw all U.S. forces from Vietnam by 1 December 1970 or face the cutoff of congressional funding for the war. Several antiwar members of the House developed companion bills, while Senator McGovern urged the administration to allow all threatened South Vietnamese asylum in the U.S. and suggested that any Americans dissatisfied with America's withdrawal from Vietnam might volunteer their own services in the war. In October, Senators Church and Hatfield devised a resolution for American withdrawal after a "reasonable interval," and Senators Harold Hughes (D-Iowa) and Thomas Eagleton (D-Mo.) prepared a bill to terminate America's entire commitment unless the Thieu regime reformed itself within sixty days.[48]

These leaders were responding to American frustration. Vietnam was being debated with a new seriousness, but the context for the discussion was a popular climate of confusion, pessimism, and ambivalence. A solid majority of Americans supported troop withdrawals and plans to strengthen the South Vietnamese to do their own fighting for the sake of an honorable settlement, although a growing number of them were dissatisfied with the president's overall Vietnam policy. Expressing little confidence in the Paris peace talks, 70 percent of those polled expected a long war, an involvement which a record 58 percent now called a mistake.[49] Given mounting reports of corruption and political repression in Saigon, an increasing number of Americans concluded that an anti-communist government would not survive in South Vietnam without American forces, and 45 percent expected a communist military victory following a U.S. withdrawal. If the center of American opinion seemed to be ambivalent, there were strong feelings on either side of it, including a sizable body that would support the president in one last attempt to win the war militarily. All sectors were frustrated. "The irony is that the American mood is as pessimistic as it is without a Dienbienphu," wrote Louis Harris, who also noted that a third of the people sampled wanted immediate and unconditional U.S. withdrawal, "a sizable figure in support of a policy that until recently was overwhelmingly held to be unthinkable and disastrous."[50]

President Nixon, put on the defensive, declared in September that he would not be affected by expressions of popular discontent. Nonetheless, the administration fought for public support. Alternating between tough and conciliatory poses, Nixon insisted that he would not be "the first President to preside over an American defeat" at the same time that he authorized reduced draft calls and said he wanted to end the war in 1970. He publicly attacked congressional critics as "defeatist," and he secretly ordered aides to link Edward Kennedy and the communist enemy.[51] Senator Goldwater declared that the Moratorium was "playing into the hands of people whose business it is to kill American fighting men," as GOP congressional leaders Hugh Scott (Pa.) of the Senate and Gerald Ford (Mich.) of the House denounced those who would "bug out" or "cut and run" from Vietnam.[52] Most colorfully of all, Vice-President Agnew dismissed critics for their "seditious drivel" and called for "positive polarization" throughout the country.[53] The White House rallied veterans' organizations and prowar groups, including an ad hoc Citizens Committee for Peace with Security which launched a "Tell It to Hanoi" advertising campaign.

Although the Moratorium was supported by the great majority of leftists and radical pacifists, it was impugned by the words and actions of militants and street fighters who were just visible enough to be useful in the administration's characterization of dissidents as irresponsible. In particular, attention was drawn to Chicago the week before Moratorium Day. The trial of the Chicago Eight had begun late in September. The defendants had already organized a support network, "The Conspiracy," and Judge Julius Hoffman had made the courtroom a site for confrontation. The case was adopted as a *cause célèbre* by the tiny Weathermen faction, which had planned to confront Chicago anyway. On 8 October, after promises of an invasion force of 20,000, a few hundred militants in makeshift battle gear appeared in Chicago's Lincoln Park. From there they trotted off toward the Drake Hotel, where they believed Judge Hoff-man lived. The march quickly broke into a spree of vandalism through Chicago's Gold Coast area. Three days later, another 150 Weathermen tangled with police in the city's historic Haymarket Square, leaving 50 people injured and 103 arrested. That was the sum total of the promised "Days of Rage" in the Windy City. Almost the entire radical left, including the Panthers, repudiated the Weathermen's self-indulgent violence, but the very fact of their irresponsibility aroused fears among organizers of the New Mobe (apprehensions that proved to be well founded when on 14 November a gang of militants invaded the VMC office in Washington and tried unsuccessfully to extort $25,000 by threatening violence during the next day's march).

On 15 October none of that mattered. If patriotism was an abiding concern for the country, then the moratorium on business-as-usual was vested with a patriotic aura. It opened as the sun's first rays lighted a memorial service for American war dead held on the Massachusetts shore, and it spread westward with the day, attaining a diversity, pervasiveness, and dignity unprecedented in the history of popular protest. It ranged from lonely picketing to mass rallies, from public demonstrations to pri-vate conversations. Managers of businesses such as the Itek Corporation and Midas Muffler encouraged workers to take time to support the Mor-atorium. Other Americans took off on their own or discussed the war at their work places.

Boston Common hosted 100,000 people who listened to speeches and music while a skywriter sketched the peace sign overhead. New York bustled with antiwar activities involving an estimated quarter-million people. The largest number jammed Bryant Park for a rally that featured Senators Eugene McCarthy and Charles Goodell, Mayor John Lindsay, and theatrical figures such as Tony Randall and Shirley McLaine. The mayor had in fact scheduled himself at fifteen rallies that day. He had also issued an order to fly the flag at half-mast in the city, a gesture widely misun-derstood. There was no mistaking the overall mood in New York. The producer of the hit Broadway musical *Fiddler on the Roof* asked the matinée audience to join the cast in marching from the show to a rally. Many did. Comedian Woody Allen cancelled all performances of his *Play It Again, Sam*. In lower Manhattan, respectable businessmen such as New York Yankees president Mike Burke and former Johnson administration officials Bill Moyers and Roswell Gilpatric headed a memorial service in Wall Street. Commuters in Grand Central Station were offered an after-noon prayer service by teachers and students from Union Theological Seminary and the Jesuits' Woodstock College. Broadway stars led a can-dlelight procession in Times Square, and thousands jammed Fifth Avenue outside St. Patrick's Cathedral for an evening service. Holding burning candles, they sang "America the Beautiful" and prayed for the war's end. "No one wanted to leave," said a reporter. "It was almost as if they were trying to stop the clock and preserve the moment."[54]

Further down the eastern coast, Philadelphia was flooded with antiwar events, many of them endorsed by public officials. A Baltimore country judge interrupted court proceedings to allow private reflection on the war. In Washington fifteen hundred congressional aides stood in a silent vigil on the steps of the Capitol during their lunch break. The mood penetrated the House of Representatives, where members rejected an overnight session in support of the Moratorium but did hold four hours of serious floor debate on the war. There were concurrent rallies around the city during the day, and in the evening Coretta Scott King led perhaps forty thousand citizens in a solemn candlelight procession from the Washington Monument to the White House.

The day passed into the central South, where the Moratorium was largely ignored, and the Midwest, where it was widely observed. Thirty people prayed in the town square of Hudson, Ohio. Chicago organizers claimed that 100,000 participated in teach-ins, vigils, leafletting, and rallies. The mayor abstained. At least ten thousand citizens, including Hubert Humphrey, gathered in downtown Minneapolis. Housewives in Duluth distributed antiwar leaflets at traffic intersections, and the Oshkosh Public Library put up a Vietnam War display. There were teach-ins at many colleges and universities. Students at Bethel College in North Newton, Kansas, tolled the campus bell once every four seconds in honor of each American killed in Vietnam. The pealing continued for days.

Westward, over three thousand people braved a six-inch snowfall in Denver in order to march to the state capitol, and a half-dozen people read the names of U.S. war dead on the steps of the Wyoming state capitol in Cheyenne. On the Pacific coast some twenty thousand southern Californians converged for programs on the UCLA campus, while several thousand more at the University of Southern California heard Ralph Abernathy of the SCLC. Actors picketed a movie set in Hollywood, women planted memorial flowers at a veterans' cemetery in West Los Angeles, and students at Whittier College—Nixon's alma mater—lit a "flame of life" intended to burn until the war's end. Across the ocean some GIs on patrol showed their solidarity with domestic dissidents by wearing black armbands.

The Moratorium was a national demonstration, teach-in, and memorial service. The national VMC avoided defining any political agenda, although Sam Brown did claim that the "common denominator" of the myriad programs was for "withdrawal from Vietnam no later than December 1st of next year."[55] Instead, the main force of the Moratorium was the willingness of ordinary and respectable citizens to conduct collective actions that indicated their wish "to have done with Vietnam" and to restore domestic harmony.[56] The breadth and depth of that sentiment was captured by the media. In their accounts the day expressed, as the CIA had feared it would, a profound sense of patriotism.

Infused with a spirit of sadness and loss, most Moratorium activities were less angry than distressed. The violence of a few incidents was offset by the tragedy of a young couple in Morristown, New Jersey, who returned from antiwar ceremonies at Glassboro State College and asphyxiated themselves in their automobile. Suicide notes conveyed their despair, and the man's sister reported simply, "He was against the war."[57] One reporter recorded feeling "a central stillness" in the Moratorium. "People felt deeply, their experiences were intimate; yet there was an open sense of sharing," as great collectivities of people of all ages and backgrounds "behaved as individuals: that was the uniqueness."[58] For a day, people throughout the nation found ways to express their longing to move beyond Vietnam and its related domestic divisions and toward a reinvigorated sense of belonging and togetherness.

The Moratorium reflected the changing nature of the war for America. With U.S. troops headed home, and given the general consensus that Saigon could not survive without them, continuing warfare was hard to defend in terms of upholding national security and international credibility. At an unparalleled moment of military retreat, with the risk of political defeat, Vietnam became a metaphor for a struggle over the national identity. It expressed a nation longing to find meaning in its losses—something more than empty humiliation. Participation in the Moratorium implied that it was all right and even patriotic to be against the war, that it was not a betrayal of earlier sacrifices to want to stop the carnage, that divisive misjudgment could be redeemed by getting beyond the conflict. Intervention, although it was attacked, was not the issue. Who would rule in Saigon, although it was discussed, receded in importance. "The very cohesion of American society is at stake," observed the *New Republic*.[59] At issue was the identity of the American people, as it was expressed in national symbols and myths.

On that level, primarily, the Moratorium was challenged. National veterans' organizations such as the American Legion urged Americans to fly the flag on 15 October as an expression of loyalty, and in the following weeks the flag became established more firmly than ever as the main symbol of the government's war policy. South Dakota war supporters bombarded a vigil in Spearfish with leaflets reading "America—Love It Or Leave It," and the city editor of the Waterbury (Connecticut) *Republican* was fired for publishing the names of area war dead in defiance of newspaper policy. Schoolteachers in various parts of the country were criticized for wearing black armbands in class. The Bank of America dismissed a veteran employee for participating in Moratorium Day activities. "No one can tell," a reporter wrote, "how many people were ostracized, or persecuted, or dismissed from their jobs, or prosecuted on trumped-up charges, or run out of town because of their opposition to the war, but there undoubtedly were many thousands of them altogether."[60]

Such reactions were part of a campaign for Americanism, a kind of ownership of the war, which was encouraged by the White House. The Moratorium exposed a deep stratum of American disaffection and undercut the administration's plans to force a dictated peace on the North Vietnamese through major military escalation after 1 November. The president "was as bitter and disappointed as I ever saw him," recalled Nixon's longtime aide, H. R. Haldeman.[61] The White House reiterated its commitment to U.S. troop withdrawal and a measured approach to a "just peace," and it fired the controversial Selective Service Director Lewis Hershey; but, at the same time, it also assailed its critics as defeatists, if not subversives. Vice-President Agnew demanded that Moratorium leaders repudiate a congratulatory letter issued by Hanoi, insisting that their failure to do that would expose them as communist stooges. In any case, the critics were "ideological eunuchs" and "an effete corps of impudent snobs," mixed in with "hardcore dissidents and professional anarchists."[62] Agnew did not spare the television news media. He accused them of distorting administration policy and war reports, and he manufactured a partisan "stab-in-the-back" legend by claiming that W. Averell Harriman, the former U.S. peace negotiator and now critic of the war, had "swapped some of the greatest military concessions in the history of warfare for an enemy arrangement on the shape of the bargaining table."[63] Transportation Secretary John Volpe added that dissidents were "Communist or Communist-inspired," and Governor Ronald Reagan of California responded that at least they were "lending comfort and aid to the enemy."[64]

The administration's counteroffensive made the critics rather than the war the central issue in the national debate over Vietnam. Even the plight of American POWs was enlisted, as Nixon encouraged millionaire Dallas electronics manufacturer H. Ross Perot to form United We Stand in support of the administration's approach and the safe return of U.S. prisoners. The Citizens Committee for Peace with Freedom in Vietnam repudiated any "premature" American withdrawal from Vietnam, and the chief of the National Guard urged the country's guardsmen to demonstrate their opposition to antiwar actions. A number of educators, veterans' leaders, and conservative activists agreed in early November to sponsor an "Honor America" week of parades and rallies during 9–16 November. Many of the holiday ceremonies were local and low-key, in effect an extension of the October mood of concern. Others were boisterous and belligerent. Through the joint efforts of the administration, conservative groups, and veterans' organizations, hundreds of thousands of Americans marched in explicit support of the president, sporting flag pins and waving what *Newsweek* called the "ubiquitous sign"—"America, Love It Or Leave It."[65] Bob Hope and Art Linkletter were honorary co-chairmen of a National Unity Week. "It's pretty hard for good, nice people to demonstrate," said Hope, [but] if we ever let the Communists win this war we are in great danger of fighting for the rest of our lives and losing a million kids, not just the 40,000 we've already lost."[66]

On 3 November, a week before Veterans Day, President Nixon in a nationally televised speech set the tone for the well-orchestrated attempt to win the public. After detailing several previously confidential diplomatic moves, the president concluded that the United States had only two choices in Vietnam. One was an "immediate, precipitate withdrawal," which he rejected on the grounds that it would set off wholesale communist massacres in the South, create "divisive recrimination" at home, and result in "a collapse of confidence . . . not only in Asia but throughout the world." The second alternative was to "search for a just peace through a negotiated settlement if possible" and Vietnamization if necessary. Nixon adroitly shifted responsibility for any future failure from himself to his critics. "North Vietnam cannot defeat or humiliate the United States," he promised. "Only Americans can do that." At the same time, he dismissed antiwar critics as a vocal minority which, if allowed to prevail over reason and popular will, would endanger America's very "future as a free society." In the most telling phrase of the speech, he appealed for support from "the great silent majority" of citizens.[67]

The president regained the political initiative with that address, masterfully phrased and presented, and effectively exploited. Within forty-eight hours, over 52,000 telegrams reached the White House, nearly all in support of the administration (it was revealed later that many of them were generated by organized Republican party workers). A Gallup poll indicated that 77 percent of Americans backed the president's policies, with only 6 percent in opposition, and that by a six-to-one margin people agreed with him that antiwar protests actually harmed the prospects for peace.[68] Politically sensitive dissenters backed off. Antiwar members of Congress criticized the slow pace of withdrawal but joined with the great majority of their colleagues to endorse the president's approach. Senator Fulbright postponed hearings on Goodell's "Vietnam Disengagement Act," ostensibly in order to avoid arousing controversy when the nation was on an "outward course" from Vietnam.[69]

Liberal antiwar dissidents could scarcely believe that Nixon had turned popular opinion around so quickly and easily. The fact that he could overwhelm the whole thrust of the October protest in a half-hour speech was "inconceivable," said an antiwar organizer; it was impossible that the power and promise of the Moratorium could be "totally erased" in a short television address.[70] He missed a critical point. The president had used his command of the media to give a specific political focus to undifferentiated national anxiety, a tactic which the Vietnam Moratorium Committee had deliberately avoided.

The administration's counteroffensive complicated the attempts of liberal and radical antiwar dissidents to cooperate on the plans for a Mobilization Against the War in November. That had been an explicit part of White House strategy, but it was hardly necessary.[71] The differences between the two factions were already deep and substantial. Some radical activists in the New Mobilization Committee clung to the old hope that the antiwar movement could revitalize a left-wing "popular front" that would transform American life, whereas liberals in and out of the VMC concentrated on the single issue of ending the war and preventing further presidential interventions. Moreover, even radical pacifists in the New Mobe who shared that liberal aim could not guarantee an absence of extremism or factionalism in a mass demonstration. After all, laughed Sidney Lens, it was "REALLY a broad coalition. We range from the Trots to the Chicago police."[72] Liberals in the VMC, on the other hand, insisted on the most decorous and respectable kind of protest, one which would not alienate their principal targets in "middle America."[73] This was a real concern in light of past mobilizations and of developments on the radical left.

The organizers of the Moratorium and the New Mobe were divided by another factor, less dramatic than the ideological ones but every bit as important. This was a difference in political strategy and resources. Mass demonstrations were very costly—a heavy drain not only on the money but also on the energy and time available to local antiwar groups. In Mobe theory, investment in the streets paid off with maximum public exposure. In Moratorium theory, on the other hand, limited resources could be used most effectively on the local level. There, where they would contribute to sustaining relationships among people who knew and trusted one another, they might generate enduring public programs. The conflict between the two organizations over ideological orientations therefore reflected a difference of organizational style and strategy. Cooperation between them was possible only because of a core of people to whom the two approaches seemed complementary.

There was also a basic conflict over dates, since both organizations had long scheduled actions in the middle of November. On 21 October the VMC and the New Mobe announced that they would plan separate but complementary actions for 13–15 November, with the Moratorium concentrating on local activities and the New Mobe focusing on mass actions in Washington and San Francisco. Nixon's speech raised the stakes for both groups, casting them as a common enemy, and in the days just prior to the demonstrations they cooperated. The Moratorium's organizational expertise and national influence was needed, particularly as the government was withholding march permits, but its leaders could not imagine anything more catastrophic than a replication of the Battle of Chicago under the undisciplined auspices of the New Mobilization. Accordingly, it was only after hard negotiations promised a disciplined, nonviolent demonstration and agreement was reached on a roster of speakers that the VMC and New Mobe coordinated their efforts.

By this time, however, many antiwar liberals had distanced themselves from the November mobilization. Former ambassadors Harriman and Kennan both warned that the demonstration would inhibit rather than spread antiwar opposition. Several members of Congress declared that they would not back the Mobe until it had purged itself of known communists, although Lowenstein held firm. The media peppered New Mobe leaders with so many questions regarding the likelihood of violence that at a press conference Sidney Lens finally screamed out: "Why the hell don't you ask the man who is really committed to violence, Richard Nixon, whether he intends to continue the massacres in Vietnam? If all of us on this podium lived a thousand years we couldn't perpetrate as much violence as Nixon does in one day. Ask your questions of him, not us."[74] The point was, of course, that the dissenters and not the war had become the paramount news issue.

Behind Lens' outburst were exhaustive efforts to plan a smooth operation: raising large funds, transporting and accommodating hundreds of thousands of people who would arrive at different times to feed into various facets of the action; negotiating permits for each segment; contracting stage and sound equipment and toilet facilities; coordinating speakers and major entertainers; organizing hundreds of legal marshals and medical personnel; communicating with the media; preparing and distributing detailed instructions not only about directions but for personal deportment. Not least important was the recruiting and training of some four thousand marshals who were to keep the peace in the face of provocations from the extreme right and, especially, the ultra-left. Many marshals were trained by Quaker groups such as the AFSC and A Quaker Action Group before they arrived in Washington, but they and others recruited on the spot were also instructed at a District of Columbia center. All of this required a host of committees, a coalition steering committee, and overall an experienced team: Ron Young of the FOR as project coordinator, Brad Lyttle and Fred Halstead on logistical arrangements.

Stewart Meacham was responsible for the March Against Death, which set the tone for the whole.[75] It had been his idea, drawn from the experience of reading the list of war dead at a rally in the spring. Here there would be no abstract list but rather 45,000 individuals, each one of them the symbol of a real death. They began to gather near Arlington National Cemetery. Late in the afternoon, led by seven drummers playing a funeral roll, the marchers left the cemetery area and crossed the Arlington Memorial Bridge in solemn single file, each person carrying a lighted candle and a placard inscribed with the name of a dead GI or a destroyed Vietnamese village. They strode silently into raw winds and a biting November rain, more than a thousand of them each hour, and on to the White House. In the wet stillness, facing blinding security lights, each citizen paused to shout the name drawn on his or her placard, and then continued in the procession down Pennsylvania Avenue and on to the west steps of the Capitol. Each in turn, the marchers placed their placards in waiting coffins and blew out their candles. Navy Second Lieutenant Donald Droz was the first of the dead to be memorialized, and his name was laid to rest that night by his twenty-three-year-old widow, Judy.

The March continued for thirty-six hours—in the darkness of Wednesday night, through the following day, to mid-morning Friday. In a war already too rich in drama and pathos, it was the most moving testimony yet offered to the thousands of individual men and women enfolded in a nation's anguish. National Security Council aide William Watts, working late in Henry Kissinger's offices, glanced outside at the line of marchers. As he watched, his wife and children filed past the window. Flushed with emotion, he contrasted their sentiments with his work.[76] The ordeal had come to this, and Watts was in a position to know that it would go much further.

Early on Thursday, while the memorial march proceeded along the Mall, an ecumenical prayer service for peace was conducted at National Cathedral by religious leaders including William Sloane Coffin and Eugene Carson Blake, head of the World Council of Churches. During the day Dr. Benjamin Spock led a demonstration at the Justice Department to protest the trial of the Chicago Eight. At Dupont Circle in the city's near northwest, militants incited violence when several hundred of them tried to storm police lines and attack the South Vietnamese embassy until they were driven back. The skirmish did not bode well for an orderly march on the next day, even as several hundred thousand peace-seekers were approaching the city in a kind of pilgrimage of petition.

Perhaps a half-million Americans gathered on Saturday morning, crowding onto the Mall from the west side of the Capitol to the Washington Monument. They came, with great ambition but shrinking hope, to "rescue the nation from the warmakers" and effect America's immediate withdrawal from Vietnam and the construction at home of "a society committed to Life and Freedom."[77] Mostly they came, one suspected, because they felt obligated to do something and because they wanted to be part of this memorable event. Gathering behind the coffins left at the Capitol after the March Against Death, the crowd formed a human wave that flowed down Pennsylvania Avenue to within a block of the White

House and then turned south along Fifteenth Street to the grounds of the Washington Monument. For five hours people flooded into the Mall. It was the largest protest demonstration in American history, with a size and diversity that not even the participants could comprehend.

Overwhelmingly white and mostly young, the marchers exhibited unusually good spirits despite the cold, grey skies and intermittent showers. Few listened to the speakers—Coretta Scott King, Senators McGovern and McCarthy, and a number of others. But the crowd perked up considerably when the cast of the Broadway hit musical *Hair* sang selections from the show. Then, joining singers Pete Seeger, Mitch Miller, and Peter, Paul, and Mary, for ten minutes the throng chanted John Lennon's haunting appeal: "All we are saying / is give peace a chance." With gripping power, the words rolled back from the Washington Monument plaza to the steps of the Capitol and up the side streets where thousands of other marchers were backed up, physically unable to squeeze onto the Mall. More than any speech or slogan, the chant, with its almost hypnotic force, reflected the curiously tribal, even spiritual, nature of the March. It was "more a celebration than a protest," said one participant.[78] Except that they got their "high" from a common moral purpose, these slightly older people could almost feel they were at another Woodstock.

In the mass of humanity that spilled across central Washington, militant activists were either ignored or isolated. On the Mall a group dumped records seized during a raid on a Boston draft board office into the Reflecting Pool, but nearby FBI agents declined to arrest them. A few radical zealots flew Vietcong flags and called for revolutionary violence, but they were contained by parade marshals and were merely tolerated by the crowd. Late in the evening, while the great bulk of the crowd headed homeward, a few thousand yippies, zealots, and sympathizers rioted at the Justice and Labor Department offices, provoking police into clearing a wide section of downtown Washington with tear gas. The incident was noted in the press, but it was correctly described as an exception to a massive demonstration conducted with seriousness and responsibility.

"A growing feeling of 'what's the use?'"

"It was the best, it was the biggest, it was the last of the antiwar demonstrations," wrote columnist Nicholas Von Hoffman. A parallel action in San Francisco was also a peaceful record-breaker. The joint mobilization was followed by the usual attacks on activists for allegedly provoking violence or abetting communism, but those were to be expected. More disheartening was the president's calculated deafness. U.S. war policy would not be made in the streets, he repeated. With the White House barricaded by hundreds of buses parked bumper-to-bumper,

Nixon ostentatiously turned his back on the crowd, letting it be known that he planned to watch a televised football game during the demonstration. "If it cannot convince the men who make war and peace they can't safely go on with the conflict," Hoffman continued, "then no amount of marching, praying or singing will change their minds."[79] November 1969 was not the last Vietnam demonstration, perhaps not even the largest, but its scale would not be repeated for a year and a half.

Of course, the mobilization had been designed to win the minds and hearts of the American people as well as those of their leaders. Like the Moratorium, it received generally fair and appreciative commentary from the newspapers. Unlike the October event, it was not covered live on TV, and even the limited news accounts of it associated the atypical violence with the organized demonstration: with respect to television, the administration's "terrorizing worked."[80] In any case, the action failed to win popular support for its point of view or for its sponsors.

Public opinion confounded antiwar activists. At the end of the fall peace offensive, a sampling of Americans labeled themselves doves and not hawks by 55 to 31 percent. Half of them agreed that the war was "morally indefensible." Four-fifths of them were "fed up and tired of the war" and agreed that antiwar protesters were "raising real questions which ought to be discussed and answered." And yet a plurality of the same people did not favor the October Moratorium, three-fourths of them disapproved of the November Mobilization, and three-fifths agreed with Nixon that antiwar demonstrations aided the enemy and hurt the president's chances of making peace.[81] Frustrated and unhappy, most Americans expressed less support for the war than resentment toward antiwar protesters. They wanted to quit the fighting more than ever, but not to surrender. They were tired of controversy, too, and they longed for domestic quiet. More than one observer concluded that "a decade of marching had come to an end."[82] Even among antiwar activists that feeling was pervasive. It expressed their deepening frustration with the ordeal of Vietnam which, they could not know, had reached only mid-point.

By that time it was apparent that the military was suffering from a complex variant of the national malaise. After festering for two years, organized antiwar discontent surfaced within the armed forces during 1969. It was partly an expression of congenital GI griping, but it gained a sharper edge with the influx of better-educated GIs who had lost their graduate school deferments. Disaffection was also fed by worsening racial tensions, increasing drug abuse, and a mounting contempt for the military's command system. The implication of a Special Forces unit in a murder case involving Vietnamese double agents intensified general misgivings over the freewheeling ways of the Green Berets and the corrupting politics of Saigon. Moreover, government investigators revealed that the army's own highest-ranking non-commissioned officer was running a highly sophisticated criminal operation that skimmed millions of dollars from the profits of army post exchanges and entertainment programs in the Far East. Perhaps most basically, the course of the war had compromised its rationale. As one trooper put it bluntly, "I don't want to get killed buying time for the gooks."[83] The explicitly antiwar thrust of military discontent accelerated with the momentum of U.S. troop withdrawals.

Antiwar service personnel demonstrated in the United States late in the year. Indeed, 1,365 active duty GIs signed an appeal for Americans to attend the Moratorium, and it was published as a full-page ad in the *New York Times*.[84] A hundred soldiers from Fort Hood joined in a large antiwar rally in Houston; some fifty GIs petitioned for peace and free speech on the steps of the National Archives in Washington; and several hundred paraded near Oceanside, California. In Vietnam, over a hundred soldiers at Pleiku fasted over Thanksgiving, protesting their involvement in "a senseless war that cannot be won," and military police broke up a Christmas Eve peace demonstration of forty GIs in front of Saigon's Roman Catholic cathedral.[85] Actions such as these encouraged antiwar activists to interpret military disillusionment, as they viewed civilian discontent, in terms of their own political agenda for immediate withdrawal.

The story of the Mylai massacre unfolded among this rising protest by GIs, giving a nightmarish cast to America's interior struggle over Vietnam. A succession of reports, accounts, and photographs gradually appeared, as if in slow motion, to document the fact that in March 1968, at the hamlet of Mylai near Songmy, GIs commanded by First Lieutenant William Calley had systematically herded hundreds of old men, women, and children together and gunned them down. The atrocity had been covered up within the army's chain of command and had come to light only when a combat photographer accumulated evidence of the tragedy and badgered officials and legislators to make inquiries. On 12 November the army disclosed that Calley was being detained to stand trial. Seymour Hersh's series of stories about the atrocity broke on the eve of the Mobilization. The revelation of the size and viciousness of the massacre, as well as its subsequent cover-up, provoked fundamental questions about personal military conduct, command responsibility, the nature of the war, and its impact on Americans—not to mention the Vietnamese. Government authorities tried to contain these questions by treating Mylai as an isolated and aberrant incident.

Antiwar critics seized upon Mylai as a microcosm of the larger atrocity of the war itself: "Mylai was not a criminal incident in an otherwise 'just' war," said the *Christian Century*, "it simply represents the ultimate logic of a criminal war."[86] Dissidents also interpreted the cover-up as typical of the war's corruption of national institutions, and they assailed the government's attempt to restrict responsibility to Calley and his men.

"The real crime is higher up," I. F. Stone concluded.[87] Mylai thus held a powerful and very specific meaning for critics of Vietnam policy. It was a metaphor for all that was wrong with the war and for the moral urgency of withdrawing from it immediately. Public sentiment was far from uniform. Calley was defended by many people, including prowar advocates, who seemed to share the view of antiwar critics that the lieutenant was a scapegoat for senior officials; but opinion divided as to whether Mylai was a typical or exceptional incident. The House of Representatives endorsed the latter view by passing a resolution praising U.S. troops in Vietnam. Like the growing protest from GIs, therefore, the revelation of the massacre was significant insofar as it helped to distinguish the courage and integrity of the soldier from the kind of warfare of which he was a moral victim.

For the time being, Mylai only aggravated the ambivalence of Congress and the public that found the war repugnant and yet uneasily accepted the administration's approach to peace. President Nixon's appeal to the "silent majority" apparently elicited more negative feeling against war protesters than support for further combat. Fifty-nine percent of Americans sampled in December identified themselves as members of the "silent majority," and 74 percent of them said that the term meant that "protesters have gone too far." The same poll suggested that although self-identified members of the "silent majority" regarded protesters much more negatively than other Americans did, they were "no more eager than the rest of the population to keep on fighting in Vietnam."[88] The White House recognized the contradictory elements of public sentiment, and it played upon them.

There were new investigations of the antiwar groups following the November demonstrations, and more charges of their communist links or defeatism. The president met at the White House with leaders of the "Tell It to Hanoi" campaign and gratefully accepted the 350,000 signatures that they had gathered in support of his policies. He emphasized his concern for American POWs and endorsed a quixotic attempt to airfreight supplies and POW wives to Hanoi in December.

Most important, the president kept pulling U.S. troops out of combat and reiterating the theme that America's exit was honorable. On 24 November the White House announced that the administration had reached its mid-December troop withdrawal goal three weeks earlier than planned, and two days later Nixon redeemed his earlier pledge to replace existing draft laws with a lottery system and then a voluntary army. In December the president announced that another fifty thousand U.S. troops would be returned home by 15 April, declaring that the communists had lost all hope "that division in the United States would eventually bring them the victory they cannot win over our fighting men in Vietnam."[89] With the White House apparently in control of events, elite critics like Mike Mansfield expressed their respect for Nixon's efforts. By the year's end the Democratic party chairman, Senator Fred Harris (Okla.), declared that the president had effectively neutralized Vietnam as a domestic political issue so that the war question would be of marginal political significance in 1970.

Harris' assessment, that the war was a dormant issue, accurately characterized the winter and early spring. Warfare in Vietnam became less severe. Reported North Vietnamese infiltration into the South subsided, while battlefield contacts and U.S. casualties declined to their lowest level in two years. Vietnamization was permitting American withdrawal without endangering the South Vietnamese government, the administration explained, and was therefore complementing the negotiation process. Even when Prince Norodom Sihanouk of Cambodia was overthrown and fighting erupted in his country, U.S. officials exuded optimism that the war would be ended to their satisfaction, with or without a formal treaty arrangement.

Antiwar activists were not assuaged by the administration's troop withdrawals and assurances, but they felt a gnawing sense of helplessness. Daniel Berrigan wrote to a supporter in December, "You must know by now that we are quite desperate with the war continuing in spite of all efforts to the contrary, a bad down-hill careening nightmare, entirely out of rational control."[90] To apparent futility was added tension within the movement. CALC held together despite differences among its leaders over Vietnam policy. The liberal Moratorium and radical pacifist New Mobe had been temporary allies at best, and after 15 November the coalition disintegrated. Quite aside from their own exhaustion, a hostile public, and an apparently successful administration, the antiwar coalitions had been drained of financial resources. This was especially true of the Moratorium, which had underwritten the November mobilization with significant funds. The mass demonstrations also drained local groups of money and energy, as Sam Brown and his friends had expected. Brad Lyttle and Fred Halstead knew from months of frustration that radical factionalism still threatened the New Mobe and SMC. Strong centripetal forces were disrupting both wings of the organized antiwar movement.

At first the VMC tried to keep to its original timetable of monthly escalations. Gamely, it sponsored three days of local actions during December. The response was so slight that it abandoned the moratorium format in order to concentrate on local organizing efforts for "the realism of immediate withdrawal" from Vietnam.[91] But what kind of local efforts? When someone suggested coordinating local actions in an April "Fast for Peace," Marge Sklencar pointed out that there wasn't enough commitment: "The obstacle to getting peace is not the silent majority, but the indifferent majority."[92] Independently, the FOR and CALC organized a seventy-five-day fast for peace to be held in front of the White House during Lent. The fact that they could attract only small groups from around the country highlighted the disparity between the committed and the indifferent which Sklencar had observed.

She was not encouraged by Congress, where criticism of the president was muted during the winter. The Senate Foreign Relations Committee conducted desultory hearings on administration policy in February, an exercise that gave a platform to Senate critics Harold Hughes and Alan Cranston (D-Calif.). George McGovern remained outspoken, and the Democratic Party Policy Council called for a "firm and unequivocal commitment" to a U.S. military withdrawal within eighteen months.[93] Aside from words, however, Congress seemed to offer little alternative to the president's approach of negotiation and Vietnamization.

That impasse defined the program for antiwar liberals. As envisioned in December by Sanford Gottlieb of SANE, Paule Schrade of the New Democratic Coalition, and Joseph Duffey, the new national chairman of ADA, the rebirth of antiwar efforts in the fall would be followed by a "second front" in the congressional elections of 1970. They proposed to use the structure and techniques of the Moratorium for a decentralized, bipartisan campaign to channel resources in support of local and state candidates. The theme would be "an immediate end to the Vietnam War" and the reallocation of national priorities. Although they would welcome help from students in their own districts, they did not recommend "another children's crusade."[94] Within a month they had a "Referendum '70" fund of a half-million dollars.[95] John Kenneth Galbraith and other antiwar liberals raised money for antiwar congressional candidates in the off-year elections, and in March seventeen thousand people, mostly veterans of the McCarthy and Kennedy campaigns, rallied at Madison Square Garden to build a "Fund for New Priorities." The off-year election did become a platform for dovish members of Congress like Lowenstein and new antiwar candidates like Father Robert Drinan, who had accompanied a FOR study team to Saigon, and Bella Abzug, a New Yorker who had been very active in the lobbying work of WSP.

Even so, the policy of negotiation and Vietnamization largely denied an issue to antiwar candidates. Just when antiwar liberals had coalesced around a firm demand for unilateral withdrawal, their rallying point had been undercut. Erich Fromm noted this fact in January, and he drew the conclusion that critics should shift from the military to the "political angle" of a new provisional government and self-determination in Vietnam.[96] A parallel strategy was to challenge the legitimacy of the Thieu government, for which Vietnamization was the crutch.

A strong basis for this approach was laid by the United States Study Team on Religious and Political Freedom in Vietnam when it visited South Vietnam in June 1969. The effort was organized by the FOR, which had sponsored a similar team four years earlier. Through Al Hassler it had maintained close working relations with Vietnamese Buddhists and had also put together an ad hoc Hoa Binh (peace) committee of American churchmen in 1968. The following year Hassler brought the two sets of contacts together in the form of the Study Team. With a prestigious membership and access to both South Vietnamese officials and their opposition, the team completed a report which Hassler turned into *Saigon U.S.A.*[97] The book had two thrusts. On the one hand, it made a case for the potential of an antigovernment but also anticommunist leadership, the "third solution" which Hassler had so passionately advocated. On the other, it documented the barbarous repression of the Thieu regime. In this respect it got to the bottom of the matter of Vietnam, as McGovern noted in his introduction to the book: "We do not have the right and we do not have the capacity to save a political régime abroad that does not have the respect of its own people."[98] This emphasis would grow in the liberal critique, and it would be especially strong after 1973. Ironically, Vietnamization opened the political aspect of intervention as it defused the military dimension.

In the winter and early spring of 1970, however, the dominant theme of antiwar liberals was New Priorities. It was promoted by ADA and CALC, and by SANE, which sponsored seventy-two town meetings on Vietnam, the anti–ballistic missile issue, and national priorities. In a way the theme was politically safe. It was noncontroversial, and radicals criticized it for that. To some extent, it hedged against the possible success of Vietnamization by emphasizing the cost to American society. In a deeper sense, New Priorities reflected—and was intended to reflect—the destructive impact of military intervention on national values and institutions. In this context, liberals began to question the constitutionality of the undeclared war. The Commonwealth of Massachusetts even passed a law prohibiting the dispatch of its young men into combat zones outside the continental U.S. for more than sixty days without an explicit congressional declaration of war. In the constitutional issue, moderates were able to articulate a direct threat posed to America by its own policies, a view summarized thus by Norman Cousins: "Constitutional government in the United States is being twisted out of shape from within the government itself. In the name of expediency, we have set in motion forces that have become inimical, perhaps inevitably so, to our own society."[99] Cousins' remark could be seen in retrospect as a harbinger of the next focus of the antiwar movement; but when he wrote, in March 1970, it was still a generalized apprehension. At the time, liberal opposition to Vietnam policy was, to say the least, diffused.

The New Mobe disintegrated under pressures different from those which pulled at the Moratorium. Its cohesion had derived specifically from the November action. By that time the radical left was more than ever rent by militants for whom government was now epitomized in the bogus trial of the Chicago Eight and in a predawn attack from Chicago police which left Panther leader Fred Hampton dead in his apartment bed. Late in November the militant RYM II reestablished its connection with the New Mobe, which about the same time was being pressed by another faction led by Arthur Waskow to adopt a multi-issue program resembling that of the original New Left. At a fractious mid-December planning meeting, Stewart Meacham withdrew in discouragement, and the so-called New Left caucus largely took over. During the winter the organization ceased to function, a victim of government harassment, ennui, and internal dissension.

The fact that its remnant factions were stalking the New Mobe was only further evidence that SDS had been rendered leaderless and politically ludicrous. Its seventy thousand members were little more than a mailing list. Its very name was claimed by two small, self-contained factions. Its irrelevance to the student scene left the Student Mobilization Committee, with leadership from experienced SWP and YSA hands, to fend off the advances of a New Left caucus similar to that in the New Mobe. The SMC, calling for spring antiwar demonstrations in 1970, found that student dissidents were turning inward to personal satisfactions, to rock culture, or to new causes such as environmentalism (campus demonstrations were planned for Earth Day, 22 April). It was racked by factionalism in the meantime, and its local efforts suffered from a lack of cohesive national leadership.

Sizable antiwar demonstrations were assembled in several cities on 15 April, but they largely reflected the work of local coalitions such as those in Boston, Chicago, New York, and San Francisco. Many participants spoke of "exhaustion" and "futility."[100] Moreover, some spring protests were marred by violence from the far left. A Moratorium rally in New York was aborted when militants forced their way to the stage; Harvard Square in Cambridge was subjected to vandalism. In this respect, the spring brought a continuation of the winter's disruptive direct action. A Catholic group called the East Coast Conspiracy to Save Lives sacked a Philadelphia draft board and the General Electric Corporation offices in Washington, and a group calling itself the Beaver 55 made a three-day sweep of destruction against draft boards in the Minneapolis–St. Paul area. There were isolated bombings and acts of arson. There were also attacks from the prowar right.

Much of the violence was related to the war only peripherally, if at all. A spate of it, including the burning down of the Bank of America in Santa Barbara, followed the arbitrary conviction of the Chicago Eight in February. In Judge Hoffman the trial provided a symbol of authority dedicated to the vindication of the social system; in the defendants it offered the epitome of resistance. Doubtless it was about a "state of mind," as the judge once referred to the alleged crime, an attitude of independence which became defiant as it encountered repression.[101] The trial had to do with the war only because through it the authorities and the media merged the images of violence, disrespect, and antiwar protest.

The contrast of the springtime mood, whatever its source, with that of the previous fall led the *Nation* to conclude that a "mean and mindless quality has overcome a small minority of the movement."[102] The large majority of antiwar activists who were already tired of the utter "futility of words and demonstrations" were only further demoralized by meanness in their midst.[103] The VMC formally dissolved in mid-April, its leaders declaring that the immediate need was for local organizing, electoral action, and clearly nonviolent civil disobedience. Sam Brown complained that the lack of congressional support deprived the Moratorium of the speakers which were its principal resource in challenging the "hard left." Stewart Meacham despaired that the instruments of democratic expression were "ineffective" regarding the war. Sidney Lens felt a "worn-out mood" around him. Dave Dellinger continued to defend nonviolent resistance: "Unless the movement becomes dangerous, it will become irrelevant."[104] In the spring of 1970, the radical antiwar movement was neither dangerous nor relevant.

Despite their fall offensive, the most concentrated dissent of the war, it seemed to many antiwar activists—liberal and radical—as though nothing had happened. After a year of effort, the president had effectively crafted a Vietnam policy that gave him the initiative in the face of his critics at home and the enemy abroad. The communists seemed to be stalemated in Vietnam, and antiwar activists had retreated in America. By withdrawing U.S. troops while channeling popular resentment against his critics, the president had masterfully secured the national center and reasserted executive control over the politics of the war.

Not that the policy satisfied the felt need of the country. Public support for Nixon's policies declined during the winter of 1970 until by mid-March, 46 percent of those polled favored either an immediate U.S. withdrawal or withdrawal within a year and a half, 38 percent stuck by the president, and a mere 7 percent said that they preferred military escalation.[105] George Gallup judged that the American people were divided into "two camps of roughly equal size" which differed only on the terms by which the U.S. should quit Vietnam. It was difficult to whip up enthusiasm for the war. Evangelist Carl McIntyre managed to rally about fifty thousand people in Washington on 4 April to march for military victory, and the extreme right struck with violence of its own—bombing an antiwar coffeehouse near Fort Dix and burning Philadelphia's Jane Addams Peace House, which sheltered a number of peace groups. In general, though, prowar advocacy was as mild as organized antiwar activism through the early spring. Even people who supported the war, noted dissident scientist Jeremy Stone, characterized themselves as "honorable withdrawalists."[106]

Although the Nixon administration had wrested the initiative in the United States, the political center was unstable. The president did not control events in Vietnam at all, and his attempt to gain the initiative there would change the antiwar movement.

The weight of its elements had shifted significantly, if imperceptibly, so that by the spring of 1970 the center of gravity within the opposition had moved from the radical left to those moderates and centrists whose goal was not revolution but reform, not to transform America in a revolt over Vietnam, but rather to save the society from the effects of further war. In a sense, this shift had further complicated the political identity of young radicals. Some of them explained to the North Vietnamese in the summer of 1969 that because Vietnam had become a "liberal's issue," the left had moved "toward fighting the system directly."[107] What little interest they had in the Vietnamese as a people declined in proportion to their disruption of the antiwar movement and their isolation from the American people. There the lines were being redrawn, and the country itself would gradually become realigned on the war as the president unilaterally expanded it into Indochina.

No one caught up in the movement could know that at the time, of course. Members of the movement had experienced so many ups and downs since 1965 that any new effort looked only like another futile gimmick in an apparently endless contest for the center. They were so used to thinking of "the Movement" as demonstrations and street protests, that when those techniques were formally abandoned it was easy to conclude that the movement itself had evaporated. They had tried so hard to reach the American people that when they were rejected or ignored it was natural to have, as Lens observed in his friends, "a growing feeling of 'what's the use?' "[108]

The Chicago Eight had been convicted, and federal prison authorities waited for the earlier Catonsville Nine, who were out on bail, as though it were time to put the movement away. Daniel Berrigan was due at Danbury prison on 9 April, but he didn't show up. Like his brother Philip and others of the Nine, the priest went underground. Twelve days later, federal agents forced their way into St. Gregory's Church, New York, and took Philip and another resister into custody. Father Dan evaded the FBI for four months, occasionally surfacing for rallies and frequently communicating through interviews and letters. His mother was in a hospital for part of that time, and the security people watched over her in hopes that her illness would lure their prey to capture.

Daniel Berrigan had misgivings about going under because he knew that his motives would be misrepresented. But what else was there "actually and usefully" to do, he asked? The classic logic of nonviolent civil disobedience was that one violated an unjust law but submitted to the legal process, accepting the consequence of one's actions. From where Berrigan stood, convicted, the problem was precisely that the whole legal system brought even "the most passionate conscience under the control of unchangeable, presumably beneficent, public authority"—Julius Hoffman in Chicago.[109] Citizens who paid tribute to the courts, law, and penal system of an evil system validated that regime—avatars of Adolf Eichmann in America.

With a "most passionate conscience," Berrigan believed that the Vietnam War was morally wrong. It was not merely imprudent or errant or even counterproductive—that much the government acknowledged as reasons for wanting an end to it. For the priest, it was evil in tragic proportions. Still it continued, destroying people in Indochina and distorting society in America. What was left "actually and usefully" to do?

Expressing his outrage, Berrigan had encountered an apparently indifferent public. Hostility he could understand, because it carried at least moral passion. Indifference implied moral numbness, and it seemed to characterize the great center of the people. At Catonsville and in their subsequent trial, the Berrigans had challenged what they took to be ethical apathy corroding the American spirit. The government had responded with a prison term which, it was clearly implied, would be mild and symbolic, like their disobedience. At this point Berrigan found himself challenged by more than public apathy. Absurdly, it seemed to him, he was being invited to acquiesce in the stifling of dissent by the very system that was perpetuating an unjust war. Not he, but the government should be on trial; not the burning of draft files, but the war should be judged wrong: that had been the whole and ineffectual thrust of the Catonsville court case. Well, then, not he but the government must bear the burden of his imprisonment. The priest went into hiding.

In Berrigan's choice, and beyond the ethical quandary it involved, were brought together many of the themes of antiwar activism between 1965 and 1970: the imperative to act on personal convictions, the growing concern over moral numbness in society, the obfuscation of the war as increasingly criticism itself became the issue, the topsy-turvy logic of radical extremists, and the sense that the tragedy of the war had become obscured by its absurdity. At the heart of the antiwar movement, as of its opposition, was a search for American values. The core of its disillusionment was its apparent rejection by the majority of American people, certainly by their government. Where, if not in the people and the government, were the central tenets of the national faith to be found? "America Is Hard to Find," Berrigan wrote from hiding:

Hard to find;
   wild strawberries   swans   herons   deer
     those things we long to be

. . . .
Hard to find; America
      now if America is doing well you may expect Vietnamese to
      do well   if power is virtuous the powerless will not be
      marked for death   if the heart of man is flourishing so will
      plants and wild animals   (But alas alas so also vice versa)
Hard to find. Good bread is hard to find. Of course. The hands
are wielding swords. The wild animals fade out like Alice's cat's
smile. Americans are hard to find . . .

. . . .
       P.S.   Dear friends   I choose to be a jail bird (one species is
        flourishing) in a kingdom of fowlers
                      Like strawberries   good bread
  swans   herons   Great Lakes   I shall shortly be
      hard to find
an exotic uneasy inmate of the NATIONALLY ENDOWED ELECTRONICALLY
                                INESCAPABLE ZOO
     remember me   I am
       free   at large   untamable   not nearly
  as hard to find   as America[110]

As difficult to discern, Berrigan might have added in April 1970, as the
antiwar movement in America. For the time being blurred, the lines were
being redrawn.

Part Four

The War and the American Way, 1970–1975

Ten

Persisting in Withdrawal

"Madness is an infection in the air"

Henry Kissinger and Richard Nixon were unlike in every respect except their ambition to leave their imprint on history, their views on a post-Vietnam U.S. foreign policy, their disposition to wield power, and their consequent dependence upon each other. Both self-styled realists, they felt an historical imperative to get beyond the crisis management of their Cold War predecessors and to achieve an equilibrium of world power. Without in the least minimizing the conflicts of interest and ideology among the United States, the Soviet Union, and communist China, Kissinger and Nixon were convinced that a stable working relationship was in the interest of all these great powers precisely because mutual antagonism compromised the leverage of each of them in a world of other emerging centers of influence. Nixon was well placed domestically to advocate accommodation because his tough anticommunist image afforded him initial support on the right, while détente could extend his working majority to the political center. Accordingly, the president and his national security advisor cultivated channels of discussion with the Soviet Union and China. They recognized that the Indochina conflict was an obstacle, but they hoped that its settlement might be parlayed into the process of great-power accommodation.

Nixon inherited in Vietnam the dilemma created when Lyndon Johnson turned the corner in 1968, accepting a limited investment in war without foregoing the original goal of a viable, anticommunist regime in Saigon. That was the purpose of Vietnamization. The strategy changed—the United States was mobilizing Vietnamese resources and reducing its own forces—but the policy remained the same, a line of demarcation between North and South. Militarily, the challenge was to deny offensive capability to the North Vietnamese.

In March 1970 conservative Cambodian military elements led by General Lon Nol overthrew the neutralist regime of Prince Norodom Sihanouk. Military leaders of the Nixon and Thieu governments seized the opportunity to deprive the North Vietnamese and Vietcong of their sanctuary and support base in Cambodia. U.S. planes and South Vietnamese artillery companies reinforced Cambodian army units attacking communist forces. Late in the month the Lon Nol government closed the port of Sihanoukville as a communist supply depot, and South Vietnamese forces opened their first major military engagement in Cambodia. A few days later, the communists launched an offensive of their own throughout South Vietnam. Saigon countered by attacking rest and supply sanctuaries in Cambodia until, in mid-April, its forces were streaming across the border where U.S. troops had taken up defensive holding positions. The Vietnam War had become more of an Indochina War.

Officially the United States government denied that it was involved in Saigon's decision to invade Cambodia. On 21 April the president made a special, nationally televised address, and he did not mention U.S. involvement in the operation. He simply announced that another 150,000 U.S. ground troops were scheduled to be withdrawn from South Vietnam (even though negotiations were stalled in Paris and the war seemed to be broadening).

The decline of organized antiwar opposition was illustrated by the fact that the initial, official expansion of the war into Cambodia was not seriously challenged. The lack of protest may have reflected popular willingness to allow the South Vietnamese to expand the conflict if that would help to strengthen the Saigon government.

The situation changed abruptly when, on April 30, President Nixon announced that he had ordered U.S. forces to join South Vietnamese troops in the invasion of Cambodia. This did not imply a widening of the war, the president insisted; rather, the attack was necessary to destroy the Cambodia-based command headquarters for enemy operations in South Vietnam, to disrupt enemy supply bases and lines, and thus to speed the pace of Vietnamization and U.S. troop withdrawals. Defending the invasion in personal and even apocalyptic terms, Nixon said that he would rather be a "one-term President" than accept "a peace of humiliation" which would result later in a larger war or surrender. "It is not our power but our will and character that is being tested tonight," he declared. "If, when the chips are down, the world's most powerful nation, the United States of America, acts like a pitiful, helpless giant, the forces of totalitarianism and anarchy will threaten free nations and free institutions throughout the world."[1] As he spoke, U.S. and South Vietnamese troops advanced into southeastern Cambodia in Operation Ultimate Victory, the largest allied field operation in two years. They encountered light resistance, captured some 2,000 enemy troops, destroyed 8,000 bunkers, and took large supplies of weapons.

Whatever added time the Cambodian invasion may have bought for Vietnamization, it focused disaffection with the pace of withdrawal, aroused mistrust of the administration, and brought into the open the latent issue of executive authority to make war.

Within minutes of the president's televised address, antiwar activists took to the streets in New York and Philadelphia, and protests erupted across the country in the following days. Scores of campuses from Maryland to Oregon rocked under a wave of marches and rallies marked by a sense of betrayal: the war was being expanded under the pretense of ending it. Critical reaction on Capitol Hill was swift and sharp, with warnings of "an impending constitutional crisis."[2] Nixon had his back to the wall. During a meeting on 3 May, he coached aides to stand tough. Congressional supporters should be persuaded to accuse his detractors of "giving aid and comfort to the enemy," he said, emphasizing the point: "—use that phrase." Nixon continued, "Don't worry about divisiveness. Having drawn the sword, don't take it out—stick it in hard. . . . Hit 'em in the gut. No defensiveness."[3] Kissinger later recalled that the commander in chief was "somewhat overwrought."[4] Other aides thought he was on the verge of a nervous breakdown.

Protests grew larger and more volatile. Twenty leaders of the New Mobe had met at the end of April in an effort to reconcile their differences and regroup the movement. In the midst of a "heavy political discussion," word came of the Cambodian invasion.[5] Pulling together with a new sense of urgency, the activists called for a major demonstration in Washington on 9 May. Brad Lyttle and Fred Halstead headed to the capital to handle local arrangements, while others activated the antiwar network by phone. Meanwhile, protests erupted spontaneously. A thousand University of Cincinnati students marched from the campus to a sit-in downtown, for instance, and large numbers of dissidents rallied at federal buildings in Nashville and Chicago. The great majority of protests were peaceful, although violence erupted at the University of Maryland and at Ohio University, and Stanford University students battled police in the worst rioting in the school's history. On 2 May, radical students attending a Black Panther support rally at Yale University appealed for a national student strike to demand an immediate U.S. withdrawal from Vietnam. The idea was endorsed by seven Ivy League student newspapers, in a joint editorial, as well as by the National Student Association, the SMC, and the New Mobe. Two days after the Yale meeting, Ohio national guardsmen fired into a milling crowd of students at Kent State University, killing four, wounding thirteen, and raising the American crisis to a new level of anguish.

The Kent State killings ignited anger which the White House only aggravated with the gratuitous comment that "when dissent turns to violence it invites tragedy."[6] Within days, about 1.5 million students left classes, shutting down about a fifth of the nation's campuses for periods ranging from one day to the rest of the school year. Georgia state colleges suspended classes for two days; Governor Reagan closed the University of California system for five days; and Pennsylvania ordered its state universities to cease operations indefinitely. Forty-four percent of the country's colleges recorded peaceful protests, and 57 percent reported that the Cambodian invasion had made a "significant impact" on them.[7] It was easily the most massive and shattering protest in the history of American higher education.

Incidents of violence occurred at only 4 percent of the country's schools, less than the broader university protests of 1969, and indeed the dissidents themselves absorbed the brunt of violence. On 14 May, Mississippi state police and national guardsmen attacked a dormitory at Jackson State University, killing two students. About that same time, young George Winne, Jr., walked onto Revelle Plaza at the University of California, San Diego with a placard saying "In the name of God, end the war." Dousing himself with gasoline, Winne lit a match and was engulfed in flames. "He was never in any demonstrations," said his mother. "He was just too sensitive."[8]

Stirred by both the invasion and the Kent State shootings, more than 100,000 people gathered in Washington on short notice, while rallies took place in other cities. Early on 9 May, President Nixon spontaneously visited the crowd near the Lincoln Memorial. He talked with a small knot of young people about football, higher education, and lessons of history. "He just kept rambling," one recalled, "and he didn't make any sense."[9] Neither did the demonstration. Most antiwar liberals and elite dissidents avoided it, apprehensive that it might prove to be explosive, and the few who did attend were excluded from speaking. Radical leaders argued over who should speak and what should be done, while tens of thousands of demonstrators milled about and a Black Panther contingent led chants of "Fuck Nixon." Halstead and Lyttle had created a corps of five hundred marshals trained in nonviolent action (in addition to three thousand other marshals whose job was to keep order). They were prepared for a massive campaign of civil disobedience, but no one could agree on a plan of action. Several experienced New Mobe leaders were absent, and direction of the rally fell to Dave Dellinger, Rennie Davis, Arthur Waskow, and Robert Greenblatt, who had not been present at the April planning meeting. The program dissipated into a "super-picnic," from which would-be supporters drifted away in disillusionment.[10] There were no suggestions for ongoing actions, and certainly no plans for coherent organization. "Of course," said a radical in a related demonstration, "I don't know what we could have done even WITH organization."[11] Direction was hard to find.

Acknowledging that the May demonstration was a fiasco, the remnants of the New Mobilization Committee nonetheless continued in motion along their various trajectories through the summer of 1970. When New Mobe leaders joined an SCLC march in Atlanta late in May to memorialize killings at Kent State, at Jackson State, and in Augusta, Georgia, there seemed to be the basis for a multi-issue alignment of black and antiwar forces. A Strategy Action Conference was scheduled in Milwaukee on 27–28 June to explore that possibility. Meanwhile, a separate meeting of nearly fifteen hundred activists was held by the Cleveland Area Peace Action Council on 19–21 June to plan a single-issue antiwar program. Heavily influenced by the SWP and YSA, and fending off disruptive SDS radicals, the Cleveland conference constituted itself as the National Peace Action Coalition (NPAC).[12] Although it welcomed antiwar supporters of any political bent, it limited its program to orderly demonstrations.

For much of the movement, the Milwaukee meeting which convened a week later was a direct repudiation of the Cleveland approach. On paper, the Strategy Action Conference was supported by an impressive spectrum of liberal and radical groups. In fact, the range was so broad as to be irreconcilable. Although established antiwar groups were represented among the eight hundred participants, there were also factious radical groups. Sid Peck and the others who signed the conference call hoped for a broad coalition of students, welfare rights organizations, Black Panthers, labor, and antiwar activists. They also intended to go beyond demonstrations to "strategies and tactics ... to stop the war."[13] Few of the workshops at the conference dealt with future antiwar activity, though, and these were dominated by proposals to confront what was presumed to be an imminent expansion of the conflict. Perhaps the most imaginative was formulated by Arthur Waskow: "liberation collectives and brigades" around the country would conduct "long marches" to Washington, where they would "liberate" the city from the war machine. Someone observed dryly, "We're not trying to liberate Washington, what we really want to liberate is ourselves."[14] The bickering led to no program of formal action. It did suggest that the radical left was still wedded to a multi-issue coalition and fascinated by the politics of disruptive action, epitomized in the Weathermen's "Declaration of War" against the U.S. government and the offer of Huey Newton, a Black Panther leader, to provide Vietnamese communists with "an undetermined number of troops to assist in the common fight against American imperialism."[15]

That was empty rhetoric; but the summer brought a good deal of real, if random, violence. Attacks on draft boards had become so commonplace that the Selective Service System reported an average of more than one antidraft action per day during the first eight months of the year.[16] Bombs were set off at federal installations and military recruitment offices from the Bronx to Santa Barbara, the worst incident being a midnight explosion late in August at the Army Mathematics Research Center of the University of Wisconsin, which killed a thirty-three-year-old researcher. Such undirected violence only underscored the hollowness of militant antiwar activism.

Radical pacifists were in a quandary. Waskow rued the lack of discipline which had spoiled the May demonstration. Even Dave Dellinger reconsidered the relationship between nonviolent revolutionary action and violence. "It is time," he conceded, "that the no longer New Left take a serious look at where it is going and what it is becoming." Certainly it was time "to stop playacting at violent revolution."[17] Still, the idea of dramatic action persisted. Waskow's proposal for "long marches" was discussed in the National Action Group in July, where it divided pacifist leaders. A majority rejected confrontation as "politically disastrous," but the notion of crisis-building remained attractive to Rennie Davis and Sid Lens, and to Brad Lyttle, who recommended it for the spring of 1971. Lens and Lyttle at least, and doubtless Waskow and Dellinger, assumed that confrontation could be disciplined, and that this would make a difference in its impact.[18] Thus, the ideal of radical action lingered on without a radical constituency.

Daniel Berrigan was still elusive when the NAG pacifists met, "as hard to find as America." From hiding, he wrote a letter to the Weathermen (he called them "Weather People"). They were larger than life, he acknowledged, because they had been endowed by the public with a mythology of fear and madness. The priest observed that "*madness is an infection in the air,*" and he agreed that its primary source was the war itself; but he warned, "the movement has at times been sickened by it too."[19]

Berrigan recalled that the Catonsville Nine had undertaken sabotage "long before" the Weathermen had adopted that tactic. On the other hand, he reminded his "brothers and sisters" in the underground that the Nine had intended it as a tool of communication—a way to dramatize the "pernicious" effect of the war on American values. Cautioning the Weathermen (gently) that "a revolution is interesting insofar as it avoids like the plague the plague it promised to heal," he appealed to them (respectfully) to abjure the violence and distortion of truth which the war embodied and to embody the humane values which alone justified rebellion.[20] In August, FBI agents captured Berrigan on Block Island, off the coast of Rhode Island, and he was sent to Danbury Prison. His words to the Weathermen, more than his imprisonment, signalled that the era of unbridled radical activism was nearly over.

This fact was not yet clear in the weeks following the invasion of Cambodia, and so the image of militancy provided a foil with which to mobilize prowar support. The explosion of antiwar opposition during May 1970 precipitated a counterforce. In St. Louis twenty thousand people marched on behalf of the administration, and at Princeton University two thousand faculty members and students signed a letter approving the Cambodian invasion. There were other prowar demonstrations, and often they were physical and violent. On 8 May hundreds of construction workers in hard hats attacked antiwar protesters in New York's financial district, injuring seventy people. Soon afterwards, some building trades-men and longshoremen joined a pro-administration rally along Wall Street, jeered Mayor John Lindsay for his antiwar sentiments, and assailed luckless long-haired young men who got in their way. They were sup-ported by union leader Peter Brennan and AFL-CIO leader George Meany. Both hard hats and white-collar Wall Street office workers sporadically demonstrated their national loyalty for the next three weeks, crowning their efforts with a parade of 100,000 people on 20 May. Construction workers in Buffalo and elsewhere organized demonstrations in support of the president and the flag, and three hundred of them attacked a student peace rally at Arizona State University. Gratefully, the White House set up a well-publicized meeting between the president and supportive union leaders. Nixon was rewarded with a hard hat imprinted with the words "commander-in-chief."

The prowar mobilization of laborers illustrated the class lines that antiwar activists had encountered before. Contemporary observers inter-preted them as the great failure of the white, middle-class antiwar move-ment—what Jimmy Breslin termed "its arrogance toward people who work with their hands for a living and its willingness not only to ignore them, but to go even further and alienate them completely."[21] In the eyes of white, working-class America, agreed the Reverend Andrew Greeley, Nixon and Agnew were "ANTI-Establishment figures," while the antiwar movement appeared as an Establishment movement that ridiculed the symbols and values of patriotic Americans.[22] Policy-shaping elites in Wall Street and on Ivy League campuses might be shifting in their attitudes toward the war, Breslin noted, but "nobody bothered to inform the steamfitters in the country that the signals had been changed."[23]

These class divisions had a profound effect on the makeup of domestic antiwar forces. According to contemporary opinion analysts, antiwar sen-timent in the United States flowed in two currents. One represented "a tiny fraction" of the population that was "highly educated, articulate, and visible."[24] The second consisted of an undereducated body of the polit-ically marginal lower classes who were much more numerous, and whose opposition to Vietnam policy was not only plastic and pragmatic but also colored by strong antipathy toward antiwar dissidents who transgressed the boundaries of conventional political debate and symbolism. Their hostility was evidently widespread, for, when people were asked to rate a set of political groups and leaders along a scale that ranged from ex-tremely negative to highly positive feelings, they placed antiwar protes-ters in the most negative category. Indeed, 53 percent of even those people who favored immediate withdrawal from Vietnam denigrated the protesters.[25] It was the abiding irony of the antiwar opposition that its most assertive advocates were held in such contempt not only by a population that increasingly termed the war a mistake, but also by many of those who supported their policies. No matter what they did, activists never escaped the grip of that irony.

The images of street protest probably contributed to the hostility elicited by antiwar activism. The movement was in transition, however. Appearing to withdraw in the summer of 1970, it persisted with less visibility but with growing support from moderate political elements and elites in the society as it focused increasingly on constitutional issues and congressional constraints. Already in May significant numbers of elite and college-educated Americans were led to interpret the war as a constitutional crisis over executive power.

Angry over the invasion of Cambodia and fearful of domestic unrest, large numbers of liberals and elite dissidents attacked the administration and demanded antiwar action from Congress. Theodore Hesburgh of Notre Dame and Robert Goheen of Princeton were among thirty-seven presidents of major universities who urged Nixon to designate a terminal date for U.S. intervention. Two hundred fifty career officers in the State Department and the Foreign Service sent a joint letter of protest to Secretary of State William Rogers. Several leading Harvard University faculty members, including Thomas Schelling and Edwin Reischauer, met privately with their colleague Henry Kissinger to announce that they were breaking with administration policy, and several National Security Council staff members quit Kissinger's service in protest.

Historian Robert Beisner sensed movement without direction. "I don't think there's ever been a time since the founding of this nation—including even the days of Fort Sumter," he told his students, "when the future direction of this country has been more problematical and unpredictable than right now."[26] Normally apolitical groups, including Nobel science laureates, entertainment celebrities, musicians, architects, and publishers, were coalescing in opposition to the continuation of the war. Mostly they petitioned their government, but prominent local leaders in Oakland encouraged people to redeem and boycott U.S. savings bonds until the war ended.

Most important, dissidents turned to Congress, which, after the invasion of Cambodia, was inundated by the heaviest volume of telegrams on record. Overwhelmingly the messages were in opposition. Five days after Nixon announced the "incursion," the Senate Foreign Relations Committee accused him of usurping the legislature's war-making power and denounced the "constitutionally unauthorized, Presidential war in Indochina."[27] The charge, though quickly dismissed by the White House, began to take root. The president of the Amalgamated Clothing Workers

Union demanded congressional constraints on the president. The American Civil Liberties Union abandoned its apolitical tradition to campaign for an immediate end of the war on the grounds that it was not constitutionally declared and therefore deprived Americans of their civil liberties. Several new groups formed to enjoin congress to reassert its constitutional war-making powers. To this end, some faculty members at the University of Rochester launched a National Petition Committee of prominent intellectuals; 25 military officers on active duty formed a Concerned Officers Movement; 325 Asian experts and about 1,000 lawyers lobbied in Washington. Earl Warren, a former chief justice of the U.S. Supreme Court, told them that there was "no crisis within the memory of living Americans" comparable to the one enveloping the country.[28] "The presidency is out of control," charged the *Christian Century*.[29] The challenge for America became ever more widely perceived as "nothing less than the survival of constitutional democracy," and the antiwar movement, its orientation shifting now from the streets to congressional politics, embraced a national symbol which would become increasingly important in the following five years.[30]

The Nixon administration was shocked by the breadth and anger of the outburst, especially after the killing of students; typically, it responded with ambivalence. For a while a siege atmosphere enveloped the White House. "We feared more demonstrations, more Kent States, an immobilized nation," one aide said. Kissinger recalled that "the fear of another round of demonstrations permeated all the thinking about Vietnam in the Executive Branch that summer—even that of Nixon, who pretended to be impervious."[31] Although Agnew lashed out at critics as a "hard core of hell-raisers" and "charlatans of peace," the administration tried to blunt the force of antiwar discontent with reassurances.[32] On 5 May, the president pledged that U.S. troops would not advance more than twenty-one miles into Cambodia without congressional approval. Three days later, Nixon promised that all American forces would be withdrawn from Cambodia by the end of June. Questioned about antiwar protesters, he declared that he agreed "with everything that they are trying to accomplish."[33] Toward the end of the month, the administration announced that U.S. ground forces would be withdrawn from Cambodia within four weeks, but that U.S. air attacks would continue on an open-ended basis. By presidential fiat, America would participate in the new war in Cambodia, but in the least vulnerable way.

This tactic reduced the clamor, as the intensity of fighting in Indochina diminished and casualties on all sides fell to the lowest levels since 1966, but it did not quell the domestic pressure for a definitive end to intervention. Congressional sentiment altered dramatically in May, and the Senate became open to proposals to set a specific date for total U.S. withdrawal from Vietnam. Within days of the invasion, a number of senators made the most serious bipartisan attempts yet to reverse U.S. intervention. Republican John Sherman Cooper (Ky.) and Democrat Frank Church developed a resolution cutting off funds for U.S. military operations in Cambodia after 30 June, while Republican Mark Hatfield and his Democratic colleague George McGovern devised an amendment to a military authorization bill that would cut off all funding for U.S. military operations in Southeast Asia after 31 December 1970.[34] Antiwar liberals in the FCNL and WILPF immediately geared up for a major lobbying effort. Late in June, the Senate voted to repeal the Tonkin Gulf resolution in a symbolic show of its displeasure over the course of the war. Early the following month it adopted a modified form of the Cooper-Church amendment which prohibited the expenditure of monies for U.S. ground forces in Cambodia and Laos. The McGovern-Hatfield resolution moved through the upper chamber during the summer and became the focal point in the congressional war debate.

The Senate was responding to a current of public opinion which produced eddies of individual and local protest throughout the summer. Some of them were quite personal, as when the eighteen-year-old Miss Montana resigned her title rather than accede to the demand of the Miss America Pageant organizers that she quit criticizing the war, or when a marine lieutenant in Vietnam assailed Nixon's policy in a public letter to his father, Senator William Saxbe (R-Ohio). Some acts were collective, as when *Life* magazine came out for total withdrawal by the end of 1971, or when the National Urban League and the NAACP demanded immediate termination of the war. In any case, these actions reflected public opinion. Popular opposition to antiwar demonstrations continued, and the removal of U.S. combat troops from Cambodia bolstered the administration's credibility; but widespread disaffection from the war was not assuaged. Opinion polls in June suggested that Americans opposed sending GIs "to help Cambodia" by 58 to 28 percent, favored a December 1971 deadline for total withdrawal by 44 to 35 percent, and wanted more than ever (58 to 24 percent) to pull U.S. forces out, even if the South Vietnamese government collapsed.[35]

Liberals and moderates, adults and students, attempted to channel public war-weariness into congressional and electoral action. Sam Brown and Ripon Society vice-president Michael Brower organized Project Pursestrings to support the Cooper-Church and McGovern-Hatfield legislation. It coordinated lobbying in Washington, promoted local committees in key states, and prepared newspaper and TV ads. Its fifteen-member Washington staff worked closely with a Citizens Committee for the Amendment to End the War formed by former attorney general Ramsey Clark and other liberal leaders in order to mobilize grassroots support for withdrawal by a fixed date. Project Pursestrings shared its office with Continuing Presence in Washington, an organization started by Dartmouth students, and with Law Students Against the War. The ADA, AFSC, and CALC brought supporters to Capitol Hill. Other groups lobbying for antiwar legislation included the several hundred members of the Corporate Executives Committee for Peace, the Pillsbury Committee to End the War (formed by twenty-six food company executives in Minneapolis), the Concerned [Military] Academy Graduates, and the Committee of Planning Professions to End the War in Vietnam. "At no other time in the history of country," wrote a Quaker lobbyist, "had so many Americans brought their concerns directly to their elected representatives, and perhaps at no other time had the machinery of our government been brought so close to a halt due to the numbers of people crowding the corridors and offices of government buildings."[36]

The Cambodian invasion also revived interest in electoral politics for new national priorities, which was the liberal version of building a multi-issue coalition around the war issue. Leon Shull reminded ADA chapters that the elections remained "the main battle."[37] Several groups raised funds for House candidates or provided subsistence for student volunteers working in campaigns. The Movement for a New Congress (MNC) operated out of Princeton to field thousands of student workers in the primaries, where it counted successes for Bella Abzug, Edward Koch, and a few others. Anticipating the summer campaign, the MNC also conducted voter registration drives, especially in California and Michigan, prepared position papers and voting analyses for candidates, and developed regional and local committees. According to the Bipartisan Congressional Clearinghouse, which was formed in May to identify peace candidates and link them with volunteers and antiwar groups, by midsummer some forty national organizations were working for the sake of "peace politics."[38] "There's no central headquarters, no 'angel' financing them," explained the *New Republic.* "But there's an abundance of energy and common goals—ending the war and setting new social priorities."[39]

The McGovern-Hatfield resolution to cut off funding for the war at the end of the year epitomized the way that liberal and moderate opponents were adapting to Vietnamization. In place of immediate withdrawal, they increasingly demanded that U.S. intervention be terminated by a fixed date (often called a "date-certain"). According to public opinion analysts, this was what the American people appeared to want. The principal challenge for antiwar dissidents seeking public support was, in the words of one McGovern advisor, to make "a clear distinction between an irreversible, time-limited withdrawal" and "the President's reversible, no-time-limit withdrawal."[40] As Philip Jessup put it, the need was to define an "intermediate policy" between the demand for immediate withdrawal and Nixon's plans for open-ended conflict.[41]

The administration fought back hard during the summer to retain full presidential power over U.S. war policy. Artfully, the White House undercut its opposition by insisting that it was in fact ending the war and by identifying its detractors with anti-American values and subversive purposes. William Safire recalled a major change in the mood of the president, who seemed to conclude that his critics could be useful "as the villain, the object against which all of our supporters could be rallied."[42] As public pressure died down in the wake of the Cambodian invasion, Nixon became concerned more with isolating his critics than with mollifying them.

The administration accordingly stepped up covert police surveillance and harassment of the antiwar movement. At Nixon's behest, White House aide Tom Charles Huston developed a plan to coordinate the operations of the government's principal security agencies and commit "clearly illegal" acts of surveillance, wiretapping and burglary.[43] Nixon personally justified more aggressive police infiltration, not with any claim of communist involvement in antiwar activism, but rather on the grounds that antiwar dissidents "were developing their own brand of indigenous revolutionary activism which is as dangerous as anything they could import from Cuba, China or the Soviet Union."[44] FBI Director Hoover was reluctant to risk his Bureau in operations that he considered more beneficial to rival security agencies, though, and rather than overrule him, Nixon rescinded his endorsement of the Huston Plan.

Still, aggressive efforts in police spying proceeded unhindered. The CIA's Operation Chaos and the FBI's Cointelpro were expanded in scope and intensity. Hoover gave Bureau agents greater latitude in their wiretapping operations and lowered the age of campus informants from twenty-one to eighteen, while field offices in at least Minneapolis and San Diego cooperated with local businessmen and right-wing vigilantes in attacking dissidents. According to one estimate, 40 percent of FBI field work by the fall of 1970 was devoted to political investigations, with 95 percent of it concentrated on leftist politics.[45] Agents were encouraged to conduct conspicuous investigations of local activists in order to "enhance the paranoia endemic in these circles" and "get the point across that there is an FBI agent behind every mailbox."[46] The whole effort suggested a paranoia corroding the administration itself, part of the infection which Daniel Berrigan sniffed in the air.

Administration leaders seized upon images of American nationhood more aggressively than ever. They assembled a lavish "Honor America" day celebration in Washington on the Fourth of July, and they arranged to turn over the crypt of the Capitol to H. Ross Perot and his campaign on behalf of American POWs. Making the American flag the very touchstone of prowar patriotism, the president and his supporters took to wearing flag jewelry, and the publishers of the *Reader's Digest* distributed sixty-eight million flag decals. Leaders in CALC suggested that Flag Day be used as an occasion to "rededicate the flag" so as to prevent it from becoming a partisan emblem. The flag was being "desecrated," complained author and critic Alfred Kazin. It was being "worn to divide our people, to start fights and to end conversation," and, most of all, to "cover up the many things that are wrong and that everyone knows are wrong."[47] His words were dissipated in an atmosphere highly charged with conflict over vital national symbols. Meanwhile, prowar patriots attacked the peace sign, which had been inherited from the Campaign for Nuclear Disarmament. Throughout the summer, the American Legion, the John Birch Society, and right-wing organizations charged that the peace symbol was a communist design, an anti-Christian insignia, or a medieval "witches' font."[48]

With support for the war flagging, the administration made Vietnam a symbol of the integrity of the presidency and of the nation's core values. The result was calculated divisiveness. "Polarization is no longer an adequate word for what is happening in America these days," observed a liberal commentator. "Try words like splintering, fragmentation, disintegration: these tell the story a little better. This nation is more broken in its relationships, more shattered in spirit, than at any time since the Civil War. All our institutional glue has come unstuck."[49] "We've got the Left where we want it now," the President told Kissinger in early August. "All they've got left to argue for is a bug-out, and that's their problem."[50] The struggle for control in the wake of the Cambodian invasion intensified the bitter "them vs. us" mentality that already characterized the regime. "It didn't matter who you were or what ideological position you took," recalled a White House staffer. "You were either for us or against us, and if you were against us we were against you."[51] What was now at issue in the war, Henry Kissinger told a group of newspaper editors, was not merely the future of this presidency, but rather "the problem of authority in this society altogether." Nixon declared that Vietnam was essentially a test of domestic "confidence in our judgment and in our leadership."[52]

Apparently relying on authority rather than political balance to hold the country together, the administration turned defiantly to deal with its congressional challenges. The president shored up his constituency in the House with the help of Democratic leaders like Speaker John McCormack (D-Mass). He made special attempts to isolate antiwar senators and dilute end-the-war amendments, claiming inherent constitutional power to do whatever he deemed necessary to protect U.S. troops. Senate minority leader Hugh Scott urged Congress to "leave the President alone."[53] Partisans attacked the loyalty and patriotism of dovish senators. Agnew, for one, charged Democratic critics with breeding "a whimpering isolationism," accused "the Fulbright claque" of giving "comfort" to the enemy, and called the McGovern-Hatfield resolution a "blueprint for the first defeat" in American military history.[54] The administration won the contest when the amendment failed in a 55-39 vote on 1 September, and the government's military commitment in Indochina remained open-ended.

Antiwar liberals were seemingly defeated after months of sustained and concentrated effort. The president could congratulate himself on having stemmed the most serious legislative attempt ever made to shut down an American war. In its effort to retain discretionary authority, the executive branch had further reinforced the impression that national policy was to withdraw from the war. It bought time for Vietnamization and a more regional conflict, but it also laid the basis for intensified popular frustration should these plans fail to bring peace.

Indeed, the president's legislative victory was deceptive. Having formerly challenged an iconoclastic minority, the White House had now been brought to bay by congressional opponents reflecting broad public disaffection. Instead of addressing the source of its problems, public weariness with continuing war, the administration remained preoccupied by its opponents. In particular, it attacked the most vulnerable and impotent sector of criticism, the antiwar left, and in doing so it employed the kind of arbitrary and unconstitutional methods which subsequently would bring it into conflict with Congress.

Hardly noticed in the victory-or-defeat polarization of issues, the contest over the war had shifted. The relative weight of the elements of opposition had changed perceptibly. From a protest of the liberal left, antiwar activism moved further toward the center of American politics in 1970, and it seriously penetrated the Democratic party and Congress. Since the demonstrations of the previous autumn, the number of people favoring immediate withdrawal had doubled. Support for the president's approach eroded through April, and the invasion of Cambodia crystalized the pervasive skepticism and dissatisfaction. By late June polls showed that nearly half the population favored getting out immediately and only 15 percent favored staying in. The administration rode out the crisis by pulling back from Cambodia, continuing troop withdrawals, and going on the offensive politically; but pessimism over the course of the war remained. Moreover, dissent was spreading among middle-class and college-educated people, although it was also strong among minority groups—especially Jews and blacks—and lower income groups.[55]

The issues on which the opposition was focused were changing, too. The feeling was growing among liberal, moderate, and elite dissidents that Vietnam signified a dangerous abuse of presidential powers. In June nearly two thirds of the people polled thought the president should get congressional approval before again sending troops into Cambodia. During the summer, while antiwar members of the House tried to legislate limits on Nixon's war, Jacob Javits (R-N.Y.) and a few other senators introduced legislation to establish definite constraints on the president's war-making power. In the eyes of ever more critics, Vietnam loomed as a test of constitutional accountability.

Although it was not clear at the time, the antiwar movement which the president challenged during the spring and summer of 1970 was developing a new configuration. Radical activists were more fragmented than ever. Liberals, on the other hand, were more integrated into and dependent on national institutions such as the Democratic party and Congress. Although somewhat reconstituted, the opposition failed in a frontal contest with the president, and the administration managed to retain public tolerance to the constitutionally unfettered war. There was a price. Fighting to build domestic support and to shatter its opponents, the White House showed a willingness to employ corrosive and even extralegal attacks on its critics, whom it equated with the enemy abroad. The result would be the worst of two worlds—a slow defeat in Indochina, and a domestic conflict with which retreat would be covered. The war would be transformed from a test of Washington's international credibility into a test of America's domestic institutions and decision-making structures.

"A number of pure causes no longer so pure, and a lot of naïve people no longer so naïve"

In this war no victory was definitive, at home or abroad, and Vietnam remained a canker in the body politic. It continued to fester, erupting with surprising force in the spring of 1971 and again in 1972. Frustration mounted among the American people despite accelerated troop withdrawals, although there was neither an issue nor an organized movement capable of mobilizing discontent into effective political action.

In Indochina ground fighting continued at low levels compared to the previous years, while the air war intensified. Military losses fell on both sides, although civilian casualties remained at least two hundred per day. By October, the United States had fewer troops in Vietnam and was suffering fewer casualties itself than at any time in half a decade. The North Vietnamese prepared for a protracted war, pending a major offensive. The United States feverishly strengthened the ARVN as it reduced its own forces.

Each side advanced an occasional diplomatic overture, but neither gave way on the central question of political control in the South. Nixon and Kissinger feared that their attempts to negotiate stable relations with the Soviet Union and China would be jeopardized by seeming weakness in Vietnam, and they hoped that a great-power détente might isolate North Vietnam, forcing a compromise peace that would give the South a chance to establish viable independence. Therefore, although both men were anxious to quit the conflict, they would not yield on the key political issue. The fighting in Vietnam ground on.

A flurry of action marked the Paris peace talks in mid-September when the communists introduced an eight-point program proposing that the PRG and Hanoi would negotiate the return of U.S. POWs in return for an American announcement of withdrawal by 30 June 1971. They also indicated that they would be willing to participate in a coalition government in Saigon, but only if Thieu were first removed. Washington responded in a nationally televised broadcast on 7 October, when the president offered what he termed a major new initiative for peace. It included a cease-fire in Indochina, the immediate release of all POWs, the convocation of a great-power conference on Indochina, and the creation of a political process which would express the will of the South Vietnamese people.

Nixon's proposal did not interest the North Vietnamese, but it encouraged elite dissidents and moderates in America. The editors of the *New York Times,* as well as leading Democratic critics such as Averell Harriman and Cyrus Vance, praised the president's offer, while several antiwar members of Congress joined Senator Charles Percy (R-Ill.) to sponsor a resolution lauding Nixon's terms as "fair and equitable."[56] Buoyantly, the president told a news conference the day after his speech that the domestic support showed the North Vietnamese that they could not "wait for political division in the United States to get them at the conference table what they cannot win on the battlefield."[57]

The great majority of leading antiwar dissidents were appalled at the ease with which Nixon outflanked his critics. The *Christian Century* termed the president's initiative more of "a major propaganda victory" then a serious diplomatic proposal.[58] The very absence of incisive commentary led the liberal editors of *War/Peace Report* to worry that leading American opinion-shapers and politicians still didn't understand "what the war is all about."[59] The implications were clear, thought Sidney Lens: Washington intended to stalemate the war until it could conclude a "Korea-formula" that would guarantee "almost total victory" for its side. In the meantime, Lens added, the administration's ploy was immobilizing antiwar liberals and fashioning "a false concept of 'national unity.' "[60]

The president was out to make unity real. Anticipating the off-year elections, he hit the campaign trail for two weeks, starting in mid-October. He called repeatedly for "the great silent majority" to help him "win a just peace in Vietnam," and to avoid "an American defeat which would bring on another war."[61] Nixon did not identify critics as communists. Instead, he appealed for popular support against the "violent and radical few, the rock throwers and the obscenity shouters," who pretended to be for peace when they were really out to "tear America down." His jaw set, the president pronounced that those "who carry a 'peace' sign in one hand and throw a bomb or a brick with the other are the super hypocrites of our time."[62] Spotting a group of antiwar protesters outside the San Jose Coliseum late in the month, Nixon jumped on the hood of his car and waved his arms over his head, his fingers fixed in a "V-for-Victory" sign, until aroused demonstrators tossed stones at his limousine. As his car sped off, Nixon told his aides gleefully, "That's what they hate to see!" In the closing days of the campaign, he repeatedly referred to the San Jose incident as indicative of the "viciousness of the lawless elements" that he intended to crush.[63]

The presidential challenge set the tone for a new round of official intimidation and harassment. Senate and House internal security committees stepped up investigations of radicals. In Kent, Ohio, a federal grand jury absolved the Ohio National Guard for its role in the death of four students and charged twenty-five student activists, including the president of the Kent State student body, with crimes related to the spring disorders. The Internal Security Division of the Justice Department opened a full-scale offensive in which, between 1970 and 1973, nearly two thousand witnesses were subpoenaed before 100 grand juries in 84 cities and 36 states.[64]

Despite its vigorous campaign, the White House failed to convert public resentment of antiwar dissidents into an electoral endorsement for its war policies. Three leading Senate doves were felled in November— Charles Goodell (R-N.Y.), Albert Gore (D-Tenn.), and Joseph Tydings (D-Md.)—but about that many hawks were defeated too. SANE's old nemesis, Thomas Dodd, was replaced by a moderately liberal Republican, Lowell Weicker. Adlai Stevenson III (D-Ill.) and John Tunney (D-Calif.) came into the Upper Chamber more critical of war policy than the incumbents they replaced. There was not much change in the House; but of the twelve representatives who lost their seats, ten had been administration supporters. Some of the newcomers were outspoken peace advocates, notably Democrats James Abourezk (S. Dak.). Bella Abzug (N.Y.), Ronald Dellums (Calif.), Robert Drinan (Mass.)., Romano Mazzoli (Ky.), William Roy (Kans.), and John Seiberling (Ohio). Allard Lowenstein was defeated in Nassau County, New York, as was Andrew Young in Atlanta. The successful challengers tended to be younger and more issue-oriented than the representatives they replaced, but few candidates had made the war central to their campaigns. The 1970 election was characterized by a great deal of ticket-splitting, and in any case the official Democratic party position on Vietnam hardly differed from Nixon's. Although Vietnam was popularly identified as the country's principal problem, it appeared to play only a small part in the voting. The election was largely a standoff on the war.

Protest continued intermittently through the autumn. There had been a fresh note in September, when 150 members of Vietnam Veterans Against the War (VVAW) conducted a three-day sweep from Morristown, New Jersey, to Valley Forge, Pennsylvania, in what they called Operation

Raw (for Rapid American Withdrawal). Outfitted in combat fatigues and carrying plastic M-16 rifles, the vets patrolled the countryside with a mock viciousness—"taking" and "torturing" prisoners and "shooting down" everyday Americans—that was intended to confront the countrymen with the war's horror. "Your silence is killing us," their signs said, and "the best way to keep faith with our fighting men is to BRING THEM BACK ALIVE—NOW!"[65] Shortly afterwards, a number of other antiwar veterans, supported by civilians such as former senator Ernest Gruening and Jane Fonda, announced the convocation of a national Citizens Commission on War Crimes in order to take testimony from ex-Vietnam servicemen to show that atrocities like Mylai were consistent with U.S. military tactics.

Following the November elections there appeared some new antiwar groups around the country, as well as more petitions and joint statements, attacks on draft boards, attempted boycotts of war-related corporations, and individual examples of conviction; but the pattern was all too familiar to activists, who, after investing years in the movement, still felt unable to convert antiwar actions into a politically effective national campaign. They seemed to have lost to Vietnamization whatever leverage they had had previously. Many were weary and defensive. "I was tired of the whole affair," remembered William Sloane Coffin, Jr. "I was fed up with the war, already the longest in our history, and I was tired of fighting Nixon."[66] Only a sixth of BEM's three thousand members were paying their dues now, and the organization was in debt. It closed its Washington office. Large parts of the antiwar movement seemed to be irrelevant, or even at cross-purposes. *Commonweal* observed late in the summer that "the peace movement aims not only to persuade but also to resist"; however, the moral obligation of resisting the war seemed to undermine the political efficacy of persuasion.[67] Quandary engendered despair. As early as September, after an extended tour among antiwar activists in Michigan, a SANE organizer reported that dissidents were demoralized and confused. Everywhere he went, he said, "I always meet the question, 'What should we be doing now?' "[68] Mostly what was done in the fall of 1970 was to regroup and plan for the winter and spring.

Even before the election, SANE and other groups created a National Coalition for a Responsible Congress to work on electoral politics after the vote. For liberals the election results promised only more of the same. Patently, this was not sufficient: something had to be done to slice through the vague, immobilizing hope for peace. Antiwar liberals and clerics developed an Interfaith Campaign to Set the Date (subsequently Set the Date Now, or STDN), hoping to build popular support for an expected congressional initiative to set 4 July 1971 as the definitive end of U.S. intervention. The project was in place by December. It was aimed especially at religious constituencies, and it had the support of the FOR,

SANE, CALC, and some Protestant and Jewish groups that regarded Vietnamization as a mercenary policy which would perpetuate violence in Vietnam indefinitely.[69]

On the antiwar left, the summertime breakup of the New Mobe had left a vacuum in leadership. The National Peace Action Committee, created at Cleveland with SWP leadership, sponsored a series of modest antiwar demonstrations in mid-November and anticipated a large one the following spring. Meanwhile, seventy or eighty independent radicals and radical pacifists followed up their June meeting in Milwaukee with a second one held 11–13 September. Acting on a proposal from Stewart Meacham, they formed yet another multi-issue coalition. Their governing assumption was that since all forms of injustice were aggravated by the war, occasional mass demonstrations could be supplemented by action in connection with other issues. They called themselves the National Coalition Against War, Racism, and Repression (NCAWRR) to give a semblance of form to the collection of social causes they endorsed and predicated a "gigantic action" featuring nonviolent civil disobedience for the spring of 1971—"if the war is still on," as Sid Lens put it.[70]

The NCAWRR program was too vague and, for some, too threatening to be the focus of effective coalition activity; it was succeeded in the fall by the People's Peace Treaty (PPT). This novel project had originated in the idea of getting a wide variety of citizen groups to hold direct discussions with the Vietnamese about the conditions necessary for peace. A broadly representative delegation from Minneapolis–St. Paul to Paris early in the summer provided a model. In the autumn the notion of people-to-people contacts was taken up with North Vietnamese and PRG representatives, who were particularly responsive when Washington rejected their October initiative. Meanwhile, in August, the National Student Association had adopted a suggestion by Rennie Davis which initiated the People's Peace Treaty (the NSA barely rejected Davis' project to shut down Washington the following May). A delegation of fifteen student leaders would be sent to North and South Vietnam, carrying with them a draft peace treaty which they would discuss with Vietnamese students. Upon their return they would present their peace treaty to a large student convocation as a way of initiating a process of ratification on campuses nationwide.[71] The group was scheduled to leave in November and return the following month. It occurred to several activists that the student-initiated peace treaty might be broadened into a national campaign.

The idea was fleshed out in an October workshop at Arch Street Meetinghouse in Philadelphia. The first phase would be teach-ins on the subject of a People's Peace Treaty. The point was not to take sides in Vietnam, but rather to define the peace that the government would not assay. The campaign would escalate in mid-April 1971, when local groups would say "no" to further war in various ways, and it would culminate in May

with massive nonviolent actions calling on the government to accept a
people's peace. Since the project would implicitly challenge the Logan
Act, which prohibited citizen diplomacy, it would in principle involve "the
entire movement in civil disobedience." Perhaps by thus challenging the
government's exclusive authority, the campaign could even help to "revolutionize the society."[72] The whole idea, worked out in the isolation of
the Quaker meeting house, elicited optimism and confidence among
those present. Early in November the concept was adopted by groups
including CALC, WSP, SANE, and the NSA. It was to be an educational
campaign that might cut through the "facade" of Nixon's peace proposals
and help people to understand the real terms on which peace could be
obtained. It was understood to be complementary to the Campaign to
Set the Date.

Critics, whether liberal or radical, now agreed that the war in Vietnam
was immoral. From John Kenneth Galbraith to Dave McReynolds, they
feared that the American system was out of control, "gone berserk,"
as McReynolds said. It needed to be restructured, Galbraith thought,
to reflect a sense of national purpose beyond bureaucratic inertia.[73]
Whether they supported a fixed date for withdrawal or promoted a People's Peace Treaty, dissidents agreed that Americans must understand
Vietnamization as promising "another full generation of violence, dissension, and recrimination."[74] Whether they felt called upon to persuade
or to resist, to rely on political pressure or disruption, they assumed that
peace had to originate in popular demand. "We're going to take ourselves
out of that war as a people," they told themselves, "if we have to do it
brick by brick, one institution at a time."[75]

Still, the old quarrel over the tactics of disruptive militancy continued
to rankle. A few zealots on the periphery of the movement advocated
revolutionary terrorism. A number of activists endorsed aggressive risk-
taking, such as attacking draft board offices, or conceded tacit support
through their very silence. Increasingly, though, respected radicals and
pacifists condemned any appearance of violence. There were widespread
complaints that the tactics of "draft-file superstars" and "new terrorists
for peace and justice" were repugnant, impractical, and politically counterproductive.[76] Bronson Clark of the AFSC argued that violence even
against property is essentially an "anti-democratic . . . centralized" form
of power.[77] His judgment was echoed by others. Dave McReynolds acknowledged that Al Hassler had been correct the previous summer in
saying that the response to the Cambodian invasion was "too apocalyptic."[78] Antiwar theologian Rosemary Reuther made a distinction between Dan Berrigan's resistance, which she could support "as a small
piece of a very complicated process of social change," and his tendency
"to absolutize this type of action," which she found "very unhelpful."[79]
Leaders in the Catholic Worker, WRL, FOR, and various Quaker groups

lauded the motives of the Catonsville Nine but rejected their tactics. Wrote Howard Zinn to Berrigan: "There is a lot of self-searching going on these days among everyone you meet. . . . The Weatherman timetable is too short, leading to desperate acts. We need a timetable longer than theirs and shorter than the liberal reformers."[80] For many activists the time had been already too long.

In the last weeks of 1970, the enthusiasm and activity of the antiwar movement seemed to shrivel. The decade was closing inconclusively. Dissidents complained about a pervasive "moral fatigue," a sense of futility if not despair.[81] They had deployed nearly every manner of protest—from self-immolations to bombings and from petitions to demonstrations—but the fighting continued. More Americans than ever called the war a mistake, and yet it only droned on. Uncounted but numerous activists quit protest either for personal fulfillment or for related reform enterprises, such as women's liberation and environmental activism. Yippie leader Jerry Rubin went into a prolonged sulk when his girlfriend ran off with another antiwar organizer. His personal life was falling apart, he said: "Suddenly the movement was over and where were we?"[82] Dedicated radical pacifist Martin Jezer and some of his friends left New York City for a Vermont farm. If they "simply gave up," they had the consolation, denied to Rubin, that "if we couldn't budge society, we did at least change ourselves." They could at least live in a manner that did not "coerce or exploit other people or the environment."[83]

The decade was ending, and so was an era. The civil rights movement, the New Left, the youth culture all seemed to be over: there were *"a number of pure causes no longer so pure, and a lot of naive people no longer so naive."*[84] The only thing that went on without interruption was the war. Large numbers of dissidents faded into private pursuits or alternate reforms as they concluded that they could neither stop it, nor live as serious citizens with it.

In the frustration of the Nixon years, particularly between September 1970 and April 1972, most of those who remained active against the war shed whatever naïveté they might have had. Their organizations declined. They lost some of their constituencies and funding, and much of their initiative and visibility. Vietnam gradually left the front pages of the newspapers. As the administration negotiated détente with China and the Soviet Union, the war ceased to threaten an international crisis. Troop withdrawals and the new course of superpower relations left the president freer to expand his air war in scope and intensity.

On the other hand, the longer the nation intervened directly in Vietnam, the stronger was the national sense that the war was wrong for any number of reasons, and the more general was skepticism about or contempt for governing authority. The decline of organized activism but masked the myriad ways in which discontent seeped through American life during these years, moving people to conclude that a total military withdrawal was in the nation's best interest, and abetting the suspicion that the war was corroding American values and institutions, including its constitutional order. While street actions diminished during 1970–1972, antiwar dissonance expanded through the population and escalated among the nation's elite. While Vietnam waned as an international crisis, it intensified as an institutional issue that increasingly focused upon the presidency. By the fall of 1971, polls suggested that popular confidence in American leaders had declined to a record low, and general opposition to the war was greater than at any time in the previous decade.[85] For dissidents the problem was that this opposition was "diffuse, often ill-informed and lacking in direction."[86] In a sense, the organized antiwar movement gave way to a pervasive antiwar mood.

". . . the enemy. He is us"

The Nixon administration continued both to remove American troops from Vietnam and to shore up the Saigon regime in the opening days of 1971. On 3 January, the president signed a congressional resolution repealing the Tonkin Gulf resolution, and shortly afterwards he indicated that American ground combat would end by May. Concurrently, however, U.S. air attacks across Indochina increased in frequency and severity, and the Pentagon announced that 100,000 U.S. troops would remain in South Vietnam on an open-ended "security mission."[87] On 1 February, the U.S. command in Saigon announced that 20,000 South Vietnamese troops were invading Laos in order to interdict North Vietnamese supply lines along the Ho Chi Minh Trail. Although no American ground forces entered Laos, there was no doubt that Operation Lamson 719 was inspired and subsidized by the United States. Its bombers, including Guam-based B-52s, pounded the Laotian jungle for days prior to the invasion; its helicopter pilots ferried the South Vietnamese into battle; and its soldiers took up defensive blocking positions for the ARVN forces.

Initially, the South Vietnamese offensive destroyed sizable arms and supply caches, heightening the confidence of South Vietnamese troops. Within three weeks, however, the North Vietnamese launched a counterattack that broke Saigon's offensive and sent the ARVN reeling back across the border. Officials in Saigon and Washington modified their initial claims of success but maintained that the invasion had weakened Hanoi's ability to continue the war. Administration supporters alleged that the news media had hampered the invasion and distorted the defeat, and Agnew accused the "arrogant" and "frustrated" Senator Fulbright of contributing to allied failure.[88]

Opinion polls in the wake of the offensive into Laos indicated that a plurality of Americans (46 to 41 percent) disapproved Nixon's handling of the war. Public approval of his handling of the presidency fell to 51 percent, the lowest point reached in his first term, whereas support for the McGovern-Hatfield amendment to end the war by a fixed date climbed to a record 73 percent.[89] Perhaps fifty thousand people demonstrated in Washington within two days of the invasion. Nationwide protests were muted, though, almost resigned. Some journalists attributed the relatively mild reaction to the fact that U.S. ground combat forces were not involved. Others explained it as a newly conservative orientation on campuses and among the public. Critics blamed the absence of stronger protest on deepening popular apathy and the genius of the White House in merchandising its policy as the route to honorable peace. This was the president's "momentary glory," wrote James Wechsler. "He has broken the spirit of the vast number of his countrymen who loathe the war but now feel helpless to do anything about it."[90] San Francisco columnist Arthur Hoppe told his readers of his gut reaction when he first heard of the failure of the South Vietnamese invasion:

Without thinking, I nodded and said, Good. And having said it, I realized the bitter truth: Now I root against my own country.

This is how far we have come in this hated and endless war. This is the nadir I have reached in this winter of my discontent. This is how close I border on treason.

I don't root for the enemy. I doubt they are any better than we. I don't give a damn any more who wins the war. But because I hate what my country is doing in Vietnam, I emotionally and often irrationally hope that it fails.[91]

There was no record of how many other loyal citizens had become resentful witnesses to the war.

The administration continued to reduce U.S. ground forces at the same time that it intensified the bombing campaign. On 7 April, Nixon announced the withdrawal of another hundred thousand troops by December; but he rejected congressional demands that he set a date for total withdrawal, insisting that national honor required the United States to give the South Vietnamese a "reasonable chance to survive as a free people."[92] The White House played variously upon fears of a communist victory and bloodbath, the dangers of a postwar right-wing backlash, and the need to guarantee the safe return of American POWs (whose numbers increased as the air war intensified). The president reserved the right to bomb North Vietnam as long as Hanoi held American prisoners, and he alluded to the need for a postwar American residual force in South Vietnam. The vice-president warned against precipitate withdrawal because it would provoke the political right, and he labeled critics as "home-front snipers" who demeaned the honor of front-line GIs.[93] American soldiers continued to be sacrificed meanwhile, as the number of war dead exceeded forty-five thousand in late April.

Although troop withdrawals were the main key to defusing the war issue, administration credibility was bolstered also by its association with the POW issue and by its China policy. Popular concern for American prisoners of war was natural, and White House efforts on their behalf were appropriate. Insisting that the welfare of POWs was an apolitical "humanitarian" and national concern, Nixon sent a former astronaut abroad in the fall of 1970 to elicit support for a prisoner exchange. In mid-November, Secretary of Defense Melvin Laird disclosed that a specially trained U.S. commando team had made a daring but unsuccessful attempt to rescue American prisoners held at a North Vietnamese camp near Son Tay. The president personally reassured POW wives that he would not rest until their husbands were safely back in the U.S. A ground swell of public sympathy generated campaigns to collect Christmas mail for POWs, to send letters to Hanoi demanding the release of prisoners, and to keep their fate before the public—programs which the White House facilitated as much as possible. The matter became implicitly political, however, as the administration identified itself and its policy with POWs. The "Tell It to Hanoi" committee sponsored a national tour by former prisoners who described North Vietnamese atrocities, while war critics were accused of impeding the release of American POWs or glossing over their brutal treatment. For their part, Americans captured in Vietnam were hostages to the national interests of both Hanoi and the United States.

Moreover, the administration skillfully deflated the fear that Vietnam would escalate like Korea into a Sino-American war. In April it announced an exchange of table tennis teams in friendly competition between the U.S. and the People's Republic of China. This modest initiative marked the first break in a generation of Sino-American hostility, and it raised expectations of more significant developments. The move was applauded especially by liberals in the foreign policy-shaping elite who had worried that the Indochina air war might incite Chinese intervention. Nixon countered that the breakthrough could be attributed to the tenacity of the U.S. stand in Vietnam. Ironically, the president used improved relations with China in order to rally support for an independent South Vietnam originally conceived to block Chinese communist expansion. "What was billed as the Asiatic Armageddon now dissolves into a Ping Pong tournament," wrote I. F. Stone. "So why go on with the killing? What's left of the war but inertia?"[94]

One might have concluded, early in 1971, that the antiwar movement also was propelled by inertia. Under pressure from some of its members to become more active, BEM reopened its Washington office and renewed its lobbying efforts on the Hill. Liberals in SANE, ADA, and a new, self-styled citizens' lobby called Common Cause urged the government to set a terminal date for intervention but otherwise offered no new initiatives (unless an ADA recommendation to impeach the president were to be taken seriously). All three organizations arrayed Vietnam alongside their domestic concerns. In mid-January 1971, George McGovern opened the 1972 presidential campaign with a peace plank. Later in the month he and Edmund Muskie both called on Nixon to set a date for withdrawal, and Senate doves introduced legislation mandating an end to intervention by 31 December. A similar measure was introduced in the House in February, and the date-certain approach was adopted as a congressional objective, along with domestic priorities, by the Democratic Policy Committee. In some sense, liberals were trying to prevent the war from further eroding the Great Society. Their efforts continued through the spring, but they were overshadowed by the demonstrative left.

Various elements of the movement's left wing still clung to the single-minded goal of immediate withdrawal, the elusive hope for a broad peace and justice coalition, the popularization of the People's Peace Treaty, or, on the fringe, a disposition to disruptive action. Partisans of these approaches contended with one another during the winter of 1970–71 even as they sought uneasily to form a united front against the war. Loosely aligned, they spawned a series of domestic actions in the spring.

Immediate withdrawal—"Out Now!" was the rallying cry of the National Peace Action Coalition, which was heavily influenced by the Trotskyist SWP. At a conference in Chicago's Packinghouse Labor Center, 4–6 December 1970, some twelve hundred delegates, mainly from local NPAC and SMC groups, projected a week of antiwar actions which would culminate in disciplined mass demonstrations in Washington and San Francisco on 24 April 1971. The date was challenged at one point by a number of NCAWRR activists who had just returned from a meeting on Vietnam in Stockholm, where plans were laid for international demonstrations in May. In the lobby of the Labor Center, while people waited inside, NPAC leaders debated with Sid Peck, Sid Lens, Ron Young, and others who wanted to defer a decision on the date to a later meeting. When it became clear that an impasse had been reached, NPAC proceeded with its original plan, rejecting the People's Peace Treaty in the process.[95] The YSA and SMC subsequently adopted the NPAC program as their own.

The dispute over a date involved differences which could not be resolved by the three hundred delegates at the NCAWRR conference of 8–10 January. One faction, led by Rennie Davis and Dave Dellinger, wanted to stage (presumably disruptive) direct action in Washington. Another faction, with Sid Peck and Ron Young as spokesmen, urged a mass demonstration which would include orderly nonviolent civil disobedience. Virtually no one supported the NPAC program. As so often in the past, the price of a nominal coalition was the promise of miscellaneous unspecified activities. It was agreed only that there would be "multi-issue action" in Washington during 1–8 May in relation to "racism, poverty, unemployment, repression, sexism, inflation, taxes and a demand to implement the [People's] peace treaty."[96] Early in February the NCAWRR was reconstituted by its leaders as the People's Coalition for Peace and Justice (PCPJ) in order to coordinate actions which would begin early in April, in tribute to Martin Luther King, Jr., and culminate in May. The organizing core of the coalition was the Fifth Avenue Peace Parade Committee.

The creation of PCPJ took place just prior to an Ann Arbor conference called by the National Student Association to ratify the draft treaty which student leaders had discussed in Vietnam. By then the invasion of Laos had generated such anger that over sixteen hundred students attended the conference. By that time, too, Rennie Davis and a few others (who had come to be known as the MayDay Collective, or Tribe) were ready with an alternative proposal: on 1 May the government would be given two days to accept the People's Peace Treaty, and if it did not, a mass demonstration would close down Washington. Davis had been convinced for months that the war could be brought home only by creating a crisis "atmosphere of struggle."[97] The key to the treaty concept was not merely education but enforcement, he argued, and that meant confrontation. The MayDay project was adopted by those who remained at the conference into its second day, although it was not endorsed by the NSA. Davis now had a mandate of sorts for massive disruptive action in the nation's capital. Moreover, through the People's Peace Treaty, he could link that activity to the remnant radical pacifist coalition now calling itself PCPJ. In effect, because of the deadline feature of his proposal, as of 3 May the date-certain approach implicit in the original treaty campaign would become immediate withdrawal.

On the eve of the Ann Arbor conference, someone in the PCPJ wrote: "The period of quiet waiting seems about to end. . . . Spring is coming!"[98] For the time being, though, turmoil was turned inward on the left. There now were two dates for a major spring action, several unreconciled tactics, diverging goals, and deep recriminations. Radical pacifist Dave McReynolds mistrusted the Trotskyists altogether and preferred the May date to align with the worldwide actions planned by the Stockholm Conference. Equally, however, he mistrusted Rennie Davis, who he thought "should be removed as coordinator," with the PCPJ separated from the MayDay Collective: "Either we are for nonviolent civil disobedience or not. . . . The one thing that will be deadly is ambiguity about the May events. I get the strong impression that . . . Rennie turned around and organized his own base at Ann Arbor and is now trying to impose his own scenario in Washington."[99] The NPAC and PCPJ offices were in the same Washington building, he noted elsewhere, but "no one talks to anyone in the elevator."[100] The PCPJ itself was divided between the MayDay group and pacifists associated with NAG. There were serious tensions in the AFSC, WILPF and FOR. In McReynolds' apprehension was a microcosm of the movement.

Mistrust was aggravated by external pressure. In January the government indicted activists who, it was said, had plotted to vandalize draft boards, destroy the heating systems of federal buildings, and kidnap Henry Kissinger. The indictment was widely understood in the movement to be a trumped-up threat.[101] In February the FBI tried surreptitiously to forestall an SMC conference. Organizations were known to be infiltrated, phones tapped. One trusted neither the mail nor unfamiliar activists. Stewart Meacham warned friends "to operate under the assumption that big brother is listening." Above all, he appealed, they must not be ruled by fear: "If we fail this spring, how can we ever hope to find the energy and the unifying principle to act effectively together again?"[102]

Desperately, a small caucus of pacifists bridged the mistrust late in February. Meacham, Dellinger, and Quaker pacifist Bob Levering were present, and the formula for even tenuous cooperation came from McReynolds: the PCPJ would support the NPAC demonstrations in Washington and San Francisco on 24 April, but it would organize lobbying and other activities in Washington during the following week; people then would be trained in nonviolent civil disobedience in anticipation of an attempt by the MayDay Tribe to block Washington streets on 3 May. The Tribe and NPAC "entered into a tacit agreement to simply stay out of each other's way," as Fred Halstead recalled.[103] On this fragile platform the movement prepared for April.

The spring campaign opened on 26 March with an appeal from Protestant church leaders for withdrawal by a fixed date. Under the auspices of the AFSC, CALC, and the FOR, about 170 of them had flown to Paris, where they had consulted with all the parties represented in the negotiations. Throughout Holy Week, protests came predominantly from the religious community—pastors who preached Palm Sunday sermons on the war or conducted vigils and fasts; 80 clergymen who were arrested when they tried to plant a charred cross in front of the White House; seminarians who chained themselves together at the Justice Department on Good Friday; Robert McAfee Brown and his son, who were arrested with others at a Berkeley draft board.

April began with rallies around the country linked to the theme of a "Long March" against the war and for domestic justice. This was the PCPJ theme. That the agenda attracted sponsorship from civil rights and poor people's advocates in the SCLC and the National Welfare Rights Organization suggested the extent to which the war was felt to repress social programs in the United States. The alignment with those organizations also illustrated the continuing effort of the antiwar movement to transcend its middle-class base. Student body leaders meanwhile sent another appeal to the president. There were demonstrations in various cities. A campaign to "unsell the Vietnam war" (stimulated by a CBS special on "The Selling of the Pentagon") enlisted forty New York advertising agencies which donated print ads, TV commercials, and radio spots worth an estimated million dollars. Women from WSP developed innovative guerrilla theater: in Kentucky they employed portable "tiger cages" to dramatize reported prisoner abuse in South Vietnam; in Evanston, Illinois, they trespassed on an Army security center to "spy on spies"; in Grand Rapids, Michigan, they lay down in a shopping mall to simulate a Laotian air attack.[104] Local actions such as these, and a national one by antiwar veterans, generated momentum which crested on 24 April.

Estimates of the size of the Washington demonstration that day varied from 200,000 to half a million, and the crowd was at least comparable to that of the November 1969 Mobilization, even though troop withdrawals had taken place in the meantime. Approximately 125,000 gathered in San Francisco—the largest West Coast demonstration in history, according to *Newsweek*.[105] Formally sponsored by Trotskyists and liberals in NPAC, the twin demonstrations had surprisingly broad support. The Washington march was endorsed by twenty-six members of Congress, including seven senators. The ADA and SANE were sponsors, along with many other liberal organizations and trade unions. Indeed, Teamsters Union officials served as parade marshals. The authorities were even relatively cooperative in making arrangements. Fred Halstead was again working on logistics, and his task had never been easier.

Blessed by good weather and a minimum of government harassment, and led by a young veteran in a wheelchair, people filled Pennsylvania Avenue in a pleasant mood. For about a third of them, this was their first demonstration. Banners and signs identified a wide spectrum of citizen groups. At the Mall radicals were all but absent from the platform. Speakers included Coretta King, Congresswoman Bella Abzug (D-N.Y.), Senator Vance Hartke (D-Ind.), the Reverends William Coffin and Ralph Abernathy, former senator Ernest Gruening, and veteran Lieutenant John Kerry (who would become a U.S. senator from Massachusetts). The crowd was relaxed, its demeanor orderly and even gentle. It was the kind of demonstration "that the cops could have brought their children to" (at least one did), observed *Time*.[106] Still, there was no disguising the underlying pessimism and outright despair. In 1969, declared National Student Association president David Ifshin, protesters had believed that the war would be over soon. "That feeling isn't here today," he told the crowd. "We know it's going to go on and on."[107] The demand for immediate withdrawal was perhaps less political than emotive.

To many observers the April demonstration seemed to reestablish the antiwar movement as an organized, national force; but beneath the surface there were crosscurrents. Just before the rally McReynolds worried about the "divisions" between NPAC and PCPJ. Somewhat ruefully, he marvelled that the Trotskyists had established themselves as a "respectable peace movement." He felt nervous about the week leading up to 3 May because it was not clear "to what extent the May Day Collective is genuinely committed to nonviolence and to what extent it is taking the adult movement for a ride."[108] That uncertainty remained as, in the days following the march, activists from PCPJ, FOR, CALC, AFSC, and WILPF lobbied on the Hill for a date-certain end to the war and conducted orderly civil disobedience at the Selective Service headquarters, the Justice Department, and the Department of Health, Education and Welfare. On 28 April four legislators introduced the People's Peace Treaty as a House resolution. Toward the end of the week, several thousand (mainly young) people from the MayDay Collective began to assemble in the city with the intention of trying to shut down the capital of a nation at war.

The plan was to use massive nonviolent direct action at bridges and street intersections in order to tie up Washington traffic, paralyze the city, and confront American leaders with the choice: "End the War or face social chaos."[109] The government beat them to the punch. At dawn on Sunday 2 May, federal officials launched an anticipatory strike against those young people who remained from an all-night rock festival near the Jefferson Memorial, scattering the crowd and making a few hundred arrests. During the day several thousand youths gathered at area universities and churches to prepare for disruptive actions on Monday.

Federal authorities were more than ready for them on 3 May. Directed by Deputy Attorney General Richard Kleindienst (who, in turn, was reporting to the president), city police backed by national troops swept the downtown area as helicopters hovered overhead. Marines, some of them manning machine guns with live ammunition, were assigned to secure the Justice Department and other federal buildings, while flak-jacketed troops patrolled the streets in scenes that to a *Newsweek* reporter "seemed more appropriate to Saigon in wartime than Washington."[110] Indeed, a Nixon aide called the operation a "military attack."[111] Small groups of protesters darted about in confusion, trying to obstruct traffic one moment and avoiding police and tear gas the next. There was violence, but police brutality was not so common as arbitrary arrest. Seven thousand people, including several hapless federal workers and shoppers, were arrested and incarcerated in the Washington Coliseum and RFK Stadium.

Nonetheless, scattered MayDay forces defied the government again on 4 May, when they marched on the Justice Department and courted further arrests. The following day the Tribe's remaining couple of thousand activists held a rally at the Capitol, which was broken up by police over

the objections of Bella Abzug and other speakers. By then, the larger
dream of sparking a nationwide work moratorium on 5 May had fizzled
along with their hopes of shutting down Washington and its war.

Rennie Davis was taken into custody on Monday. He conceded failure
but noted that the city had been in a state of siege: "It wasn't Saigon, but
was a taste."[112] The euphoria of having fought and survived led a few
activists to claim victory. In fact, the demonstrators had responded with
remarkable discipline and nonviolence, as they had been coached to do,
and there was a huge discrepancy between the threat they posed and
the treatment they received. Moral courage was not the same thing as
political impact, however, and once again the image of recalcitrance belied the reality of moral indignation. Most antiwar liberals and elite dissidents distanced themselves from the MayDay disruptions. Within the
pacifist left, evaluations of the event differed sharply; but that only ac-
centuated the fact that, as McReynolds acknowledged, the organized
movement was split and "perplexed beyond measure."[113]

A bare majority of Americans supported the administration's handling
of the demonstrators, although a small group of critics led by Senator
Edward Kennedy denounced the draconian measures.[114] Certainly, the
president himself felt more combative. Even as federal troops patrolled
the streets near the White House, Nixon talked with his aides about
hiring Teamster goons to beat up antiwar demonstrators. "These people
try somethin'," he told H. R. Haldeman, "bust 'em."[115] In the wake of
what he perceived as a victory, the president told White House assistant
Charles Colson what he really wanted to do with his opponents: "One
day we will get them—we'll get them on the ground, where we want
them. And we'll stick our heels in, step on them hard and twist—right,
Chuck, right?" Kissinger "knows what I mean," Nixon continued, "just
like you do it in the negotiations, Henry—get them on the floor and step
on them, crush them, show them no mercy."[116]

As he had done eight months before, the president misdiagnosed his
and the nation's problem. The difficulty was not his challengers, whatever
their tactics. At issue was the national undercurrent of disaffection they
carried into confrontation. This mood could not be cut away by force or
even talked aside forever. It had to be understood, and an eloquent appeal for understanding had been made in the capital just before the mass
demonstration there. The fact that the plea was carried to Washington by
Vietnam veterans was indicative of how far the malaise of the war had
spread.

Antiwar veterans had become a real force during the winter and spring
of 1971 for two related reasons: they forced the issue of war crimes, and
they took the initiative in calling for a decisive end to the conflict. Neither
thrust was new in 1971, of course, but both were much more visible
than before.

A Citizens Commission of Inquiry into U.S. War Crimes in Vietnam had been founded in February 1970 with support from Quakers, clergy, lawyers, and veterans. In the fall it planned hearings that would lead to a national inquiry: the Winter Soldier Investigation. Not only was this a query in wintertime, it enlisted men who were willing to relive in public the pain of war for the sake of their country and comrades in arms: neither summer soldiers nor sunshine patriots they.

In December 1970 the Citizens Committee convened a hearing in a Washington hotel where veterans testified to widespread, officially condoned atrocities in Vietnam. On the basis of three hundred pages of those hearings, in January 1971 several officers asked the military to convene a formal court of inquiry into war crimes. By that time the trial of Lieutenant Calley was in progress and provided a foil for the soldiers' revelations. At the end of the month, from 31 January through 2 February 1971, VVAW conducted its own national inquiry in a Howard Johnson motel in Detroit. The project was funded with help from CALC, BEM, Emil Mazey of the United Auto Workers, Jane Fonda, and the music group Crosby, Stills and Nash. Over a hundred veterans and POWs unburdened themselves of grisly memories: tortured prisoners, murdered civilians, destroyed villages, and indiscriminate firing and bombing. They related attempts by the military to quash reports of atrocities, decent treatment at the hands of the enemy, and even their criticism of the war itself. Several hundred Vietnam veterans from the U.S. and Canada listened. The published edition of the hearings was dedicated, *"America . . . See what you've become, Amerika."*[117]

There was indeed growing apprehension that national institutions were being corroded. Revelations of military spying on civilian antiwar activists mounted throughout the winter. In March anonymous burglars released to the press documents stolen from a local FBI office in Media, Pennsylvania, which demonstrated the unprecedented scope of government surveillance and harassment. Frequent reports of war-related corruption, together with a legacy of misinformation about the conduct of the war, strained popular confidence in the government. In March, 69 percent of those polled said that they felt that they were not being told "all they should know" about the war, leaving Nixon with what George Gallup called "a giant-sized 'credibility gap'" comparable to that suffered by Lyndon Johnson.[118]

It was not just that people mistrusted the administration; many of them could not trust their own society. In April nearly half of those sampled said that the escalation of internal crises was "likely to lead to breakdown" within the U.S., and a third declared that traditional ways of living in America were not working.[119] The country was beginning "to fall apart," Congresswoman Bella Abzug wrote in her diary; it was undergoing a "moral convulsion."[120] As if to cap the sense of inverted values and moral crisis, Lieutenant Calley was found guilty late in March and sentenced to life at hard labor.

Public reaction to Calley's conviction was swift, angry, and overwhelming. Citizens, especially in the South and West, who normally supported the administration, denounced the government for punishing Calley and announced their opposition to a war in which policymakers prosecuted soldiers for doing their duty. Waves of protest letters poured into Washington; several local draft board officers resigned; two radio stations stopped broadcasting army enlistment advertisements; the Kansas State Senate passed a resolution urging Nixon to free the lieutenant; and a heroic "Ballad of Lieutenant Calley," set to the tune of "The Battle Hymn of the Republic," sold a quarter-million copies within a week.[121]

Both combat veterans and antiwar activists criticized the government for making a scapegoat of Calley. If he had committed a crime, they said, then the guilt ran up the entire chain of command. Several representatives urged the House Armed Services Committee to open public hearings on war crimes charges. Hans Morgenthau, among others, placed the responsibility squarely with the political leadership and lamented the lack of will to settle the nation's "moral and political accounts." For some citizens, the conviction had a reverse twist: "If he is guilty, they say, so are we. He is, and we are."[122]

The uproar over the Calley conviction both advertised and aggravated a larger crisis within the military that was manifested in antiwar sentiment, pervasive racial tensions, and violent resentment toward the command system. From whatever causes, there had been a significant drop in morale and combat responsiveness since 1967. The frequency of AWOL and desertion and the number of requests for discharge for reasons of conscientious objection escalated wildly, reaching record highs in 1971. Drug abuse became epidemic, stockade and brig rebellions frequent. "Fragging" (attacking fellow soldiers, usually superiors, with fragmentation grenades or other weapons) increased by a factor of 2.6 from 1969— by a factor of 5 when figured against total troop strength.[123] There was no way to number the incidents of personal recalcitrance, quiet resistance, or "search-and-evade" tactics by small units on patrol. The integrity of the military itself was eroding.

The crisis within the armed forces accelerated Washington's plans to shift from the draft to an all-volunteer army; and, in a circular way, the dismantling of the draft further discredited the Selective Service System and devalued the prospect of military service in Vietnam. Who wanted to be, as Lieutenant John Kerry put it in April, "the last man to die in Vietnam? How do you ask a man to be the last man to die for a mistake?"[124] Draft resistance and disparities in eligibility for exemption raised problems for the Selective Service, but nothing damaged it more than the rapid growth after 1969 of hundreds of draft counseling centers and legal advisory groups which seized upon the failure of local draft boards to abide by legal and administrative regulations. With thousands of ordinary antiwar citizens serving as draft counsellors, the system became swamped with so many protests and appeals for reclassification that by 1971 it fell apart "in shambles."[125] The Nixon administration claimed credit for lowering draft calls, introducing a lottery system for draft liability, and finally ending the draft in 1972, but those changes were less a matter of principle than a response to the fact that Selective Service had been shredded by a combination of mismanagement, federal court rulings, and citizen opposition. Efforts to reform and then to end the draft only underscored the conclusion reached by more and more Americans: that the future of Vietnam was not worth the lives of American boys or the social cohesion of American society. By the spring of 1971 war-weariness and the wish to be done with Vietnam was pervasive.

Loyal antiwar veterans acted. On Lincoln's Birthday they staged a small rally outside the White House, where they threw their medals and service ribbons over the fence toward their former commander in chief. They didn't want to be called heroes, they said. They didn't want "to call evil good."[126] That rally was a precursor of the mid-April campaign sponsored by VVAW, "Dewey Canyon III" (named to spite the code name for the operation into Laos). The organization now had over two thousand veterans on its membership rolls. On 18 April several hundred of them, together with a delegation of Gold Star mothers, marched to Arlington National Cemetery, but federal officials refused to let them hold a wreath-laying ceremony. Undeterred, two hundred returned the following day and were admitted. For the next three days, VVAW activists conducted mock search-and-destroy operations downtown; attempted to turn themselves in to Pentagon officials for committing war crimes; were arrested for milling about the Supreme Court building with demands that the Court rule on the war's constitutionality; and testified before the Senate Foreign Relations Committee, which was investigating ways to end the fighting. Millions of television viewers heard Lieutenant Kerry explain that he and his friends had come to the Capitol with "one last mission— to search out and destroy the last vestige of this barbaric war, to pacify our own hearts, to conquer the hate and the fear that have driven this country these last ten years and more, so when thirty years from now our brothers go down the street without a leg, without an arm, or a face, and small boys ask why, we will be able to say 'Vietnam' and not mean a desert, not a filthy obscene memory, but mean instead the place where America finally turned and where soldiers like us helped it in the turning."[127]

Finally, on 23 April, seven hundred veterans marched from their campsite on the Mall to the west steps of the Capitol, where each man solemnly announced his name and unit and then threw his medals over a makeshift fence toward the nation's seat of authority.[128] Quite simply, the veterans had "identified the enemy. He is us."[129] The phrase was adapted from Walt Kelly's comic strip character, Pogo, who had used it to describe the problem of environmental pollution. But it was especially poignant coming from soldiers who had found it so very difficult to identify the enemy in the field.

The VVAW protest carried the weight of tested patriotism, seeming to arise from the Vietnam conflict itself. It conveyed no ideology except love of country. It did not represent a political demand so much as it expressed disillusionment and the anguish of anger turned inward: ". . . the enemy. He is us."

That same feeling was spreading throughout the nation. Calvin Trillin found it when he returned to Kansas, which he had surveyed in 1967. "I don't think you could find a hawk around here if you combed the place and set traps," a small-town newspaper editor told the visiting journalist. The same people who earlier had argued for military escalation and opposed negotiations called for military disengagement and withdrawal, and they did so "with the same sense of patriotism and same distaste for demonstrators that they had when they believed in military victory." In part, Trillin explained, peace had become the position of the president, whom they supported as loyally in 1971 as they had in 1967. Partly, too, Kansans opposed antiwar activists at least as much as they opposed the war because they detested all forms of anti-government public protest and because this compounded resentment allowed them to distinguish what they believed now "from what the war protesters were so despised for believing a few years ago."[130] The protesters may have been right. But Kansans refused to concede that possibility because they wanted so much to believe that their government was not wrong.

For a growing number of Americans, the war itself was wrong. That feeling was the real problem for the administration. In June a record 61 percent of those polled said that the war was a mistake, and a month later they believed by 65 to 20 percent that the U.S. withdrawal should continue "even if the government of South Vietnam collapsed."[131] The issue and the anxiety were not about Vietnam but over the United States. For many it was a question of national values. In this vein, writer Norman Podhoretz reassessed his thinking about Vietnam. Having never believed anything good could come from a clear American defeat, he wrote, "I now find myself—and here is the main source of my own embarrassment in writing about Vietnam—unhappily moving to the side of those who would prefer just such an American defeat to a Vietnamization of the war which calls for the indefinite and unlimited bombardment by American pilots in American planes of every country in that already devastated region."[132] To sensitive consciences like his, Vietnamization seemed to have left America just as culpable and therefore morally vulnerable as it had been during the ground war, precisely because it evaded the destruction to which it contributed.

Slowly, antiwar activists concluded that they were in a new phase of the struggle, that Vietnamization had changed the situation in both Vietnam and the United States. They knew that a sizable majority of Americans had drifted into opposition to the war. They felt that the country was seething with an "uneasiness and anxiety" which was rooted in the war and in its corrosive effects on American society.[133] They believed that the government was "not responding as it should to normal political processes" and was courting a fundamental crisis of state.[134] They could not see, though, that there was any prospect of converting the antiwar mood of the nation into a political force capable of overcoming the president's determination to continue the war—at least not without plunging finally into that crisis.

Eleven

Normalizing Dissent

"There's a feeling that the Senate ought
to tell the President that we should
get the hell out of the war"

Used to being a frustrated minority and seeming to succumb regularly to White House initiatives, antiwar activists found it difficult to appreciate the extent to which the political system itself was beginning to carry the popular antiwar mood. Throughout 1971, however, the president found himself periodically challenged by Congress and then, the following year, in the electoral arena. Nixon repeatedly beat back or outflanked his opponents, but in so doing he lay the basis for a confrontation over constitutional authority and, ultimately, legitimacy. So fluid and unpredictable was the administration's approach, and so great were the resources at its command, that political challengers found it difficult to identify issues on which to mount sustained opposition. Nonetheless, two foci developed early in 1971: the corruption of the Thieu regime and the goal of a terminal date for American intervention.

The focus on Thieu was given public definition on the antiwar left. It was not uniquely there, of course, nor was it new. For years the AFSC and especially the FOR had advocated the Buddhist "Third Force" as an alternative to the dependent, divisive regime in power. The FOR and other groups had also promoted the efforts of Don Luce to expose the torture of political prisoners in the South, and they had made the "tiger cages"—brutal holding pens which Luce had discovered—the symbols of Saigon's repression.[1] Denouncing Thieu as a tyrant, his regime as corrupt, and the war as a crime, supporters of the People's Peace Treaty promoted its ratification on college campuses and in city halls. They were seeking, in effect, to circumvent the exclusiveness of governmental negotiations by generating a popular definition of peace terms. Their campaign reinforced other programs which stressed the hypocrisy of relying on the Saigon regime for Vietnamese self-government when that regime was itself the real barrier to a peace settlement.

A second antiwar front was opened on 26 February with the Set the Date Now Campaign, scheduled to run through July. For this purpose the FOR, CALC, and AFSC aligned over twenty Catholic, Protestant, and Jewish organizations, which were joined by SANE, Common Cause, ADA, and the VVAW. In March the coalition sponsored a visit to Paris by 171 people, who returned to lobby for a definitive end to American military commitment within the year.

By the time the campaign was launched, its program was at the center of Democratic politics. In the House, William Ryan and twelve other representatives introduced a resolution to complete withdrawal by 30 June; Bella Abzug and thirty-one others designated the Fourth of July. In the Senate a new version of the McGovern-Hatfield bill targeted 31 December for total withdrawal of U.S. forces. A number of Democrats opposed the idea and stood behind the president, but plainly they were losing influence within their own party. On 22 February, the Democratic Policy Committee identified U.S. withdrawal from Vietnam by the end of the year as an objective of the Ninety-second Congress. The following month Democratic leaders reiterated the demand, and in April about twenty House dissidents, headed by New York's Bella Abzug and Benjamin Rosenthal, organized a traveling team to rally support for a date-certain withdrawal.

This stance seemed pretty timid to radical activists, but it was the first commitment from a responsible body in a major national party to a full and final U.S. pullout. For the moment it did not pose a challenge to the operation of foreign policy. Rather, it reflected a gnawing popular desire for reassurance that the war was in fact going to end. The force of that mood was captured in April in the hyperbole of Republican senator Hugh Scott. "You don't see any hawks around here," said the minority leader. "The hawks are all ex-hawks. There's a feeling that the Senate ought to tell the President that we should get the hell out of the war."[2]

Dissidents tried to get Congress to do just that. On 2 June a group of Washington leaders, including Clark Clifford and Paul Warnke, announced their intention to lobby for legislation that would set a date for American withdrawal by 31 December 1971. The idea of a cutoff date was backed by members of the foreign policy elite such as Ambassador Harriman, by the country's prestige press, and by the U.S. Conference of Mayors, among others. As numerous antiwar proposals were introduced in Congress, Senators McGovern and Hatfield reintroduced their resolution for an American withdrawal by the end of the year as an amendment to a draft extension bill. Representatives Lucien Nedzi (D-Mich.) and Charles Whalen (R-Ohio) introduced parallel legislation in the House. Senate majority leader Mansfield drafted a nonbinding resolution calling upon the president to negotiate an immediate cease-fire that would be followed by the phased withdrawal of U.S. troops in tandem with the release of American POWs, and a total American withdrawal within nine months of the return of the last prisoners. These proposals marked an aggressive effort to separate America's honorable withdrawal from Vietnam from the administration's commitment to the survival of the Thieu regime.

The force of elite protest grew when, on 13 June, the *New York Times* began to publish the Defense Department's secret history of American decision-making in Vietnam prior to 1967, known popularly as the *Pentagon Papers.* Appearing sensationally in the *Times,* the *Washington Post,* and then in a string of leading urban dailies, the account documented what antiwar critics had said all along: that the United States government, in its effort to maintain an anticommunist regime in Saigon, had shown little concern with Vietnamese wishes and had systematically deceived its own people about its behavior and intentions. Thus the Pentagon's own history, at least as it was interpreted in the *New York Times* and other newspapers, directly contradicted the official myth of America as a reluctant intervener in Vietnam's affairs. Although its analysis ended with 1967, it inevitably enlarged doubts over President Nixon's credibility.

The White House was shocked by the appearance of the *Pentagon Papers.* Initially, it shrugged off the documents as the low-level bureaucratic memoranda of a Democratic administration, but within a few days Kissinger and other aides persuaded the president that the unauthorized publication would expose him as "a weakling."[3] Goaded into action, Nixon ordered the Justice Department to block the public release of the Defense Department study and to identify and punish those responsible for divulging the account to the press. For the first time in American history, the government tried to use the power of prior restraint to bar publication of information on the grounds that it was injurious to the national security. The newspapers complied with a restraining order, and attorneys for the *New York Times* argued before the Supreme Court not that restraint was unconstitutional, but rather that the government had failed to show that publication would damage national security. By a vote of six to three, the Court rejected the administration's suit and allowed continued publication of the *Papers,* which by then was eagerly awaited.

In the meantime, former Defense Department intelligence analyst Daniel Ellsberg publicly acknowledged that he was responsible for the release of the study. Within days, he and an associate, Anthony Russo, were charged by the Justice Department with unauthorized possession of government documents and ordered to appear before a grand jury. For the antiwar movement Ellsberg provided a hero—a man who had risked his career on behalf of truth and public disclosure. The White

House understood that. With Nixon, Kissinger concluded that "there are forces at work bent on destroying this government," and the two identified Ellsberg as the symbol if not the agent of those forces within the eastern establishment and the Democratic party.[4] Determined to wreck Ellsberg's reputation, the president ordered White House agents to do whatever was necessary to discredit him and other prominent dissidents, in line with a strategy for electoral victory in 1972 devised by Patrick Buchanan: the Democrats were to be divided between elite liberals and hard-hat conservatives. White House aide G. Gordon Liddy would conclude by the fall that "we weren't [merely] in for a campaign in '72; it would be war." He explained, "There was no doubt in my mind that the United States was at war internally as well as externally," and the enemy within had to be destroyed at all costs.[5]

The controversy over the *Pentagon Papers* introduced new strains in the relationship of the government and the press, and it aggravated the tensions among the leadership at a time when popular antiwar sentiment seemed to be mounting. In midsummer, various polls indicated that a record-high percentage of the American people regarded the war as a mistake, and that the president's credibility rating had sunk to a level comparable to that of his predecessor.[6] Nonetheless, congressional dissidents were unable to convert this sentiment into effective legislation.

In June, the Senate rejected the McGovern-Hatfield deadline of 31 December for total withdrawal by a 55-42 vote, and the House defeated the companion Nedzi-Whalen bill 254-158. Late in the month, the Senate passed Mansfield's nonbinding resolution; but the House rejected it, and, after a month of argument, a conference committee produced an administration-approved compromise that eliminated any hint of a withdrawal deadline. There seemed to be no political handle, no leverage with which dissidents in Congress could challenge the administration's policy that, by its own account, was winding down the war—honorably.

Through the summer and into the fall, the organized antiwar movement continued to contract and to dissipate its resources in divided tactics. Al Hassler responded to an appeal from the United Buddhist Church by framing an appeal to *all* the combatants to "Stop the Killing." Circulated through the International FOR, of which he was executive secretary, the appeal amounted to a cease-fire. Other activists argued that a political settlement must precede a cease-fire or, alternatively, that the United States should simply retire from Vietnam. Many liberals, including those in SANE, ADA, and the FCNL still lobbied for a date-certain withdrawal. Allard Lowenstein tried to rally antiwar youth behind an antiwar presidential candidate for 1972. The Committee to Unsell the War unleashed a full-blown, Madison Avenue campaign of newspaper copy and radio and TV ads which protested Nixon's war without suggesting any alternative. Religious pacifists in the FOR, AFSC, CALC, and WRL made plans for a solemn witness to the death toll in Vietnam, which they projected for the fall. Liberal dissidents could agree only that the war they all abhorred was likely to continue indefinitely. Thus, when CALC recalled in August at its first national conference that the founders "never thought that the war would drag on this long," the organization was converted from an emergency clearinghouse to a permanent body.[7] At the same time, "About Vietnam" was dropped from its name, freeing Clergy and Laymen Concerned to address a variety of issues.

Antiwar radicals patched over the antagonism between NPAC and PCPJ without really soothing the tensions between them. A July convention of NPAC roiled with "mindless political in-fighting." Militants from SDS even had to be physically removed from the Hunter College hall when they disrupted the meeting.[8] The organization reverted to the SWP formula of mass demonstrations for immediate withdrawal. Meanwhile, the PCPJ continued to promote the People's Peace Treaty virtually without media coverage. The organization was mired in intramural confusion— dogged by arguments over the tactics of the MayDay Tribe and diverted by a host of causes, including poverty, racial injustice, feminism, and (in the aftermath of riots at Attica penitentiary) the prison system. Relationships among radicals were rent by charges of elitism and male chauvinism. The pressure was not just the war, as Tom Hayden later recalled. "We had become isolated, self-enclosed in a universe of political rather than human life. In this sealed universe, social relationships were contained within organizations, language turned to jargon, disputes were elevated to doctrinal heights, paranoia replaced openness, and the struggle to change each other became a substitute for changing the world."[9] Debilitating tension plagued even pacifists who had a more identifiable heritage than radicals and a stronger sense of community. The problem was not just the war; it was a stifling atmosphere that affected everyone in search of personal and social identity—liberals as well as radicals. But it was Vietnam that caged the quest and distorted it.

Some antiwar radicals followed Staughton Lynd's example in turning away from the war issue to address America's mounting economic problems. Others simply quit the movement, like yippie activist Abbie Hoffman, who was tired of government harassment as well as the "petty ugliness" and "bail fund hustles" of left-wing activism.[10] A few Roman Catholic activists tried to struggle on, but they suffered a major defeat when twenty-eight of them were led by a government agent into a raid on a draft board office in Camden, New Jersey, that turned out to be an FBI trap. Vexed by government authorities and divided by personal and political animosities, antiwar radicals maintained no semblance of a united front.

For half a decade antiwar activists had been divided between a radical left and a liberal wing: each a loose, eclectic alliance. They had in common only the fact that they all struggled to contain and reverse U.S. war policy in Vietnam—that and their collective status as a self-conscious minority. In 1971 radicalism virtually evaporated, and liberal, even moderate, elements came to predominate. There was now something of a political base and a popular antiwar mood with which to work, but dissidents still could not find a way to convert strong antiwar sentiment into an explicit policy of complete and total withdrawal. From all appearances, antiwar activists had been vindicated in their judgment that the war had been imprudent and wrong, but they could not persuade the nation to court explicit defeat.

The Nixon administration, on the other hand, refused to contemplate the prospect of a clear national failure in Vietnam. Instead, it persisted in Vietnamization, hoping that a powerful South Vietnamese army supported by U.S. air power and residual ground forces would maintain an anticommunist regime in Saigon, with or without a negotiated settlement in Paris. The strategy addressed three key fronts.

Domestically, the president counted on holding his established congressional supporters in line, keeping his opposition divided and off balance, and courting public acquiescence by the continuous reduction of U.S. ground forces in Vietnam (more rapidly than his military advisers thought prudent). In September troop strengths were down to 220,000.

Militarily, the president counted on air power to check communist forces while a stable South Vietnamese defense was built. Armadas of B-52 strategic bombers regularly pounded communist supply lines and troop concentrations throughout Indochina, and U.S. fighter-bombers periodically struck North Vietnam on the pretext that they were defending those U.S. combat forces which remained in South Vietnam. Using the Pentagon's own figures—and much of the air war was kept secret— a Cornell University study team concluded in November that the Nixon administration had unleashed more bomb tonnage upon Indochina in its thirty months than the Johnson administration had dropped in four years (the total was said to be three times the tonnage expended by the U.S. in World War II).[11]

Internationally, in 1971 Nixon and Kissinger appear to have counted on an emerging great-power condominium with the Soviet Union and China to isolate North Vietnam and induce a Korea-like settlement. Meanwhile, the Paris talks were continuing in a perfunctory way. On 1 July, communist negotiators surprised the U.S. government when they put forward a seven-point peace program that promised the return of U.S. POWs by 31 December 1971, in return for an American promise of total withdrawal of its forces and its support for the Thieu regime. The White House derisively dismissed the proposal for not guaranteeing the safety of remaining U.S. combat forces, and although the president acknowledged that the release of U.S. prisoners was one of his major goals, he insisted that the overriding U.S. objective was to maintain an anticommunist regime in Saigon.[12] Meanwhile, Kissinger flew secretly to China, in a move that the administration hoped would outflank both Hanoi and domestic critics.

Nixon revealed the Kissinger mission in a televised address on 15 July. He announced that he himself would visit China by May 1972 as a step toward normalizing relations between the two powers. Except on the far right, his supporters were euphoric. Even antiwar liberals were pleased. Senator Scott, dazzled by the president's diplomatic artistry, suggested that Nixon's visit would induce Hanoi to compromise. Apparently, the Republican minority leader had changed his mind: the Senate would not have to tell the president to get out of the war after all.

Even though the antiwar critics were politically ineffective, the president, for all of his political and diplomatic success, failed to mollify the country's antiwar mood. The public still wanted out of Vietnam. Revelations of war-related corruption continued to make the news, some of them directly implicating the Saigon regime in drug trafficking and other crimes. Despite frantic warnings from the White House, Thieu insisted on running as the lone candidate in the elections scheduled for October: pretensions to democratic politics in South Vietnam were plainly farcical. Americans sampled in November wanted to get out of Vietnam by a three-to-one margin. They rejected the idea of maintaining a residual U.S. force there by 55 to 32 percent, opposed using U.S. bombers on behalf of postwar South Vietnam by 57 to 29 percent, and overwhelmingly objected to providing a billion dollars in aid to Saigon. A record 65 percent said that the war was "morally wrong." Louis Harris concluded from his polls that the patience of the American public with the war had "collectively worn out."[13] Numerous commentators agreed.

Antiwar dissidents in Congress returned to the contest in the fall. Senate doves achieved only the passage of a diluted version of the non-binding resolution originally proposed by Senator Mansfield, which called on the administration to withdraw its forces from Indochina "at the earliest practicable date" following the release of POWs.[14] House leaders blocked a direct vote on even this measure. Finally, on 10 November, antiwar House members managed to pass a modified version of the Senate bill, declaring that the American purpose ought to be the withdrawal of all forces from Indochina by a "date certain" following a prisoner exchange. After a few days of debate, Senate and House conferees agreed to attach the modified Mansfield amendments to a military procurement bill.

Although President Nixon signed the bill, he declared that he would disregard the Mansfield amendment and any other legislative riders intended to constrain his prerogatives as military commander in chief. Angrily, Senator Frank Church replied that the amendment was "now part of the law, and, as such, is not subject to dismissal by the President," and a group of antiwar lawyers tried to sue the president for "flouting" the legislature.[15] Antiwar legislators could not sustain their attack on the president, however, even when he most blatantly dismissed their efforts. Late in November, Senator John Sherman Cooper, although an opponent of the war, declared that it was fruitless to proceed because no congressional amendment could be drafted that would "clearly present the issue" of congressional opposition to the president's plans for a long-term U.S. residual force in Vietnam.[16] The president had fended off dissident legislators, even as he revealed a troubling disdain for constitutional procedures and congressional powers.

Nixon had good reason to conclude that the congressional challenge did not represent a significant political threat. South Vietnam seemed to be stronger as U.S. troops withdrew, and the communists were held in check. By the end of the year, summit meetings were scheduled for Beijing and Moscow. And public disaffection remained unfocused, leaving the administration with a free rein.

Ad hoc demonstrations against the war continued during the autumn. There were local marches, interfaith prayer vigils, petitions from national church and civic bodies, consumer boycotts, referenda, and individual witnesses. In Pittsfield, Massachusetts, the position of immediate cease-fire and withdrawal carried a referendum by 70 percent. A troop of fifteen entertainers, led by Jane Fonda and Donald Sutherland, took a show to antiwar coffeehouses near military bases in the U.S. and the Pacific. At the halftime ceremonies of a University of Michigan home football game in October, Vietnam veterans lined the sidelines and a hundred thousand fans stood as the band played "Taps" and an announcer read a prepared statement calling for a date-certain end to the war. The most striking expression of public feeling came in San Diego, where local activists and military personnel organized a referendum on preventing the USS *Constitution* from sailing to its battle station in the Tonkin Gulf. Citizens voted by an almost 80 percent plurality to detain the ship in port. When the *Constitution* departed under tight security, nine crewmen jumped ship and sought sanctuary in a local church. Another thousand sailors from the sister ship USS *Coral Sea* petitioned Congress to prevent their vessel from leaving port in Alameda. Still, such expressions did not add up to a national movement.

Coalition efforts were unimpressive. The PCPJ Moratorium on 13 October involved no more than 50,000 people nationally. Perhaps twice as many demonstrators turned out for local actions called by NPAC for 6 November, but this program too was disappointingly small.[17] Between those two events, the PCPJ sponsored an "Evict Nixon" action in Washington. National coordinator Rennie Davis had publicized it as a second MayDay, and District of Columbia police were ready for ten thousand activists. No more than five hundred protesters followed Davis and Dellinger from a small rally toward the White House, however, and when they met the police they quietly sat down in the street and were arrested. The opposing forces "clashed like two powder puffs."[18]

Evaluations of the movement at the end of the year, both by the media and by activists, had a postmortem quality. Dave McReynolds reported a "down mood" among activists, and Amy Swerdlow of the WSP added that "*any* involvement of people now on any level is an achievement."[19] Pacifist Gordon Zahn concluded: "We stand in the antechamber of a dying antiwar movement." The core peace groups were holding, he wrote, but the rest seemed to be "peeling off."[20]

In some respects, Zahn was correct. The FOR peaked at a membership of 23,000 in 1972, about a third more than in 1969 (and almost twice that of 1963), and the WRL was up to some 15,000. The AFSC was not a membership organization, of course, but probably it was included in the "core" groups to which Zahn referred. A second layer of organizations closely allied to the pacifist ones, and with much overlapping membership, had mostly peaked in 1969 and then declined in membership: SANE was down from 24,700 to 21,500 members; WILPF from 12,300 to 8,000; CALC from 31,200 to 23,000; BEM had surged from 3,000 to 11,000 between 1970 and 1971, only to decline to 4,200 by April 1972. These were liberal groups, and they were losing constituents, probably from a receding feeling of urgency. Radical groups such as SDS had virtually ceased to exist, and even the tightly knit SWP was fading. On the other hand, in 1972 there was growth in a third layer of the antiwar movement which included groups for whom the war was the only raison d'être. The very moderate Another Mother for Peace rose to 236,000. An association which made few demands on its members, it nonetheless linked small clusters of women in thousands of communities. The much more activist VVAW claimed nearly 20,000 members (including 2,500 on active duty in Vietnam).[21] Moreover, political debates suggested that an end to the war was assumed to be national policy, the outstanding issue being the rate and terms of withdrawal. What worried Gordon Zahn and his friends was the declining organizational base from which to mobilize the widespread antiwar sentiment.

More than ever, that base lacked coherence at the center. There were disputes even in VVAW, where John Kerry and others resigned as coordinators. The PCPJ was in total disarray. It was $100,000 in debt; it had lost the FOR and CALC in May (the AFSC had no formal connection); and it disintegrated after Stewart Meacham left in the fall to become Quaker international affairs representative in Singapore. Brad Lyttle had served as a full-time staff member since February 1971 because the organization offered the only hope of an effective coalition, but by November he had given up. The leaders, notably Dellinger, had simply gone along with the "adventurists" of the MayDay Tribe, Lyttle wrote, and that had destroyed the organization. In December, NPAC rejected an appeal from Sandy Gottlieb of SANE, among others, to engage in the coming election. It opted instead for yet another demonstration in the spring of 1972, but then the very coordinators who had proposed that tactic resigned.[22] The PCPJ and NPAC finally severed their relationship and faded into independent sets of mailing lists. The era of coordinated radical street action was over.

Beyond surface turmoil and endemic frustration, activists wrestled with difficult issues of moral and political judgment. Within the WRL, for example, Roy Kepler complained to Dave McReynolds that coalitions invited dangerously simplistic thinking. He also objected to an article in which his friend seemed to compromise on the total rejection of violence. In reply, McReynolds defended selective participation in coalitions—certainly he had opposed some, and he argued that there were different degrees of violence. Although all violent acts were morally wrong, he felt, they did not all carry the same weight of social responsibility. The article which stimulated the correspondence had been written in Hanoi. It reflected McReynolds' sense of the disparity between the magnitude of the North Vietnamese military campaign and the American air war, on one hand, and the relative merits of national liberation and U.S. intervention, on the other. The radical pacifist personally rejected the use of violence, but he felt a particular responsibility for the injustice committed by his own country. Besides, it was his political judgment that whatever the outcome of a struggle within Vietnam, it could not be settled as long as the United States intervened there.[23]

Al Hassler engaged in a similar correspondence, not only with McReynolds but also with Dick Fernandez of CALC and others. The particular issue was the "Appeal to All Combatants to Stop the Killing," which called for an immediate cease-fire, release of all POWs, and preparation for a general political settlement—a campaign which Hassler had initiated early in the year in response to his Buddhist contacts. The appeal was taken up by Mary Temple and others, who formed the U.S. Committee to End the Killing, which included former deputy defense secretary Cyrus Vance and former University of California president Clark Kerr. The Vance-Kerr group was attracted especially because the appeal did not single out the United States as at fault.[24] Hassler pressed the appeal because its universality squared with his understanding of pacifist morality. Besides, he could not imagine pacifists refusing Vietnamese Buddhist supplications for an end to the killing. More to the point in his correspondence, however, was Hassler's political judgment. He argued that it was "sheer fantasy" to suppose that Nixon would cut loose from Thieu or, given the low troop level projected for the summer of 1972, to think that he could be dislodged from the presidency. There simply was not enough leverage to set the date now or in the foreseeable future. Without a cease-fire, the killing would continue indefinitely.[25]

Fernandez, on the other hand, was actively involved in the Set the Date Now Campaign. He did not suppose that U.S. departure would end the killing: "There will be, whenever we decide to leave . . . a terrific power struggle." He guessed that the communists would win, but he felt that could not be as bad as the repression and destruction wrought by Saigon with U.S. air support. In any case, he insisted, a cease-fire would not end America's presence or its will to maintain a pliable regime in the South, and therefore a cease-fire would not "remove the root cause of the current conflict." The United States could not ordain the future of Vietnam. The administration's will to do so had to be challenged, and that was the point of imposing a specific date for withdrawal.[26]

To be sure, similar discussions were being carried on by thoughtful Americans who were neither activist nor pacifist—citizens in and out of government. The debates within the antiwar movement had particular significance: they contravened the image of activists as altogether simplistic, ideological, or anti-American; they explained some of the division among like-minded dissidents; they revealed the frustration of a situation laden with moral ambiguity and devoid of political leverage; and they evoked the commitment which enabled the movement to persist.

The president had only to look across the street to assess organized activism in November. Outside the White House religious pacifists from the FOR, CALC, WILPF, and AFSC staged a three-week human tableau to portray the "Daily Death Toll" in the continuing air war. There were arrests and detentions, but interest in the drama was minimal and participation dwindled, accenting the sense that protest was futile and that nonviolent direct action was "not currently very fashionable or exciting."[27]

The state of national sentiment at the end of 1971 was illustrated by the response to a punishing five-day air attack on North Vietnam that Nixon ordered on Christmas Eve. Protest was almost incidental and appropriately surrealistic. On 26 December sixteen VVAW members seized the Statue of Liberty in New York harbor, while in coordinated strikes elsewhere a few other veterans briefly occupied the Betsy Ross house in Philadelphia, blockaded the Lincoln Memorial in Washington, and barricaded themselves in the South Vietnamese consulate in San Francisco. After days of tension, the vets left their harbor prize, insisting that they had succeeded in putting the war "back on Page One, where it belongs."[28] Of course, it was the veterans and not the war that made the news.

Media emphasis on Vietnam waned. With the war "scaling down," said a newspaper editor, "it's hard to justify front-page coverage."[29] Only 15 percent of Americans polled in December 1971 felt that Vietnam was the country's foremost problem. Most people worried more about the economy.[30] Even the POW issue was muted. The president promised the families of prisoners that he would "eventually succeed" in winning the release of their loved ones; but North Vietnam had attached that issue to the condition that the U.S. abandon its support of Saigon, and White House aides pressed organized groups concerned with the prisoners to ease up on their activities.[31] The number of U.S. combat forces was down to 184,000, and another 45,000 were due home within two months. The air war escalated further and the political issue remained at a stalemate, but those matters were neither newsworthy nor targets for large public demonstrations.

Antiwar activists expressed "cynicism and despair," trapped as they were in an impossible situation. "In 1965," explained a CALC leader, "the American people knew there was a war, and we had to convince people it was wrong. In 1972, people know the war is wrong, but we have to convince them that there is a war."[32] As the president had hoped, Vietnamization was not only turning the fighting over to the South Vietnamese, it was encouraging Americans to turn the fate of Vietnam over to him. Indeed, one of the effects of Nixon's policy was to change the meaning of war in the United States. If by "war" one meant vulnerability to death and destruction, then Vietnam seemed to be virtually over for Americans. If by "war" one meant unleashing death and destruction on others, however, there seemed to be no end in sight.

"The Presidency is what is on the line"

As the new year opened, Democratic leaders tried to carry Vietnam from congressional to electoral politics. Presidential aspirant Edmund Muskie said that it was time for America to quit Southeast Asia regardless of the consequences, and he promised "as close to an immediate withdrawal from Vietnam as possible" if he were elected.[33] George McGovern urged the administration to set a date of 1 June for the final withdrawal of all U.S. forces. Even Hubert Humphrey asserted that "our most urgent, immediate need is to end the war and do it now," adding, "Had I been elected, we would now be out of that war."[34] Nixon was ready for the contenders. In his view the issue was not simply to end a war, but to build a lasting peace, and the only way to do that was through strong executive leadership. "The Presidency," he declared early in the year, "is what is on the line."[35]

The incumbent seized the initiative on 25 January when he revealed that he and Kissinger had been conducting secret negotiations with the North Vietnamese for six months and that the only remaining problem was Hanoi's insistence on the prior overthrow of the Thieu regime. He then outlined a new offer, proposing that within six months of a diplomatic agreement, the U.S. would withdraw all its forces from Vietnam at the same time as all POWs were exchanged, a cease-fire went into effect throughout Indochina, and new South Vietnamese elections were held under international supervision and with the participation of the PRG. The one thing not envisioned in the plan was to abandon Saigon, which, Nixon declared, "the United States of America will never do."[36]

That had been the central issue all along, and so the communists were unappeased. The North Vietnamese government denounced the president's revelations of secret negotiations, demanding that the United States drop its support of Thieu and set a date for final withdrawal. Within a month the peace talks collapsed. On 23 March they were suspended indefinitely.

At home the president capitalized on his January proposal. Calling upon the country to unite behind his new peace offer, Nixon urged critics to avoid saying anything that "might give the enemy an incentive to prolong the war until after the election."[37] Senators Muskie and Humphrey meekly welcomed Nixon's initiative, and the nation's prestige press uniformly applauded it. Polls reflected a surge of public confidence in the administration. Publicly, Dave McReynolds conceded that Nixon's offer left "the peace movement badly shaken." After all, he wrote privately, the president "accepted what we thought was the key point in our demands—the exchange of our prisoners for the withdrawal of our troops."[38]

The administration was not taking chances, though. In a memo written to his top aides just after his January address, Nixon called for "a massive counterattack on the partisan critics" who still challenged his presidency over the war. Insisting that the issue be put in patriotic terms, he framed the White House line: "We have done everything but offer surrender to the enemy. They want the United States to surrender to the Communists. ... [T]hey are consciously giving aid and comfort to the enemy. They want the enemy to win and the United States to lose."[39] Acting on Nixon's orders for "the attack line," H. R. Haldeman and Henry Kissinger virtually repeated the president's words in public, while other aides began to plan covert action against antiwar activists. The president meanwhile took the high road, departing on a historic state visit to China in hopes of fashioning a new era of peace through superpower détente.

When he returned on 28 February, his public image as a peace-seeker had been greatly enhanced. The bombing in Indochina had escalated sharply (U.S. planes conducted as many raids on North Vietnam in the first three months of 1972 as in the whole previous year), but by comparison with troop withdrawals and the president's dramatic China trip, the air war did not make news. Hardly a hundred thousand GIs remained in Vietnam. Still, there were certain stubborn facts: the political issue in Vietnam was not being negotiated; sky-borne destruction was escalating; and it was an election year. Domestic criticism not only continued but broadened to include more Democratic politicians and religious liberals. Protesters focused on the air war and its corporate support, and dissent became more sharply moral in tone.

Inevitably, as the war affected Americans less directly, those who remained concerned emphasized its impact on the Vietnamese—its moral aspect. In January an interfaith coalition, including CALC and the National Council of Churches, sponsored an "Ecumenical Witness for Peace" in Kansas City. The assembly of over six hundred religious leaders, a third of them Catholic, condemned Vietnamization as "fundamentally immoral" and demanded that Congress cut off funding for the war.[40] Concern over moral numbness in the people seemed to be more sharply etched than ever, and the Eichmann motif returned as some activists compared the institutionalized, personally dissociated air war with Hitler's gas chambers. Thus, when a group of Catholic radicals in Honolulu entered Hickam Air Force base and poured blood on strategic maps of Indochina, one of their leaders promised, "Some day people will feel, when they hear the word 'Hickam' what others in history have felt when they heard the word 'Auschwitz.'" The National Federation of Roman Catholic Priests condemned "the immorality of the automated air war" and the "antiseptic" evil of the "electronic battlefield."[41]

By the time of the Ecumenical Witness, leaders of the core antiwar groups had developed a coherent sense of direction as a result of their reassessment of the war itself. They had become clear that the bombing campaign was not only a concomitant to Vietnamization but had in fact supplanted previous combat strategy. Their analysis was given definitive form by Fred Branfman, who had spent four years in Laos. For two years, beginning in March 1967, he had been an educational advisor of the International Volunteer Service, and then he had devoted another two years to reporting the plight of Laotian refugees and researching the air war. With this background, he was chosen to direct Project Air War, an information center founded by the Indochina Education Council.[42]

The Vietnam conflict had undergone such a major change that it deserved to be called a "Third Indochina War," Branfman argued. The prototype of the new warfare could be seen in the devastation of the Plain of Jars in Laos, beginning in 1969. This was total war, he insisted: it was directed at civilians as well as at military forces, and it was waged throughout Indochina. Its dimensions were secret or at least unacknowledged. For the United States it was low-risk warfare in which Asian ground troops mainly provided support for automated air power. It was waged with "a completely ahuman kind of mentality." The challenge of the peace movement was to confront the American people with the reality of the new "Orwellian" war.[43]

These ideas had been widely circulated in the movement toward the end of 1971, and they were carefully weighed in a large NAG meeting,

11–12 January 1972.[44] Branfman presented his analysis of the air war. Then Sid Peck reported on a recent visit with several Indochinese delegations in Paris. The consensus there, he found, was that the U.S. was tied to Thieu, who was increasingly isolated in the South. Peck concluded that the movement should try to isolate Nixon on the issue of support for Saigon. Discussion yielded a threefold program for the year: to mount a broad educational program on the air war; to publicize it in the 1972 electoral campaign, working with Set the Date Now; and to target protest actions in April and May at air bases and corporations making components for automated warfare. "Perhaps we have to begin again as if it were another war"—that was the mood: "a new war."[45]

A small working group hammered out details of the program, based on a Brad Lyttle prospectus, and formed a task force to develop it further.[46] Rather than create a new umbrella coalition, the liberal pacifist groups tamed the PCPJ for their purpose, moving it from Washington to New York and cutting its staff to one paid worker. Essentially, it ceased to be a pretender to a broad-based, independent coalition and became instead the instrument of the cooperating groups. At the same time, their focus on automated warfare and the "military/corporate complex" enabled the PCPJ to echo the multi-issue concern that had motivated earlier attempts at coalition: "We do not view ourselves now as simply a 'peace' movement," it still claimed, "but as a coalition for ending the war and also changing America."[47]

That rhetoric was as old as the movement and as current as the trial of the Harrisburg Seven, which lasted from February to April. Charged with conspiring on bizarre plots, such as the kidnapping of Kissinger, and prosecuted on evidence supplied by a paid FBI informer, the defendants were not Jerry Rubins or Abbie Hoffmans. They included the Reverend Philip Berrigan and other dedicated radical pacifists who evoked an outpouring of support from people who believed they had been framed. Forty days of rallies culminated on 1 April with demonstrations in Harrisburg, Pennsylvania, by perhaps ten thousand people united in the memory of Martin Luther King's nonviolent struggle against war, poverty, and repression. The trial gave the movement a needed lift, which peaked when a hung jury resulted in a mistrial, and it also provided a fresh symbol of the apparent relationship of the war and social injustice.

The Campaign to End the Air War intended to make that connection, but not in a merely rhetorical sense. Its program included, for example, a CALC project to challenge Honeywell, maker of antipersonnel weapons, at its stockholders' meetings. CALC was experimenting self-consciously with action targeted at the intersection of political and economic systems. It was moving from generalized protest—"a shotgun effect"—to "a style that struggles for specific clear objectives."[48] Similarly, the air war campaign was grounded in researched information. Branfman's Washington-based Project Air War and the related Indochina Resource Center was one source. In Cambridge, Massachusetts, an Ad Hoc Military Build-Up Committee was formed to document the increase in air and naval forces accompanying the withdrawal of ground troops. Other material came from the National Action/Research on the Military-Industrial Complex (NARMIC), a program developed by the AFSC in 1970 to study commercial and university war contractors, military strategy, and weapons systems. With a budget of over $37,000, it subscribed to relevant journals and directories as well as a computerized service for aerospace industries, but its staff also trained local organizers to do their own research.[49] It quickly became an information base for CALC and local groups attempting to monitor and influence defense contracting, and it also prepared reports and a widely distributed slide show on the automated battlefield.

With its preparation for a Campaign to End the Air War, the antiwar movement was somewhat reorganized and reoriented. Allan Brick reported to the FOR that "we have learned a lot about how media-conditioned mass movements can be dissolved almost overnight if there is no solid information and analysis in the heads of their morally concerned activists."[50] Nonetheless, through the early spring of 1972, the movement appeared to be stalled. It was still divided over spring actions, and its new program lacked a focal point.

Suddenly there was action. On 30 March, North Vietnam launched a major offensive across the demilitarized zone toward the provincial capital of Quangtri, while further south its troops menaced cities in the central highlands and Saigon in the Delta. Deploying tanks, heavy artillery, and mobile antiaircraft missiles, the communists advanced in the face of U.S. air strikes and South Vietnamese forces. The main part of Saigon's army held to defensive positions and avoided pitched battles, even as President Thieu declared that the "decisive" struggle of the war was under way.[51]

Determined to check the communist offensive, the United States dramatically stepped up the air war in South Vietnam and extended it northward without pretending to restrict bombing to military targets. The communist assault was a last, desperate attempt to wreck Vietnamization and seize a military advantage before President Nixon's scheduled trip to Moscow in May, the White House said—"one last throw of the dice."[52] The administration claimed the right to bomb anywhere in Indochina, without prior congressional authorization, on the grounds that it was protecting remaining U.S. troops, although the White House reassured worried members of Congress that it would not reintroduce U.S. ground combat troops into South Vietnam. On 15 April, for the first time since

1968, Hanoi and Haiphong were bombed. Fred Branfman was scared when he heard the news: all the restraints were loosed, and any form of escalation was possible.

Unexpectedly, the country rediscovered its capacity for protest. Reflecting the plans of the Campaign to End the Air War to target corporate support of the war effort, there was picketing, demonstrating, and stockholder action against companies such as IBM, Honeywell, General Electric, and Raytheon. Campuses came alive to the crisis. Demonstrations on 22 April which had been projected by NPAC months before were now timely. A New York rally attracted the largest crowd in two years, and marchers returned to the streets of Washington, San Francisco, Gainesville, Madison, Los Angeles, and other cities. Innumerable protests were locally initiated, and often they were imaginative. Pacifists in the Philadelphia area organized a canoe flotilla in an attempt to establish a nonviolent blockade against the movement of U.S. war material to Indochina, and seven seamen from the USS *Nitro* jumped overboard to join the protest. In Vietnam, early in the month, fifty soldiers attached to the army's 196th infantry briefly refused patrol duty in a dangerous sector south of the demilitarized zone, shouting:

> We're not going; this isn't our war; we're not going out in the bush.
>
> Why should we fight if nobody back home gives a damn about us?
>
> Why the hell are we fighting for something we don't believe in?[53]

Antiwar sentiment escalated among the country's elite, with expressions of opposition from the presidents of eight Ivy League colleges, for example, and the bishops of the United Methodist Church. Swedish prime minister Olof Palme led European protests against the U.S. bombing campaign. In the United States public opinion polls in late April showed only a narrow 47 to 44 percent margin of support for the escalation, while a plurality of 71 to 23 percent favored legislation aimed at cutting off funds for U.S. military involvement in Vietnam after 31 December if American POWs were released.[54]

Even in the face of the battlefield emergency, congressional opposition grew sharply. The FCNL, ADA, SANE, CALC, and WILPF monitored legislation and coordinated lobbying efforts in Washington and among local constituencies. Another Mother for Peace appealed to its members, *"You must do something!"*[55] The Church-Case Amendment for a December date-certain was coming to a vote. Another bill already introduced in the Senate and House would have cut off all air attacks in Indochina. Senator Mansfield protested the bombing escalation and called for complete U.S. withdrawal. It was "time for Vietnamization to fish or cut bait," he said.[56] Senators Edmund Muskie (D-Me.), Edward Kennedy (D-Mass.), and others called for an immediate halt to all bombing of North Vietnam and for the resumption of peace talks around the issue of U.S. withdrawal. House majority whip Thomas P. (Tip) O'Neill (D-Mass.) attacked the bombing increase as a "dangerous escalation" of the war, and promised to sponsor a measure to cut off funding.[57]

The Nixon administration nonetheless held firm, claiming success in Vietnam and appealing for patience. On 25 April the White House announced that peace talks would resume in May. The next day the president declared that Vietnamization had "proved itself sufficiently" that another 20,000 GIs would be brought home within two months, but he declared that the escalated bombing would continue until the North Vietnamese military offensive was broken. The communists "will fail in their efforts to conquer South Vietnam militarily," he promised. "Their one remaining hope is to win in the Congress of the United States and among the people of the United States the victory they cannot win among the people of South Vietnam or on the battlefield of South Vietnam."[58]

The North Vietnamese advances continued. By the end of April, they had surrounded Kontum despite heavy U.S. bombing, and the South Vietnamese command reported the country's highest losses of the war. On 1 May, Saigon abandoned Quangtri without a fight. Disintegrating in panic, the remnants of its Third Division fled, along with thousands of civilians, down Route 1 toward Hué, the ancient imperial capital already swollen with perhaps 300,000 refugees. President Thieu announced a major shakeup in his command; but U.S. military leaders advised Washington that the situation in the Central Highlands was deteriorating rapidly, that the North Vietnamese had already destroyed years of pacification efforts, and that the fighting morale of the South Vietnamese armed forces was evaporating. On 3 May, Senator John Stennis (D-Miss.) voiced his belief that North Vietnam was winning the war. Nixon increased the naval and air forces in the region.

The issue was joined, and antiwar pressure broadened. Twenty-two labor leaders called for a June conference in St. Louis in order to establish a Labor for Peace organization that would press for an immediate end to involvement. The nonpartisan League of Women Voters called for immediate and total American military withdrawal, a demand also made in a joint letter by the presidents of some sixty midwestern universities. The National League of Families of American Prisoners and Missing in Southeast Asia, which had long supported the administration, voiced displeasure that the POW issue remained unresolved. Reflecting a general sense of crisis, the antiwar coalition called for local actions in an "Emergency Nationwide Moratorium" on 4 May which was sponsored by several members of Congress. Columnist James Reston expressed concern about Nixon's effectiveness under extreme stress, given his penchant for "unpredictable behavior."[59]

The president struck back hard on 8 May. With his entire policy on the verge of collapse, Nixon ordered the mining of all North Vietnamese ports and river systems and the increased bombing of North Vietnamese roads and rail lines in order to "interdict" communist supply lines and halt the offensive.[60] The president warned that U.S. naval forces would search and seize ships bearing arms to North Vietnam and that mining and bombing would end only with the return of American POWs and the conclusion of an internationally supervised cease-fire. For the first time, the president made no mention of the need for a prior political settlement in South Vietnam. He also made no attempt to involve Congress in his decision, merely notifying a few congressional leaders of his escalation minutes before he announced it. Risking the possibility of a clash with Russia and China, Nixon told his top advisers that he would "stop at nothing to bring the enemy to his knees."[61]

Stunned and divided by the President's actions, Congress waited anxiously for Moscow's response while another round of protest swept the country. Antiwar liberals from ADA, the National Education Association, and various trade unions convened an emergency convocation in Washington, pressing Congress to set a date for total withdrawal from Vietnam. The city councils of Sacramento, California, and Fort Wayne, Indiana, passed resolutions in opposition to continuation of the war. Spontaneous marches, demonstrations, and teach-ins erupted in scores of places around the country. On college campuses there were more protests during May than had taken place following the Cambodian invasion two years earlier. Ten thousand people conducted a peaceful torchlight procession to the state capitol in Madison, Wisconsin. Thousands of dissidents caused massive traffic jams on highways at Chicago, Boulder, Albuquerque, and elsewhere. Demonstrations were sometimes accompanied by civil disobedience. One hundred fifty arrests resulted from a protest religious service in the Capitol rotunda by activists from CALC, and eleven nuns were arrested in an antiwar action in New York's St. Patrick's Cathedral. Ten Phoenix women gained entrance to Williams Air Force Base and chained themselves together on a runway before they were hauled away. Proceedings in the House of Representatives were disrupted by a tape recording of heavy aircraft, played from the gallery.

Although there were isolated incidents of violence, the protests against the May escalation reflected controlled anger. For all their breadth, demonstrations were smaller in size and less volatile than those of previous years. *Time* speculated that seven years of fruitless protest had led to exhaustion. *Newsweek* ventured that there was this time more caution among the politicians and more of "a sense of futility" among the demonstrators.[62] "What I protest," said Amherst College president John William Ward, after being arrested in a sit-in at an Air Force base in western Massachusetts, "is there is no way to protest. I speak out of frustration and despair. I do not think words will change the minds of men in power who made these decisions."[63] Whatever his motives, Ward could no longer constrain his feelings.

Indeed, many elite dissidents courted visibility with new élan during the May protests. Nineteen members of Congress, including Senators Edward Kennedy and John Tunney, joined a thousand citizens in a public protest on Capitol Hill. Several of Kissinger's aides openly denounced Nixon's decision as "fruitless and ill-conceived" and resigned, while some former top civilian leaders in the Pentagon, including Cyrus Vance, Paul Warnke, and Alaine Enthoven, scored the president's action as "dangerous, wrong, and ineffective."[64] Former secretary of defense Clark Clifford objected to it in an appearance before the House Foreign Affairs Committee. Jane Briggs Hart, the wife of Senator Philip Hart (D-Mich.), announced her refusal to pay income taxes in conscientious objection to the air war. Hundreds of national celebrities marched on the Capitol to demand that Congress vote to end U.S. involvement in Vietnam. When the legislature did not act on their petition, they sat down in the Capitol and were arrested *en masse*. The outburst culminated in a Washington rally of ten thousand, sponsored by the antiwar coalition, at which Bella Abzug urged Nixon's impeachment.

That idea had begun to get serious consideration. It had been broached following the 1970 Cambodian invasion and had been revived by Congressman Paul McCloskey (R-Calif.) and a few others in early 1971, but it did not gain force until the spring of 1972, when many critics concluded that the president was fighting to maintain the Saigon government at the expense of American institutions. In the aftermath of the May escalation, political figures as different as Eugene McCarthy and Richard Daley declared that Nixon had exceeded his constitutional powers. Journalist Tom Wicker called the President an "unchecked Caesar."[65] Antiwar dissidents complained that Washington's war—and its attendant police surveillance, executive excesses, and military secrecy—was corrupting the very processes of American democracy. In the view of leading intellectuals such as Margaret Mead and Michael Novak, "For an increasing number of Americans the enemies are not overseas. They are now in Washington."[66] Wrote William Stringfellow, a leading religious antiwar critic, "We ought to have learned that the issue is not war, or that the issue is no longer the war." As Vietnam now threatened the survival of American constitutional democracy, he concluded; "the present outcry to 'stop the war' [must] be translated 'impeach the President.' "[67]

Representatives Bella Abzug and William F. Ryan of New York introduced impeachment resolutions in the House, while Princeton University law professor Richard A. Falk and several others established a National Committee for Impeachment in an effort to generate grassroots support.

The Committee purchased space in the *New York Times* for an ad which was run over the objections of angry pressmen who called it "traitorous" and "detrimental to the boys in Vietnam and the POWs."[68]

Proposals for impeachment were premature in May 1972. Whatever excesses could then be charged to the president could not be construed clearly as "high crimes and misdemeanors," although knowledge of the secret bombing of Cambodia would later tie his Vietnam policies to the impeachment process. Indeed, by Nixon's own account, the war was being brought to a painful but successful conclusion in a way that would vindicate the presidency and bring with it the world's best hope for credible American power and thus lasting peace. A week before the 8 May escalation, Nixon told a group of Texas supporters that the communists must not be allowed to win in Vietnam because that would cause the presidency to "lose respect" in the eyes of the world and thus cause a loss of respect for American will and power. Soberly, he promised "I will not let that happen."[69] It was the supreme irony of his administration that when he uttered those words Nixon already had authorized the actions that would cost him his office eighteen months later. White House aides were finalizing plans to break into the Democratic National Committee headquarters at Washington's Watergate complex in order to photograph key documents and tap phones. That was accomplished late in the month. A second raid on 17 June was interrupted by Washington police, and the stage was set for a new drama in the struggle over the presidency.

The full dimensions of Watergate were effectively covered up for the rest of the year, and the president emerged from the May protests apparently in command at home and abroad. Apprehensions that his escalation of the war would jeopardize détente with the Soviet Union were quickly dispelled by the Russians themselves. Amidst perfunctory objections to the new bombings, they welcomed Nixon to Moscow late in the month for the formal signing of the SALT I arms limitation agreement. Large numbers of Americans felt "a distinct change of mood," a relief from pent-up frustration. The momentum of protest could not be sustained, and Congress declined to challenge the executive branch. "Rarely if ever in the long and lamentable history of the Viet Nam War have the attitudes of the American public shifted so abruptly as they have in the recent weeks," reported *Time* magazine.[70] In April, two-thirds of the country was gripped in "a deepening sense of gloom and frustration" regarding the war; but approval of the president's war policies rose to 59 percent by mid-May, and in early summer his handling of the presidency received the highest approval rating since November 1969. In this respect, too, talk of impeachment was premature.

With much reason for confidence, therefore, the president appeared before a joint session of Congress on 1 June to report on his trip to the

Soviet Union. He thanked Congress for its continuing support of his Vietnam policy, but he gave no hints as to where the United States and the war were now heading. There had been some progress toward a settlement during his conversations with Russian leaders, Nixon said, but he declined to provide details for fear that it would "jeopardize" the search for peace.[71] Foreign policy was an executive privilege.

"The normalization of dissent"

In the Far East the White House aggressively exploited its advantage, deploying enormous military power on behalf of Thieu's beleaguered forces. Early in the summer the lines on military maps—sterile images that masked ferocious combat—stabilized as the North Vietnamese forces held stubbornly to the ground they had seized in the northern provinces and Central Highlands while South Vietnamese troops bravely attempted major counteroffensives to regain the provincial capitals of Kontum and Quangtri. The human cost was staggering. Perhaps 100,000 North Vietnamese and 25,000 South Vietnamese died during and shortly after the spring offensive. The number of civilian casualties was incalculable. Senator Kennedy, who had begun to study them in 1970, estimated that at least 25,000 South Vietnamese civilians had died in the spring offensive and its immediate aftermath and that another 55,000 were wounded.

North and South, the area was deluged by airborne devastation. "The bastards have never been bombed," Nixon told his top aides, "like they're going to be bombed this time."[72] The administration doubled the strength of U.S. fighter-bomber forces in Indochina, tripled the size of the U.S. carrier force, and quadrupled the number of B-52s. Although only 39,000 U.S. troops remained in Vietnam, that many more manned the U.S. naval task force in the Tonkin Gulf, and another 50,000 maintained seven air bases in Thailand. Nixon loosened the restrictions that Lyndon Johnson had established on the air war. By mid-July, U.S. planes were conducting over 300 strikes a day against North Vietnam alone, ranging close enough to the Chinese border to provoke Beijing's first formal protest since 1968, and night raids were directed against Hanoi for the first time in the war. Within a three-day period in August, while the Republican National Convention met at Miami Beach, U.S. planes launched 1,000 strikes on both sides of the demilitarized zone. If this was the Third Indochina War, it was all that Fred Branfman had feared.

Peace talks resumed in Paris. Although still deadlocked around the central question of the war—who would rule in Saigon—both sides were increasingly anxious for a settlement. There was some basis for movement. One of the things Nixon had not told Congress was that Kissinger, in his discussions with the Russians, had made it clear that the United

States would permit North Vietnamese troops to remain in the South after a cease-fire. The administration wanted to separate military from political issues as the basis for negotiation. Perhaps sensing that the Americans were ready to forego direct support of Thieu, Moscow and Beijing encouraged Hanoi to negotiate seriously, and there was reason to do so. By mid-September the offensive had been checked, and North Vietnam had sustained enormous destruction. On the other hand, American military analysts concluded, large numbers of communist troops had continued to infiltrate the South; they held about two-thirds of South Vietnam's northern provinces, and they could sustain fighting at the current rate for at least two more years under the same bombing levels. Moreover, Kissinger was anxious to get beyond Vietnam and on to global affairs.

In September he provided an opening to North Vietnamese negotiator Le Duc Tho when he agreed to a tripartite commission that would supervise the elections and political arrangements in the South following a cease-fire. The commission would include representatives of the Saigon government, the PRG, and neutralists. Probably calculating that with the presence of communist military forces in the South, the political legitimacy accorded to the PRG would seriously undercut Saigon, Le Duc Tho on 8 October dropped the demand for the prior removal of Thieu from the government. Working feverishly from this basis, the negotiators arrived at the outlines of an accord by 23 October. Saigon rejected it, but on 26 October the North Vietnamese announced that Washington had agreed to an immediate cease-fire, total U.S. troop withdrawal within sixty days, immediate steps toward the release of POWs, an end to U.S. political involvement in South Vietnam, and a South Vietnamese political settlement in which the PRG would have legitimate status. Thus forced into the open by Hanoi, the administration's package virtually conceded failure to drive the North Vietnamese back by bombing, but it also offered a more substantial prospect for peace than the proposal made by presidential candidate George McGovern earlier in the month. By the end of October, rational comparisons were irrelevant to the election.

George McGovern had known air war through service as a bomber pilot in World War II, for which he received the Distinguished Flying Cross. Subsequently, he had completed a doctorate in history and become a college professor. He left teaching to help rebuild the Democratic Party in South Dakota, and from that base he entered the House of Representatives, where he established a consistently liberal record. After failing in a bid for a Senate seat in 1960, he directed the Food-for-Peace program for President Kennedy until 1962, when he won in his second attempt at the Senate. From early 1965 he voiced opposition to military escalation in Vietnam. Although he was an unexciting, dry speaker, there was an attractive no-nonsense quality about the man that inspired confidence among people who were inured to hype. The other early contenders for the Democratic nomination, notably Edmund Muskie and Hubert Humphrey, were critical of the continuing Indochina War, but the South Dakota senator had attacked it first and most explicitly. He, more than they, enlisted the support of antiwar dissidents.

Already in December 1971, Sandy Gottlieb had tagged McGovern as a preferred candidate who could couple a clear stand on the war with a platform of social and economic priorities, "a kind of new populism."[73] SANE endorsed the senator in January. By that time the coalition behind the Campaign to End the Air War had identified electoral politics as a high priority, and it implicitly supported McGovern. Business Executives Move for a Vietnam Peace endorsed him in April, and the following month BEM also pledged $50,000 to defeat twelve key prowar members of Congress whom it identified as the "deadly dozen."[74] By June, WILPF found that McGovern's campaign was giving hope to otherwise discouraged members, and Dave McReynolds reported that long-time anarchists in the WRL were urging people to work in the election campaign. McReynolds himself felt that he could vote not merely against Nixon but, "for once, *for* something."[75] As activists entered the McGovern campaign, they dissipated the resources of antiwar organizations and indirectly contributed to the perception that they were on the decline. The core groups were nonetheless confident that McGovern's effort to clarify the war issue paralleled their own, and they also valued his candidacy as leverage on the Democratic party. The *Guardian* rightly observed that the McGovern campaign signified "the normalization of dissent."[76]

Antiwar efforts during the summer were an extension of the Campaign to End the Air War. They were largely related to the AFSC's Indochina Summer Project, an umbrella program for public information, nonviolent direct action, and political action. The principal antiwar groups cooperated on the project, which relied on them for outreach. As the summer program unfolded, it was subject to the vicissitudes of voluntarism and the divisions in American society. A troubling incident took place in July, when a number of Washington black politicians challenged an ad hoc demonstration in support of antiwar legislation. Movement leaders were called upon to negotiate with the obstructionists, while two thousand women and children braved the District of Columbia's worst rains in thirty years to join Joan Baez and WILPF activists holding hands in a "Ring Around the Congress." Although the eclecticism of the movement left it vulnerable, diversity was also a resource. The summer project drew on a wide variety of materials: various topical papers and pictorial displays, AFSC films, the NARMIC slide show, CALC's *American Report,* booklets produced by Project Air War, a digest of the *Pentagon Papers* by Tom Hayden, and a poignant anthology of Laotian *Voices from the Plain of Jars.*[77] Direct action during the summer included CALC's Honeywell project and pacifist attempts to interdict U.S. ammunition ships with flotillas of pleasure craft. Political action included legislative lobbying in conjunction with the FCNL, meetings with delegates to the national nominating conventions, and organized testimony at Democratic party platform hearings.

The platform adopted by the Democrats in July called for the "immediate and complete withdrawal" of U.S. forces from Indochina.[78] McGovern was nominated on the first ballot. He vowed to halt the U.S. bombing of Indochina upon his inauguration and to withdraw remaining U.S. troops within ninety days, leaving U.S. air power in Thailand only long enough to guarantee the safe return of American POWs. Declaring that it was "the time for reconciliation," the candidate promised amnesty for draft resisters after U.S. troops and POWs were safely back in America, and opposed war-crimes trials for government officials or military personnel.[79]

By this time, the public had been exposed to a series of war-related disclosures. In June it was revealed that Lt. General John Lavelle had deliberately concealed a two-year covert air war in Indochina by systematically filing false reports. About the same time, it was reported that the CIA and the Air Force had used weather modification techniques against North Vietnam and that during 1966 and 1967, American military forces tried to build huge fire storms in the guerrilla-dominated "Iron Triangle" region northwest of Saigon. These incidents added credibility to North Vietnamese charges in July that U.S. planes were destroying the fragile Red River dike system, thereby threatening the country with flooding and starvation. The U.S. government denied the charges; but independent French and Swedish news teams documented them, and these revelations elicited strong international complaints. Defiantly, Nixon conceded that North Vietnam's dike system had been hit on a dozen occasions, but he insisted that the damage was minor and unintentional. Critics were unappeased. Several Democratic senators asserted that the attacks had been targeted, and a committee of prominent international lawyers protested that for the United States even to consider destroying the irrigation system indicated how far it had "departed from the principles and purposes of the United Nations Charter" and a decent respect for the opinion of humankind.[80]

Other stories raised the spectre of corrupted institutions and values: reports of CIA and Saigon involvement in Southeast Asian drug trafficking, exposure of Operation Phoenix (a CIA program to subvert the Vietcong, which included assassination), and disclosures of American-subsidized political repression in South Vietnam. In August, a Senate subcommittee concluded that Army spying on civilians during the 1960s had been unprecedented in scope, although (since so many records had been destroyed) its real dimensions were unknown. The trial of Daniel

Ellsberg and Anthony Russo over the *Pentagon Papers* enlarged evidence of governmental malfeasance. Antiwar protests built upon these accounts.

By far the most controversial summer actions were two trips to North Vietnam by Jane Fonda and former attorney general Ramsey Clark. Although active in the antiwar struggle since 1969, Fonda did not emerge fully in the political spotlight until July 1972, when she made a much-publicized visit to Hanoi. After touring bomb-damaged parts of the country and talking with some American POWs, she made a special report over Hanoi radio in which she testified to the good treatment of the prisoners and called upon U.S. airmen to quit the bombing. Fonda's broadcast provoked a furor in the United States. The State Department formally rebuked her. Veterans' organizations and conservative politicians urged a consumer boycott of her movies, and some members of Congress charged her with treason. That tempest was still swirling when Ramsey Clark visited Hanoi and reported on the damage being wrought by the air strikes. Traveling as part of an international commission assembled to assess war damage in North Vietnam, Clark agreed with Fonda that the bombing should be halted immediately. White House officials dismissed him as a fool or a communist stooge, and the Veterans of Foreign Wars urged the government to charge both him and Fonda as "traitorous meddlers in official Government security."[81]

Jane Fonda returned not only to the United States but to Tom Hayden, who in a sense had come back to America. Following the trial of the Chicago Eight, Hayden had retired to Berkeley. For a while he searched for self-understanding in a small radical commune, but the intensity of collective self-criticism drove him out and alone to Los Angeles. Gradually, painfully, a sense of perspective returned, and with it purpose. At Immaculate Heart College he was given a seminar to teach on Vietnam— not the politics but the people. He and his students produced graphic displays that were responses to their own discoveries. By the fall of 1971, he was offering similar courses at other area institutions. Meanwhile, he was close to the Ellsberg trial in Los Angeles, and began to reduce the *Pentagon Papers* to a popular summary. He was edging back to the Hayden of Port Huron, to a Left that was of and not against America.

He was teaching his class at a Claremont college on 1 April 1972 when he heard of the North Vietnamese offensive. It seemed to him that Vietnamization had been destroyed abroad and was now vulnerable in the United States. With his portable display he formed the Indochina Information Project and helped the McGovern people in an effort to inform and arouse people. Tom Hayden was back in Middle America, and he was not alone. He had met Fonda in February. She was fresh from a tour of military bases and was speaking on Vietnam with a slide show even more political than his. Over the next few months they fell in love, and when she returned from North Vietnam they cemented their relationship by designing an intensive speaking tour to revive awareness of the war, register voters in opposition to Nixon, and "move the antiwar forces out of their growing isolation and into the mainstream."[82] Thus was born the Indochina Peace Campaign (IPC).

Working closely with CALC, Fonda and Hayden added medical aid for Indochina to their agenda and took to the road. They opened on 3–4 September at the Ohio State Fair in Columbus and in Dayton. Together, with former POW George Smith and folksinger Holly Near, they undertook an eight-week tour of seven states in the industrial Northeast that seemed vital to McGovern's electoral chances, averaging four presentations a day and reaching ninety-five cities. On the platform Hayden appeared restrained, Fonda passionate. Both of them renounced slogans in favor of well-developed explanations, and they stressed their patriotic sentiments. They were taking back the flag.

Surprised and delighted, they found that audiences were overwhelmingly receptive to an approach that was both "very American" *and* supportive of Vietnam's revolutionary communists. Antiwar activism "does not mean condemning your country," Hayden insisted, "but means that it must be rescued and changed."[83] Looking ahead, the IPC portrayed Vietnam as "*the focal point* in the worldwide struggle against American imperialism," and insisted that radical dissent was a form of patriotism. For the short term, it promoted McGovern's candidacy, or at least tried to insure that "*no* candidate has a mandate to continue the war" after the election.[84]

That caution was well advised. McGovern's campaign had fumbled almost immediately when it was disclosed that his running mate, Senator Thomas Eagleton of Missouri, had a record of hospital treatment for nervous exhaustion. After considerable confusion, Eagleton was replaced on the ticket by Sargent Shriver (director of the Peace Corps under Kennedy and of Johnson's War on Poverty program), but McGovern's popularity fell precipitously. His indecisiveness, subsequent attempts to placate conservative elements in the party, and statements on Vietnam were adroitly exploited by the GOP, which redirected the campaign from the issue of Nixon's policy to the alleged weakness of his opponent's position and character.

Republican stalwarts seized the initiative even before their convention in August. When McGovern declared that as president he would go to Paris and Hanoi in order to negotiate a settlement and secure the release of American POWs, he was castigated as "begging" for peace (the image was later recalled in the Republican party platform) and prolonging the war.[85] The Democratic nominee was identified with stereotypic antiwar activists and his whole party with the prospect of defeat and betrayal. Upon Ramsey Clark's return from Hanoi, for instance, Nixon campaign manager John Mitchell called on McGovern to repudiate the man "who has spent the last week broadcasting Communist propaganda" (and whom the senator had mentioned as a possible successor to FBI Director Hoover).[86] As activists made plans to demonstrate at the Republican National Convention in August, Senator Robert Dole publicly asked Mc-Govern to "get in touch with his anti-war supporters and let us have our convention in peace."[87]

As a matter of fact, the GOP capitalized on attempts to disrupt its convention by a freewheeling group of self-styled "zippies" who attracted a mélange of people interested mostly in drugs, nudity, and music. Their plans had been disparaged throughout the movement since January, but to no avail, and most antiwar groups simply stayed away. Jane Fonda, Rennie Davis, and Daniel Ellsberg tried to introduce a note of rational criticism at the convention, and Dave Dellinger fasted to protest both the war and the undisciplined dissenters. A thousand-member VVAW contingent marched through Miami Beach in silence because, as an organizer explained, "there's nothing more to say."[88] Nonetheless, with the memory of Chicago in 1968, the image of outrageous counterculture was in some degree transferred to the Democratic campaign.

Republicans pointedly assailed the Democrats' commitment to rapid withdrawal from the war. Secretary of Defense Laird urged the platform committee to reject "policies of planned weakness, of white-flag waving and of abandonment of our nation's role in helping to maintain peace."[89] The committee adopted a Vietnam resolution that not only lauded the president's efforts but also warned against a Democrat "act of betrayal."[90] Nixon struck the same note in accepting his party's nomination: he would "not stain the honor" of the American sacrifice for Vietnam, he would never forget the plight of American POWs in North Vietnam, and he would never "join our enemies in imposing a Communist Government" in South Vietnam.[91] White House officials also attacked the media for alleged bias in reporting the war. With the help of right-wing advocacy groups such as Accuracy in Media, Inc., presidential aides like Patrick J. Buchanan accused the major television networks of broadcasting with a consistently antiadministration bias.

Combining attacks on Democrats and the media with covert, even illegal, actions and a series of indictments against antiwar critics, the administration kept its challengers off balance. At the same time, it secured popular expressions of support from conservative associations and even, in a reversal of its 1971 position, the U.S. Conference of Mayors. The White House also played on the prisoners of war issue. POW bracelets became the rage of the new fashion season. Inscribed with the name, rank, and date of capture of each of the country's 1,600 known POWs or MIAs (missing in action), over a million bracelets were sold by a Los Angeles–based group called Voices in Vital America (VIVA), which earlier had functioned as the prowar Victory in Vietnam Association. Although the bracelets were merchandised and bought as a heartfelt expression of concern for the prisoners, the campaign served to identify compassion with partisan loyalty.

By the end of the summer, McGovern was reeling toward the electoral margin. His party was not as cohesive as the president's (now augmented by supporters of Governor Wallace, who had been shot in a June assassination attempt), and he was not nearly as well funded. While Nixon distanced himself from controversy, and even from the press, McGovern and the Democratic party were subjected to critical scrutiny by the news media. McGovern was opposed by an overwhelming majority of newspapers, apparently being tarnished with the image of personal irresoluteness and irresponsibility on the war, if not a lack of patriotism, and out of tune with the conservative sensibilities of the electorate. Public opinion analyst Daniel Yankelovich found, for example, that while nearly a fourth of the electorate identified McGovern as "radical" or "very liberal," only 2 percent of the voters categorized themselves in those terms.[92]

Congressional dissidents also were turned back in the summer, just when support for congressional legislation to end the war seemed to be gaining ground. The House Foreign Affairs Committee narrowly approved legislation to cut off funds for U.S. military action against North Vietnam by 1 October, and in another close vote (49–47) the Senate adopted a defense appropriation amendment to end funding for the war, concurrent with the release of POWs, within four months of passage. The House rejected the October end-the-war bill on 10 August, however, and related legislation in the Senate bogged down. In September the congressional reversal turned into a rout. House and Senate conferees scrapped the appropriation amendment. Shortly afterwards, the House defeated a similar amendment, and when the original one was reintroduced, the Senate defeated it, completely reversing itself and cutting off antiwar efforts on the Hill.

There were other signs of caution. In one, the Senate gingerly circled the troubling case of General Lavelle. Testimony before the Senate Armed Services Committee seemed to establish the fact that the general had directed and covered up the two-year bombing of North Vietnam entirely outside the established chain of command. The crucial question was whether the president knew about Lavelle's secret air war. Suspicion lay heavily upon the White House, but the committee could not establish conclusive links and dropped the matter. Similarly, the congressional investigation of Watergate was halted in early October.

Early in the fall Senator McGovern attempted to spur his lagging presidential campaign. He hammered away at Thieu's dictatorship and the immorality of the air war, assailed Nixon's bombing policies, and said he would effect the earliest possible peace. The great weight of his campaign rested on his promise to end the war quickly. On 10 October the Democratic candidate vowed that within ninety days of his inauguration he would halt U.S. bombing of North Vietnam and military aid to South Vietnam, arrange to remove remaining U.S. troops, and send his vice-president to Hanoi to speed the release of American POWs. He also promised greater federal support for war veterans, and "an opportunity to come home" (he declined to use the word *amnesty*) for draft exiles and resisters.[93]

McGovern was immediately trapped in a cross fire of criticism. Within his own party, George Wallace dismissed his proposals as disgusting, while W. Averell Harriman complained that the war could be ended faster by simply cutting off aid to Thieu. Republicans were contemptuous. Secretary of Defense Laird described McGovern's program as a declaration of "unconditional surrender" and derided the senator as a "spokesman for the enemy."[94] The administration picked the Democrat apart on the amnesty issue. Addressing representatives of POW and MIA families, Nixon said that amnesty for draft-law violators was "the most immoral thing" he could imagine, and in an election-eve address he identified three major issues in the campaign: "We stand for peace with honor versus peace with surrender. We stand for a strong America versus a weak America. We stand for no amnesty for draft dodgers and deserters."[95]

By this time reports of progress in the Paris peace talks had surfaced. On 25 October several major newspapers published reports of an accord between the United States and North Vietnam. On the next day Hanoi announced the terms of agreement that Washington had accepted. Perceiving a threat to the survival of his regime, Thieu denounced the settlement as a suicidal coalition with the communists. The whole process stalled. Desperate to keep negotiations open, Kissinger acknowledged in a news conference on 26 October that a diplomatic breakthrough had occurred and said that, although some minor problems remained to be solved, final negotiations should be concluded soon. "We believe," he declared, "that peace is at hand."[96]

The administration's compromise package was so couched that it could be interpreted as "peace with honor." The extent to which it undercut Thieu was not altogether clear—not even to the president, who calculated that continued assistance would give the regime a fighting chance.[97] The agreement could be laid alongside the initiatives with China and the Soviet Union to form a pattern of peacemaking. Even though it had been rebuffed by Saigon, therefore, it reinforced already strong popular mistrust of McGovern and support for the president. Americans sampled in late September polls regarded the incumbent as "more sincere, believable" than his challenger by 59 to 20 percent.[98] On election eve, they believed Nixon more likely than McGovern to effect an earlier end to U.S. involvement in Vietnam by 43 to 33 percent, and felt that Nixon was more likely to move the world closer to peace by 61 to 22 percent.[99] In sum, the great majority of Americans in the fall of 1972, business and newspaper leaders included, looked upon President Nixon—rather than Senator McGovern—as the country's best prospect for peace.

Not surprisingly, McGovern was overpowered in a record 49 states and in a 61.7 to 37.5 percent popular landslide. As Nixon understood quite well, and antiwar critics to the contrary notwithstanding, the election issue was not the Indochina War. McGovern had been repudiated, but so had the war and, given the public expectation of a postwar communist victory, there was little support for even the Saigon government. The issue was the presidency.

Moreover, and perhaps the most important, antiwar dissent had been normalized in 1972. Opposition to Nixon's Vietnam policy had been channeled into the national election, and the Democratic party had adopted an explicitly antiwar platform. Although they lost the presidential election, the Democrats gained in Congress, winning two Republican seats for a 56-42 edge in the Senate and holding a 239-192 majority in the House.[100] Dissidents had weathered a blistering attack on their patriotism; but the administration had raised expectations of forthcoming peace higher than ever, and Nixon was convinced that Congress would move quickly to cut off funding when it convened in January, a view in which the Joint Chiefs of Staff concurred. As long as the war continued, the presidency was still on the line.

Showdown

Fighting did not seem to abate after the election. The peace compromise arduously crafted by Kissinger and Le Duc Tho appeared to have been shattered by the resistance of President Thieu. Hanoi launched large-scale ground attacks, while on election eve U.S. B-52s set a record for saturation bombing. Following his reelection, Nixon entered what Kissinger recalled as "the strangest period in [his] Presidency. . . . as if victory was not an occasion for reconciliation but an opportunity to settle the scores of a lifetime."[101] He was both combative and withdrawn, isolated from the public and all but his closest aides. The president reassured Saigon and told Kissinger to lay its objections on the table in Paris. Both men felt that a modicum of accommodation was required to bring Thieu along; and Nixon, conscious that domestic support was evaporating, was especially anxious for a settlement. When talks resumed toward the end of November, each side hardened its position. Although agonizing bargaining over the next few weeks returned them almost to the original compromise, Kissinger became convinced that the North Vietnamese were stalling. Le Duc Tho suspended the talks on 13 December and returned to Hanoi, allegedly for consultation. Insofar as the public could tell, therefore, nothing had changed after the American election, except that the sticking point was more clearly than ever the survival of the Saigon government.

Thus the political issue shifted from military disengagement to withdrawal of support from Thieu. Convinced that the war would last as long as Washington insisted on subsidizing a friendly regime in Saigon, antiwar critics argued for a final end to U.S. aid to the regime they had long identified as the main obstacle to peace. Kissinger's compromise and Thieu's rejection of it provided critics with a rallying point. Hans Morgenthau, for example, conceded that any political settlement was "virtually certain to doom the Thieu regime," but argued that this was no longer a sufficient reason for the United States to reject a peace agreement.[102] The Lawyers Committee on American Policy Towards Vietnam formally appealed to Nixon to sign the October agreement.

That became the major thrust of antiwar activity—to lobby Congress to put pressure on the administration to sign its own peace program. "Sign Now!" became the rallying slogan for the IPC, SANE, WRL, WILPF, WSP, and CALC. Over Thanksgiving, antiwar religious leaders agreed to mobilize their constituents on Capitol Hill on 3–4 January. The impasse in peace negotiations seemed to cast a glaring light on the political and moral contradictions of Vietnamization: the assumption that Saigon could accomplish with only material aid what had been denied to American prowess, and the subsidizing of Vietnamese to fight a war "that we believe is not worth our own lives."[103]

Suddenly, dramatically, the bombing was escalated again. No one in the United States was more impatient and frustrated with the course of events in Vietnam than Richard Nixon. When negotiations broke down in mid-December, he bludgeoned North Vietnam with twelve days of the most concentrated aerial bombardment in the war. American B-52s and fighter-bombers pounded Hanoi and the port city of Haiphong from 18 December to January, except for a thirty-six-hour pause at Christmas. Although intended for military and industrial targets, the attack struck a Polish freighter, the Egyptian consulate, the civilian airport, residential districts, and North Vietnam's largest hospital. Reportedly some 2,200 civilians were killed in what was widely called the "Christmas bombing."

While he delivered this massive threat to Hanoi, Nixon turned to Saigon with both a carrot and a stick. He personally assured Thieu of continued support and promised that a peace agreement would be enforced; but he also warned the South Vietnamese president in no uncertain terms that only acceptance of the negotiated compromise could preempt a congressional cutoff of assistance, a threat which the White House regarded as altogether real. Thieu defiantly resisted the settlement which he believed would leave him vulnerable and dishonored. Doubtless, he hoped that the bombing would soften Hanoi's demands.

The White House pressured Saigon secretly—by the back door, as it were. The massive bombing of Hanoi was up front. Conceding that "there is no way whatever that we can mobilize public opinion behind us," President Nixon refused to explain or seek public approval for the devastation he had unleashed.[104] He did not even bother to speak about it with congressional leaders until 5 January, and then he left them without allowing any questions.

Sinking further into a deep melancholy, Nixon retreated into seclusion and sullen anger while a storm of protest broke in public, in Congress, and overseas. Danish and Australian dockworkers refused to unload American ships. Demonstrators in Kent, England, insulted U.S. Ambassador Walter Annenburg during a Christmas carol concert, and anti-American street demonstrations broke out in places from Bangladesh to West Berlin. The governments of Italy, Sweden, Belgium, Austria, and the Netherlands lodged formal protests. The Canadian House of Commons voted unanimously to deplore the air attacks and urge their cessation. Australia cut off aid to the Thieu government.

In the United States some 3,000 people demonstrated in New York City, and there were actions and antiwar religious ceremonies elsewhere (in the Far East an Air Force captain who already had flown 150 sorties over Indochina declared that he could no longer participate in the mass destruction in good conscience, and some communications officers in Okinawa refused support services for the bombing). Public protests were small and unimpressive in comparison to previous outbursts, but Congress was flooded with mail. Expressions of strong indignation came from the articulate elite and the press. A widely quoted dispatch from a French correspondent cited "carpet bombing" of heavily populated areas in Hanoi and Haiphong; the description, though exaggerating the devastation, evoked the terror bombing of London and Dresden in World War II. Daniel Bell and Nathan Glazer called the bombing a Nazi-like *"Schrecklichkeit"* commenting that Nixon was treating the American people "as if they were the subjects of a totalitarian state."[105] What was troubling was not only the inhumanity of the air raids but their arbitrariness. Columnist James Reston complained of the President's "war by tantrum."[106]

The Christmas bombing fueled criticism that the president was exceeding his constitutional authority (not to mention good judgment), an apprehension which Nixon had inflamed by a sweeping postelection executive reorganization and impounding of congressionally appropriated funds. Concurrent with the air attack, moreover, there were further revelations of war-related corruption, notably eight years of systematic smuggling of heroin sewn into the bodies of dead American soldiers returned home, and new rumors of links between the Watergate burglars and the Committee to Re-Elect the President.

Major peace groups, reporting more outraged phone calls than at the time of the Cambodian invasion, turned to Congress. Forty-one religious leaders, including fourteen Catholic, Methodist, and Mennonite bishops, issued a joint Christmas pastoral letter denouncing the president for aborting the peace and calling for a religious convocation in Washington on 3–4 January 1973 on behalf of an immediate cessation of bombing, the signing of the October peace agreement, and a congressional cutoff of war funding if peace were not completed by Inauguration Day, 20 January. Wrote religious pacifist John M. Swomley, Jr., "There must be a showdown, and it will come—if it comes—when the Congress reconvenes."[107]

Shock and anger mounted on Capitol Hill. The president had unilaterally intensified the war with unaccountable ferocity. What the administration regarded as an instrument of diplomacy seemed to legislators very much like war. Expressing the prevailing sentiment in Congress, Senator George Aiken (R-Vt.) described his "shock, dismay, and disbelief" over the bombing decision, and he complained that one "might as well be on another planet" as to get critical information from the White House.[108] Senator William Saxbe (R-Ohio) suggested that Nixon had "left his senses," and even Senate minority leader Hugh Scott said that he was "heartsick and disappointed" with the bombing.[109] Shortly after the start of the Christmas bombing, Senate majority leader Mike Mansfield promised that he would press for legislation to end the war immediately upon the reopening of the Ninety-third Congress, and significant support for the idea circulated around the Hill. Of seventy-three senators polled, forty-five indicated that they opposed the bombing and would support legislation to end the war regardless of White House policy.[110] Even in the House, which had provided the mainstay of congressional support, majority leader Wilbur Mills (D-Ark.) warned that legislation to end the war in 1973 would be passed unless the administration stopped the fighting soon.

Nixon had understood that the bombing would provoke a showdown when he launched the air offensive. "How long do you think the Congress will appropriate money for South Vietnam after we begin bombing again?" he had asked John Ehrlichman. "Six months?" The aide estimated that if Congress concluded that the South Vietnamese were preventing a peace agreement, it would cut off funds "in half that time." Nixon nodded in assent.[111] In taking the risk, the administration tried to keep its options open by expressing its willingness to cancel the attack in return for serious negotiations along lines opened on 23 November. This was reiterated to Hanoi during the bombing campaign. On the day after Christmas, it appeared that the gamble might pay. The North Vietnamese agreed to resume negotiations on 8 January, implicitly on American terms. Arrangements were quickly confirmed and announced. The New Year opened quietly in Hanoi.

Not so in Washington. Recalling the October debacle in negotiations, Kissinger and Nixon were constrained from revealing their hopes until peace truly was "at hand," and so a showdown still loomed on Capitol Hill. There the promised religious convocation of 3–4 January mustered 2,300 protesters who lobbied their elected representatives. House Republicans loyally voted 137-7 to support the administration; but a caucus of Democratic representatives voted 154-75 to cut off funds for military operations in Indochina contingent only on the return of POWs and a safe withdrawal of U.S. troops, and Senate Democrats followed suit, voting 36-12.[112] Senate majority leader Mansfield promised that antiwar Democrats would obtain the nation's "complete disinvolvement." Speaker of the House (and longtime administration supporter) Carl Albert (D-Okla.) agreed to support fellow Democrats in reestablishing congressional control over questions of war, peace, and public spending.[113] The stage was set for a confrontation with the president.

The country was on hold. Rumors of an impending settlement multiplied, but that had happened before. On 15 January the president announced that the United States was unilaterally suspending offensive military action against North Vietnam because of progress in the Paris peace talks; but in South Vietnam fighting intensified as both sides grabbed territory in anticipation of an imminent cease-fire. On 19 January, two key proadministration senators, Barry Goldwater and John Stennis, pointedly warned President Thieu that he would risk a cutoff of U.S. aid by sabotaging a peace agreement (part of a White House secret campaign to secure Saigon's acquiescence, the warning appeared to be directed equally to the president).

The next day brought Richard Nixon's second inauguration, and his assurance that Americans stood "on the threshold of a new era of peace."[114] While Republican revellers celebrated the renewal of the president's mandate, Leonard Bernstein conducted Haydn's *Mass in Time of War* in a "plea for peace" concert at National Cathedral, where Eugene McCarthy and the dean of the cathedral, the Reverend Francis B. Sayre, called for an end to the war. A hundred thousand antiwar protesters gathered in Washington, and thousands of other dissidents held rallies in Chicago, San Francisco, and Seattle. The demonstrations were subdued, expectant, and yet apprehensive that the promise of peace might yet be withdrawn.

At 10:00 P.M. on 23 January, simultaneously with statements in Hanoi and Saigon, the president announced over national television that Kissinger and Le Duc Tho had initialed an agreement "to end the war and bring peace with honor in Vietnam and South Asia."[115] An internationally supervised cease-fire was scheduled for 7:00 P.M. eastern standard time, 27 January. Within sixty days America's remaining 23,700 troops would be withdrawn and her prisoners of war returned. The United States would continue to aid Saigon, which Nixon identified as "the sole legitimate government" and the defender of South Vietnamese self-determination. The president said nothing at the time about the status of the demilitarized zone, South Vietnam's political prisoners, the presence of North Vietnamese troops in the South, or the political status of the PRG, and Kissinger was hard pressed to explain how the January settlement differed from the aborted October agreement. As both the president and his national security advisor understood, those details were no longer at issue. Politically, they claimed to have achieved "peace with honor." Actually, the point was that American military engagement had ended. It was a time not so much for analysis or moralizing as for acceptance, less for jubilation than for relief.

Following the announcement, Kissinger returned to his home. About midnight he received a phone call from Nixon, moodily ensconced in the Lincoln Sitting Room of the White House. The caller admonished him not to be discouraged by the enormous letdown likely to follow success. "There were many battles yet to fight," Kissinger recalled Nixon saying, and his aide "should not weaken." The tired advisor concluded that the president "really was addressing himself."[116] Henry Kissinger knew his chief well enough to understand the mood, but he could not then appreciate its prescience.

Twelve

Closing the Circle

"At the end of the tunnel is a tunnel"

About forty middle-aged men and women had among them maintained a silent vigil for 369 consecutive Saturdays in front of the Stevens building at the often windswept corner of State Street and Michigan Avenue in Chicago. Deciding to "give peace a chance," they put down their placards on the last Saturday of January 1973. They were not sanguine. "We expect to be back," said one.[1] Antiwar dissidents were relieved but apprehensive, glad for the end of direct U.S. military intervention even though they understood that the conflict in Vietnam would continue. Although painfully aware that thousands of Vietnamese political prisoners languished in the South, they welcomed the return of American POWs.

As combat troops drifted back to the United States, more than six hundred prisoners of war came home. They were feted with parades, celebrations, and lavish gifts. Intimate family reunions were aired on public television. Some of the released pilots praised the president for liberating them with honor, alleged that antiwar critics had prolonged their imprisonment, and condemned the idea of a postwar amnesty. Several of them publicly claimed to have been mentally and physically tortured by their North Vietnamese captors. When Jane Fonda accused them of lying, she elicited outrage. The actress retreated somewhat from her charge, but she was excoriated nonetheless, formally censured by the Indiana State Senate and burned in effigy by University of California students. The issue was not really the veracity of accounts of torture; at stake was the unblemished heroism of the POWs. The *Christian Century* judged that they provided the nation with a desperately needed "expiation of guilt."[2] That was perhaps too theological and too cynical an assessment of popular opinion, but there were others who also resented what Robert Lifton called a "carefully manipulated spectacle."[3] If the

348

POWs were exploited, it was because they filled a national need: they were about all that could be salvaged from the war.

Very few Americans felt like celebrating the peace accord itself. Most of those polled were relieved; many felt a gnawing sadness. Overwhelmingly, they regarded the whole affair as a mistake, one that should not be repeated even though it was widely assumed that the Saigon government would succumb to communist political pressure.[4] Politicians reacted with gratitude for the end of overt U.S. military involvement, and with cynicism about both the feasibility of the peace agreements and administration pledges not to intervene further. Senator Church announced plans for legislation banning the reintroduction of combat units in Indochina, although Senator Mansfield cited private assurances from Kissinger that no secret understandings were attached to the accords.[5] Like the public, political leaders generally assumed that even though the war in Indochina was far from over, it was no longer an American contest.

That assumption eroded the antiwar movement. Many activists felt "rather lost," Dave McReynolds conceded, without the "one great unifying factor—the Vietnamese war." Pacifist Fay Honey Knopp explained to Daniel Berrigan that for years the antiwar movement had brought "meaning and direction" to many people who now needed "to take time off to get heads and minds . . . together" and to experiment with other ways of organizing their lives.[6] "There would always be a small core of activists," said the chairman of the Lansing (Michigan) Area Peace Council; but the day of the big demonstration was over. She doubted that there was any issue that could bring the movement together again.[7]

Nonetheless, activists were convinced that Vietnam remained an issue. They regarded the Paris accords as a counterfeit peace "as yet ambiguous as best," a fragile, jerry-built set of contradictions. It was "a ceasefire, not a settlement." Explained Business Executives Move for a Vietnam Peace, "The question of who rules South Vietnam—which is what the war was all about—is left unsettled."[8] Dissidents drew a distinction between the end of overt American combat and continuing U.S. intervention in the struggle for power in Indochina. The Nixon administration had withdrawn from the fighting, but it had not abandoned its political objective of an allied, anticommunist South Vietnam. In that respect, peace was still elusive and Vietnam yet an American dilemma: "at the end of the tunnel is a tunnel."[9]

That observation aptly conveyed the sense of indefinitely protracted struggle with which activists received the Nixon peace. It was penned in notes for a February meeting on strategy and the future program of the Indochina Peace Campaign, one of a number of meetings held by the major peace organizations from November 1972 through the winter. From those consultations emerged the antiwar organization, program, strategies, and self-understanding that lasted through the spring of 1975.

For all that dissidents knew at the outset, the conflict could have continued for another decade.

The reorganization of the movement confirmed changes underway for at least two years, probably four. As antiwar sentiment seeped through the public and found increasing expression in Congress and in the McGovern campaign, the organized movement appeared to decline. Certainly it lost visibility. In fact, though, it was reorienting itself to a new political situation and adopting the tactics of persuasion and legislative pressure. The weight of liberal constituencies in the movement increased. After the radical left imploded and then disintegrated, elements of the liberal left (including former New Left leaders like Hayden and Lynd but also elements of ADA) began to work their way back into the system. Furthermore, as the mentality of wartime crisis declined, Vietnam ceased to be a useful issue for left-wing coalition politics. As a result, for example, the IPC separated social justice issues from its focus on Indochina. The cease-fire confirmed these trends. It left the movement with a liberal pacifist coalition in the National Action Group, a left-liberal Indochina network in the Indochina Peace Campaign, and a new liberal coalition in the Coalition to Stop Funding the War. These elements cooperated informally throughout most of 1973 until they were brought together formally in October.

The pacifist membership groups—the FOR, WRL, and smaller ones such as the Catholic Peace Fellowship and Movement for a New Society (Philadelphia)—held solid, although along with the AFSC they began to experience financial problems. Some of their leaders formed a close-knit team which had worked together in NAG since the 1968 Chicago convention debacle. Twenty-seven of them gathered in November at the FOR headquarters in Shadowcliff, a graceful mansion overlooking the Hudson at Nyack. Richard Deats of the FOR and Dave McReynolds of the WRL had called the meeting. Those present included Carl Zitlow of the FOR, Ron Young, previously with the FOR but now peace education secretary of the AFSC, Trudi Young and Dick Fernandez of CALC, Tom Cornell of the Catholic Peace Fellowship, Jim Forest of the FOR and CPF, Brad Lyttle, and Dave Dellinger. For two days they reviewed the situation in the wake of the McGovern defeat. The consensus was that they needed to get beyond the "negative image of the movement" and think in terms of "long-term efforts."[10] They agreed to meet with some regularity in order to align the pacifist wing.

The issue-oriented peace groups which had been founded before the war—WILPF, SANE, and WSP—had stabilized somewhat during 1972, but they anticipated further attrition during 1973, as did groups formed in opposition to the war, such as CALC, BEM, and VVAW. In fact, the membership of SANE and CALC would slip by about 50 percent during the year. The VVAW had peaked at about 20,000 veterans. The membership of Another Mother for Peace would plummet by 60 percent during 1973. The National Peace Action Committee and Student Mobilization Committee maintained what Fred Halstead called "skeletal structures," which meant that they ceased to play any real role.[11] The People's Council for Peace and Justice remained a convenient fiction: Dave Dellinger was personally valued by even those colleagues he had frustrated, and the PCPJ was a useful way to relate war and social justice.

That relationship had changed significantly since the halcyon days of the late 1960s when radicals thought they could forge a left-wing coalition around the war issue. Rather, the reverse had been the case: the war had transformed radicalism into divisive slogans and images which no sooner appeared to be on the cutting edge than they became anachronistic. By September 1971 a number of social justice radicals associated with Staughton Lynd were trying to put together a New American Movement (NAM), something of a successor to the National Conference on New Politics of 1967 but explicitly opposed to "one-shot demonstrations" and "sterile debate between 'elitists' and 'anarchists.'" The Left had to "start over," Lynd believed. It had to stop living "off the glory of the Third World Struggles" and to "fight clearly for the interests of the majority of the American people."[12] A year later, the NAM had a few regional branches, and its interim committee called a national conference. Its supporters clearly wanted to create a current of democratic socialism that would be a force within and not counter to American political culture. Significantly, the interim committee endorsed the Indochina Peace Campaign.

Following the Hayden-Fonda whirlwind effort on behalf of McGovern, the IPC was given a more enduring basis with two "resource centers" in Boston and Los Angeles. It was not designed to be an organization with interests of its own, Hayden emphasized. Instead, its regional centers would service a network of activities in a grassroots campaign of political education about foreign affairs. It would concentrate on Indochina. Although its rationale was to challenge the U.S. intervention in the Third World, it would interpret that policy as having warped authentic national values and institutions. That is why the NAM endorsement was significant: it suggested the self-conscious reentry of some New Left leaders into American political life.

The Christmas bombing of North Vietnam strengthened the resolve and relevance of both the IPC and the pacifist groups, and it also stimulated the formation of a broad Campaign to Stop Funding the War (CSFW), which would provide the organizing base of antiwar effort for the next two years. Representatives of ten Washington religious peace groups, SANE, ADA, and the National Education Association met on 29 December 1972. They recognized that "the House is the key" to getting the administration in check.[13] On the basis of FCNL research, they identified about seventy members of Congress who might be susceptible to pressure. By the time the group met again on 5 January, liberal philanthropist Stewart Mott had underwritten most of its projected budget. Within another week there were enough contacts to begin building coalitions in congressional districts, an office was established with phones and a small staff, and Edward Snyder of the FCNL and A. Dudley Ward of the United Methodist Church were supervising the project. They had about $50,000, mostly from Mott, and a mailing list of some 700,000 donors to McGovern's presidential campaign. The senator's office, ADA, SANE, UAW, and WILPF were fully involved, along with Curtis Gans. The coalition quickly expanded to some forty organizations, including the AFSC, WRL, CALC, and BEM, and later Common Cause. It was a low-visibility program to rally local pressure on House members from seventy swing districts to support legislation cutting off war funds in February—truly a Coalition to Stop Funding the War.

With the outcome of the Paris negotiations still in doubt, staff members worked feverishly, varying their approach district by district and making as many contacts as possible. They assumed that the bombing would elicit a new constituency of disillusioned people that their established contacts could mobilize. By the time they were fully underway, however, the peace accord had been signed and the situation had changed. Now the issue was U.S. support of Thieu in what was assumed to be a long struggle for power. The challenge was to monitor the cease-fire and "serve notice to Nixon that re-involvement would not be tolerated by the American public." Accordingly, the Coalition's intensive short-term legislative project was replaced "precisely *because* [since] vigilance would be relaxed in the euphoria over the achievement of a cease-fire, it was especially important to remain in action."[14] In the following months the CSFW, under the capable direction of Jan Orloff, developed the most systematic and sophisticated lobbying effort of the antiwar movement.

Antiwar organizations were aligned not only structurally but also in terms of goals and strategy. Their basic challenge was clarified by McGovern's defeat and then by the peace accord itself: American military withdrawal was implicitly contingent on continued support for Saigon (privately, Nixon had been explicit about that). To the president that meant peace "with honor." To dissidents it portended a return to the pre-1965 policy of intervening through a proxy war and building a client state from the outside, except that the situation had changed in at least three respects: the threat of Chinese expansion no longer obscured the issue; the struggle for power now embroiled all of Indochina on terms militarily disadvantageous to the United States; and the American public was reluctant to support overt military commitments. The problem for dissidents was to popularize their interpretation so that they could bring popular disaffection with the war just ended to bear on any further, covert intervention. In this sense Vietnam remained a tunnel "at the end of a tunnel."

With this understanding, antiwar activists identified three related political goals: to implement the peace accords, to end the bombing of Cambodia and military aid to Lon Nol, and to publicize the plight of political prisoners in South Vietnam.

At the center of this cluster of objectives was the peace accord. Hans Morgenthau predicted in November 1972 that the political future of South Vietnam would be decided on "the same hamlet and jungle battlefields" where it had been fought for years and that without U.S. air power Thieu would lose what he could not win with it.[15] The critical point in Morgenthau's analysis was that Saigon remained at war in the South and not merely against the North: the very legitimacy of the regime in power was at issue. American dissidents all assumed that Thieu would not submit to free elections and could not survive them. He was the symbol of a dependent government, not of the Vietnamese people. Accordingly, they concluded, the United States could implement the provision for self-determination in the peace accord only by disengaging itself from the Thieu regime. In particular, it must withhold further military and political assistance. The same line of argument was extended to the Lon Nol government in Cambodia, except that there the crisis was compounded by the twin tolls of American bombing and Khmer Rouge atrocities.

The campaign to free an estimated 200,000 political prisoners held by Saigon had further ramifications. It had always reflected genuine concern for the rights and well-being of Vietnamese dissidents. But while before the cease-fire it had been coupled with the return of American POWs, afterwards it had the political value of further discrediting Thieu's legitimacy. Moreover, within the antiwar movement it aligned leaders who differed about the Buddhist Third Force. Al Hassler and Don Luce gave a high priority to freedom for political prisoners in South Vietnam because they believed that this would strengthen the noncommunist opposition to Thieu, which was the only alternative to total communist rule in the South. Dave McReynolds supported the campaign because it discredited the Saigon regime, although he thought the Third Force more illusory than ever. Despite conflicts of opinion, the movement was coalescing around shared objectives.

Peace groups agreed also on objectives that suggested their aspiration to get beyond opposition to war: reconstruction in Vietnam, a general amnesty at home, and new national priorities in foreign and domestic policy.

Under the January peace accord, the United States committed itself to help in the reconstruction of North Vietnam, and this became a subordinate legislative goal for several antiwar groups. Meanwhile, nongovernmental assistance was channeled to the people of Vietnam. Since 1971 the AFSC had sponsored a Quaker medical team which assisted civilian casualties in the Quangngai Province of the South at a cost of nearly $2 million. Late in the spring of 1973, the agency organized a fund to restore Bachmai hospital in Hanoi, which had been destroyed in the Christmas bombing.[16] Giving succor to the victims of war reflected universal values and an attempt to move beyond political polarization, a tone characteristic of the IPC's stress on the humanity of the Vietnamese. Similarly, Daniel and Philip Berrigan criticized Fonda and other activists for dismissing out of hand charges that POWs had been tortured. They asked Hanoi for a categorical accounting. "In a wretched sort of way," Daniel Berrigan wrote in April, "our whole past decade is placed in question by this; whether we can suddenly stomach torture, as long as it is inflicted by the good guys on the bad guys." Not that they expected the North Vietnamese to confess to human rights violations; rather, it was important to get "on record" their total opposition to violence against human beings.[17]

Amnesty for draft resisters and violators of military laws was urged as a first step both in reconciling the nation to itself and in reordering national priorities. A mere pardon was unacceptable, said VVAW veterans: "We are not asking for forgiveness."[18] If America was truly to come to terms with the tragedy of the war, it would have to accept both those who had served and those who had resisted in any form. Robert Pickus, among others, demurred, arguing that unconditional amnesty should be reserved for conscientious objectors who had accepted the penalties of the law. Nonetheless, universal and unconditional amnesty was a high priority for the FOR, WRL, and AFSC. It was endorsed by other peace groups and church-related agencies also, and during the spring CALC created two alliances of amnesty-related groups, at the same time distributing large quantities of literature and trying to convert draft counseling services to work with potential amnesty recipients and their families.[19]

Beyond the immediate effects of the war lay the long term. Vietnam had limited the "horizons—and the emotions"—of even many in the peace movement and had obscured the vision of an alternative national security based on world order.[20] Since 1970, Hassler had put his greatest effort into a program called Dai Dong, an impressive effort of the International FOR to mobilize a worldwide constituency for environmental action. That still was his highest priority. SANE was anxious to get on with issues around which it had been created—disarmament agreements, the reduction of international tension, and now conversion from a war economy. The IPC wanted to see a break with the Cold War polarization of issues that had led to repeated intervention in the internal and anticolonial struggles of Third World nations. Leaders in ADA were ready to tackle the social programs of the Great Society which Vietnam had derailed. There was latent ambiguity here, as Trudi Young acknowledged when she reported that CALC staff were eager to work for "changes we seek but don't yet have a blueprint for."[21] "New priorities" was less a clear agenda than a desire to get beyond Vietnam. Still at stake was a matter of identity—of the nation and of those who challenged the war.

As they worked out their goals and strategies, activists reflected on their earlier efforts. By this time there had been voiced nearly every charge against the government and every claim for it which would surface in the next generation. The evaluations of 1973 were accordingly self-conscious, although they did not constitute a systematic analysis. Expressed in the midst of a still unresolved war, they were marked by a pervasive sense of noble failure. Why had activists, for all they had assayed and endured, been unable to reverse policy so widely resented among the people? Granted that never before in the country's history had "so many citizens challenged so central a government policy," as Michael Walzer observed, *"why didn't the peace movement win?"*[22] There was no single, comprehensive answer in 1973, but many chance remarks and partial explanations added up to a surprising degree of consensus.[23]

Perhaps the protest movement had been isolated by its middle-class character and had relied too much on the ephemeral enthusiasm of students. Perhaps it had been isolated also by a counterculture associated with it and by rhetoric that had smacked of being, if not anti-American, disdainful of national symbols and values. Its partisanship for peace had been so intense that it had tolerated elements which romanticized North Vietnam and the Vietcong. It had accepted uncritically activists who identified the United States with the terrible reality of the war it waged but interpreted the NLF only by its stated ideals. With a few exceptions, however, those had not been the steady leaders of the movement. More often they had been hangers-on, and that led to other observations.

It was widely assumed that the movement's effectiveness had been compromised by its association with political radicalism, which in turn had spawned militant extremists. The Vietnam crisis had been too much clouded by the language of revolution in America. The antiwar movement had been too often used by radical groups for their own ends. In the view of Michael Harrington, among others, the problem with that association had been that radical interpretations were wrong. In the view of Tom Hayden, the problem was that the movement had been fragmented by internal interests and conflicts. In the view of many, the radicalism of the 1960s had carried a distinctively romantic, personal, and moralistic quality which glorified spontaneity and feeling at the expense of thought. Its adherents, preoccupied with transforming their own consciousness, had eschewed realism about both the war and the political consequences of well-intentioned witness.

It was generally conceded that the movement had been disorganized and fractured—in part, by social currents extraneous to the war—and that it had been too crisis-oriented. Many now recognized that the strategy of mass demonstrations had been a surrogate for long-term, hard political organizing. Although the war had been a moral crisis, its resolution required a political solution. Instead, the movement had rocked from demonstration to demonstration and too often had merely reacted to events—the initial escalation, the Tet offensive, the invasions of Cambodia and Laos, the Christmas bombings. As though peace were always just around the corner, moral sensibility would generate action, and light was not only energy but force. Seeking to exploit crises but vulnerable to them, the movement had been subverted and disrupted by government harassment, its message undercut by official dissimulation.

On the other hand, it seemed clear in retrospect that the government's response had undermined its own legitimacy. Activists had called official credibility into question, legitimating protest and resistance. This in turn had contributed to a greater degree of political accountability. Moreover, if the antiwar movement had reacted to events, it had thereby built up skepticism; if it had suffered from moralism, it had given public ethics a political value. It had been fragmented, but it had helped to polarize the political center and the growing establishment, thereby creating a venue for political action.[24]

Leading activists concluded in 1973 that they had been rejected because they had forced open issues for which the public was not prepared to accept responsibility—the devastation which had leveled Vietnam and the war's subversion of American society. If Washington's claim to peace with honor was any indication, they felt, the nation had not yet confronted itself in Indochina. The way that the January accord was heralded was, in the words of Rosemary Reuther, "the demonstration in the last analysis of the American messianic self-image."[25] How could the people have accepted antiwar protest if they could not accept national failure? Perhaps—and this was the thrust of Hayden's widely accepted analysis— just perhaps, the people could have accepted failure if the tragedy had been explained coherently and without the rhetoric of moral indictment. Even yet, it might not be too late to confront still unresolved issues with "an unshakeable confidence in the American people, which means confidence in ourselves."[26] Invariably, as activists evaluated their efforts, they were led further into the contest over the meaning of Vietnam for American life and history.

Most dissidents had insisted all along that Vietnam had been the logical and not accidental result of Cold War interventionism. They argued that a proper understanding of the tragic error in Indochina was necessary in order to redirect American policy from deterrence and intervention to disarmament and popular self-determination. "We have to learn and teach the lessons of Vietnam well," Hayden wrote for the Indochina Peace Campaign. "It was not our war but it is our peace."[27] Those "lessons" would not easily be digested by the public. The country was too broken and dispirited to confront the disaster in ways that would yield meaningful conclusions. Dave Dellinger enjoined antiwar activists to help their fellow Americans pass through "some dark night of the soul." Other peace leaders talked about compassion, atonement, forgiveness, and healing in "this period of something-less-than-peace" when the nation, still divided, was "permeated with the odor of war."[28]

In Washington the president was also concerned to define the lessons of the war. A national leader anxious to leave his imprint on history, Nixon publicly claimed credit for bringing America "peace with honor," and attacked his critics for having impeded the triumph of his policies. The president believed that antiwar dissidents were "going to be lost souls." He recalled thinking that "they basically are haters, they are frustrated, they are alienated—they don't know what to do with their lives." With the peace settlement, he thought, antiwar critics had gotten "their comeuppance" and were "really in for some heavy depression." In January he told Kissinger, "Our enemies have now been exposed for what they really are. They are disturbed, distressed, and really discouraged because we succeeded, and now we have to start to play to those who are willing to give us somewhat of a break in writing the history of these times."[29] On Nixon's orders, a group of White House aides met on 23 January in order to seal the administration's "victory over the critics" and solidify the popular belief that the Christmas bombing had brought about the president's "peace with honor."

Speechwriter Pat Buchanan set the tone. "The Far Left has been banging away at us for years. ... It's because of them that this war lasted longer than it should have. Now is the time to nail them to the wall." Kissinger objected that he did not want to make internal attacks sound like a claim to victory because that would only encourage the North and South Vietnamese to follow suit, which would help to unravel the peace agreement. White House staffers William Safire and Ray Price complained that an overt attack on critics would only make the president look like a "sore winner." Nonetheless, Haldeman and the majority agreed that the administration and its supporters should attack antiwar critics and advance the position that Vietnam was "a war fought for the right reason to the right result." Otherwise, Haldeman warned, the president would personally seize that line in his determination to control the national memory of the war, and this could jeopardize the domestic consensus required to sustain the anticommunist governments in Saigon and Phnompenh.[30]

"A relevant and powerful response"

Whether a justification of the war and an attack on its critics was to be orchestrated by the White House or personally conducted by the president was altogether irrelevant in the winter and spring of 1973. The whole discussion misread the peace movement, whose extreme left wing had long since disintegrated and whose remnant was now working toward a congressional strategy. Indochina policy increasingly became linked to a judicial and legislative challenge based not on the merits of Vietnam but, rather, on the misconduct of the administration. Antiwar critics played a role in that challenge, but their efforts were so integrated with political ones and the issues of foreign policy were so interwoven with those of executive malfeasance that the administration was never able to manufacture a plausible target. Peace activists understood this. "Nixon right now needs an enemy," Dave McReynolds observed in July, but the activists declined "to play the role."[31]

Early in February, while a federal grand jury under Judge John Sirica investigated the burglary of the Democratic National Headquarters at the Watergate complex during the previous year, the Senate established a select committee on campaign practices to conduct its own inquiry. In late March, it began to appear that the crime was more than an isolated incident. One of the culprits, former CIA operative James McCord, stated that White House superiors had pressed him and the others to plead guilty and remain silent. Chief White House counsel John Dean, sensing that he was being set up as a scapegoat, began to negotiate with Justice Department investigators, while acting FBI director L. Patrick Gray admitted that he had personally destroyed evidence taken from the White House office safe of Watergate burglar E. Howard Hunt. In the meantime, the federal judge presiding over the *Pentagon Papers* trial released a Justice Department memorandum implicating Hunt and G. Gordon Liddy, another former White House staffer and Watergate burglar, in a break-in at the office of Daniel Ellsberg's psychiatrist.

Shaken by the spreading scandal, the president fired Dean, announcing on 30 April that White House aides H. Robert Haldeman and John Ehrlichman and Attorney General Richard Kleindienst had resigned their positions and that incoming attorney general Elliot Richardson would assume responsibility for the administration's own Watergate investigation. Making an emotional plea for help in protecting the office of the president, Nixon vowed that he knew nothing of the planning or the cover-up of the Watergate burglary. His claims were not compelling: a plurality of Americans polled believed that the president knew of the break-in and the subsequent deception.[32] Congressional cloakrooms buzzed with talk of impeachment, and Senator Fulbright predicted that the Senate would reassert its authority. "I think we have come to disaster by executive government," he said, and now Congress had to "reassert its traditional role."[33]

Nixon had become his own worst enemy, just as the administration opened efforts to contain the growing force of the communists in Indochina. Late in April reconnaissance flights over North Vietnam were renewed and mine-clearing operations in its coastal waters were suspended. Earlier, bombing was intensified in Cambodia, involving about sixty B-52 bombing runs and 250 fighter-bomber strikes daily. Despite mounting congressional objections, the president said that he would keep up the attacks until the communist Khmer Rouge quit. Administration spokespeople argued that the president was constitutionally empowered to continue bombing this "lingering corner of the war" as an extension of his "residual authority" as military commander in chief.[34]

Challenge to that authority mounted. The Lawyers Committee on American Policy Toward Vietnam attacked the bombing as a violation of U.S. treaty obligations, while Robert Drinan and three other congressmen filed suit in a Boston federal district court to stop the bombing on the grounds that it was an unconstitutional usurpation of congressional war-making power. Congresswoman Elizabeth Holtzman (D-N.Y.) independently filed a lawsuit against the bombing. Meanwhile, a dozen B-52 crewmen wrote letters to various members of Congress, complaining that the Cambodian bombing made them no more than "mercenaries."[35]

Clearly, the president's authority would be tested in Congress. Some activists considered making Watergate their main emphasis but decided instead to utilize the opportunity to press for cessation of the bombing and an end to intervention. Since, as Al Hassler conceded, there was no longer a constituency for demonstrations or mass protests, antiwar activists had little "muscle" of their own.[36] They had to rely on Congress. Leaders of the CSFW met on 30 April and concluded that a cutoff of funding for the Cambodian bombing had "the best immediate chance for success and should be given top priority."[37] The Coalition became the clearinghouse for lobbying efforts directed at congressional swing votes.

Congress responded, the more vulnerable to pressure because public opinion reportedly opposed the bombing by a two-to-one margin.[38] Angered by the president's unilateral air war and no longer liable to the charge that opposition would be construed as undercutting American GIs, the House on 10 May prohibited the use of funds for U.S. combat operations in Indochina, and shortly afterward the Senate restricted expenditures for the Cambodian bombing. Antiwar activists found the legislation delightfully "astonishing," but Attorney General Richardson had boasted that the administration would find other funding sources. Nixon's press secretary declared that the air war would continue despite congressional opposition.

The president had weathered earlier congressional challenges to his war policies, but 1973 was different. In this round, the foreign policy issue increasingly shaped up as a constitutional issue because it was inextricably bound to the Watergate scandal. Attorney General Richardson named Archibald Cox, a Harvard University law professor, as special Justice Department prosecutor in the case, and the Senate Committee took testimony detailing White House attempts to involve the CIA in the Watergate cover-up. Twenty-five Republican conservatives, including Senator Barry Goldwater, formally complained that Nixon's mishandling of the crisis was harming the country and the GOP. Fighting to protect his presidency, Nixon invoked national security. On 22 May he conceded in a nationally televised address that former aides had concealed some aspects of the burglary in deference to his concern for security, and shortly thereafter he was applauded by ex-POWs at a White House dinner when he stressed the need to protect state secrets in the national interest. A few weeks later, secrecy itself became a constitutional issue when it was revealed that the president had covertly recorded his conversations. Nixon claimed executive privilege for the recordings until finally, after a wave of protest, he agreed to leave the question of their status to the courts.

Meanwhile, the administration stepped up the bombing of Cambodia, now consumed by civil war and social revolution. American planes unleashed more lethal tonnage in the five months after the Paris accords than they had dropped in the preceding three years of war. It was not enough to stem the Khmer Rouge, but it was too much for Congress, which voted late in June to cut off funding for the bombing altogether. Nixon vetoed the bill. Within days, however, he signed into law a compromise measure curtailing the air war by 15 August.

It was a signal victory for the president's opponents. Congress finally had halted funds for military action. The FCNL noted that moderates and conservatives had come over "for the first time."[39] Still, the compromise left a bad taste: if the devastation were not warranted, why let it continue for even a day? Congresswoman Holtzman carried her suit for an immediate bombing halt to the Supreme Court, which ruled against her. A committee of the U.S. Catholic Conference condemned the bombing as useless and immoral, while Catholic pacifists rallied in Washington with a new exercise in nonviolent resistance. On 6 July four Sisters of Notre Dame de Namur entered the White House on a standard tour and then dropped to their knees to pray the Lord's Prayer in protest. For the next six weeks, other dissidents prayed in "kneel-ins" that produced 158 arrests and numerous unexpected expressions of sympathy.[40]

Aside from a mid-June demonstration of 2,500 people against the bombing, during the summer of 1973 there was little public protest of intervention. The CSFW reviewed the spring successes in Congress and, again with financial support from Stewart Mott, determined to concentrate on challenging assistance for Saigon. All antiwar groups reported sagging levels of contributions, however, and nonpacifist ones continued to lose members. Dick Fernandez resigned as CALC director in June, citing his need for personal growth and family time. Dissidents complained about public indifference to Vietnam, whether it derived from rising conservatism, war-weariness and economic problems, or from a simple wish to put it behind. Indeed, the big news in 1973 was an oil embargo applied by an international cartel of producers. The antiwar movement was in "a painfully ambiguous situation," wrote John McAuliff, an officer of the AFSC and IPC: there was a "paradoxical sense of weakness and isolation at the moment of greatest triumph."[41]

Frustrated activists followed the revelations of earlier government attacks on them, details of which mounted during the summer. John Dean's testimony before the Senate Watergate committee in June depicted an almost paranoid White House staff repressing dissent, even by illegal means. There were new details of illegal surveillance and harassment by the CIA, FBI, and IRS. In August, for example, eight leaders of Vietnam Veterans Against the War challenged the conduct of their Gainesville, Florida, trial on charges of conspiring to disrupt the 1972 Republican convention. They raised an objection on the grounds that two FBI agents had been found sitting with electronic surveillance devices in a closet adjacent to their defense attorney's office.[42] The presiding judge refused to throw out the government's case, but the jury acquitted the men a few weeks later. This was the eighth major antiwar conspiracy case brought to trial and lost by the Justice Department's Internal Security Division. It became increasingly clear that the administration's attack on antiwar critics was only part of a broader pattern of arbitrary, secretive, and illegal activity.

Perhaps the most disturbing revelation of official Vietnam-related misconduct surfaced in mid-July when the Senate Armed Services Committee unmasked the secret air war against then-neutral Cambodia between March 1969 and May 1970 which had been hidden by the White House and the Pentagon. While Nixon had solemnly testified to his respect for Cambodian neutrality, the Air Force had conducted 3,640 sorties there with the loss of untold American lives (incalculable because the deaths were reported as occurring in Vietnam). The secret air war struck many constitutional experts as more serious than even the Watergate disclosures, and Congressman Drinan submitted an impeachment resolution on the last day of the month. The White House fought back, claiming that the action was pursuant to the president's power to protect U.S. troops in Vietnam. Nixon even took pride in it. He did not explain the systematic falsification of military records or the circumvention of Congress; it was as if he were oblivious to the fact that the issue had shifted from the conduct of the war to the question of accountability.

Early in autumn, attention centered again on Watergate and control of the White House tapes, although by October the administration was under fire from a new direction. Vice-President Agnew was faced with charges of corruption. On 11 October he resigned office, agreeing to plead no contest to tax evasion charges and to accept fines in order to avoid prison. House minority leader Gerald R. Ford was nominated and confirmed as vice-president. Agnew had scarcely departed when the U.S. Appeals Court in Washington ruled that the president must turn over subpoenaed White House tapes to Judge Sirica. Nixon attempted to evade the ruling with a scheme that provoked the opposition of special prosecutor Cox. Blocked by his own appointee, Nixon ordered Cox dismissed and the special prosecutor's office closed, but Attorney General Richardson and his top assistant resigned rather than execute the president's directive. By the time Justice Department aide Robert Bork agreed to do his bidding, Nixon had incurred furious congressional and public anger. Public approval of his handling of the presidency fell to 27 percent. Telegrams of protest flooded Congress in what a Western Union official called "the heaviest concentrated volume on record."[43] The president's impeachment was now taken seriously.

Nixon retreated to new line of defense, agreeing to turn over the tapes to Judge Sirica and to name Leon Jaworski as the new special prosecutor. At the same time, he warned House Republicans that weakening the presidency would jeopardize the European alliance (at a time when an Arab-Israeli war had broken out and threatened a fresh Soviet-American confrontation), and he promised there would be no new "bombshells" in the Watergate case. That proved to be less than reassuring when the White House claimed that two of the nine subpoenaed tapes had never actually been recorded and when it became clear that eighteen minutes from a conversation between the president and Haldeman had been inexplicably erased. The issue of accountability was compounded by a growing question of credibility. In November, Congress addressed both issues by overriding a presidential veto to pass the War Powers Act, which asserted explicit congressional controls over presidential war-making powers.

With the administration mired in its own defense, antiwar activists persisted in the last months of 1973 to demand a total end to American intervention in Indochina. Dissidents, even those who previously had been skeptical of traditional politics, understood that the issues of accountability and credibility were their main leverage. Wrote Stewart Meacham: "Vietnam, when we come right down to it, is too much for us. The crimes are monstrous and beyond our reach, emotionally. I can dimly imagine what it would be like to do the Watergate thing, but I really cannot imagine the reality of a napalmed or a carpet-bombed village. ... [Watergate] crimes are accessible to us emotionally; they trigger a relevant and powerful response."[44] Leading activists concluded that the conflict with the administration had "forced the rest of the establishment to take sides," so that it was possible to "pursue tactics designed to persuade the powerful—like pressuring congresspeople—who could not be made to listen in 1964."[45] Indeed, there was a widespread feeling that, despite the lack of a mass constituency, the chances for success in finally ending intervention were now greater than ever.

Early in the fall they concentrated on the political prisoner campaign. All of the peace groups cooperated in an International Day of Concern for political prisoners on 23 September, a project proposed by Don Luce. Local constituencies were reached, the national news magazines picked up the story, and special attention was given to Congress. Indeed, CSFW district contacts in Los Angeles persuaded Representative Edward Roybal (D-Calif.) to introduce legislation preventing the use of U.S. funds for Saigon's police and prison system, and then the national office helped to build support for it among other House members. At the same time, the Coalition promoted similar legislation by Senator James Abourezk (R-S. Dak.) and lobbied against aid measures promoted by the administration. The senator expressed his appreciation for the CSFW effort, which, he said, had built "a foundation of support" that could eventually carry Congress.[46]

A similar confidence within the antiwar movement led to its first truly united campaign. It was put together at Germantown, Ohio, where on 26–28 October a meeting of 215 activists from 15 national organizations and 24 states produced "an overwhelming consensus" on a "united strategy" for the coming year. They simply voted to continue the successful approach: "day to day community work" coordinated with congressional lobbying for the release of Saigon's political prisoners and an end to U.S. aid to the Thieu regime. They agreed to share resources, sponsor common programs, and hold joint actions—all in support of the CSFW effort. This was to be an ongoing campaign, not a new coalition, and it would be coordinated by the ad hoc group that had sponsored the International Day of Concern.[47] If there was no longer a constituency for mass protests, the converse was that the situation now seemed ripe for traditional pressure politics: *"for the first time the antiwar movement has acquired the objective capacity to actually end US* [sic] *involvement in Indochina."*[48]

The activists at Germantown concluded that the antiwar movement, although smaller and less visible than at any time since Nixon took office, could go beyond raising public awareness or staging symbolic protests. It could exercise "decisive weight" in decision-making by pressing the war issue upon a Congress and a public increasingly alienated from the executive branch. Amnesty, impeachment, and solidarity with the Vietnamese were all important, it was agreed, but they were all peripheral to legislative pressure. There was residual radicalism around, especially in New York City. It took the VVAW out of the mainstream of the antiwar movement, and it disrupted the IPC in the spring of 1975. But it was isolated. "At the end of the tunnel," the movement finally had put together a stable coalition with realistic objectives.

"Muffling silence"

The 1973 Nobel Peace Prize was awarded to Henry Kissinger and Le Duc Tho for their work in negotiating peace for Vietnam. Kissinger said that he was pleased to accept the award in recognition of "the central purpose of President Nixon's foreign policy—the achieving of a lasting peace."[49] That was diplomatic. It was also representative of public opinion, which for the most part had distanced itself from the war, enveloping in a muffling silence both the past ordeal of America and the current one in Indochina. Le Duc Tho deferred the prize until real peace came to Vietnam. That was realistic.

Certainly, if the measure were death in combat, peace was still a stranger in that hapless land. On the October day that Kissinger responded to the Peace Prize announcement, the government in Saigon announced that since the conclusion of the Paris accords the South Vietnamese had suffered 54,895 casualties, including 1,650 civilians and 9,700 soldiers killed. It estimated the number of communist dead at about 35,000. The Vietcong claimed that 6,000 civilians had been killed and 30,000 arrested and tortured by Saigon. Even allowing for blatant error, this was no cease-fire. The concurrent devastation in Cambodia, from both bombing and civil war, was incalculable.

In truth, American withdrawal from combat in Vietnam never had been synonymous with peace. President Thieu had quickly seized the initiative, attempting to oust communist forces from as much of the countryside as possible. Refusing to accord political legitimacy to South Vietnamese communists and attacking nonaligned groups and dissidents, he brushed the political settlement aside and polarized the country for a final confrontation. For their part, the communists had never accepted Thieu's regime or the division of the country as final. Although North Vietnam refrained from a large-scale offensive throughout 1973, regrouping its forces and emphasizing political activity in the South, it clearly was committed to renewed warfare if that were necessary and when the time was ripe. In January 1974, on the eve of the first anniversary of the Paris peace accord, Thieu ordered his troops to attack the territory of the Provisional Revolutionary Government. War was on again in earnest, and the White House did its best to support its client state.

American withdrawal from combat had not meant an end to intervention. Nixon had privately guaranteed Thieu that the United States would underwrite his government, and he had provided Saigon with enormous supplies of military equipment and a large force of military advisors (whose status was simply redefined as civilian). Indeed, the Pentagon had provided $284.7 million of military assistance during 1973, about three-fourths of the total for the previous year. As Saigon launched its new offensive, the White House asked Congress for an additional $600 million in military aid for the 1974 fiscal year ending 30 June, and a month later it proposed another $1.45 billion for the 1975 fiscal year.[50]

The aid debate took place against the background of deepening economic crisis and pressure to trim the budget, but in the foreground was the question of Saigon's legitimacy, in view of charges that it was a corrupt police state. Ambassador Graham Martin in Vietnam and proadministration groups in the United States were encouraged to attack the news media and all opponents of aid as selling out the South. A delegation sponsored by the right-wing American Security Council toured South Vietnam in February. It claimed that the government held no more than 25,000 political prisoners and that the only threat to the South Vietnamese came from the "outpouring of propaganda" by "purveyors of bias" desperate to see Thieu fall.[51] From Saigon, Ambassador Martin complained of "numerous inaccuracies and half-truths" in America and declared that Hanoi was trying to use "remnants of the American peace movement" to win congressional support for its policies.[52] In January, Martin had met five critics who were in South Vietnam for two weeks under the leadership of George Webber, president of New York Theological Seminary and chairman of CALC's National Steering Committee. Upon its return, the group renewed claims of American-financed repression, which were verified soon afterwards by Amnesty International. The ambassador sent Webber a photograph of thirty-two children killed in a communist mortar attack, charging the theologian and his associates with responsibility for the deaths because they had failed to use their "great influence in Hanoi."[53] The ambassador's insensitivity was matched only by his naïveté.

Congress was unimpressed. In March the Senate rejected an administration request for $474 million in supplemental aid for Saigon, and on 4 April the House followed suit. Antiwar activists were thrilled. Pressure had been mounted by the ADA, CSFW, and FCNL, working with a broad coalition of peace groups and churches, together with labor, agricultural, and environmental organizations (even if public concern could not be aroused over the struggle in Vietnam, special interests could be mobilized to cut loose from it). In the winter Tom Hayden and Jane Fonda had conducted teach-ins for congressional aides, who proved to be helpful with the spring vote. The most effective lobbying came from congressional critics, though, and they surprised themselves. After the vote, Representative Dellums stood in the night air outside the Capitol and repeated, "I can't believe it."[54] Nor could the White House: two weeks after the House vote, the Pentagon announced that it was shifting $226 million in its accounts to provide additional military aid to the South Vietnamese.[55]

Economics surely played an important part in the congressional shift, along with growing doubts about Saigon, but mistrust on Capitol Hill was aggravated by a winter flurry of revelations and charges: that the Joint Chiefs of Staff had operated a spy ring within the National Security Council, that the military had deliberately underestimated communist strength during the Johnson years, and that there had been systematic corruption in the Pacific area PX system. By circumventing the congressional mandate to scale down military funding, the administration only confirmed apprehensions of its unaccountability.

Nixon now was enmeshed in the Watergate scandal. Since January, former aides had pled guilty to various charges or been indicted, while the president had alternately feigned compromise and resisted attempts to secure the White House tapes. At the end of April, he released 1,200 pages of tapes, "blemishes and all." Within days, analysis revealed a host of discrepancies, contradictions, and omissions in the edited version. What it did document unequivocally was a White House style which conservative columnist James J. Kilpatrick read with "shame, embarrassment, disgust, and chagrin."[56] The staunchly proadministration *Chicago Tribune* called for Nixon's departure, either by resignation or impeachment. Frustrated and on the verge of losing control, the president declared that he would release no more tapes and would resist further subpoenas for them. On 9 May the House Judiciary Committee announced that it would open formal hearings on impeachment.

Throughout the first half of 1974, meanwhile, antiwar leaders vacillated between optimism about Nixon's political demise and frustration with fading interest in Indochina. It was hard to keep the war clearly in view. The news media seemed to be indifferent toward Southeast Asia, and activists were dispersing into collateral causes. Even peace effort implied more than Vietnam. The AFSC and CALC were cooperating to block the development of the B-1 Bomber, and CALC was beginning to study U.S. connections with repressive regimes in Chile and the Philippines. The threads of social and economic forces reinforcing militarism had grown more elusive, Ron Young wrote to Sandy Gottlieb, and "we may help stop this war only to find our country already involved in similar wars in other places."[57] A field representative of SANE spent ten weeks in Connecticut and concluded that liberals there were "interested in many issues and truly knowledgeable about few."[58]

As long as the White House tried to sustain the government in Saigon, therefore, it provided the single issue on which antiwar dissidents could rally; and Nixon's Indochina policy became more vulnerable as his leadership was compromised by Watergate. The constitutional and war issues were inextricably knotted together, and only Congress could cut through them.

Leading activists understood this, and so despite their differences they continued to direct their efforts toward Capitol Hill. Funded through 1974 by Stewart Mott and employing several full-time staff members, the CSFW now coordinated the lobbying of over thirty organizations, including ADA and Common Cause. It worked with the American Federation of Teachers, the National Women's Political Caucus, the Ripon Society, and the Conference of Mayors. It coordinated pressure in Washington with the work of scores of local groups. Members of the rural Norfolk Peace Group, for instance, wrote letters to local newspapers, editorialized on radio and television, and held biweekly slide shows throughout northeastern Nebraska. After a two-month tour of the country during the early winter, Don Luce reported that local activists were keeping the war issue alive in a population that preferred to make it "unreal, far away, and something to forget." From their efforts, Luce said, he had gained "a warm feeling for the strength and goodness I have seen," and fresh hope for success.[59]

By mid-May, AFSC peace education leaders felt "for the first time" that they could realistically anticipate an end to intervention. Constituent pressure on Congress was "virtually all" against aid to Saigon, they were told, and the FCNL and CSFW could look back on a series of lobbying efforts that had met with success: an aid to the bombing of Cambodia, the cutoff of aid to Thieu's police and prison system, and cuts in military appropriations for South Vietnam. Although flushed with new hope, they were not sanguine. If America did not disengage in the near future, they feared, "the war could be with us for another generation." It seemed all the more critical to identify continued aid as prolonging the victimization of the Vietnamese.[60]

In an effort to personalize that suffering, peace activists developed a dramatic and, for many, poignant metaphor: the tiger cage, so named for cells in which political prisoners were held in Vietnam. Demonstrators shackled themselves in an eight-by-ten-by-five-foot cage which they had placed at the east entrance to the Capitol. There, from 24 June to 24 August, they fasted, a few at a time, on behalf of the Vietnamese. Tourists gaped or offered quiet support; there was very little hostile or abusive comment. It was quiet street theater, the demonstrators said, an attempt not so much to change a policy as to break the public silence in a small way. Similar exhibits were set up in other cities. The tiger cage represented the activists' sense of their helplessness to break through the veil of apparent unconcern, one of them recalled, and as well their deep indignation about the "muffling silence" of the war which America still abetted.[61] The tiger cage was more than a simulation of prison conditions in Vietnam; it was to many a metaphor for the peace movement—caged inside America.

In the Capitol, behind the tiger cage, the struggle over military assistance and foreign policy continued. In May the Senate rejected another supplemental aid request. In June the House cut food aid requests for South Vietnam and Cambodia, in part because of evidence that the funds were being used for military and police purposes. The next month House and Senate conferees trimmed the administration's fiscal year 1975 military request for Saigon to $1 billion, and in August it was cut further to $700 million. Senator Muskie voiced congressional sentiment when he said bluntly that South Vietnam was nothing more than "a bleeding sore."[62] Congress was responding to economic pressure, to continued revelations of executive mendacity, to a widespread belief that the war was no longer an American responsibility. It was now up to Saigon. The legislature was finally abandoning the elusive policy of four administrations that had been determined to maintain—unilaterally if necessary—an independent, anticommunist regime in South Vietnam.

The war and the constitutional issues remained bound together. Even as Congress rejected Nixon's Indochina policy, it moved inexorably toward repudiating the president. After an initial bout of partisanship, the House Judiciary Committee plodded for weeks through the administration's record of malfeasance and misconduct, while special prosecutor Jaworski took his case for access to the White House tapes directly to the Supreme Court. The president's supporters dwindled amidst a midsummer hemorrhage of revelations of criminal misconduct, convictions of former aides, and finally a unanimous Supreme Court decision turning the tapes over to government prosecutors. Late in July the Judiciary Committee voted three articles of impeachment, detailing charges which ranged from the obstruction of justice to the misuse of government agencies and the willful defiance of lawful subpoenas (but rejecting a charge of unconstitutionally waging the secret war against Cambodia). Impeachment proceedings were scheduled for 19 August.

Nixon at first insisted that he would not resign, and he conceded nothing. Then, on 8 August, the president explained to an estimated ninety million television viewers that he was resigning his position because he no longer had "a strong enough political base in the Congress to justify continuing."[63] A classic understatement, it was also typical of an era in which reality had been systematically obscured.

"Saying no to 'one more time'"

Promising that "our long national nightmare is over," Gerald Ford succeeded to the White House.[64] The price of order was to be unsettled questions and undefined issues. Ford projected a spirit of continuity and compassion. He insisted that he would pursue Nixon's policies in Indochina; but at the same time he declared his support for a partial, "earned" amnesty for draft resisters and deserters as a way to help bind the nation's wounds. Ford's language implied that amnesty was a form of forgiveness, and it cut in two directions. Scarcely a month after assuming office, the new president granted his predecessor a full pardon and immunity for crimes committed during his presidency on the grounds that Nixon had suffered enough.

The pardon was greeted with incredulity and hostility. In Grand Forks, North Dakota, a judge released a man charged with drunken driving, saying that the law was on a holiday. Hundreds of federal convicts appealed for executive clemency on the grounds that they had suffered enough. Americans polled opposed the pardon by two-to-one, and the Senate passed a resolution urging Ford to refrain from further pardons in Watergate-related cases until the judicial process had been exhausted.

Antiwar activists shared the pervasive suspicion and resentment of Nixon's pardon. They understood, moreover, that his removal did not end involvement in Indochina. Congress had dislodged "the discredited Big Un from the catbird seat," wrote Daniel Berrigan, "but the sponsorship of chaos, torture, tiger cages, goes on."[65] Intervention was systematic, explained Dave McReynolds: "It is the system, not individuals, that needs to be impeached. Our target was never an individual—Nixon or anyone else. It was and is the system we want to change."[66] Critics of intervention were therefore not surprised when Ford affirmed his determination to maintain allied governments in Cambodia and South Vietnam, although they were pleased to find that Congress remained responsive to pressure for continued cuts in requested military aid. That remained a major focus of peace movement activity.

Another was amnesty. McReynolds identified the crux of the amnesty issue early in the fall, warning that it should be sharply distinguished from Nixon's pardon. There was no trade-off here, the pacifist wrote: "the one thing we should be clear on is that Nixon, the law-evader and law-breaker, is not in the same category as those men who, by their courage, upheld the law, the constitution, and the conscience of a nation by refusing service in the Vietnam war."[67] The pardon, whatever its merits, was a form of forgiveness; amnesty was a form of restoring social relationships without prejudice of guilt. That was not the way that Ford saw it.

In mid-September the president announced the establishment of a program of conditional amnesty for draft resisters, evaders, and military deserters. Identified as "earned re-entry," the Ford program required returnees to take a loyalty oath, undertake two years of alternative service, and submit to periodic review by a Clemency Board headed by former New York senator Charles Goodell. It was an ersatz compromise too heavy with administrative machinery and too light on understanding. Veterans' groups and prowar nationalists attacked it for acknowledging the very possibility of forgiveness, while antiwar critics and amnesty advocates denounced its presumption of guilt. Officially, resisters to military service were being invited to work their way back into good standing with society; from the critics' point of view, resisters to the war had exercised their only options in a society divided over the merits of the war.

Urging evaders and deserters to boycott the program, antiwar critics pressed all the more aggressively for a universal and unconditional amnesty for all. In reality, however, they conceded that this would not be possible until the American people fully and directly considered their national responsibility for the war. That was precisely what most Americans were eager to avoid.

Thus, in trying to rally support for unconditional amnesty, the dissidents faced the larger challenge of sustaining popular interest in the war issue. Many of them felt that they were shouting at the deliberately deaf, and they were tired of it. Young Massachusetts activist Peter Barrer, for one, declared that he was temporarily withdrawing from antiwar effort because there was "too much work and not enough satisfaction in return. I am most tired of persuading, energizing, pushing exhausted co-workers to do this or that. I felt enormously discouraged to watch the personal lives of friends, whose political persistence I admired, shredded by inattention. . . . [I] am frightened of that happening to me, and I am determined not to participate when it happens to others."[68] For four years, Barrer said, his life had been defined by his political work. Now that was over. The "sense of temporary urgency" was gone, and things appeared differently. "The struggle for a more humane society will be a very long one, and during it I will lead my own life, too." Barrer was typical of many activists who felt the need to pursue familiar concerns through more personal communities and less formal programs. Adapting to the absence of mass constituencies, they developed small nuclei—groups such as Philadelphia's Movement for a New Society or the radical Catholic Jonah Houses—as means for sustaining themselves in the long struggle for a "more humane society."

Meanwhile, the war in Indochina continued, and with it the issue of American involvement. This was the focus of antiwar political efforts coordinated by the CSFW through the fall. Activists across the country conducted a "Week of Concern" in October to call attention to the plight of Saigon's political prisoners and the need to cut off aid to Indochina. There were tiger cage vigils, church services, films and speakers, rice-and-water dinners. In Portland, Oregon, the mayor made the observance official. Demonstrators found themselves in concert with Congress, which continued to cut administration requests for assistance to Cambodia and South Vietnam and restricted the use of appropriated funds.

Repeated requests by the administration for military aid in 1974 were predicated on unrealistically optimistic assessments of Saigon's strength and communist weakness, in part a consequence of misinformation about ARVN combat losses.[69] One result of the requests was to encourage president Thieu in an equally unrealistic expectation of significant American assistance. Thus, in spite of economic chaos, the regime did not adapt to changes in either the political or the military situation in South Vietnam, and both worsened. In neighboring Cambodia the Khmer Rouge controlled the countryside, leaving the pro-American government of Lon Nol bunkered in the capital of Phnompenh.

Suddenly, at the end of December, the North Vietnamese attacked the village capital of Phuoc Long province at the southern end of the Central Highlands. Within two weeks they had taken the whole province. The scope of defeat led President Thieu to further tighten the reigns of repressive domestic power and stimulated additional opposition in Saigon. Nearly fifty Vietnamese legislators signed a letter to the American president in their own blood, requesting that he withdraw all support from Thieu.

Throughout the winter months the Ford administration nonetheless pressed for military aid in a vain hope of averting military catastrophe. Although warned by the congressional leadership that legislative approval would "be extremely difficult, if not impossible" to win, the president nonetheless asked Congress at the end of January for an additional $222 million in assistance for Cambodia and $300 million for South Vietnam.[70] The funds were essential to restore the military balance and promote peace negotiations, the White House claimed. Grasping at threads as though they were lifelines, Ford proposed to cease all support for South Vietnam after two years if Congress would meet his immediate request.

"The problems of Southeast Asia are not going to be solved by more ammunition," concluded Senator Henry "Scoop" Jackson, long a Democratic supporter of the war effort, and he spoke for most of his colleagues. Twelve senators and seventy representatives endorsed a mid-February letter to Ford which urged that it was time to phase out all U.S. aid and to "extricate ourselves from the situation in Southeast Asia once and for all." The president tried to circumvent strong congressional opposition through parliamentary maneuvers and warnings that time was running out, but to no avail. On 12 March the House Democratic caucus decisively rejected the aid package, and House speaker Carl Albert cautioned that any further requests "will be defeated all the way." Calmly, Senator Mansfield observed that America and the world were at "the beginning of an end of an era."[71]

In large measure, Washington was prepared to accept the passage of the era. The strength of that attitude could be measured in the positions taken by those who had once been bulwarks of the war effort: Senator Jackson, for example, who dismissed the Thieu regime as "repressive"; Senator John Tower (R-Tex.), who concluded that Cambodia was "not salvageable"; Senator Goldwater; and Governor George Wallace of Alabama. A clear national consensus had emerged. Gallup reported that 80 percent of the country opposed the aid request, partly out of fiscal conservatism but mostly from fear of further involvement.[72]

A curious double vision characterized national discussion of Vietnam early in 1975. Looking to the past, political leaders and commentators mostly agreed that the war had led to economic inflation and incredible abuses of official power. They differed about the responsibility for national failure and tried to fix the blame anywhere—on the antiwar opposition, the news media, or the Vietnamese themselves—rather than on the incumbent U.S. government. Looking to the future, they sought to put the war behind them as quickly as possible. Past commitments could not be redeemed, they concluded, and the country should not be mortgaged to them. Only incidentally, however, did the partisans on the assistance issue discuss the immediate present, the crisis in Indochina. Their circumspection was understandable, for the current war raised the question of precisely how the United States was going to accept defeat in Southeast Asia, and that was the question that policymakers and politicians had avoided since 1954. Further assistance to South Vietnam was to be denied not only out of the perception that it was the end of an era but in order to make it so.

For the remnant of antiwar activists, the aid issue was an opportunity to end the intervention: it was "saying no to 'one more time.' "[73] They now found themselves expressing a national mood. Beginning in mid-January, as CSFW representatives lobbied on Capitol Hill, Catholic pacifists undertook a twenty-day protest by reading the terms of the Paris peace agreements on the White House grounds. On the anniversary of the 1973 peace accord, 25–27 January, some two thousand dissidents descended on Washington in a self-styled Assembly to Save the Peace Agreement. The title identified the point that had separated the executive branch and its critics for two years. From Nixon to Ford, the agreement had been interpreted as a cease-fire which left the Thieu government in place as the only legitimate government in a sovereign South, and assistance to Saigon had been predicated on that assumption. To antiwar

critics the accord implied an end to American interference and an opening for a coalition, including South Vietnamese communists and neutralists, from which the future of the South would evolve. In this view
the peace terms had been vitiated by Thieu's intransigence, reinforced
by the promise of American aid.

The Assembly to Save the Peace Agreement was the last gathering of
the movement, and it was different from the rest. Forty percent of those
who registered were engaging in a Washington action for the first time.
Nearly evenly divided between men and women, about 30 percent were
students, 23 percent white collar workers, and 13 percent full-time activists. Three-fifths were between 20 and 35 years of age; a fifth were 35
to 50. On Saturday they attended programs at George Washington University, which included a session on the current situation in Indochina;
group meetings; a showing of the newly released antiwar film, *Hearts
and Minds*; and a major plenary. Sunday opened with a Buddhist-Chris-
tian-Jewish worship service on campus, followed by another film and
meetings on antiwar strategy and organizing. An evening "Convocation
for Peace" at the New York Avenue Presbyterian Church was followed by
a candlelight walk to Lafayette Park across from the White House. On
Monday the participants were briefed by legislators and CSFW staff, and
then they lobbied in the Senate and House office buildings. At noon they
took time out for remarks by a few legislators and some songs on the
Capitol steps. It was that simple. There was no march, no confrontation,
no open-ended workshop on social ills. There were neither radical
speeches nor counterculture events. The Assembly did not fit the prevailing image of an antiwar protest. Even so, its participants epitomized
the whole course of the movement and their memories recapitulated it.

The faces on the platforms were not all American. The participation
of a member of the Swedish parliament reflected the legacy of European
protest since the Campaign for Nuclear Disarmament in Britain and the
first International Days, as well as the hospitality provided to American
draft resisters and AWOLs abroad. The presence of several exiled Vietnamese recalled the FOR's early promotion of the Buddhist Third Force,
as well as the movement's continuing contacts with Vietnamese in Saigon,
Hanoi, and Paris.

Mostly, though, it was an American Assembly. Here yet one more time
were the organizations that antedated the nation's involvement in Vietnam: the FOR, AFSC, WILPF, WRL, and FCNL. They had provided much of
the initiative for the reconstruction of the modern peace movement in
the late 1950s and had been the core of antiwar activism. As sponsors
of the Assembly to Save the Peace Agreement, they were represented
among its organizers, leaders, and participants. John McAuliff of the AFSC
was a principal organizer. Frances Crowe of the AFSC and WILPF spoke
on Saturday, and there were many WILPF members present. Ron Young

chaired the Sunday evening session (since working with Al Hassler in the FOR, he had become AFSC peace education secretary). Roy Finch, a former executive secretary of the WRL, lobbied on Monday, and FCNL director Ed Snyder helped with the legislative briefing.

A contingent from the New Jersey chapter of SANE was a reminder of that organization which had entered the public arena to challenge decision-makers on nuclear testing and had taken on Vietnam. WSP also had formed around the nuclear issue and then challenged the war. Bella Abzug had been led from WSP activism into politics; now she participated in the Assembly as a congresswoman.

The principal speaker Saturday night was the venerable I. F. Stone, an early critic of both nuclear arms policy and Indochina intervention. He was an embodiment of policy-shaping elite—journalists and academics, critics and commentators—that had challenged official accounts of the effects of nuclear testing and then of Vietnam. Lippmann, Morgenthau, Niebuhr, Fall, Kennan, Chomsky, Galbraith, Schlesinger, and other liberals had become increasingly critical of Cold War liberal assumptions. They had divided the political establishment and won defections from it (like Daniel Ellsberg and Morton Halperin, who were at the Assembly). They had offered an alternative source of information and authority to the Republic. Here at the January gathering the audience heard not only Stone but also Frances FitzGerald, Richard Falk, and Richard Barnet.

Barnet interpreted foreign policy somewhat more radically than most of those critics, and he was closer to the activists. He was associated with the Institute of Policy Studies from which Arthur Waskow and Marcus Raskin had tried to connect the intellectual elite with action politics in order to create an alternative to institutionalized liberalism in the Democratic Party. Their New Politics had bred confusion in the antiwar movement, but it also had reflected a pervasive sense that Vietnam itself exemplified the very foreign and domestic priorities whose reorientation it preempted. Anxiety over that dilemma had gripped ADA, another agency which mediated between the intellectual and political communities in opposition to the war and which was represented at the Assembly by Ruth Lederer, among others.

Responsibility for organizing the Sunday night candlelight walk to the White House rested with an AFSC group called Nonviolent Action Training. To older activists, it might have recalled Larry Scott's 1957 creation of CNVA as a direct action program against atmospheric testing. Scott also had helped to found A Quaker Action Group, which had supervised many of the direct action projects of the antiwar movement before dissolving into the Movement for a New Society (1971). These pacifists had been radical in the sense that they applied direct action and civil disobedience in witness to their convictions and in order to challenge public apathy on specific issues.

In turn, they had stimulated pacifists who were radical in the sense that they envisioned the overall transformation of American values—the group that formed around Dave Dellinger's *Liberation* collective of the late 1950s. In the next decade the ever more revolutionary rhetoric and program of radical pacifism had become divisive, not only within the collective but within the antiwar movement. If Dellinger was at the Assembly, it was not recorded.

David Harris was there. He spoke at the noontime rally on the steps of the Capitol. Recently deported from Saigon along with several other activists present, Harris had helped to extend civil disobedience to draft resistance. The evolution from individual refusal of military service to the burning or turning in of draft cards had taken conscientious objection from personal conviction to organized resistance, and from universal pacifism to selective objection. Prominent intellectuals had courted complicity in resistance to allegedly illegitimate authority, and several church bodies had endorsed selective objection to war.

Indeed, one of the more significant trends of the period had been the creation of a network of religious activists. First responding to the civil rights crisis, leaders like William Sloane Coffin and Robert McAfee Brown had been converted to the antiwar cause. They had increased in number, enlisting consistent Jewish support and growing Catholic cooperation. Moreover, Catholic radical pacifism had grown from seeds set by Tom Cornell and others in the CPF, nourished in the reflections of Thomas Merton, and stimulated by the examples of Daniel and Philip Berrigan. At an early point CALC had mobilized ecumenical opposition to the war. Religious activists had given the movement important access to the public. They had also shared its agonizing debates over morality, strategy, and rhetoric. A pastoral call to attend the 1975 Assembly was signed by CALC's former director, Richard Fernandez, and other of its leaders. Its current director, Don Luce, participated in the workshop on organizing.

The Assembly had been endorsed also by Ralph Abernathy. Now president of the SCLC, he had been with Martin Luther King, Jr., SNCC, and CORE when direct action and civil disobedience were first employed on a wide scale to challenge the legitimacy of racist institutions. Their initial success had reinforced radical pacifism and stimulated the social conscience of middle-class whites. The frustration and division of civil rights organizations in the mid-1960s had been carried into the peace movement along with King's leadership, and race and war had been entwined in the turbulence which followed his assassination. The civil rights movement had broadened, meanwhile, into disparate claims for rights from other social and cultural minorities, women, and youth, but it had not led to the formation of all-encompassing left-wing coalitions.

The rights of blacks had been but one of many student concerns in the 1960s. Even Vietnam had aroused the campuses only sporadically, and then not necessarily against the war. Social protest from students had captured attention disproportionately, though, and it had been especially volatile. Initially, it had been fed by the test-ban issue and by the civil rights movement. When the fledgling SDS had offered a comprehensive critique of Cold War liberalism, it had created the image of a cohesive New Left (which it then had tried to fulfill). The author of SDS's Port Huron Statement was prominent in the 1975 Assembly: no one could have represented the previous decade of youthful radicalism better than Tom Hayden.

Initially committed to participatory democracy in the form of community organizing, SDS had taken up the issue of Vietnam in 1965 at I. F. Stone's urging, then shied away from a leadership role in the movement. Into the vacuum had come both the disciplined Old Left of the CP and the SWP, and a mélange of radicals who linked the NLF to an indiscriminate American revolution. In their train floated the counterculture. For some radicals Vietnam had been a synonym for opportunity in crisis, a chance to head a left-wing coalition. For others, notably Tom Hayden and Rennie Davis after their 1967 trip to Hanoi, it had been a cause. In either case, radicalism had spawned a militant fringe. The motifs of madness and moral numbness that had surfaced in the late 1950s seemed to be confirmed a decade later, and with them the ever stronger imperative to the morality of personal action. Many activists had taken recourse in mass demonstrations, others in individual or organized civil disobedience. Mounting pressures had exploded in the 1968 Battle of Chicago and rumbled on to the 1971 May Day action. By this time Hayden had isolated himself, while the radical left turned inward and then dissolved as a social movement.

Another participant in the 1975 Assembly had been close to those events. Ron Young had known disagreement and tension in the FOR, and he had helped to coordinate several demonstrations, including the 1969 Mobilization. He had suffered through the problems of building coalitions. For how many hours had he debated exclusion and nonexclusion, acceptable slogans, and speakers' rosters? In how many meetings had he, Dave Dellinger, Stewart Meacham, Brad Lyttle, Dave McReynolds, and Fred Halstead struggled over the terms of cooperation? So much effort had gone into training marshals and containing militants—even so, the informal NAG that had been formed to impose more discipline on demonstrations after 1968 had not availed in the MayDay action following the 1971 march on Washington.

Young could remember, too, the corrosive effect of government surveillance, harassment, and political espionage, including illegal acts by the CIA and FBI. As the war effort had stifled domestic social programs, the executive branch had stifled dissent. Not only the movement but also political critics had felt the effects of that repression. At the Assembly to

Save the Peace Agreement, fresh revelations were shared by Daniel Ellsberg. In the audience was Frank Wills, the guard who had stumbled on the break-in at Watergate.

Aside from Tom Hayden, none of the radical leaders of the late 1960s was on the program of the Assembly to Save the Peace Agreement in 1975. Clearly, the movement had not disappeared, but it had changed. It had seemed paradoxical that organized activism had become weaker despite an influx of Vietnam veterans into it and the rise in antiwar sentiment among the people that had been dramatized as early as the 1969 Moratorium. In those days Vietnamization seemed to have deprived the war of popular legitimacy and the movement of political leverage.

And yet for at least four Assembly speakers—Bella Abzug, Ron Dellums, Robert Drinan, and James Abourezk (since 1972 a senator)—the political system had begun to open up by 1970, for they had been elected to the House then. A principal address on Sunday evening was made by George McGovern, whose 1972 presidential contest had normalized dissent on the war. Elizabeth Holtzman and Thomas Harkin (D-Iowa), who participated in the Assembly, were among numerous antiwar candidates elected to Congress in the wake of that campaign. Indeed, after 1974 the saying went, "Scratch a new House member and you're likely to find an old peace activist."[74] By then a more responsive Congress had made possible the legislative campaign of the Campaign to Stop Funding the War. The director of the CSFW, Larry Levin, and a staff member, Jaqui Chagnon, participated in the Assembly. As a CSFW project, it was an expression of the reconstructed peace movement.

For many participants the emotional high point of the weekend was the film *Hearts and Minds*. It was produced by Peter Davis, whose *Selling of the Pentagon* had stimulated an attempt to "Unsell the War" with volunteer help from the advertising industry. Cells of activism had formed in innumerable business and professional groups in the previous decade—none more visible than those among entertainers. From poet Robert Lowell to actress Jane Fonda, or from Peter, Paul, and Mary to Leonard Bernstein, with Alan Ginsberg and Bob Dylan along the way, Vietnam had involved many streams of American culture.

Tom Hayden, like others, had recaptured something of his original vision. In the IPC he and Jane Fonda had invested the faith in an informed people which he had carried earlier into Newark, New Jersey. Holly Near had toured the country with them, singing, "Oh, America, / I now can say your name, / Without feeling bitter, / Without feeling shame." Before the Assembly's candlelight walk on Sunday evening, Near stood before a microphone with Joan Baez, who as a high school girl had discovered her first social cause in the nuclear issue. As they sang, the crowd joined in: "Stop the funding, Lord, Kum-ba-ya ... No more killing Lord, Kumba-ya ... Oh Lord, Kum-ba-ya." At the noon rally on Monday, Pete Seeger shared a newly written song which ended with the refrain, "Nixon down and Thieu to go." Seeger and Baez concluded the program as the crowd sang: "Implement the Peace, Lord, Kum-ba-ya; Implement the Peace, Lord, Kum-ba-ya." The Assembly to Save the Peace Agreement had in some respects recaptured the tone with which the movement had begun. A lot had been added in the lyrics.

In the following weeks the CSFW continued pressing its opposition to military assistance in Indochina. The war still seemed interminable, a feeling reinforced by the administration's overt commitment to the Thieu and Lon Nol regimes. This alliance, concluded the *Nation,* was "the politics of obsession." Dissidents could hope at most that American withdrawal from Vietnam might lead to a nationalist Third Force government in Saigon and an internal political accommodation with the communists that could finally end the war. That was what the Assembly had meant by "saving the peace agreements." Through the late winter it seemed to be a possibility, for leading peace advocates still anticipated four to six years of struggle. They scarcely expected an early and definitive conclusion to the ordeal in Vietnam.

"Such joy and such dismay collide"

The end came with shocking suddenness. By March the North Vietnamese had fielded large forces in the South, backed with enormous stockpiles of supplies. On 10 March they attacked and quickly overran Banmethuot in the Central Highlands. Pleiku and Kontum fell soon afterwards, as the South Vietnamese retreat degenerated into a rout. Large units of government troops were trapped. The rest fled southward along with some hundred thousand refugees, shedding their uniforms, dropping their weapons, and abandoning an area traditionally identified as the spiritual source of Vietnamese nationhood. North Vietnamese forces entered Hué on 25 March and pressed on toward Danang, where authority was in shreds and desperate refugees sought access to departing military planes. On 30 March the communists occupied the city, a decade after U.S. marines had opened the ground war there. The way to Saigon was blocked more by a mass of refugees than by a defensive force.

President Thieu vowed to protect the southern provinces, and he formed a national war cabinet for this purpose; but actually Saigon was ruled by panic. Its airport was jammed by people seeking escape, and foreign consulates were flooded with visa requests. Unwilling to concede the reality of defeat, Ambassador Martin insisted that the capital was in "no danger." General Frederick Weyand concluded from a special fact-finding visit that the South Vietnamese Army had the "spirit and capability to defeat the North Vietnamese," and Kissinger unveiled a plan of continued U.S. aid to South Vietnam over a three-year phase-out period.[75]

The aid issue became an exercise in responsibility-mongering. During the March offensive, the chairman of the Joint Chiefs of Staff complained that South Vietnam had its back "against the wall" mainly because of congressional funding cutbacks, and Secretary of Defense James Schlesinger insisted that Saigon would have been more successful had Congress been "less niggardly."[76] Eleven days after the fall of Danang, President Ford declared in a nationally televised address that he was requesting $722 million in military aid and $250 million in economic assistance for South Vietnam in order to facilitate a settlement between Saigon and Hanoi: such was the strength of denial. Some opponents of aid still held out the prospect of a negotiated settlement: such was the power of hope.

Attitudes in America no longer affected events in Indochina, though. In the bloodiest fighting in three years, North Vietnamese forces closed in on Saigon, where the regime was coming apart. It was Thieu himself who faced reality first. On 21 April he resigned the presidency and left the country, instructing his chosen successor to negotiate an end to the war. Five days earlier the military government of Lon Nol had surrendered to the insurgent Khmer Rouge in Cambodia.

Official denial of the inevitable confused American plans for evacuation. There were innumerable examples, but the saddest was Operation Babylift, a plan to airlift Vietnamese infants and children for adoption in the United States. Compassion and politics were intermingled. Predictions of a "bloodbath" following communist victory had been recycled from Vietnam through Washington and back again for years, at least partly in support of aid requests, and they had produced a sense of desperation on both sides of the Pacific. Accompanied by a public relations fanfare that rivalled the 1973 release of American POWs, several hundred Vietnamese children were flown to America in the first two weeks of April, while thousands of Americans offered to adopt them.

The babylift had elements of high drama and selfless generosity: on 5 April, President and Mrs. Ford personally welcomed a planeload of 325 Vietnamese children ferried to San Francisco in a quarter-million-dollar charter flight subsidized by an American businessman. Unfortunately, the operation was compromised by political motives, apparently being used to generate American sympathy for the crumbling regime and further military assistance.[77] In addition, Operation Babylift was marked with tragedy, as on 4 April a C-5A transport crashed shortly after take-off from Saigon, with the loss of over 200 children. Compassion, political manipulation, and unintended human disaster: the program seemed to be a last, sorrowful symbol of the war effort. "Only in America could the babylift be conceived," wrote one critic. "Nations have stolen children before, and nations have rescued children, but to steal children while *believing* that we are rescuing them—only in America."[78] Granting the humanitarian motives with which the babylift—and previously the war—were received by the American public, critics argued that both had been accompanied by a tragic naïveté and unwillingness to face reality. "There's a lot of blood on American hands," wrote a Catholic journal, "and it is not going to be washed away by grand gestures."[79] That was a theme with which dissidents would identify their postwar responsibilities: "Someone has got to help Americans confront and accept remorse," wrote one. "Someone has got to help Americans to weep."[80]

As the end drew more and more clearly into view, the opportunity for remorse was preempted. The Ford administration softened its criticism of Congress. When Kissinger announced plans for a final, orderly evacuation of Americans from Saigon, for example, he said that he accepted congressional rejection of aid requests "without recrimination or vindictiveness."[81] Shortly afterwards, on 23 April, the president called for national reconciliation as he told a cheering audience at Tulane University that the war was "finished as far as America is concerned."[82] Senator Goldwater agreed that the country should forego attempts to assign blame: it was best, he said, to "forget this unfortunate happening, learn our lessons from it, and promise never to repeat them."[83] He did not explain how lessons could be drawn from a forgotten experience.

For the time being, events overtook memory. South Vietnamese forces reeled backward. The Vietnamese legislature ousted Thieu's hand-picked successor and named General Duong Van Minh to conclude the war on communist terms, but negotiation was declined. Saigon was no longer anyone's to give, the communists seemed to say: it would be taken.

Americans and Vietnamese were being flown out of Tansonnhut air base the day that Ford spoke at Tulane, although Ambassador Martin had not yet faced reality, and the evacuation was still unofficial. Early on 29 April, Tansonnhut came under such heavy fire that fixed-wing evacuation became impossible, and still the final airlift was delayed. When helicopter evacuation was ordered at last, what was supposed to have been a smooth, four-hour operation turned into a twenty-one-hour nightmare that juxtaposed the terror and panic of the civilians and the courage of the military personnel at Tansonnhut and in Saigon. The last helicopter lifted away from the embassy roof at 7:53 A.M. on 30 April, barely hours before the communist tanks rumbled into the city. At midday General Minh surrendered the government and its military forces to the conquerors, whose appearance was greeted with an eerie silence.[84] In Washington, President Ford pleaded for national unity and a moratorium on the politics of recrimination, explicitly closing a chapter in the American experience.

After more than a decade of effort, antiwar activists reacted to the war's end with an uneasy blend of relief, joy, and sadness. Peace celebrations took place, but they were muted. Some 50,000 people filled the

Sheep Meadow in New York's Central Park on 14 May, but it seemed to observers that the strictures of speakers such as Congresswoman Bella Abzug and Elizabeth Holtzman were lost in the mellowness of the spring day. South of San Francisco, middle-aged women, businesspeople, and professionals who had been the backbone of local antiwar activism gathered and quietly welcomed the end of fighting in Vietnam. Students at nearby Stanford University showed little interest.

Only a few antiwar radicals publicly applauded the communist victory. Overwhelmingly, opponents of the war agreed that it was the only way to end the prolonged suffering it had engendered, but most of them assumed that the "malevolent repression" of the Thieu and Lon Nol regimes would give way to a more or less benevolent totalitarianism—"a liberation without liberty."[85] That turned out to be an abstract understatement when measured against the thousands of Vietnamese incarcerated for years in "reeducation camps," the more than a million of them who fled into diaspora, and the perhaps six million Cambodians massacred in the Khmer Rouge holocaust. Whether those were the costs of defeat or of the war itself was a question for the future. For the present, in 1975, there was a leaden peace weighted with the immediate results of the war: perhaps fifty-eight thousand Americans dead or missing, over a million Vietnamese dead, innumerable veterans mentally disoriented, over five million acres of land defoliated, the lovely Plain of Jars turned into a wasteland, villages smashed and villagers dislocated, ancient tribal cultures dissolved, the social fabric of three nations rent, the continuity of historical change violently ruptured.

Paul Mayer recalled that his heart was filled with conflicting emotions: "bitterness, joy, weariness, exhilaration." Searching for an appropriate simile, Arthur Waskow looked back to ancient Jewish celebrations of peace in which were included bitter herbs symbolic of the human costs incurred and still to be paid. Barbara Deming wrote simply, "Such joy and such dismay collide in me."[86]

In that somber mood, some peace advocates looked ahead. Those who were still active were precisely the ones who were most committed to peace beyond the end of war. "The public and the media have every reason to be skeptical about a peace movement that opposes war only when the war is going the wrong way," the AFSC's Ed Lazar advised. The CSFW evolved over some years into the Coalition for a New Foreign Policy, as a small core of peace advocates continued to work for social change.[87] In the following decade they would challenge U.S. intervention in support of repressive regimes abroad, take up the campaign to limit nuclear arms once more, and become involved in issues of economic justice at home and in the developing world. There was a basis for thinking about such issues in systemic terms now, of seeing relationships where before there were only discrete issues or ideological stances. There was available experience in political action, in mobilizing pressure on issues with only selective use of public demonstrations. The broad antiwar movement had become a small peace movement again, and its constituent organizations now had to set new agendas and cultivate new constituents until new issues formed the basis for fresh national coalitions in the 1980s. There would be a major campaign for a "freeze" in nuclear arms development, for example. There would be another against interventionism in Central America, and then the prevalent slogan, "No More Vietnams" would recall the past.

In the spring of 1975, Vietnam was immediate, and it was regarded by peace advocates as a precious if bitter heritage. As imperative as national reconciliation might seem, there was a danger of forgetting the source of division. Sheldon Wolin worried about a "politics of oblivion" that would drown memory. In that way "lies disaster," warned Robert McAfee Brown.[88] The administration had finally withdrawn America from Vietnam, an IPC member remarked, but it could not easily "withdraw Vietnam from America."[89] Washington had been defeated in Vietnam, observed Noam Chomsky, but it was only bruised at home, and it would try to obscure or dominate the history of the war, which, if properly understood, condemned the decision-making process itself. Others laid the responsibility on the nation as a whole, even on the errors of the antiwar movement: "there is enough blame for everybody," the *Nation* editorialized.[90] Unless the war was thoroughly understood and responsibility accepted, its ghosts would haunt the Republic for decades. Wrote Marine veteran W. D. Ehrhart:

> We are the ones who have to live
> with the memory that we were the instruments
> of your pigeon-breasted fantasies.
> We are inextricable accomplices
> in this travesty of dreams:
> but we are not alone.

> We are the ones you sent to fight a war
> you did not know a thing about—
> those of us that lived
> have tried to tell you what went wrong.
> Now you think you do not have to listen.[91]

Despite all of the difference in their wartime experiences, both the most sensitive fighting men and the most serious antiwar critics had faced directly the issues that perhaps most Americans had repressed in what columnist Garry Wills called "an ever-more-difficult *willed* ignorance."[92] For the antiwar movement, no less than for veterans like Ehrhart, the war had been an ordeal endured for the nation. For them, as for him, the effort to convey "what went wrong" was to be the last campaign.

That effort was never pursued with any coherence. Most activists needed a respite as much as their fellow citizens. For those who had enough energy—or who had made a vocation of advocacy—other issues claimed attention. Activism had priority over reflection. Nor was it then possible to agree on what had happened, much less what it meant. "There never was a war that was not inward," poet Marianne Moore had written of an earlier time.[93] In 1975 the views of peace advocates varied with their feeling-entangled memories. The movement's understanding of Vietnam and America was as complex as its collective experience. It was perhaps enough to leave interpretation to the next generation, which, after all, would have to live with the record of this one. Sufficient, surely, that the nation and the citizens who challenged its futile war in Indochina had endured their common ordeal.

Reflections

The Antiwar Movement and America

Charles Chatfield

"The time has come for a fresh examination of the main issues"

"Hard to find." Of the two decades of peace activism ending in 1975, the ordeal of the Vietnam War in America is the most difficult to understand. The era seemed, at the time, to be one of unadulterated discord. Even then, however, the most acute observers could identify two broad motifs within the cacophony around them. The dominant one pitted the Johnson and Nixon administrations against their antiwar critics in a contest for and against intervention in Indochina. It resounded mainly in the public arena and was an attempt to win the political center of the country. There were permutations on this theme as the distribution of opinion and power in the government changed and as political strategies of both sides shifted. The White House lost that contest, but the antiwar movement did not win it. The choices were not clear-cut. Both administrations subordinated clarity about policy alternatives to the preservation of executive discretion. Moreover, the withdrawal of public support for the war effort did not take place in direct relation to the strength of organized protest.

The explanation for this apparent paradox introduces a second motif: the tensions within the antiwar movement. In this internal contest there were no winners, although radicalism disintegrated and the liberal wing emerged dominant. For the most part, issues were obscured by a shifting coalition of disparate elements, by varying moral and political outlooks, and by a persistent impulse to subordinate all differences in the interest of ending the war. The national ordeal never was adequately defined, either in the public fora or in the movement itself.

Even to describe the period as one of struggle and contest is to accept the impression of a polarized society, assumed by both defenders and opponents of intervention. In the depths of the war, the view of "us" against "them" was a controlling image in political and moral discourse, an extension perhaps of the Cold War rationale that led to Vietnam in the first place. It was a way of thinking, latent until called forth by the war itself, when it became a principle of explanation. Ironically, it was a mode of thought that was largely vitiated by the multiplicity of conflict in the United States and Indochina although it has nonetheless dominated subsequent interpretation of the period. That the image was once pervasive is a measure of its historical validity, and yet somehow the description does not satisfy. One wants to understand conflict as a process, to view polarization in the context of national development.

Perhaps the fact that America was so "hard to find" in the 1960s offers a clue to forms of struggle beyond simple polarities. From start to finish, the Vietnam War was characterized by obfuscation. Militarily, it was pursued with a ferocity so out of proportion to the defined objectives that it was justifiably condemned as immoral. Politically, throughout the war and for whatever reasons, the White House attempted to relegate its opposition and the issues themselves to the periphery. Antiwar critics therefore felt alienated not only *from* but *by* their government. Those dissidents were themselves caught up in a shifting coalition of social causes which lost in clarity what they gained in intensity by being associated with the war issue. Accordingly, the arbitrary military and political conduct of the war intersected with swirling currents of social and intellectual change to produce a crisis of order and authority unknown to the United States since the Civil War. At the time, the source of social chaos was widely understood to reside in protest, preeminently antiwar protest. In retrospect, however, the crisis atmosphere in America can be understood in terms of the interaction of the antiwar movement with a more or less unresponsive government. Changes within the movement itself were affected by the extent to which the political system was responsive to protest. This interaction becomes clear only when the years of most intense domestic conflict, from about 1967 through 1971, are seen within the larger period and society.

"We are not all of a mind on this." Bernard Fall once observed that there were many wars in Vietnam—multiple dimensions to the conflict. Similarly, there were many antiwar movements in America. Protest had many masks, so different that some observers contended that there was no such thing as *an* antiwar movement. William Stringfellow doubted its existence in 1969, and he opposed the war. Shortly after the November Mobilization, he wrote in *Christianity and Crisis* that "the war protests

of the past few years have been spasmodic, haphazard, frustrated, fatigued and incoherent." They were all of that. Antiwar activists did not establish a single directing organization, coordinated leadership, or ideology. They drew on varied constituencies. They offered contradictory critiques of American society and foreign policy. They argued among themselves almost as bitterly as they excoriated those they held responsible for the war. As Stringfellow knew, however, his observation was a reflection of the character of the peace and antiwar movement rather than a denial of its existence.

There was after 1955, in fact, a definable body of Americans who sought new initiatives in disarmament and the international order that would reverse the nuclear arms race and reduce Soviet-American tensions. Drawing on established peace societies such as the American Friends Service Committee, the Fellowship of Reconciliation, the Women's International League for Peace and Freedom, and the War Resisters League, peace advocates added specialized campaigns such as SANE and CNVA (and also Women Strike for Peace and the Student Peace Union), whose primary achievement was to draw attention to the issue of atmospheric nuclear testing. After 1965 many of these same people sought to reverse Washington's military involvement in Vietnam. Few foreign policy dissidents dared hope at the outset to assemble a massive campaign against intervention. They were joined nonetheless by countless citizens who improvised an identifiable antiwar movement of disparate groups, leaders, followers, and tendencies. It was more assembled than it was organized. It functioned as a movement of movements.

Its constituent organizations were national, regional, and local, with only loose connections among the levels or the groups. Many of them were nuclei of people within professional or civic bodies. Most were ephemeral, leaving only traces of their activity. The size of the movement is very difficult to estimate, since only a few national organizations had definable memberships. Their combined known membership probably was between forty and eighty thousand people in 1962 and increased to three or four hundred thousand a decade later. Most of that growth came from the addition of new organizations such as Vietnam Veterans Against the War, Clergy and Laity Concerned, and Another Mother for Peace. The figure does not include coalitions, covert groups such as the Resistance, or political ones like the Socialist Workers Party. Moreover, the total number includes groups as different as CALC and AMP: the former was a network for specific projects, the latter a largely nominal grouping. The memberships themselves were not particularly significant (although changes in any definable group were instructive) because dissent grew at mostly local levels, often spontaneously, and faded there. In this broad sense, probably several million citizens were involved in antiwar activity. The assembling of increasingly large crowds through 1969 was impressive, but even so, the impact of public demonstrations depended more on media coverage than on mere numbers. Most important, especially after 1971, dissatisfaction with war policy was multiplied and channeled through a labyrinth of citizen networks.

Liberals and leftists, men and women, blacks and whites, students and established intellectuals, clergy and laity: countless citizens passed in and out of the antiwar movement. Its core was indelibly middle class and well educated. It was a typically American reform effort—a voluntary crusade attracting adherents and impelling them to act out of a felt personal responsibility for social wrongs. The tendency to define political obligation in terms of personal morality, and the assumed value of action per se, contributed to the movement's persisting problems with poor organization, lack of discipline, and intermittent participation. It proved very difficult to mount sustained political pressure, and the temptation to attribute frustration in this regard to the system itself or to the government only exacerbated a sense of moral isolation from society. On the other hand, this same personal and moral quality gave the movement the fluidity, adaptability, and irrepressibility that enabled it to survive and metamorphose in a struggle that none of the dissidents had anticipated.

"A new ... alignment for peace." Building on small, established groups, the resurgent peace movement of 1955–1963 was essentially a form of public advocacy. It focused attention on atmospheric testing, and it organized through a liberal coalition. Political liberals in SANE, for instance, sponsored conferences, developed newspaper advertisements, popularized expert testimony, and organized letter-writing campaigns. Even the radical pacifists in the CNVA applied nonviolent direct action mainly for its symbolic value in dramatizing the nuclear arms issue. The great majority of actions were low-key and informational, although gradually the movement became more aggressive and turned to mass demonstrations, prayer vigils, and nonviolent civil disobedience. Then, with the signing of the 1963 test-ban treaty, the coalition began to dissolve.

By that time, intensified civil rights campaigns, heightened sensibility to the Third World, and the rise of a new and youthful left began to shift the weight of elements in the peace movement, motivating activists to put themselves on the line for their beliefs. Some peace advocates joined early critics among the articulate elite to criticize U.S. intervention in Vietnam, but the movement did not undergo a significant change until 1965. Then the sudden escalation of military involvement in Vietnam precipitated an abrupt change in focus from the generalized Cold War to the specific conflict. As American intervention assumed massive proportions, the peace movement rapidly evolved an antiwar thrust and offered leverage to the gathering dissent.

The tactics of the movement changed, but not suddenly. At the outset they represented an extension of the antinuclear campaign, emphasizing persuasion (as in teach-ins) and political pressure. Between 1965 and 1967 protest remained largely respectful, its tactics designed to build an antiwar consensus. Facing hostile prowar majorities, most activists talked, taught, and marched without disruption. A few burned their draft cards— or, in extreme cases, themselves—in symbolic demonstrations of their willingness to atone for their country's alleged wrongdoing.

Almost from the outset, however, there was a sharp note of disillusionment with Lyndon Johnson, who had campaigned against Goldwater on a peace platform and had identified himself with the social programs of the Great Society. Congressional reluctance to confront the issues in Vietnam and evidence of official dissimulation served to heighten the frustration. In the face of a war escalating indefinitely and an apparently unresponsive political system, dissidents challenged the credibility and implacability of the government. The tone of protest became sharper, even theatrical, like that of the concurrent civil rights and black power movements. The emphasis of dissident strategy turned from an attempt to influence key policy-shapers to the mobilizing of massive demonstrations.

"A growing feeling of 'what's the use?'" By 1967 the weight and initiative in the antiwar movement had shifted to the left. It was attracted there by the social turbulence that now swirled around the war issue, and it was driven there by the apparent inflexibility of national policy. By the fall of 1968, opponents of the war were afflicted with despair (encouraged by political responses in the spring, they felt disillusioned in the summer). Anguish deepened through the next two years. There seemed to be no recourse, nothing that had not been tried. The dissenting judgment on the war appeared to have been vindicated—Vietnamization was a response to popular disaffection—and yet the devastation continued, even expanded, with no indication that the United States was about to abandon its original political objectives. Distorted judgment in that period was not limited to antiwar activists; it was a national malaise.

Between 1967 and 1971 dissidents aligned sporadically in attempts to reverse U.S. military policy in Vietnam, but they could not agree on what that implied. Their purpose was clear; their direction was not. The war and the protest against it alike became tokens of what was wrong in America. Public policy debate was freighted with symbolism, and rising disaffection was diffused. The antiwar movement reacted, expanded, or contracted in intensity as U.S. policy in Indochina varied. It appeared to abandon its function as an advocate of alternative policy and emerged in an adversarial role.

There was a self-conscious shift "from protest to resistance," although it was never as aggressive as it was portrayed. The overwhelming majority of antiwar actions remained peaceable and restrained. Dissidents mainly petitioned, prayed, marched, picketed, published, and worked through the political system. Quite plainly, however, a notable minority of activists escalated their protest in nonviolent sit-ins, occupation of draft boards and ROTC installations, and organized draft resistance. The number of draft-card burnings rose to a few thousand, and there were a few dozen recorded instances of flag-burning. Nonetheless, tactics remained in general both nonviolent and symbolic.

With the country trapped between a racial crisis at home and military failure abroad, a relatively small number of extremists resorted to physical attacks on the institutions and representatives of domestic authority. Infatuated with the romantic anarchism of yippies or the rebel mystique of the Weathermen, some militants called for mass disorder and street actions, and a few argued for outright violence. Whenever possible, they attached themselves to the periphery of the antiwar movement. Such was the air of moral crisis that a few radical pacifists courted confrontation on the assumption that it could be kept nonviolent. To a surprising degree it was, but the exceptions made the media—notably in Chicago in 1968 and at the MayDays of 1971. Although the great majority of antiwar activists condemned violence and continued to pray and petition, a very small number of extremists sought to "bring the war home," detonating bombs, attacking police, and committing vandalism. The pseudorevolutionary fantasy played itself out, but not before it had been attached to the public image of the antiwar movement.

The revolutionary rhetoric of radical leftists, the actions of militant extremists, a counterculture fringe, nonviolent civil disobedience, and organized draft resistance: protesting the war increasingly meant resisting authority, and it was portrayed as being more confrontational than it actually was. In particular, the Nixon White House deliberately heightened and exploited confrontation. The administration's carefully crafted strategy of attacking critics while withdrawing troops, combined with the exhaustion of the radical left—and the nation—seemed to brake the momentum of opposition. Countless dissidents drifted off into other reform endeavors or became passive. Ironically, the dispersal of street dissidence facilitated antiwar efforts within Congress and the Democratic party, even though it left many protesters with a sense of failure.

"A relevant ... response."   The movement never regarded itself as exclusively adversarial, of course. The ADA, SANE, and Allard Lowenstein's campaign to dump Johnson functioned within the political system. Even as confrontation reached its apogee in the streets of Chicago in 1968, critics within the Democratic convention hall challenged the war through conventional strategies of persuasion and electoral politics. Nixon's winning campaign that year was predicated on his achieving peace, and Humphrey's loss intensified efforts to reform the Democratic party. The Moratorium of the following year was an essentially liberal strategy.

By that time a broad grouping of antiwar liberals and elite policy critics was in a position to bring the movement more fully into the political mainstream. It was not only that radicalism had disintegrated; the political system had become more responsive.

This could be seen throughout the country, where independent local groups were organized on political lines. They were not tabulated in the declining memberships that so distressed national peace organizations. Rather, they reflected pervasive discontent with the war. Gradually, this was directed into congressional politics. Through the McGovern candidacy it was normalized in the Democratic party. With the demand for withdrawal by a specific date, it was pursued in the legislature. In 1973 activists on the national level developed a systematic lobbying effort around the issue of military assistance for Saigon. They helped to link war-related corruption and arbitrary policies such as the bombing of Cambodia to the issue of presidential unaccountability, which reached its nadir in the Watergate scandal. So enmeshed with other national issues was the war, and so integrated with other advocacy groups were Vietnam dissidents, that the antiwar movement became all but invisible.

These shifts in composition and approach were matters of emphasis. The personalized and heterogeneous peace and antiwar movements of 1955–1975 encompassed a wide range of tactics, from polite letter-writing to terrorist bombings, from quiet prayer vigils to horrific self-immolations, from reasoned analysis to fiery rhetoric. Lacking any central direction or agreed-upon strategy, the choice of action was determined mostly by personal impulses; but it was strongly influenced by the political conduct of the war and the degree to which the political system itself accommodated protest.

"A number of pure causes no longer so pure"

"No way to relate." Antiwar activists contributed to the growth of public disaffection with the war and helped to give it focus, but they were unable to harness it. At least prior to the 1973 peace accord, they did not establish themselves as a positive reference point for the many politicians and millions of people whose early support of the war turned into resentful neutrality. The opportunity certainly seemed to be there. According to public opinion polls, domestic opposition to Washington's Vietnam policies consistently spread through two parts of American society. On the one hand, there existed a small but vibrant antiwar movement, extremely articulate and politically active. On the other hand, there was a much larger body of people (some analysts estimated that it was sixty times the organized antiwar movement) who opposed U.S. military engagement but refused to make their dissent public.

The two groups differed with respect to class and culture. Organized opposition to the war came mainly from middle-class, college-educated whites, materially comfortable and motivated by largely moral considerations. Politically liberal and sympathetic to social justice causes, antiwar activists were also tolerant of changes in popular culture, sexual mores, and race relations. In contrast, the great majority of Americans favoring disengagement from Vietnam were a people apart. According to public opinion analysts, the greatest number of them were in the lower economic class, often women and blacks, with grade-school educations and low-prestige jobs. Politically inarticulate and generally isolationist, these disaffected citizens opposed the war as a waste of men and money and had little confidence in the democratic sensibilities of the Vietnamese people, North or South. Suspicious of most authority, they seemed ambivalent in the face of cultural change, but they made no secret of their dislike for active protesters and street demonstrators.

The connection with civil rights groups was a special case. It antedated and stimulated the organized antiwar movement. In the early 1960s, SNCC inspired radical activists; but it was ruptured by an internal crisis, and the emphasis on black power precluded any real cooperation with that organization. Martin Luther King, Jr., briefly became a cementing force in the movement, but the connection was very much weakened by his assassination. In any case, civil rights groups had political problems and agendas of their own.

Middle-class antiwar activists made some lackluster attempts to rally working-class Americans to their side. Although they repeatedly tried to organize around the idea of a coalition of the disaffected, radical sectarianism and self-interest invariably proved to be disruptive, and in any case cooperation was limited to specific antiwar actions. Some of the SDS militants who, like Tom Hayden, migrated into northern urban ghettoes in a sincere attempt to facilitate community organization carried with them opposition to the war. Some radical pacifists marched into marginal neighborhoods to mobilize people there against exploitation and war. The Socialist Workers party worked hardest to draw supporters from the trade unions into demonstrations, and with some success. For the most part, however, there were few serious attempts to convert lower-class dissent into an active antiwar force. Although radicals tended to romanticize blacks and poor whites, for the most part working-class Americans were regarded as inert and inaccessible.

Potential supporters of the antiwar movement may have been alienated by qualities they associated with militant radicals who, although not representative, got much media exposure: a kind of romantic egoism, political indiscipline, an orientation toward action regardless of consequences, argumentative sectarianism, and disdain for venerated national symbols. The movement was most visible between 1967 and 1971 when it was least conventional and, therefore, least acceptable to many Americans. Antiwar activists took to the streets in impressive numbers then. They even penetrated government offices and corporate boardrooms, but they failed to mobilize the American laboring class or even the middle class.

According to contemporary opinion analysts, most people responded to the Vietnam War as they did to other foreign policy developments— not out of a knowledge of the situation, but rather in response to cues issued by respected reference groups. Normally, political guidance is provided by political parties or religious and social affiliations. During the war years, however, the country's traditional reference groups divided, the leadership of consensual policy was fragmented, and public opinion on the war issue became ambivalent. Theoretically, the breakup of traditional reference groups should have provided antiwar activists with an extraordinary opportunity to establish their own movement as a respected opinion-shaping base, but its organizational style and cultural image appear to have fixed it in popular thought as a deviant force on the margin of national life. Antiwar tactics specifically addressed the political mainstream after 1971, but they were perforce less visible and could not reshape the popular mythology surrounding war-related activism. In various ways, organized protest was affected by the pervasive discontent on which it fed.

"A lot of naïve people no longer so naïve." By 1973 there was general consensus among activists that earlier, radical attempts to form coalitions around domestic issues had been a serious distraction. The liberal wing of the movement was dominant then, among pacifists as well as in its traditional bastions such as SANE and Americans for Democratic Action. These activists were inclined to concentrate on their basic middle-class constituency, to work through the established political system, and to regard earlier anxiety about their class orientation as another diversion from the peace effort. They concluded that the movement had left itself vulnerable in other ways as well, notably its stereotyped association with so-called anti-Americanism and the counterculture.

Abuse of revered national symbols did accompany opposition to the war, although it occurred mainly on the periphery of organized activity and was misunderstood. It took forms such as street theater, unfurling Vietcong flags, spilling blood on Selective Service files, burning draft cards, and even some violence against war-related public property. Predictably, this cultural agitprop infuriated large numbers of Americans and antagonized some elements of the movement. It was counterproductive insofar as it did not take seriously the myths and symbols that defined America, doubtless conveying a sense that the war and the national ordeal were not taken seriously either. That was deeply offensive to many people who anguished over Vietnam.

In a more profound and almost certainly more usual sense, the den-

igration of popular symbols reflected the activists' own indignation—
even anger—that patriotism was draped around an unjust war. If so-
called Americanism itself had not been used as a cultural weapon, it
could have been put in quotation marks to describe antiwar rhetoric:
anti-"Americanism." Draft-card burning clearly had this force, particularly after it was made a federal offense. The connotation was similar to
the occasional inversion of the flag, an international signal of distress.

Unfortunately for activists, distress was generic in the 1960s. Symbolism was used to challenge social and cultural conformity in general, and
it offered no distinction between rejection of a dominant, even if oppressive, lifestyle and a specific, if repressive, foreign policy. This left the
antiwar movement vulnerable to extraneous attack, since the contest over
the war was waged more on the level of symbols than on issues. The
recognizable peace sign itself was subjected to tortuous exegesis designed to convert it from an affirmative to a negative image. Moreover,
it proved very difficult to condemn the war as immoral without impugn-
ing the morality of the nation, or the leadership as distinct from the
people. The problem was aggravated by activists' pervasive concern with
popular anomie (the motif of moral numbness) and complicity (the Eichmann motif). "Madness is an infection in the air," Daniel Berrigan wrote,
and it obscured all distinctions.

Negative images were indiscriminately associated with dissent itself,
especially those of violence and disorder. In reality, violence was seldom
employed in antiwar protests. In was used mostly by local right-wing
activists or police, especially prior to 1967. In that year disruptive street
actions and attacks on draft board property began to increase in frequency and, more important, in notoriety. Concurrently the country
experienced worsening racial crisis and campus unrest. Governing authorities, growing apprehensive about the relation of domestic violence
and Vietnam, made serious attempts to infiltrate security agents in the
antiwar movement, both for surveillance and harassment. Not until 1968–
1971 did the connection between violence and the antiwar movement
become salient in American politics. Militancy did increase then. With
the disintegration of the radical left and the rise of groups such as the
Weathermen, some dissidents detonated bombs, set fire to buildings, and
attacked police. Still, it is difficult to correlate the actual growth of antiwar violence with the sharp rise in official concern at the time. According
to a 1970 study conducted by Treasury Department officials Eugene Ros-
sides and G. Gordon Liddy, there were 4,358 bombings in the United
States from January 1969 to April 1970, of which 36 percent could be
attributed to specific sources and 20 percent to antiwar dissidents. Otherwise, there are no federal figures which attribute violence to the war
issue.

In spite of lacking concrete evidence, the Nixon administration consistently identified antiwar protest with domestic violence and terrorism, particularly after it failed to link the movement to communism. Ironically, some administration officials used agents provocateurs to incite antiwar activists to violence or encouraged prowar enthusiasts to inspire citizen attacks on dissidents. The Nixon White House made a determined effort to discredit and destroy the antiwar movement, and it identified dissent with violence so effectively that it made the legitimacy of protest itself a political issue.

Government officials and prowar partisans also routinely attacked antiwar activists as being either communist-inspired or a source of encouragement to Vietnamese communists and, thus, a force prolonging the war. Doubtless some radical leaders naïvely romanticized Hanoi (as the White House knowingly romanticized Saigon); but despite their most energetic efforts, investigative agencies failed to find any evidence to the charge that dissenters were either inspired or manipulated by communists. Exhaustive studies prepared for both Johnson and Nixon concluded instead that even radical elements in the movement were indigenous American idealists, however perverse they might seem. Indeed, by the 1970s the word "commie" conveyed cultural and social deviance more than political subversion.

Similarly, there is no evidence that protest prolonged the war. Certainly the war continued despite dissident attempts to end it. The fact that Vietnamese communists periodically proclaimed their appreciation of the antiwar movement does not mean that they depended on it. To suppose so is to confuse cause-and-effect with parallel causes and to perpetuate the underestimation of Vietnamese will and capacity which itself contributed to American defeat. The charge that the movement prolonged the war rests on the assumption that it sapped the will of the nation to fight (or that the Vietnamese thought it did) and that the contest could otherwise have been won. In fact, it seems likely that most Americans concluded that the effort was futile and counterproductive, and withdrew their support accordingly. In this sense, it was the people themselves who were "no longer so naïve" about the war.

Nonetheless, the antiwar movement was vulnerable to unwarranted charges of abetting violence and communism. It was extraordinarily large and diverse. It was organized to attract dissidents, not to discriminate among them. Included in its number were a relatively few who were prepared to emulate the violent acts of what Fred Halstead aptly called "plate glass revolutionaries" and others who proffered a romantic version of Maoist revolution. Moreover, its public image was formed when those elements were most visible and domestic confrontation most intense.

Much of the difficulty in defining the movement's image was a consequence of its association with suspect causes. This challenge antedated the war in SANE's experience, and it surfaced repeatedly in the coalition

politics of the movement. The notion of excluding anyone from demonstrations on the basis of ideology could be interpreted as accommodating
the "we-they" polarization that underlay the war itself. Moreover, the
intensely personal morality of many activists made the exclusion of any
form of witness ethically tenuous. On the other hand, inclusiveness carried practical penalties. The association of radical, countercultural, and
anti-"American" images with antiwar demonstrations aggravated divisiveness and made the movement vulnerable to attack.

The major peace groups adapted to their dilemma in three ways. First,
they tried to distinguish between slogans and behavior, accepting demonstrators under any banner as long as they conducted themselves in an
orderly manner. Second, they developed elaborate crowd controls, including thousands of specially trained marshals, in order to impose a
measure of discipline and to intercede between demonstrators and their
detractors. Third, they tried to sequence events so as to make alternatives available to people whether they chose to express their views, conduct nonviolent civil disobedience, or court nonviolent confrontation.
Throughout the period both activists and security forces learned a great
deal about controlling large popular demonstrations, but movement leaders could not preclude all violence or offensiveness. Nor could they insure that the media would accurately convey their cause. In fact, theirs
was not purely an antiwar movement. It was connected—partly in reality
and certainly in the popular mind—with other domestic change movements, and that relationship determined in a large measure both its
vulnerability and its force.

"The antiwar movement is something that has been happening to America"

The significance of the antiwar movement depends upon what it is
measured against, of course, and evaluation is laden with anomalies.
Leading activists never believed that they could literally stop the war, and
yet they did not relent in their struggle to do so. Indeed, they even
cultivated the impression that public opposition could reverse official
policy. The Johnson and Nixon administrations insisted that they would
not respond to protest, and yet both adapted their policies to pressure
from dissenters. Public opinion surveys indicated that the American people consistently resented the antiwar movement but increasingly agreed
with its arguments and conclusions.

The very contradictions in the movement and in reactions to it suggest
dissonance. Probably it helped to transform the war in Southeast Asia
into a protracted domestic struggle which, when compounded by related
social turmoil, produced a crisis in the American social and political
order. Certainly antiwar activists confronted their people and leaders with

fundamental questions about democratic politics and national interest. In order to assess the role of the movement, then, it is useful to view it in several contexts.

"The Presidency is on the line." Both Lyndon Johnson and Richard Nixon believed that the presidency was "on the line," challenged both by the conflict in Vietnam and by domestic controversy. Each perceived the stakes differently. For Johnson the national consensus and Democratic coalition required for the Great Society was endangered as much by polarization as by defeat. For his successor, either prolonged war or ignominious loss jeopardized the "grand design" for international order and realistic U.S. leadership in it. Accordingly, each walked a thin edge on the war issue, probably perceiving his options to be very limited. For both, presidential discretion was important and would be threatened by substantial popular dissent, especially if it were translated into political terms. Consequently, as much as they might dislike it, they could hardly avoid letting their conduct of the war be affected by organized protest.

In some respects it constrained them. Thus Johnson refused to mobilize the country by calling up the reserves, largely out of fear of aggravating domestic division. When he was finally convinced in 1968 that the people would not support an indefinite war, he set a ceiling on it. Nixon's 1969 plan to deal North Vietnam a savage military blow was inhibited by domestic dissent, and his heralded Vietnamization was almost certainly encouraged by it. His bombing campaign in Cambodia was curtailed by Congress, which finally put enormous pressure on him to secure a peace accord. Ford's attempt to sustain Saigon with military assistance was frustrated by a Congress that was fortified by antiwar lobbying. Understood in any but the most narrow sense, the antiwar movement contributed to the congressional shift on Indochina, directly through electoral politics and the Democratic party and indirectly by marshalling alternative sources of information and by demonstrating.

The movement created other constraints on the government. Both wartime administrations were eroded by defections (in Nixon's case, as a response to the mining campaign of 1972). Although officials doubtless made independent judgments on the merits of policy, they likely were influenced by a gathering consensus among the articulate elite. Moreover, as Melvin Small has shown in *Johnson, Nixon, and the Doves,* loyal aides and even the presidents themselves were psychologically drained by the skepticism and hostility to which they and their families were subjected. Aggressive protest contributed at least to political and personal fatigue.

Conversely, active dissent induced both presidents to overextend themselves. Increasingly entrenched, Johnson made ever more extravagant claims for the war effort. This fostered the intense disillusionment that followed Tet in 1968 and forced him to choose between an escalating war and the cohesiveness of the political center. Nixon's Vietnamization initially thwarted dissent, but it also introduced continued pressure to extricate the nation from the war once and for all. His subsequent invasions of Cambodia and Laos, and even the massive Christmas bombing, were responses to that pressure. They were also a series of calculated risks in defiance of it. While denying that protest had any real import, each administration mobilized supporters, denigrated critics, and went to great lengths to discredit antiwar activists. Nixon was driven by his hatred of them to approve the covert and criminal aggressiveness that ultimately brought down his presidency and its Indochina policy. In short, the White House, no less than its organized opposition, contributed to political confrontation.

"A three-front war." The contest was for the political center, which seemed to have a mind of its own. The independence of the public frustrated both the antiwar movement and the executive branch. Certainly, in every available opinion poll, majorities of Americans condemned activists as frivolous, communist, or responsible for prolonging the war. Nonetheless, the polls indicated that growing numbers of people endorsed the dissidents' contentions that the communists would eventually triumph in Vietnam, that the war was proving too costly to the United States, and that the prospect of communist success was more tolerable than open-ended conflict. With respect to public opinion, the antiwar movement functioned both directly and indirectly.

From many angles, critics exposed error and self-deception in the government's public statements. As they did so, they accented a general anxiety over the trustworthiness and sagacity of governing authority— what Fulbright aptly called "the arrogance of power." From the outset, dissidents launched a moral and political challenge to official policy and the reasoning behind it. Early critics, such as Walter Lippmann and Hans Morgenthau, put policymakers on the defensive, and initial dissent tilted the balance against any Korea-like settlement that would involve an open-ended U.S. presence to guarantee Vietnam's permanent partition. Journalists and scholars challenged the government's understanding of Indochina. Religious leaders raised ethical objections to policy. Radical critics attacked it as counterrevolutionary globalism, a consequence of the country's decision-making structure and dominant interests. Originating among members of the policy-shaping elite, criticism of the war spread to prestigious universities, major journals of opinion, the Democratic party, the business community, and Congress. It came to include even officials like Secretary of Defense Clark Clifford. With the publication of the *Pentagon Papers,* the government itself was in a sense co-opted for the antiwar critique. The organized antiwar movement actively assembled critics into a network of dissent which offered an alternative source of information and authority on Vietnam and divided national leadership on the merits of the war. In all these respects activists affected public opinion directly.

They also consciously moved the issue from elite to popular fora, but in so doing they reduced complex relationships to polar alternatives. Conflicts regarding not only Vietnam but other social issues were played out in mass demonstrations and symbolic actions. Accordingly, national leaders voiced not only dissenting judgments about the war but also apprehensions about the impact of polarization and disorder on American institutions. It is altogether possible that as dissonance within the governing circles was fed back to the public, confidence in national policy waned further, in turn making more feasible the election of antiwar candidates and, thereby, a more responsive political system. It may indeed be that rather than converting the nation to its point of view, organized protest helped to coalesce public disaffection and to channel it into the political process on many levels. Such an effect was possible only because of the historical conjunction of antiwar and other movements of protest.

"The Movement, like society, has run amok." From 1955 on, more and more citizens were learning from related experiments in social change. By the early 1960s a resurgent peace movement converged with political liberalism, radicalism revitalized in a New Left, and a civil rights movement imbued with an interfaith revival of the social gospel. Reform efforts created a base of material resources, adaptable ideas, experienced organizers, and networks of supporters. Together they animated a lively sense of idealism: they contributed to the range, tone, energy, and momentum of the opposition which crystalized around escalating intervention in Vietnam.

Although interaction with other social reform impulses contributed synergistic power to the antiwar movement, it also aggravated an inherent division there. Nominally, the split was between liberals and radicals, but those labels do not convey a sense of the issues because both wings were in flux, and neither was fixed by a governing ideology or stable constituency. Still, there was an irreducible difference in the ways they approached the Vietnam War. Some activists fresh from peace and civil rights campaigns viewed American intervention in Indochina as a mistake, an aberration that had to be corrected through public education and electoral action so that the United States could resume its quest for international order and domestic reform. They were in this measure liberals. Other activists, especially from the Old and New Left, viewed Vietnam as a counterrevolutionary war of American aggression that sprang from the elitist and self-interested culture of American capitalism, which they wanted to transform for the sake of social and international justice. Their approach was at least in this sense radical.

Together, antiwar liberals and radicals believed that American military intervention in Vietnam was wrong and that Washington bore the principal responsibility for effecting a peace settlement. Beyond that basic agreement they divided. Often their difference was expressed in strategic quarrels on the relative merits of immediate or negotiated withdrawal, of organization around the single issue of the war or on multiple social issues, and of various techniques for effecting change, such as persuasion, conventional politics, mass demonstrations, or confrontation. Prolonged and often esoteric quarrels over strategy only obscured the main line of division. Antiwar liberals saw the war as a policy issue, antiwar radicals as a means toward revolutionary social change. The former tried to de-escalate and then end U.S. military involvement, while the latter challenged intervention in an attempt to transform the distribution of power and privilege in America. One side saw Vietnam as a crisis in a democracy that it wanted to save; the other viewed the war issue as an opportunity to redeem society from falseness and corruption. The lines were not neat (there were liberals, after all, who also wanted to redistribute power and privilege), the alternatives not necessarily exclusive. Nonetheless, antiwar rhetoric often masked a debate over America.

For the most part, that division was understood only by a small core of activists. The antiwar movement provided a focal point for large numbers of Americans who for one reason or another opposed the war but were not involved in protest organizations. Organized activism related millions of otherwise disconnected people to a single issue. This was its raison d'être: to mobilize public opposition to the war.

The opposition to this war was also linked to the liberalization of popular culture. Wars tend to breed cultural conformity and conservative politics, but the Vietnam War was different. In varying measure, the antiwar movement aligned the organized disaffection of blacks, women, and students. It also competed with these groups and others, such as environmentalists. It included a few activists who thought themselves the harbingers of a counterculture, many who emphasized individual autonomy and alternative group loyalties, and a majority that questioned authority at a root level.

These social demands and cultural trends were part of what Ronald Lora, in *America in the '60s,* has aptly called "a revolt against traditional cultural authorities." They included challenges to conventional wisdom about religion, scientific objectivity, national security, the sources of poverty, the infinite durability of the environment, and adult, white, and male dominance. Some of these causes enlisted specific groups—increasingly blacks, established intellectuals, students, and women. They sprang up independently before the war and perhaps would have run their courses without it, becoming more or less institutionalized in the normal process of social change. They were tenuously related to Vietnam by activists who perceived the effort to end the war as part of the struggle for a more open society. The pursuit of that social and cultural goal led to confusion and severe tension, and it also corroded the ethic of authority, whether in protest organizations, in delegated civic responsibility, or in the military chain of command.

What is liberation to some is disintegration to others, however. By 1971 a plurality of Americans agreed that domestic disunity was a greater problem than the war itself. Insofar as protest contributed to domestic strife (or the impression of it), it contributed to that war-weariness which ultimately impelled the nation to withdraw. The alignment of antiwar activism with other social and cultural change likely reinforced a popular impression that protest itself was a social problem. Therefore the antiwar movement and the war were resented for the same reason: they were eroding familiar values and institutions. Ironically, then, Vietnam threatened the quite different social values of both activists and traditional citizens. Given the perception that the antiwar movement was contributing to social dissonance, it was understandable that a public impatient with Vietnam declined to endorse demonstrative protest.

"We mean to speak the weight of our whole lives." The most distinctive quality of organized opposition to the war was its moral thrust. Vietnam intensified the dissatisfaction with pragmatic liberal realism and the anxiety over moral numbness which had surfaced with respect to nuclear arms. The war was widely condemned as immoral, not only on the universal grounds of pacifism but in terms of "just war" ethics—by Reinhold Niebuhr as much as A. J. Muste, by Hans Morgenthau as well as Daniel Berrigan. Policy was challenged on moral grounds, especially after 1968 when military victory was implicitly abandoned. As American troops were withdrawn, Indochinese became the only combatants—and civilians—at risk. For those who followed events, the question was more clearly what U.S. policy was doing to others. The issue of war-related public morality was brought home in the latter years of the Nixon administration when the events surrounding Watergate joined it to the issue of accountability. Throughout the period the moral criterion was the only common denominator in the antiwar movement, where it was pressed incessantly.

Calling the war "immoral" was a form of rhetoric—an abstract shorthand for "terribly wrong." The administration countered that the conflict was a matter of honor and obligation: hence moral. Offsetting ethical claims tended to undercut the force of abstractions. To that extent the nation lost familiar value-laden reference points. Words such as communism, containment, democratic government, free world, peace, and victory became too obviously manipulative, and too often contradicted by reports from Southeast Asia. Notions such as patriotism, loyalty, and national honor were imbued with ambivalence as the antiwar movement associated them with dissent. It was little wonder, then, that the public was benumbed by abstract words naming alternative moralities. In this environment it was hardly ironic that skepticism about war was extended to exhortations for peace. It was appropriate for *Commonweal* to advise the graduating class of 1975 that its fight would be against cynicism.

The obverse of public ethics was the morality of personal responsibility. Whatever its sources in American culture, this was a strong current in the 1960s. Early in the decade it impelled black students to take repression upon their own shoulders, and some white students perceived racism as a shared responsibility. The sense of personal accountability for social injustice surfaced in the Peace Corps and community service. It was extended to Vietnam. Especially among the pacifist and youthful elements of the antiwar movement, it was joined to an ethics of action: the notion that belief must find expression in behavior, that decision is the epitome of morality, that to witness outweighs results.

This attitude was characteristic of the so-called romantic radicalism of the period. Its attraction was felt mainly among young people, although it was also inherent in radical pacifism. Doubtless it was profoundly therapeutic when activists were oppressed by the apparent futility of their efforts. Apparently relegated to the periphery of their society and alienated from their government, they could at least witness to the truth as they knew it: *"at least it was something to do."* Still, the emphasis on personal morality aggravated the problems of already isolated activists. It could not only motivate activism but also rationalize withdrawal from politics. To the extent that action justified itself, the test of political impact was eroded. To the extent that the transformation of character became an all-absorbing goal, the organizational bonds required for sustained public action were snapped.

Such moralism never dominated the antiwar movement as a whole. Liberals, including leading pacifists, and even radicals in the Communist party and Socialist Workers party did try to mount politically effective campaigns, although they might rely on mass demonstrations to do so. Again they faced the difficulty of coalition politics. Theirs was a hydra-headed movement. The established peace groups had to reconcile differences not only among themselves but also with a series of ephemeral groupings, each with its own floating constituency. More or less together, they reacted to whatever crisis promised to unify them and give them access to the public. Under circumstances beyond their control, activists often appeared to be leaderless, their movement politically unstable. Nonetheless, at the core there was staying power and remarkable persistence, due in part to a coterie of dedicated, even professional, organizers and in part to the intractable fact of the war itself.

"Our problem is in America, not in Vietnam." The problems associated with building a coalition against the war thus derived partially

from the diversity and intensity with which individuals gathered in the hope of improving the quality of American society. In the midst of a despondent reflection on the fragility of the movement in 1973, an activist noted that someone had counted seven hundred volunteer groups in Massachusetts that were dedicated to various causes. What a dynamic society, she thought! The antiwar movement was a part of that dynamism.

The fabric of American society was dramatically rewoven in the two decades after 1955. Racism was at least mitigated. Student life-styles and curricula were altered. The status of women was reexamined. The Democratic and Republican coalitions began to realign. The executive branch was constrained by the 1973 War Powers Act. A large number of new peace organizations were formed which continued after the war, such as SANE, the Council for a Livable World, the World Without War Council, the Center for War/Peace Studies, the Fund for Peace and its project centers, and the Campaign to Stop Funding the War (under various names). Those concerned themselves mainly with foreign policy. Clergy and Laity Concerned and Common Cause bridged over to domestic issues. A number of other organizations stimulated peace research and education, or international exchange. All of them were complemented by a plethora of associations addressing civil rights, environmental, and feminist issues, or by cells of socially concerned professionals—civil servants, business people, physicians, psychologists, scientists, entertainers, educators, historians. Throughout the period there seemed to be a cycle of social consciousness, protest, campaigns, and long-term organization for concrete goals. The process was accompanied by turbulence, as old social patterns were rent and refashioned.

Whatever forces were acting elsewhere in American society, the war had at least two major effects on it. First, the war touched all domestic conflicts, charging them with high tension and obscuring the issues around which national identity was being redefined. Second, the antiwar movement interacted with the process of social reconstruction. Voluntarism in opposition to the war mushroomed, especially on the local level. Often it was only loosely connected to national organizations—perhaps to receive information, raise funds, or send demonstrators to a mobilization. Indeed, local activists sometimes resented the fact that their resources were drained to support national actions. All this citizen activity suggests that the movement in the broadest sense was not so peripheral to the American mainstream as its leaders feared. Its history on the national level reflected efforts in the American interior—in church meetings, college teach-ins, congressional offices, city street actions, curbside vigils, and divided families—where most Americans struggled among themselves over Vietnam.

"A test of will and purpose"

Just as Vietnam distorted domestic change, it clouded international issues. The peace advocates of 1955–1963 intended to promote alternatives to Cold War policy. They identified national with international security and fostered a cooperative approach to world order. They were genuinely concerned about nuclear testing, but they also hoped to parlay that issue into a fresh approach to international relations. Instead, their larger vision was subsumed in their immediate campaign. Moreover, multilateralism was weakened as the test ban was taken up by the government, where it was framed in bilateral negotiations and related to an ongoing arms race. By that time the peace coalition was becoming converted to an antiwar movement in reaction to the escalating Vietnam War.

Again the larger vision of peace through internationalism suffered. The war intensified the competition of world views, even among dissidents themselves. Foreign policy realists advocated a more modest assessment of American capacity and a larger sense of international complexity. Antiwar liberals, as they became increasingly sensitive to the implications of a national security state, sought to demilitarize foreign policy. For radicals Vietnam was the litmus test of U.S. counterrevolutionary intervention in emerging Third World nations. Except for a small number of academic peace researchers, few dissidents identified Vietnam as a symptom of global disorder among competitive sovereign states or called for the reconstruction of that system, although historically that was the philosophical ground of the peace movement. Vietnam itself was too compelling, too daunting. Peace meant primarily an end to intervention in Indochina, and that required unilateral American action.

At the same time, though, protracted involvement in Indochina helped to change frames of reference. Realists such as Kennan and Fulbright, Niebuhr and Morgenthau identified limits to the exercise of power which were ethical as well as logistical. Pacifists and internationalists perceived in Indochina the intersection of a classic Cold War conflict between Sino-Soviet and American blocs with Third World anticolonialism (already gaining bloc form as the North-South debate over disparities in regional development) and also internal struggles for power among Vietnamese, Cambodians, and Laotians. If peace advocates romanticized the liberation movement as they challenged a simplistic anticommunist rationale for intervention, many of them were led during and after the war to appreciate the complexity of the conflict and the mixed motives of the belligerents. Subsequently, they tried to apply their understanding to the larger international system and the problems of relating peace and justice, order and change, on a global scale.

Meanwhile the world changed, making the whole war effort increasingly irrelevant to American national interests. The United States had attempted to erect a bulwark against what it interpreted as the expansion of Soviet and, especially, Chinese communism among formerly colonial nations. As fighting escalated, the merit of extending containment to Southeast Asia was bitterly contested in principle and in terms of its feasibility. That is, the tenets of Cold War liberalism were both extended to and challenged in Vietnam (as they had been extended to and challenged in the nuclear arms race). By 1972, Washington was actively stabilizing its relations with Russia and China, which were, in turn, understood to be at odds with one another. Whether or not an independent, anticommunist regime in South Vietnam was ever viable, it was no longer a primary factor in the calculation of U.S. national security. American policy in Indochina was bankrupt by that time, in any case. The political problem faced by the Nixon administration was to liquidate the investment with a minimum of political loss—to save face especially at home but, given the administration's large design for world order, also abroad. Although "peace with honor" disguised defeat, it was not in the nature of the administration to recognize that fact, nor in its interest to acknowledge it.

Precisely in this respect, the antiwar movement played its major role. It kept open the prospect of an American defeat as a national option. Never a popular position, disengagement—and even policy failure—was discussed in public from the start. It is perhaps ironic that President Nixon could not accept defeat (although he acknowledged the limits of power), since it was by withdrawing troops, stabilizing relations with China, and overextending his constitutional authority that he undercut support for even noncombatant intervention. Well before he left office, the public had conceded failure and cut its losses.

Although the acceptance of potential defeat cannot be attributed directly to organized protest, antiwar activists had kept the prospect before the nation for a decade. They had been compelled to argue in a society at war that the highest form of patriotism was criticism, even resistance. They had called upon their countrymen to accept defeat when the nation's military forces remained intact, even powerful, in the field. At a time when their presidents called for victory over communist aggression or peace with honor, critics could offer nothing more than the acceptance of failure with dignity. Inevitably, they antagonized a large body of their fellow citizens.

In fact, however, people withdrew their support for the war effort as they rejected victory as a meaningful goal in Vietnam. In this measure the public gravitated to the central point of organized protest—its distinction between the warfare and the policy for which it was waged. To call the war immoral was in this sense more than a rhetorical device. It was to say that the goal of creating and sustaining an independent, anticommunist government in South Vietnam was illusory—that the terrible toll taken in Indochina could not serve even American security, much less peace in Vietnam or order in the world. The carnage had no justifiable purpose: in uncounted variations, that was the clarion message of the antiwar movement. It was frequently obscured by the way that activists presented themselves and more often by the way they were portrayed by policymakers. The question of purpose in Vietnam was turned into a multifaceted test of will in the United States.

Martin Luther King, Jr., and many other activists observed, when confronted with allegations of protest violence, that in objective terms the United States was employing devastating and indiscriminate violence in Indochina. It was imposing its will as though that were a goal in itself: this was the point of their opposition to the war. But those were not objective times, and it still is difficult to reflect on King's words without raising extremely painful questions that go to the heart of national identity and purpose. It was, and perhaps still is, easier to pretend that dissent was merely the rhetorical expression of malcontents whose tactics contradicted or obscured their plea for peace—to treat the challenge of antiwar dissidents as willful or trivial rather than to answer it.

There gathered in the United States between 1955 and 1975 the largest domestic opposition to a warring government in the history of modern industrial society. Originating in a small-scale protest against Washington's Cold War policies, specifically against the atmospheric testing of nuclear weapons, it exploded after 1965 into a sustained challenge to military intervention in Indochina. Overwhelmingly, antiwar dissidents regarded the decision on Vietnam as a definition of American purpose. They were idealists, and they identified their ideals with their nation. This is why they tried so desperately to reach the public. It is also why they were so vulnerable to popular rejection and apathy. They felt intensely that they shared the ordeal of the war—for the nation. They argued that the core issue was not the future of democracy in Vietnam: that, they insisted, was beyond the purview of the United States. The critical issue was the purpose of the American people. The antiwar movement did not force the United States to quit the war. Its political significance was, instead, that it persistently identified that choice as the essential issue of American foreign policy and national identity.

Notes
Bibliography
Index

Notes

Designations for Depositories

AFSC	American Friends Service Committee headquarters	MLKC	Martin Luther King, Jr., Center for Nonviolent Social Change
Bancroft	Bancroft Library		
BLMH	Bentley Library, Michigan Historical Collections	NYPL	New York Public Library
		SCPC	Swarthmore College Peace Collection
BPL	Boston Public Library		
CHSL	Chicago Historical Society Library	SFNO	SANE/Freeze National Office
CNSS	Center for National Security Studies	SHSW	State Historical Society of Wisconsin Library
Cornell	Cornell University, Olin Library	Syracuse	Syracuse University, George Arents Library
FCNL	Friends Committee on National Legislation	Tamiment	Tamiment Library, New York University
Georgetown	Georgetown University	UCSD	University of California, San Diego
Hoover	Hoover Institution on War, Revolution and Peace	UNC	University of North Carolina, Southern Historical Collection
JFKL	John F. Kennedy Presidential Library		
LBJL	Lyndon Baines Johnson Presidential Library	Virginia	University of Virginia, Alderman Library
LC	Library of Congress, Manuscript Division	Yale	Yale University, Sterling Library

1. Regenerating Concern

1. Quoted in "Best Defense? Prayer," *Time,* 27 June 1955, 17. See Stephen E. Ambrose, *Eisenhower: The President* (New York: Simon and Schuster, 1984), 2: 256–57.

2. "The New Era in Destructive Capacity," *New Republic,* 28 Feb. 1955, 3. See Ralph Lapp, "A Confused Alert—But Even a Good One May Be Obsolete," *Life,* 27 June 1955, 48.

3. James P. Warburg, *Turning Point Toward Peace: A Challenge to Candidates* (New York: Current Affairs Press, 1955), 34; also Herbert S. Parmet, *Eisenhower and the American Crusade* (New York: Macmillan, 1972), 406–7.

4. Vera Micheles Dean, "The Atom: Fall-out and Break-Through," *Foreign Policy Bulletin* 34 (1 Apr. 1955): 112.

5. Robert Divine, *Eisenhower and the Cold War* (New York: Oxford Univ. Press, 1981), 154–55.

6. The United Nations Association was a small group formed by leaders of the League of Nations Non-partisan Association (the full name) to coordinate wartime support for a UN. It largely absorbed its parent body, emerging as the American

Association for the United Nations (1945) which evolved into the present United Nations Association of the United States of America (1965). See Robert A. Divine, *Second Chance: The Triumph of Internationalism in America During World War II* (New York: Atheneum, 1967).

7. Wesley T. Wooley, *Alternatives to Anarchy: American Supranationalism since World War II* (Bloomington: Indiana Univ. Press, 1988), 47–53; Jon A. Yoder, "The United World Federalists," in Charles Chatfield, ed., *Peace Movements in America* (New York: Schocken, 1973), 100. For a thorough treatment of these developments, see Paul Boyer, *By the Bomb's Early Light: American Thought and Culture at the Dawn of the Atomic Age* (New York: Pantheon, 1985).

8. Lawrence S. Wittner, *Rebels Against War: The American Peace Movement, 1933–1983* (Philadelphia: Temple Univ. Press, 1984), 165, 171–72; Milton Katz, *Ban the Bomb: A History of SANE, the Committee for a Sane Nuclear Policy, 1957–1985* (New York: Greenwood, 1986), 13; Wooley, *Alternatives to Anarchy,* 59–82.

9. "Internationalism and American Foreign Policy," in Charles Chatfield and Peter van den Dungen, eds., *Peace Movements and Political Cultures* (Knoxville: Univ. of Tennessee Press, 1988), 216; emphasis in the original.

10. Norman Thomas, in *Post War World Council Newsletter* (Feb. 1955): 3.

11. *New York Times,* 26 May 1955, 18; cited hereinafter as *NYT.*

12. American Friends Service Committee (AFSC), *Speak Truth to Power: A Quaker Search for an Alternative to Violence* (Philadelphia: AFSC, 1955), 25, 50. See Lawrence S. Wittner, *Rebels Against War,* 230–31. Among the authors of the AFSC pamphlet who would be active in the subsequent peace and antiwar movements were Stephen G. Cary and Robert Pickus, who were principally responsible for it, Jim Bristol, Robert Gilmore, Milton Mayer, A. J. Muste, and Clarence Pickett.

13. Chester Bowles, *The New Dimensions of Peace* (New York: Harper, 1955), 377, 244.

14. Norman Cousins, "Worse Than the H-Bomb," *Saturday Review* 35 (31 Dec. 1952), 20, quoted in Milton S. Katz, "Norman Cousins: Peace Advocate and World Citizen," in Charles DeBenedetti, ed., *Peace Heroes in Twentieth-Century America* (Bloomington: Indiana Univ. Press, 1986), 178.

15. Otto Nathan and Heinz Norden, eds., *Einstein on Peace* (New York: Simon and Schuster, 1960), 635–36.

16. Linus Pauling, *No More War!* (New York: Dodd, Mead, 1958), vii.

17. Bowles, *New Dimensions of Peace,* 319; I. F. Stone, *The Haunted Fifties* (New York: Vintage, 1969), 120.

18. Stone, *The Haunted Fifties,* 107. See Herbert S. Parmet, *The Democrats: The Years After FDR* (New York: Macmillan, 1976), 153–59; Allen J. Matusow, *The Unraveling of America: A History of Liberalism in the 1960s* (New York: Harper and Row, 1984), 3–13; and Robert Booth Fowler, *Believing Skeptics: American Political Intellectuals, 1945–1964* (Westport, Conn.: Greenwood, 1978).

19. Warburg, foreword, "The Dawn of Peace?" *Christian Century* 72 (11 May 1955): 559; "Emerging 'Cold Peace'," *Nation,* 3 Sept. 1955, 186.

20. Muste, "We Complete Our Second Year," *Liberation* 2 (Feb. 1958): n.p.; and "Tract for the Times," editorial in *Liberation* 1 (Mar. 1956): 6; emphasis in the original. See Muste, "A Strategy for the Peace Movement," *Liberation* 7 (June 1962): 7–8.

21. James Farmer was then race relations secretary of the Fellowship of Reconciliation (FOR). Bayard Rustin succeeded him in that post after serving as youth secretary. Other key founders of CORE were FOR-member Bernice Fisher, who was secretary-treasurer of CORE, and George Houser, who held an FOR

staff position. CORE originally referred to the Committee on Racial Equality in Chicago (1942). See Jo Ann Ooiman Robinson, *Abraham Went Out: A Biography of A. J. Muste* (Philadelphia: Temple Univ. Press, 1981), 109–37.

22. C. Wright Mills, *The Causes of World War III* (New York: Simon and Schuster, 1958), 94.

23. Orlie Pell, "Conscientious Objectors Protest Civil Defense," *Four Lights* 15 (Jan. 1956): 1; emphasis in the original. See Dorothy Day et al., "The Demonstrators' Statement," *WRL News* (July–Aug. 1955): 3; "Pacifists Demonstrate, Educate on C.D. Day," *Fellowship* 21 (1 July 1955): 25; Ammon Hennacy, *The Book of Ammon* (Salt Lake City: privately printed, 1965), 286–87; and Mel Piehl, *Breaking Bread: The Catholic Worker and the Origin of Catholic Radicalism in America* (Philadelphia: Temple Univ. Press, 1982), 214–15.

24. Muste, "Tract for the Times," 4.

25. Among its editorial board were several individuals who would play important roles in the subsequent peace and antiwar movements, notably A. J. Muste, Bayard Rustin, Sidney Peck, Robert Pickus, Robert Gilmore, and, of course, David Dellinger.

26. Muste, "Tract for the Times," 4–6; emphasis in the original.

27. Ibid.; David Dellinger, "The Here-and-Now Revolution," *Liberation* 1 (June 1956): 17–18.

28. David Dellinger, "They Refused to Hide," *Liberation* 2 (July–Aug. 1957): 6; Muste, "We Complete Our Second Year," n.p.; and "Tract for the Times," 6.

29. Muste, "Tract for the Times," 4.

30. *Liberation* was preceded in 1954 by Irving Howe's *Dissent.* A. J. Muste and Sidney Lens were contributing editors to both magazines, which together "portended important changes in the political climate of the mid-1950s," in the view of Irwin Unger, *The Movement: A History of the American New Left, 1959–1972* (New York: Dodd, Mead, 1974), 17. The advent of *Liberation* was thus not an isolated event.

31. Muste, "Tract for the Times," 5. See Albert Bigelow, *The Voyage of the Golden Rule: An Experiment with Truth* (Garden City, N.Y.: Doubleday, 1959), 42.

2. Coalescing Organization

1. Stone, *The Haunted Fifties,* 90.

2. *NYT,* 20 Sept. 1956, 1; 16 Oct. 1956, 1; and 27 Oct. 1956, 1.

3. Robert Divine, *Blowing on the Wind: The Nuclear Test Ban Debate, 1954–1960* (New York: Oxford Univ. Press, 1978), 112.

4. Norman Thomas, *The Prerequisites for Peace* (New York: Norton, 1959), 79; "Shut the Gates of Hell!" *Christian Century* (2 Apr. 1958): 395–96.

5. George Kennan, "A Chance to Withdraw Our Troops in Europe," *Harper's,* Feb. 1958, 38–39.

6. "An Editorial," *Journal of Conflict Resolution* 1 (Mar. 1957): 2; also Cynthia Earl Kerman, *Creative Tension: The Life and Thought of Kenneth Boulding* (Ann Arbor: Univ. of Michigan Press, 1974), 46–48, 68–71.

7. Quoted in John Minnion, *The CND Story* (London: Allison and Busby, Ltd., 1983), 15.

8. Pauling, *No More War!* 180–99.

9. Nevil Shute, *On the Beach* (New York: Morrow, 1957), 311. The lines on the title page of the book are from Eliot's "The Hollow Men," in *Collected Poems 1909–1935* (New York: Harcourt, 1936). The film version starred Gregory Peck, Anthony Parker, Fred Astair, and Ava Gardner.

10. *NYT,* 6 June 1957, 1; Ambrose, *Eisenhower,* 198–99; "What's Back of the 'Fall-Out' Scare," *U.S. News and World Report,* 7 June 1957, 25.

11. Milton Katz, *Ban the Bomb,* 21–22.

12. Lawrence Scott, quoted in Milton S. Katz and Neil H. Katz, "Pragmatists and Visionaries in the Post–World War II American Peace Movement: SANE and CNVA," in Solomon Wank, ed., *Doves and Diplomats: Foreign Offices and Peace Movements in Europe and America in the 20th Century* (Westport, Conn.: Greenwood, 1978), 268. See Wittner, *Rebels Against War,* 242–47; and Milton Katz, *Ban the Bomb,* 22.

13. Lawrence Scott, quoted in Neil H. Katz, "Radical Pacifism and the Contemporary American Peace Movement: The Committee for Nonviolent Action, 1957–1967" (Ph.D. diss., Univ. of Maryland, 1974), 32.

14. Bigelow, *Voyage of the Golden Rule,* 25.

15. Homer Jack statement, 22 Nov. 1957, box 16, Homer Jack Papers, SCPC. Regarding other actions cited, see "WILPF takes 10,000 Signatures to White House," *Four Lights* 17 (October 1957): 1; and Bigelow, *Voyage of the Golden Rule,* 39–41.

16. Homer Jack statement, 22 Nov. 1957, p. 2, box 16, Jack Papers, SCPC.

17. Donald F. Keys, quoted in Milton S. Katz, "Peace, Politics and Protest: SANE and the American Peace Movement, 1957–1972," (Ph.D. diss., St. Louis Univ. 1973), 70, n. 15.

18. Minutes of 24 Sept. 1957 SANE meeting, SANE Washington Logbook, 1957–1959, SFNO.

19. *NYT,* 23 Nov. 1957, 1. According to Stephen Ambrose, three members of the Gaither commission were so alarmed that they recommended a preventive war against the Soviet Union. *Eisenhower,* 2: 434.

20. Quoted in Milton Katz, "Peace, Politics and Protest," 189; Jerome Grossman, "Editorial," *Peace Politics Newsletter,* no. 1 (Oct. 1963): 2; "First Step to Where?" *Bulletin of the Atomic Scientists* 19 (Oct. 1963): 2; and I. F. Stone, "Why and How Did Peace Suddenly Break Out?" *I. F. Stone's Weekly* 11 (2 Sept. 1963): 1.

21. Erich Fromm, in meeting minutes of 24 Sept. 1957 SANE meeting, SANE Washington Logbook, 1957–1959, SFNO.

22. Fromm, quoted in Milton Katz, "Peace, Politics and Protest," 77; and Shotwell, in minutes of 2 Dec. 1957 SANE meeting, SANE Washington Logbook, 1957–1959.

23. Norman Cousins to Trevor Thomas, 13 June 1958, box 20, SANE Records, SCPC, quoted in Milton Katz, "Peace, Politics and Protest," 118. For Larry Scott's comment, see Milton Katz, *Ban the Bomb,* 46.

24. Robert Gilmore, in minutes of 19 Sept. 1958 SANE executive committee meeting, SANE Washington Logbook, 1957–1959, SFNO.

25. See Norman Thomas, *The Prerequisites for Peace* (1959), 75–76. The case was dismissed on the grounds that the petitioners did not show specific injury to themselves and that aliens suffering injury had no standing in a U.S. court.

26. Bigelow, *Voyage of the Golden Rule,* 47, 112.

27. The incident and long trial are recounted in Earle Reynolds, *The Forbidden Voyage* (New York: McKay, 1961). Reynolds was eventually defended by Joseph Rauh, who secured a disallowance of conviction on appeal (29 Dec. 1960).

28. "The Fall-Out Suits Seek Court Intervention (December 1958—Progress Report)," in Bigelow, *Voyage of the Golden Rule,* appendix C, 282. See Norman Thomas, *The Prerequisites for Peace,* 75–77; and "Conscience Goes to Court," *Christian Century* 75 (16 Apr. 1958): 461.

29. "They Feel It in Their Bones," *Nation,* 19 Apr. 1958, 334.

30. George Gallup, *The Gallup Poll: Public Opinion, 1935–1971,* 3 vols. (New York: Random House, 1972), 2: 1541, 1552.

31. *NYT,* 5 May 1958, 21.

32. Arthur M. Schlesinger, Jr., "The Challenge of Abundance," *Reporter,* 3 May 1956, 9–11.

33. Thomas C. Schelling and Morton H. Halperin, *Strategy and Arms Control* (New York: Twentieth Century Fund, 1961), 141–42. On the broad shift among liberal intellectuals to support of arms control, see Duncan C. Clarke, *Politics of Arms Control: The Role and Effectiveness of The U.S. Arms Control and Disarmament Agency* (New York: Free Press, 1979), 10–28; Lawrence Freedman, *The Evolution of Nuclear Strategy* (London: Macmillan, 1981), 95–103, 191–207; Michael Mandelbaum, *The Nuclear Question: The United States and Nuclear Weapons, 1946–1976* (New York: Cambridge Univ. Press, 1979), 54–98; and Robin Ranger, *Arms And Politics, 1958–1978: Arms Control In A Changing Political Context* (Toronto: Gage, 1979), 3–49.

34. James E. King, "Strategic Surrender: The Senate Debate and the Book," *World Politics* 11 (Apr. 1959): 418–22.

35. *NYT,* 4 June 1959, 1.

36. Lewis Mumford, "Moral Emergency," *Fellowship* 24 (1 Jan. 1958): 22; Eugene Rabinowitch, "The First Year of Deterrence," *Bulletin of the Atomic Scientists* 3 (Jan. 1957): 6; also, Parmet, *The Democrats,* 156–58.

37. Quotation from a member of the Wisconsin Liberal Club (a Student League for Industrial Democracy [SLID] chapter) in George R. Vickers, *The Formation of The New Left: The Early Years* (Lexington, Mass.: Lexington Books, 1975), 26. See Milton Cantor, *The Divided Left: American Radicalism, 1900–1975* (New York: Hill and Wang, 1978), 185; Unger, *The Movement,* 1–24; Edward J. Bacciocco, Jr., *The New Left in America: Reform To Revolution, 1956–1970* (Stanford: Hoover Institution Press, 1974), 1–20; Maurice Isserman, *If I Had a Hammer: The Death of the Old Left and the Birth of the New Left* (New York: Basic Books, 1987); and James Miller, *"Democracy Is in the Streets": From Port Huron to the Siege of Chicago* (New York: Simon and Schuster, 1987), 21–31.

38. Michael Walzer, "Dissent at Thirty," *Dissent* 31 (Winter 1984): 3. Walzer was recalling his days as a graduate student in political science at Harvard.

39. Howard Metzenberg, "Student Peace Union, Five Years Before the New Left" (honors thesis, Oberlin College, 1978), 16–18.

40. Ken Calkins, "The Student Peace Union," *Fellowship* 26 (1 Mar. 1960): 5.

41. Dan Cohen, "Manifesto for the New Era," *SPU* (Student Peace Union) *Bulletin* (Jan. 1960): 3.

42. Ibid., 6; and Cohen, "Our Communist Line," ibid., 3.

43. Clayborne Carson, *In Struggle: SNCC and The Black Awakening of the 1960s* (Cambridge, Mass.: Harvard Univ. Press, 1981), 12.

44. Ibid., 23.

45. Martin Oppenheimer and George Lakey, *A Manual for Direct Action: Strategy and Tactics for Civil Rights and All Other Nonviolent Protest Movements* (Chicago: Quadrangle, 1964).

46. Mike Parker to Pete Salmon et al., 30 Apr. 1960, folder 22, box 1, Student Peace Union (SPU) Records, SHSW; Ken Calkins to David McReynolds, 5 March 1960, carton 3, War Resisters League (WRL) Records, SCPC. For the breadth of the new actions, see Wittner, *Rebels Against War,* 262–75.

47. Vickers, *The Formation of the New Left,* 51.

48. Metzenberg, "Student Peace Union," 44.

49. Minutes of 27–28 Aug. 1960 SPU national planning meeting, folders 28, 29, box 1, SPU Records, SHSW. At the time, the CND logo was also referred to as the "lollipop."

50. C. Wright Mills, "Letter to the New Left," in Pricilla Long, ed., *The New Left: A Collection of Essays* (Boston: Porter Sargent, 1969), 25.

51. Jack Newfield, *A Prophetic Minority* (New York: New American Library, 1966), 83. The membership figure is given in Miller, *"Democracy Is in the Streets,"* 39.

52. Lewis Coser et al., "The Committee of Correspondence: A Statement," Mar. 1960, in Committee of Correspondence Folder, Social Protest Project (SPP), Bancroft. The signators to this statement—including Kenneth Boulding, Paul Goodman, Michael Harrington, S. I. Hayakawa, Robert Heilbroner, Robert Maynard Hutchins, Seymour Melman, Walter Millis, Barrington Moore, Lewis Mumford, Charles Osgood, and Gilbert White—were quite representative of the liberal wing of the peace movement. The Bear Mountain meeting was held on 10–13 March.

53. "Why the Committees of Correspondence?" n.d., ca. spring 1960, Sidney Lens Papers, CHSL; form letter, Stephen Cary et al., 25 May 1960, box 22, SPU Records, SHSW; and Lewis Coser et al., "The Committee of Correspondence: A Statement," Mar. 1960, SPP, Bancroft. Lens used the plural, "Committees," because he assumed a network of local ones such as he tried to create in Chicago. The steering committee of the national committee included a substantial core of pacifists—Stephen Cary, Robert Gilmore, Stewart Meacham, A. J. Muste—and, in addition, H. Stuart Hughes, Russell Johnson, David Riesman, and Harold Taylor.

54. "The Candidates and the Politics of Peace," *Nation,* 6 Feb. 1960, 109–10.

55. Niebuhr, "Foreword," to Harrison Brown and James Real, *Community of Fear* (Santa Barbara, Calif.: Center for the Study of Democratic Institutions, 1960), 5; and John C. Bennett, "How My Mind Has Changed," *Christian Century* 76 (23 Dec. 1959): 1502.

56. Matusow, *The Unraveling of America,* 11. For a perceptive analysis of liberal realism and its adaptability, see also Robert Booth Fowler, *Believing Skeptics.*

57. Theodore H. White, *The Making of a President* (New York: Atheneum, 1961), 117.

58. Board of Directors Policy Statement, "Standards for SANE Membership," 26 May 1960, SANE Washington Logbook 1960–62, SFNO, and Norman Cousins and Clarence Pickett, memo re "Implementation of the May 26th Policy Statement," 29 July 1960, SANE Washington Logbook 1960–62. See Wittner, *Rebels Against War,* 258–61 and, for a full account of the 1960 controversy, Katz, *Ban the Bomb,* 45–64.

59. Sandy Gottlieb to Norman Cousins, 18 Oct. 1960, carton 2, 1977 accession, SANE Records, SCPC.

60. Letter, Robert Gilmore to SANE, 27 June 1960, in *Survival* (11 July 1960): 3, in carton 2, 1977 accession, SANE Records, SCPC; Muste to Alfred Hassler, 3 Jan. 1961, Hassler transfile 2, Fellowship of Reconciliation (FOR) Records, SCPC; Muste, "The Crisis in SANE: Act II," *Liberation* 5 (Nov. 1960): 7–8; and Nathan Glazer, "The Peace Movement in America—1961," *Commentary* (Apr. 1961): 292–93. Pauling at the time was being individually harassed by Dodd's committee. See Katz, *Ban the Bomb,* 52–54, 56–58.

61. *NYT,* 26 May 1960, 11; and U.S. Congress, Senate Internal Security Subcommittee of the Committee on the Judiciary, *Communist Infiltration in the Nuclear Test Ban Movement,* 86th Cong., 2d sess., 1960. That report was contradicted by another from the House Un-American Activities Committee.

62. Sanford Gottlieb, "Summary: Third National Conference of the National Committee for a SANE Nuclear Policy," p. 3, SANE Washington Logbook, 1960–62, SFNO.

63. "Fifteen Years in Hell is Enough!" *Christian Century* 77 (3 Aug. 1960): 892.

64. John F. Kennedy, quoted in Robert A. Divine, *Foreign Policy and Presidential Elections: 1952–1960* (New York: Watts, 1974), 210.

65. The Lesson of the Campaign," *Nation,* 12 Nov. 1960, 357; and "The Candidates and the Politics of Peace," 109.

66. David Alan Rosenberg, "The Origins of Overkill: Nuclear Weapons and American Strategy, 1945–1960," *International Security* 7 (Spring 1983): 66.

67. "Number One Issue," *Commonweal* 73 (11 Nov. 1960): 166.

68. "The Box Score Is the Thing," *Saturday Review* 43 (30 Jan. 1960): 24.

69. TOCSIN statement quoted in "The Contagion of Conviction," *Nation,* 17 Dec. 1960, 466; Glazer, "Peace Movement in America—1961," 296.

70. "The Contagion of Conviction," 466.

71. Jim Peck, "Biggest Civil Disobedience Action," *WRL News* (May–June 1960): 2; and A. J. Muste, "The 500 Who Didn't Hide," *Liberation* 5 (May 1960): 3–4; emphasis in the original.

72. David Reisman and Michael Maccoby, "The American Crisis: Political Idealism and the Cold War," *Commentary* 29 (June 1960): 466.

3. Making a Transition

1. Barry M. Goldwater, *Why Not Victory?: A Fresh Look at American Foreign Policy* (New York: McGraw-Hill, 1962), 152, 154, 159.

2. Richard M. Nixon, Speech in Seattle, Wash., 27 Oct. 1961, in *NYT,* 28 Oct. 1961, 2.

3. The World Law Fund, originally the "Fund for Education Concerning World Peace Through World Law," was a special project of the Institute for International Order. Its sponsors represented mainly leaders in professional fields.

4. "Memorandum Outlining a Major National Campaign to Build Support for Alternatives to the Threat of War as the Central Thrust of American Policy," attached to Norman Thomas form letter, 11 Sept. 1961, folder 5, box 8, SPU Records, SHSW.

5. "Memorandum Outlining . . . ," p. 2; Norman Thomas to Stewart Meacham, 15 Dec. 1961, carton 20, World Without War Council (WWWC) Records, SPP, Bancroft.

6. Midge Decter, "The Peace Ladies," *Harper's,* Mar. 1963, 49; and flyer, "Women, Strike for Peace!" 1 Nov. 1961, Women Strike for Peace (WSP) Records, SHSW; emphasis in the original.

7. Penny Blim, letter to the editor, *Nation,* 13 Jan. 1962, 20.

8. Decter, "Peace Ladies," 48; Elise Boulding, "The Task," *Women's Peace Movement Bulletin* 1 (18 Feb. 1962): 1; Boulding, "What Every Woman Knows," *Women's Peace Movement Bulletin* 1 (19 May 1962): 1. See also the WSP entry in *New University Thought* 2 (Spring 1962): 62.

9. Snell Putney and Russell Middleton, "Some Factors Associated with Student Acceptance or Rejection of War," *American Sociological Review* 27 (Oct. 1962): 658. See Roy Finch, "The New Peace Movement, Part II," *Dissent* 10 (Spring 1963): 140.

10. Memorandum by Leo Szilard to "A Selected Group of Well-Informed Persons," 22 Mar. 1963, box V-4, Leo Szilard Papers, UCSD. Also, see Leo Szilard, "Are We on the Road to War?" *Bulletin of the Atomic Scientists* 18 (Apr. 1962):

23–30; and "'Peace Lobby' Launched," *War/Peace Report* 2 (Aug. 1962): 7. For a full and insightful treatment of Szilard, see Barton Bernstein, "Introduction," in Helen Hawkins et al., eds., *Toward a Livable World: Leo Szilard and the Crusade for Nuclear Arms Control* (Cambridge, Mass.: MIT Press, 1987), xvii–lxxiv.

11. Unger, *The Movement,* 83. Unger assesses the number of student demonstrators as 5,000; Vickers estimates 8,000 in *Formation of the New Left,* 52. The fullest description of the event is in Metzenberg, "Student Peace Union," 74–78.

12. Steven V. Roberts, "'Something Had to Be Done,'" *Nation,* 194 (3 Mar. 1962): 189. Also I. F. Stone, *In A Time of Torment* (New York: Vintage, 1968), 357–59.

13. Dellinger, "Growing Pains in the Anti-War Movement," *Liberation* 7 (Apr. 1962): 15.

14. Michael Harrington, "The New Peace Movement," *New Leader* 14 (20 Aug. 1962), 8.

15. Quotations from "The Port Huron Statement," in Miller, *"Democracy Is in the Streets,"* 361, 333. The complete Statement is accessible in Miller, 329–77, and in Judith Clavir Albert and Steward Edward Albert, eds., *The Sixties Papers: Documents of a Rebellious Decade* (New York: Praeger, 1984), 176–97. See also Kirkpatrick Sale, *SDS* (New York: Vintage, 1974), 49–55.

16. Alfred Hassler to Sidney Lens, 7 Sept. 1962, Sidney Lens Papers, CHSL; and Michael Parker to David McReynolds, n.d. [ca. late Sept. 1962], folder 5, box 6, SPU Records, SHSW.

17. Paul Goodman, "Declaring Peace Against the Governments," in *Drawing the Line: The Political Essays of Paul Goodman,* ed. Taylor Stoehr (New York: Dutton, 1979), 124; David Dellinger, "Growing Pains," 14; and see Goodman, "'Getting Into Power': The Ambiguities of Pacifist Politics," *Liberation* 7 (Oct. 1962): 5.

18. Riesman to Altbach, 8 Aug. 1962, SPU Records, SHSW; and see Harrington, "New Peace Movement," 8.

19. Finch, "New Peace Movement, Part II," 145.

20. "The Political Peace Race," *War/Peace Report* 2 (Sept. 1962): 9; and Paul Booth, *Peace Politics: A Study of the American Peace Movement and the Politics of the 1962 Congressional Elections* (Ann Arbor, Mich.: Peace Research and Education Project, sponsored by the Swarthmore College Peace Research Committee, Feb. 1964), 51.

21. *NYT,* 2 Mar. 1962, 5; and *NYT,* 18 Apr. 1962, 22.

22. *NYT,* 26 Mar. 1962, 18; and Goldwater, *Why Not Victory,* 162.

23. SANE, "The U.S.-Cuban Crisis," 24 Oct. 1962, carton 7, WWWC Records, SPP, Bancroft.

24. Later researchers found that hardly 2 percent of students actively asserted their views during the crisis and that a solid majority of the overwhelmingly proadministration students believed that those few dissenters were justified in protesting. Mark Chesler and Richard Schmuck, "Student Reactions to the Cuban Missile Crisis and Public Dissent," *Public Opinion Quarterly* 28 (Fall 1963): 471, 476.

25. National Information Memo, no. 15, 4 Nov. 1962, 1, WSP Records, SHSW.

26. H. Stuart Hughes, "On Being a Candidate," *Commentary* (Feb. 1963): 125; Jerome Grossman, "Is Politics a Legitimate Activity for Pacifists?: 'By All Means!'" *Fellowship* 29 (1 May 1963): 22; Norman Thomas, *Post War World Council Newsletter* (Nov. 1962): 4.

27. Memorandum by Norman Thomas, 13 Nov. 1962, box 1, Turn Toward Peace (TTP) Records, SCPC; and Donald B. McKelvey, "Random Thoughts After Cuba," SPU *Discussion Bulletin* 4 (Spring 1963), box 25a, SPP, Bancroft; National Infor-

mation Memo, no. 15, 4 Nov. 1962, 2, WSP Records; and Harold Taylor, "Cuba and the Peace Movement," Dec. 1962, Cuba folder, carton 15, WWWC Records, SPP, Bancroft.

28. Jack Newfield, "The Cuban Crises and the Peace Movement," *Common Sense* 4 (1 Dec. 1962): 2.

29. National Information Memo, no. 15, 4 Nov. 1962; 3, WSP Records, SHSW (emphasis in the original); Tom Hayden, "Cuba and the USA," *Common Sense* 4 (1 Dec. 1962): 12.

30. *Washington Witness: The Newsletter of The Peace Action Center* 18 (Nov. 1962): 1; and Merton to Dan Berrigan, 27 Nov. 1962, Daniel and Philip Berrigan Papers, Cornell.

31. Norman Cousins, *The Improbable Triumvirate: John F. Kennedy, Pope John, Nikita Khrushchev* (New York: Norton, 1972), 78–110; Milton Katz, *Ban the Bomb,* 83. For a full account of the negotiations from 1954 to 1963, see Harold Karan Jacobson and Eric Stein, *Diplomats, Scientists, and Politicians: The United States and the Nuclear Test Ban Negotiations* (Ann Arbor: Univ. of Michigan Press, 1966).

32. The speech is reproduced in Allan Nevins, ed., *The Burden and the Glory: John F. Kennedy* (New York: Harper and Row, 1964), 53–56.

33. Cousins, *The Improbable Triumvirate,* 135, 132.

34. I. F. Stone, "Why and How Did Peace Suddenly Break Out?" *I. F. Stone's Bi-Weekly* 11 (2 Sept. 1963): 1.

35. Quoted in Milton Katz, "Peace, Politics and Protest," 189; Grossman, "Editorial," 2; "First Step—To Where?" *Bulletin of the Atomic Scientists* 19 (Oct. 1963): 2.

36. Quoted from Stewart Alsop and Charles Bartlett, "In Time of Crisis," *Saturday Evening Post,* Dec. 1962, 20.

37. Charles Bolton, "A Program for the Future," *Nation,* 2 Nov. 1963, 14; Homer Jack, "Next Steps in the American Peace Movement," SANE Washington Logbook, SFNO, 1963.

38. Vickers, *Formation of the New Left,* 52; Philip Altbach, "The Quiet Campus," *New Leader* 46 (5 Aug. 1963): 12. A nominal SPU office continued for a few years.

39. Eleanor Garst, National Information Memo, no. 2, 3 Oct. 1963: 1–2, WSP Records, SHSW.

40. Milton Katz, *Ban the Bomb,* 87–89. Cousins remained on SANE's national board, and Pickett was named an honorary sponsor. Donald Keys moved up from his position as program secretary, as Jack became director of the Department of Social Responsibility of the Unitarian Universalist Association of the United States and Canada, although he remained on SANE's board.

41. King quotation from *NYT,* 5 Aug. 1962, sec. 6, p. 11.

42. *NYT,* 16 July 1963, 1; 6 May 1963, 59.

43. *NYT,* 15 Nov. 1963, 34.

44. Sanford Gottlieb, quoted in Milton Katz, "Peace, Politics and Protest," 198–99.

45. David McReynolds, quoted in Neil H. Katz, "Radical Pacifism and the Contemporary American Peace Movement: The Committee for Nonviolent Action, 1957–1967," 143–44.

46. Memorandum by Norman Thomas, 9–10 March, 1963, pp. 2–3, carton 3, WWWC records, SPP, Bancroft.

47. Thomas, "Peace Demonstrations: Evaluation with Recommendations," 7 June 1963, p. 3, SANE Washington Logbook, 1963, SFNO; and Robert Pickus, quoted in Steve Thiermann "To Those Concerned," 19 Nov. 1963, carton 3, WWWC Records, SPP, Bancroft; emphasis in the original. For a useful summary

analysis of the state of organized peace activism in 1963, see Charles Bolton, "A Program for the Future," *Nation,* 2 Nov. 1963, 179–81.

48. *America and the New Era* (SDS pamphlet, June 1963), 14; and Bacciocco, *The New Left in America,* 132.

49. Richard Flacks, "Some Thoughts on the Current Scene," *PREP Newsletter,* no. 1 (May 1963): 10, in carton 4, WWWC Records, SPP, Bancroft.

50. Donald Widman, "Politics and Peace: An Answer to Carleton," SPU *Discussion Bulletin* 4 (Fall 1963): 41, box 25a, SPP, Bancroft.

PREP signified the Peace Research and Education Project, an SDS operation which originated during winter 1962–63. Directed by Richard Flacks, a graduate student in sociology at the University of Michigan, PREP served as a clearinghouse for international information and a hothouse for SDS foreign policy ideas. Sale, *SDS,* 82, 152–55.

51. "The Test Ahead," *Progressive* 27 (Sept. 1963): 5; emphasis in the original.

52. Notes, Turn Toward Peace national staff meeting, 9–10 Sept. 1963, p. 2, attached to form letter by Joe Tuchinsky and Charles Tupper, 17 Sept. 1963, carton 20, WWWC Records, SPP, Bancroft.

53. Flacks, "Some Thoughts on the Current Scene," 9; and Wini Breines, *The Great Refusal: Community and Organization in the New Left: 1962–1968* (New York: Praeger, 1982), 16.

54. Harrington, "New Peace Movement," 7.

55. Charles D. Bolton, "Alienation and Action: A Study of Peace Group Members," *American Journal of Sociology* 78 (Nov. 1972), 540, 557; and Finch, "New Peace Movement, Part II," 139.

56. Allen Ginsberg, "Howl," in Ginsberg, *Allen Ginsberg: Collected Poems, 1947–1980* (New York: Harper and Row, 1984), p. 126.

57. See Theodore Adorno, *The Authoritarian Personality* (New York: Harper and Row, 1950); Erich Fromm, *Escape from Freedom* (New York: Holt, Rinehart and Winston, 1941); Lewis Coser and Irving Howe, *The American Communist Party* (Boston: Beacon, 1957); Clinton Rossiter, *Marxism: The View from America* (New York: Harcourt, 1960); Daniel Bell, *The End of Ideology* (New York: Collier, 1961); and, for a perceptive treatment of the liberal preoccupation with ideology, Fowler, *Believing Skeptics.*

58. Fromm, *The Sane Society* (New York: Rinehart, 1955), 357.

59. Pickus, "Speak Truth to Power: A Revolutionary Approach in the Search for Peace," *Progressive* (Oct. 1955), 8.

60. Cousins, quoted in Divine, *Blowing on the Wind,* 151; and Muste, "Getting Rid of War," in Nat Hentoff, ed., *The Essays of A. J. Muste* (New York: Simon and Schuster, 1967), 387–89.

61. Lewis Mumford, *In the Name of Sanity* (New York: Harcourt, 1954), 3; Robert Steed, "Dorothy Day Among Pacifists Jailed," *Catholic Worker* 24 (July–Aug. 1957): 1.

62. C. Wright Mills, *The Causes of World War III,* 47, 81; and Mills, "Program for Peace," *Nation,* 7 Dec. 1957, 420, 424.

63. *Post War World Council Newsletter* (May 1961): 3.

64. "Howl," in *Collected Poems,* 131.

65. Mumford, *In the Name of Sanity,* 5.

66. Mills, *The Causes of World War III,* 48, 74, 76.

67. Bigelow, *Voyage of the Golden Rule,* 47, 112.

68. Roberts, " 'Something Had to Be Done'," *Nation,* 3 Mar. 1962, 189.

69. Ralph E. Lapp, *Kill and Overkill: The Strategy of Annihilation* (New York: Basic Books, 1962), 154. See also his critique of technological-political elites in

The New Priesthood: The Scientific Elite and the Uses of Power (New York: Harper and Row, 1965).

70. Flyer, "Student Action: For a Turn Toward Peace," 16–17 Feb. 1962, folder 11, box 8, SPU Records, SHSW; emphasis in the original.

71. "The Port Huron Statement," Miller, *'Democracy Is in the Streets,"* 334.

72. Paul Goodman, "Declaring Peace Against the Governments," 125; and Thomas Merton, "Peace: A Religious Responsibility," in *Breakthrough to Peace* (New York: New Directions, 1962), 102.

73. Thomas Merton, *The Nonviolent Alternative* (New York: Farrar, Straus and Giroux, 1971), 130.

74. Ibid., 161.

75. Lewis Mumford, "The Morals of Extermination," *Atlantic Monthly,* Oct. 1959, 40; and Stephen Carey and Robert Pickus, "Rejoinder," *Progressive* 19 (Oct. 1955): 24.

76. Stewart Meacham, "The Voice of the People," *Nation,* 21 Feb. 1959, 162.

77. Mike Parker and Bill Caspery to Allen Brick, 21 Oct. 1960, folder 3, box 1, SPU Records, SHSW.

78. Arthur Waskow to David Riesman, 7 June 1962, box 14, Arthur Waskow Papers, SHSW.

79. The HUAC incident is treated as formative in the rise of the Berkeley New Left in Bacciocco, *The New Left in America,* 26–27; Miller, *'Democracy Is in the Streets,"* 46; and Unger, *The Movement,* 45–46. *Operation Correction* is not mentioned.

80. "The Port Huron Statement," in Miller, *'Democracy Is in the Streets,"* 374.

81. Regarding this aspect of black power (and pentecostal) movements, see Luther P. Gerlach and Virginia H. Hine, *People, Power, Change: Movements of Social Transformation* (Indianapolis: Bobbs-Merrill, 1970), esp. 99–109.

82. Norman Cousins, *Present Tense: An American Editor's Odyssey* (New York: McGraw-Hill, 1967), 266.

83. Bigelow, *Voyage of the Golden Rule,* 47, 112; Baez, quoted in "Joan Baez Gets Award," *CTA Reports* 3, no. 8 (Nov. 1983): 1.

84. Dorothy Hutchinson, "Mother's Day at the A.E.C.," *Christian Century* 76 (6 May 1959): 554; and Jerome D. Frank and Earl H. Hash, "The Making of a Peace Activist," *War/Peace Report* 5 (Apr. 1965): 9.

85. Merton, *Breakthrough to Peace,* 10, 222.

86. "The Port Huron Statement," in Miller, *'Democracy Is in the Streets,"* 332.

87. Sarah Evans, *Personal Politics,* 102; also Cantor, *The Divided Left,* 192.

88. Stanley Aronowitz, "When the New Left Was Young," in Sohnya Sayres et al., eds., *The 60s Without Apology* (Minneapolis: Univ. of Minnesota Press, 1984), 18. See Dick Cluster, "It Did Make a Difference," in Dick Cluster, ed., *They Should Have Served That Cup of Coffee* (Boston: South End Press, 1979), 119; Irwin Unger describes "meaning" as a focal point in *The Movement,* 38–39.

89. John P. Diggins, *The American Left in the Twentieth Century* (New York: Harcourt, 1973), 157.

90. Lawrence Lipton, *The Holy Barbarians* (New York: Messner, 1959), 283, 167, 170.

91. Marty Jezer, *The Dark Ages: Life in the United States, 1945–1960* (Boston: South End Press, 1982), 255.

92. Matusow, *Unraveling of America,* 280–87. See Morris Dickstein, *Gates of Eden: American Culture in the Sixties* (New York: Basic Books, 1977), 3–23, 27.

93. Norman Mailer, *Advertisements For Myself* (New York: Putnam, 1959), 355, 341, 343.

94. Ibid., 353.

95. Allen Ginsberg, quoted in Milton Viorst, *Fire in the Streets: America In the 1960s* (New York: Simon and Schuster, 1979), 75.

96. Paul Goodman, *Growing Up Absurd: Problems of Youth in the Organized System* (New York: Random House, 1956), 188; emphasis in the original.

4. Crystalizing Dissent

1. France occupied and annexed Indochina piecemeal. In 1879, Cochinchina, or the southern colonial region, was transferred to the French Ministry of Colonies, and this is a convenient date from which to trace colonial rule.

2. Bao Dai had succeeded to the throne upon the death of his father, Khai Dinh, in 1925. The young emperor was studying in France, however, and did not return to Vietnam until 1932. He was the nominal ruler of French Indochina from then until the end of World War II, so that his leadership in South Vietnam offered a semblance of legitimacy to that regime.

3. "A Costly Victory in Vietnam," *Life,* 28 Nov. 1960, 30; "Revolt at Dawn," *Time,* 21 Nov. 1960, 27; and "A Billion for Vietnam—For the U.S., Trouble," *U.S. News and World Report,* 28 Nov. 1960, 84.

4. *NYT,* 19 Feb. 1962, 1.

5. *NYT,* 16 Mar. 1962, 1.

6. *NYT,* 25 Apr. 1962, 1.

7. Bernard Fall, quoted in "Vietnam: The Unpleasant Truth," *Newsweek,* 20 Aug. 1962, 40.

8. Hans Morgenthau, "Vietnam—Another Korea?" *Commentary* 33 (May 1962): 374.

9. "Vietnam: The Unpleasant Truth," 40. Bigart's concluding survey was published in *NYT,* 25 July 1962, 1.

10. *NYT,* 28 Nov. 1962, 5.

11. Robert McNamara, "Memorandum for the President," 11 Nov. 1961, *The Pentagon Papers: The Defense Department History of United States Decision-making on Vietnam,* ed. Senator Mike Gravel (Boston: Beacon, 1972), 1: 111; cited hereinafter as *Pentagon Papers.*

12. *NYT,* 8 May 1963, 10.

13. *NYT,* 14 July 1963, sec. 6, p. 2.

14. "Foreign Policy Resolutions," *ADA World Magazine* 18 (May 1963): 3.

15. National Information Memo, no. 2, 28 June 1963, 4, WSP Records, SHSW.

16. Fred Halstead, *Out Now! A Participant's Account of the American Movement Against the Vietnam War* (New York: Monad, 1978), 20–21.

17. SANE National Board, "Policy Statement on Vietnam," 27 Sept. 1963, folder 50, box 4, SPU Records, SHSW; and "The 'Undeclared War' in South Vietnam," *SANE Report* (Oct. 1963), in SANE Action folder, SANE Washington Logbook, FSNO, 1963.

18. SPU form letter to all chapters, n.d., ca. Oct. 1963, folder 19, box 2, SPU Records, SHSW; Halstead, *Out Now!* 22.

19. "Algeria, Vietnam and Punta Del Este," *Monthly Review* 13 (Mar. 1962): 500; Annalee Stewart, "Undeclared War in Vietnam," *Four Lights* 22 (June 1962): 3; and "Vietnam Again," *New Republic,* 15 Dec. 1962, 5.

20. National Information Memo, no. 2, 28 June 1963, 4, WSP Records, SHSW; "Disaster in Installments," *Nation* 29 Jan. 1963, 43; and Robert Halfhill, in SPU *Discussion Bulletin* 4 (Fall 1963): 42; SANE resolution passed in November 1963, quoted in Milton Katz, *Ban the Bomb!* 95.

21. "Rome and Saigon," *Christian Century* 80 (4 Sept. 1963): 1067; and "Viet

Crisis Is Religious," *Christian Century* 80 (11 Sept. 1963): 1093; 10 Sept. 1963, *Congressional Record,* 88th Cong., 1st sess., 16599.

Years later, the Rev. Donald Harrington recalled that the starting point of the Vietnam Ministers Committee was when he saw the front page *New York Times* picture of the self-immolation of a Buddhist monk. "It caused me to feel that we simply were not being told the truth about what was happening there, and about what would come of our sending so-called 'advisers' to South Vietnam." Donald Szantho Harrington, conversation with Charles DeBenedetti, 5 May 1982.

22. 10 Sept. 1963, *Congressional Record,* 88th Cong., 1st sess., 16488.

23. Gail Paradise, "Coup Fells Diem," *SPU Bulletin* (Nov. 1963): 7, SPP-Bancroft; also, "What If the People, After Diem's Overthrow, Vote for Peace?" *I. F. Stone's Weekly* 11 (11 Nov. 1963): 2.

24. Walter Lippmann, "Mr. Kennedy on Viet-Nam," 5 Sept. 1963, reel 10, Walter Lippmann Papers, Yale.

25. *NYT,* 25 Feb. 1963, 1; "Viet Nam and Southeast Asia," *Report to the Committee on Foreign Relations, United States Senate* (Washington, D.C.: GPO, 1963), 9.

26. Lippmann, "Mr. Kennedy on Viet-Nam." Lippmann's views are well developed in his regular columns, Mansfield's in his speeches and committee reports.

27. "Reunifying Vietnam," *New Republic,* 14 Sept. 1963, 5.

28. *Post War World Council Newsletter* (May 1961): 3.

29. "Where Swarming Gnats Can Devour a Giant," *I. F. Stone's Weekly* 10 (21 May 1962): 1; Norman Thomas, in *Post War World Council Newsletter* (June 1962): 1.

30. "Disaster in Installments," 43.

31. WILPF statement to Kennedy et al., "Vietnam," 9 May 1962, in box 14b, Records of the U.S. Section, Women's International League for Peace and Freedom (WILPF) Records, SCPC; and editors, "Barbed Wire and Bamboo," *New University Thought* 2 (Autumn 1962): 4.

32. "Where Swarming Gnats," 1; also Howard Zinn, *SNCC: The New Abolitionists* (Boston: Beacon, 1965), 85.

33. Norman Thomas Speech MSS, 18 Oct. 1963, p. 5, at SPU-SDS meeting, box 1, Post War World Council Records, SCPC; and "No-Win in Vietnam," *New Republic,* 5 Oct. 1963, 6.

34. Quoted from Roger Hagan, "The Ngos," *Correspondent,* no. 29 (Nov.–Dec. 1963): 9 (Hagan was a Harvard-based critic with considerable influence in SDS); "Barbed Wire and Bamboo," 13.

35. Chapel Hill SPU to SPU National Office, 9 Oct. 1963, folder 3, box 2, SPU Records, SHSW.

36. "Vietnam—New Start," *New Republic,* 16 Nov. 1963, 3.

37. Gail Paradise, "Coup Fells Diem," 7; also "What If the People," 2.

38. *NYT,* 20 July 1964, 1.

39. *Pentagon Papers,* 2: 304–5.

40. *NYT,* 25 March 25, 1; and 20 Aug. 1964, 12.

41. *NYT,* 19 Feb. 1964, 1; *Pentagon Papers,* 2: 325; and Henry Cabot Lodge to Averell Harriman, 3 Mar. 1964, Memorandums for the President folder, box 1, McGeorge Bundy Aides Files, National Security File (NSF), LBJL; the spelling is Viet-nam in the original.

42. *Washington Post* (cited hereinafter as *WP*), 30 Mar. 1964, microfilm: Vietnam, 63 Public Opinion: Mar.–Dec., 1964, DOD; and Lloyd A. Free and Hadley Cantril, *The Political Beliefs of Americans: A Study of Public Opinion* (New Brunswick, N.J.: Rutgers Univ. Press, 1967), 59–60.

43. "Ain't It Awful," *Nation,* 24 Feb. 1964, 117; and Ed Snyder, "The Detente Between the United States and the Soviet Union," 18 June 1964, box 4, WSP Records, SHSW.

44. A. J. Muste and David McReynolds, "Memo on Vietnam: A Statement Prepared for the War Resisters League," attached to Charles Bloomstein form letter, 7 Aug. 1964, carton 15, WWWC Records, SPP, Bancroft.

45. *NYT,* 11 July 1964, 1–2; Sanford Gottlieb, letter to the editor, in *WP,* 27 July 1964, DOD; and Lippmann, "Our Commitment in Viet-Nam," 28 May 1964, reel 10, Lippmann Papers, Yale.

46. Mike Mansfield, memorandum for the President, 6 Jan. 1964, Memorandums for the President folder, box 1, McGeorge Bundy Aides files, NSF, LBJL.

47. Lippmann, "The Asian Balance of Power," 2 June 1964, reel 10, Lippmann Papers, Yale; and 3 June 1964, *Congressional Record* (cited hereinafter as *Cong. Rec.*), 88th Cong., 1st sess., 12399; also, Ronald Steel, *Walter Lippmann and the American Century* (New York: Vintage, 1981), 549–50.

48. Saul Schindler to Ernest Gruening, 25 Mar. 1964, printed in 28 Apr. 1964, *Cong. Rec.,* 88th Cong., 2d sess., 9297.

49. Stone, *In A Time of Torment,* 191.

50. 3 June 1964, *Cong. Rec.,* 88th Cong., 2d sess., 12609.

51. Lippmann, "Finland and Southeast Asia," 11 Feb. 1964, reel 10, Lippmann Papers, Yale; Wayne Morse, 3 June 1964, *Cong. Rec.,* 88th Cong., 2d sess., 12610; *Cong. Rec.,* 88th Cong., 2d sess., 12610; and Ernest Gruening, 10 Mar. 1964, in *Cong. Rec.,* 88th Cong., 2d sess., 4835.

52. Norman Thomas, Report of the Committee on Re-Evaluation, 30 June 1964, p. 1, box 1, TTP Records; Robert Gilmore to Anne Farnsworth, 8 June 1964, carton 1, WWWC Records, SPP, Bancroft. See also Roger Hagan, "The American Peace Movement: What Is It? What Has It Accomplished?" *Vital Issues* 13 (Feb. 1964), carton 18, WWWC Records; and Jerome Grossman, "The 'Peace' Crowd," *Nation,* 20 Jan. 1964, 66.

53. Paul Booth, "PREP Report," in *SDS Bulletin* 2 (July 1964), 6, in box 29b, SPP, Bancroft.

54. Tom Hayden and Richard Flacks, "The Peace Movement: New Possibilities?" n.d. [ca. mid-1964], 6; Dick Flacks to SDS work lists re: "New Crisis in Vietnam," 29 Feb. 1964, box 8, Records of the Students for a Democratic Society (SDS Records), SHSW; Booth, "PREP Report," 5–6.

55. Martin Boksenbaum, quoted in Michael Ferber and Staughton Lynd, *The Resistance* (Boston: Beacon, 1971), 19; cf. "Burn Draft Cards," *WRL News* (May–June 1964): 1. Armed Forces Day was 16 May in 1964.

56. Ferber and Lynd, *The Resistance,* 17–20; Nancy Zaroulis and Gerald Sullivan, *Who Spoke Up? American Protest Against the War in Vietnam, 1963–1975* (Garden City, N.Y.: Doubleday, 1984), 225.

57. "Student Committee to Send Medical Aid to the Front of the National Liberation of South Vietnam Statement," *SDS Bulletin* 2 (May 1964): 17; also, *NYT,* 15 Apr. 1964, 5.

58. *NYT,* 26 Apr. 1964, 3; Zaroulis and Sullivan, *Who Spoke Up?* 19; and 5 June 1964, *Cong. Rec.,* 88th Cong., 2d sess., 12842.

59. In July, pollster Eugene Gilbert, director of the respected Gilbert Youth Service, reported that one in three American teenagers would object to taking orders to fight in Vietnam, and that "a large minority—39 percent—thought the stand of the . . . [May Second Movement] accurately reflected the feelings of teenagers in general." Gilbert noted, however, that the majority of teenagers who objected to U.S. policy in Vietnam believed that policy "was not decisive enough."

Philadelphia Inquirer (cited hereinafter as *PI*), 24 July 1964, DOD. Regarding the political composition of the M2M Movement (often designated M-2-M) and the PLP role in it, see "Students Act for Protest on Vietnam," *National Guardian,* 21 Mar. 1964, 3; and Halstead, *Out Now!* 22–23.

60. Progressive Labor Party statement, Jan. 1965, quoted in Paul Jacobs and Saul Landau, eds., *The New Radicals: A Report With Documents* (New York: Vintage, 1966), 184.

61. Homer Jack form letter, 16 Mar. 1964, carton 20, WWWC Records, SPP, Bancroft.

62. Gail Paradise, "Our Choice in Vietnam," *SPU Bulletin* (May 1964): 7.

63. Alfred Hassler to Mr. and Mrs. Ivan Potts, 15 June 1964, Hassler transfile 4, FOR Records, SCPC. Also, "Vietnam: Symptom of a Bankrupt Policy," FOR national council meeting, 9–11 Apr. 1964, p. 1, folder: FOR, carton 12, WWWC Records, SPP, Bancroft; and "Vietnam," *Fellowship* 30 (May 1964): 2.

64. *NYT,* 6 Aug. 1964, 8. The resolution is printed in full.

65. *Los Angeles Times,* 10 Aug. 1964; and *PI,* 24 Aug. 1964, DOD.

66. *NYT,* 30 Sept. 1964, 1; and *NYT,* 25 Oct. 1964, 50; *NYT,* 27 Oct. 1964, 21; and *NYT,* 11 Sept. 1964, 19.

67. "Vietnam: The Only Answer," *Progressive* 28 (Sept. 1964): 3; and "What Few Know About the Tonkin Bay Incidents," *I. F. Stone's Weekly* 12 (24 Aug. 1964): 4.

68. David McReynolds, "Memo on Atlantic City Democratic Convention and Pacifist Action Re South Vietnam," n.d. [ca. late Aug. 1964], carton 8, WWWC Records, SPP, Bancroft; *NYT,* 18 Oct. 1964, sec. 4, p. 5.

69. David McReynolds, "I SHALL Vote for Johnson," *WRL News* no. 127 (Sept.-Oct. 1964): 2; emphasis in the original.

70. *Pentagon Papers,* 2: 350; 3: 191.

71. Mansfield, memorandum for the President, 9 Dec. 1964, Name File, NSF, LBJL.

72. "SANE Statement of Policy for 1964," attached to minutes of SANE national board meeting, 17 Dec. 1964, p. 16, SANE Washington Logbook, SFNO; emphasis in the original.

73. David McReynolds, "After the Election," *WRL News* (Nov.–Dec. 1964): 2.

74. A. J. Muste to Dwight Macdonald, 27 Jan. 1965, box 35, series 1, Dwight Macdonald Papers, Yale; emphasis in the original.

75. "Vietnam—The Continuing Campaign," *CNVA Bulletin,* 5 (25 Jan. 1965): 1; and *National Guardian,* 12 Dec. 1964, 7.

76. PREP Report, n.d., ca. late Dec. 1964, box 29, SDS Records; Sale, *SDS,* 170–72; Halstead, *Out Now!* 30–32. SDS took on singular sponsorship for an anti-Vietnam march in Washington mainly in order to finesse "the old question of how can we maintain our traditional position of openness to all sectors of the left, but avoid having the March destroyed or rendered ineffective by too close association with sectarian left-wing groups." C. Clark Kissinger, "SDS National Council," *SDS Bulletin* 3 (Jan. 1965): 15.

77. Stone, *In A Time of Torment,* 194. For SDS's growing emphasis on anti-imperialism, see Paul Potter, "Which Way SDS?" *SDS Bulletin* 3 (Oct. 1964), 25; and Bacciocco, *New Left in America,* 161.

78. "U.S. Press and Vietnam," *National Guardian,* 17 Oct. 1963, 2. "There is little for foreigners to 'win' in Vietnam," wrote another critic, "for, short of destroying perhaps a majority of the Vietnamese people, it is unlikely that we will ever succeed in moulding a Vietnam tailored to American desires." Robert S. Browne, "The Civil War in Vietnam," *Liberation* (Sept. 1964): 10.

79. "Vietnam—No Exit? *New Republic,* 7 Mar. 1964, 3; "The Serpent in the Garden," *Nation,* 11 May 1964, 469; and Lippmann, "On Viet-Nam," 22 Dec. 1964, reel 10, Lippmann Papers, Yale.

5. Consolidating Opposition

1. Joan Baez, *And a Voice to Sing With: A Memoir* (New York: Summit, 1987), 117.

2. "Annual Message to the Congress on the State of the Union, Jan. 4, 1965," in *Public Papers of the Presidents of the United States: Lyndon B. Johnson, 1965* (Washington, D.C.: GPO, 1966), 1: 3.

3. *Aggression from the North: The Record of North Viet-Nam's Campaign to Conquer South Viet-Nam* (Washington, D.C.: U.S. Department of State, Feb. 1965). This document was effectively challenged by I. F. Stone, among others. Even McGeorge Bundy regarded it in retrospect as inept. See Melvin Small, *Johnson, Nixon, and the Doves* (New Brunswick, N.J.: Rutgers Univ. Press, 1988), 32–33.

4. George C. Herring, *America's Longest War: The United States and Vietnam, 1950–1975* (New York: Wiley, 1979), 130.

5. J. T. McNaughton, 27 Jan. 1965, in *Pentagon Papers,* 3: 687; McGeorge Bundy to President Johnson, 14 July 1965, M. Bundy—Memos to the President, vol. 12, July 1965, box 4, Memorandums for the President File, NSF, LBJL.

6. Bundy, memorandum for the President, "Comments on Vietnam for Your Newspaper Visitor [Lippmann]," 19 Feb. 1965, Memorandums for the President, Aides Files, NSF, LBJL; and Bundy, 7 Feb. 1965, in *Pentagon Papers,* 3: 309.

7. Bundy, memorandum for the President, "The Demonologists Look at the Noise from Hanoi, Peking and Moscow," 20 Apr. 1965, Deployment of Major U.S. Forces to Vietnam, vol. 3, tab 44a in National Security Council History File, NSF, LBJL.

8. Bundy, in *Pentagon Papers,* 3: 313.

9. Gallup poll, in *WP,* 16 Feb., 7 Apr. 1965, n.p., microfilm: Vietnam: 63 Public Opinion: January 1965–July 1968, DOD. Harris polls from Feb. through Apr. showed a fairly consistent plurality for holding the line, with a shift from those "not sure" to both negotiating out and carrying the war to the North. H. Schuyler Foster, *Activism Replaces Isolationism: U.S. Public Attitudes, 1940–1975* (Washington: Foxhall Press, 1983), 283.

10. Mother Mary Berchmans, quoted in "Vietnam: The Treacherous Demands," *Worldview* 8 (Mar. 1965): 8.

11. Bundy, memorandum for the President, "Vietnam—Telegrams from the Public," 9 Feb. 1965, box 40, National Security Council History File, NSF, LBJL.

12. Memorandum, Chester Cooper to McGeorge Bundy, "Review of White House Mail on Vietnam," 6 Apr. 1965, Vietnam Memos folder, 1–20 Apr. 1965, box 16, National Country File/Vietnam, NSF, LBJL. According to a White House analysis, the great majority of letters came from New York City and California, followed by New England (especially in Boston area), Michigan and the Middle Atlantic states, with scarcely 18 percent submitted from the rest of the country.

13. "Many Demonstrations Decry Slaughter," *Four Lights* 25 (Mar. 1965): 1; *NYT,* 11 Feb. 1965, 6.

14. E. Raymond Wilson, *Uphill For Peace: Quaker Impact on Congress* (Richmond, Ind.: Friends United Press, 1975), 289.

15. Stewart Meacham, "Conference With a High Government Official Regarding U.S. Policy Toward Vietnam," 23 Apr. 1965, p. 5, Peace Education Division (PED) files, American Friends Service Committee (AFSC) Records, AFSC.

16. "Vietnam: A Time for Common Sense and Free Discussion," *SANE Action* (17 Apr. 1965), in SANE Washington Logbook, SFNO, 1964–65.

17. "Ideologue: Vietnam," *Free Student,* no. 2, n.d. [ca. Apr. 1965], p. 4; Daniel Berrigan, "In Peaceable Conflict," *Catholic Worker* 31 (Mar. 1965): 1.

18. "Declaration of Conscience," *Catholic Worker* 31 (Feb. 1965): 2; Halstead, *Out Now!* 67, n. 8.

19. Paul Booth to John Clayden, 4 Mar. 1965 box 33, SDS Records, SHSW.

20. Jack A. Smith, "Vietnam Protests Grow," *CNVA Bulletin* 5 (27 Feb. 1965): 2.

21. "An Appeal to Our Students," attached to "University of Michigan Teach-In Protest on the War in Viet Nam," 24 Mar. 1965, Vietnam Teach-in folder, SPP, Bancroft.

22. Marc Pilisuk, "The First Teach-in: An Insight into Professional Activism," *Correspondent,* no. 34 (Spring-Summer 1965): 8; also Louis Menashe and Ronald Rodosh, eds., *Teach-ins: U.S.A.: Reports, Opinions, Documents* (New York: Praeger, 1967), 11; and Arnold Kaufman, "A Short History of the University of Michigan Teach-in," 24–25 Mar. 1965, box 4, Arnold Kaufman Papers, BLMH.

23. "Campus, '65," *Newsweek,* 22 Mar. 1965, 53. See Richard E. Peterson, *The Scope of Organized Student Protest in 1964–65* (Princeton: Educational Testing Service, 1966).

24. Small, *Johnson, Nixon, and the Doves,* 37–38.

25. Ibid., 40.

26. Memorandum, Chester L. Cooper for Jack Valenti, "The Campus Critics and U.S. Vietnam Policy," 24 Apr. 1965, box 215, White House Central File, National Security-Defense File (EX ND 19/CO 312), LBJL; emphasis in the original.

27. See, for example, Wilson, *Uphill for Peace,* 489.

28. Charles Bloomstein, "Roundup on Vietnam," 5 Mar. 1965, carton 3, Turn Toward Peace, WWWC Records, SPP, Bancroft.

29. "Is the Escalator Out of Control? *SANE Action* (25 Mar. 1965): 2, SANE Washington Logbook, 1964–65.

30. "The National Apathetic," *Nation,* 29 Mar. 1965, 321; and Sidney Lens to Norman Thomas, 11 Mar. 1965, Sidney Lens Papers, CHSL.

31. *NYT,* 16 Mar. 1965, 1.

32. Memorandum, Chester L. Cooper to the White House, 13 Apr. 1965, box 41, Deployment of Major U.S. Forces to Vietnam, 1965, in National Security Council History File, NSF, LBJL.

33. Carle Oglesby and Todd Gitlin, "That Bright and Necessary Day of Peace," 8 Apr. 1965, pp. 1–2, carton 8, WWWC Records, SPP, Bancroft.

34. Donald Keys, quoted in Cedrick Belfrage and James Aronson, *Something to Guard: The Stormy Life of the National Guardian, 1947–1967* (New York: Columbia Univ. Press, 1978), 306.

35. Quoted in Miller, *"Democracy Is in the Streets,"* 176.

36. Martin Roysher and Charles Capper, "The March As A Political Tactic," n.d. [ca. Mar. 1965], pp. 2–3, box 9, SDS Records, SHSW.

37. Robert Gilmore to William Hefner, 26 Apr. 1965, box 1, TTP Records, SCPC; and Norman Thomas et al., "Statement on the Student March on Washington," 16 Apr. 1965, carton 2, WWWC Records, SPP, Bancroft.

38. Some estimates were as high as 25,000. Halstead, who based his figures on personal observation or averaged available estimates, gives 20,000. *Out Now!* 40.

39. Paul Potter, "The 'Incredible' War," *National Guardian,* 24 Apr. 1965, 5. See also the evaluations of Potter's speech in Halstead, *Out Now!* 41–43, and Miller, *"Democracy Is in the Streets,"* 232–33.

40. Todd Gitlin, *The Whole World is Watching: Mass Media in the Making and Unmaking of the New Left* (Berkeley: Univ. of California Press, 1980), 27; Sale, *SDS,* 191–99.

41. Quoted in Sale, *SDS,* 214.

42. Quoted in Miller, *"Democracy Is in the Streets,"* 235.

43. Quoted in *Pentagon Papers,* 3: 706.

44. Robert McCloskey, quoted in *Pentagon Papers,* 3: 460.

45. Lippmann, "The Sharpening Predicament in Vietnam," 22 June 1965, reel 10, Lippmann Papers, Yale.

46. Lippmann, "Ordeal of Decision," 8 July 1965, reel 10, Lippmann Papers.

47. George W. Ball, *The Past Has Another Pattern: Memoirs* (New York: Norton, 1982), 432–33. Similarly, when seven leading left intellectuals met with Adlai Stevenson in late June and asked him to resign as UN ambassador in protest against the war, their erstwhile hero declined with the comment, "That's not how we play the game." Thomas Powers, *The War At Home: Vietnam and the American People, 1964–1968* (New York: Grossman, 1973), 52.

48. Quoted in Eric F. Goldman, *The Tragedy of Lyndon Johnson* (New York: Knopf, 1969), 427.

49. Ibid., 450.

50. The committee was formed at a meeting called by Henry J. Cadbury, a Quaker, on 12 April and met with Senator George McGovern. Hassler transfile 4, FOR Records, SCPC.

51. Howard Schomer, "Runaway War or Deadlocked Peace," *Christian Century* 82 (4 Aug. 1965): 958; and 10 Aug. 1965, *Cong. Rec.,* 88th Cong., 1st sess., 19803.

52. "U.S. Policy in Vietnam: A Statement," *Christianity and Crisis* 35 (14 June 1965): 126.

53. Sanford Gottlieb to Benjamin Spock et al., 13 May 1965, folder: Politics, SANE, 1965–67, box 54, Benjamin Spock Papers, Syracuse.

54. Quoted in "Do It Yourself," *Nation,* 21 June 1965, 657–58; also Jack Newfield, "Respectables Fill Garden to Protest Viet War," *Village Voice,* 17 June 1965, 3.

55. Small, *Johnson, Nixon, and the Doves,* 51. Small develops the conflict between President Johnson and McGeorge Bundy over the debate and makes the case that this contributed to the latter's declining influence. Zbigniew Brzezinski and O. Edmund Clubb (both of Columbia University) also participated in the 21 May debate. Arthur Schlesinger, Jr., had been a special assistant to Johnson, 1963–64; Seymour Melman, a professor of industrial engineering at Columbia, had already been critical of the military emphasis in the economy and of the nuclear arms race.

56. "The Formation of the Inter-University Committee and a Bibliography," 1; "The Origins and Purpose of the I.U.C." n.d. [ca. mid-1966], p. 1, box 4, Kaufman Papers, BLMH; and "The Inter-university Committee for a Public Hearing on Viet Nam," Ann Arbor, n.d. [ca. June 1965], carton 2, WWWC Records, SPP, Bancroft.

57. William A. Williams, in Menashe and Radosh, eds., *Teach-ins: U.S.A.,* 189.

58. Joan Wallach Scott, "The Teach-in: A National Movement or the End of an Affair?" *Studies on the Left* 5 (Summer 1965): 85.

59. The Inter-University Committee for a Public Hearing on Vietnam continued with a modest informational program as the Inter-university Committee for Debate on Foreign Policy.

60. Mario Savio, "An End to History," in Mitchell Cohen and Dennis Hale, eds., *The New Student Left: An Anthology* (Boston: Beacon, 1966), 249.

61. The quoted adjectives are Fred Halstead's, in *Out Now!* 55.

62. Editors' preface to *We Accuse: A Powerful Statement of the New Political Anger in America as Revealed in the Speeches Given at the 36-Hour 'Vietnam Day' Protest at Berkeley, California* (Berkeley: Diablo Press, 1965), 1; Jack Newfield, "The Student Left," *Nation,* 10 May 1965, 494.

63. David Dellinger, "The March on Washington and Its Critics," *Liberation* 10 (May 1965): 6; James Petras, "Berkeley's Vietnam," *Liberation* 10 (June 1965): 32. See Robert Scheer and Warren Hinckle, "The 'Vietnam' Lobby," *Ramparts,* July 1965, 24, 21, for an elaborate construction of liberal involvement in Vietnam intervention.

64. Robert Pickus, "Vietnam Day Berkeley," 21 May 1965, transcript of tape recording, 2, box 2, TTP Records, SPP, Bancroft.

65. Norman Thomas, in "Vietnam and the Left: A Symposium," *Dissent* 12 (Autumn 1965): 396; and Thomas, in *We Accuse,* 114.

66. Staughton Lynd, "Coalition Politics Or Nonviolent Revolution?" *Liberation* 10 (June–July 1965): 19–20.

67. Robert Pickus, "Political Integrity and Its Critics," *Liberation* 10 (June–July 1965): 37–38; Alfred Hassler, "Solution," *Fellowship* 31 (Sept. 1965): 2, emphasis in the original.

68. A. J. Muste to Theodore Roszak, 23 Sept. 1965, box 49, A. J. Muste Papers, SCPC.

69. Lippmann, "Can the Question of War Be Debated?" *Newsweek,* 15 Mar. 1965, 23.

70. Commager, quoted in Menashe and Radosh, eds., *Teach-ins U.S.A.,* 323; and McReynolds, "Stanleyville–Saigon–Santo Domingo," *WRL News,* no. 131 (May–June 1965): 3; emphasis in the original.

71. David Dellinger, "Vietnam and the International Liberation Front," *Liberation* 10 (Aug. 1965): 16, 30; Paul Booth to Jeff Segal et al., 20 July 1965, box 8, SDS Records, SHSW; and "'Stop the War,'" *Free Student,* no. 3, n.d. [ca. May 1965], 14.

72. *PI,* 21 June 1965, DOD.

73. Lady Bird Johnson, *A White House Diary* (New York: Holt, Rinehart and Winston, 1970), 262.

74. Memorandum, James Thomson to McGeorge Bundy, "Thoughts on the 'Teach-in,'" 14 May 1965 folder, box 19, McGeorge Bundy, May–June 1965, in Aides File, NSF, LBJL.

75. Minutes of Cabinet Meeting of 18 June 1965, 18 June 1965 Cabinet Meeting folder, p. 33, box 3, Cabinet Papers, LBJL.

76. William Wilcox Robinson, *Los Angeles: A Profile* (Norman: Univ. of Oklahoma Press, 1968), 51–52.

77. "The McComb Anti-War Petition," in Jacobs and Landau, eds., *The New Radicals,* 249.

78. Estimate in Massimo Teodori, ed., *The New Left: A Documentary History* (Indianapolis: Bobbs-Merrill, 1969), 35; Jerry Rubin, "NCCEWVN," *Vietnam Day Committee News* 1 (Aug. 1965): 1; and Rubin, "Oct. 15–16 and the VDC," *Vietnam Day Committee News* 1 (11 Oct. 1965): 1.

79. David Dellinger, in "After Washington . . . Three Views," *CNVA Bulletin* 5 (27 Aug. 1965): 6; also Staughton Lynd and Bill Tabb, "Remarks on the NCC Convention," *Peace and Freedom News,* no. 12 (13 Dec. 1965): 1; and Norma Becker et al., "Call for a Congress of Unrepresented People to Declare Peace in Vietnam," in *ERAP Newsletter,* 14 Aug. 1965, box 12, SDS Records, SHSW.

80. Lynd, quoted in Halstead, *Out Now!* 66–67.

81. The Washington Action Project was a summer antiwar program coordinated by former civil rights leader Robert Moses Parris and CNVA and civil rights activist Eric Weinberger.

82. Memorandum, Donald Ropa and Chester Cooper to McGeorge Bundy, "The Week in Asia," 9 Aug. 1965, p. 2, Cooper File, Name File, NSF, LBJL.

83. "Turning Point for Peace?" *National Guardian,* 21 Aug. 1965, 2.

84. Jack Newfield, "Some Things Unite Them, Some Things Divide Them," *Village Voice,* 19 Aug. 1965, 3, 16.

85. Frank Emspak was a twenty-two-year-old University of Wisconsin student with strong family connections in the Old Left.

86. Milton Mayer, "A Citizen at the White House," *Progressive* 29 (June 1965): 28; emphasis in the original.

87. *The Johnson Presidential Press Conferences* (New York: Earl M. Coleman Enterprises, 1978), 1: 349.

88. In 27 July 1965, Foreign Policy Advisors folder, p. 3, box 1, Meeting Notes File (MNF), LBJL.

89. *NYT,* 30 July 1965, DOD.

90. Steven Smale, quoted in Sam Angeloff, "The Antiwar Marches and How They Happen," *Life,* 10 Dec. 1965, 114; emphasis in the original; also *National Vietnam Newsletter,* no. 2 (12 Aug. 1965), 5, in box 9, SDS Records, SHSW; "August 12 Black Day for Berkeley," *Berkeley Barb,* 13 Aug. 1965, 1.

91. *NYT,* 8 Dec. 1965, 1.

92. Louis Harris, "We Have to Finish the Job," *Newsweek,* 20 Sept. 1965, 27.

93. *WP,* 11 Oct. 1965, DOD.

94. William C. Berman, *William Fulbright and the Vietnam War: The Dissent of a Political Realist* (Kent, Ohio: Kent State Univ. Press, 1988), 44.

95. Christopher Lasch, "New Curriculum for Teach-ins," *Nation,* 18 Oct. 1965, 239.

96. Douglas Dowd to Arnold Kaufman, 29 Oct. 1965, box 4, Kaufman Papers, BLMH; also, Lasch, "New Curriculum for Teach-ins," 240–41.

97. Late in August members of Congress, outraged by highly publicized incidents of draft-card burning, enacted legislation fixing a penalty of five years in prison and up to $10,000 in fines for anyone convicted of destroying Selective Service documents.

98. Quoted in "They March, Doubting They Will Overcome," *New Republic,* 30 Oct. 1965, 9.

99. Rachel Towne to Frank Emspak, 16 Oct. 1965, folder 3, box 13, NCCEWVN Records, SHSW.

100. "Vox Vietnik Fires a Volley of Protests," *Life,* 29 Oct. 1965, 40b; and John K. Jessup, "The Answer to What the Vietniks Call a Moral Issue," *Life,* 29 Oct. 1965, 40d.

101. "And Now the Vietniks," *Time,* 22 Oct. 1965, 25a; and U.S. Senate, Internal Security Committee, "The Anti-Vietnam Agitation and the Teach-in Movement: The Problem of Communist Infiltration and Exploitation," 89th Cong., 1st sess. (Washington, D.C.: GPO, 1965), xiv–xv.

102. Thomas Dodd, in *NYT,* 21 Oct. 1965, 1; Senator Robert Byrd, in *Cong. Rec.,* 89th Cong., 1st sess., 22 Oct. 1965, 28244.

103. Russell, *Cong. Rec.,* 89th Cong., 1st sess., 18 Oct. 1965, 27253; Proxmire, *Cong. Rec.,* 89th Cong., 1st sess., 18 Oct. 1965, 27255.

104. *WP,* 30 Oct. 1965, DOD. Those polled agreed with President Johnson's decision to involve U.S. military forces in Vietnam by 2 to 1, and approved his handling of the war by 58 percent.

105. "Apocalypse," *Fellowship* 31 (Mar. 1965): 2.

106. VDC news release, n.d. [ca. early Oct. 1965], p. 2, International Days of Protest folder, SPP, Bancroft.

107. Renata Adler, "The Price of Peace Is Confusion," *New Yorker,* 11 Dec. 1965, 195; and Saul Landau, "This Must Never Happen Again," *Vietnam Day Committee News* 1 (11 Oct. 1965): 3.

108. Jeanne Riha, in *National Vietnam Newsletter,* no. 4 (9 Sept. 1965), p. 26, box 50, SDS Records, SHSW.

109. Staughton Lynd to Frank Emspak, 16 Nov. 1965, folder 12, box 7, SDS Records.

110. David S. Surrey, *Choice of Conscience: Vietnam Era Military and Draft Resisters in Canada* (Amherst, Mass.: Bergin, 1982), 40.

111. Paul Booth, "Build, Not Burn," 20 Oct. 1965, box 49, SDS Records, SHSW; also in *I. F. Stone's Weekly* 13 (1 Nov. 1965): 2.

112. Neil Haworth, memorandum to CNVA, 21 Oct. 1965, New Left Groups folder, carton 19, WWWC Records, SPP, Bancroft.

113. Dorothy Day to Dwight Macdonald, 29 Oct. 1965, series 1, box 13, Dwight Macdonald Papers, Sterling Library, Yale University; and David McReynolds to Staughton Lynd, 14 April 1969, carton 4, WRL Records, SCPC.

114. Quotations from an interview with Norman Morrison's wife, *Evening Sun* (Baltimore), 25 Nov. 1965, WSP Records, SHSW (in the *Sun's* account, the child was "beside him"); the story Morrison read was published in *I. F. Stone's Weekly* 13 (1 Nov. 1965): 3.

115. McReynolds to Lynd, 14 Apr. 1969.

116. Tom Cornell, "Life and Death on the Streets of New York," *Catholic Worker* 32 (Nov. 1965): 8.

117. *NYT,* 10 Nov. 1965, DOD; also Anthony Towne, "Immolations and Consensus: The Justification of Innocence," *Christian Century* 83 (19 Jan. 1966): 72; and Zaroulis and Sullivan, *Who Spoke Up?* 62.

118. Andrea Dworkin to Frank Emspak et al., 9 Nov. 1965, folder 2, box 8, NCCEWVN Records, SHSW.

119. Michael Locker, "The War and the Draft," 9 Nov. 1965, 4, box 29c, SDS Records, SHSW.

120. *May 2nd Movement Report,* no. 2 (30 Oct. 1965), folder 5, box 12, NCCEWVN Records, SHSW.

121. Frank Emspak to W. L. Husband, 3 Nov. 1965, folder 6, box 7, NCCEWVN Records.

122. Joan Levenson to Jerry Rubin, 8 Nov. 1965, folder 7, box 9, NCCEWVN Records. Levenson was on the NCCEWVN staff.

123. ADA press release, 11 Feb. 1965, Vietnam folder, carton 1, Americans for Democratic Action (ADA) Records, SHSW.

124. Steven M. Gillon, *Politics and Vision: the ADA and American Liberalism, 1947–1985* (New York: Oxford Univ. Press, 1987), 184.

125. Sanford Gottlieb to Clark Kissinger, 31 Aug. 1965, box 31, SDS Records, SHSW; "Washington Mobilization on Vietnam, November 27," *SANE Action,* 7 Sept. 1965, SANE Washington Logbook, SFNO, 1964–65.

126. "Minutes of Ann Arbor Meeting, 18–20 September 1965," p. 2, folder 2, box 1, NCCEWVN Records, SHSW.

127. Snyder, minutes of administrative committee meeting, 30–31 Oct. 1965, 1965 logbook of Friends Committee on National Legislation (FCNL), SCPC.

128. Sanford Gottlieb to Frank Emspak, 31 Oct. 1965, folder 6, box 12, NCCEWVN Records, SHSW.

129. Arthur M. Schlesinger, Jr., to Don Edwards, 21 Oct. 1965, folder: Protest Letters, box 4, ADA Records, SHSW; Irving Howe et al., "The Vietnam Protest,"

New York Review of Books 5 (25 Nov. 1965): 12; Michael Harrington, "Does the Peace Movement Need Communists," *Village Voice,* 11 Nov. 1965, 1.

130. Quoted in "And Now the Soulnik," *Time,* 10 Dec. 1965, 35. Robert Sherrill, "Patriotism of Protest," *Nation,* 13 Dec. 1965, 466.

131. Quoted in Halstead, *Out Now!* 115.

132. Quoted in Powers, *The War At Home,* 92; and "middle Left" quoted from Sherrill, "Patriotism of Protest," 466. Published quickly in several journals and pamphlets, Oglesby's speech became one of the most widely read statements of the early antiwar movement and a minor classic in radical criticism of the war. See "Bankruptcy of the Liberals," *Commonweal* 83 (7 Jan. 1966): 396–400.

133. Sanford Gottlieb, "Final Report," 9 Dec. 1965, March on Washington for Peace in Vietnam folder, carton 3, ADA Records, SHSW.

134. "March for Peace," *Christian Century* 82 (8 Dec. 1965): 1501–2; also "The Biggest Peace Demonstration in the History of Washington," *I. F. Stone's Weekly* 13 (6 Dec. 1965): 2.

135. *WP,* 18 Nov. 1965, DOD. Only 10 percent said that they ever felt any urge to join any public demonstration and, of that number, one-sixth said that they would like to protest against demonstrations.

136. Arnold Kaufman, "The International Days of Protest: A Strategic Disaster," n.d. [ca. Dec. 1965], box 4, Kaufman Papers, BLMH; and John C. Bennett, quoted in *War/Peace Report* 5 (Nov. 1965): 17.

137. Paul Albert and Arthur Waskow to all participants, 20 Dec. 1965, folder 36, drawer 13, Jerome Grossman Papers, BPL.

138. Report on the Convention of the National Coordinating Committee to End the War in Vietnam," n.d., submitted to the National Executive Council of the W. E. B. Du Bois Clubs of America, folder 8, box 10, NCCEWVN Records, SHSW.

139. Andrew Kopkind, "Radicals on the March," *New Republic,* 11 Dec. 1965, 15.

140. Bradford Lyttle, "N.C.C. Convention," *CNVA Bulletin* 5 (13 Dec. 1965): 3.

141. Jerry Rubin, "Proposal for the Future of the National Coordinating Committee," *Peace and Freedom News,* no. 3 (31 Dec. 1965): 2.

142. Frances Prevas, "The Convention: Observations and Reflections," *Crisis* 1 (10 Dec. 1965), 3; also Adler, "The Price of Peace," 195–202.

143. Halstead's detailed account of the NCCEWVN convention reflects a YSA viewpoint, *Out Now!* 93–120.

144. Quotations from "Minutes of a Meeting of People from the South," 24 Nov. 1965, folder 8, box 1, NCCEWVN Records, SHSW.

145. See Todd Gitlin, *The Sixties: Years of Hope, Days of Rage* (New York: Bantam, 1987), esp. 196–221 for an evocative treatment of the youth culture in relation to the political movement.

146. "Allen Ginsberg's Suggestions for November 20: Demonstration of Spectacle As Example of Communication," *VDC-March on Oakland* (19 Oct. 1965), in Michael Rossman, "An Alternative Proposal for November 20," Nov. 1965, p. 3, Vietnam Day Committee folder, SPP, Bancroft.

147. *SDS Bulletin,* special edition, n.d. [ca. Oct. 1965], p. 8, box 29b, SPP, Bancroft.

148. "VDC Reply to Gazette Series," *Berkeley Barb,* 5 Nov. 1965, 1.

149. Ira Sandperl to Marv Davidoff, 5 Nov. 1965, box 50, Muste Papers, SCPC.

150. Michael Rossman, "An Alternative Proposal for November 20," 3.

151. Jonathan Eisen, "Heads You Win, Tails We Lose: A Report on the SDS Convention," in Cohen and Hale, eds., *The New Student Left,* 309. The number of local chapters shot from 40 to 125 in 1965, and membership increased from

1,500 to 4,300. The SDS claimed 10,000 members in Dec. 1965, according to Miller, *"Democracy Is in the Streets,"* 235.

152. Gitlin, quoted in Miller, *"Democracy Is in the Streets,"* 258.

153. Quoted in Eisen, "Heads You Win," 307.

154. Peter Steinberger, "Our Aims in the Anti-War Movement," in "Campus Voice: University of Michigan SDS," 30 Nov. 1965, box 29c, SPP, Bancroft.

155. Prevas, "The Convention," 3.

156. Edward Richer, "Peace Activism in Vietnam," *Studies On The Left* 6 (Jan.–Feb. 1966): 55; emphasis in the original; Prevas, "The Convention," 3.

157. *WP,* 6 Dec. 1965, DOD.

158. *WP,* 13 Dec. 1965, DOD.

159. "Straws in the Wind," *Nation,* 27 Dec. 1965, 514.

160. *WP,* 21 Nov. 1965, p. 22, DOD.

6. Raising the Stakes

1. Memorandum, Hayes Redmon to Bill Moyers, "Public Opinion and Vietnam," 17 Dec. 1965, pp. 4–5, BDM Memos folder, September '65–Mar. '66, box 11, Bill Moyers, Aides File, NSF, LBJL.

2. *WP,* 14 June 1966, and 8 May 1966, DOD.

3. Jerome H. Skolnick, *The Politics of Protest* (New York: Ballantine, 1969), 33.

4. George Kennan, "De-Escalated War: A Necessity," *ADA World Magazine* 1 (Jan. 1966): 2–3; General James M. Gavin, "A Communication on Vietnam," *Harper's,* Feb. 1966, 17–18; see also George McGovern, "We Can Solve the Vietnam Dilemma," *World Federalist* 11 (Nov.–Dec. 1965): 14.

5. "Meeting with Foreign Policy Advisors on Bombing Pause," p. 5, 3 Jan. 1966 folder, box 1, MNF, LBJL.

6. The case for this interpretation seems good, although it remains circumstantial. See Small, *Johnson, Nixon, and the Doves,* 78; and Berman, *William Fulbright,* 56.

7. U.S. Senate, Committee on Foreign Relations, "Supplemental Foreign Assistance Fiscal Year 1966—Vietnam," part 1, 89th Cong., 2d sess. (Washington, D.C.: GPO, 1966), 354; also printed as *The Vietnam Hearings* (New York: Vintage, 1966).

8. "Answers to the Right Questions," *ADA World Magazine* 1 (Mar. 1966): 28M.

9. Walter Lippmann, "War in Asia," *Newsweek,* 14 Mar. 1966, 23; and Lippmann, "The President in the Morass," 4 Jan. 1966, reel 10, Lippmann Papers, Yale.

10. David Nevin, "The Dissent: Its Questions and Attacks on U.S. Involvement in Vietnam," *Life,* 25 Feb. 1966, 56b.

11. Robert F. Kennedy, "A Moderate Proposal: Negotiating from Reason," *ADA World Magazine* 1 (Mar. 1966): 14.

12. "Interview with Arthur M. Schlesinger, Jr." *Playboy,* 13 May 1966, 79; and John K. Galbraith, "A Bankrupt U.S. Policy," *ADA World Magazine* 1 (May 1966): 5M.

13. Quoted in Mitchell Kent Hall, "Clergy and Laymen Concerned About Vietnam: A Study of Opposition to the Vietnam War" (Ph.D. diss., Univ. of Kentucky, 1987), 17.

14. Philip Berrigan to Daniel Berrigan, 13 Jan. 1966, Berrigan Papers; and Hall, "Clergy and Laymen," 11.

15. The first board included 28 Protestants, 7 Jews, and 5 Catholics. Hall, "Clergy and Laymen," 25–26.

16. "Clergy Concerned About Vietnam," *Christian Century* (26 Jan. 1966): 99.

17. Abraham Heschel to Hans Morgenthau, 8 Apr. 1966, box 1, Clergy and Laity Concerned (CALC) Records, SCPC.

18. John C. Bennett to the Rev. John L. McKenzie, 7 Apr. 1966, box 1, CALC Records. A year later the name was changed to Clergy and Laymen Concerned About Vietnam (CALCAV), and in 1973 it became Clergy and Laity Concerned. Because of the continuity of the organization, the acronym CALC is used throughout this work.

19. John C. Bennett, "From Supporter of War in 1941 to Critic in 1966," *Christianity and Crisis* 26 (21 Feb. 1966): 13.

20. Reinhold and Ursula Niebuhr, "The Peace Offensive," *Christianity and Crisis* 25 (24 Jan. 1966): 301.

21. Casey Hayden and Mary King, "Sex and Caste," *Liberation* 11 (Apr. 1966): 35. Also, Caroline Jenness, "Women's March to Bring the Men Home Now," *Bring the Troops Home Now Newsletter* 1 (10 June 1966): 9.

22. Jack Newfield, "New Group Seeks to Wed New Politics to New Left," *Village Voice,* 17 July 1966, 24; and Arthur Waskow to Muste, 30 Mar. 1966, box 52, Muste Papers.

23. Norman Thomas to Roger Baldwin, 2 Mar. 1966, carton 2, 1977 accession, SANE Records; and Newfield, "New Group Seeks," 1.

24. Leon Shull, "Vietnam Key to '66 Politics," *ADA World Magazine,* 21 (Feb. 1966): 4.

25. Mav Davidoff to A. J. Muste and David Dellinger, 7 Jan. 1966, box 43, Muste Papers.

26. "Jerry Rubin's Future Plans," *Berkeley Barb,* 7 Jan. 1966, 2; emphasis in the original. Also printed in Jerry Rubin, "Protest & Power," *VDC News* 1 (28 Jan. 1966): 1.

27. Benjamin Spock to Sidney Lens, 30 Mar. 1966, Lens Papers, CHSL.

28. Richard Cummings, *The Pied Piper: Allard K. Lowenstein and the Liberal Dream* (New York: Grove, 1985), 319.

29. Jim Peck, "My Confrontation with President Johnson," *WIN* 2 (11 Mar. 1966): 2; and Fred Halstead, *Out Now!* 138. The Fifth Avenue Peace Parade Committee estimated 6,000 at the Waldorf-Astoria action.

30. Halstead, *Out Now!* 145. Coordinators were David Dellinger and Norma Becker.

31. Frank Emspak to Dena Clamage, 12 Jan. 1966, folder 5, box 11, NCCEWVN Records, SHSW.

32. Estimated numbers are even harder to gauge than usual, ranging from 100,000 to 200,000.

33. Jerry Rubin, "Alliance for Liberation," *Liberation* 11 (Apr. 1966): 9.

34. "Local Groups," *CNVA Bulletin,* 6 (2 May 1966), 6.

35. Staughton Lynd, "Radical Politics and Nonviolent Revolution," *Liberation* 11 (Apr. 1966): 4; and David Dellinger, "On the New Nonviolence," *WIN* 2 (11 June 1966): 13.

36. Meeting with Foreign Policy Advisors, p. 7, 28 Jan. 1966 folder, box 1, MNF, LBJL; meeting with Foreign Policy Advisors, p. 4, 24 Feb. 1966 folder, box 1, MNF, LBJL; *NYT,* 6 May 1966, 6; and *Public Papers of the Presidents of the United States: Lyndon B. Johnson, 1966* (Washington, D.C.: GPO, 1967), 1: 519.

37. Meeting with Foreign Policy Advisors on Resumption of Bombing, p. 7, 27 Jan. 1966 folder, box 1, MNF, LBJL.

38. Memorandum, Valenti to the President, 25 Jan. 1966, p. 1, Jack Valenti, 1965–1966 folder, box 12, Office Files of the President (OFP), LBJL.

39. *WP,* 19 June 1966, DOD. Of those polled 34 percent agreed that South Vietnamese wanted U.S. forces, 33 percent disagreed, and 28 percent were undecided.

40. *WP,* 3 June 1966, DOD.

41. James Cameron, "The Unquiet Americans," *New Statesmen,* 17 June 1966, 873; and "T. R. B. from Washington," *New Republic,* 25 June 1966, 4.

42. Eugene H. Methvin, "Behind Those Campus Demonstrations," *Reader's Digest,* Jan. 1966, 43.

43. "The Wrong Place," *Time,* 8 Apr. 1966, 28.

44. Jim Peck, "A Taste of Fascism in Our Own Backyard," *WIN* 2 (29 Apr. 1966): 8; Frank Emspak to Howard Schulman, 17 May 1966, folder 5, box 12, NCCEWVN Records, SHSW. See also "Violence and the Anti-war Movement," *Bring the Troops Home Now Newsletter* 1 (10 June 1966): 3.

45. "Open Season on Dissenters," *Christian Century* 83 (20 Apr. 1966): 483; *NYT,* 22 Apr. 1966, 16, and *NYT,* 29. Apr. 1966, 1; Arthur M. Schlesinger, Jr., "McCarthyism is Threatening Us Again," *Saturday Evening Post,* 13 Aug. 1966, 12.

46. J. William Fulbright, *The Arrogance of Power* (New York: Vintage, 1966).

47. Olive Mayer, "Immorality of Napalm Production Found by Aroused Citizenry," *Memo* 4 (June 1966): 7; see Maxine Shaw, "Redwood City Fights Napalm," *Catholic Worker* 32 (May 1966): 1; and "No More Napalm," *Bring the Troops Home Now Newsletter* 6 (20 June 1966): 20–21.

48. *PI,* 18 Apr. 1966, DOD.

49. David McReynolds to A. P. Beautal, 14 June 1966, box 4, WRL Records, SCPC.

50. "Our Intentions in Vietnam," *Commonweal* 84 (22 July 1966), 454; and "Genocide in Vietnam," *Churchman* 80 (Sept. 1966): 4.

51. Owen Lattimore, "The Point Beyond Decency," *Nation,* 21 Feb. 1966, 213.

52. Daniel Berrigan to the Father General, 4 June 1966, Berrigan Papers, Cornell.

53. William Fulbright to Chester Bowles, 17 June 1966, box 330, series 1, Chester Bowles Papers, Yale.

54. John C. Bennett, "It is Difficult to Be an American," *Christianity and Crisis* 26 (25 July 1966): 13, 165; Lippmann, "Heresy at Omaha," *Newsweek,* 18 July 1966, 17; also Steel, *Walter Lippmann,* 575–77.

55. *WP,* 24 July 1966, DOD.

56. Also making the trip were Bradford Lyttle (CNVA), Karl Meyer (*Catholic Worker*), Professor William Davidon (Haverford College), Barbara Deming (*Liberation*), and Sherry Thurber (a student).

57. The point was made by Barrie Thorne, "Resisting the Draft: An Ethnography of the Draft Resistance Movement" (Ph.D. diss., Brandeis Univ., 1971), 164.

58. Included were the AFSC, CORE, FOR, NCCEWVN, SDS, SANE, SNCC, CALC, WSP, WILPF, CNVA, Universities Committee on the Problems of War and Peace, New York Parade Committee, Massachusetts Pax, and Inter-University Committee for Debate on Foreign Policy. The Du Bois Clubs and YSA were not invited, but representatives were accepted.

59. Paul Lodico to Fred Halstead, 26 July 1966, quoted in Halstead, *Out Now!* 190.

60. Letter to "Dear Friend" from Douglas Dowd, 3 Aug. 1966, quoted in Hal-

stead, *Out Now!* 191. The coordination committee, under A. J. Muste, was known as the November 5–8 Mobilization Committee.

61. Joan Levenson, "Cleveland Meeting—July 22, 1966," p. 2, folder 1, box 14, NCCEWVN Records, SHSW.

62. "4-Day Mobilization Timed to Project Vietnam in Elections," *Memo* 5 (Sept. 1966): 2; and press release, n.d. ca. 10–11 Sept. 1966, box 1, National Mobilization Committee (NMC) Records, SCPC.

63. Robert Greenblatt, in "Proceedings, National Leadership Conference, Cleveland, September 10–11," p. 1, box 5, NMC Records. Greenblatt was a young assistant professor of mathematics at Cornell University.

64. Laura Foner, notes during Chicago trip, 13–16 Aug. 1966, folder 11, box 2, NCCEWVN Records, SHSW. Also, "IUC Report," *New Left Notes* 1 (23 Sept. 1966): 7.

65. Sanford Gottlieb to Robert Greenblatt, 14 Nov. 1966, p. 3, box 4, Kaufman Papers, BLMH.

66. Stewart Meacham to Carol Urner, 14 Apr. 1966, Peace Education no. 1, 1966, AFSC Records, AFSC.

67. "Changing Climate," *Time,* 2 Sept. 1966, 12.

68. *NYT,* 6 July 1966, 1; Martin Luther King, Jr., to Walter Reuther, 30 June 1966, folder 18, box 20, Martin Luther King, Jr., Papers, MLKC.

69. SNCC press release, 6 Jan. 1966, WSP Records, SHSW; published version in *National Guardian,* 15 Jan. 1966, 3.

70. Stanley Wise to Archie Brest, 11 Feb. 1966, folder: Vietnam, Student Nonviolent Coordinating Committee Records, box 150, King Papers, MLKC.

71. A. J. Muste to Peter Buch, 14 Aug. 1966, box 42, Muste Papers, SCPC (punctuation in the original, "Civil rights").

72. "SNCC-S.D.S. Joint Draft Statement," *New Left Notes* 1 (8 July 1966): 1; Carmichael, quoted in *National Guardian,* 22 Apr. 1967, 2.

73. Quoted in Marty Jezer, "SNCC Draft Protesters Arrested in Atlanta," *WIN* 2 (5 Nov. 1966): 2, 5.

74. Donaldson, quoted in Susan Goodman, "Changing the Complexion of the Peace Movement," *Village Voice,* 8 Sept. 1966, 2.

75. Peter Buch, "Editor Tours Southwest," *Bring The Troops Home Now Newsletter* 1 (8 Aug. 1966): 7.

76. Remington Rose, letter to the editor, *New Republic,* 3 Sept. 1966, 29.

77. "Hullabaloo at HUAC," *Newsweek,* 29 Aug. 1966, 16; also, "HUAC Hellzapoppin," *New Republic,* 27 Aug. 1966, 6; and "Summer Madness," *Time,* 26 Aug. 1966, 10–11.

78. David McReynolds to Douglas Dowd, 10 Aug. 1966, box 47, Muste Papers, SCPC.

79. Gloria K. Bosait, "No Peace for a Peace Marcher," *Village Voice,* 18 Aug. 1966, 7–8.

80. Bernard Fall, "Viet Nam in the Balance," *Foreign Affairs* 45 (Oct. 1966): 9.

81. Neil Sheehan, "Not a Dove, But No Longer a Hawk," *New York Times Magazine,* 9 Oct. 1966, p. 27; also printed in *Progressive* 30 (Dec. 1966): 23.

82. Richard Goodwin, "The Lengthening Shadow of War," *Christianity and Crisis* 26 (31 Oct. 1966): 239; and Goodwin, "What We Can Do About Vietnam," *New Leader* 49 (7 Nov. 1966): 12.

83. "Half Dove, Half Hawk, and Wholly Opportunist," *I. F. Stone's Weekly* 14 (26 Sept. 1966): 1.

84. Richard Trexler to Office, n.d. [ca. mid-Nov. 1966], folder 9, box 13, NCCEWVN Records, SHSW.

85. Quoted in Lawrence Lader, *Power On the Left: American Radical Movements Since 1946* (New York: Norton, 1979), 233.

86. Quoted in Jack A. Smith, "Rallies for Peace Staged in 50 Cities," *National Guardian,* 12 Nov. 1966, 1.

87. Elliot Borin, "Blown Minds Only VDC Rock Casualties," *Berkeley Barb,* 29 July 1966, 1.

88. Allen J. Matusow, *Unraveling of America,* 297; also Bacciocco, *The New Left in America,* 212–13.

89. Phil Whitten to Joan Levenson, 20 Sept. 1966, folder 1, box 10, NCCEWVN Records, SHSW; Levenson to Whitten, 3 Oct. 1966, folder 1, box 10, NCCEWVN Records.

90. *WP,* 20 Sept. 1966, DOD.

91. Seymour Martin Lipset, "Doves, Hawks, and Polls," *Encounter* 27 (Oct. 1966): 39.

92. *New York World Journal Tribune,* 11 Dec. 1966, DOD; *WP,* 18 Dec. 1966, DOD.

93. "The Painless War," *Nation,* 19 Sept. 1966, 236–37; also "The Draft: The Unjust vs. the Unwilling," *Newsweek,* 11 Apr. 1966, 30.

94. Jack Newfield, "LBJ or RFK? LSD or SDS?" *Village Voice,* 1 Dec. 1966, 28; see also Powers, *The War At Home,* 119–37. Vietnam was the center of electoral attention only in the Detroit suburb of Dearborn, where 51 percent of the voters (mostly from wealthier neighborhoods) supported administration policy and 40 percent (mostly from working-class precincts) favored a cease-fire and U.S. withdrawal in what observers termed "a class vote." "The Dearborn Referendum," *Nation,* 19 Dec. 1966, 659.

95. Minutes of Spring Mobilization Committee meeting, 18 Dec. 1966, box 47, Muste Papers, SCPC.

96. Minutes of Spring Mobilization Committee meeting, 18 Dec. 1966, box 47, Muste Papers; also A. J. Muste, "Mobilize for Peace," *Liberation* 11 (Dec. 19966), 22–25; and Paul Booth, "Cleveland Conference," *New Left Notes* 1 (16 Dec. 1966): 1.

97. Benjamin Spock to Donald Keys et al., 25 Nov. 1966, box 73, SANE Records, SCPC; and Milton Katz, "Peace, Politics and Protest," 230.

98. Homer Jack to Tudja Crowder, 20 Dec. 1966, folder: 1967 SANE, box 9, Spock Papers, Syracuse.

99. Don Newton, "SANE's MSG Seasoning," *WIN* 3 (13 Jan. 1967), 6; emphasis in the original; and *NYT,* 9 Dec. 1966, 33. [MSG referred to Madison Square Garden.]

100. Theodore Sorensen, "The Importance of Being Civil," *Saturday Review,* 26 Nov. 1966, 30.

101. "The Hard-Pressed Pacifist," *Fellowship* 32 (Nov. 1966): 2.

102. Muste, "Mobilize for Peace," 22.

103. Joe Flaherty, "The Puppets for Peace: Abduction at the Cathedral," *Village Voice,* 5 Jan. 1967, 3.

104. Memorandum, Jack Valenti to President Johnson, 18 Sept. 1966, Jack Valenti, 1965–66 folder, box 12, OFP, LBJL. Harry McPherson reported the same finding. McPherson, in Bill Moyers, memorandum to the President, 4 Aug. 1966, BDM Memos, 12 July–August 1966 folder, box 12, OFP, LBJL.

105. *CCCO News Notes* 18 (Mar.–Apr. 1966): 1.

106. *New York World Journal Tribune,* 11 Dec. 1966, DOD; *WP,* 18 Dec. 1966, DOD.

107. Richard W. Schweid, "Non-Cooperators Confront Draft," *Catholic Worker* 33 (Jan. 1967): 8.

108. Ron Young, memo to executive staff, 6 Oct. 1966, Hassler transfile 5, FOR Records, SCPC.

109. Staughton Lynd, "Escalation in Vietnam," *Liberation* 11 (Oct. 1966): 4.

110. Robert Murphy, "And Party Afterwards," *WIN* 3 (13 Jan. 1967): 4.

111. Quoted in Michael Ferber and Staughton Lynd, *The Resistance* (Boston: Beacon, 1971), 61.

7. Sharing the Crisis

1. "Getting Out," *Commonweal* 85 (23 Dec. 1966): 335.

2. Hans Morgenthau, "Freedom, Freedom House and Vietnam," *New Leader* 50 (2 Jan. 1967): 18.

3. David Dellinger, *Vietnam Revisited: From Covert Action to Invasion to Reconstruction* (Boston: South End Press, 1986): 80; chapter 8, pp. 65–82, is a republication of his 1966 report in *Liberation*.

4. Tom Hayden and Staughton Lynd, *The Other Side* (New York: New American Library, 1966).

5. Philip Berrigan to Dean Rusk, 11 Jan. 1967, Berrigan Papers, Cornell; memorandum, Sanford Gottlieb to Benjamin Spock et al., 27 Jan. 1967, folder: SANE politics, box 54, Spock Papers, Syracuse.

6. Chester Coope, oral history interview, 2: 4–5, LBJL.

7. Guenter Lewy, *America in Vietnam* (New York: Oxford Univ. Press, 1978), 64, 67.

8. Jonathan Schell, "The Village of Ben Suc," *New Yorker,* 15 July 1967, 28–93.

9. Louis Harris, "How the U.S. Public Now Feels About Vietnam," *Newsweek,* 27 Feb. 1967, 24; Foster, *Activism Replaces Isolationism,* 293.

10. Memorandum, Gottlieb to Spock et al., 27 Jan. 1967, Spock Papers, Syracuse; cf. "Danger on the Home Front," *Christian Century* 84 (25 Jan. 1967): 100.

11. Urbana, Illinois, Another Mother for Peace card, n.d., box 619-484, Public Opinion Mail/Vietnam, White House Central File, LBJL.

12. "Clergy Mobilize for Peace," *Christian Century* 84 (4 Jan. 1967): 5; see Hall, "Clergy and Laymen," 50–58.

13. Quotations from *Baltimore Sun,* 16 Feb. 1967, 2, DOD.

14. Martin Luther King, Jr., "The Casualties of the War in Vietnam," in Dr. Martin Luther King, Jr., et al., pamphlet, *Speak on the War in Vietnam* (New York: CALCAV, 1967), 8.

15. King, "Beyond Vietnam," in *Speak on the War,* 11, 15; reprinted in Clyde Taylor, ed., *Vietnam and Black America: An Anthology of Protest and Resistance* (Garden City, N.Y.: Doubleday/Anchor, 1973); see Stephen B. Oates, *Let the Trumpet Sound: The Life of Martin Luther King, Jr.* (New York: New American Library/ Mentor, 1982), 415–22; King, "An Address by Dr. Martin Luther King," March 25th Peace Parade and Rally, box 5, NMC Records, SCPC.

16. King, interview on "Face the Nation," 16 Apr. 1967, in box "Speeches," 3/67–8/67, King Papers, MLKC.

17. King, "An Address by Dr. Martin Luther King," 25 Mar. 1967 in box "Speeches," 3/67–8/67, King Papers.

18. *NYT,* 21 May 1967, 26.

19. Memorandum, John Roche for the President, 5 Apr. 1967, KI folder, box 8, Confidential File, Name File, LBJL; and Memorandum, John Roche for the President, 18 Apr. 1967, p. 1, box 29, Aides Files/Marvin Watson, LBJL.

20. "With But One Voice," *Nation,* 24 Apr. 1967, 515–16; see David Halberstam, "The Second Coming of Martin Luther King," *Harper's,* Aug. 1967, 49–50; and Oates, *Let the Trumpet Sound,* 437–42.

21. David Dellinger, "The April 15 Mobilization," *Liberation* 11 (Feb. 1967): 4; see Staughton Lynd and David Dellinger, "A Call for Noncooperation," *Liberation* 11 (Feb. 1967): 7; and Susan Sutheim, national office, to Jeff Harris, 10 Feb. 1967, box 2, NMC records, SCPC.

22. *Radio-TV Defense Dialogue: Broadcasts of 14, 15, 16 April, 1967,* p. 1, DOD.

23. New York WSP Steering Committee to James Bevel, 24 Feb. 1967, box 6, Fifth Avenue Peace Parade Committee Records, SCPC.

24. Sidney Peck, "Memorandum on Mobilization Event," 3 Feb. 1967, box 4, NMC Records, SCPC.

25. Michael Harrington, "For a Dynamic Majority," *New Leader* 50 (27 Mar. 1967): 21.

26. "Project Merrimack," 24 Apr. 1967, p. 991, CIA Document Memorandum for the Record, folder: segregated Number 1-281, File 504, Merrimack, Resistance Documents, CNSS.

27. *NYT,* 17 Apr. 1967, 1.

28. Madeline Duckles, "Spring Mobilization—San Francisco," *Memo* 5 (Apr. 1967), 2, AFSC Records, AFSC.

29. Halstead, *Out Now!* 274.

30. Memorandum, Mike Yarrow to Colin Bell, 18 Apr. 1967, p. 1, PED files, AFSC Records, AFSC.

31. Tom Cleaver, "Spring Mobilization: Two Reports," *New Left Notes* 2 (8 May 1967): 4; Amy Swerdlow, "Spring Mobilization—New York," *Memo* 5 (Apr. 1967): 5; emphasis in the original.

32. Max Lerner, "Three-Front War," *New York Post,* 26 Apr. 1967, DOD.

33. Assistant Secretary of Defense Phil Goulding, quoted in Small, *Johnson, Nixon, and the Doves,* 96.

34. Ibid., 102.

35. Rusk, quoted in *NYT,* 17 Apr. 1967, 9; and in *Wall Street Journal,* 17 Apr. 1967, DOD.

36. "1967: A Mid-Year Report," FCNL 1967 Logbook, SCPC.

37. *Baltimore Sun,* 18 Apr. 1967, 1, DOD.

38. Memorandum, Robert E. Kintner for the Attorney General, 19 May 1967 (HU 4/FG 135/PR18), Confidential File, White House Central File, LBJL; memorandum, Robert W. Komer for the President, 24 Apr. 1967 (Ex ND 19/CO 312), box 225, National Security-Defense, White House Central File, LBJL.

39. "The Dilemma of Dissent," *Time,* 24 Apr. 1967, 20.

40. "Responsible Dissent on Vietnam War," *Denver Post,* 26 Apr. 1967, DOD; "Impractical Demonstration," *Christian Science Monitor,* 19 Apr. 1967, DOD; and "It's Peace Hysteria," *Detroit News,* 30 Apr. 1967, DOD.

41. Steven P. Tczap to the President, 27 May 1967 (Genl ND 19/CO 3126/1/67), box 275, National Security-Defense File, White House Central File, LBJL; and ad from Washington State University *Daily Evergreen* attached to letter from Professor Bernard E. Bobb to Johnson, 26 May 1967 (Genl ND 19/CO 3126/1/67), box 275, National Security-Defense File, White House Central File, LBJL.

42. *Wall Street Journal,* 3 July 1967, DOD.

43. *NYT,* 13 May 1967, 4; *NYT,* 15 May 1967, 28.

44. Calvin Trillin, "The War in Kansas," *New Yorker,* 22 Apr. 1967, 101, 122.

45. *NYT,* 19 June 1967, 19.

46. Foster, *Activism Replaces Isolationism,* 297.

47. Louis Harris, "A New Sophistication," *Newsweek,* 10 July 1967, 22; and John Davies, in *Los Angeles Times,* 28 May 1967; *WP,* 14 and 16 May, 15 June 1967, DOD.

48. Peter L. Berger, "A Conservative Reflection About Vietnam," *Christianity and Crisis* 27 (6 Mar. 1967): 34–35.

49. James A. Wechsler, "Call for Silence," *New York Post,* 26 Apr. 1967, DOD.

50. "Speaking Out," *Nation,* 8 May 1967, 578.

51. Robert McAfee Brown, "Dissent in the Great Society," *Christianity and Crisis* 27 (15 May 1967): 104.

52. Sidney Peck, in minutes of meeting, 20–21 May 1967, p. 4, box 5, NMC Records, SCPC.

53. Benjamin Spock to Arnold Kaufman, 9 May 1967, box 3, Kaufman Papers, BLMH.

54. Quotations from policy statement cited in Milton Katz, *Ban the Bomb,* 105.

55. A former counsel for the United Auto workers (UAW) and active in the civil rights campaign of 1948, Joseph Rauh had fought to seat the Mississippi Freedom Democratic party in 1964 and was a pillar of ADA liberalism.

56. Statement of the Negotiation Now! Campaign, n.d. [ca. Apr. 1967], box 3, Kaufman Papers, BLMH.

57. *ADA World Magazine* (July 1967): 11.

58. Donald F. Keys to Mary Temple, 8 Sept. 1967, box 3, Kaufman Papers, BLMH.

59. "Foreign Policy Statement," adopted at national board meeting, 19–21 May 1967, folder: Tyler et al., carton 3, ADA Records; John Kenneth Galbraith to Rexford Tugwell, 17 July 1967, carton 3, ADA Records, SHSW.

60. James Wechsler, "Dissenters Divided," *Economist* 224 (8 July 1967): 109.

61. CALC had 78 chapters and a 12,000-person mailing list by June 1967. Hall, "Clergy and Laymen Concerned," 72. Fernandez' comment about the influence of Bayard Rustin and Norman Cousins is in a letter to Al Hassler, 17 May 1966, box 1, CALC Records, SCPC.

62. Phrase from AFSC Peace Education Committee Minutes, 26 Apr. 1967, p. 6, PED files, AFSC Records, AFSC.

63. Lee Webb and Richard Fernandez, codirectors, *Vietnam Summer: Organizers' Manual* (author's copy; no pagination).

64. John Fink to Vietnam Summer offices, n.d. [ca. July 1967], box 3, series 3, Vietnam Summer Records, SCPC.

65. Quotation from David Harris, *Dreams Die Hard* (New York: St. Martin's, 1982), 184. Harris does not mention the meeting with Heller and his friend.

66. Ferber and Lynd, *The Resistance,* 89, 1.

67. An early edition was entitled "A Call to Confrontation with Illegitimate Authority."

68. Mary McCarthy, *Vietnam* (New York: Harcourt, 1967), 86, and Zinn, *The Politics of History* (Boston: Beacon, 1970), 1, both quoted in Sandy Vogelgesang, *The Long Dark Night of the Soul: The American Intellectual Left and the Vietnam War* (New York: Harper and Row, 1974), 121–22, 124.

69. For a selection of these essays, see Noam Chomsky, *American Power and the New Mandarins* (New York: Pantheon, 1967).

70. Individuals Against the Crime of Silence folder, SPP, Bancroft; *NYT,* 9 July 1967, sec. 4, p. 7.

71. Linus Pauling, "Peace on Earth: The Position of the Scientists," *Bulletin of the Atomic Scientists* 23 (Oct. 1967): 48.

72. Jack Newfield, "No Taxation Without De-Escalation," *Village Voice,* 6 Apr. 1967, 6–7.

73. "Even now," read the Minuteman warning, "the cross hairs are on the

back of your necks." *Vietnam Summer News* 1 (25 Aug. 1967): 4; Abigail McCarthy, *Private Faces/Public Places* (Garden City, N.Y.: Doubleday, 1972), 284.

74. Sidney Lens contended that the burglary was committed by Chicago police agents. Lens, *Unrepentant Radical: An American Activist's Account of Five Turbulent Decades* (Boston: Beacon, 1980), 326.

75. David McReynolds, "A Letter for Our Time," *WIN* 3 (16 June 1967): 10.

76. *NYT,* 28 Aug. 1967, 60.

77. *NYT,* 8 Oct. 1967, 67; and 10 Aug. 1967, 17.

78. *NYT,* 20 Aug. 1967, sec. 6, p. 30.

79. Gitlin, "Thesis for the Radical Movement," *Liberation* 12 (May–June 1967): 35.

80. Lynd, "Lynd on Draft Resistance," *New Left Notes* 2 (19 June 1967): 1; Tom Hayden, quoted in *National Guardian,* 31 June 1967, 4.

81. *National Guardian,* 26 Aug. 1967, 6; and "Confront the Warmakers Oct. 21–22: Press Statement Issued Aug. 28," *Mobilizer to End the War in Vietnam* 2 (1 Sept. 1967): 1; emphasis in the original. At first, Mobe leaders planned to invest the Capitol, but they discarded this idea when Communist party leader Arnold Johnson and others complained that this would be tantamount to "insurrection." Minutes of 12 Aug. Administrative Committee meeting, box 2, NMC Records.

82. Robert Greenblatt, "The Peace Force: A Program for Direct Action and Radical Education," submitted to SMC, ca. May–June 1967, box 2, NMC Records; National Mobilization minutes, 20–21 May 1967, ibid.; Jack Spiegal, quoted in *National Guardian,* 27 May 1967, 16.

83. Abbie Hoffman, quoted in Naomi Feigelson, "Mobilizing for Peace—Up, Up, and Away," *Village Voice,* 31 Aug. 1967, 26; and Jerry Rubin, in *WP,* 3 Sept. 1967, DOD.

84. Jeremy Stone, "Disobedience Now! An Exchange of Views," *Commonweal* 86 (14 July 1967): 445.

85. Richard Flacks, "Some Roles for Radical in America," *Liberation* 12 (May–June, 1967): 42; and the Resistance, flyer, n.d. [ca. Oct. 1967], The Resistance folder, Tamiment.

86. Jack Newfield, "One Cheer for the Hippies," *Nation,* 16 June 1967, 809.

87. Charles Bloomstein to *Liberation* editorial board, 27 June 1967, box 5, WRL Records, SCPC; McReynolds to Dellinger et al., 13 June 1967, Lens Papers, CHSL.

88. Homer Jack, "Report on July 1967 Meeting," in box 3, Kaufman Papers; see also report in SANE national board meeting, 15 June 1967, SANE folder, June–July 1967, I, box 9, Spock Papers, Syracuse; and Sidney Lens, "The Stockholm Conference and 'Realism' in the Vietnam War," *Fellowship* 33 (Sept. 1967): 9–12.

89. Thich Nhat Hanh, *Vietnam: Lotus in a Sea of Fire* (New York: Hill and Wang, 1967).

90. Memorandum, David McReynolds to FOR Executive Committee, 2 Oct. 1967, carton 2, WRL Records, SCPC.

91. McReynolds to Alfred Hassler, 3 Aug. 1967, carton 5, WRL Records.

92. "Don't Mourn for Us . . . Organize: The Call of the National Conference for New Politics," n.d. [ca. summer 1967], p. 1, WSP Records, SHSW; and "Draft Statement on the Need for Strengthening the New Politics," n.d. [ca. Aug. 1967], p. 1, folder 36, drawer 13, Grossman Papers, BPL; emphasis in the original.

93. Farrel, Broslawsky, et al., "A Call to a New Politics," n.d., box 1, Kaufman Papers, BLMH, emphasis in the original; and Oglesby, quoted in Sanford Gottlieb,

"Report on the National Conference for New Politics Convention," p. 1, folder 36, drawer 13, Grossman Papers, BPL.

94. June Greenlief, "Static on the Left: Politics of Masquerade," *Village Voice,* 12 Oct. 1967, 5.

95. Tom Hayden, *Reunion: A Memoir* (New York: Random House, 1988), 208; on Bratislava and Hanoi, see 206–19; on the POWs, 220–41.

96. John Wilson, quoted in Robert L. Allen, "Vietnamese and Americans Discuss War," *National Guardian,* 23 Sept. 1967, 1.

97. Hayden was quoted by *Newsweek,* which cited an anonymous reporter from *Ramparts* (probably Keating). This was repeated by Stephen S. Schwarzchild, who noted that the comment reflected "the mood of the gathering," in "The New Left Meets the Real Thing," *Dissent* 15 (Mar.–Apr. 1968): 80.

98. Memorandum, Jim Leonard to all concerned, "New Tendency in the 'Anti-War' Movement?" 25 Oct. 1967, p. 4, Center for War/Peace Studies folder, carton 2, ADA Records, SHSW; and James Ridgeway, "Freak-Out in Chicago," *New Republic,* 16 Sept. 1967, 12.

99. "A Message from Dr. Spock," *New York SANE Newsletter,* Sept. 1967, SANE folder, 1967, box 9, Spock Papers, Syracuse.

100. Clarence Heller and Robert Pickus to Donald Keys, 21 Oct. 1967, box 73, SANE Records, SCPC. See also Milton Katz, "Peace, Politics and Protest," 247–73.

101. "SANE Political Action Strategy—1968," *SANE World* (Nov. 1967): 1; and Sandy Gottlieb, oral history transcript, Eugene R. McCarthy Oral History Collection, Georgetown.

102. Gottlieb, quoted in Milton Katz, "Peace, Politics, and Protest," 272.

103. Peter Steinfels, "The Case for Withdrawal," *Commonweal* 86 (22 Sept. 1967): 586.

104. Norman Cousins, "Is the National Honor Being Bombed?" *Saturday Review,* 9 Sept. 1967, 22; Seymour Melman, "Alternative Policies for Peace," *SANE World* (Sept. 1967), 2–3; emphasis in the original.

105. "'End This War'," *The Nation,* 9 Oct. 1967, 323.

106. Quoted in *Fellowship* 34 (Jan. 1968): 16. Also, *NYT,* 16 Oct. 1967, 11.

107. *WP,* 2 Oct. 1967, and 17 Oct. 1967, DOD.

108. Don Oberdorfer, "Millions See War as Error: Gallup," *WP,* 17 Oct. 1967, DOD.

109. Walter Lippmann, "The Tax Revolt," *Newsweek,* 23 Oct. 1967, 25.

110. Hall, "Clergy and Laymen," 84.

111. Quoted in "The Escalation of Dissent," *Commonweal* 86 (17 Oct. 1967): 102.

112. Robert McAfee Brown, "In Conscience, I Must Break the Law," *Look,* 31 Oct. 1967, 48, 52.

113. Quoted in Michael Useem, *Conscription, Protest, and Social Conflict: The Life and Death of a Draft Resistance Movement* (New York: Wiley, 1973), 159; see Ferber and Lynd, *The Resistance,* 78–90.

114. Quoted in William Sloane Coffin, Jr., *Once to Every Man: A Memoir* (New York: Atheneum, 1977), 244.

115. *National Guardian,* 28 Oct. 1967, 8; the numbers agree with Halstead, *Out Now!* 341–46, and Ferber and Lynd, *The Resistance,* 140–47, and are lower than some contemporary sources.

116. Quoted in Ferber and Lynd, *The Resistance,* 144.

117. Paul Goodman, "The Duty of Professionals," in Stoehr, *Drawing the Line,* 169; Maris Cakers, "Dining With Dean," *WIN* 3 (30 Nov. 1967): 4; and Michael Miles, "Tactics of Disruption," *New Republic,* 4 Nov. 1967, 10.

118. Maris Cakers, "From Dissent to Resistance!" *Mobilizer To End The War In Vietnam* 2 (1 Sept. 1967); 6; and Keith Lampe, "On Making a Perfect Mess," ibid., 3.

119. Dorothy Schmeling, oral history transcript, p. 5, McCarthy Collection, Georgetown.

120. Bruce Jackson, "The Battle of the Pentagon," *Atlantic Monthly,* Jan. 1968, 39. For an evocative dramatic narrative of the confusions at the Pentagon, see Norman Mailer, *The Armies of the Night* (New York: New American Library, 1968); but also see Halstead, *Out Now!* 335–39, and Zaroulis and Sullivan, *Who Spoke Up?* 137–43.

121. Estimates of the number of protesters remaining overnight vary widely, and of persons arrested from 647 to 693. The Mobe counted 675 arrested and booked and another some 200 arrested but not jailed (Halstead, *Out Now!* 339). The above narrative is constructed from both secondary and primary accounts.

122. *NYT,* 27 Oct. 1967, 3; see *Radio-TV Defense Dialogue,* 23 Oct. 1967, p. 1, DOD; Barry Goldwater, "'Peace' Demonstrators Showed Hate for U.S.," *Philadelphia Bulletin,* 29 Oct. 1967, DOD.

123. *NYT,* 29 Nov. 1967, 2; and "Antiwar Protests: A Weapon for Communists," *U.S. News & World Report,* 13 Nov. 1967, 12.

124. *PI,* 4 Dec. 1967, and *New York Post,* 18 Dec. 1967, DOD.

125. *The Johnson Presidential Press Conferences,* 2: 870; and SRS, "Memorandum for the Record: Project Resistance, 8 Oct. 1967, folder: Merrimack Resistance documents, segregated nos. 1–281, CNSS.

126. Jim Forest to Daniel Berrigan, 5 Dec. 1967, Berrigan Papers, Cornell; emphasis in the original.

127. Michael Harrington, "A Question of Philosophy, a Question of Tactics," *Village Voice,* 7 Dec. 1967, 6.

128. Jerry Rubin, "We Are Going to Light the Fuse to the Bomb," Village Voice, 6 Nov. 1967, 7; Davidson quoted in Bacciocco, *New Left in America,* 197.

129. Emmett John Hughes, "The Smell of Crisis," *Newsweek,* 13 Nov. 1967, 29.

130. "Man-Made Misery and God's Promise," *Christian Century* 84 (17 Dec. 1967): 1,944; "The Administration," *Time,* 15 Dec. 1967, 23; Lady Bird Johnson, *A White House Diary,* 592; "A New Revolution?" *Commonweal* 87 (29 Dec. 1967): 397; *Life,* 20 Oct. 1967, 4; "Changing Views on Vietnam," *Saturday Evening Post,* 28 Nov. 1967, 90.

131. Quoted in Albert Eisele, *Almost to the Presidency: A Biography of Two American Politicians* (Blue Earth, Minn.: Piper, 1972), 284; and Richard T. Stout, *People* (New York: Harper, 1970), 117. See also Eugene R. McCarthy, *The Year of the People* (Garden City, N.Y.: Doubleday, 1969), 286–89.

132. "Selecting a President," *Nation,* 27 Nov. 1967, 546.

8. Turning a Corner

1. Louis Harris, quoted in "Sizing Up the Public on the War," *Business Week,* 24 Feb. 1968, 37; also *Washington Star,* 26 Jan. 1968, DOD.

2. Memorandum, McGeorge Bundy for the President, "A Commentary on the Vietnam Discussion of November 2," 10 Nov. 1967, p. 1, under 2 Nov. 1967, President's Appointment File, LBJL.

3. Harrison Salibury, oral history transcript, 1: 29, LBJL.

4. Townsend Hoopes, *The Limits of Intervention* (New York: McKay, 1969), 98.

5. "Should We Get Out of Vietnam?" *Good Housekeeping,* Jan. 1968, 15.

6. *Chicago Daily News,* 25 Oct. 1967; and *Washington Post,* 29 Oct. 1967, DOD.

7. Notes on the President's Meeting with Bob Lucas, 14 Aug. 1967, Notes on Meetings-President folder, 1967, box 1, Office Files of George Christian, LBJL.

8. Jim Jones to the President, meeting with Secretaries Rusk et al., pp. 3–4, 4 Nov. 1967 folder, box 2, MNF, LBJL.

9. The CIA report is reprinted in full in Charles DeBenedetti, "A CIA Analysis of the Anti-Vietnam War Movement: October 1967," *Peace and Change* 9 (Spring 1983): 35–39; emphasis in the original.

10. McGeorge Bundy for the President, 10 Nov. 1967, pp. 4–5; Jim Jones to the President, meeting with Secretaries Rusk et al., pp. 3–4, 4 Nov. 1967 folder, box 2, MNF, LBJL.

11. McGeorge Bundy memorandum for the President, 10 Nov. 1967, pp. 6–7, LBJL; emphasis in the original.

12. Paul Douglas to John Roche, 21 Aug. 1967, ND 19 (CO 312), box 722, White House Confidential File, LBJL.

13. Quoted in Zaroulis and Sullivan, *Who Spoke Up?* 145.

14. *Public Papers of the Presidents of the United States: Lyndon B. Johnson, 1967* (Washington, D.C.: GPO, 1968), 2: 1186.

15. Arthur Schlesinger, Jr., *The Bitter Heritage* (New York: Houghton Mifflin, 1967), 116.

16. George Kennan, quoted in ibid., 115.

17. An informal group of specialists recommended policy change in late 1967; the Committee of Concerned Asian Scholars was formed on 23 March 1968 in Philadelphia. "The Asian Experts Discover Vietnam," *Nation* (15 Apr. 1968): 507.

18. As in so many other demonstrations, the real significance was outreach. In this case, the action was followed up by plans for a coalition of women's groups from several churches, WSP, WILPF, and other groups which had participated in the parade. "Minutes of Program and Action Committee Meeting," 21 Feb. 1968, PED Records, AFSC.

19. Memorandum, Liz Carpenter to Mrs. Johnson, "The Eartha Kitt Invitation," 19 Jan. 1968, Women's Doer Luncheon, 1/8/68/ folder in file 2, box 45, location 4D, Liz Carpenter's Subject Files, Social File, LBJL.

20. Seymour Melman, ed., *In the Name of America* (New York: Clergy and Laymen Concerned About Vietnam, 1968); Richard A. Falk, ed., *The Vietnam War and International Law* (Princeton: Princeton Univ. Press, 1967).

21. Hall, "Clergy and Laymen," 91–92. Some 30,000 copies of the book were distributed to the public.

22. Harvey Cox, "Who's Next?" *Commonweal* 87 (2 Feb. 1968), 524; and Martin Jezer, "If This Be Conspiracy...," *WIN* 4 (31 Jan. 1968): 8.

23. *New York Post,* 23 Dec. 1967, DOD.

24. President Johnson, in meeting with Secretary Rusk et al., 8 Apr. 1967, 8 Apr. 1968 folder, box 2, MNF, LBJL.

25. Quoted in "The Slaughter Goes On," *New Republic,* 24 Feb. 1968, 13.

26. "Doublethink in Vietnam: To Destroy Is to Save," *Christian Century* 85 (21 Feb. 1968): 220; also Godfrey Hodgson, *America in Our Time* (New York: Vintage, 1976), 356.

27. *NYT,* 6 Mar. 1968, 1.

28. Gillon, *Politics and Vision,* 211, 217, and for interpretation, 223–30.

29. Foster, *Activism Replaces Isolationism,* 299.

30. Eden Lipson, oral history transcript, 30, McCarthy Collection, Georgetown.

31. Eugene McCarthy, *The Year of the People,* 294.

32. Jerome Grossman to Mr. and Mrs. Victor Sidel, 29 Mar., 15 Apr. 1968, folder 6, drawer 10, Grossman Papers, BPL.

33. Don Peterson, oral history transcript, p. 4, McCarthy Collection, Georgetown.

34. Stout, *People,* 122, 134.

35. Mary Schramm, oral history transcript, p. 3, McCarthy Collection, Georgetown.

36. Louis Harris in *WP,* 25 Mar. 1968, 16; George Gallup, ibid., 2 May 1968, p. G-1. The 74 percent support for the war in February represented an immediate post-Tet surge of opinion, but support dropped also from the more representative December 1967 figure of 61 percent.

37. Quoted in Hoopes, *Limits of Intervention,* 204.

38. Harry McPherson, oral history transcript, 16–17, LBJL; also, McPherson, *A Political Education* (Boston: Little, Brown, 1972), 433–34.

39. Cyrus Vance, summary of notes, 26 Mar. 1968, p. 2, box 2, MNF, LBJL. See also Chester L. Cooper, *The Lost Crusade: America in Vietnam* (New York: Dodd, Mead, 1970), 465; Hoopes, *Limits of Intervention,* 64–65; and Herbert Y. Schandler, *Lyndon Johnson and Vietnam: The Unmaking of a President* (Princeton: Princeton Univ. Press, 1977), 311–12.

40. Dean Acheson, summary of notes, 26 Mar. 1968, p. 2, box 2, MNF, LBJL; George Ball, in ibid.

41. *I. F. Stone's Weekly* 16 (29 Apr. 1968): 2.

42. Quotation from signs carried in antiwar parade, in Jonathan Eisen, "Peace and Politics in the Park," *Commonweal* 88 (17 May 1968): 254; emphasis in the original.

43. Memo, Linda Morse et al., 20 May 1968, in Student Mobilization Committee folder, file 5, SCPC.

44. Stanley Aronowitz, "The Radical Dilemma," *Guardian,* 4 May 1968, 6.

45. *NYT,* 9 Apr. 1968, DOD.

46. See, for example, Richard Pfeffer, ed., *No More Vietnams? The War and the Future of American Foreign Policy* (New York: Harper and Row, 1968).

47. Bill Gilbert, "The Great World and Millersburg," *Saturday Evening Post,* 20 Apr. 1968, 40.

48. Calvin Trillin, "The Last Peaceful Place," *New Yorker,* 20 Apr. 1968, 175.

49. John Kenneth Galbraith, "Politics in 1968 and the Liberal Response," p. 2, 1968 Convention folder, carton 1, ADA Convention, ADA Records, SHSW.

50. *NYT,* 13 Feb. 1968, 26.

51. *NYT,* 31 Mar. 1968, 53.

52. Memorandum of Conversation, Meeting with Hubert Humphrey et al., 3 Apr. 1968, p. 1, box 6, LBJ Famous Names/Robert Kennedy, White House Famous Names File, LBJL. See Lyndon Baines Johnson, *The Vantage Point: Perspectives of the Presidency, 1963–1969* (New York: Holt, Rinehart and Winston, 1971), 422.

53. *NYT,* 23 June 1968, 2.

54. Daniel Berrigan, *Night Flight to Hanoi: War Diary with Eleven Poems* (New York: Harper, 1971), xvi. Also, Francine du Plessix Gray, *Divine Disobedience: Profiles in Catholic Radicalism* (New York: Vintage, 1971), 45–133; and, for a dramatic version, Daniel Berrigan, *The Trial of the Catonsville Nine* (Boston: Beacon, 1970).

55. Dorothy Day to Daniel Berrigan, 31 May 1968, Berrigan Papers, Cornell.

56. David Halberstam, "Bargaining with Hanoi," *New Republic,* 11 May 1968, 14.

57. *NYT,* 25 Apr. 1968, 29.

58. Clifford National Security Council meeting, 22 May 1968, box 1, Clark

Clifford Papers, LBJL; see also *NYT,* 9 July 1968, 1–2. Clifford was recalling, imperfectly, stanza 52 of "Sir Andrew Barton." See Francis James Child, ed., *The English and Scottish Popular Ballads* (New York: Dover 1965), 3: 345.

59. Cabinet meeting of 26 June 1968, p. 3, Cabinet meeting, 26 June 1968 folder, box 14, Cabinet Papers, LBJL.

60. *Baltimore Sun,* 3 June 1968; *WP,* 19 Aug. 1968; *Philadelphia Evening Bulletin,* 23 Aug. 1968, DOD.

61. *NYT,* 13 Mar. 1968, 17; and *WP,* 25 Aug. 1968, DOD.

62. *NYT,* 11 Aug. 1968, 54.

63. Benjamin Spock to Norman Thomas, 15 July 1968, box 11, Spock Papers, Syracuse; also, William Sloane Coffin, *Once to Every Man: A Memoir* (New York: Atheneum, 1977), 274–77; Lynn Z. Bloom, *Doctor Spock: Biography of a Conservative Radical* (Indianapolis: Bobbs-Merrill, 1972), 304–22. All the defendants except Marcus Raskin (principal author of "The Call to Resist") were convicted and sentenced to two years in prison and $5,000 in fines.

64. "Either/Or in 1968," *Guardian,* 30 Mar. 1968, 8.

65. Tom Hayden, quoted in Stewart Meacham, memorandum to those concerned, 28 Mar. 1968, PED files, AFSC Records, AFSC.

66. Flint Anderson et al., to Philip Berrigan, 1 Mar. 1968, Berrigan Papers, Cornell.

67. Unger, *The Movement,* 160.

68. "The Birth of the Yippies," *WIN* 4 (15 Feb. 1968): 16; and Martin Jezer, "The Yippies Are Coming!" *Liberation* 12 (Feb. 1968): 8.

69. Phil Ochs, "Have You Heard? The War is Over!" *Village Voice,* 23 Nov. 1967, 16, 38.

70. Abbie Hoffman, "The 1968 Election," *WIN* 4 (15 Mar. 1968): 5.

71. Jerry Rubin, "I Am the Walrus!" *WIN* 4 (15 Feb. 1968): 4.

72. Tom Hayden, quoted in Maris Cakers, "Report of Press Conference in New York City by Dave Dellinger and Tom Hayden, Saturday, June 29," box 2, NMC Records, SCPC.

73. Ibid.; Halstead makes the case that they acted independently, *Out Now!* 408.

74. Dellinger, Summary of Administrative Meeting held at Ohio Area Peace Action Council, Cleveland, 20 July 1968, p. 3, in NMC Records, SCPC.

75. Hayden credits Albert Camus with the phrase, *Reunion,* 297.

76. C. D. Brennan to W. C. Sullivan, 9 May 1968, Folder I-14, Socialist Workers Party, National Security Studies Records, CNSS.

77. J. Edgar Hoover to SAG, Albany, 5 July 1968, New Left/COINTELPRO, 1968–1971, file: I-17/a, CNSS.

78. SAC/Cincinnati to Hoover, 3 June 1968, CNSS.

79. San Antonio SAG to SOG, 27 Aug. 1968, CNSS.

80. Arthur M. Schlesinger, Jr., *Robert Kennedy and His Times,* 825, 851.

81. J. Edgar Hoover, wire to Johnson and Department of the Army and Secret Service, 24 Aug. 1968, HU 4 Freedoms folder, box 57, Confidential File, White House Central File, LBJL. Hoover warned that the disruption was planned to send the delegates into the streets, "where they will be met with massive antiwar demonstrations . . . to disrupt and discredit the democratic process." One source of the FBI's intelligence was a forthcoming article in *Saga* magazine.

82. *NYT,* 28 Aug. 1968, 36.

83. Lowenstein, Memorandum, "Al's Account of His Attempt to Second the Nomination for Julian Bond at the Democratic National Convention," n.d. [ca. Aug. 1968], box 56, Allard Lowenstein Papers, Southern Historical Collection,

University of North Carolina at Chapel Hill; Arthur Miller, "From the Delegates' Side," in Walter Schneir, ed., *Telling It Like It Was: The Chicago Riots* (New York: New American Library, 1969), 45.

For fuller accounts of the convention and related events, see Daniel Walker, *Rights in Conflict: A Report Submitted by Daniel Walker, Director of the Chicago Study Team, to the National Commission on the Causes and Prevention of Violence* (New York: Bantam, 1968); Lewis Chester et al., *An American Melodrama: The Presidential Campaign of 1968* (New York: Viking, 1969); Hayden, *Reunion,* 293–326; Todd Gitlin, *The Sixties: Years of Hope, Days of Rage* (New York: Bantam, 1987), esp. 322–36; Zaroulis and Sullivan, *Who Spoke Up?* 175–208. Also Paul R. Miller, "The Chicago Demonstrators: A Study in Identity," *Bulletin of the Atomic Scientists* (Apr. 1969): 3–6; and Paul Miller, "Revolutionists Among the Chicago Demonstrators," *Bulletin of the Atomic Scientists* (Feb. 1970): 16–21.

84. *NYT,* 24 Aug. 1968, 1.

85. Richard Goodwin, quoted in Jack Newfield, "The Streets of Daleyland," in Schneir, ed., *Telling It Like It Was,* 110; and "When a 2-Party System Becomes a 1-Party Rubber Stamp," *I. F. Stone's Weekly* 16 (9 Sept. 1968): 3.

86. Gitlin, *The Sixties,* 334.

87. *NYT,* 18 Sept. 1968, 1; and 31 Aug. 1968, 10.

88. *NYT,* 3 Sept. 1968, 34; and 5 Sept. 1968, 1; also Hodgson, *America in Our Time,* 370–75.

89. *NYT,* 2 Nov. 1968, 27; and 16 Sept. 1968, 1.

90. Walker, *Rights in Conflict,* 5; Stone, "2-Party System," 1.

91. Gitlin, *The Sixties,* 338.

92. *Guardian,* 16 Nov. 1968, 6; and 26 Oct. 1968, 3; and Sale, *SDS,* 478–83.

93. Rennie Davis and Tom Hayden, "Politics After Chicago," Sept. 1968, p. 1, Vietnam File, SCPC.

94. Martin Jezer, "Notes from a Vermont Farmer," *WIN* 4 (15 Nov. 1968): 4.

95. Philip Berrigan, "Exchange of Views on Burning of Draft Files," *New Politics* 7 (Fall 1968): 22. For the Milwaukee Fourteen action, see Charles Meconis, *With Clumsy Grace: The American Catholic Left, 1961–1977* (New York: Seabury, 1979), 27–32.

96. *Guardian,* 28 Dec. 1968, 10.

97. Hoover to SAG/Albany, 9 Oct. 1968, folder: I-17/a New Left COINTELPRO, 1968–1971, CNSS.

98. Memorandum, Richard Helms to the President, "Student Unrest," 4 Sept. 1968, pp. 21, 25, 32, Intelligence File folder, NSF, LBJL.

99. In 18 Sept. 1968 Cabinet Meeting folder, box 15, Cabinet Papers, LBJL.

100. U.S. Senate, Final Report of the Select Committee to Study Governmental Operations with Respect to Intelligence Activities [Church Committee Report], 94th Cong., 2d sess., 2: 98. The U.S. Justice Department penetrated its agents so deeply among radical activists that a government operative served as "grand marshal" of yippie activities in Washington. Indeed, on one occasion, this agent requested FBI protection for Jerry Rubin and Abbie Hoffman out of fear that "someone may try to kill them and this would be tragic for everyone." Unsigned memorandum to Attorney General Ramsey Clark, 30 Oct. 1968, box 45/Yippies, Warren Christopher Papers, LBJL.

101. Kim Moody, "The GI Resistance," *New Politics* 7 (Spring 1968): 65.

102. Frank Cormier, *LBJ: The Way He Was* (Garden City, N.Y.: Doubleday, 1977), 260.

103. Halstead, *Out Now!* 433; *Task Force* 1 (25 Oct. 1968): 1 [this was a San Francisco area GI antiwar paper].

104. Christopher Wren, "Protest in the Ranks," *Life,* 15 Oct. 1968, 32, 31. See Edward F. Sherman, "Dissenters and Deserters," *New Republic,* 6 Jan. 1968, 23–25.

105. Ferber and Lynd, *The Resistance,* 169–84.

106. David Osher (New York Resistance), quoted in Ferber and Lynd, *The Resistance,* 159.

107. Sanford Gottlieb to Paul Olynyk, 15 July 1968, 1977 addendum, box 12, SANE Records, SCPC.

108. "Machiavellianism Parading as a Search for Peace, *I. F. Stone's Weekly* (21 Oct. 1968): 4, 1, emphasis in the original. Cf. "If It Goes on for Two More Years," *Economist* 22 (19 Oct. 1968): 48; and "Vietnam: Serious Talks," *War/Peace Report* 8 (Dec. 1968): 15.

109. *NYT,* 29 Sept. 1968, 74; 21 Sept. 1968, 16; and 16 Oct. 1968, 30.

110. *NYT,* 25 Aug. 1968, 91.

111. *NYT,* 12 Oct. 1968, 29.

112. Benjamin I. Page and Richard A. Brody, "Policy Voting and the Electoral Process: The Vietnam War Issue," *American Political Science Review* 66 (Sept. 1972): 983.

113. *NYT,* 3 Dec. 1968, 20; and 8 Dec. 1968, 84.

114. John Kenneth Galbraith to Chester Bowles, 3 Dec. 1968, box 330, series I, Bowles Papers, Yale.

9. Redrawing the Lines

1. Walter Lippmann, "The Crux in Vietnam," *Newsweek,* 2 Dec. 1968, 27.

2. Henry Kissinger, *The White House Years* (Boston: Little, Brown, 1979), 74. the interpretation of Nixon's attitudes is drawn also from his memoirs and speeches, as well as from the accounts of his aides.

3. Richard Nixon, quoted in Curt Smith, *Long Time Gone: The Years of Turmoil Remembered* (South Bend, Ind.: Icarus Press, 1982), 213, 217.

4. Henry Kissinger, *Years of Upheaval* (Boston: Little, Brown, 1982), 94.

5. Richard Nixon, *RN: The Memoirs of Richard Nixon* (New York: Grosset and Dunlap, 1978), 291; Egil "Bud" Krogh, quoted in David Frost, *I Gave Them a Sword* (New York: Morrow, 1978), 286.

6. Paul Potter, notes of a meeting on the future of Mobe, n.d. [ca. late Jan. 1969], p. 13, box 3, Student Mobilization Committee to End the War in Vietnam (SMC) Records, SHSW. The CALC paper was "The Reconciliation We Seek," Hall, "Clergy and Laymen," 117.

7. Earl Craig, executive director, temporary steering committee minutes of the St. Louis meeting of 24 Nov., 29 Nov. 1968, box 2, Kaufman Papers, BLMH.

8. George McGovern, *Vietnam Today,* CALC pamphlet, ca. 3–5 Feb. 1969, CALC Records, SCPC.

9. Arthur M. Schlesinger, Jr., quoted from statement of 26 Feb. 1969, in ADA Foreign Policy Committee folder, carton 1, ADA Records, SHSW. Schlesinger was then a national vice-chairman of ADA. The Coalition was launched at a Washington conference, 26–27 Feb. and was sponsored by the AFSC, ADA, FOR, FCNL, SANE, SCLC, WSP, WILPF, Federation of American Scientists, the Central Conference of American Rabbis, and three protestant churches.

10. Harold Willens, untitled memo, n.d., ca. Jan. 1969, carton 3, Business Executives Move for Vietnam Peace (BEM) Records, SCPC.

11. "Vietnam and the Future of the American Empire: Washington Mobilization, February 3–5, 1969," *Issues & Actions* (13 Jan. 1969): 1.

12. "Against the Misuse of Science—An Appeal by M.I.T. Scientists," *Bulletin of the Atomic Scientists* 25 (Mar. 1969): 8.

13. Kenneth Keniston, *Youth and Dissent: The Rise of a New Opposition* (New York: Harcourt, 1971), 354–57.

14. Klaus Mehnert, *Twilight of the Young: The Radical Movements of the 1960s and Their Legacy* (New York: Holt, Rinehart and Winston, 1976), 42.

15. See, for example, John E. Mueller, *War, Presidents, and Public Opinion* (New York: Wiley, 1973), 149; Richard R. Lau, Thad A. Brown and David O. Sears, "Self-Interest and Civilians' Attitudes Toward the Vietnam War," *Public Opinion Quarterly* 42 (Winter 1978): 476, 479; and E. M. Schreiber, "Opposition to the Vietnam War Among American University Students and Faculty," *British Journal of Sociology* 24 (Sept. 1973): 295.

16. Harris Wofford, *Of Kennedys and Kings* (New York: Farrar, Straus and Giroux, 1980), 448; William J. McGill, *The Year of the Monkey: Revolt on Campus, 1968–69* (New York: McGraw-Hill, 1982), 54.

17. Minutes of the Administrative Committee of the National Mobilization Committee, 7 Dec. 1968, box 2, NMC Records, SCPC.

18. *I. F. Stone's Weekly* 17 (27 Jan. 1969): 1.

19. Rennie Davis in notes of meeting, n.d. [ca. late Jan. 1969], p. 5, box 3, SMC Records, SHSW.

20. Lawrence Scott, quoted in minutes of NAG meeting, 11 Feb. 1969, p. 1, 1969, PED files, AFSC Records, AFSC.

21. *WP*, 7 Apr. 1969, A-4.

22. *National Observer*, 14 Apr. 1969, in SANE Washington Logbook, SFNO, 1969.

23. Hugh Sidey, "The Right of the Individual vs. the Right of the Group," *Life*, 9 May 1969, 4.

24. Richard Nixon, quoted in Curt Smith, *Long Time Gone*, 217.

25. Athan Theoharis, *Spying On Americans: Political Surveillance from Hoover to the Huston Plan* (Philadelphia: Temple Univ. Press, 1978), 16.

26. Memo re "Action in Washington, December 17–18, 1969," 21 May 1969, in minutes of 20 May 1969 meeting, WILPF Records, SCPC.

27. *Public Papers of the Presidents of the United States: Richard Nixon, 1969* (Washington, D.C.: GPO, 1969), 373, 372 (hereinafter cited as *PPP: RN, 1969*).

28. *PPP: RN, 1969*, 374–75.

29. *NYT*, 22 Aug. 1969, 4.

30. Daniel Berrington to Thomas M. Haberle, 20 June 1969, Berrigan Papers, Cornell.

31. Andrew Kopkind, "Vietnam and the Big Lie," *New Statesman*, 16 May 1969, 680.

32. The home was that of Harold Tovish, the date probably mid-April. Jerome Grossman to Tovish, 24 Nov. 1969, folder 15, drawer 11, Grossman Papers, BPL.

33. The project was authorized by MassPAX on 1 June on the condition that there be a "semantic change" to eliminate "strike" but retain the dimension of "work stoppage." Minutes of MassPAX executive meeting, 1 June 1969, folder 24, file 3, Grossman Papers, BPL.

34. Jerome Grossman, "A Proposal for a Deadline Strike to end the War in Vietnam," n.d., ca. 20 Apr. 1969, folder 1, drawer 11, Grossman Papers, BPL.

35. Grossman, in minutes of MassPAX meeting, 1 June 1969, p. 5, file 3, box 6, Vietnam Moratorium Committee (VMC) Records, SHSW; Sam Brown et al., form letter to congressmen, 1 July 1969, box 2, VMC Records. Although in *Moratorium: An American Protest* (New York: Tower, 1970), 33–34, Paul Hoffman

wrote that the initial target date was changed from September late in the summer, the October date appears in the original Grossman proposal.

36. Paul Glusman, "One, Two, Three . . . Many SDS's," *Ramparts,* Sept. 1969, 10. The "Weatherman" line is from Bob Dylan's "Subterranean Homesick Blues."

37. On the committee were individuals from the New York Parade Committee, WSP, the "Conspiracy" (Rennie Davis), *Liberation* (Dellinger), CALC, Cleveland Area Peace Action Council (CAPAC), SWP, CP, Chicago Peace Council (CPC), AFSC, New York WSP, and several independent or local groups. Only three were under thirty, and one one was from a student group. Leadership of the New Mobe was vested in Fay Knopp (AFSC) and Abe Bloom (Washington SANE) as project directors for Washington with Sidney Peck and Stewart Meacham as cochairpersons there. Rennie Davis was counterbalanced by Sylvia Kushner (CPC) as project directors in Chicago with Douglas Dowd and Sid Lens as cochairmen. Dellinger was named (largely nominally) liaison coordinator, and other local groups were trusted to act on their own. Halstead, *Out Now!* 467, 472.

38. Stewart Meacham, "Why Washington?—Why Now?" *New Mobilizer,* no. 2 (25 Sept. 1969): 2.

39. Carl Oglesby, "Notes on a Decade Ready for the Dustbin," *Liberation* 14 (Aug.–Sept. 1969): 5–6, 14; Staughton Lynd, "A Program for Post-Campus Radicals," ibid., 44.

40. Abbie Hoffman, *Soon to be a Major Motion Picture* (New York: Putnam, 1980), 243.

41. *PPP: RN, 1969,* pp. 427–28.

42. Gallup, *WP,* 1 July 1969, 21. Harris reported his rating at 47 percent excellent to good, 45 percent fair to poor, *PI,* 11 Aug. 1969, DOD.

43. Seymour M. Hersh, *The Price of Power: Kissinger in The Nixon White House* (New York: Summit, 1983), 118; also, Nixon, *RN,* 393.

44. "Vietnam: One Week's Dead," *Life,* 27 June, 1969, 20–32.

45. Nixon, *RN,* 393.

46. H. R. Haldeman, *The Ends of Power* (New York: Times Books, 1978), 98; Hersh, *The Price of Power,* 126.

47. "Special Information Report (Special): 15 October 1969 Activities," 10 Oct. 1969 [CIA document released to author, 1985].

48. *NYT,* 29 Sept. 1969, 4; ibid., 9 Oct., 10.

49. Harris, *PI,* 5 Oct. 1969, DOD; Gallup, *WP,* 5 Oct. 1969, DOD.

50. Harris, *New York Post,* 30 Oct. 1969, DOD; Quoted in "Americans on the War: Divided, Glum, Unwilling to Quit," *Time,* 31 Oct. 1969, 13; Gallup, *PI,* 12 Oct. 1969, DOD; Harris noted that southerners and George Wallace supporters were both more opposed to troop withdrawals than the rest of the country and more convinced that the communists would succeed following a U.S. withdrawal. He speculated that resentment among these groups could jeopardize Nixon's "Southern middle American strategy" for reelection.

51. *NYT,* 2 Oct. 1969, 18, and 27 Sept. 1969, 1; Magruder, *An American Life,* 80.

52. *NYT,* 16 Oct. 1969, 19; 1 Oct. 1969, 1.

53. Agnew, quoted in Peter N. Carroll, *It Seemed Like Nothing Happened: The Tragedy and Promise of America in the 1970s* (New York: Holt, Rinehart and Winston, 1982), 6–7.

54. "Oct. 15: A Day to Remember," *Newsweek,* 27 Oct. 1969, 34.

55. "Transcript of Sam Brown's appearance on 'Face the Nation,'" Oct. 1969, CBS-TV, in box 2, VMC Records, SHSW.

56. "The Unsilent Opposition," *New Republic,* 15 Nov. 1969, 9.

57. Quoted in "Oct. 15: A Day to Remember."

58. Robert Lewis Shayon, "TV-Radio," *Saturday Review,* 8 Nov. 1969, 41.

59. "The Unsilent Opposition," 9.

60. Richard Harris, "Annals of the Law: A Scrap of Black Cloth, II," *New Yorker,* 24 June 1970, 37.

61. Haldeman, *Ends of Power,* 98.

62. *NYT,* 31 Oct. 1969, 25; 20 Oct. 1969, 1, 2.

63. *NYT,* 14 Nov. 1969, 1.

64. *NYT,* 1 Nov. 1969, 1; 23 Oct. 1969, 53.

65. "'Love It . . . Or Leave It,'" *Newsweek,* 24 Nov. 1969, 34.

66. "Parades for Peace and Patriotism," *Time,* 21 Nov. 1969, 26; "Nixon's Unsilent Supporters," *Time,* 21 Nov. 1969, 25.

67. *PPP: RN, 1969,* 907, 908, 902, 907, 909, 908, 909.

68. *NYT,* 5 Nov. 1969, 11.

69. *NYT,* 6 Nov. 1969, 11; 19 Nov. 1969, 1.

70. Ken Hurwitz, *Marching Nowhere* (New York: Norton, 1971), 155, 159.

71. Jeb Stuart Magruder, *An American Life* (New York: Atheneum, 1974), 89. According to plans drafted by White House aide Dwight Chapin, the administration would divide liberal and radical antiwar activists by attacking the latter as violence-prone, "less rational" subversives, while drawing the former "back into the fold of the national consciousness."

72. Sidney Lens, quoted in Francine due Plessix Gray, "The Moratorium and the New Mobe," *New Yorker,* 3 Jan. 1970, 45.

73. Jerome Grossman to T. R. Blake, 28 Oct. 1969, folder 14, drawer 11, Grossman Papers, BPL.

74. Lens, *Unrepentant Radical,* 356.

75. Susan Miller (Episcopal Peace Fellowship) had administrative responsibility for the March Against Death, with the assistance of Trudi Young, wife of Ron Young of the FOR.

76. William Watts, quoted in Hersh, *The Price of Power,* 131.

77. "Official Statement Written for and Adopted by the New Mobilization Committee," *Fellowship* 35 (Nov. 1969): 4. The New Mobe estimated 800,000; the police 250,000; and others from 300,000 to 700,000. Halstead, who was jointly in charge of logistics, notes that the 4,000 chartered buses alone would have brought 200,000 people. *Out Now!* 520.

78. *Guardian,* 22 Nov. 1969, 5.

79. "It was the Best, Biggest, and Last," *WP,* 16 Nov. 1969, B-7.

80. Small, *Johnson, Nixon, and the Doves,* 190.

81. Harris, *Chicago Tribune,* 10, 13 Nov. 1969; Gallup, *PI,* 13 Nov. 1969, in DOD; Harris, "Americans on the War," *Time,* 31 Oct. 1969, 13.

82. Francine du Plessix Gray, "The Moratorium and the New Mobe," 42.

83. Quoted in "A New GI: For Pot and Peace," *Newsweek,* 2 Feb. 1970, 24.

84. The soldiers authorized the use of their names and military identification in the Sunday edition, 9 Nov. 1969, cited in Halstead, *Out Now!* 504.

85. *NYT,* 28 Nov. 1969, 18.

86. "Carnage and Incarnation," *Christian Century* 86 (24 Dec. 1969): 1633.

87. *I. F Stone's Weekly* 17 (15 Dec. 1969): 1.

88. Harris, *PI,* 15 Jan. 1970, DOD.

89. Address to the Nation of 15 Dec., in *PPP: RN, 1969,* 1028.

90. Daniel Berrigan to Estelle Holt, 9 Dec. 1969, Berrigan Papers, Cornell.

91. VMC form letter, 2 Jan. 1970, box 6, VMC Records, SHSW.

92. Marge Sklencar, quoted in Francine du Plessix Gray, "The Moratorium and the New Mobe," 42.

93. *NYT,* 10 Feb. 1970, 1.

94. Form letter, 5 Dec. 1969, box 4, VMC Records, SHSW.

95. "Nixon's Loyal Opposition," *Nation,* 19 Jan. 1970, 35.

96. Memo, 3 Jan. 1970, box 3, VMC Records, SHSW.

97. Alfred Hassler, *Saigon U.S.A.* (New York: Baron, 1970). The team included Representative John Conyers, Jr. (R-Mich.), the Reverend Robert F. Drinan (dean of the Boston College Law School), John de J. Pemberton (national secretary of the ACLU), retired admiral Arnold E. True, Mrs. Anne McGrew Bennett, Methodist bishop James Armstrong, Rabbi Seymour Siegel, the Reverend Peter Jenkins (general secretary of the FOR in Britain), and FOR officers Alfred Hassler and Allan Brick (as executive director of the project).

98. Hassler, *Saigon U.S.A.,* x.

99. Norman Cousins, "Laos," *Saturday Review,* 21 Mar. 1970, 82.

100. "Antiwar Movement to Go 'Local'?" *War/Peace Report* 10 (May 1970): 20.

101. Hayden, *Reunion,* 346. Bobby Seale's case was separated from that of the others. John Froines and Lee Weiner were acquitted. The rest were found guilty of incitement but not conspiracy. Even before the verdict they were jailed on 159 counts of contempt of court, all but 13 of which were overturned on appeal (as was the case itself).

102. "Remember November," *Nation,* 4 May 1970, 516; James Wechsler, "New Left vs. New Right: The False Choice," *Progressive* 34 (May 1970): 15, 13.

103. "Anti-War Movement to Go 'Local'?" 20.

104. Sam Brown, "The Politics of Peace, *Washington Monthly* 2 (Aug. 1970): 42; Stewart Meacham to Dan Seeger, 31 Mar. 1970, Young file, carton 4, FOR Records, SCPC; Sidney Lens to Anne Draper, 26 Apr. 1970, box: Antiwar Activities 1971, Lens Papers, CHSL. Dellinger, "April 15: Telling Off the Taxman," *WIN* 6 (15 May 1970): 22, 24.

105. Gallup, *WP,* 15 Mar. 1970, DOD.

106. Ibid.; Stone, quoted in *Northern Virginia Sun,* 17 Mar. 1970, DOD.

107. Franz Schurmann, "'Where are you now that we *really* need you,'" *Ramparts,* Aug. 1969, 16.

108. Sidney Lens to Anne Draper, 26 Apr. 1970, box: Antiwar Activities 1971, Lens Papers, CHSL.

109. Daniel Berrigan, "From the Underground #1,"in Daniel Berrigan, *America Is Hard to Find* (New York: Doubleday, 1972), 52.

110. From Daniel Berrigan, "America Is Hard to Find," in Berrigan, *America Is Hard to Find,* 15–16.

10. Persisting in Withdrawal

1. *PPP: RN, 1970,* 410, 409.

2. *NYT,* 2 May 1970, 1; Albert Gore, quoted in ibid.

3. Quoted in William Safire, *Before the Fall* (Garden City, N.Y.: Doubleday, 1975), 189.

4. Kissinger, *White House Years,* 487.

5. Sidney Peck, "May Ninth," Sept. 1970, National Coalition file, Vietnam file, PED files, AFSC Records, AFSC.

6. *NYT,* 5 May 1970, 1.

7. Richard E. Peterson and John A. Bilorusky, *May 1970: The Campus Aftermath of Cambodia and Kent State* (Berkeley: Carnegie Commission on Higher Education, 1974), 15, 17–18.

8. George Winne, Jr., quoted in McGill, *Year of the Monkey,* 37. For two detailed studies of campus unrest, see DeWitt Blamer and LaMar Palmer, *The Strike at Washington State University: An Example of Nonviolent Confrontation* (Wash-

ington State Univ.: Office of Student Affairs, Aug. 1970), and Mitchell K. Hall, "A Crack in Time: The Response of Students at the University of Kentucky to the Tragedy at Kent State, May 1970," *Register of the Kentucky Historical Society* 83 (Winter 1985): 54.

9. "New Dimensions for Dissent," *Economist* 235 (16 May 1970), 42.

10. Jeremy Brecher, "Thoughts for the Next Crisis," *Liberation* 15 (June 1970): 19.

11. Quoted in Calvin Trillin, "U.S. Journal: Fort Dix, New Jersey," *New Yorker,* 6 June 1970, 46; emphasis in the original.

12. National coordinators of NPAC were Jerry Gordon of the Cleveland Area Peace Action Council, James Lafferty of the Detroit Committee to End the War Now, Ruth Gage-Colby of WILPF, Don Gurewitz of SMC, and John T. Williams, a Teamster official in Los Angeles.

13. Sidney Peck, "Cleveland Anti-War Conference," memorandum, n.d. [ca. June 1970], box 17, SMC Records; "Dear Brothers and Sisters," 9 June 1970 [conference call], box 17, SMC Records. The call was signed by Dave Dellinger (The Conspiracy), Trudi Young (WSP), Dick Fernandez (CALC), Stewart Meacham (AFSC), and Sidney Peck.

14. "A Proposal for … the Disruption/Liberation of Washington," n.d. [ca. June 1970], PED files, AFSC Records, AFSC; "New Mobe Undecided on Program," *Guardian,* 4 July 1970, 3, 7, 10; Halstead, *Out Now!* 563–68 (the Cleveland conference), 568–69 (the Milwaukee conference).

15. Huey P. Newton, "Letter to the National Liberation Front of South Vietnam (With Reply)," 29 Aug. 1970, in Taylor, ed., *Vietnam and Black America,* 290. See pp. 293–35 for an appreciative reply from the deputy commander of communist forces in the South, 31 Oct. 1970.

16. *NYT,* 8 Sept. 1970, 5.

17. David Dellinger, "A Time to Look at Ourselves," *Liberation* 15 (Aug.–Oct./Autumn 1970): 6, 74.

18. Minutes, National Action Group, 31 July 1970, PED files, AFSC Records, AFSC.

19. Daniel Berrigan, "Letter to the Weathermen," in Berrigan, *America Is Hard to Find,* 96; emphasis added.

20. Ibid., 92–98.

21. Jimmy Breslin, "One Way to End the War," *New York* 3 (22 June 1970), 28.

22. Andrew Greeley, "Turning Off the People," *New Republic,* 27 June 1970, 15; emphasis in the original.

23. Breslin, "One Way to End the War," 28.

24. Philip E. Converse and Howard Schuman, "'Silent Majorities' and the Vietnam War," *Scientific American* 222 (June 1970), 24.

25. Ibid.

26. Robert Beisner, "On Student Reaction to the Indochina Crisis" [class lecture of 7 May 1970], in *North American Review* 7 (Fall 1970): 58.

27. *NYT,* 5 May 1970, 1.

28. Quoted in "Two Gatherings," *New Yorker,* 30 May 1970, 24.

29. "A Shattered Trust," *Christian Century* 87 (13 May 1970), 587.

30. "The President's Power—and the People's," *Progressive* 34 (June 1970), 3; see also Pete Hamill, "Letter from the Fever Zone," *New York* 3 (25 May 1970), 33; and "The Southeast Asian Crisis That Will Not Go Away," *Fellowship* 36 (July 1970): 2.

31. Magruder, *An American Life,* 123; Kissinger, *White House Years,* 968.

32. *NYT,* 23 May 1970, 1; and 4 June 1970, 1.

33. *PPP: RN, 1970,* 414.

34. Hatfield and McGovern introduced the bill with Harold Hughes and Robert Goodell.

35. Gallup, *NYT,* 7 June 1970, 49; *WP,* 5 May 1970; Harris, Gallup, *NYT,* 14 June 1970, 5; Harris, *Chicago Tribune,* 17 Aug. 1970, DOD.

36. Camille Marker, "Washington Visitation Report 1969," p. 7, in box 2, PED files, AFSC Records, AFSC.

37. Quoted in Joseph Duffey, "National Chairman Memo," n.d. [ca. June 1970], Vietnam folder, carton 3, ADA Records, SHSW.

38. "Honoring America," *New Republic,* 11 July 1970, 6.

39. Ibid., 5.

40. Milton J. Rosenberg et al., *Vietnam and the Silent Majority: The Dove's Guide* (New York: Harper and Row, 1970), 151–52; all italicized in the original.

41. Ibid., 152; *WRL News* (July–Aug. 1970): n.p., in Tamiment.

42. Safire, *Before the Fall,* 308.

43. Huston's draft report of June 1970, quoted in Theoharis, *Spying on Americans,* 25.

44. Nixon, quoted in Frank J. Donner, *The Age of Surveillance* (New York: Knopf, 1980), 265.

45. Nick Egleson, "The Surveillance Apparatus," in Paul Cowan et al., *State Secrets: Police Surveillance in America* (New York: Holt, Rinehart and Winston, 1974), 17.

46. FBI document, quoted in Kenneth O'Reilly, *The FBI, HUAC, and the Red Menace* (Philadelphia: Temple Univ. Press, 1983), 218.

47. Alfred Kazin, "The Flag Business," pp. 1–2, in Harken, Publication of Publishers for Peace, Emergency on Cambodia-Laos-Vietnam War folder, June 1970, Tamiment.

48. *NYT,* 3 Aug. 1970, 30.

49. Alan Geyer, "A Need for Nationhood," *Worldview* 13 (July–Aug. 1970): 3.

50. Quoted in Kissinger, *White House Years,* 969.

51. Safire, *Before the Fall,* 308; quoted in J. Anthony Lukas, *Nightmare* (New York: Viking, 1976), 15.

52. Kissinger, quoted in Marvin Kalb and Bernard Kalb, *Kissinger* (Boston: Little, Brown, 1974), 169; Nixon, quoted from 18 Feb. 1970 speech, *PPP: RN, 1970,* 149.

53. *NYT,* 18 Aug. 1970, 1.

54. *NYT,* 11 Sept. 1970, 20; *NYT,* 18 Aug. 1970, 1.

55. Robert Chandler, comp., *Public Opinion: Changing Attitudes on Contemporary Political and Social Issues* [A CBS News Reference Book] (New York: Bowker, 1972), 167–83.

56. *NYT,* 9 Oct. 1970, 1. The Percy resolution was supported by Mansfield, Church, Cooper, Hatfield, McGovern, and Hughes, among others.

57. "Replies to Reporters' Questions About Reaction to Address on Southeast Asia, 8 Oct. 1970," *PPP: RN, 1970,* 830.

58. "A Way Out?" *Christian Century* 87 (21 Oct. 1970): 1244.

59. "Nixon, the Viet Cong, and the 'Third Force,'" *War/Peace Report* 10 (Nov. 1970): 13.

60. Sidney Lens, "Nixon's Peace Plan Is a Camouflage for Vietnamese Surrender," *American Report* 1 (30 Oct. 1970): 4. *American Report* was founded as a CALC journal.

61. *PPP: RN, 1970,* 890; 854, 827, 934.

62. Ibid., 934, 1060, 1035, 865, 1035.

63. Quoted in Jonathan Schell, *The Time of Illusion,* 130, 1026.

64. Although these grand juries returned 400 indictments, mostly on conspiracy charges, the proceedings yielded a conviction and plea-bargaining rate of only 15 percent, compared with 65 percent in all federal criminal cases. Donner, *Age of Surveillance,* 355–56.

65. Quoted from Sydney H. Pendleton, "Vietnam Veterans' Long March for Peace," *Fellowship* 36 (Nov. 1970): 1; and "Operation RAW," n.d., box 3, Vietnam Veterans Against the War (VVAW) Records, SHSW; emphasis in the original.

66. Coffin, *Once To Every Man,* 308.

67. "Taking Fr. Berrigan Seriously," *Commonweal* 92 (7 Aug. 1970), 380.

68. Burt Cantrell report on 31 Aug.–3 Sept. 1970 trip, in box 12, 1977 accession, SANE Records, SCPC.

69. The Campaign to Set the Date was initially headed by Allan Brick of the FOR, but by January 1971 Herschel Halbert was listed as director of Set the Date Now (STDN). See *American Report* 1 (25 Dec. 1970): 1, and "Toward Peace in Indochina," an STDN brochure, n.d. [ca. Dec. 1970], carton 2, 1977 accession, SANE Records.

70. Sidney Lens, "National Coalition Against War, Racism and Repression: Why It Was Formed!" box: Antiwar Activities 1969–71, Lens Papers, CHSL. See also press release of the National Coalition Against War, Racism, and Repression, 16 Oct. 1970, and related materials under People's Coalition for Peace and Freedom, Vietnam file, PED files, AFSC Records, AFSC. An interim committee included Meacham, Sidney Peck, Douglas Dowd, Roberto Elias (Chicago Moratorium), and Thierrie Cook (Seattle Liberation Front). William Douthard was named national coordinator.

71. Ron Young, "Report on a Meeting in Washington, D.C. November 5, 1970," folder: People's Peace Treaty folder, PED files, AFSC Records, AFSC.

72. "Summary of Weekend Workshop on Spring Action Proposals," 16–17 Oct. 1970, Vietnam-NAG file, PED files, AFSC Records, AFSC.

73. David McReynolds, "What the Movement Has Learned," *WIN* 7 (15 Feb. 1971): 8; John Kenneth Galbraith, "The Plain Lessons of a Bad Decade," *Foreign Policy,* no. 1 (Winter 1970–71): 41, 45.

74. "Toward Peace in Indochina," n.d. [ca. Dec. 1970], SANE Records, SCPC.

75. Interview with Bob Greenblatt, "The People's Peace Treaty and May First," *WIN* 7 (15 Feb. 1971): 22.

76. Gordon C. Zahn, "Terrorism for Peace and Justice," *Commonweal* 93 (23 Oct. 1970): 84; Mark Morris, "Organize Don't Burglarize," *WIN* 6 (1 Oct. 1970): 21; and Charles Derber, "Terrorism and the Movement," *Monthly Review* 22 (Feb. 1971): 41.

77. Bronson Clark, "The Grave of Revolution," *AFSC Quaker Service Bulletin* (Winter 1970): 6.

78. McReynolds, "Comments on Al Hassler's Critique of New Mobe Program Suggestions," 10 Sept. 1970, p. 2, Hassler transfile 2, FOR Records, SCPC.

79. Rosemary Reuther, "The Discussion Continues," *Commonweal* 92 (4 Sept. 1970): 431.

80. Howard Zinn to Daniel Berrigan, 12 Oct. 1970, Berrigan Papers, Cornell.

81. William Stringfellow and Anthony Towne, "A Christmas Card from the FBI," *Commonweal* 93 (15 Jan. 1971): 364.

82. Jerry Rubin, *Growing (Up) at Thirty-Seven* (New York: M. Evans, 1976), 4, 2.

83. Martin Jezer, *WIN* 7 (15 Feb. 1971): 4, 3.

84. James Finn, "After Vietnam—What?" *American Report* 1 (29 Jan. 1971): 4; emphasis added.

85. *NYT,* 5 Nov. 1971, 48, 1.

86. R. G., "Nixon's 8-Point Peace Plan for Re-Election," *Liberation* 16 (Feb. 1972): 2.

87. *NYT,* 7 Jan. 1971, 1.

88. *NYT,* 1 Apr. 1971, 16.

89. *Baltimore Sun,* 31 Jan. 1971, DOD.

90. James Wechsler, "A Time of Numbness," *American Report* 1 (26 Feb. 1971): 4.

91. Arthur Hoppe, "To Root Against Your Own Country," published in *San Francisco Chronicle,* quoted in *War/Peace Report* 11 (Apr. 1971): 13.

92. *NYT,* 8 Apr. 1971, 1.

93. *NYT,* 2 Apr. 1971, 15.

94. "Peace Is Still a Long, Long March Away," *I. F. Stone's Bi-Weekly* 19 (3 May 1971): 4.

95. *Guardian,* 19 Dec. 1970, 4; "Spring Antiwar Activities, 1971" [proposal passed by NPAC convention, 4–6 Dec. 1970], box 18, SMC Records, SHSW; Halstead, *Out Now!* 584–87.

96. "Summary report of the National Coalition Conference, Chicago, Jan. 8–10, 1971," file: PPT, People's Coalition for Peace and Justice (PCPJ) Papers, SCPC.

97. Quoted in Carl Davidson, "War Protests Set for May," *Guardian,* 23 Jan. 1971, 4. The spring action was referred to variously as MayDay, May Day, and Mayday; the latter, although least used, is the most appropriate word—a signal of distress.

98. "PCPJ Memo," 5 Feb. 1971 [Ron] Young carton 1, FOR Records, SCPC.

99. David McReynolds to David Dellinger, 15 Feb. 1971, carton 8, WRL Records, SCPC.

100. David McReynolds, "It May Not Be a Wedding But They Are in Bed Together," *WIN* 7 (1 Apr. 1971): 16.

101. In Apr. 1972, with the trial jury deadlocked, a mistrial was declared.

102. Stewart Meacham to Lorena J. Tinker, 5 Mar. 1971, under People's Coalition for Peace and Justice, Vietnam file, PED files, AFSC Records, AFSC.

103. Halstead, *Out Now!* 598.

104. *Memo* 1 (Apr. 1971): 12.

105. *Newsweek,* 3 May 1971, 24. The San Francisco organizers estimated 300,000 people.

106. "Protest: A Week Against the War," *Time,* 3 May 1971, 10.

107. Ibid., 11.

108. David McReynolds to Clancy Sigal, 22 Apr. 1971, carton 8, WRL Records, SCPC.

109. *Mayday* (1971): A Tactical Manual, p. 24 (author's copy).

110. "The Crowd in the Cage," *Newsweek,* 17 May 1971, 24.

111. Ray Price, quoted in Small, *Johnson, Nixon, and the Doves,* 217.

112. "The Word from Washington," *Progressive* 35 (June 1971): 12.

113. David McReynolds, "Wanted: Those Over Thirty," *Fellowship* 37 (June–July 1971), 2.

114. A few years later, the federal courts concurred in this criticism. In January 1975, a District of Columbia court awarded $12 million to 1,200 citizens in recompense for suffering unlawful arrest during the MayDay demonstrations. It was at that time the largest civil judgment ever awarded, and the first in which damages were awarded directly for the violation of the citizens' constitutional rights. "Paying for Mayday," *Newsweek,* 27 Jan. 1975, 46.

115. Quoted in Hersh, *Price of Power,* 427n.

116. Charles W. Colson, *Born Again* (Old Tappan, N.J.: Chosen Books, 1976), 45.

117. *The Winter Soldier Investigation: An Inquiry into American War Crimes* (New York: Beacon, 1972), an abridged transcript of the hearings; emphasis added. Guenter Lewy argues that some of the testimony was compromised, *America in Vietnam,* 316–17.

118. *WP,* 23 May 1971, DOD.

119. Albert H. Cantrill and Charles W. Roll, Jr., *Hopes and Fears of the American People* (New York: Universe Books, 1971), 32–33.

120. Bella Abzug, *Bella!* (New York: Saturday Review Press, 1972), 35, 107; "The Harrisburg Indictments," *Commonweal* 93 (5 Feb. 1971), 435.

121. Bernard Asbell, "The Day America Could Have Used a Psychiatrist," *Today's Health* 49 (Aug. 1971): 27–29.

122. Hans Morgenthau, "Calley and the American Conscience," *New Leader* 54 (19 Apr. 1971): 5; "Calley: Thee and We," *Progressive* 35 (May 1971): 6.

123. Official figures for the incidence of fragging are cited in Lewy, *America in Vietnam,* 156; AWOL, desertion, and conscientious objection rates are given in John Helmer, *Bringing the War Home: The American Soldier in Vietnam and After* (New York: Free Press, 1971), 39, and David Cortright, *Soldiers in Revolt: The American Military Today* (Garden City, N.Y.: Doubleday/Anchor Books, 1975), 11.

124. Quoted in "Protest: A Week Against the War," 13.

125. Lawrence M. Baskir and William A. Strauss, *Chance and Circumstance: The Draft, the War and the Vietnam Generation* (New York: Knopf, 1978), 68.

126. *American Report* 1 (19 Feb. 1971): 1.

127. Quoted in Zaroulis and Sullivan, *Who Spoke Up?"* 357–58.

128. "Another Plan for Peace," *America* 1 (7 May 1971): 474.

129. Al Hubbard, "Winter Soldier Offensive: Phase 3," n.d. [ca. Feb. 1971], in box 6, VVAW Records, SHSW. Walt Kelly recalled that the phrase "We have met the enemy and he is us" was reduced from the introduction to his *Pogo Papers* (New York: Simon and Schuster, 1952–53), in which, speaking of environmental pollution, he had written, "we shall meet the enemy, and not only may he be ours, he may be us." Mrs. Walt Kelly and Bill Crouch, Jr., eds., *The Best of Pogo* (New York: Simon and Schuster, 1982), 224.

130. Calvin Trillin, "War Without Hawks," *New Yorker,* 22 May 1971, 68.

131. *Baltimore Sun,* 6 June 1971, DOD. *PI,* 18 Aug. 1971, DOD (the 65–20 percent figure in July compared to 60–26 percent in April); Cantrill and Roll, *Hopes and Fears,* 40.

132. Norman Podhoretz, "A Note On Vietnamization," *Commentary* 51 (May 1971): 8.

133. David Hawk, in *Christianity and Crisis* 31 (3 May 1971): 83.

134. "The Kooks Nobody Noticed," *I. F. Stone's Bi-Weekly* 19 (17 May 1971): 4.

11. Normalizing Dissent

1. See Don Luce, "An Open Letter to the People of Viet Nam," *American Report* 18 (June 19971): 2, 8.

2. Quoted in "'You Don't See Any Hawks Around Here,'" *Newsweek,* 19 Apr. 1971, 27.

3. Harry R. Haldeman, with Joseph DiMona, *The Ends of Power* (New York: Times Books, 1978), 110. "Henry," Haldeman noted, "really knew how to get to Nixon."

4. Quoted in Colson, *Born Again,* 58.

5. G. Gordon Liddy, *Will* (New York: St. Martin's, 1980), 182, 194.

6. *NYT,* 6 June 1971, 52; *NYT,* 27 June 1971, 1.

7. Robert S. Lecky, "CALC after Ann Arbor: Peace Efforts Renewed," *American Report* 1 (3 Sept. 1971): 6.

8. Chuck Fager, "Coalition Capers," *WIN* 7 (1 Sept. 1971): 15.

9. Hayden, *Reunion,* 435.

10. Quoted in *Guardian,* 29 Sept. 1971, 13; and Abbie Hoffman, "I Quit," *WIN* 7 (1 Sept. 1971): n.p.

11. *NYT,* 8 Nov. 1971, 6.

12. *NYT,* 17 Sept. 1971, 2.

13. Harris, *WP,* Nov. 1971, DOD; Harris, *Chicago Tribune,* 11 Nov. 1971, DOD.

14. *NYT,* 1 Oct. 1971, 5.

15. *NYT,* 18 Nov. 1971, 1; and 21 Nov. 1971, sec. 4, p. 5.

16. *NYT,* 24 Nov. 1971, 1.

17. The movement's estimates for 6 Nov. are in Halstead, *Out Now!* 651; but far lower figures were given in the contemporary press.

18. "Son of Mayday," *Newsweek,* 8 Nov. 1971, 45.

19. David McReynolds to Bill Sutherland, 3 Dec. 1971, carton 9, WRL Records; Swerdlow, quoted in minutes of a NAG meeting, 17–18 Dec. 1971, in Young carton 1, FOR Records, SCPC.

20. Gordon Zahn, "Who Are We? Where Are We Going?" *Fellowship* 38 (Jan. 1972): 7.

21. All these figures are drawn from archival records and correspondence. They are only approximate and reflect assessments at different months of a given year.

22. These were Ruth Gage-Colby, Jerry Gordon, James Lafferty, and John Williams—four of the five NPAC coordinators. *Guardian,* 8 Dec. 1971, 3.

23. Roy Kepler to David McReynolds, 8 Dec. 1971, and McReynolds to Kepler, 15 Dec. 1971, carton 9, WRL Records; McReynolds, "Reflections from Hanoi," *WRL News* (Sept.–Oct. 1971): 3–4.

24. "Why the Response of Peace Leaders to the 'Appeal To All Combatants' Can Be Crucial in Ending the Killing in Indochina," 11 Nov. 1971, issued by the U.S. Committee to End the Killing in Indochina. *Fellowship* 37 (Jan. 1972): 5.

25. Quotation from Al Hassler to John Swomley, 19 Nov. 1971, Young carton 1, FOR Records, SCPC; but, for the formulation of his argument, see especially Hassler to Richard Fernandez, 21 Oct. 1971, in box 3, CALC Records, SCPC; and Hassler to Fernandez, 19 Nov. 1971, Young carton 1, FOR Records.

26. Quotation from Fernandez to E[ugene] C[arson] Blake et al., "End the Killing or U.S. Withdrawal," 6 Oct. 1971, box 3, CALC Records, SCPC; but see also Fernandez to Hassler, 8 Nov. 1971, Young carton 1, FOR Records, SCPC.

27. David McReynolds to James Wechsler, 1 Dec. 1971, carton 9, WRL Records, SCPC.

28. *NYT,* 29 Dec. 1971, 32.

29. Quoted in *NYT,* 20 Oct. 1971, 78.

30. Gallup, *PI,* 18 June 1971, DOD.

31. *NYT,* 29 Sept. 1971, 16.

32. Quotations from Arnold S. Kaufman, "A Strategy for Radical Liberals," *Dissent* 18 (1971–72): 393; and minutes of NAG meeting, 17–18 Dec. 1971, NAG file, PED files, AFSC Records, AFSC.

33. *NYT,* 6 Jan. 1972, 22.

34. *NYT,* 11 Jan. 1972, 1.

35. *PPP: RN, 1972,* 12.

36. Ibid., 43.

37. Ibid., 193.

38. *NYT,* 8 Feb. 1972, 1; memo, David McReynolds, "Vietnam: Endless War," 14 Feb. 1972, in Hassler Transfile 2, FOR Records, SCPC.

39. Hersh, *Price of Power,* 486.

40. "Ecumenical Witness: Withdraw Now!" *Christian Century* 89 (26 Jan. 1972): 81; for positions taken by the assembly, see "A New Ecumenical Witness Against War," *Fellowship* 38 (Feb. 1972): 2.

41. Jim Douglass, quoted in *American Report* 2 (31 Mar. 1972): 3; National Federation, quoted in *NYT,* 17 Mar. 1972, 20; David McReynolds, "The Air War, Or the Banality of Evil," *WRL News* (Jan.–Feb. 1972): n.p.

42. The Indochina Education Council was created by agencies of the United Church of Christ, the United Presbyterian Church in the U.S.A., and the United Methodist Church. It operated also an Indochina Resource Center that made academic expertise and information accessible to Congress, peace groups, and journalists.

43. Quotations from "The Third Indochina War: An Interview with Fred Branfman," *Liberation* 17 (Apr. 1972): 21; Branfman, "The Indochina War," *Memo* 2 (Feb. 1972), 3; see also Branfman, "The Era of the Blue Machine, Laos: 1969–," *Washington Monthly,* July 1971, 9; reprinted in *Indochina Chronicle,* no. 6–7 (15 Oct. 1971): 1.

44. About 30 leaders were present, representative of some 18 groups including the FOR, CALC, WRL, WSP, WILPF, NARMIC, and AFSC. "Report of NAG meeting, 11–12 Jan. 1972," NAG file, PED files, AFSC Records, AFSC.

45. "It's time," *Opposition: Air War,* no. 1 (30 Mar. 1972): 1.

46. It was referred to alternately as the Campaign to End the Air War, the Campaign to Stop the Air War, and Project Air War.

47. Flyer, "What Is the People's Coalition for Peace and Justice," n.d. [ca. spring 1972], file 1, PCPJ Papers, SCPC.

48. *Honeywell Campaign: Organizing Manual* (New York: CALC, Apr. 1972), 5.

49. "NARMIC," 1 Sept. 1970, program description in Narmic file, PED files, AFSC Records, AFSC.

50. Allan Brick, "The Ongoing War," *Fellowship* 38 (1 Jan. 1972): 4.

51. *NYT,* 6 Apr. 1972, 1.

52. *NYT,* 9 Apr. 1972, 1.

53. Quoted in *NYT,* 13 Apr. 1972, 1.

54. Gallup, *NYT,* 26 Apr. 1972, 9.

55. Memo to key AMP leaders, 19 Apr. 1972, AMP folder, box 2, PCPJ Papers, SCPC.

56. *NYT,* 5 Apr. 1972, 1.

57. *NYT,* 20 Apr. 1972, 1.

58. *PPP: RN, 1972,* 552, 553.

59. *NYT,* 7 May 1972, IV, 15.

60. *PPP: RN, 1972,* 585.

61. Nixon, *RN,* 606.

62. "Clamor and Caution," *Newsweek,* 22 May 1972, 24.

63. Ibid.

64. *NYT,* 12 May 1972, 20; and 14 May, sec. 4, p. 12.

65. *NYT,* 9 May 1972, 41.

66. Dale Anderson et al., "The Bombing of America," *Christianity and Crisis* 32 (15 May 1972): 115.

67. William Stringfellow, "Impeach Nixon Now," *Commonweal* 96 (26 May 1972): 281.

68. *NYT,* 1 June 1972, 27.

69. Quoted in *NYT,* 1 May 1972, 1.

70. "The President Buys More Time—And Some Hope—on the War," *Time,* 12 June 1972, 16; see *NYT,* 14 May 1972, 28.

71. *NYT,* 2 June 1972, 1.

72. Richard Nixon, in House of Representatives Judiciary Committee tape of 29 June 1972 meeting, quoted in *NYT,* 30 June 1974, 27.

73. Sanford Gottlieb, "Some Proposals for George McGovern's Primary Campaign," 27 Dec. 1977, carton 1, 1977 accession, SANE Records, SCPC.

74. *NYT,* 12 June 1972, 32.

75. David McReynolds to Roy Kepler, 27 June 1972, carton 7, WRL Records, SCPC.

76. "Independence," *Guardian,* 21 June 1972, 8.

77. "The AFSC Indochina Summer Project," 26 May 1972, a proposal for AFSC meeting, Vietnam, Projects file, PED files, AFSC Records, AFSC; Fred Branfman, comp., *Voices from the Plain of Jars: Life Under an Air War* (New York: Harper and Row, 1972).

78. *NYT,* 13 July 1972, 22.

79. George McGovern, *An American Journey* (New York: Random House, 1974), 117.

80. Philip C. Jessup, form letter, 16 Aug. 1972, in Vietnam War folder, box 36, Jessup Papers, LC; Lawyers Committee, open letter to UN Secretary-General, ibid.

81. *NYT,* 24 Aug. 1972, 9.

82. Hayden dates Fonda's return in the spring of 1972, in Hayden, *Reunion,* 448.

83. Tom Hayden, "The IPC: A Working Paper," Mar. 1973, pp. 19, 2, 24, folder: Pamphlets folder, carton 3, Indochina Peace Campaign (IPC) Records, SHSW; emphasis in the original; also Tom Hayden, untitled draft article, n.d. [ca. Nov. 1972], in box 11, Staughton Lynd Papers, SHSW.

84. IPC memo, n.d. [ca. early Oct. 1972], box 1, PCPJ Papers, SCPC; emphasis in the original.

85. *NYT,* 1 July 1972, 1.

86. *NYT,* 13 Aug. 1972, 31.

87. *NYT,* 17 July 1972, 18.

88. Quoted in Joseph Kraft, "Anti-War Movement Flounders in Miami," *Baltimore Sun,* n.d. [ca. Aug. 1972], DOD.

89. *NYT,* 16 Aug. 1972, 10.

90. *NYT,* 20 Aug. 1972, 5.

91. *NYT,* 24 Aug. 1972, 1.

92. *NYT,* 27 Aug. 1972, 34.

93. *NYT,* 11 Oct. 1972, 1.

94. *NYT,* 12 Oct. 1972, 40, 1; Melvin Laird quoted in *NYT,* 25 Sept. 1972, 42.

95. *PPP: RN, 1972,* 987, 1119.

96. *NYT,* 27 Oct. 1972, 1, 37.

97. Kissinger insisted when discussing these negotiations in his memoirs that he, his aides, and the president sincerely believed that the agreement provided adequately for Saigon's political future. He believed it would have succeeded if American assistance had continued, which is to say if executive authority had not been undermined by Watergate. See especially Kissinger, *White House Years,* 1470. It is not altogether clear what form and extent of assistance were anticipated, but in any case the view formed a convenient rational for Saigon's defeat in the event that aid was insufficient.

98. George Gallup, *The Gallup Poll: Public Opinion, 1972–77* (Wilmington, Del.: Scholarly Resources, 1978), vol. 1, *1972–75,* 62.

99. Harris, *WP,* 2 Nov. 1972, DOD. No matter how strongly the electorate favored Nixon's war policies, most Americans did not expect them to work. Although they approved of the president's handling of the war by 59–33 percent, nearly half thought that the South Vietnamese government would collapse following America's final withdrawal, and when asked about South Vietnam's status in 1977, 38 percent said that they expected the country to be governed by communists and another 33 percent anticipated a coalition government. In the fall of 1972, in other words, a large majority of Americans already expected and accepted an outcome in Vietnam which they had long fought to oppose. *NYT,* 26 Nov. 1972, 18; *WP,* 2 Nov. 1972, and 14 Dec. 1972, H2, all DOD.

100. There was, in addition, one independent in the House and one in the Senate where also one was listed independently as a conservative Republican. U.S. Bureau of the Census, *Statistical Abstract of the United States: 1988* (108th edn.), Washington, D.C., 1987, 242.

101. Kissinger, *White House Years,* 1406.

102. Hans Morgenthau, "Kissinger's Next Test," *New Leader* 55 (13 Nov. 1972): 6.

103. Roger Shinn, "Our Cause is Not Just," *Christian Century* 89 (1 Nov. 1972): 1103.

104. Nixon, *RN,* 1972, 722.

105. Daniel Bell and Nathan Glazer, "The Shame of Richard Nixon," *New Leader* 56 (22 Jan. 1973): 3; emphasis in the original.

106. *NYT,* 27 Dec. 1973, 39.

107. John M. Swomley, Jr., "Amnesty and Reconciliation," *Christian Century* 59 (27 Dec. 1972): 1322.

108. George D. Aiken, *Aiken: A Senate Diary* (Brattleboro, Vt.: Stephen Greene, 1976), 134–35.

109. *NYT,* 30 Dec. 1973, 1.

110. *Congressional Quarterly,* 21 Dec. 1972, 1.

111. John Ehrlichman, *Witness to Power: The Nixon Years* (New York: Simon and Schuster, 1982), 315.

112. *NYT,* 3 Jan. 1973, 1; 5 Jan. 1973, 1, 5.

113. *NYT,* 4 Jan. 1973, 1.

114. *NYT,* 21 Jan. 1973, 1.

115. *NYT,* 24 Jan. 1973, 1.

116. Kissinger, *White House Years,* 1475.

12. Closing the Circle

1. Shirley Lens and Lillian Hayward, "Chicago Women for Peace: Law Vigil," *Chicago Tribune*; reprinted in *Memo: Women for Peace* 3 (Spring 1973): 25.

2. "A Temporary Expiation of Guilt," *Christian Century* 40 (21 Mar. 1973): 331.

3. Robert Lifton, quoted in *NYT,* 28 Mar. 1973, 47.

4. *The Harris Survey Yearbook of Public Opinion 1973* (New York: Louis Harris and Associates, 1976), 264, 275–77, 281, 282, 289, 290; 1973 Gallup, *The Gallup Poll, 1972–77,* 1: 93–94.

5. *NYT,* 25 Jan. 1973, 1; 27 Jan. 1973, 1.

6. Fay Honey Knopp to Daniel Berrigan, 24 June 1973, Berrigan Papers.

7. Mrs. Betsy Homan, quoted in "Has the U.S. Heard the Last of the 'Peaceniks'?" *U.S. News and World Report,* 30 Apr. 1973, 55.

8. Quotations from Pat Jordan, "Vietnam: Our Peace is Christ," *Catholic Worker* 34 (Feb. 1973): 1; "Vietnam: Beyond the Ceasefire," the WRL Executive

Committee, 28 Jan. 1973, box 2, PCPJ Papers (italicized in original); and *BEM News Notes* (5 Feb. 1973): 1, in carton 2, BEM Records. Similarly, see "Rejoice, Rejoice," *New Republic,* 3 Feb. 1973, 10; and "Editorial," *Pax,* n.d. [ca. Feb. 1973], p. 3, box 1, Chicago Peace Council (CPC) Records, CHSL.

9. From L.A. Center [of IPC], "notes on strategy and programs for Detroit conference," Conference National Meeting folder, Detroit, 16–18 Feb. 1973, carton 11, IPC Records, SHSW.

10. Notes of NAG meeting, 20–21 Nov. 1971, attached to FOR executive committee minutes, 11 Dec. 1972, FOR Records, SCPC.

11. Halstead, *Out Now!* 703.

12. Staughton Lynd to Mrs. Carol Bernstein, 28 Sept. 1971, folder 10, box 9, Lynd Papers, SHSW; and Lynd, "New American Movement: A Way to Overcome the Mistakes of the Past," n.d. [ca. Sept. 1971], folder 9, box 11, Lynd Papers. Alice Lynd worried that the acronym NAM might be confused with Vietnam or with the National Association of Manufacturers.

13. Minutes of meeting of 29 Dec. 1972, in Edward Snyder to Dudley Ward, 2 Jan. 1973, folder: CSFW 1973, Friends Committee on National Legislation (FCNL) Records, FCNL.

14. Jan Orloff, "Final Project Report," 21 Mar. 1983, folder: Final Project Report, Coalition to Stop Funding the War (CSFW) Records, SCPC; emphasis in the original.

15. Morgenthau, "Kissinger's Next Test," 6.

16. AFSC medical assistance to the communist population has become a source of controversy. The agency maintains that no more than 15 percent of its wartime medical aid was channeled to the NLF or North Vietnamese, and this under government license. John Sullivan, "An AFSC Reflection . . . ," May 1988, 5 (author's copy).

17. Daniel Berrigan to Jim Forest, 9 Apr. 1973, Berrigan Papers, Cornell.

18. "Position Paper" [on amnesty], VVAW folder, SPP, Bancroft.

19. The two alliances were the Interreligious Task Force on Amnesty and the National Council for Universal and Unconditional Amnesty, the latter representative of both religious and secular groups at national and local levels.

20. "SANE staff recommendations to the committee on the Future of SANE," 18 Nov. 1972, SANE Records, SCPC.

21. Trudi Young, "National CALC program staff memo," Jan. 1974, file 21, CALC Records, SCPC.

22. Michael Walzer, "The Peace Movement," *New Republic,* 10 Feb. 1973, 24.

23. This synopsis of the movement's self-evaluation draws upon minutes and resolutions, publications and correspondence for the period. Only direct quotations are cited.

24. Generally assumed, this point was made explicitly in "An Anti-War Decade: The Fruits of Protest," *Focal Point* (15 Sept.–1 Oct. 1973), box 3, PCPJ Papers, SCPC.

25. Rosemary Reuther, "America the Beautiful," *American Report* 3 (12 Mar. 1973): 12.

26. Tom Hayden, "Some Thoughts on Peace," May 1973, Arizona folder, carton 9, IPC Records, SHSW.

27. Hayden, "Vietnam: The Struggle for Peace, 1972–1973," n.p., introduction, Feb. 1973, in Pamphlets folder, carton 3, IPC Records.

28. David Dellinger, quoted in *NYT,* 18 Feb. 1973, 60; "The Challenges of Peace," *Progressive* 37 (Mar. 1973): 3; "Editorial," *Pax* (Feb. 1973): 3, box 1, CPC Records, CHSL.

29. Nixon, *RN,* 685, 714, 757.

30. Quotations from Safire, *Before the Fall,* 673–74.

31. David McReynolds to William Hendrickson, 20 July 1973, in carton 4, WRL Records. McReynolds was explaining why movement leaders were not going to get involved in a drive to impeach Nixon.

32. *NYT,* 19 Apr. 1973, 1.

33. J. William Fulbright, quoted in *Face the Nation: Transcripts, 1973* (Metuchen, N.J.: Scarecrow, 1975), 16: 99.

34. *NYT,* 29 Mar. 1973, 1.

35. *NYT,* 3 May 1973, 14.

36. Al Hassler to Guy Gipson, 1 May 1973, Hassler transfile 9, FOR Records, SCPC.

37. *Indochina Chronicle* [of the Indochina Resource Center], no. 27 (31 Aug. 1973): 3.

38. Gallup poll, cited in *NYT,* 13 May 1973, 5.

39. *Legislative Update* (29 June 1973).

40. When six of those arrested were brought before federal judge (and former Indiana Republican congressman) Charles W. Halleck, he read their offense, recited their prayer, and then declared that "there's no way I'd have any one of these people spend one day in jail." Quoted in Mobi Warren, "Unauthorized Prayer," *Fellowship* 39 (Sept. 1973): 31.

41. John McAuliff, "How to End a War That's Already Over," *Indochina Program Newsletter,* no. 16 (12 Apr. 1973): 1.

42. *NYT,* 9 Sept. 1973, sec. 4, p. 3.

43. Quoted in *NYT,* 24 Oct. 1973, 31.

44. Stewart Meacham, "Why Watergate? Why not Vietnam?" *AFSC Quaker Service Bulletin* 54 (Fall 1973): 6.

45. "An Anti-War Decade," *Focal Point* (15 Sept.–1 Oct. 1973), box 3, PCPJ Papers, SCPC.

46. James Abourezk to Larry Levin, 18 Oct. 1973, CSFW Records, SCPC.

47. The organizations represented at the Germantown Conference included the AFSC, CALC, CPF, CSFW, FOR, IPC, PCPJ, SANE, WILPF, WRL, Episcopal Peace Fellowship, Indochina Resource Center, and Vietnam Resource Center. "Indochina Conference: Official Report" (Germantown, Ohio: 26–28 Oct. 1973), Indochina Conference folder, carton 11, IPC Records, SHSW.

48. Ibid.

49. *NYT,* 17 Oct. 1973, 10.

50. *NYT,* 28 Jan. 1974, 24; 20 Jan. 1974, 4; 25 Feb. 1974, 1.

51. *NYT,* 27 Feb. 1974, 4.

52. *NYT,* 9 Mar. 1974, 3; 18 Mar. 1974, 6.

53. *NYT,* 16 Apr. 1974, 9; 21 Apr. 1974, sec. 2, p. 2; *American Report* 4 (15 Apr. 1974): 1.

54. "Aid Defeat Examined," *Focal Point* 1 (15 May 1974): 1.

55. *NYT,* 17 Apr. 1974, 8; 18 Apr. 1974, 2.

56. *NYT,* 10 May 1974, 17.

57. Ron Young to Sanford Gottlieb, 7 Feb. 1974, SANE Records, SCPC.

58. Tom Howarth, "Ten Months in Connecticut" (1 Mar. 1973–1 Jan. 1974), p. 4, SANE Washington Logbook, SFNO, 1974.

59. Don Luce to Carol [?] et al., "The Country and the War—1974," 18 Mar. 1974, folder: IPC Mobile Education Project, carton 1, IPC Records, SHSW.

60. John McAuliff, quoted in Minutes of the Peace Education Committee, AFSC, 17–19 May 1984, in AFSC/NPED Committee file, PED files, AFSC Records, AFSC.

61. Diane Norman, "Breaking the Silence on the 'Peace' in Vietnam," *Center* 8 (Jan.–Feb. 1975): 2, 5–6; see also Carol Bragg, "Carol Bragg Sums Up Tiger

Cage Vigil and Fast," *Peacework* 24 (Oct. 1974), Peacework folder, carton 8, IPC Records, SHSW.

62. *NYT,* 26 July 1974, 8.

63. Richard Nixon, "Address to the Nation Announcing Decision to Resign," 8 Aug. 1974, *PPP: RN, 1974,* 627.

64. *NYT,* 10 Aug. 1974, 1.

65. Daniel Berrigan, form letter, Aug. 1974, Berrigan Papers, Cornell; "Big Un" [*sic*] in original.

66. David McReynolds, "After the Fall," *WRL News* (Sept.–Oct. 1974), n.p.

67. Ibid.

68. Peter Barrer, "Why I'm Changing My Way of Working," *Peacework* (Nov. 1974): 7, in Peacework folder, carton 8, IPC Records, SHSW.

69. Detailed in Arnold R. Isaacs, *Without Honor: Defeat in Vietnam and Cambodia* (Baltimore: Johns Hopkins Univ. Press, 1983), 310–13.

70. *NYT,* 28 Jan. 1975, 29, 5.

71. *NYT,* 27 Jan. 1975, 5; 10 Feb. 1975, 3; 7 Mar. 1975, 1; 13 Mar. 1975, 1; and 17 Mar. 1975, 3.

72. *NYT,* 28 Jan. 1975, 16; 12 Mar. 1975, 1; 21 Feb. 1975, 8; and 9 Mar. 1975, 18.

73. "Saying No to 'One More Time'," *Christian Century* 92 (5–12 Feb. 1975): 99.

74. The phrase was attributed without citation to columnist Mary McCrory.

75. *NYT,* 4 Apr. 1975, 1, 10; 27 Mar. 1975, 1.

76. *NYT,* 20 Mar. 1975, 1; 21 Mar. 1975, 10.

77. See the report in *NYT,* 13 Apr. 1975, sec. 4, p. 41; and also the account in Isaacs, *Without Honor,* 395–97.

78. James S. Kunen, "Slow Down," *New Times,* 2 May 1975, 6.

79. "Involvement's Last Hours," *Commonweal* (25 Apr. 1975): 67.

80. Michele Clark, "The Politics of Guilt," *WIN* 20 (8 May 1975): 10.

81. *NYT,* 18 Apr. 1975, 15.

82. *NYT,* 24 Apr. 1975, 1.

83. *NYT,* 28 Apr. 1975, 18.

84. For a detailed description of the evacuation and of the fall of Saigon see Isaacs, *Without Honor,* 447–87.

85. Hendrick Hertzberg, in "The Collapse of America's Indochina Empire," *WIN* 11 (1 May 1975): 7.

86. Arthur Waskow, "Celebration and Mourning," *WIN* 11 (8 May 1975): 11; Paul Mayer and Barbara Deming, in "The Collapse of America's Indochina Empire," 7.

87. The renamed CSFW merged in 1976 with the Coalition on National Priorities and Military Policy to form the Coalition for a New Foreign and Military Policy, which a decade later became the Coalition for a New Foreign Policy.

88. "On 'Forgetting' Viet Nam," *Christianity and Crisis* 35 (23 June 1975): 154.

89. "Notes on the Future of the IPC," n.d. [ca. Mar. 1975] (author's copy).

90. "Operation Self-Deception," *Nation,* 26 Apr. 1975, 483.

91. W. D. Ehrhart, "A Relative Thing," in *To Those Who Have Gone Home Tired: New & Selected Poems* (New York: Thunder's Mouth Press, 1984), 18.

92. Garry Wills, in "The Meaning of Vietnam," *New York Review of Books* 22 (12 June 1975): 24.

93. From "In Distrust of Merits," *A Marianne Moore Reader* (New York: Viking, 1961), 45.

Bibliography

The references in this bibliography are selected for their contribution to the formulation and development of the volume. They are the materials most important to the construction of the narrative and interpretation of the antiwar movement and its context from 1955 to 1975, and are known to have been used by Professor DeBenedetti (having been cross-checked against his original manuscript and files of source notes) or were consulted by the assisting author. The reader is referred to the text and notes for sources specific to most particular events, speeches, and publications of opinion.

Manuscripts

Multiple Depositories

The Swarthmore College Peace Collection. Swarthmore, Pennsylvania, is the single most important archive on peace and antiwar movements. The major independent document groups consulted there include the records of the following organizations: Another Mother for Peace; Business Executives Move for Vietnam Peace; Clergy and Laity Concerned; Committee for Nonviolent Action; Friends Committee on National Legislation; Fellowship of Reconciliation; National Coalition Against War, Racism and Repression; National Committee for a Sane Nuclear Policy; National Mobilization Committee to End the War in Vietnam; People's Coalition for Peace and Justice; Postwar World Council; Student Peace Union; Vietnam Summer; Women's International League for Peace and Freedom; War Resisters League; and Women Strike for Peace.

The papers of Homer Jack, Staughton and Alice Lynd, and A. J. Muste were also valuable sources. In addition, the smaller holdings in Collective Document Group A were used for Center for Defense Information, Council for a Livable World, Coalition to Stop Funding the War, Indochina Peace Campaign, National Coordinating Committee to End the War in Vietnam, National Mobilization Committee, Physicians for Social Responsibility, Turn Toward Peace, and Vietnam Veterans Against the War.

The State Historical Society of Wisconsin Library, Madison, is another major archive with respect to opposition to the Vietnam War. Consulted were the records of the following groups: Americans for Democratic Action, Detroit Committee to End the War in Vietnam, Fifth Avenue Parade Committee, Indochina Peace Campaign, National Coordinating Committee to End the War in Vietnam, Students for a Democratic Society, Student Mobilization Committee to End the War in Vietnam, Student Peace Union, Vietnam Moratorium Committee, Vietnam Veterans Against the War, Women Strike for Peace, New Mobilization to End the War in Vietnam, Vietnam Mobilization Committee. The Staughton Lynd Papers and the Arthur Waskow Papers were also valuable.

The Lyndon Baines Johnson Presidential Library, Austin, Texas, is an indispensable repository regarding government interaction with citizen protest. Most useful for this study were the following files: Aides File, Cabinet Papers, Clark Clifford, Famous Names, George Christian, Meeting Notes, McGeorge Bundy

Aides, Name File, National Security, Office Files, Office Files of George Christian, Office Files of the President, Presidential Appointment, Social, White House Central and White House Confidential. The Oral History Interviews with Chester Cooper, Clark Clifford, Henry McPherson, John Roche, Harrison Salisbury, and Cyrus Vance were also helpful.

Other archives holding multiple collections of value for this study include:

The Bancroft Library, University of California, Berkeley: the Social Protest Project, and the World Without War Council (formerly Turn Toward Peace) Records

The Chicago Historical Society Library, Chicago, Manuscripts Division: the Chicago Peace Council Records, the Illinois Committee to Repeal the Draft, and the Sidney Lens Papers

The Hoover Institution on War, Revolution and Peace, Stanford, California: the New Left Collection, and the David Shoup Collection

The Library of Congress, Manuscript Division, Washington, D.C.: the Democratic Study Group Records, the Philip Jessup Papers, and the Reinhold Niebuhr Records

The Martin Luther King, Jr., Center for Nonviolent Social Change, Atlanta: the Martin Luther King, Jr., Papers, and the Student Nonviolent Coordinating Committee Records

The Sterling Library, Yale University: the Chester Bowles Papers, the Walter Lippmann Papers, and the Dwight McDonald Papers

The Tamiment Library, New York University: the Emergency Committee on the Cambodia-Laos-Vietnam War, and the journal *Resistance*

Specific Collections

The American Friends Service Committee Records, American Friends Service Committee headquarters, Philadelphia

The Daniel and Philip Berrigan Papers, Special Collections, Olin Library, Cornell University

The Center for National Security Studies, Washington

The Friends Committee on National Legislation Records, Friends Committee on National Legislation, Washington

The Jerome Grossman Papers, Department of Archives and Manuscripts, Boston Public Library, Boston

The Arnold S. Kaufman Papers, Michigan Historical Collections, Bentley Library, Ann Arbor

The John F. Kennedy Presidential Library, Waltham, Massachusetts

The Allard Lowenstein Papers, Southern Historical Collection, University of North Carolina, Chapel Hill

The Eugene R. McCarthy Oral History Collection, Georgetown University

The Hans J. Morgenthau Papers, Manuscript Division, Alderman Library, University of Virginia, Charlottesville

The SANE Washington Logbooks, SANE/Freeze National Office, Washington

The Benjamin Spock Papers, George Arents Library, Syracuse University

The Leo Szilard Papers, Special Collections, University of California, San Diego

The Norman Thomas Papers, Manuscripts Division, New York Public Library

Published Documents

The *Congressional Digest, Congressional Quarterly,* and *Congressional Record* were used in connection with specific issues. The annual volumes of *Public Papers of the Presidents* (Government Printing Office, Washington, D.C.) were studied for all the years of the Lyndon Johnson and Richard Nixon administrations and for the first year of the Ford Administration. A few published documents of particular importance to this study are included in the list of published books and articles.

Newspapers and Periodicals

The *New York Times* was studied for the entire period. Further newspaper accounts, notably the *Washington Post* and the *Philadelphia Inquirer*, were obtained from the useful News Clipping and Analysis Service, Secretary of the Air Force, Department of Defense.

The periodical literature can be divided into three categories. First, selected national journals were followed throughout the period. These include news magazines such as *Life, Look, Newsweek, Time,* and *U.S. News and World Report.* They include also national journals of political and cultural commentary such as the *Atlantic Monthly, Center Magazine, the Christian Century, Christianity and Crisis, Commentary, Commonweal, Dissent, Harper's, I. F. Stone's Weekly* [subsequently *Bi-Weekly*], the *New Leader, the New Republic,* the *New Statesman,* the *New Yorker,* the *Progressive,* and the *Saturday Review of Literature.* They include also periodicals which reflected particular constituencies, notably *ADA World Magazine,* the *Bulletin of Atomic Scientists, Commonweal,* and the *National Guardian* [after 1970 the *Guardian*], *New Left Notes* [in the mid-sixties], and *Ramparts.* In a class by itself but very useful was the *Village Voice.*

Second, numerous national journals were consulted only for isolated articles or on specific events. Most of these are not listed, even though articles from them may be cited in the text. A few articles which represent professional assessments of the antiwar movement are included in the list of secondary published works.

Third, there was a large quantity of periodical literature published by antiwar and related organizations. Most of these often ephemeral periodicals are not identified here but can be found in the manuscript collections of the organizations with which they were affiliated. Listed below is a selection of those journals which were followed for the entire period or that part of it for which they were published. The organization that published a particular periodical is listed in parentheses, together with the period for which the journal was most useful, if this was limited.

AFSC Quaker Service Bulletin (American Friends Service Committee)
American Report (Clergy and Laity Concerned, 1971–73)
The Catholic Worker (The Catholic Worker Movement)
CCCO Notes (Central Committee for Conscientious Objectors, from the mid-sixties)
CNVA Bulletin (Committee for Non-Violent Action, through 1966)
Fellowship (Fellowship of Reconciliation)
Focal Point (Indochina Peace Campaign, 1973–74)
Four Lights (Women's International League for Peace and Freedom)
Indochina Program Newsletter (Indochina Peace Campaign, 1971–75)
Liberation
National Information Memo (Women Strike for Peace)
The Resistance (The Resistance, 1971–72)
SANE World [originally published as *SANE Action*] (SANE, 1965–69)
SPU Bulletin (Student Peace Union, 1960–66)
War/Peace Report (1965–73)

WIN
Worldview
WRL News (War Resisters League)

Selected Books and Articles

Abzug, Bella. *Bella!* New York: Saturday Review Press, 1972.

Aiken, George D. *A Senate Diary.* Brattleboro, Vt.: Stephen Greene, 1976.

Ambrose, Steven E. *Eisenhower: The President.* New York: Simon and Schuster, 1984.

Andrews, Bruce. *Public Constraint and American Policy in Vietnam.* Beverly Hills, Calif.: Sage, 1976.

Bacciocco, Edward J. *The New Left in America: Reform to Revolution, 1956–1970.* Stanford: Hoover Institution Press, 1974.

Baez, Joan. *And a Voice to Sing With: A Memoir.* New York: Summit, 1987.

Bailey, George. "Television War: Trends in Network Coverage of Vietnam, 1965–1970," *Journal of Broadcasting* 20 (Spring 1976): 147–58.

Ball, George G. *The Past Has Another Pattern: Memoirs.* New York: Norton, 1982.

Bannan, John, and Rosemary Bannan. *Law, Morality, and the Courts: Peace Militants and the Courts.* Bloomington: Indiana Univ. Press, 1975.

Baskir, Lawrence M., and William A. Strauss. *Change and Circumstance: The Draft, The War and the Vietnam Generation.* New York: Knopf, 1978.

Belfrage, Cedric, and James Aronson. *Something to Guard: The Stormy Life of the National Guardian, 1947–1967.* New York: Columbia Univ. Press, 1978.

Berkowitz, William R. "The Impact of Anti-Vietnam Demonstrations Upon National Public Opinion and Military Indicators." *Social Sciences Research* 2 (Mar. 1973): 1–4.

Berman, Jerry J., and Morton M. Halperin, eds. *The Abuses of the Intelligence Agencies.* Washington, D.C.: Center for National Security Studies, 1975.

Berman, Ronald. *America in the Sixties: An Intellectual History.* New York: Harper and Row, 1970.

Berman, William C. *William Fulbright and the Vietnam War: The Dissent of a Political Realist.* Kent, Ohio: Kent State Univ. Press, 1988.

Bernstein, Barton. "Introduction." In Helen Hawkins et al., eds., *Toward a Livable World: Leo Szilard and the Crusade for Nuclear Arms Control,* pp. xvii–lxxiv. Cambridge, Mass.: MIT Press, 1987.

Berrigan, Daniel. *Night Flight to Hanoi: War Diary with Eleven Poems.* New York: Harper, 1971.

———. *The Trial of the Catonsville Nine.* Boston: Beacon, 1970.

Bigelow, Albert. *The Voyage of the Golden Rule: An Experiment with Truth.* Garden City, N.Y.: Doubleday, 1958.

Bloom, Lynn Z. *Doctor Spock: Biography of a Conservative Radical.* Indianapolis: Bobbs-Merrill, 1972.

Bolton, Charles D. "Alienation and Action: A Study of Peace Group Members." *American Journal of Sociology* 78 (Nov. 1972): 537–61.

Booth, Paul. *Peace Politics: A Study of the American Peace Movement and the Politics of the 1962 Congressional Elections.* Ann Arbor, Mich.: Peace Research and Education Project, 1964.

Boyer, Paul. *By the Bomb's Early Light: American Thought and Culture at the Dawn of the Atomic Age.* New York: Pantheon, 1985.

———. "From Activism to Apathy: The American People and Nuclear Weapons, 1963–1980." *Journal of American History* 70 (Mar. 1984): 837–44.

Braestrup, Peter. *Big Story: How the American Press and Television Reported and*

Interpreted the Crisis of Tet 1968 in Vietnam and Washington. New Haven, Conn.: Yale Univ. Press, 1978.

Breins, Wini. *The Great Refusal: Community and Organization in the New Left: 1962–1969.* New York: Praeger, 1982.

Brodie, Bernard. *Vietnam: Why We Failed in War and Politics.* New York: Macmillan, 1973.

Brooks, Robin. "Domestic Violence and America's Wars: An Historical Perspective." In Hugh Davis Graham and Ted Robert Gurr, eds., *The History of Violence in America: Historical and Comparative Perspectives,* pp. 529–50. New York: Praeger, 1969.

Brown, Robert McAfee. *Vietnam: Crisis of Conscience.* New York: Association Press, 1967.

Bunzel, John A. *Anti-Politics in America: Reflections on the Anti-Political Temper and Its Distortions of the Democratic Process.* New York: Knopf, 1967.

Burstein, Paul. "Senate Voting on the Vietnam War, 1964–1973: From Hawk to Dove." *Journal of Political and Military Sociology* 7 (Fall 1979): 171–82.

Burstein, Paul, and William Feurdenburg. "Changing Public Policy: The Impact of Public Opinion, Antiwar Demonstrations, and War Costs on Senate Voting on Vietnam War Motions." *American Journal of Sociology* 84 (July 1978): 99–122.

Burton, Michael G. "Elite Disunity and Collective Protest: The Vietnam Case." *Journal of Political and Military Sociology* 5 (Fall 1977): 169–83.

Cantor, Milton. *The Divided Left: American Radicalism, 1900–1975.* New York: Hill and Wang, 1978.

Cantrill, Albert H., and Charles W. Roll, Jr. *Hopes and Fears of the American People.* New York: University Books, 1971.

Capps, Walter H. *The Unfinished War: Vietnam and the American Conscience.* Boston: Beacon, 1982.

Carroll, Peter N. *It Seemed Like Nothing Happened: The Tragedy and Promise of America in the 1970s.* New York: Holt, Rinehart and Winston, 1982.

Carson, Clayborne. *In Struggle: SNCC and the Black Awakening of the 1960s.* Cambridge, Mass.: Harvard Univ. Press, 1981.

Chandler, Robert, comp. *Public Opinion: Changing Attitudes on Contemporary Political and Social Issues.* New York: Bowker, 1972.

Chester, Lewis. *An American Melodrama: The Presidential Campaign of 1968.* New York: Viking, 1969.

Chomsky, Noam. *American Power and the New Mandarins.* New York: Pantheon, 1967.

———. *For Reasons of State.* New York: Random House, 1973.

———. *The Trials of the Resistance.* New York: New York Review, 1970.

Christian, George. The President Steps Down. New York: Macmillan, 1970.

Clavir, Judith, et al. *The Sixties Papers: Documents of a Rebellious Decade.* New York: Praeger, 1984.

Clecak, Peter. *Radical Paradoxes: Dilemmas of the American Left, 1945–1970.* New York: Harper, 1974.

Cluster, Dick, ed. *They Should Have Served that Cup of Coffee.* Boston: South End Press, 1970.

Coffin, William Sloane. *Once to Every Man: A Memoir.* New York: Atheneum, 1977.

Colson, Charles W. *Born Again.* Old Tappan, N.J.: Chosen Books, 1976.

Commanger, Henry Steele. *The Defeat of America: Presidential Power and the National Character.* New York: Simon and Schuster, 1974.

Cooney, Robert, and Helen Michalowski, eds. *The Power of the People: Active Nonviolence in the United States.* Culver City, Calif.: Peace Press, 1977.

Cooper, Chester L. *The Lost Crusade: America in Vietnam.* New York: Dodd, Mead, 1970.

Cormier, Frank. *LBJ: The Way He Was.* Garden City, N.Y.: Doubleday, 1977.

Cortright, David. *Soldiers in Revolt: The American Military Today.* Garden City, N.Y.: Doubleday/Anchor, 1975.

Cousins, Norman. *The Improbable Triumvirate: John F. Kennedy, Pope John, Nikita Khrushchev.* New York: Norton, 1972.

————. *Present Tense: An American Editor's Odyssey.* New York: McGraw-Hill, 1967.

Cowan, Paul. *The Making of an Un-American: A Dialogue with Experience.* New York: Delta, 1970.

————. *State Secrets: Police Surveillance in America.* New York: Holt, Rinehart and Winston, 1974.

Cummings, Richard. *The Pied Piper: Allard K. Lowenstein and the Liberal Dream.* New York: Farrar, Straus and Giroux, 1973.

Dean, John. *Blind Ambition: The White House Years.* New York: Simon and Schuster, 1976.

DeBenedetti, Charles, ed. *Peace Heroes in Twentieth-Century America.* Bloomington: Indiana Univ. Press, 1986.

DeBenedetti, Charles. *The Peace Reform in American History.* Bloomington: Indiana Univ. Press, 1980.

Dellinger, David. *More Power Than We Know: The People's Movement Toward Democracy.* Garden City, N.Y.: Doubleday, 1975.

————. *Revolutionary Nonviolence: Essays by Dave Dellinger.* New York: Doubleday, 1971.

————. *Vietnam Revisited: From Covert Action to Invasion to Reconstruction.* Boston: South End Press, 1986.

Dickstein, Morris. *Gates of Eden: American Culture in the Sixties.* New York: Harcourt, 1973.

Divine, Robert A. *Blowing on the Wind: The Nuclear Test Ban Debate, 1954–1960.* New York: Oxford Univ. Press, 1978.

————. *Eisenhower and the Cold War.* New York: Oxford Univ. Press, 1981.

————. *Foreign Policy and Presidential Elections: 1952–1960.* New York: Watts, 1974.

Donner, Frank J. *The Age of Surveillance.* New York: Knopf, 1980.

Ehrlichman, John. *Witness to Power: The Nixon Years.* New York: Simon and Schuster, 1982.

Eisele, Albert. *Almost to the Presidency: A Biography of Two American Politicians.* Blue Earth, Minn.: Piper, 1972.

Ellsberg, Daniel. *Papers on the War.* New York: Simon and Schuster, 1972.

Evans, Sara. *Personal Politics: The Roots of Women's Liberation in the Civil Rights Movement and the New Left.* New York: Knopf, 1979.

Fairclough, Adam. "Martin Luther King, Jr., and the War in Vietnam." *Phylon* 45 (Mar. 1984): 19–39.

Ferber, Michael, and Staughton Lynd. *The Resistance.* Boston: Beacon, 1971.

Finn, James. *Protest: Pacifism and Politics.* New York: Random House, 1968.

Fisher, Randall M. *Rhetoric and American Democracy: Black Protest Through Vietnam Dissent.* Lanham, Md.: Univ. Press of America, 1985.

Foster, H. Schuyler. *Activism Replaces Isolationism: U.S. Public Attitudes, 1940–1975.* Washington: Foxhall Press, 1983.

Fowler, Robert Booth. *Believing Skeptics: American Political Intellectuals, 1945–1964.* Westport, Conn.: Greenwood, 1976.

Free, Lloyd A., and Hadley Cantril. *The Political Beliefs of Americans: A Study of Public Opinion*. New Brunswick, N.J.: Rutgers Univ. Press, 1967.

Fromm, Erich. *The Sane Society*. New York: Rinehart, 1955.

Frost, David. *I Gave Them a Sword: Behind the Scenes of the Nixon Interviews*. New York: Morrow, 1978.

Fulbright, William J. *The Crippled Giant: American Foreign Policy and Its Domestic Consequences*. New York: Random House, 1972.

Gallup, George. *The Gallup Poll: Public Opinion, 1935–1971*. New York: Random House, 1972.

———. *The Gallup Poll: Public Opinion, 1972–77*. Wilmington, Del.: Scholarly Resources, 1978.

Garrow, David J. *The FBI and Martin Luther King, Jr.* New York: Penguin, 1981.

Gelb, Leslie H., and Richard K. Betts. *The Irony of Vietnam: The System Worked*. Washington: Brookings Institution, 1979.

Gillon, Steven M. *Politics and Vision: The ADA and American Liberalism, 1947–1985*. New York: Oxford Univ. Press, 1987.

Gitlin, Todd. *The Sixties: Years of Hope, Days of Rage*. New York: Bantam, 1987.

———. *The Whole World is Watching: Mass Media in the Making and Unmaking of the New Left*. Berkeley: Univ. of California Press, 1980.

Goldman, Eric F. *The Tragedy of Lyndon Johnson*. New York: Knopf, 1969.

Gray, Francine du Plessix. *Divine Disobedience: Profiles in Catholic Radicalism*. New York: Vintage, 1971.

Halberstam, David. *The Making of a Quagmire: America and Vietnam During the Kennedy Era*. New York: Knopf, 1964.

Haldeman, Harry R., and Joseph Dimong. *The Ends of Power*. New York: Times Books, 1978.

Hall, Mitchell Kent. "Clergy and Laymen Concerned About Vietnam: A Study of Opposition to the Vietnam War." Ph.D. diss., Univ. of Kentucky, 1987.

Halperin, Morton, and Robert Borosage. *The Lawless State: The Crimes of the U.S. Intelligence Agencies*. New York: Penguin, 1976.

Halstead, Fred. *Out Now! A Participant's Account of the American Movement Against the Vietnam War*. New York: Monad, 1978.

Harris, David. *Dreams Die Hard*. New York: St. Martin's, 1982.

Hassler, Alfred. *Saigon U.S.A.* New York: Richard W. Baron, 1970.

Hayden, Tom. *Reunion: A Memoir*. New York: Random House, 1988.

———. *Trial*. New York: Holt, Rinehart and Winston, 1970.

Hayden, Tom, and Staughton Lynd. *The Other Side*. New York: New American Library, 1966.

Heath, G. Lewis, ed. *Mutiny Does Not Happen Lightly: The Literature of the American Resistance to the Vietnam War*. Metuchen, N.J.: Scarecrow, 1976.

Heath, Jim F. *Decade of Disillusionment: The Kennedy-Johnson Years*. Bloomington: Indiana Univ. Press, 1975.

Helmer, John. *Bringing the War Home: The American Soldier in Vietnam and After*. New York: Free Press, 1971.

Hensley, William E. "The Vietnam Anti-War Movement: History and Criticism." Ph.D. diss., Univ. of Oregon, 1979.

Herring, George C. *America's Longest War: The United States and Vietnam, 1950–1975*. New York: Wiley, 1979.

Hersh, Seymour M. *The Price of Power: Kissinger in the Nixon White House*. New York: Summit, 1983.

Hezong, Arthur. *McCarthy for President*. New York: Viking, 1976.

Hoffman, Abbie. *Soon to be a Major Motion Picture*. New York: Putnam, 1980.

Hoffman, Paul. *Moratorium: An American Protest.* New York: Tower, 1970.

Holsti, Ole, and James Rosenau. "Vietnam, Consensus, and the Belief Systems of American Leaders." *World Politics* 32 (Oct. 1979): 1–56.

Hoopes, Townsend. *The Limits of Intervention.* New York: McKay, 1969.

Horowitz, Irving. *The Struggle is the Message: The Organization and Ideology of the Anti-War Movement.* Berkeley, Calif.: Glendessary Press, 1972.

Hurwitz, Ken. *Marching Nowhere.* New York: Norton, 1971.

Isaacs, Arnold R. *Without Honor: Defeat in Vietnam and Cambodia.* Baltimore: Johns Hopkins Univ. Press, 1983.

Isserman, Maurice. *If I Had a Hammer . . . : The Death of the Old Left and the Birth of the New Left.* New York: Basic Books, 1987.

Jacobs, Paul, and Saul Landau, eds. *The New Radicals: A Report with Documents.* New York: Vintage, 1966.

Jacobson, Harold Karon, and Eric Stein. *Diplomats, Scientists, and Politicians: The United States and the Nuclear Test Ban Negotiations.* Ann Arbor: Univ. of Michigan Press, 1966.

Jezer, Martin. *The Dark Ages: Life in the United States, 1945–1960.* Boston: South End Press, 1982.

The Johnson Presidential Press Conferences. New York: Earl M. Coleman Enterprises, 1978.

Johnson, Lyndon Baines. *The Vantage Point: Perspectives of the Presidency, 1963–1969.* New York: Holt, Rinehart and Winston, 1971.

Joseph, Paul. *Cracks in the Empire: State Politics in the Vietnam War.* Boston: South End Press, 1981.

Kalb, Marvin, and Bernard Kalb. *Kissinger.* Boston: Little, Brown, 1974.

Karnow, Stanley. *Vietnam: A History.* New York: Penguin, 1983.

Kasinsky, Renee G. *Refugees from Militarism: Draft-Age Americans in Canada.* New Brunswick, N.J.: Transaction Books, 1976.

Katz, Milton S. *Ban the Bomb: A History of SANE, the Committee for a Sane Nuclear Policy, 1957–1985.* New York: Greenwood, 1986.

———. "Peace, Politics and Protest: SANE and the American Peace Movement, 1957–1972." Ph.D. diss., St. Louis Univ., 1973.

Katz, Milton S., and Neil H. Katz. "Pragmatists and Visionaries in the Post–World War II American Peace Movement: SANE and CNVA." In Solomon Wank, ed., *Doves and Diplomats: Foreign Offices and Peace Movements in Europe and America in the Twentieth Century,* pp. 265–88. Westport, Conn.: Greenwood, 1978.

Katz, Neil H. "Radical Pacifism and the Contemporary American Peace Movement: The Committee for Non-Violent Action, 1957–1967." Ph.D. diss., Univ. of Maryland, 1974.

Kearns, Doris. *Lyndon Johnson and the American Dream.* New York: Harper, 1976.

Kendrick, Alexander. *The Wound Within: America in the Vietnam Years, 1945–1974.* Boston: Little, Brown, 1974.

Keniston, Kenneth. *Young Radicals: Notes on Committed Youth.* New York: Harcourt, 1968.

———. *Youth and Dissent: The Rise of a New Opposition.* New York: Harcourt, 1971.

Kennan, George F. *Russia, the Atom, and the West.* New York: Harper, 1959.

Kerman, Cynthia Earl. *Creative Tension: The Life and Thought of Kenneth Boulding.* Ann Arbor: Univ of Michigan Press, 1974.

Kissinger, Henry. *The White House Years.* Boston: Little, Brown, 1979.

———. *Years of Upheaval.* Boston: Little, Brown, 1982.

Lake, Anthony, ed. *The Legacy of Vietnam*. New York: New York Univ. Press, 1976.

Larner, Jeremy. *Nobody Knows. Reflections on the McCarthy Campaign of 1948*. New York: Macmillan, 1978.

Lens, Sidney. *Unrepentant Radical: An American Activist's Account of Five Turbulent Decades*. Boston: Beacon, 1980.

Lewy, Guenter. *America in Vietnam*. New York: Oxford Univ. Press, 1978.

———. *Peace & Revolution: The Moral Crisis of American Pacifism*. Grand Rapids, Mich.: Eerdmans, 1988.

Liddy, G. Gordon. *Will*. New York: St. Martin's, 1980.

Litwak, Robert S. *Detente and the Nixon Doctrine: American Foreign Policy and the Pursuit of Stability, 1969–1976*. New York: Cambridge Univ. Press, 1984.

Lora, Ronald, ed. *America in the '60s: Cultural Authorities in Transition*. New York: Wiley, 1974.

Lyttle, Bradford. *The Chicago Anti-Vietnam War Movement*. Chicago: Midwest Pacifist Center, 1988.

Magruder, Jeb Stuart. *An American Life*. New York: Atheneum, 1974.

Mailer, Norman. *Advertisements for Myself*. New York: Putnam, 1959.

———. *The Armies of the Night*. New York: New American Library, 1968.

Mandelbaum, Michael. *The Nuclear Question: The United States and Nuclear Weapons, 1946–1976*. New York: Cambridge Univ. Press, 1979.

Matusow, Allen J. *The Unraveling of America: A History of Liberalism in the 1960s*. New York: Harper and Row, 1984.

McCarthy, Abigail. *Private Faces/Public Places*. Garden City, N.Y.: Doubleday, 1972.

McCarthy, Eugene E. *The Year of the People*. Garden City, N.Y.: Doubleday, 1969.

McGill, William J. *The Year of the Monkey: Revolt on the Campus, 1968–69*. New York: McGraw-Hill, 1982.

McGovern, George. *Grassroots: The Autobiography of George McGovern*. New York: Random House, 1977.

McPherson, Harry. *A Political Education*. Boston: Little, Brown, 1972.

Meconis, Charles. *With Clumsy Grace: The American Catholic Left, 1961–1977*. New York: Seabury, 1979.

Mehnert, Klaus. *Twilight of the Young: The Radical Movements of the 1960's and Their Legacy*. New York: Holt, Rinehart and Winston, 1976.

Menashe, Louis, and Ronald Rodosh, eds. *Teach-ins, U.S.A.: Reports, Opinions, Documents*. New York: Praeger, 1967.

Merton, Thomas. *The Nonviolent Alternative*. New York: Farrar, Straus and Giroux, 1971.

Metzenberg, Howard. "Student Peace Union, Five Years Before the New Left." Honors thesis, Oberlin College, 1978.

Miller, James. *"Democracy Is in the Streets": From Port Huron to the Siege of Chicago*. New York: Simon and Schuster, 1987.

Minnion, John. *The CND Story*. London: Allison and Busby, 1983.

Morgenthau, Hans J. *Truth and Power*. London: Pall Mall, 1970.

———. *Vietnam and the United States*. Washington: Public Affairs Press, 1965.

Mueller, John E. *War, Presidents, and Public Opinion*. New York: Wiley, 1973.

Newfield, Jack. *A Prophetic Minority*. New York: New American Library, 1966.

Nixon, Richard. *RN: The Memoirs of Richard Nixon*. New York: Grosset and Dunlap, 1978.

Oates, Stephen B. *Let the Trumpet Sound: The Life of Martin Luther King, Jr.* New York: New American Library/Mentor, 1982.

Oberschall, Anthony. "The Decline of the 1960s Social Movements." In Louis Kriesberg, ed., *Research in Social Movements: Conflict and Change*. Greenwich, Conn.: JAI Press, 1977.

O'Reilly, Kenneth. *Hoover and the Un-Americans: The FBI, HUAC, and the Red Menace.* Philadelphia: Temple Univ. Press, 1983.

O'Rourke, William. *The Harrisburg 7 and the New Catholic Left.* New York: Crowell, 1972.

Parmet, Herbert S. *The Democrats: The Years After FDR.* New York: Macmillan, 1976.

————. *Eisenhower and the American Crusade.* New York: Macmillan, 1972.

The Pentagon Papers: The Defense Department History of United States Decisionmaking on Vietnam. Ed. Senator Mike Gravel. Boston: Beacon, 1972.

Peterson, Richard E. *The Scope of Organized Student Protest in 1964–65.* Princeton, N.J.: Educational Testing Service, 1966.

Peterson, Richard E., and John A. Bilorusky. May 1970: The Campus Aftermath of Cambodia and Kent State. Berkeley, Calif.: Carnegie Commission on Higher Education, 1974.

Piehl, Mel. *Breaking Bread: The Catholic Worker and the Origin of Catholic Radicalism in America.* Philadelphia: Temple Univ. Press, 1982.

Powers, Thomas. *The War at Home: Vietnam and the American People, 1964–1968.* New York: Grossman, 1973.

Quigley, E. *American Catholics and Vietnam.* Grand Rapids, Mich.: Eerdmans, 1968.

Rader, Dotson. *"I Ain't Marchin' Any More!"* New York: McKay, 1969.

Ranger, Robin. *Arms and Politics, 1958–1978: Arms Control in a Changing Political Context.* Toronto: Macmillan, 1979.

Raskin, Marcus B., and Bernard B. Fall. The Viet-Nam Reader: Articles and Documents on American Foreign Policy and the Viet-Nam Crisis. New York: Random House, 1965.

Reynolds, Earle. *The Forbidden Voyage.* New York: McKay, 1961.

Robinson, Jo Ann. *Abraham Went Out: A Biography of A. J. Muste.* Philadelphia: Temple Univ. Press, 1981.

Rosenberg, Milton J. *Vietnam and the Silent Majority: The Dove's Guide.* New York: Harper and Row, 1970.

Rothman, Stanley, and S. Robert Lichter. *Roots of Radicalism: Jews, Christians, and the New Left.* New York: Oxford Univ. Press, 1982.

Rubin, Jerry. *Growing (Up) at Thirty-Seven.* New York: Evans, 1976.

Safire, William. *Before the Fall.* Garden City, N.Y.: Doubleday, 1975.

Sale, Kirkpatrick. *SDS.* New York: Vintage, 1974.

Salisbury, Harrison E. *Vietnam Reconsidered: Lessons from a War.* New York: Harper and Row, 1984.

Schandler, Herbert Y. *Lyndon Johnson and Vietnam: The Unmaking of a President.* Princeton: Princeton Univ. Press, 1977.

Schell, Jonathan. *The Time of Illusion.* New York: Knopf, 1976.

Schlesinger, Arthur, Jr. *The Bitter Heritage: Vietnam and American Democracy, 1941–1966.* Boston: Houghton Mifflin, 1967.

————. *Robert Kennedy and His Times.* Boston: Houghton Mifflin, 1978.

Schuman, Howard. "Two Sources of Antiwar Sentiment in America." *American Journal of Sociology* 78 (Nov. 1972): 513–36.

Skolnick, Jerome H. *The Politics of Protest.* New York: Ballantine, 1969.

Small, Melvin. *Johnson, Nixon, and the Doves.* New Brunswick, N.J.: Rutgers Univ. Press, 1988.

Smith, Curt. *Long Time Gone: The Years of Turmoil Remembered.* South Bend, Ind.: Icarus Press, 1982.

Stavis, Ben. *We Were the Campaign: New Hampshire to Chicago for McCarthy.* Boston: Beacon, 1970.

Steel, Ronald. *Walter Lippmann and the American Century.* New York: Vintage, 1981.

Stone, Gregory, and Douglas Lowenstein, eds. *Lowenstein: Acts of Courage and Belief.* New York: Harcourt, 1983.

Stone, I. F. *The Haunted Fifties.* New York: Random House, 1969.

———. *In a Time of Torment.* New York: Vintage, 1968.

———. *Polemics and Prophecies, 1967–1970.* New York: Random House, 1970.

Stout, Richard T. *People.* New York: Harper, 1970.

Sullivan, Michael P. *The Vietnam War: A Study in the Making of American Policy.* Lexington: Univ. Press of Kentucky, 1985.

Surrey, David S. *Choice of Conscience: Vietnam Era Military and Draft Resisters in Canada.* New York: Praeger, 1982.

Szulc, Tad. *The Illusion of Peace: Foreign Policy in the Nixon Years.* New York: Viking, 1978.

Taylor, Clyde, ed. *Vietnam and Black America: An Anthology of Protest and Resistance.* Garden City, N.Y.: Doubleday/Anchor, 1973.

Teodori, Massimo, ed. *The New Left: A Documentary History.* Indianapolis: Bobbs-Merrill, 1969.

Theoharis, Athan G. *Spying on Americans: Political Surveillance from Hoover to the Huston Plan.* Philadelphia: Temple Univ. Press, 1978.

Thorne, Barrie. "Resisting the Draft: An Ethnography of the Draft Resistance Movement." Ph.D. diss., Brandeis Univ., 1971.

Unger, Irwin. *The Movement: A History of the American New Left, 1959–1972.* New York: Dodd, Mead, 1974.

U.S. Congress. Senate. Internal Security Subcommittee. *The Anti-Vietnam Agitation and the Teach-in Movement: The Problem of Communist Infiltration and Exploitation.* 89th Cong., 1st sess., 1965.

———. Internal Security Subcommittee. *Communist Infiltration in the Nuclear Test Ban Movement.* 86th Cong., 2d sess., 1960.

———. Select Committee to Study Governmental Operations with Respect to Intelligence Activities. *Final Report.* 94th Cong., 2d sess., 1976.

———. Committee on Government Operations. *Riots, Civil and Criminal Disorders: Hearings Before the Permanent Subcommittee on Investigations.* 91st Cong., 2d sess., 1970.

Useem, Michael. *Conscription, Protest, and Social Conflict: The Life and Death of a Draft Resistance Movement.* New York: Wiley, 1973.

Vickers, George R. *The Formation of the New Left: The Early Years.* Lexington, Mass.: Lexington Books, 1975.

The Vietnam Hearings. New York: Vintage, 1966.

Viorst, Milton. *Fire in the Streets: America in the 1960s.* New York: Simon and Schuster, 1979.

Vogelgesang, Sandy. *The Long Dark Night of the Soul: The American Intellectual Left and the Vietnam War.* New York: Harper and Row, 1974.

Walker, Daniel. *Rights in Conflict: A Report Submitted by Daniel Walker, Director of the Chicago Study Team, to the National Commission on the Causes and Prevention of Violence.* New York: Bantam, 1968.

Warner, Nichlas. "The American Anti-War Movement, 1965–1972: Its Birth, Growth and Maturity." B.A. thesis, Australian National University, 1972.

Waterhouse, Larry, and Mariann Wizard. *Turning the Guns Around: Notes on the GI Movement.* New York: Praeger, 1971.

Wattenberg, Ben J. *The Real America: A Surprising Examination of the State of the Union.* Garden City, N.Y.: Doubleday, 1974.

White, Theodore H. *America in Search of Itself: The Making of the President, 1956–1980.* New York: Harper and Row, 1982.

Wilson, E. Raymond. *Uphill for Peace: Quaker Impact on Congress.* Richmond, Ind.: Friends United Press, 1975.

Witcover, Jules. *85 Days: The Last Campaign of Robert Kennedy.* New York: Putnam, 1969.

Wittner, Lawrence S. *Rebels Against War: The American Peace Movement, 1933–1983.* Philadelphia: Temple Univ. Press, 1984.

Wofford, Harris. *Of Kennedys and Kings: Making Sense of the Sixties.* New York: Farrar, Straus and Giroux, 1980.

Woodstone, Norma Sue. *Up Against the War: A Personal Introduction to U.S. Soldiers and Civilians Fighting Against the War in Vietnam.* New York: Tower, 1970.

Young, Nigel. An Infantile Disorder? The Crisis and Decline of the New Left. London: Routledge and Kegan Paul, 1977.

Zaroulis, Nancy, and Gerald Sullivan. *Who Spoke Up? American Protest Against the War in Vietnam, 1963–1975.* Garden City, N.Y.: Doubleday, 1984.

Zinn, Howard. *SNCC: The New Abolitionists.* Boston: Beacon, 1965.

Index

An American Ordeal
was composed in 10 on 12 ITC Garamond Light on a
Mergenthaler Linotron 202 by Brevis Press; printed
by sheed-fed offset on 50-pound acid-free Glatfelter
B-16 Natural, Smyth-sewn and bound over binder's
boards in ICG Arrestox B and notch bound with paper
covers by Thomson-Shore, Inc.; with dust jackets and
paper covers printed in 2 colors by Thomson-Shore,
Inc.; designed by Kachergis Book Design, Inc.; and
published by SYRACUSE UNIVERSITY PRESS,
Syracuse, New York 13244-5160.